Edward Gibbon, Luminous Historian

EDWARD GIBBON,
LUMINOUS
HISTORIAN
1772–1794

Patricia B. Craddock

The Johns Hopkins University Press
Baltimore and London

For David and Patty

© 1989 The Johns Hopkins University Press
All rights reserved
Printed in the United States of America

The Johns Hopkins University Press
701 West 40th Street
Baltimore, Maryland 21211
The Johns Hopkins Press Ltd., London

The paper used in this publication meets the minimum requirements
of American National Standard for Information Sciences—
Permanence of Paper for Printed Library Materials, ANSI z39.48-1984.

Library of Congress Cataloging–in–Publication Data

Craddock, Patricia B.
  Edward Gibbon, luminous historian, 1772–1794.

  Sequel to: Young Edward Gibbon.
  Bibliography: p.
  Includes index.
    1. Gibbon, Edward, 1737–1794. 2. Historians—
England—Biography. 3. Gibbon, Edward, 1737–1794.
History of the decline and fall of the Roman Empire.
4. Rome—History—Empire, 30 B.C.—476 A.D.
5. Byzantine Empire—History. I. Title.
DG206.G5C7 1989   937'.0072024   88-45416
ISBN 0-8018-3720-0 (alk. paper)

Contents

Preface

This book completes the biographical study of Edward Gibbon begun with my *Young Edward Gibbon* (1982). It begins with the year of Gibbon's first sustained work on the *Decline and Fall*, 1772, and concludes with the historian's death and an account of the reputation of both man and work. Although Gibbon's history was frequently discussed, edited, and reprinted in the first seventy years of the nineteenth century, no one tried to compete with the book he had written about himself. Between 1853 and 1874, the German classicist Jacob Bernays worked intermittently on what promised to be an excellent book-length study of Gibbon in five chapters, one of which would have been biographical; but it was unfortunately never completed. A full-scale biographical study of Gibbon that was more than a recapitulation of the memoirs was not even attempted until 1878, when J. Cotter Morison contributed a volume on Gibbon to the "English Men of Letters" series. Even Morison's biography does not attempt to go beyond the published materials, which were then limited to what was included by Lord Sheffield in his five-volume edition of Gibbon's *Miscellaneous Works* (1814). But Morison reorganizes and sometimes reinterprets the Sheffield material and devotes two of his ten chapters to an interpretation and evaluation of the *Decline and Fall*. He provides less a new perspective on Gibbon's life than a new perspective on what a biography of Gibbon might be. No other biography or book-length study of Gibbon was published in the nineteenth century.[1]

At the end of the nineteenth century, however, new impetus was given to Gibbon studies by two events: scholars were given access to the manuscript materials that had been unavailable under the terms of the first Lord Sheffield's will, and J. B. Bury's great new edition of the *Decline and Fall* inspired new interest in Gibbon's masterpiece. During the two decades after commemoration of the centennial of his death (1894), the complete texts of the drafts of the memoirs; better texts of Gibbon's letters (and more of them); G. B. Hill's hostile, but contextually exhaustive, edition of the traditional text of Gibbon's autobiography; and various other Gibboniana followed.[2] These materials were greeted as major literary events in both England and the United States. Henry James's comment, unique in manner, is typical in content:

> What shall I say of . . . our having at last the text, delicious and incomparable, of his Autobiography and Letters? . . . The oddity of the whole story of our perverted possession of him is only equalled by the beauty— there is no other name for it—of what relenting fate has at last restored to us. . . . What has lately happened is of a nature to make [a taste for Gibbon] in general so much stronger than ever that I feel a double pang at having to leave untouched one of the most rounded little romances of the literary life.[3]

The first biography of the twentieth century, however, was concerned with new interpretations rather than the new materials. An expansion of a 1907 essay in a volume called *Pioneer Humanists*, J. M. Robertson's 1925 biography was, like Morison's, a contribution to a series, "Life-Stories of Famous Men." Treating Gibbon as a Rationalist hero, Robertson is much annoyed with some of his predecessors, notably Morison, for complaining that Gibbon was insensitive to Christianity. Gibbon appreciated Christianity fully, as a political phenomenon, Robertson argued. "If the power to learn were as common as the habit of reading, or even of reading Gibbon, the *History of the Decline and Fall of the Roman Empire* would be the most educative, politically, of all historical works," although Gibbon achieves "sociological explanation" only in the fifteenth and sixteenth chapters, which have contributed to the longevity of his history. In portraying Gibbon's life, Robertson utilizes some of the new biographical materials published by John Meredith Read in his *Historic Studies in the Pays de Vaud* (1897), and readers recognized the freshness of his portrayal of Gibbon in youth.[4] Robertson also explicitly discusses something he identifies as a British historiographical tradition, comparing Gibbon, Macaulay, and Carlyle.

But the new materials were not used extensively until the thirties. Between 1932 and 1937, three book-length studies of Gibbon's life and work were published. The earliest, G. M. Young's, is based on fresh sources and incorporates wide-ranging knowledge of the period and of literary and historical materials valuable for an understanding of Gibbon's masterpiece, but it is undocumented and focused on Gibbon's accomplishments rather than on his experiences. It remains valuable for many passing insights into the man and the work. R. B. Mowat's 1936 biography is a narrative account almost exclusively devoted to Gibbon the man; Mowat does not analyze the works at all. This modest work is based principally on the *Autobiographies*, which it often paraphrases closely, and on Read. It was immediately overshadowed by the first full-scale modern biography of Gibbon, that of D. M. Low (1937). Low had already edited Gibbon's journal for the years 1761–63, with an exhaustive biographical introduction (1929). For the first time, a biographer was prepared to amplify and correct Gibbon's statements about his life and at the same time to place the *Decline and Fall* in two contexts: the author's life and times, and the history of historiography. For fifty years it has justly remained the definitive biography.

But in those fifty years, new materials for biography have become available. Furthermore, new ideas about history and its history, as well as new perceptions of authorial authority in both history and autobiography, have arisen. Book-length studies of Gibbon have taken various forms: studies of the history, with attention to the biography as its background (Giarrizzo 1954, Swain 1966, Jordan 1971, Baridon 1977b, Gossman 1981, Burrow 1985); biographical essays incorporating new opinions on the life and the history, but relying on previously published accounts of the life (Joyce 1953, E. J. Oliver 1958, de Beer 1968, Parkinson 1973); and, of course, studies of the history essentially unconcerned with the life (Fulgum 1953, Bond 1960, D. M. Oliver [diss.] 1969, Marks [diss.] 1975). (W. B. Carnochan's 1987 *Gibbon's Solitude* reached me too late for consideration here; it seems to fall into the second of these categories.)

The present volume, like *Young Edward Gibbon*, attempts to do something new, not to refute or reject the accomplishments of its predecessors. I have tried to incorporate the new material and new interpretations into a simultaneous study of the life and work, one that would complement Gibbon's own portrayal of himself as the historian of the Roman Empire by portraying both the process of composing a great history and the complex human who composed it. Gibbon did *not* imagine that he was the Roman Empire, but because he did not finish the final draft of his memoirs, he has encouraged us to think that he was not a man, but a role—the historian, the Gibbon. Certainly he worked hard to gain title to that role, but when he actually was the historian, he was, like anyone else, distracted, supported, or inspired by other desires, problems, feelings, needs, issues, and experiences. I believe that in rejecting the completed draft (E) of his memoirs, which portrays his whole life as a preparation for, and pendant to, the achievement of the *Decline and Fall*, Gibbon himself authorizes my approach.

Like the first volume of my biography, then, this one attempts to portray both the man and the historian. It argues that the perception of himself as historian gradually had an effect on the human qualities that had characterized the young Edward Gibbon, working, with other experiences, a change in his behavior that is not entirely admirable. But his less amiable traits of behavior and character must still be understood, not only in the context of the greatness of his task and achievement, but also in that of a continuing capacity to bestow and accept love and kindness where he knew they would not be rejected.

The other major effort of this volume is to portray the historiographical development within the *Decline and Fall*, which is in part, but only in part, the development of its narrator. In each chapter of the present volume, Gibbon's work on the portions of the *Decline and Fall* probably composed during the period in question is treated as one of the events and activities of his life at that time. Yet this book is not an analysis of the *Decline and Fall*, and there is no attempt to establish direct causal connections between events in Gibbon's personal or public life and his changing methods and views as a historian. What is attempted here is to show that the history—composed, after all, in two countries, in varying circumstances, and over the course of at least seventeen years—reveals gradual changes of perspective and method that are as much events in the author's life, as they occur, as changes of domicile or acquisition of friends, property, or position. There are indeed some parallel developments in the history and in the man; for example, I show that both acquire a more liberal view of excellence in women and a more complex perspective on the relationship between Christianity and civilization. But the attempt here is to portray the simultaneous developments in the man as historian and the man as man, without necessarily claiming causal relationships between the two processes. Similarly, Gibbon's other writings are a part of his personal history and are incorporated in this study as events in his life.

As in the previous volume, I have translated all foreign-language quotations for the reader's convenience (if the translation is not my own, that is indicated). The original is provided in the notes, except for readily available passages from Gibbon's own letters and *Miscellaneous Works*. Again, I am deeply indebted to my predecessors, editors and interpreters alike. Two of the scholars whose influence has been most important to me, Irvin Ehrenpreis and F. A. Pottle, are no longer here to see this new product of their instruction, but I wish nevertheless to record my continuing gratitude for the good fortune of knowing them and learning from them. I have been equally fortunate in two friends who have read this manuscript in draft and whose advice has made it less imperfect: Dr. Margaret Craddock Huff, my sister, of Northeastern University and Episcopal Divinity School, and Dr. Joan E. Hartman, professor and chair of English, College of Staten Island, City University of New York. I am grateful, too, to many lovers of Gibbon who have encouraged my work. Perhaps it is new evidence of the diminishment of humankind (or the expansion of human knowledge) that my biography of Gibbon has required almost exactly as many years as his study of the Roman Empire.

Acknowledgments

First, I am deeply grateful to the National Endowment for the Humanities, for a research fellowship that supported the first draft of this volume in 1985–86. I am also grateful to the Endowment and to the Guggenheim Foundation for the fellowships that supported the research for this volume and for its predecessor, *Young Edward Gibbon*, as well as to the American Council of Learned Societies for a summer travel grant that permitted me to consult the Gibbon collections in Lausanne. The following persons and institutions have kindly permitted me to quote manuscript materials: the Archives Cantonales Vaudoises, the Beinecke Rare Book and Manuscript Library (Yale University), the British Library, the East Sussex Record Office, John Murray, the Presidents and Fellows of Magdalen College (Oxford University), and the Pierpont Morgan Library, New York. For permission to reproduce the Walton portrait of Gibbon (1774), I thank the National Portrait Gallery, London; permission to reproduce the engraving of the Romney portrait (1781) and sketches by Lavinia Countess Spencer (1785) was kindly granted by the Trustees of the British Museum.

ONE

DECLINE AND TRIUMPH,
1772–1776

O N E

Study and Society

n 1791, in the comfortable house in Lausanne he had once shared with his friend Georges Deyverdun, enjoying the privileges of lionhood as the fruit of fame, Edward Gibbon, "the celebrated historian," received a letter from an old friend, Ann Benazet, née Allen. After introducing Mr. Owen,[1] a friend of her son's, to Gibbon, she remarks that she finds old friends more valuable every year. "I know not if tis the same with you, as with me, probably not, as I am exactly in mind, & Sentiments, what I was twenty years ago. you I remember made it your System, to change imperceptibly, as times and things change round you."[2] Gibbon, who was still at work on his *Memoirs* when he received her letter, makes no mention in them either of this friendship ("we both pretended to be Sentimental whilst Children," Ann recalls, "perhaps really were so") or of the quality of character to which he had once laid claim. But imperceptible change—perhaps he actually used the word *insensible* as he does so often in the *Decline and Fall*—is exactly what the observer, following the transformation of the young gentleman of letters into the historian of the Roman Empire, must trace. The modest, clubbable, but somewhat silent,[3] undistinguished man in his thirties who settled down in his new London lodgings to write a great history seems very different from "the Historian," the domestic and social dictator of Lausanne, the acknowledged star of the historical constellation of a historical age, whose voice, according to one witness, "at the slightest hint of opposition," could swell to "as manly a bass as [Charles] Fox or [Richard] Sheri-

3

dan."[4] As "historian" of the historian, Gibbon himself tells us of a life in which all events and attitudes led, directly or indirectly, to the one great purpose and achievement. In so doing, he tells us an important truth about that life, a truth developed, confirmed, and revised by subsequent biographers such as D. M. Low and Joseph Swain. But Mrs. Benazet gives us a clue to a different perspective on that life as it was lived, a clue that Gibbon himself seems once to have held and then to have abandoned. In becoming the historian of the Roman Empire, Gibbon adopted the supreme role of his life, the one that gave it both subjective and objective meaning, but he also "imperceptibly" reduced his choices and rigidified his personality and his way of life. These changes affected the history itself, probably for the better, but problematically; they affected the man still more problematically.

Despite such excellent studies of the historian as those cited above (to which one might add also the older biographies by Robertson and Young), accounts of Edward Gibbon the man, the person who wrote the history, have largely perpetuated two mythical characterizations. The first is akin, ironically, to the myth of James Boswell (who passionately hated Gibbon), that of the petty, contemptible person who somehow managed to produce a great book. Boswell, however, is often seen as intellectually contemptible; not so Gibbon. Condemnations center on his moral and emotional qualities.[5]

The second myth, which was perhaps originally intended to counteract the ill effects of the first, is similar to it in its flattening of Gibbon's emotional life and in its patronizing attitude to him as a human being. It portrays Gibbon as one of the luckiest of men, fortunate even in his apparent misfortunes.[6] The latter myth characterizes many admirers of the history and even of the autobiography; the former usually affects attitudes toward the history as well as toward the historian, and is in part a reaction to an inferred author within the history and behind its narrator, or to Gibbon's unromantic self-portrayal in the *Memoirs*.

The revisionist attitude of admirers of the history who reject the myth that Gibbon's life was a scholarly idyll can go to the opposite extreme, taking the view that Gibbon's personal life was irretrievably marred, with the history either the cause of or the sole compensation for a miserable existence. Some valuable recent studies of the history and of Gibbon as historian have proposed, in passing, this view of his personality and emotional life. "The limitations of the man and consequently of the mind are painfully obvious" (yet essential to the production of the great work). "To create 'the historian of the Roman Empire' Gibbon paid dearly . . . in loneliness, frustration, unfulfilled love" (but "if the price of genius was high, Gibbon paid it willingly"). "The History was the only achievement of a life of failure and renunciation."[7]

To untangle and reconcile the various truths, half-truths, and errors of these incompatible positions, past and present, it is useful to examine in detail the gradual process by which Gibbon identified himself with Rome, with the narrator of the history, and with the role of great man, celebrity, and sage to which his writing it seemed to entitle him. But it is also essential constantly to challenge the view that he reduced or inflated himself in these ways by emphasizing the affectionate, appreciative, self-critical, generous, scholarly man who was also Edward Gibbon. Though his personal faults and weaknesses were accentuated by success, his virtues were not eliminated; they were, in fact, in some ways also accentuated. If he adopted with pleasure and relief the sobriquet and social niche of "the historian," if he exploited a happy temperament (influenced, perhaps, by his aunt, Catherine Porten, the "true mother of [his] mind")[8] that led him to revel in life's gifts instead of bewailing its limitations, it is perhaps unnecessary as well as ungenerous to condescend to him as incapable of great suffering or supreme joy. He "imperceptibly" adapted himself so completely to new circumstances and conditions that in the end he lost his ability to tolerate difference or opposition and in some instances failed to see that he himself was an appropriate object of his own irony. Yet in many other cases, even to the end of his life, he acknowledged ludicrous aspects of his own role in the human comedy with wit and good humor; and the emotional crises of his later life— deaths of friends, the loss of the France that was in some ways his intellectual home, his own illness—revealed the character beneath the role. It was Walter Bagehot who first quipped that Gibbon thought he *was* the Roman Empire,[9] but even David Jordan and Michel Baridon, in their balanced, though different, appraisals, regard the man who emerges from the trials of Gibbon's youth as sufficiently characterized (after one allows for his politics) by his identification with his historical task. With Leo Braudy, they have perceived and pursued the development of the historian within the history, but the corresponding and complicating changes outside it must also be explored.[10]

As Gibbon literally and figuratively made himself the historian of the Roman Empire, he had to continue to be an eighteenth-century English gentleman, a (step)son and nephew, a friend, a landowner, and for a while a member of government as well as of "society." He chose, moreover, to maintain more intellectual roles than we sometimes give him credit for. His library[11] indicates interests ranging from ballet to beekeeping, from farce to anatomy, in addition to the enormous range of subjects he found useful, if only by way of analogy or amplification, in the history itself. It is the task of the present volume to relate the development of all these other aspects of Gibbon's career as a man to his career in the role of historian and, most especially, to the gradual developments within the history itself.

After Gibbon's father died in 1770, nearly two years elapsed in the settlement of the first difficulties of the estate and in preparation for a new life of bachelor independence.[12] To this period, with the three years immediately preceding, Gibbon attributes the preliminary studies for his history. Though his chronology in the autobiography is far from exact, it is loosely reliable, and we may readily accept that he had read not only the original records, but the secondary authorities he later cites, such as Muratori, Tillemont, Lardner, Sigonius, Maffei, Baronius and Pagi, and the Theodosian code (*Memoirs* 147). But before he was able to "disentangle [himself] from the web of rural œconomy," remove himself and his books to London, and establish "a mode of life agreable to [his] wishes,"[13] the only writing preparatory to the *Decline and Fall* that we are certain Gibbon produced is the "rough draught" to which he refers in the *Decline and Fall* (*DF* chap. 30, 4:283, n. 88 [86]).[14] Because he also tells us that the "first rough manuscript" of the history (except for certain specified chapters, not including chapter 30) was used as printer's copy, we can infer that what he wrote in 1771 was something less than a full-scale draft. It was probably similar to the extant "Outlines of the History of the World for the Period 800–1500," and it is a plausible hypothesis that such "outlines" were complete for the entire fifteen-century period of the *Decline and Fall* before he began to write the first chapter: it was always his practice to "revolve . . . all that [he] knew, or believed or had thought on the subject" before seeking new information (*Memoirs* 98).[15] Much of the last quarter of 1772 was spent in choosing and redecorating his new house in London, but "no sooner was [he] settled in [his] house and library than [he] undertook the composition of the first Volume of [his] history" (*Memoirs* 155).

In the *Memoirs* he describes with obvious satisfaction the general pattern of his life as he began to write:

1773 January-1783 September - I had now attained the solid comforts of life, a convenient well-furnished house, a domestic table, half a dozen chosen servants, my own carriage, and all those decent luxuries whose value is the more sensibly felt the longer they are enjoyed. These advantages were crowned by the first of earthly blessings, Independence: I was the absolute master of my hours and actions: nor was I deceived in the hope, that the establishment of my library in town would allow me to divide the day between Study and Society. Each year the circle of my acquaintance, the number of my dead and living companions, was enlarged. To a lover of books the shops and sales in London present irresistible temptations; and the manufacture of my history required a various and growing stock of materials. . . . By my own choice I passed in town the greatest part of the year: but whenever I was desirous of breathing the air of the Country, I possessed an hospitable retreat at Sheffield place in Sussex, in the family of Mr Holroyd, a valuable friend, whose character, under the name of Lord Sheffield, has since been more conspicuous to the public (*Memoirs* 154–55).

Accurate and revelatory though this paragraph is, it conceals as much as it reveals, and in particular, it blends together periods of Gibbon's life that by imperceptible degrees came to differ greatly.

It conceals, of course, all the petty complications of daily life, including the delays of the carpenters, painters, and upholsterers working on 7 Bentinck Street, his much-loved house in London. The year 1773 had begun with the sad duty of caring for the effects and arranging the funeral of James Scott, a relative of Gibbon's stepmother's who had been of great service to the Gibbons during the financial crisis precipitated by Gibbon's father's mismanagement.[16] After the elder Gibbon's death, Gibbon's tireless and efficient friend John Holroyd, later Lord Sheffield, became his principal financial adviser, and neither Gibbon nor his stepmother saw so much of Mr. Scott as they had done for a time. Nevertheless, Gibbon accepted and carried out his obvious obligation unhesitatingly; it included comforting and advising his stepmother when they met in London in mid January. Indeed, he wrote to Holroyd, "I have kept so close to Mrs G that I don't know a Syllable of news" (*Letters* 1:359).[17] Gibbon had also undertaken various commissions for the Holroyds, who were coming to town later in the winter, most particularly taking Mrs. Holroyd's watch to the jeweler and seeking a footman and stables for their London sojourn. One might infer that little time was available for the Roman Empire, yet there is one tiny hint that Gibbon's mind was not entirely on the eighteenth century. The watchmaker's name was James Tregent. The spelling of this French name should have been straightforward to Gibbon, but instead he chooses to spell it "Trajan" and quips, "some relation I presume of the Emperor" (*Letters* 1:360).

On February 5, 1773, his attorney drew up the lease between Gibbon and Charles Heath that officially gave Gibbon his own London residence, and on February 11 he was at last able to write to his stepmother from Bentinck Street. His patience cannot have been too severely tried by the "cursed upholsterers," for he decided on the house about December 11 and was only ten or eleven days late by the timetable he proposed on December 21: "I shall set out next Thursday [Christmas Eve] for Holroyd's, stay about a fortnight, send up for my books and *young* Housekeeper about the middle of next month, and get into my new Habitation towards the end of it" (*Letters* 1:355–56). We may easily imagine the satisfaction with which he looked around his new library, at the bookcases painted white (with an "Adamic" frieze) and the light blue wallpaper trimmed with gold (*Letters* 1:353). Presumably it was about this time that he purchased

the 150 pens (100 of them large) for which he was billed in 1773 by
Richard Green of 154 Fleet Street.[18]

But at first, Gibbon tells us, everything about the book itself was
"dark and doubtful." He had not even settled on the title of the work,
or "the true æra of the decline and fall of the Roman Empire, the
limits of the Introduction, the division of the chapters, and the order
of the narrative." He had long ago taken the first step preliminary to
the writing of the history, in the 1771 outline or draught.[19] His second
preliminary step, completed prior to May 1774, was to write a brief
essay summarizing his theme. A version of this essay was eventually
published as the conclusion of volume 3 of the *Decline and Fall*. These
"General Observations on the Decline of the Empire in the West"
have often disappointed Gibbon's admirers, especially those unaware
of their early date of composition,[20] and the essay has supplied ammunition to Gibbon's detractors; but it has also been admired and
praised, and Gibbon himself obviously remained sufficiently satisfied
with it to award it a climactic place in his history. Both its value and
its weaknesses rest, I think, on the same circumstance: it is Gibbon's
earliest recorded response to his great modern predecessors as philosophic historians of Rome, especially Montesquieu. As such, the
"General Observations" are both a tribute and a debate.

Gibbon was of course familiar with Montesquieu's famous little
book, *Considérations sur les causes de la grandeur des Romains et de leur
décadence*. Montesquieu's general influence on him is discussed not
only by Gibbon himself, in the *Memoirs*, but by many other scholars.[21]
In fact, Montesquieu was clearly the most important Enlightenment
influence on Gibbon. But the *Decline and Fall* would not exist if
Gibbon had been entirely satisfied with Montesquieu's sketch. The
"General Observations," therefore, were necessary to him as a means
of defining not only what he had learned from Montesquieu, but what
more there was to be said.[22] In the event, Gibbon came to differ more
strongly from Montesquieu than these early remarks suggest, principally because he approached his material not only as an apprentice
"sociologist" of history,[23] but also as a historian proper. It is probable
that he completed these "General Observations" in some form no
later than July or August 1773,[24] for either they or the early chapters
of the history to which they were preliminary must be the "things I
wish to finish, and for which my Library is absolutely requisite" of
which he wrote to his stepmother, Dorothea Gibbon, on July 31.

His usual practice was to write his chapters before adding the
notes, though he sometimes used the facing pages of a manuscript to
make either notes for notes, or the notes themselves.[25] Of course he
often added or corrected notes, as well as text, in the process of
seeing the work through the press. The last footnote to "General
Observations," for example, must have been written after 1776.[26] But

in general, as we shall see, Gibbon's notes represent a kind of dialogue with the text, as well as its factual bulwark. In this dialogue, it
should be noted, Gibbon uses and portrays secondary as well as
primary sources.[27] More than half the citations in the *Decline and Fall*
credit writers of the sixteenth through the eighteenth centuries.[28] Yet
neither in the "General Observations" nor in their notes is there an
explicit reference to Montesquieu, and the only reference to Voltaire,
who is also an implicit participant in this conversation, is to the *Siècle
de Louis XIV* and deals with modern sieges, not with Voltaire's historical ideas. In general, Gibbon expects his readers to recognize allusions to the arguments and occasionally to the texts of the literary
historians of the modern period, and of course to literary classics both
ancient and modern.[29] Nevertheless, we might have expected a general reference to Montesquieu here, if the "General Observations" had
been published as the introduction to the history. Instead, Gibbon
invokes Montesquieu implicitly: "The rise of a city, which swelled
into an Empire, may deserve, as a singular prodigy, the reflection of
a philosophic mind. But the decline was the natural and inevitable
effect of immoderate greatness" (*DF* ch. 38, 4:173). The "philosophic
mind" was clearly Montesquieu's. The thesis, too, is Montesquieuan—
closer, in some ways, to Montesquieu than to the *Decline and Fall* as
actually written. But it is already Montesquieu with a difference, or
differences.

Part of the early difference between Gibbon's view of Rome's fall
and Montesquieu's is attributable to Voltaire, but the rest is Gibbon
himself. Michel Baridon has well analyzed the way in which Gibbon
united "the two great currents of French Enlightenment historiography":

> Before [Gibbon], the two axes of research did not converge.
>   There was the law, and there were customs, Montesquieu and Voltaire.
> The one will move from the theory of institutions to a theory of history,
> the other from revolt against the dominant ideology to a philosophy of
> history.[30]

Voltaire helps Gibbon avoid the excesses of "l'ésprit de système,"
rigid determinism. But Gibbon is not content with Voltaire's own
philosophical determinism, in which, Gibbon believed (as we shall
have occasion to see more fully later), Voltaire is often deceived by
his very skepticism and also by his determination to subordinate
events to principles.

Gibbon's own perspective is revealed in the organization of his
argument. Most paragraphs of the "General Observations" have a
structure typical of Gibbonian deliberative prose: the false or incomplete thesis precedes the true one. Error has its full opportunity to
influence the reader, but the weight of both argument and rhetoric

supports its opponent. Thus the Greeks attributed the Roman successes to fortune rather than merit, but a wiser Greek, Polybius, has
explained "the deep foundations of the greatness of Rome"—competition for honor, a balanced constitution, citizen soldiers, incorporation
of former enemies, military skills, and the spirit of a people "incapable of fear and impatient of repose" (*DF* chap. 38, 4:172–73). Thus
also "the decay of Rome has been frequently ascribed to the translation of the seat of empire," but in fact the "foundation of Constantinople more essentially contributed to the preservation of the East
than to the ruin of the West" (*DF* 4:174–75). Christianity, directing
itself to a future life, contributed to the decline and fall, but though
"the decline of the Roman empire was hastened by the conversion of
Constantine, his victorious religion broke the violence of the fall, and
mollified the ferocious temper of the conquerors" (*DF* 4:175). At this
stage, however, Gibbon recognizes the provisional character only of
rejected historical positions; the final views seem to require no further
questioning.

The other paragraph in this section of the "General Observations"
begins with the allusion to Montesquieu already quoted. The next
sentence, a famous one, continues the organic metaphor and concludes that "the stupendous fabric yielded to the pressure of its own
weight" (*DF* 4:174). But when Gibbon moves away from metaphor,
the principal self-defeating greatness seems to be not that of the
Empire itself, but that of the Roman legions. They became too
powerful to be denied luxuries that then undermined their power. In
this, too, he follows Montesquieu, who had observed that long after
other strengths were lost, the Romans retained their military strength.
But "in this later period . . . they even filled the corps of national
troops with barbarian soldiers. . . . formerly, their constant policy was
to keep the military art for themselves and deprive all their neighbors
of it. . . . Finally, the Romans lost their military discipline and went
so far as to abandon their own arms."[31]

It is clear, then, how persuasive Gibbon found Montesquieu as he
sat down to review his own perspective on the subject he had chosen.
It is also clear, however, that he leaves room for both chance and
human decisions to influence events. The materials, not only in this
paragraph, but in the preceding ones about Roman greatness, show
Gibbon's interest, even at this point, in issues not defined by Montesquieu. For example, a paragraph about the successes of the Republic
notes a missed opportunity and an inherent weakness: "The ambitious design of conquest, which might have been defeated by the
seasonable conspiracy of mankind, was attempted and achieved; and
the perpetual violation of justice was maintained by the political
virtues of prudence and courage" (*DF* chap. 38, 4:173). We may
compare Montesquieu, who says that the Romans conquered "not only

by means of the art of war but also by their prudence, wisdom, and constancy, and their love of glory and country." Gibbon omits "wisdom" and insists on noting the basic injustice. "It is not chance that rules the world," in Montesquieu's view. "There are general causes, moral and physical, which act in every monarchy, elevating it, maintaining it, or hurling it to the ground. All accidents are controlled by these causes."[32] The Romans were ruined because "good laws, which have made a small republic grow large, become a burden to it when it is enlarged. . . . [Rome] lost its liberty because it completed the work it wrought too soon."[33] The conclusion that the other nations' failure to achieve "seasonable conspiracy" contributed to the Roman success (hardly the action of an inevitable law) is Gibbon's.

In reflecting on Montesquieu's analysis of the fall, Gibbon had the advantage of knowing Montesquieu's later work, the *Esprit des lois*. In it, Montesquieu explains more clearly the kinds and variety of impersonal causes that influence human history, including climate, religion, and customs. "Gibbon was the first historian to make use of this discovery." With its help, he could "dismiss the Pyrrhonists, the providentialists, and the political moralists."[34] He prepares to do so here, but as he had already suggested in his youthful *Essai*, he never abandoned the idea of other kinds of causes as well, or the complications of empirical fact that made application of these causes impossible in many cases.[35]

Montesquieu scatters observations about the relationship between the Roman fate and the prospects for modern Europe throughout the *Considerations*. But, as David Jordan suggests, the influence of Voltaire's didactically philosphic history is the strongest presence in the last six paragraphs of the "General Observations," which conclude, notoriously, that we *may* "acquiesce in the pleasing conclusion that every age of the world has increased, and still increases, the real wealth, the happiness, the knowledge, and perhaps the virtue, of the human race" (*DF* 4:181).[36] But it is important that this "pleasing conclusion" has been previously limited, rather severely, to technology alone, among the three "improvements of society" (technology, individual geniuses such as poets and philosophers, public institutions such as laws and commerce). Thus Gibbon's comment, in context, by no means amounts to a wholehearted assent to the idea of progress.

Despite his failure to pay sufficient tribute to the science of the Arabs,[37] Gibbon appreciates technological progress, particularly of a fundamental kind, such as improvements in agricultural methods. He illustrates the "arts" that can never be lost by two examples: the scythe and the abandonment of cannibalism. As the power to feed ourselves increases, the temptation to feed on each other decreases, and "war, commerce, and religious zeal"—a scourge, a blessing, and a folly—have spread these gifts ever more widely throughout the world.

It is in this limited sense that we can see continual progress in human history. But the other two "improvements of society" are vulnerable: private genius and public industry may be extirpated.

Before exploring this minimal case of progress, Gibbon proposes three reasons why Europe should not suffer the fate of the Roman Empire (in this essay characterized by him as "a deluge of Barbarians"). He acknowledges that "these speculations" may prove "doubtful or fallacious" (*DF* 4:179). The "speculations" certainly resemble the perspective of Voltaire—Jordan calls them "didactic and superficial, clearly in the style of Voltaire"—but Jordan sees Gibbon's reservations and qualifications only as a sign of lack of enthusiasm for standard *philosophe* doctrine;[38] I think we may see Gibbon's position, even here, as somewhat different in kind as well as degree. The security of military science against barbarian attack, and the pious hope that technological advance will always be accompanied by "proportionable improvement in the arts of peace and civil policy" (*DF* 4:79), as in the case of Russia, suggest, it is true, an excessive and facile optimism; but it is only a hope, and Gibbon's survey of distinctions between modern Europe and the Roman Empire includes many issues much closer to the heart of his own subject. The first point, for example, is the Romans' inadequate knowledge of the north and east. They did not suspect that revolutions in China, by putting pressure on the northern hunters and shepherds, "poor, voracious, and turbulent," could affect the "peace of Gaul or Italy" (*DF* 4:176). This allowance for the rest of the world is certainly Voltairean, and Gibbon explicitly rejects Montesquieu's conclusion that the barbarians had ceased to come from the north because population had been reduced. But Gibbon's presentation also foreshadows, however dimly, his later view that the change from a civil society based on herds and hunting to one based on agriculture and commerce is the key to an escape from the problem represented in Roman history, the incompatibility of barbaric and civic virtues. Religious fanaticism of the individualistic kind—"enthusiasm"—continues, however, to threaten this resolution.[39] These important points are developed in the *Decline and Fall*.

The second section of this analysis of Europe's safety from barbarians, moreover, is only nominally directed to dangers from without. The real protections from the fate of the Empire apply to internal faults. Because Europe is a coalition of states rather than a single empire, the tyranny or incapacity of particular leaders cannot have such devastating consequences as in the world state. Each state is kept ready for war by "temperate and undecisive contests" that, regardless of the victor, leave Europe itself unconquered.[40] Oddly, but perhaps at the time accurately, Gibbon clearly believed that the application of science to warfare had increased defensive capabilities more than offensive ones. It is here that he invokes and criticizes Voltaire:

"Historians may indignantly observe that the preparations of a siege would found and maintain a flourishing colony; yet we cannot be displeased that the subversion of a city should be a work of cost and difficulty, or that an industrious people should be protected by those arts, which survive and supply the decay of military virtue" (*DF* 4:179, with n. 9). In the note to this passage, he quotes Voltaire's comments about the cost of the armaments for the siege of Turin, which conclude with the observation with which Gibbon begins.[41]

Not all the footnotes to the "General Observations" were written as Gibbon wrote the text, as we have seen, but some certainly were. The first four, for example, deal with the Greek debate about the Roman achievement used by Gibbon as the introduction to the "Observations." The fifth is clearly related to Gibbon's debate with Richard Hurd about the Book of Daniel, carried on in the summer of 1772.[42] In fact, the terms of Daniel's prophecy help to explain the strained metaphor that concludes Gibbon's first paragraph: "the images of gold, or silver, or brass, that might serve to represent the nations and their kings, were successively broken by the *iron* monarchy of Rome" (*DF* 4:173).

Several of the notes at the end of the "Observations," on the other hand, must have been added in preparation for publication in 1781, or at any rate, after 1776. The sixth note refers to *Mémoires sur les Chinois,* first published in 1776; the seventh gives cross-references to the earlier volumes of the *Decline and Fall;* the fifteenth is the one that refers to the *five* great voyages commissioned by George III (the fifth in 1776). The eighth note deals with America: "America now contains about six millions of European blood and descent; and their numbers, at least in the North, are continually increasing. Whatever may be the changes of their political situation, they must preserve the manners of Europe; and we may reflect with some pleasure that the English language will probably be diffused over an immense and populous continent." While the second sentence of this note suggests a composition date during the American Revolution, the first could have been written in 1771. In any case, it is difficult to see the marked differences in attitude some writers have attributed to Gibbon's references to America in 1771 and 1781 respectively.[43]

Other notes deal with savage man (10–14), and it would be interesting to know whether Gibbon thought of this extreme contrast when he began his study of a lost civilization or when he was preparing to publish it. In either case, it is clear that Gibbon had no belief or interest in the hypothesis of the noble savage; he qualifies his description ("naked both in mind and body, and destitute of laws, of arts, of ideas, and almost of language") only by saying: "Fancy or perhaps reason may still suppose an extreme and absolute state of nature far below the level of these savages, who had acquired some arts and instruments" (*DF* 4:179–80 n. 10). He makes no reference to Rousseau, but there is a note citing "the learned and rational work" of A. Y. de Goguet on the origin of human arts and technology. Gibbon's contrast of civilization not with barbarism but with savagery is necessary to his extremely cautious version of the doctrine of progress.[44]

As Gibbon began to write, then, he took a view of his subject that included its instructive value for his contemporaries, in this resembling not only Voltaire but Bolingbroke and the humanist and classical historical tradition. But as Gibbon wrote, he abandoned for the most part this species of overt, impersonal didacticism. For his scenic and narrative approach, the most important feature of these "General Observations" is their identification of the weaknesses of Rome of which he was aware at the beginning of his history. They may be summarized as follows: the Romans' fallacious sense that their world was the world; a dangerous unity under a single monarchy unbalanced by other powers; a reliance on military virtue, which inevitably decays as it succeeds; a religion that neglected social virtues; competition among monarchs only in luxury. The three great introductory chapters develop all these points, directly or indirectly.

No one knew, at first, about Gibbon's historical project, at least so far as we can tell from the extant letters. But the new resident of Bentinck Street was by no means a recluse. Business, society, and family were distractions variously acceptable and predictable, but those whose image of Gibbon is that of the vast sedentary figure whose hat remains unused throughout a month-long visit to a friend's country estate[45] will be surprised by another distraction of which Gibbon complains in March—"this abominable fine weather which will not allow me a quiet hour at home, without being liable to the reproaches of my friends and my own conscience." He hates being driven from his "own new, clean comfortable dear house"; "if it would but rain, I should enjoy that union of study and society, in which I have always placed my prospect of happiness" (*Letters* 1:362). Clearly Holroyd is one of the friends who insists on Gibbon's taking advantage of the weather, though Holroyd is currently employing "his great soul and his little body" entirely on the subject of tithes. An unhappier distraction is the illness of Gibbon's aunt and foster mother, Catherine Porten: "Mrs. Porten is, I much fear in a very bad Way: her old Complaint, but the fits more violent and more frequent. We shall not possess her long!" (*Letters* 1:362–63). Yet, two months later, "her spirits are still good" (*Letters* 1:365). It seems probable that Aunt Kitty's ills were seasonal, for in the summers she was well enough for various expeditions, and she lived until 1786.

The business that most occupied Gibbon in the spring of 1773 was the attempt to sell an estate at Lenborough. Gibbon inherited so many debts from his father, especially including £17,000 owed to

Gosling's Bank, for which the bank was pressing the heir, that it seemed advisable to him and to Holroyd to sell enough property to clear them, even if he could not obtain a very good price for the land. The first idea was to sell it by auction, and a sale was scheduled for May 24. But the estate failed to bring the reserve price (£20,000). There then began a Restoration comedy that lasted for years, not to Gibbon's amusement. On June 12, a man named, implausibly, Lovegrove, characterized by Gibbon as "a rich brutish honest horse Dealer," agreed to purchase Lenborough for that price, "after a very hard battle in which he squeezed from me a promise of throwing him back a hundred for trouble &c." But he would not agree to pay for the property before November. As it turned out, Gibbon's characterization was wrong by at least one word—"honest." His sanguine hope that the matter was settled was unfounded; in fact, Lenborough was not sold until December of 1783 (and then not to Lovegrove), and it ultimately brought only £15,600, with unspecified further charges against that amount yet to pay. Gibbon ruefully remarked on that occasion, "Sure I have been peculiarly unfortunate in my connections of business, for in good truth, Winton, Lovegrove, and Sir H. Burrard are more than should fall to the share of one man" (*Letters* 3:382). But in 1773 Gibbon could think the most pressing of his inherited financial burdens settled. "By Michaelmas," he wrote to his stepmother, "I shall be a clear though a poor man" (*Letters* 1:368—poor because all the purchase money would be consumed in paying off the mortgage and another debt incurred by his father).

Sometime during the spring of 1773, Gibbon and three friends— George Wilbraham, Godfrey Bagnall Clarke, and Booth Grey—decided on a project of an entirely different nature. They commissioned their portraits from Henry Walton—four copies of each (one copy of Gibbon's is in the National Portrait Gallery, London). Gibbon sent his own copy of the painting of himself to his stepmother on July 13. Because he was writing to apologize for a long silence and to announce a further delay in a projected visit to her, the portrait was a timely gift, an acceptable surrogate for its subject. During June and July, Gibbon remained in London writing as the town grew "empty." As long as Parliament sat, Gibbon took an interest in its deliberations and sometimes attended them late into the night. Thus he welcomed this "dull" summer period, which allowed him more regular hours, as well as more time for writing, and which was soon enlivened by a very acceptable visitor, his old friend from Lausanne, Georges Deyverdun.

Deyverdun, who was Gibbon's closest male friend during his adolescent years in Lausanne and who had collaborated with him on several literary projects in the sixties, was earning his living by "bearleading" the eighteen-year-old earl of Chesterfield in his travels on

the four great ages of the world, is reached only in the concluding third of the chapter. In a passage often erroneously quoted to support the idea that Gibbon thought benevolent dictatorship the best form of government and the age of the five emperors the best example of such a dictatorship,[53] Gibbon ironically paraphrases the recent characterization of the world's worst age by his friend William Robertson.[54] Gibbon acknowledges the paradox that the period in which ordinary men had suffered least was that in which a vast number had been governed by absolute power in the hands of leaders both virtuous and wise. The reigns of the Antonines "are possibly the only period of history in which the happiness of a great people was the sole object of government" (DF chap. 3, 1:84). But this praise is qualified heavily: these princes "deserved the honour of restoring the Republic, had the Romans of their days been capable of enjoying a rational freedom," and at best, the general happiness was fatally unstable, hanging on "the character of a single man" (DF chap. 3, 1:86). The chapter, and the portrait of "unfallen" Rome, ends with two paragraphs about the bitterness of this state for free people: the Romans, who remembered and revered freedom, suffered more exquisitely from their slavery to imperial monsters (DF chap. 3, 1:87) than did peoples who had never been free; the vastness of the Roman world permitted no escape within civilization as they knew it. " 'Wherever you are,' said Cicero to the exiled Marcelus, 'remember that you are equally within the power of the conqueror' " (DF chap. 3, 1:90).

Gibbon was aware from the beginning that he might have begun his account of the declining empire at a point earlier or later than the one he selected, including its birth; some possibilities are specifically rejected by him (the division of the Empire into Eastern and Western, the establishment of Christianity), and others ignored or cited in the history as critical points *within* the decline, for example, the reign of Valens, in which the Visigoths crossed the Danube. In particular, his account of the five good emperors rhetorically echoes Montesquieu's account of the period from the death of Gallienus to that of Probus, when "four great men . . . by a great stroke of luck, succeeded each other [and] reestablished an empire that was about to perish."[55] This echo suggests that Gibbon has considered and rejected beginning his account in the third century.

The reasons he chose to begin as he did were, we may conclude, both literary and philosophical. No matter how much one accepts the organic metaphor for the history of empires, it becomes a mere truism to begin the progress toward death with birth. Within that metaphor, maturity must be allowed for, after all, and Gibbon mentions it in his preface, characterizing the age of Trajan and the Antonines as that in which "the Roman monarchy, having attained its full strength and

maturity, began to verge towards its decline" (*DF* Preface of the
Author, l:xxxix). Also, Montesquieu, Machiavelli, Voltaire, and Tacitus united to invite Gibbon to consider the Empire as progress past,
as well as decline from, the Republic, at least insofar as the Republic
must already have fallen in virtue to permit the establishment of the
Empire. Voltaire's proposal of the period as a peak of civilization
required development and correction. Gibbon's own subject, as Ian
White has valuably pointed out, is not the peaks, but the valleys
between—"chronic history."[56] A valley is defined as such, however,
by the existence of peaks. The age of the Antonines really did offer
a fair prospect,[57] especially from the perspective of Roman citizens,
even though it was built on ruins, and subject to ruin.

To emphasize the contrast and maintain the Roman perspective,
Gibbon sometimes relegates the clues to ruin to the footnotes. But
the impulse that lay behind the whole history is expressed in the text
as well: "On that celebrated ground [the seven hills of Rome and their
environs] the first consuls deserved triumphs, their successors adorned
villas, and *their* posterity have erected convents" (*DF* chap. 1, 1:23,
with n. 81 [76]). It has been claimed that in "these first three chapters
we find most of what is essential in Gibbon."[58] This claim is much
too strong. But it is true that everything in these three chapters is
essential to Gibbon's theme and that they require a careful, precise
reading, appreciative of the ironic perspective and elegiac tone, to be
fully understood. Gibbon's introduction could hardly foreshadow all
that he was to learn and conclude about his subject in the next
fourteen years, and it was the section he was most interested in
revising after the history was completed. Nevertheless, it remained
remarkably satisfactory as a preparation for the remaining sixty-eight
chapters.

The literary advantages of Gibbon's introduction require little discussion. The three chapters provide one side of the strong static frame
with which he surrounds the narrative proper, a frame tentatively
completed with the static chapters 15 and 16 in the first volume, and
finally completed with the three chapters on the ruins of the city that
close the whole history (69–71). They are essential to the establishment of the complex response he desires in his reader: on the one
hand, the appreciation of magnificence, the recognition of human
ability and achievement, the greatness irretrievably lost; on the other,
the cost of that magnificence, the limitation of that ability, the
building made possible by the ruin. After these three chapters, readers have two necessary points of reference before them: the greatness
achieved by absolute power and a unified world, with its vulnerability;
and the greatness open to shared power and a free world, with its
greater vulnerability.

The first three chapters of the *Decline and Fall*, exclusive of notes,

are about 30,000 words long, and we may estimate that he wrote about
70,000 words to bring them to their present state (*Memoirs* 155–56).
On a good day, he could write three folio pages—about 1,500 words
(*Letters* 2:19). These chapters represent, then, at least forty-five writing days, and probably much more. Of course he would not have
written continuously. Each chapter represents much thought and rereading, as well as a composition process that included the formation
of whole paragraphs in the mind before putting pen to paper (*Memoirs*
159). As we have seen, Gibbon was experiencing both pleasant and
unpleasant distractions as he wrote. Nevertheless, it seems possible
that he would have had time to compose and recompose the three
chapters and even to add their notes before departing for Bath and
Cornwall on August 16.

We know that he "always closed his studies with the day, and
commonly with the morning" (*Memoirs* 179), bearing in mind, of
course, that in eighteenth-century parlance, the morning ended at
dinner time, and not necessarily at noon. This habit was already
established when he lived in Bentinck Street, and it was not only
during Deyverdun's visit that he combined study with society. Indeed,
it was during the summer of 1773 that he became a friend of Sir
Joshua Reynolds and Oliver Goldsmith and improved his acquaintance
with David Garrick and George Colman into friendship. In a letter of
August 7, he remarks that his clubs, "Boodles and Atwoods[,] are no
more," and he almost gloats over the "delicious solitude" he is enjoying: "My Library, Kensington Gardens, and a few parties with new
acquaintance who are chained to London, (and among whom I reckon
Goldsmith, and Sir Joshua Reynolds,) fill up my time" (*Letters* 1:373).
Before the *beau monde* left London for the summer, Gibbon had been
in the habit of giving "the prettiest little dinners in the world" (*Letters*
1:373). But even when he dined alone, he would, during the good
weather, "walk till dark in *my* Gardens at Kensington" before returning home for supper and bed (*Letters* 1:375). With what satisfaction
he departed for Cornwall—his father's financial disasters apparently
settled, his acquaintance in London increasing, and most of all, his
book well begun—we can readily imagine.

It is not likely that the book advanced during the period he spent
with his cousins at Port Eliot in Cornwall (which lasted at least to the
end of September and was quickly succeeded by other visits, so that
he did not return to London until October 17). But his certainty that
writing the history was his true work is obvious from two pieces of
evidence. First, when asked to edit Lord Chesterfield's letters for
publication, he declined, as we can hardly imagine his doing in the
difficult years between his return from Italy and his father's death. (It
is true that he was influenced, at least in part, by a fear that the
family's opposition to the project and his friendship with Deyverdun

would make the latter's position difficult if he accepted the task—
Letters 1:377–78.) Second, he alludes in a letter to Holroyd to "the
prosecution of my great Work," in an obvious tone of confidence
(*Letters* 1:377). This is the first extant reference to the history. His
mentioning it in a letter—his letters to Holroyd were usually shared
with all the other adults at Sheffield Place—suggests that he was no
longer concerned to keep the project entirely secret.

While at Port Eliot, which had no library, Gibbon explored other
interests. He was hoping that his cousin would offer him a seat in
Parliament, though he was convinced by the end of the visit that
Eliot had no such intention. And he enjoyed, in his own way, the
natural beauties of the place. He renewed his acquaintance with his
cousins, especially the children. Still, he cannot have been sorry when
the six weeks ended and he could escort his stepmother back to Bath,
take an excursion to visit the Guises and the bishop of Llandaff (Shute
Barrington), and return to London. On Sunday, October 24, however,
he was off again—this time to the Holroyds at Sheffield Place. His
visit there lasted until early December. His stepmother's hopes were
aroused by news she received from there: "The intelligence you received of fair Eyes, bleeding hearts, and an approaching Daughter in
law, is all a very agreable Romance," he wrote. "A pair of very
tolerable Eyes [those of Elizabeth Fuller] I must confess made their
appearance at Sheffield, and what is more extraordinary were accompanied by good sense and good humour, without one grain of affectation. Yet still I am *indifferent*, and she is *poor*" (*Letters* 1:380). So
much for romance. Yet even this response suggests what will later be
more apparent: with his father's financial problems nearly settled
(however Draconian the method), Gibbon was no longer certain that
he did not wish to marry. Even Miss Fuller had not been ruled out: a
number of allusions to her (under the name of "Sappho") appear in
subsequent letters; she did not marry until 1781.

The first year of Gibbon's life as the historian of the Roman Empire
was drawing to a close. In retrospect, and at the time, it was one of
the happiest of his life. Not only had he achieved the way of life he
had long desired, in which study and society were comfortably combined, but he was succeeding in both. He knew that the work he was
producing was the best of his life. As for society, he was enjoying the
company of all his best male friends, both Swiss and English, and the
approbation and affection of several surrogate mothers and sisters.
His financial worries were apparently all but over. Without the pain
of restless ambition, he could look forward to still fairer prospects.

TWO

Finding a Voice

ibbon took only a few holidays between his return to London in December 1773, and September 1775. Apart from two weeks in Bath, five at Sheffield Place during the summer of 1774, and a total of no more than three weeks devoted to short expeditions to visit various friends, he seems to have been in London almost continuously for twenty-one months. This is the gestation period of an elephant, and of the remaining portions of the first volume of the *Decline and Fall*—not, perhaps, an unduly slow schedule. Yet he could remark, in September 1774, "I have not by many degrees been so diligent as I intended" (*Letters* 2:30). If the demands of study were satisfying and powerful, the demands of society were equally so. In study, he had found his style, his role as narrator, his voice. In society, he was still relatively silent—an observer, not a participant. But as his confidence that he had found a place in the social world grew, so did his distractions from his vocation as historian.

His first extant letter of 1774 is written, typically, from one of his clubs—though Gibbon remained "clubbable" throughout his life, there are perhaps more references to his activities at various clubs and coffee houses during this period than at any other period of his life. Whist, a favorite amusement in Lausanne, was one of the attractions, but there were others. While Parliament sat (mid January to late May, except for an Easter recess; mid November to Christmas),[1] Gibbon was restless when nothing of interest was going on there ("our Committee of the Catch Club has done more business this morning than

22

all those of the house of Commons since their last meeting"—*Letters*
2:1). Not a Member, he frequented the Visitors' Gallery of that
"school of civil prudence" (*Memoirs* 156). Contemporary politics might
be useful to the historian of the ancient world, but other new activities
had no such rationalization. New acquaintances in the world of theatre, art, and literature were increasing. We hear of dinners with
Garrick, Colman, and Goldsmith, and, in an episode that reminds
one of young Boswell's efforts to hiss down David Mallet's *Elvira*,[2]
Gibbon and his friends went in a body to insure a good reception for
Colman's *Man of Business* at its first performance on January 29 at
Covent Garden. But Gibbon's focus is very different from Boswell's;
Gibbon gives an account not of the actions, persons, and setting of
the episode, but of the "cause" they were supporting: "Between
friends, though we got a Verdict for our Client, his Cause was but a
bad one. It is a very confused Miscellany of several Plays and Tales,
sets out brilliantly enough, but as we advance the Plot grows thicker
the Wit, thinner, till the lucky fall of the Curtain preserves us from
total Chaos" (*Letters* 2:2). In other words, his response to his own
experience is analytical, not narrative.

The most gratifying possible result of these new friendships, however, was at first denied to Gibbon. In March, Goldsmith proposed
him for membership in the famous Literary Club.[3] He was black-
balled—we do not know by whom (but not by Boswell, who was not
in London). This setback does not seem to have discouraged Gibbon—perhaps he did not know he had been proposed—and it was
only temporary. We do not know exactly when he became a member
of the Club, but the delay was little more than a year at most, for
Gibbon was present at the meeting of April 7, 1775,[4] the first for
which records of attendance exist. Goldsmith—D. M. Low suggests
that their friendship may have rested on a common interest in fine
clothes—was probably not his sponsor, for Goldsmith died only a
month after the meeting at which Gibbon was defeated. But Gibbon
now had other friends among the club members, especially Sir Joshua
Reynolds, whom he visited frequently.

Other new groups were more immediately hospitable. On March 8
Gibbon was admitted to the degree of Master Mason in the Lodge of
Friendship No. 3.[5] Though he signals this election only by a Masonic
joke—"administration keep their Secret as well as that of Free Ma-
sonry, and as Coxe profanely suggests, for the same reason" (i.e.,
nothing to reveal—*Letters* 2:7)—Gibbon was pleased enough with this
new source of fellowship to continue his membership for many years,
even after he returned to Lausanne to live.[6]

Other old friends, and family affection, continued to occupy his
time as well. He dined frequently with his Aunt Kitty, now retired as
a landlady for Westminster students and "grow[ing] younger every

day" (*Letters* 2:22). In February he and Kitty made plans for an Easter expedition to Bath to visit Mrs. Gibbon. "Mrs. P[orten] . . . looks forward to Easter," Gibbon wrote to the latter, "as the Jews to their Messiah. I flatter myself that her hopes will be better founded" (*Letters* 2:5). He also saw frequently his uncle Sir Stanier Porten, the Fullers, including "Sappho," and his old friends of the Romans and Boodles.

But some of his distractions were disturbing. The "horse jockey" Lovegrove (*Letters* 2:1), far from paying for Lenborough earlier than his promised date of November, had still failed to reach agreement with Gibbon on various peripheral issues of the sale. More—each time Gibbon agreed to a proposal of Lovegrove's, Lovegrove reneged and made a different proposal. Or so at least Gibbon perceived the matter. The difficulty was that the only way to force Lovegrove to comply with his agreement was to take the case to Chancery, and Gibbon, with a proto-Dickensian dread of that court, sought to avoid it by almost any means. Buriton, too, presented certain difficulties, as the tenant pressed for repairs that were not necessarily a part of the lease. Holroyd, of course, advised and supported Gibbon in all these estate difficulties. Of a meeting planned between himself, Lovegrove, and their attorneys, Gibbon wrote to Holroyd, "Your presence . . . would be received as the descent of a Guardian Angel" (*Letters* 2:7). Generally speaking, that angel descended whenever requested to do so, but in this case, the meeting did not occur. Two months later, Gibbon was more desperate, and at last began to perceive the truth about his supposedly settled financial problem: "For God's sake, send me Advice," he wrote to Holroyd. "I seem to be in a much worse situation than before I agreed with him" (*Letters* 2:17).

By mid March 1774, there was a new topic for concern, though it is clear that Gibbon was not yet much exercised by it. That topic was America. Both Holroyd and Godfrey Bagnell Clarke, Gibbon's closest English friends and most trusted advisers, were apparently ardent Tories on the American question. "The mildness of Clarke is rouzed into military Fury [by Gage's reports from New England]; but he is an old Tory, and you are a Native of the Bog [Irish]. I alone am an Englishman, a Philosopher, and a Whig," says Gibbon. This comment concludes a letter that, despite Holroyd's interest, contains no news about America: "You may suppose that nothing very important can have occurred since you left Town: But I will send you some account [of] America after Monday, though indeed my anxiety about an old Manor takes away much of my attention from a New Continent" (*Letters* 2:6). The same tone continues until Gibbon himself is given reason to feel responsibility for the public weal, as we shall see. In 1774, in any case, the gravity of the American situation was by no means clear to everyone. "American business is suspended and almost forgot," Gibbon wrote to Holroyd in mid April. "The other day we had a brisk report of a Spanish War. It was said they had taken one of the Leeward islands. It since [tur]ns out that we are the Invaders, but the invasion [is] trifling." Besides, there was "great news from India" (*Letters* 2:13, 10). Despite this complacency about American calm, Gibbon was aware, apropos of Lenborough, that "a dead Calm [is] sometimes more fatal than a storm" (*Letters* 2:17).

The most distressing distraction, however, affected Gibbon neither politically nor financially, but as a friend. Near the end of March, he and his friend Godfrey Clarke enjoyed a pleasant dinner with the latter's father, who "goodnaturedly" joined the young men "at a Tavern, a thing he had not done for many years before." Two days later, the elder Clarke, though "a thin little Man, as abstemious as a hermit," was "destroyed by a stroke of apoplexy" as he stepped into his coach to go out to dinner (*Letters* 2:10). He was only sixty-one, and Gibbon's friend, unlike Gibbon himself, had enjoyed his father's friendship and confidence. A feeling stronger even than the love of letters preoccupied Gibbon for several weeks, and it is only when Clarke seems somewhat to have recovered that Gibbon resumes his cheerful tone. He is touchingly pleased that he is the friend whose company means most to Clarke; if there is vanity in his assumption of the role of comforter, there is also sincerity, signaled clearly by his sacrifice not only of society but even of study to Clarke's needs, and by his writing to Clarke, when they were separated during the first weeks of Clarke's bereavement, "almost every post." With his usual touch of self-mockery, Gibbon wrote to his stepmother, "The pleasure of being of service to an afflicted friend, may make *even* the Country agreable" (*Letters* 2:15).

The city was unusually hard to leave, not only because of the demands of the Roman Empire, but because Deyverdun had arrived in it for a brief stay. Deyverdun had "been forced to quit" his position as tutor-companion to the young Lord Chesterfield "by the little Peer's strange behaviour" (nature unspecified). But he had a new charge, Lord Middleton, with whom he was scheduled to go abroad in May. "It's an unworthy office for him," Gibbon wrote, "but Lord M appears a very tame bear, and if we can fix a quiet annuity, he may after this Tour enjoy ease and independence for the rest of his life" (*Letters* 2:12). On April 13 Clarke left town. A week later, Gibbon's apology to Sheffield for not writing included not only "the aversion to Epistolary Conversation, which it has pleased the Daemon to implant in my nature," but the demands of being "a very fine Gentleman, a Subscriber to [a] Masquerade," who is "now writing at Boodle's in a fine Velvet Coat with ruffles of My Lady's chusing," and also "a Historian: and in truth when I am writing a page, I not only think it a sufficient reason of delay, but even consider myself as writing to you" (*Letters* 2:14).

If his comments to his correspondents are proportionate to his interest, the philosophical historian seems to have felt a very considerable interest in an empty spectacle, the Boodle's masquerade at the Pantheon. "We have a great deal of Money and consequently of taste," he told Dorothea Gibbon. "Flying Bridges, transparent temples and eighteen thousand Lamps in the Dome are the general subject of conversation." It is true that he adds, "For my own part I subscribe but am very indifferent" (*Letters* 2:15–16). Yet he not only attended, but took his aunt with him (*Letters* 2:17), and stayed at the Pantheon until five in the morning. To Holroyd, Gibbon wrote of "the Triumph of Boodles. Our Masquerade cost two thousand Guineas, and a sum that might have fertilized a Province, (I speak in your own style) vanished in a few hours; but not without leaving behind it the fame of the most splendid and elegant Fête, that was perhaps ever given in a seat of the Arts and Opulence" (*Letters* 2:16).

Despite the masquerade and the demands of friendship, Gibbon continued to function as historian. On the day after the masquerade, it is true, he slept until ten, "took a good Walk, and returned home to a more rational entertainment," the visit of three friends for dinner. Other days were also lost. But on good days, such as May 24, he "wrote three folio pages" before dinner (*Letters* 2:19). Though we cannot know which pages they were, we may assume that he was making significant progress on the central chapters of the first volume, in which, after he had solved the problems of style and structure necessary to complete the first three chapters, he "advanced with a more equal and easy pace" (*Memoirs* 156).

Chapters 4–7 of the *Decline and Fall* describe the period between the death of Marcus Antoninus (A.D. 180) and the celebration of the secular games (248) by Philip as a wavelike sequence of apparently hopeless degradation of the Empire and apparently recovered prosperity. This period includes at least three emperors of whom posterity has sometimes thought better than Gibbon does: Septimius Severus, Severus Alexander, and Maximinus I. But throughout, Gibbon seeks to show that, despite apparently crucial distinctions among the qualities of the various emperors, distinctions, moreover, which he carefully analyzes and memorably dramatizes, the reality is that the Roman Empire was becoming constantly less Roman and constantly more subject not just to the whims of an individual, but to the whims of an individual selected by mercenary soldiers. Good emperors and bad, strong emperors and weak, contribute to this pattern. In these chapters Gibbon makes many generalizations about what we would call sociology and political science, usually, though not always, as a part of the introduction or conclusion of a chapter or section. His continued inspiration by, and even reliance on, Montesquieu, is apparent in this interest in history as a source of generalizations about social orders and organizations. But his appraisals of the characters, his appreciation of the crucial scenes and lines of action, and his acceptance of even bad evidence when it is the only evidence, using it to vivify the narrative even when it is necessary to qualify or retract it in the notes, places him also in the classical narrative tradition.

The organization of these four chapters emphasizes the similarities among the events they are concerned with. Narrative chapters, they are organized around characters, that is, they begin with an expository introduction (except for chapter 4, which follows three chapters of exposition) and then provide a "character" of the next emperor or candidates for emperor, a narrative of the events of his succession and reign, a character of his rival or an analysis of his own errors of character and policy, often with further expository sententiae, a narrative of his death, and a concluding evaluative commentary.[7] Some chapters include several such units, with the effect of increasing the pace of the narrative: the hapless empire seems to change hands with febrile rapidity. In these chapters, the "useful prejudices" that make the Empire a society begin to dissolve, and its disintegration consequently accelerates.[8]

In sixty-eight years of decline, there are fifteen emperors. Marcus Antoninus's unworthy heir, Commodus, is followed by the senate's excellent choice, Pertinax, whose murder by the Praetorian guards is followed immediately by the auction of the Empire to the highest bidder, Julian. After his death, Julian's dear-bought prize is contended for by three able generals, and civil war seems to be the destiny of the Empire, but Septimius Severus easily overcomes his rivals. His reign brings peace and strength to the Roman domain, but at a cost to present freedom and future security. As in the age of the Antonines, however, Septimius Severus's contemporaries are unaware of the "secret poison," and though his sons contend with each other, Caracalla, the victor, retains the loyalty of the troops. Gibbon takes a wholly negative view of Caracalla; for the first time, the Romans' "peculiar felicity . . . that the virtue of the emperors was active, and their vice indolent" fails (DF chap. 6, 1:148). Gibbon's reluctance to praise a successful military dictator, and his distinction between passively and actively destructive emperors, illustrate the humanistic and moralistic arguments of the early volume of the history,[9] yet these views are compatible with, even preparation for, the more original and complex analysis of the whole issue of heroism that, as we shall see, is a theme of his last three volumes. Gibbon has already discovered one of the devices by which he simultaneously maintains suspense, accuracy, and a sense of impending doom: constantly to point out to the reader depths or disasters experienced by the Romans "for the first time." Thus, advantages of which we, like the Romans, have hardly been aware are perceived at the very moment when they have been lost.

Both the literary pleasure of variety and the historical theme of the limited power of individual emperors require that the differences between Caracalla and his successors, and among those successors, be made clear to the reader, yet readers must also see those differences as powerless to effect real change in the direction of the Empire. Caracalla's first successor is Macrinus, one of the Praetorian prefects, who is soon rejected by both army and senate. After his death, two cousins of Caracalla's, children of his mother's sister's daughters, succeed in turn, Elagabalus and Alexander Severus. Elagabalus is an effete monster; Alexander succeeds as a youth of seventeen, dominated by his mother, Mamaea. Alexander's reign lasted thirteen years, a relatively long period, and was "represented in the *Historia Augusta* as a resuscitation of senatorial power."[10] Gibbon saw the resuscitation as an illusion and the reign as a welcome but ultimately meaningless respite in the collapse of the Empire into anarchy. Rhetorically, Gibbon still seems at times to write in the humanistic tradition in which individual heroes and villains control history. Of Alexander he comments: "The pride and avarice of his mother cast a shade on the glories of his reign; and by exacting from his riper years the same dutiful obedience which she had justly claimed from his unexperienced youth, Mamaea exposed to public ridicule both her son's character and her own" (*DF* chap. 6, 1:171). Nevertheless, the sixth chapter can end, like the third, with a portrayal of the "general happiness of the Roman world." It is easy to see why Gibbon hesitated in choosing the point at which to begin his history. It is also easy to see why he preferred, for the contrast with collapsing Roman power and culture, the age of Nerva, Trajan, and the Antonines, over this doubtful respite during the reign of a woman and an unheroic youth. "The personal characters of the emperors . . . can interest us no further than as they are connected with the . . . Decline and Fall of the monarchy" (*DF* chap. 6, 1:171). Yet such qualities as their personal avarice affect all their subjects as economic beings and may poison even a "generous" action like extending citizenship to all free men.[11]

Throughout these chapters, whatever the temporary successes and virtues of a particular emperor, Gibbon's analyses of army, finances, and the fatal dependence of the constitution on the character of the ruler continue to provide the "philosophic observer"—narrator or reader—with a double perspective on the Roman world. Thus, after several illustrations of the disadvantages of hereditary monarchy, the unworthy sons of worthy fathers, Gibbon begins the seventh chapter by noticing the opposite danger, the placing of the power of election de facto in the hands of the army. Chapter 7 is devoted to showing that in the Roman world, in which the "daring hopes of ambition were set loose from the salutary restraints of law and prejudice," the "meanest of mankind might . . . [be] raised by valour and fortune to a rank in the army, in which a single crime would enable him to" obtain the throne (*DF* 1:182–83). This is Gibbon's introduction to the five-year reign of the first barbarian emperor, the giant Maximin, or Maximinus I. J. B. Bury (n. 11) finds Gibbon too harsh in his judgment of Maximin, but today's conventional judgment, as represented by the *Oxford Classical Dictionary*, could as well support Gibbon's view, that his virtues were only those of a great soldier. For Gibbon, the issue is the same as it would have been for the senators: a peasant, a Thracian, a man elevated even in the army principally because of his great physical strength, did not belong on the throne of the Empire.

The career of Maximin also illustrates, in Gibbon's view, the continuing and fatal indulgence displayed by the emperors toward the soldiers. When Maximin confiscates the independent revenues of the cities for the imperial treasury, Gibbon sees this as the result of his "avarice, stimulated by the insatiate desires of the soldiers." Bury complains that Gibbon is unfair here: "One can feel little indignation that the amusements of the populace should have been postponed for the defence of the empire. Gibbon hardly seems to realize that Maximin's warfare was serious" (*DF* chap. 7, 1:88, with n. 18). This debate between domestic and military demands on the public treasury sounds strangely familiar, and we may note, as Bury does not, that Gibbon regards the money as required not for legitimate, but for *insatiate*, demands by the army. Nevertheless, it is clear that here, as in the case of Severus, Gibbon is concerned to show that a powerful emperor and restoration of military virtues—especially temporarily—does not mean that the decline of the Empire has ceased—even temporarily. Only those who attempt to preserve or restore the *idea* of Rome gain credit with Gibbon for delaying its fall. For him the heroic gestures of the reign occur in the Senate. And they are feeble. They begin with the selection of the Gordians as senatorial emperors in opposition to the "barbarous Maximin" (*DF* chap. 7, 1:190), now declared a mere usurper.

Gordian I, proconsul of Africa and of senatorial rank, was a scholar and consul, who was "above fourscore years old" when he "reluctantly accepted the purple"—"a last and valuable remains of the happy age of the Antonines, whose virtues he revived in his own conduct, and celebrated in a elegant poem of thirty books." His son, proclaimed emperor with him, also demonstrated both social and studious virtues: "Twenty-two acknowledged concubines, and a library of sixty-two thousand volumes, attested the variety of his inclinations; and

from the productions which he left behind him, it appears that both
. . . were designed for use rather than for ostentation" (*DF* 1:190–91).
To these senatorial emperors, Rome and Italy rallied. "A new spirit
had arisen. . . . The senate assumed the reins of government, and,
with a calm intrepidity, prepared to vindicate by arms the cause of
freedom" (*DF* 1:193). It was as well that it had, for "while the cause
of the Gordians was embraced with such diffusive ardour, the Gordians themselves were no more" (*DF* 1:194). In this emergency, the
senate proclaimed two new emperors from its own ranks, and when
the people were restive, added a caesar, the thirteen-year-old grand-
son of Gordianus I. This coalition succeeded in inspiring the murder
of Maximin by his despairing troops, but the two new emperors,
Balbinus and Maximus, were murdered by the Praetorian guards, and
the thirteen-year-old caesar, who then became the emperor Gordian
III, died at nineteen. Moreover, the reign of Gordian III necessarily
represents the qualities, not of his own character, but of his advisers,
among whom the Praetorian prefects were most important. The second of these was Philip, "an Arab by birth, and consequently, in the
earlier part of his life, a robber by profession." Philip assassinated and
supplanted the last of the Gordians, thus ending the brief resurgence
of senatorial influence.

   Earlier (*DF* chap. 5, 1:129–30), Gibbon had cited with total approval and agreement Montesquieu's analysis of the distinction between Roman civil wars and those of modern Europe, that is, that
the Romans contended only for a change of masters and not for a
cause they felt to be their own. Gibbon does not recur to that point
with reference to the Gordians' cause surviving them, though this
might seem to be the exception that tests Montesquieu's rule. Instead,
Gibbon inserts "the ingenious, though somewhat fanciful, description, which a celebrated writer of our own times [Montesquieu] has
traced of the military government of the Roman empire" (*DF* 1:207).[12]
To this description Gibbon appends three notes that suggest, first,
that Montesquieu's description of the government of Algiers as an
aristocracy is inaccurate—"Every military government floats between
the extremes of absolute monarchy and wild democracy"; second, that
a better analogy for the military government of the Roman Empire is
available ("the military republic of the Mamelukes in Egypt"); and
third, that the *Historia Augusta* is self-contradictory, and therefore
patently false, in the account on which Montesquieu relies. The last
point is typical of Gibbon's objection to the factual inaccuracy or
indifference of all the philosophes, whether of the line of Montesquieu or of that of Voltaire. But the first two, the classification of the
form of government and the choice of historical analogy for it, suggest
that his views of history have begun to distinguish themselves more
clearly from those of Montesquieu, not by rejecting that great prede-

cessor's kind of thinking, but by extending or correcting it, sometimes by Montesquieu's own views as expressed in the *Esprit des lois*.

Chapter 7 ends with another retrospective survey of the Empire, as Philip's celebration of the secular games at Rome commemorates the millennium of the founding of the city. "The magnificence of Philip's shows and entertainments dazzled the eyes of the multitude. The devout were employed in the rites of superstition, whilst the reflecting few revolved in their anxious minds the past history and the future fate of the empire" (*DF* 1:209). Gibbon, taking with him the reader, is among the reflecting few. In the first four centuries, the Romans acquired "the virtues of war and government"; in the next three, with the assistance of fortune, they applied those virtues to obtain "an absolute empire over many countries of Europe, Asia, and Africa." But the last three hundred years "has been consumed in apparent prosperity and internal decline. The nation of soldiers, magistrates, and legislators, who composed the thirty-five tribes of the Roman people, was dissolved into the common mass of mankind," indistinguishable from those who had "received the name, without adopting the spirit, of Romans." The only free men were the members of the mercenary army, and by their "tumultuary election, a Syrian, a Goth, or an Arab was . . . invested with despotic power over the . . . country of the Scipios." Yet "to the undiscerning eye," Philip's power seemed as great as that of any of his predecessors. "The form was still the same, but the animating health and vigour were fled," and the barbarians would soon discover that the Empire had declined (*DF* chap. 7, 1:209–10).

Three things should be noted about Gibbon's summary: the Christians are not mentioned; the barbarians discover, rather than create, the Roman decline; and it is the spirit, not the size, of Rome that appears to be at fault, particularly its surrender of Roman citizenship and identity to the "common mass of mankind" and of the power of election to the mercenaries. Not clear here is the role of individual, or even collective, character: what moral flaws or political errors were inescapable, and which were culpable? For the moment, Gibbon sets such questions aside. What he has not set aside is a sense of the significance of economic pressure on historical events, a point he may have been particularly conscious of because of the current American complaints about taxation.[13] He chooses the end of the reign (chapter 6) of the least bad of these fifteen princes (in his view), Alexander Severus, to survey the "finances of [Rome], from the victorious ages of the commonwealth to the reign of Alexander Severus." Unfortunately, economic information is hard to come by, says Gibbon, betraying his reliance on literary sources: "History has never perhaps suffered a greater or more irreparable injury than in the loss of that curious register bequeathed by Augustus to the senate, in which that experienced prince so accurately balanced the revenues and expenses of the Roman empire. . . . We are reduced to collect a few imperfect hints from such of the ancients as have accidentally turned aside from the splendid to the more useful parts of history" (*DF* chap. 6, 1:173). But Gibbon is perfectly capable of transcending this limitation. He combines ancient history and geography (Tacitus and Strabo) with a modern traveller's account to make a convincing inference that the taxes collected by Rome from its subject states amounted to a major portion of their revenue:

> Augustus once received a petition from the inhabitants of Gyarus, humbly praying that they might be relieved from one third of their excessive impositions. Their whole tax mounted indeed to no more than one hundred and fifty drachms, or about five pounds; but Gyarus was a little island, or rather a rock, of the Aegean Sea, destitute of fresh water and every necessary of life, and inhabited only by a few wretched fishermen. (*DF* chap. 6, 1:174)

Gibbon's notion of economic history is not yet informed by the reading of his friend Adam Smith, but he uses his own talent for perceiving connections among disparate materials, and the common sense or intuition he so often substitutes for theorizing, to come to a preliminary understanding of the importance of economic factors in political history. A recurrent theme in these early chapters is the pressure on the emperors (or emperor-candidates) to buy the affections and support of the mercenary soldiers and the consequent discouragement to two classes Gibbon much preferred, landowners and tradesmen. This "digression" on the finances of the Empire is the only major departure from chronology in chapters 4 through 7 of the history.

By the end of May, Gibbon had probably completed these seven chapters. As he turned to survey Rome's enemies, in chapters 8 and 9, he was interrupted by a surprising visitor, his pious Aunt Hester, the devoted follower of William Law and, in the family tradition, the successful rival of Gibbon's father for his grandfather's affection and fortune (*Memoirs* 20).[14] Hester Gibbon, Lord of the Manor of Newhaven, patroness of two schools, and a woman of independent means as well as strong religious conviction, was too important to ignore or offend, but hardly a congenial figure either to Gibbon or to his stepmother.[15] Gibbon obviously expected Dorothea to enjoy his slightly catty "tale of Wonders." In his letter he makes a story of it— his surprise at learning that Dorothea had arrived in London unannounced—naturally he assumed that "Mrs. Gibbon" was Dorothea— his indignation that his stepmother was not staying at his house, his discovery of the true identity of this Mrs. Gibbon:

> I immediately went to Surry Street where she lodged, but though it was no more than half an hour after nine, the Saint had finished her Evening

Devotions and was already retired to rest. Yesterday morning (by appointment) I breakfasted with her at eight o'Clock, dined with her to-day at
two [that is, unfashionably early] in Newman Street [at Catherine Porten's
house], and am just returned from setting down. She is in truth a very
great curiosity; her dress and figure exceed every thing we had at the
Masquerade. Her language and ideas belong to the last Century. However
in point of Religion she was rational that is silent. (*Letters* 2:17)

This visit amounted to a reconciliation, or at least to a new stage in
the relationship between nephew and aunt, more than three years
after her brother's death. Hereafter she remained in touch with Gibbon, seeking his advice and support (or rather, Holroyd's through
him), especially with respect to her Sussex estate.

After this brief interlude of familial attention, Gibbon seems to
have devoted himself during June to the *Decline and Fall*, almost
without other business. Two very brief notes to Holroyd and a letter
to Dorothea Gibbon at the end of the month are the sole signs of life
from "one Edward Gibbon a Housekeeper in Bentinck Street," as he
apologetically admits to his stepmother. A visit from Edward Eliot
and Eliot's sister Mrs. Bonfoy, with a report that Mrs. Gibbon had
been unwell, roused him to write; as usual, his procrastination as a
correspondent did not apply to a letter necessary for the comfort of a
sick friend.[16] In the letter, he reports three other family engagements,
formed at the insistence of Catherine Porten: dinners on three con-
secutive Sundays given by Catherine, by Gibbon himself, and by Sir
Stanier Porten in honor of an old family friend and her new husband,
"an old Swiss Officer about seventy, a Man of family, but with as
little money as character who most probably married her for a fortune
which he now begins to discover was spent to his hands [that is,
before he touched it]. . . . The Baronne is more ridiculous, and will I
fear be more miserable than ever" (*Letters* 2:16–17).

Such an image of marriage might seem to encourage Gibbon's
notorious cynicism on the subject of women in the first portions of
the *Decline and Fall*,[17] but he was also watching a romance. His uncle
Stanier, now fifty-eight, had met at his sister's "a good agreable
Woman Miss Wybolt" (she was Gibbon's age—thirty-seven). "The
under Secretary is seriously in love with her, and seriously uneasy that
his precarious situation precludes him from happiness. We shall soon
see which will get the better Love or reason. I bet three to two on
love" (*Letters* 2:22). He would have won the bet; Sir Stanier and Miss
Wybault were married six months later. But of course neither the
comic nor the romantic match was uppermost in his mind; what he
was really thinking of, as he for the first time acknowledges to his
stepmother in this letter, was his writing, "which may perhaps produce
something next year either to tire or amuse the World," he tells her.

By this time he was probably more than half done with the first volume of the history. Chapters 8 and 9 are quite different from their predecessors; they suspend the action of the history and provide brilliant pictures of Rome's eastern and western enemies, the Germans and the Persians. To give these pictures their fullness and energy, Gibbon combines evidence from various periods, a methodological crime for which he has often been reproved by his successors.[18] But it is fair to notice that he acknowledges that the picture is a composite, and, further, to see that what he is representing is, as it were, a Platonic image of these nations—what they meant, over time, to the Romans, not the history of their national characters and constitutions. Despite the criticism, these chapters have been much applauded and certainly much enjoyed.

These two chapters heighten the suspense and drama of Rome's fate by characterizing her enemies, and they enrich the temporal, spatial, and sociological variety of the book. Effortlessly reaching back into the mythical past of the Persians and Babylonians, and forward to the cities and towns of modern Germany, the chapters provide for the reader that extraordinary sense of vastness, variety, and vivacity that gave the history the popularity of a novel or essay. But more particularly, they show that the author had already planned his history as an analysis of the relationship between ecclesiastical and political history, or of the sociology of religion; that he perceived a pattern in the history of empires that is related more to narrative than to scientific laws, and that his romantic spirit was by no means dead. They also illustrate his dawning, but not yet fully achieved, interest in the stages of society, which differs, as J. G. A. Pocock has shown (1981), from the theory of his contemporary Adam Ferguson, to which it is related. And they show, I think, that with gathering courage and success—with eight chapters complete—Gibbon was willing, and indeed able, to take on his admired master Tacitus at his own game.

The chapter on Persia may be seen as a miniature parallel of the history of Rome, from Romulus to Constantine, with two important reversals. The prehistory is disposed of in a few paragraphs, but it provides a context in which even the Roman Empire is a fleeting phenomenon. The principal emphasis is on historic times, specifically the dynasty of the Sassanids. The founder of this dynasty is one of the hero-figures who delay and vary the downward trajectory of civilization in the *Decline and Fall*. It is noticeable that already Gibbon is capable of praising virtue (as he sees it) wherever it is found, even in a "barbarian" or bishop. But Artaxerxes has a fatal flaw, in the account of which Gibbon both foreshadows the Christian history that concludes the first volume of the history and illustrates how narrative can examine the relationships among individual merit, "immoderate greatness," and social institutions that must be understood, in his view, in order to understand the fall of a state.

But if this account precisely anticipated Gibbon's as yet unwritten discussion of Christianity and Rome, the latter would be much less powerful. Instead, Gibbon inverts chronology in the order of his presentation and eschews irony. The account of Zoroastrianism precedes that of the secular events of Artaxerxes' reign, and in the transitional description of the Zend Avesta, Gibbon foreshadows his account of the Koran and hints at his opinion of all sacred books: "In that motley composition, dictated by reason and passion, by enthusiasm and by selfish motives, some useful and sublime truths were disgraced by a mixture of the most abject and dangerous superstition" (*DF* chap. 8, 1:218). Artaxerxes imposes monotheistic intolerance, encourages a large and greedy body of priests, and allows religion and the priesthood to influence secular policy. "The majesty of Ormusd [Zoroastrian deity], who was jealous of a rival, was seconded by the depotism of Artaxerxes, who could not suffer a rebel; and the schismatics within his vast empire were soon reduced to the inconsiderable number of eighty thousand" (*DF* 1:220). If we are inclined to overlook analogies to the other great religions Gibbon will treat, his notes prod us to think of them: "Notwithstanding all their . . . protestations . . . the Mahometans have constantly stigmatized [the Zoroastrians] as idolatrous worshippers of the fire" (*DF* chap. 8, 1:216, n. 18 [13]); "Both Hyde and Prideaux affect to apply to the Magian, the terms consecrated to the Christian hierarchy" (n. 22 [17]); "The divine institution of tithes exhibits a singular instance of conformity between the law of Zoroaster and that of Moses" (n. 24 [19]). But with all the inherent faults of an intolerant religion, including the massacre or terrorizing of the disaffected, "the religion of Zoroaster . . . was not productive of any civil commotion" and even served as a unifying force. It differed markedly from Christianity in its concern for this world:

> There are some remarkable instances in which Zoroaster lays aside the prophet, assumes the legislator, and discovers a liberal concern for private and public happiness, seldom to be found among the grovelling or visionary schemes of superstition. Fasting and celibacy . . . he condemns with abhorrence, as a criminal rejection of the best gifts of providence. The saint, in the Magian religion, is obliged to beget children, to plant useful trees, to destroy noxious animals, to convey water to the dry lands of Persia, and to work out his salvation by pursuing all the labours of agriculture. (*DF* 1:216)

Of course, Gibbon himself was as far from Magian as from Christian sainthood, but what is important to the reader of the *Decline and Fall* is the preparation for the indictment of Christian asceticism in chapter 15.

The reigns of the great Sassanids form an interval in the Persian annals comparable to the reigns of the five good emperors in the annals of Rome. Gibbon's concluding summary contrives both to convey the inevitability of their defeat and to present them as formidable opponents for Rome. They fail, he says, because their "designs were too extensive for the power of Persia, and served only to involve both nations in a long series of destructive wars and reciprocal calamities." The Persians—"long since civilized and corrupted"—lack both the hardiness and independence of the Germanic barbarians and the science of warfare that defended ancient Greece and Rome and defends modern Europe. But—a significant but, Gibbon leads us to believe, by beginning the concluding paragraph of the chapter with it—"the nobles of Persia, in the bosom of luxury and despotism, preserved a strong sense of personal gallantry and national honour." As with the contrast of the secular sainthood of the Magi and Christian asceticism, this is a direct reflection on Rome's loss of "useful prejudices" and citizen soldiers (*DF* chap. 8, 1:228–29).

The romantic conclusion of the Persian chapter is followed by a carefully matter-of-fact opening for the chapter on the Germans, in which Gibbon is very conscious of the need to compete with his master Tacitus.[19] Despite or because of the Tacitean model, however, this chapter is one of the most "sociological" in the first volume. In it Gibbon wrestles with the incompatibility of freedom and civilization, or rather, he acknowledges the advantages of barbarism for the former and tries to analyze why the barbarian way of life is nevertheless not to be preferred.

Gibbon first concedes that climate had some effect—difficult to determine and easy to exaggerate—on the German body and character, encouraging larger stature and "a kind of strength better adapted to violent exertions than to patient labour" (*DF* chap. 9, 1:233). Then he indulges himself and his reader with a retelling of Olaus Rudbeck's heroic romance of Germanic origins from the children of Noah. But when he moves from hypotheses, philosophical or romantic, to concrete information, he notes that the Germans lacked letters, iron, and money. Without the first, they could not have either a reliable history or the capacity to extend their experience beyond themselves. The "*illiterate* peasant . . . rooted to a single spot, and confined to a few years of existence, surpasses but little his fellow-labourer the ox in the exercise of his mental faculties" (*DF* 1:236).[20] "Money . . . is the most universal incitement, iron the most powerful instrument, of human industry; and it is very difficult to conceive by what means a people, neither actuated by the one nor seconded by the other, could emerge from the grossest barbarism" (*DF* 1:238). Savages, in Gibbon's view, are uninterested in social or technological change, and nomadic warriors, in particular, waste the resources of the earth: "The same extent of ground, which at present maintains, in ease and plenty, a million of husbandmen and artificers, was unable to supply an hun-

dred thousand lazy warriors with the simple necessaries of life" (*DF*
1:240). As Pocock points out in the article cited above, though Gibbon is influenced by Ferguson's four-stage view of cultural change, he
reduces the four virtually to two, by associating agriculture to the
mercantile, civilized economy and by equating hunters, shepherds,
and savages. In Gibbon's version of the theory, a farmer differs from
a merchant, a savage from a hunter-shepherd, but not nearly so much
as the two middle stages differ from one another. Gibbon has often
been criticized for continuing to use external barbarians as the typical
threat to civilization in an age when they no longer affected the
civilized world, but in recognizing nomadic barbarians as a continuing
danger, he may have had a crucial point.[21] According to Fernand
Braudel, they indirectly continued to threaten modern Europe: "The
'barbarians' who were a real danger to civilization belonged almost
entirely to one category of men: the nomads. . . . when a dispute
arose among these horse- and camel-men . . . or a drought or population increase drove them out from their pasturage, they invaded their
neighbours' lands. . . . The nomads . . . represent an exceptional case
of a long parasitical existence."[22]

Gibbon portrays the Germans, then, as a typical case of the rival
social order most dangerous to the two fundamentals of civilization,
agriculture and trade. But he does not portray them wholly negatively.
As Michel Baridon (1977a) has most fully and carefully discussed,
Gibbon's perspective as a "philosophe" is greatly enriched by his
recognition of the appeal of the "Gothic." The Germans, for example,
"found some compensation for this savage state in the enjoyment of
liberty. Their poverty secured their freedom, since our desires and
our possessions are the strongest fetters of despotism" (*DF* chap. 9,
1:241). After surveying their laws, which permitted their magistrates
to redistribute all the land in their districts annually but not to punish
malefactors with death, imprisonment, or even blows, Gibbon concludes that they must have been "destitute of industry and the arts,
but animated with a high sense of honour and independence" (*DF*
1:244).

Given their preparation for war by nature and culture, it seemed to
Gibbon to require explanation that the Germans so long failed to
affect the power of the Empire, and he devotes the concluding pages
of the chapter to showing that "their progress was checked by their
want of arms and discipline, and their fury was diverted by the
intestine divisions of ancient Germany" (*DF* chap. 9, 1:250). In passing, he makes a comment revelatory about his strategy in presenting
the history. In the introductory chapters, Gibbon had emphasized the
universal peace and the almost effortless power that characterized
the empire under the five good emperors. Hadrian and the elder
Antoninus experienced only "a few slight hostilities"; Marcus and his

generals "obtained many signal victories" (*DF* chap. 1, 1:9), dispatched in a single sentence. From the perspective of the Capitol, we
infer, Rome seemed comfortably invincible. But suddenly we learn
here in the ninth chapter that the "general conspiracy" of the Germans and Sarmatians during the reign of Marcus "terrified the Romans" (*DF* chap. 9, 1:253). There is no inconsistency—this was the
occasion of Marcus's victories—but to obtain a complete view, the
reader must respond first to one perspective, then to the other, and
finally to the simultaneous knowledge of both. As H. H. Milman
warns, "The estimate which we are to form, depends on the accurate
balance of statements in remote parts of the work; and we have
sometimes to correct and modify opinions, formed from one chapter
by those of another. Yet . . . the mind of the author has already
harmonized the whole result to truth and probability."[23] Although
Gibbon's narrative methods change and develop in the course of the
history, it is striking that this utilization of multiple, mutually chal-
lenging perspectives characterizes them almost from the first. It
permits him to give clear and powerful shape to his enormous subject.

The tenth chapter is summed up by its opening and closing sentences: "From the great secular games celebrated by Philip to the
death of the emperor Gallienus, there elapsed twenty years of shame
and misfortune" (*DF* chap. 10, 1:256). "We might suspect that war,
pestilence, and famine had consumed, in a few years, the moiety of
the human species" (*DF* chap. 10, 1:303). For Rome these twenty
years represent an uninterrupted sequence of defeat by strangers and
oppression by tyrants at home. But the chapter has sections with a
curiously cheerful effect, especially those on the Goths, proleptically
treated as the sovereigns of a civilized Italy. Such tonal effects support the view of those who see the *Decline and Fall* as having for
subtext, from the very beginning, the rise of modern Europe.[24] This
theme, already present in the second chapter's anticipation that "the
fierce giants of the north" would "mend" the Roman breed, restore
freedom, and with freedom, after ten centuries, "taste and science"
(*DF* 1:64), as the metaphors imply, is consistent with the portrayal of
decline because it proposes not a total replacement of one breed or
civilization with another, but a transformation—mending, restoration—of one society into another, with both gains and losses.[25]

Before Gibbon left for his July holiday at Sheffield Place, he had
probably completed ten chapters of his history. We may readily sur-
mise that he discussed not only his work so far but plans for the future
during his six weeks with the Holroyds in Sussex. His return to
London was precipitated by a crisis. "Sir Edmund's intelligence was
but too well founded," he reported to Holroyd (*Letters* 2:23); Godfrey
Clarke was seriously—as it proved, mortally—ill. For the next week
and a half Gibbon wrote to Holroyd of no other subject. Probably the

Roman Empire also suffered neglect, though Gibbon's habit of early
rising and ability to concentrate may have permitted him to continue
work. Much of his time was certainly spent either with Clarke or
with Clarke's family.

With the first message of hope about Clarke, it is true, Gibbon
betrays a lively interest in his own comfort ("If you have an Irish *cream
cheese* to spare, Bentinck street is ready to receive it"). But it is not
until Clarke's recovery is "perfect, may it be lasting," that Gibbon
devotes much attention to another subject, and then that subject is
his friend Holroyd's intention to seek election to Parliament, not from
a friendly borough, but from the county. Gibbon thinks the effort
unlikely to succeed, but if Holroyd decides to make the attempt,
Gibbon also has some suggestions as to how to pursue his candidacy.
It will be remembered that Gibbon was the veteran of several parliamentary campaigns, though he himself had been defeated in his only
previous effort to win a seat.[26] Cheese and Holroyd's parliamentary
ambitions figure largely in Gibbon's correspondence for the rest of the
month.

With September an epoch in Gibbon's life came to a climax.
Henceforth he would hold new responsibilities, familial, literary, and
political. About the first of the month, Edward Eliot visited him and
asked him to serve as guardian to his children and executor of his
will. This vote of confidence in his ability as a man of affairs and his
goodwill as a cousin pleased Gibbon, and he readily "consented to
accept an office which indeed I consider as an essential duty of social
life" (*Letters* 1:32). If he could not help remembering that Eliot controlled several seats in Parliament, he did not allow himself to dwell
on the memory. He returned contentedly enough to the Roman Empire. We can be fairly sure, in fact, that he progressed into the
eleventh chapter, in which the Roman arms are again successful,
because on September 9, he describes himself as "destroying an army
of barbarians." He had every incentive to do so, for a distinguished
publisher wished to publish his book. On September 6 he wrote to
Holroyd, "I have conversed with Cadell and find him ready and even
willing. He proposes next March (if I am prepared) and 750 Copies.
Deliberamus" (*Letters* 2:30). It was not Gibbon's first book, but it had
already been refused by his "timid friend Mr. Elmsley" (*Memoirs* 157),
who had published his *Observations on the Sixth Book of the Aeneid*, and
in any case Strahan and Cadell were a distinguished firm, who published Hume and were about to publish Adam Smith. Their willingness not only to publish this ambitious book by a virtually unknown,
though experienced, author, but to do so at their own risk and on
generous terms, must therefore have been a welcome vote of
confidence.

But Gibbon's satisfaction in this achievement, this opportunity to speak to the world at last in his own language and voice and at length, paled for the moment beside the next event of the month. *"Turn over* [the page]," he wrote to Holroyd on September 10. *"Great things await you."* Eliot had offered him an *independent* seat in Parliament. "You may suppose my answer, but my satisfaction was a little damped when he added that the expence of the election would amount to about £2400, & that he thought it reasonable that we should share it between us." This difficulty resolved—Eliot would pay all, and Gibbon would repay his share to Eliot's son John when John, then thirteen, came of age, or make John his heir—Gibbon was entirely delighted. "This is a fine prospect open[ing to] me and if, next spring I should take my seat and pub[lish] my book, it will be a very memorable Æra in my life" (*Letters* 2:32). As he wrote when he passed on the news to his stepmother, "After such intelligence I could add nothing but what would be flat and insipid" (*Letters* 2:34).

The two rival formulations of the ideal life in Gibbon's letters and memoirs are "study and society" and "study, society, and business." By "business" he does not mean caring for his estates and investments, but participating in the public life of his country. In his *Memoirs*, written after the completion of the history, he twice asserts that the writing of a great book should be regarded as a great action;[27] families should be prouder of their kinship to a great poet or novelist than of their kinship to a king or general. But Gibbon often betrays uneasiness with such heroes of contemplative life; in spite of himself, we might say, he admires the active heroes more. The reconciling type, the one that could clearly win the approval of a man like his father as well as a man like himself, is the author-statesman—Julius Caesar, Marcus Aurelius, Julian. Perhaps Gibbon himself was about to join this line.

THREE

Ominous Developments

or the remainder of September, Gibbon's prospects appeared totally unclouded, but clouds were gathering, for both the British and the Roman empires. In Gibbon's private life, an uncharacteristic euphoria was quickly to be replaced by problems and even loss. But at first none of this was apparent to the historian, who, it has been remarked, was no prophet.[1] He looked around at good news on all sides: his friend Clarke's health was "infinitely better"; his friend Holroyd's parliamentary schemes, though contrary to Gibbon's best judgment, were not untenable; the visit to Mrs. Gibbon in Bath, for which his stepmother was impatient (although it would "most wonderfully delay the fall of the Roman Empire"), would be a pleasant occasion shared with the Holroyds, who also had elderly relatives living in Bath; even his financial affairs were in a state of calm, and renewed meetings with Hester Gibbon, who had descended on London for another ten-day stay, boded well for the financial interests of her only Gibbon relative (*Letters* 2:34–35). Perhaps she, like the two old ladies who loved him, his faithful aunt Catherine Porten and his stepmother, was pleased by his parliamentary prospects. There is a hint, in a letter of Catherine to Dorothea, that the two had schemed affectionately to bring Eliot to offer the seat to Gibbon: "I take the first opportunity to rejoice with you upon the Prospect we have of our Friend making a figure in Parliament, I own I flatter my Self as I am sure you do," wrote Aunt Kitty. "Why it was not done sooner and several other things upon that Subject I defer till I have the Pleasure of seeing You."[2]

Gibbon could therefore afford to spend a weekend at Sheffield Place to discuss Holroyd's prospective campaign. Accordingly, he went to Sussex on Friday, September 30—and on that very day, Parliament was unexpectedly dissolved.[3] Gibbon would become a "senator" not in the spring, as he had anticipated, but almost immediately, in the general election.

In the country, however, he was not immediately aware of this turn of fortune. His friend Clarke sent a message to him that arrived on Saturday, October 1, but his sponsor, Edward Eliot, was unable to reach him and apparently complained about it to Mrs. Gibbon, the first intimation to Gibbon of the difficulties of being patronized, however benignly. In fact, Gibbon had not neglected to seek out Eliot. Though there was hardly time for Gibbon to get to Cornwall, and his presence there was far from necessary to his election, he wrote to his cousin offering "*to fly*" there. His affectionate stepmother was concerned lest he miss his opportunity. "If you will answer for Mr. Eliot's intentions I will answer for his power," Gibbon told her (*Letters* 2:35). He writes calmly, but he makes it clear that he cared deeply about the proposed seat. A touch of the long-suppressed romantic youth appears, indeed, in his declaration that "before his offer I could contentedly have borne my exclusion; but I could not now support the disappointment, and were it to happen, I would instantly and for ever leave this Kingdom" (*Letters* 2:36). And he admits to Holroyd that while he and Clarke are both expecting news of their election (Clarke for Derbyshire), Clarke does so "with much more Philosophy," that is, less excitement (*Letters* 2:36).

Fired by election fever, Holroyd decided to seek election for Sussex despite Gibbon's advice to go slowly, and Gibbon therefore changed his "cold counsels . . . into warm wishes" (*Letters* 2:37). Holroyd's candidacy was difficult in two important ways; he lacked the endorsement of the county meeting, and he had neither long residence nor strong ties in Sussex. Gibbon's opinion gives a clear view of his political position at this time, uninfluenced by hopes of sinecures or fears of revolution. In his opinion, Holroyd should seek the endorsement—and plan to abide by the determination—of the county meeting: "I am a great friend to County meetings. . . . They form a happy medium between the Junto's of Grandees in town, and the Mob-archy of the rout of freeholder[s], and preserve the peace of the County, without sacrificing it's independence" (*Letters* 2:34). Gibbon has often been accused of losing a youthful or lifelong liberalism under the pressure of the French Revolution, or worse, of sacrificing it for the benefits of a sinecure under Lord North's government. But the limits of his enthusiasm for democracy were marked long before he entered the political arena—they can be seen in his summary of Blackstone (1765) and even in his "Lettre sur le gouvernement de Berne" (1758 or 1763, probably the latter), the document most clearly showing the freedom-loving side of Gibbon's political views.[4] The remark in this 1774 letter shows again that Gibbon is a centrist, dreading "mobarchy" and condemning not only despotism, but the rule of "juntos of grandees"—small groups of very powerful persons. Some writers have enrolled the author of the *Decline and Fall* in the cause of revolution; others have seen him as admiring despotism, at least when it is benevolent; still others see the politics of the history as belied by the behavior of Gibbon the man.[5] These very contradictions, as well as a close examination of *all* the evidence, will convince most readers that Gibbon never was either a favorer of violent revolution or acquiescent in any form of "slavery," including, or especially, "the servile equality of despotism" (*Letters* 1:343).

Holroyd was more conservative politically than Gibbon, and when the county meeting endorsed two other candidates, he decided to stand anyway. By mid October, however, Holroyd had decided to give up his lost cause: Gibbon was helping him to compose a letter of withdrawal for the papers. Soon afterwards, Gibbon was elected M.P. for Liskeard, an event he announced to his friend with a certain pomposity intended as tact. But Gibbon found a much more supportive tone when writing of his friend's disappointment in later letters: "By this time I suppose your Election over and would bet two to one that Sir James has carried it; a lucky circumstance for you, he will fill the place, and some years hence when you have shaken off the *novus homo* you may assert the liberty of the East [that is, Holroyd's end of the county]" (*Letters* 2:39).

The *Decline and Fall* would have been in danger of neglect had Gibbon had no other distraction but the election. In fact, he had several others: Holroyd's wife, Abigail, the first and perhaps the dearest of Gibbon's honorary sisters, was ill, and Gibbon's letters not only to the Holroyds, but to Mrs. Gibbon, recur frequently to her health. He affectionately insisted that Holroyd bring her to stay in Bentinck Street for a few days at the end of October and suggested that they all—Aunt Kitty would travel with Gibbon in his chaise— then go to Bath. Meanwhile, Deyverdun had returned to London with Lord Middleton. In the event, Deyverdun, Aunt Kitty, and Gibbon started for Bath on November 9. "We mean to live with you and upon you, but as Mrs P is large and your house is small, I should think that if you procured us two bedchambers and a dining Room in the neighbourhood of Charles Street *we should have more room to swing a cat,*" Gibbon wrote cheerily to Dorothea Gibbon (*Letters* 2:41; emphasis Gibbon's).

With all this, however, Gibbon must have continued writing the history during the last three months of the year. A few later writers have betrayed envy of Gibbon's scholarly ease; oddly, they say he did not have to work, as if the writing of a great history were mere play.[6] They mean, of course, that he did not have to earn a living by some task other than writing the history, such as teaching. But of course he did have to work, not only at the writing itself, but in the roles of M.P., landowner, and concerned friend and relation. If he did not have distraction of assigned tasks, he lacked also not only the conveniences of modern scholarship, but even those available to others in his own time: he had no amanuensis, no university affiliation, no student assistants, no public library. The *Decline and Fall*, especially this first volume, remains a triumph of industry as well as ability and opportunity. In October, in a week and a half in November, and in December, Gibbon must have managed to complete chapters 11–14 of the history, for the last two (15 and 16), a volume in themselves, and thrice rewritten by Gibbon before the end of June 1775, would have given him more than enough to do in the new year.

Chapters 11–14 have an ironic structure. After destruction had come within sight of Rome, the fortunes of the city and the empire took a dramatic turn for the better. "It was saved by a series of great princes, who derived their obscure origin from the martial provinces of Illyricum" (*DF* chap. 1, 1:304). In the next thirty years, "Claudius, Aurelian, Probus, Diocletian and his colleagues . . . deserved the glorious title of Restorers of the Roman world." In this Gibbon echoes Montesquieu. But unlike Montesquieu, Gibbon does not see this restoration as adequate, complete, or essential. The high praise has a hollow ring when we discover that it is only in military discipline and consequent strength with respect to frontiers and "foreign and domestic enemies" that the Empire has been restored. While "the virtues of Claudius, his valour, affability, justice, and temperance, his love of fame and of his country, place him in that short list of emperors who added lustre to the Roman purple," the account of these virtues is suspect because it comes from interested witnesses, and his reign, however glorious, lasted less than two years. Its brevity is emphasized in Gibbon's portrayal, in contrast, say, with the even shorter reign of Julian, which Gibbon expands to fill parts of three chapters. As for Claudius's successor, Aurelian, he reigned "only four years and about nine months; but every instant of that short period was filled by some memorable achievement" (*DF* chap. 11, 1:314). Yet his severe disposition was such that his "love of justice often became a blind and furious passion" (*DF* chap. 11, 1:339), and he died by the hand of "a general whom he had always loved and trusted. . . . regretted by the army, detested by the senate, but universally acknowledged as a warlike and fortunate prince" (*DF* chap. 11, 1:340). Though Gibbon makes much of the peaceful and constitutional interregnum after

Aurelian's murder, the reigns of Tacitus, Probus, Carus and his sons are at best marked by military success or the mere "theatrical representation" of restored liberty. "The triumph due to the valour of Probus was conducted with a magnificence suitable to his *fortune*" (*DF* chap. 12, 1:361; emphasis added), says Gibbon significantly, and immediately points out that the "desperate courage of about fourscore Gladiators" marked the occasion with a rebellion, "disdaining to shed their blood for the amusement of the populace." Probus, too, was murdered by his own soldiers, Carus died naturally (Gibbon believes) but after only ten months, and both of his sons, made caesars though unworthy of the Empire, were dead within eighteen months of their father's death.

The most impressive evidence of a restored empire, in Gibbon's view, is the reign of Diocletian and the colleagues with whom he shared his power and responsibilities. "Like Augustus, Diocletian may be considered as the founder of a new empire" (*DF* chap. 13, 1:378). But his reign, to which Gibbon devotes a chapter, introduced many destructive innovations and failed to restore Roman civilization with Roman power. "It is almost unnecessary to remark" (Gibbon remarks) that "the progress of despotism had proved very unfavourable to genius, and even to learning. The succession of Illyrian princes restored the empire, without restoring the sciences" (*DF* chap. 13, 1:422). Law, physic, poetry, and history were alike silent or feeble. "A languid and affected eloquence was still retained in the pay and service of the emperors. . . . The declining age of learning and of mankind is marked . . . by the rise and rapid progress of the new Platonists," who, Gibbon believes, "scarcely deserve a place in the history of science" (*DF* chap. 13, 1:423–24). Thus this apparent restoration is, in Gibbon's view, ultimately an irrevocable step toward the destruction of Rome.

Politically and economically, as well as culturally, Gibbon finds Diocletian's constitutional innovations distasteful and—even when unavoidable—destructive. He symbolizes this perspective by the note on which he begins his account of Diocletian. Diocletian is the first emperor to come from the class of the slaves—"and, after the death of Numerian, the slave, by the confession and judgment of his rivals, was declared the most worthy of the Imperial throne." Like Augustus, Diocletian is characterized by Gibbon as duplicitous, lacking in "splendid" virtues, but a supremely able politician:

> a vigorous mind, improved by the experience and study of mankind; dexterity and application in business; a judicious mixture of liberality and economy, of mildness and rigour; profound dissimilation under the disguise of military frankness; steadiness to pursue his ends; flexibility to vary his means; and above all the great art of submitting his own passions, as well as those of others, to the interest of his ambition, and of colouring his

ambition with the most specious pretences of justice and public utility. (*DF* chap. 13, 1:378)

His associates were skillful generals, but two of them were brutal and the third was weak. Thus when Diocletian's health forced him to abdicate, the Roman world was "afflicted by five civil wars" in the next eighteen years, and the turbulence was ended not by a restoration of Roman greatness, but by the domination of Constantine. Moreover, Diocletian's policies included the settlement of conquered barbarians in Roman territories, so that "multitudes of secret enemies, insolent from favour, or desperate from oppression, were introduced into the heart of the empire" (*DF* chap. 13, 1:391). Under Diocletian, even "the image of the old constitution" preserved in the Senate was obliterated, as he "resolved to deprive that order of its small remains of power and consideration" (*DF* chap. 13, 1:409). The Praetorians, once the scourge of the Empire but now the only remaining sign of importance for the city of Rome, "were insensibly reduced, their privileges abolished, and their place supplied by two faithful legions of Illyricum." Most fatally, the emperors ceased to treat Rome as their capital.

In 303, "the arduous work of rescuing the distressed empire from tyrants and barbarians" was complete, and a triumph was celebrated in Rome to mark this success and the twentieth anniversary of Diocletian's accession. Yet Gibbon's view of this triumph is ironic, and the tone of his account is tinged with melancholy, because the triumph "was the last that Rome ever beheld. Soon after this period, the emperors ceased to vanquish, and Rome ceased to be the capital of the empire" (*DF* chap. 13, 1:406–7). The city was no longer holy, and its Senate, "losing all connexion with the Imperial court and the actual constitution, was left a venerable but useless monument of antiquity on the Capitoline hill" (*DF* chap. 13, 1:410). It is easy to understand why some readers have supposed that Gibbon idealized the Republic, and why others think he is insufficiently appreciative of the accomplishments of Diocletian. But what we see clearly enough, as Mortimer Chambers, among others, has pointed out,[7] is that Gibbon fully appreciated the profound constitutional change effected by Diocletian, and that, however clear-eyed his recognition of the faults of the real constitution of the Republic, and the further faults of its "image" as preserved by Augustus and his successors, he knew that the hope of a balanced government permitting freedom to each according to his capacities—freedom to choose work and preserve life and property for the masses; and similar freedoms, plus freedom of thought, with responsibility for sharing government, for an elite— disappeared when Rome became openly a monarchy in the Persian style. We might expect that Gibbon's tendency to write as a Roman senator would have been exaggerated by his new role as a "British senator," and we might hope that he would be aware of the constitutional developments in process in his own age, as George III aspired to restore powers to the monarch that had fallen into abeyance during the two preceding reigns. But though there are many passages in the *Decline and Fall* that tempt the (American) reader to invidious comparisons between the policies and actions of George III and the Romans, they do not cluster in the periods of Gibbon's political independence, or disappear when he himself is a supporter of Lord North's government. Indeed, an American revolutionary leader, Henry Laurens, amused himself while imprisoned in the Tower by "copying extracts from the *Decline and Fall* and comparing them with the events of the American war,"[8] that is, showing that they revealed the folly of the British position. The most striking instance of Gibbon's "eye on America," in the opinion of an advocate of this theory, must have been written when Gibbon was a member of the Board of Trade and the author of a pamphlet supporting the Government's position.[9] A more persuasive view is that Gibbon's ideas of Roman politics were more deeply held and more independently developed than his ideas of the politics of his own age. The influence, therefore, is more likely to be from the history to Parliament, not from Burke to the history. Here, Diocletian's constitutional changes were far more important to Gibbon than America's. We shall be able to condemn his short-sightedness when the two constitutions have had equally long-lasting effects.

In the new Roman disposition, monarchy was indeed restored, or rather, reached a new level of blatancy. Though there were two augusti and two caesars (more or less), each of the emperors was more absolutely and obviously a monarch than Augustus or his successors, even those who were tyrants. All the emperors aspired to rival the others—and the Great Kings of Persia—in magnificence. In Gibbon's view, Diocletian, like Shakespeare's Henry IV, expected that "an ostentation of splendour and luxury would subdue the imagination of the multitude . . . and that habits of submission would insensibly be productive of sentiments of veneration." The new system, despite its successes, was divisive and expensive:

> He multiplied the wheels of the machine of government, and rendered its operations less rapid but more secure. . . . In their civil government, the emperors were supposed to exercise the undivided power of the monarch. . . . Notwithstanding these precautions, the political union of the Roman world was gradually dissolved. . . . Instead of a modest family of slaves and freedmen, such as had contented the simple greatness of Augustus and Trajan, three or four magnificent courts were established in the various parts of the empire, and as many Roman *kings* contended with each other and the Persian monarch for the vain superiority of pomp and luxury. (*DF* chap. 13, 1:413–14)

Thus the Roman subject had less freedom, even though the Empire had less unity. The contrast with Gibbon's opening references to the united culture, but political division, of modern Europe, is all but explicit.

Gibbon reserves his full description of the new constitution for its "season of full maturity and perfection" under Constantine, and he acknowledges that Diocletian managed his revenues "with prudent economy": "he deserves the reproach of establishing pernicious precedents, rather than of exercising actual oppression" (*DF* chap. 13, 1:415). Nevertheless, the sense that the new Empire had declined from its predecessor is strongly maintained throughout this chapter; the next chapter, devoted to civil wars, cruelty and ingratitude among the emperors and caesars, and the eventual triumph of Constantine, confirms that sense. Licinius is certainly contemptible, in Gibbon's view, both for incapacity and for cruelty and ingratitude. But when, as a defeated old man, he sues for life and is granted it, but is later accused of treason, Gibbon's contempt for him is mingled with pity. "According to the rules of tyranny, he was accused of forming a conspiracy, [but] . . . we may perhaps be allowed, from his weakness, to presume his innocence" (*DF* chap. 14, 1:475–76). With this victory, the unification of the Empire under a single ruler, and Constantine's outrageous edict—quickly repealed—overthrowing all the laws enacted in Licinius's reign, Gibbon concludes his account of Constantine's rise to power, which, Gibbon says, has been minutely related "not only as the events are in themselves both interesting and important, but still more as they contributed to the decline of the empire by the expense of blood and treasure, and by the perpetual increase as well of the taxes as of the military establishment" (*DF* chap. 14, 1:476).

The last sentence of chapter 14 seems to lead to an account of Constantine's reign, but Gibbon has been preparing for something else. Chapters 15 and 16, which conclude the first volume of the history, contain his celebrated analysis of the pre-Constantinian success of Christianity and his revisionist (though far from unprecedented) view of the persecutions suffered by the infant church. Christians, hardly mentioned in the first eight or nine chapters of the history, are gradually brought to the reader's attention in the course of chapters 10 through 14. The references are still infrequent, but they could perhaps be shown to occur at an imperceptibly accelerating pace. In chapter 11, a note suggests, for the first time, that the emperors were aware of the Christians' existence; Aurelian tells the senate, "One should imagine . . . that you were assembled in a Christian church, not in the temple of all the gods" (*DF* chap. 11, 1:320 n. 45 [38]). As we approach the age of Constantine, a few references to the Christians even achieve the dignity of the text, for example, in

the account of a peasant revolt in Gaul (287), "we are *not* disposed to
believe that the principal leaders Aelianus and Amandus were Christians, or to insinuate that the rebellion, as it happened in the time of
Luther, was occasioned by the abuse of those benevolent principles
of Christianity which inculcate the natural freedom of mankind" (*DF*
chap. 13, 1:384; emphasis added). In general, however, the reader of
chapters 1–14 could easily forget that Gibbon's history has occupied
itself with the first centuries of the *Christian* era. But as we have
already seen, Gibbon has carefully prepared our minds to reject the
intolerance, asceticism, lack of patriotism, superstition, and fanaticism
that he saw in the early Christian culture; he is ready to present as his
culminating argument in the book, which after all might not go
beyond the present volume, an attack on mutual inhumanity among
the nations of Christian Europe.

But he can hardly have begun the writing of the two climactic
chapters in 1774. October was disturbed by politics, November by
travel, and at the end of the month, by the beginning of Gibbon's
parliamentary duties. In November, also, with Gibbon's return from
Bath, it became clear that his friend Clarke, five years younger than
himself, was dying, only a few months after Gibbon had been comforting him in his mourning for his father's unexpected death. Gibbon
and Clarke had been friends for ten years, and now it was clear that
Gibbon could do nothing for his friend except accept the trusteeship
of his estate, which had to be settled to avoid its transmission to an
"idiot Brother." Two other concerns also affect the close of the year,
though very differently—politics and marriage. All three matters took
decisive turns at the close of 1774 and the beginning of 1775.

In the opening weeks of the parliamentary session, Gibbon tried
to prepare himself to speak. In a sense, he had nothing to lose, for no
one knew of the great work in progress, and therefore, presumably, no
one would have been surprised if his maiden speech had been less
than impressive. Many other country gentlemen had published a
pamphlet or two in their youths, and other "young" members were
venturing forth. Too many, in fact—"Hartley Sir W Maine and some
other new Members lost their maidenheads with very little credit.
Once or twice I was a little lewd but am now well pleased that I
resisted the praemature temptation" (*Letters* 2:45). It has been thought
that Gibbon's silence requires special psychological explanation.[10] But
his inability to bring himself to speak in Parliament was certainly
increased by the response he saw to other feeble efforts. Thomas
Hutchinson describes one, early in January 1775—"Mr Innes, a new
member, made a short blundering speech. . . . He kept the house in
a roar by his odd manner."[11] Thus we do not have to suppose patho-
logical shyness on Gibbon's part, or (extrapolating from his parliamentary silence and Boswell's grudging sneers about his conversation in

Johnson's presence) assume that he was silent in conversation. On the contrary, Gibbon spoke much, and apparently well, in private discussions on public affairs.[12] But at first he had two reasons not to seek the floor in Parliament: he was not particularly well informed on current issues, and he had not made up his mind about his own positions. In America, the great subject, Gibbon had hitherto taken no more than a casual interest, an interest perhaps inspired more by the fervor of his politically minded friends than by his own sense of its importance. Now, like the scholar he was, he decided that in order to speak he needed more information. But, unlike a shy recluse, he sought it among both books and men.[13]

In the manuscript catalogue of his library compiled in 1777, some 150 works are listed (among a total of 1,920) that were published between 1770 and 1775, inclusive, and which therefore must have been bought by Gibbon (not his father) at or near the time of their publication.[14] These books, if they are representative of his book purchases at the time, show that he was adding to his library at least as many books dealing with America and Parliament as with Rome and her neighbors, though of course he had previously acquired the "tools of his trade," the books dealing with Roman history. His new purchases include proceedings of the American Continental Congress, books by and about Americans, and records of parliamentary actions and debates. Several books about Massachusetts, published in the sixties, he acquired at this time from the royal governor of the colony, Thomas Hutchinson. Gibbon seems to have attempted to read arguments from both sides, Burke *and* Johnson, for instance; and Arthur Lee, Franklin, Hutchinson, and Isaac Mauduit among the Americans. The history of Parliament and the reports of committees on disputed elections (Gibbon was appointed to such a committee in February) were the only topics connected with public affairs that competed with America for Gibbon's attention, as revealed by his book purchases.

Among men, Mauduit was the American expert Gibbon first sought out. On December 6, he dined at Benjamin Letthieullier's with Mauduit and Sir Thomas Miller—all three opposed to North's policies in America.[15] (Mauduit, like Hutchinson, was a Tory loyalist, but at this time they hoped that a compromise could be reached between the colonists and the mother country.)[16] Gibbon invited Mauduit, Miller, and Letthieullier to dine in Bentinck Street on December 13, together with his friend John Thomas Batt (a friend, too, of Samuel Johnson's and "most well-known people of his day").[17] Batt was one of the two or three people who saw portions of the *Decline and Fall* in manuscript (*Letters* 2:81)—Deyverdun, and probably Holroyd, being the others—and Gibbon probably invited Batt because of general confidence in his judgment, not specifically because of his position on America. On December 23, Hutchinson wrote in his journal: "I walked into the city to Mr Mauduit's. Mr Gibbons, a Member of Parliam^t came in, to be informed of what passed between Mr Grenville and the Colony Agents, when the Stamp Act was passed; for Charles Fox, he said, had charged Mr Grenville with smuggling that Act through the House."[18] Gibbon's attempt to be both conscientious and independent of mind is striking here, consistent with his almost romantic portrayal of the Roman Senate's last stand (with the Gordians). On America, Gibbon found both Mauduit and Hutchinson valuable sources of information and opinions; certainly they influenced his views.[19] Speaking of a meeting with Mauduit, Gibbon remarked, "he squeaks out a great deal of sense and knowledge, though after all I mean to think *perhaps* to *speak* for myself" (emphasis added), and went on, "I likewise (at his house) conversed with Governor Hutchinson, with whom I mean to get acquainted" (*Letters* 2:51).

Gibbon's pursuit of American informants was delayed not only by the parliamentary recess, but by an old enemy, the gout. It was a mild attack, but no doubt made it less convenient to walk into the City to visit Mauduit. Meanwhile, he pursued another campaign by proxy. His Uncle Stanier's December romance had perhaps reminded Gibbon that it was not too late for him to marry. But it was marriage that entered Gibbon's head, not romance. While he was in Bath, he seems to have authorized his stepmother to consult Anne Portman, another elderly widow, about approaching the family of a young woman Gibbon might have considered marrying. But he had not yet met, or at least did not know well, the young woman in question. "If the general idea should not startle Miss, the next consultation would be, how, and where the Lover may throw himself at her feet, conte[mplate] her charms, and *study her character*" (emphasis Gibbon's), he wrote to Dorothea Gibbon. "After that we may proceed to more minute enquiries and arrangements" (*Letters* 2:48–49).

But before this moment of high romance or low comedy could occur, the matchmakers encountered difficulties. Gibbon's own description of the negotiation (from his perspective) deserves quotation and comparison with the highflown, but sincere, letters he had written to Suzanne Curchod without any need for intermediaries. The comparison is not flattering to his more mature self. But the letter does show a warm and honest relationship with his stepmother, and it indicates where his values were—not in overthrowing religion, but in replacing it, as he thought, with character, allowing for "decency and toleration":

> Surely no affair was ever put into better hands than mine has been [Gibbon wrote to Dorothea Gibbon]. Your skill and friendship, I am not surprized at, but Mrs Portman is a most excellent procuress, and The Lady Mother has given as proper an answer as could be expected. There

is only one part of it which distresses me, *Religion*. It operates doubly, as
a present obstacle and a future inconvenience. Your evasion was very able,
but will not prudence as well as honour require us being more explicit in
the *suite*. Ought I to give them room to think I should patiently conform
to family prayers and Bishop Hooper's sermons. I would not marry an
Empress on those conditions. I abhor a Devotee, though a friend both to
decency and toleration. . . . After all, what occasion is there to enquire
into my profession of faith. It is surely much more to the purpose for them
to ask how I have already acted in life, whether as a good son, a good
friend, whether I game, drink, &c. (*Letters* 2:49)

He adds assurances that he is not a gamester and no longer a heavy
drinker (as in his militia days). As to women, "I give you my honor,
that I have not either with [Miss F—— Fuller?] or with any other
Woman, any connection that could alarm a Wife." Fortune might
prove an issue, for Gibbon's was encumbered still by his father's debts.
"Above all things, I think [my fortune] should not be *magnified*. . . .
You see how serious I am in this business."

What we see, perhaps, is how purely it is a business—he makes
several jocular references to the "well furnished [marital] Market"
(*Letters* 2:54). When the negotiation fell through, however, he was
indifferent, because he was absorbed in a much more significant loss.
On December 26, Clarke died. "You will easily suppose that the
shock however expected, and the hurry of melancholy business, have
swallowed up the remembrance of any lesser disapointment, and indeed engross all my thoughts" (*Letters* 2:52). It is nearly two weeks
later before Gibbon responds to Mrs. Gibbon's report, and the tone of
his comment is interesting:

> The Willow Garland you sent me has not much disconcerted my
> Philosophy, and indeed the Sanctity of the Lady had a little prepared me
> for, and reconciled me to the disappointment. . . . I should hope that . . .
> we might, either now or hereafter, find the opportunity of retrieving our
> first miscarriage.—Sir Stanier and Lady Porten exhibit a very pretty
> picture of conjugal fondness and felicity and yet they have been married
> very near three Weeks. (*Letters* 2:54)

The resemblance of Gibbon's play to Restoration Comedy is complete
with this concluding "sentiment," but there is a certain subtle interplay between the hero of this marriage farce and the otherwise urbane
and humane narrator of the *Decline and Fall*. Porson long ago remarked
with stinging wit that the treatment of Christianity in the *Decline and
Fall* suggested revenge for personal injury,[20] and this rejection in the
name of religion was, of course, only one more in a series of such
injuries experienced by Gibbon. More significantly, I think, the whole
situation helps to account for a rather noticeable difference between
Gibbon's treatment of women in the first volume of the history and
his treatment of them thereafter. His portrayal of both the faults and

virtues of women in this volume is much more conventional and traditionally misogynistic than it will later become, when his customary comfortable relationship with intelligent women is restored. Later he will be criticized for tolerating sexual activity in women and for insensitivity to the sufferings of ravished virgins, but he will not assume that female courage is artificial, or that only "angels in the house" are excellent women.[21]

Parliament recessed on December 23. Clarke's affairs occupied Gibbon and Clarke's other executor, Thomas Skipwith, for the first week in January 1775, and Gibbon had the gout. But he found time and energy to participate in games of chess at the Chess Club in St. James's, and to spend ten days at Up-park, seat of his old friends the Fetherstonhaughs, where he had expected to see Lady Fetherstonhaugh's brothers, but instead "found Lord Egremont and fourscore fox hounds" (*Letters* 2:56). On his return journey he spent some time with his agent at Buriton and left affairs there in a much less awkward position: "The Troubles of Buriton are perfectly composed, and the Insurgents reduced to a state though not a temper of submission" (*Letters* 2:56). Perhaps these military metaphors were inevitable, for when Parliament reconvened and Gibbon returned to his writing, military matters were of course paramount in both. Instead of his usual feeble excuses for not having written, he could say to Holroyd, "The fate of Europe and America seems fully sufficient to take up the time of one Man and especially of a Man who gives up a great deal of time for the purpose of public and private information" (*Letters* 2:57).

The new source of information on America was of course Governor Hutchinson. On January 20 Gibbon and Mauduit called on Hutchinson in the evening and arranged to dine together on the 23rd. According to Hutchinson, they "desired to see [him] on American affairs." Many of the guests met again on the 24th. "Dined with Mr Mauduit, [two others], and Mr Gibbons—the two last Members of Parliament, both for supporting the authority of Parlt, but ready to any reasonable concession." And on the 29th, "Dined with Mr Gibbons, Mr Lethueiller, Member for Andover, Clarke, &c. . . . Mr Gibbons speaks of a design to attaint 14 or 15 of the Provincial Congress."[22] Hutchinson, accustomed to importance and to the conversation of knowledgeable people, shows the value he placed on Gibbon's talk in choosing his views and information, among all those present, to record on both these occasions.

By the end of the month, Gibbon could write: "I think I have sucked Mauduit and Hutcheson very dry, and if my confidence was equal to my eloquence and my eloquence to my knowledge, perhaps I might make no very intolerable Speaker. At all events I fancy I shall try to expose myself" (*Letters* 2:57). He would have spoken in support

of Lord North's Government, "which *in this instance* I think the cause
of England" (*Letters* 2:56—Gibbon's emphasis), but would presumably
have urged planning that was more wide-ranging than North's practice
and as much conciliation of the colonists as was compatible with
"firmness."[23] Apparently Holroyd replied to his friend's rather complacent self-deprecation with a vigorous "Speak, and be damned." Gibbon writes on February 8, "I am not damned according to your
charitable wishes, because I have not acted," that is, spoken in Parliament (*Letters* 2:59). But it is rather interesting to inquire what Holroyd's "charitable wishes" imply: he cannot have objected to what
Gibbon planned to say, because they agreed. It seems possible that
he did not think his friend should attempt to speak, or at least not
yet. But perhaps he meant only, "Get on with it."

February was so full of the British Empire that it is hard to see
how Gibbon found time to pursue the Roman Empire. In fact he was
at work on two long chapters, presently about one-seventh of the first
quarto volume of the history and supported by more than three hundred notes, which in their first draft were far longer: "the fifteenth
and sixteenth Chapters have been reduced by three successive revis-
als from a large Volume to their present size" (*Memoirs* 156). It must
be remembered that each "revisal" had to be written out anew by the
author's own hand. He did not use "scissors and paste," as we can
easily determine from the extant drafts of at least three works that
he revised extensively, the *Essai*, the "Weights and Measures of the
Ancients," and, of course, his memoirs. Instead, he copied out again
even passages he retained verbatim.

All work on the history during these busy weeks must have been
done in the early morning, sometimes after a long night in the House
of Commons. A committee to which Gibbon had been appointed,
"always sits from ten to three and a half after which that day [Monday,
February 6] I went into the House and sat till three in the Morning,"
he reports (*Letters* 2:59). But for the time being he found this strenuous
schedule stimulating and assured himself that in learning how political
power works, he was acquiring "the first and most essential virtue of
an historian" (*Memoirs* 156). Holroyd's view of his friend's activity is
reflected in a letter he received in April; "I am glad to hear that
Gibbon is so attentive to his duty in Parliament—in the intervals &
recesses he must be if possible more entertaining."[24]

Gibbon's hopes of bringing himself to speak were dissipating.
Though he now felt "tolerably prepared as to the matter," he "dreaded
exposing [him]self in the manner" (*Letters* 2:63) and thought himself
not "armed by Nature or education with the intrepid energy of mind
and voice" necessary to a form of argument in which pure volume
sometimes outweighed sense (*Memoirs* 156). In the end he found his
silence inglorious and inexplicable on at least one occasion: "alas

throughout that public business I have remained silent and notwith-standing all my efforts chained down to my place by some invisible unknown invisible power" (*Letters* 2:64). But to infer that he was seriously unhappy in his inglorious silence, even though it reduces him to stuttering on this occasion, is, I think, quite unnecessary. He was conscious that his "timidity was fortified by pride" (*Memoirs* 156), and his accounts of the debates, votes, decisions, and prospects of Parliament are copiously scattered with intimations of a sense of proud proprietorship: "We" voted an address; "we expect next Tuesday to be a great day"; "our" general divisions are estimated; even "In a few days *we* [emphasis added] stop the ports of New England." The form is, of course, commonplace, but it is striking to the reader of the letters, especially when juxtaposed with Gibbon's usual narrative per-spective of detached observer and with his preference of the first-person singular for the expression of his own views.

If we compare Gibbon's retrospective account of these debates, written when he was composing his memoirs, with his descriptions to Holroyd at the time, we can see how much Gibbon was associating himself in 1775 with the major actors in the political events of the day. We can also see the intrusions of his personal views and doubts, and the disappearance of both as he achieved historic distance. From his letter to Holroyd of February 8:

> There was such an inundation of speakers . . . that neither Lord George Germaine nor myself could find room for a single word. The principal Men both days were Fox and Wedderburne, on the opposite sides, the latter displayed his usual talents. The former taking the vast compass of the quaestion before us discovered powers for regular debate which neither his friends hoped nor his Enemies dreaded. We voted an address (304 to 105) of lives and fortunes declaring the Massachusets Bay in a State of Rebellion. More troops but I fear not enough go to America to make an army of 10000 Men at Boston, three Generals Howe, Bourgoyne and Clinton. In a few days we stop the ports of New England. I cannot write Volumes, but I am more and more convinced that with firmness all may go well: yet I sometimes doubt Lord N. (*Letters* 2:59)

Gibbon does not appear to notice that it is comical to equate the silence of an unknown backbencher with that of the secretary of state for the American colonies. Yet a narrator with historical perspective takes over for the next two sentences, with one revealing exception, "before *us*." Gibbon's firmness as part of the group and doubts in his own person are sufficiently clear from the remainder of the passage. Clearly he is caught up by the enthusiasm of the debate and believes for the time in the power of this senate, but his skeptical intelligence is not entirely convinced. He is confused and impressed by the blos-soming of Fox in opposition—Fox, after all, was twelve years younger than the silent Gibbon.

In the autobiograhical passage, on the other hand, both enthusiast
and skeptic are silenced, or rather judged and transcended by the
philosophic historian:

> [Lord North,] who could wield with equal dexterity the arms of reason
> and ridicule . . . was seated on the Treasury bench between his Attorney
> and Solicitor General . . . *magis pares quam similes:* and the minister might
> indulge in a short slumber whilst he was upheld on either hand by the
> majestic sense of *Thurlow*, and the skillful eloquence of *Wedderburne*. From
> the adverse side of the house an ardent and powerful opposition was
> supported by the lively declamation of *Barrè*, the legal acuteness of Dun-
> ning, the profuse and philosophic fancy of *Burke* and the argumentative
> vehemence of *Fox*, who in the conduct of party approved himself equal to
> the conduct of an Empire. By such men every operation of peace and war,
> every principle of justice or policy, every question of authority and free-
> dom was attacked and defended; and the subject of the momentous con-
> test was the union or separation of Great Britain and America. (*Memoirs*
> 212–13)

Throughout February and March, Gibbon continued to be en-
grossed in politics, especially America. To the surprise and encour-
agement of the American party,[25] Gibbon sat and voted with Wilkes
on the question of the Middlesex election (if Wilkes were declared
elected for Middlesex, the American party gained another vote and a
powerful voice). But Gibbon seems much more motivated by a liking
for Wilkes's company—earlier, when Wilkes was ill, he had remarked,
"we shall lose much amusement" (*Letters* 2:24)—than by "Patriotism,"
or so we may infer from his calmly amused report that "before the
end of the debate, [Wilkes] fell fast asleep" (*Letters* 2:61). It was an
issue on which a number of Lord North's supporters voted against
the Government. For the first three weeks of the parliamentary session, Gibbon continued to seek out Hutchinson, who records Gibbon's
dissatisfaction with Lord North's leadership in his journal (February
18): "I called early upon Mr Gibbon, Bentinck Street. He laments the
want of a more general plan: says that in all great affairs since Lord
North's Administration this has been the case. Members who are
independent, and not obliged to follow the Minister, are at a loss
what part to take, for want of a more thorough knowledge of what is
to be the next measure, &c."[26] Yet even in this period Gibbon did
not devote himself exclusively to the affairs of empires. He took time
for social occasions, including cards, and for the last two weeks of
March, he was agreeably interrupted by a visit from the Holroyds.
Assessing his life as an M.P. at the Easter recess, he wrote to his
stepmother: "It is upon the whole an agreable improvement in my life
and forms just the mixture of business of study and of society which
I always imagined I should, and now find I do like. Whether the

House of Commons may ever prove of benefit to myself or Country is another quaestion" (*Letters* 2:63).

This praise is so temperate that it is not surprising to find Gibbon in April wholeheartedly dismissing America and Parliament to return to Rome: "I have resumed my History with vigour and adjourned Politicks to next Winter" (*Letters* 2:64). In addition, April saw dinners and conversation with Aunt Kitty, Deyverdun, and Lord North, renewed attention to Clarke's estate, and Gibbon's presentation at Court: "My presentations passed graciously, and I am glad that I can now walk about the Rooms on a footing with other people" (*Letters* 2:65).

One of the dinners with Lord North was at the Cambridges in Twickenham. Gibbon dined there two days in succession (April 18 and 19). The second dinner was also attended by Johnson and Boswell and has been made famous by the latter, who takes occasion to sneer at Gibbon for not defending historical writing when Johnson disparaged it. But to Gibbon, the earlier dinner, at which Lord North was the star, was the more noteworthy: "If they turned out Lord N tomorrow they would still leave him one of the best Companions in the Kingdom" (*Letters* 2:66). By this time, Gibbon, as a member of the famous Literary Club resident in London, would have seen—and heard—Johnson frequently; the conversation that Boswell reports so vividly may have seemed routine to him.[27] And Boswell portrays the whole company as greeting one of Johnson's outrageous remarks with restraint rather than argument: "We sat in a comical sort of restraint, smothering a laugh, which we were afraid might burst out."[28] Perhaps Gibbon was similarly amused by Johnson's views of history.[29] Perhaps, as Boswell suggests, he preferred not to compete with "the black bear,"[30] whether or not he thought his abilities unequal to the competition. Certainly Gibbon was regarded as an agreeable companion by others; indeed, one of the members of the Club, who disliked Gibbon's history and especially his style, nevertheless had high praise for his conversation: "I always thought his Familiar Conversation the most Valuable Part of his Character, as well as the most agreeable *Feature* about him."[31]

When Parliament reconvened in May, Gibbon took up again his interest in America. Though Hutchinson records only one meeting with him that month (May 6), it was a dinner given by Gibbon in Bentinck Street, one of the "prettiest dinners in the world" he prided himself on giving at times; Hutchinson said he had "seldom met with a more agreeable party, or more profitable subjects of conversation." All the guests except Hutchinson and Sir Stanier Porten were Members of Parliament, and "it seemed generally agreed that the American affairs made not the least disturbance in any part of the Kingdom."[32]

Six weeks later, all of them, including Gibbon, were less sanguine, as Hutchinson reports: "Mr Gibbon called. He says many who were strong for the measures of Parliament, are much discouraged by the news from America, they having been made to believe there would be no action. I think in general, he will be in Opposition: dropped something like Ld Chatham's being a necessary man in such difficult cases."[33] America had forced itself upon the attention even of the man with the most inclusive historical perspective. But until the end of May, Gibbon remained detached or hopeful on the subject of reconciliation with the American colonies: describing the debate on the New York remonstrance, for instance, he comments, "In this season and on America the Archangel Gabriel would not be heard. On Thursday an attempt to repeal the Quebec bill, and then to the right about, and for myself having supported the British I must destroy the Roman Empire" (*Letters* 2:69). Indeed, he seems as much interested in a charming Pomeranian puppy, named, in honor of the donor's residence, Bath ("Gibbon would be ambiguous and Dorothea disrespectful"), as in either empire: "Her figure and coat are perfect, her manners Genteel and lively, and her teeth (as a pair of ruffles have already experienced) most remarkably sharp. She is not the least fatigued with her Voyage, and compleatly at home in Bentinck Street" (*Letters* 2:70). But on May 28 news arrived of the battle of Lexington, and Gibbon, like all those who had hoped to assert the authority of Parliament without (what they considered) civil war, was much concerned. He hastened to Hutchinson, who comforted him with the idea that the insurgents would have to return to their farms in May to sow "Indian corn the great sustenance of the Province" (*Letters* 2:71).

This defeat was from Gibbon's point of view the most ominous development of the whole period: "I have not courage to write about America. We talk familiarly of Civil War Dissolutions of Parliament, Impeachments and Lord Chatham. The boldest tremble, the most vigorous talk of peace. And yet no more than sixty five rank and file have been killed. . . . Gage has plenty of provisions . . . &c *hopes* he is not in danger of being forced" (*Letters* 2:75). A peaceful settlement seemed hopeless.

Gibbon's financial affairs were also very disturbing. None of his concessions succeeded in moving Lovegrove either to complete or to relinquish the purchase of Lenborough. On July 3 Gibbon wrote to Holroyd, "My tranquillity is disturbed by constant fretting, the Goslings must grow impatient and the purchase money melts away in interest. Where, when, or how will this end? For God's sake send me some effectual advice" (*Letters* 2:77–78). Deyverdun was off on his travels again, and the marriage negotiations had apparently ceased (Gibbon's only comments on the subject of marriages are cynical: on Sir Richard Worsley's engagement to "the youngest Miss Fleming:

love and £80000" [*Letters* 2:76]; "the Dutchess of Bedford made regular proposals of marriage to the young Earl Cholmondely and was as regularly refused" [*Letters* 2:79]). The fair prospects of the previous summer had sadly dimmed.

But Gibbon's tone was on the whole elated. It was too early to despair about America, Holroyd could advise him about business, Deyverdun had prospects of settlement, and his own way of life, with Parliament adjourned, was again that of study and society, a pattern, he would later discover, more truly congenial to him than the variant "study, society, and business" with which he had been experimenting. At the end of June, he was able to deliver the manuscript of the *Decline and Fall* to his publishers. He planned to spend the summer "correcting and composing," but there are reports of dinner engagements, and "when I am tired of the Roman Empire I can laugh away the Evening at Foote's Theatre" (*Letters* 2:78). Holroyd had fears even about the Roman Empire, but Gibbon knew better:

> Your apprehensions of a precipitate work &c, are perfectly groundless. . . . The *head* is now printing? true: but it was write [sic] last year and the year before. . . . As to the tail it is perfectly formed and digested (and were I so much given to self content and haste) it is almost all written. The ecclesiastical part for instance is written out in fourteen sheet, which I mean to refondre [recast] from beginning to end. . . . Batt and Deyverdun have read and observed. . . . I print no more than 500 copies of the first Edition, and the second (as it happens frequently to my betters) may receive many improvements. So much for Rome, now for Ireland [that is, Holroyd's affairs]. (*Letters* 2:81)

Thus Gibbon spent the summer of 1775 in his library, enjoying the company of Bath ("pretty, impertinent fantastical all that a young Lady of fashion ought to be" [*Letters* 2:84]) and correcting proofs: "many blemishes of style, which had been invisible in the manuscript, were discovered and corrected in the printed sheet." He says he was neither "elated by the ambition of fame; nor depressed by the apprehension of contempt"—the latter is certainly true. And surely he did not anticipate the degree of fame that was to come, though he knew he had selected his subject well and developed it with "diligence and accuracy." He even "flattered [him]self that an age of light and liberty would receive without scandal, an enquiry into the *human* causes of the progress and establishment of Christianity" (*Memoirs* 157). In that expectation, he later felt, he had been too optimistic.

FOUR

Christianity Confronted

he last two chapters of volume 1 of the *Decline and Fall*, those which Gibbon was still revising as the printers began work on the beginning of the history, were of course to be the most hotly debated portions of the work. Heralded by some as a courageous contribution to the Enlightenment campaign against organized religion, damned by others as a cowardly, furtive attack on divine truths and simple faith,[1] they were, in Gibbon's own view, neither. Gibbon's ostensible purpose in chapter 15 was to examine the natural and social—the human—causes of the spread of the Christian religion; in chapter 16, he proposed to reduce to historical dimensions the mythicized accounts of the early Christian martyrs. But the two chapters also have a common function—to treat the Christian church as a phenomenon of general history, not a special case admitting supernatural explanations and disallowing criticism of its adherents. Each of these chapters climaxes in an indictment of the institutional church of modern Europe, first for supplanting in an unnecessarily destructive way the great culture that preceded it, and second for the outrage of religious intolerance and warfare.

Unlike the theologian, Gibbon believed, the historian has the "melancholy duty" of discovering "the inevitable mixture of error and corruption which [Religion] contracted in a long residence upon earth, among a weak and degenerate race of beings" and of remembering that "truth and reason" rarely triumph easily in this world. He therefore proposes five "secondary" causes that "favoured and assisted" the rapid growth of the church, deferring with polite irony to the "obvious" primary cause, "the convincing evidence of the doctrine itself, and . . . the ruling providence of its great Author" (*DF* chap. 15, 2:2).

His "becoming submission" in calling his five causes only "secondary" had the probably unexpected effect of opening him to accusations of cowardice and dishonesty. Readers such as John Whitaker, who perceived that Gibbon really felt that human causes were primary rather than secondary, believed that to suggest that Christianity's success could be explained without divine intervention was to threaten, or attempt to threaten, the faith of innocent adherents and the success of the institution in the present. "You have . . . exhibited Deism in a new shape, and in one that is more likely to affect the uninstructed million, than the reasoning form which she has usually worn. . . . And I can only deplore the misfortune, and a very great one I consider it, to the highest and dearest interests of man among all your readers."[2] Many accused Gibbon of attempting to *cause* "the Decline and Fall of the Christian Church." In this context Gibbon's response to the religion of his proposed wife (see above, p. 52) and his relationships with a number of sincerely religious persons are revealing. He thoroughly approved of "decency and toleration," not only for nonreligion, but for religion.[3] He expected his aunt, his stepmother, Suzanne Curchod Necker, William Robertson, the Wartons, and various other friends and acquaintances of greater and lesser religious sophistication, but undoubted religious faith, to be able to read his history with approval, and in fact, they did so. How?

In the first place, Gibbon clearly did not think that his depiction of the historical nature and function of the Church would threaten it as an institution of modern life. He may have hoped to reform that institution in certain ways by indicating discrepancies between its professions and its actuality, but throughout the history, as many scholars have now demonstrated in various ways, Gibbon is anxious to retain such "useful prejudices" as religion offers to civil life. He even hints that some of the virtues of early Christianity, for example, its charity, have been neglected by those who profess to continue it. Contemporary (Protestant) Christianity has been purged, he seems to suggest, of many of the absurdities of the early Christians.[4] But it retains one of the worst, intolerant zeal in the pursuit of opinions, a point to which he returns in chapter 16. In the nineteenth and twentieth centuries, after it was conceded that religion was legitimately the object of historical inquiry and the subject of natural and social laws, a number of writers asserted that only the tone and manner of chapter 15 prevented its endorsement by Christians as "a Christian history, written in the most Christian spirit of candour."[5] Unlike Voltaire, Gibbon neither expects nor desires to "écraser l'infâme."

Nor, I think, did he hope or expect to deceive anyone about his own beliefs, except readers so naive, or pure in heart, that his protestation about secondary causes would enable them to read his history without discomfort or challenge to their belief. (The *Decline and Fall* has in fact had at least a few such readers, as well as readers charitable enough to be willing to accept Gibbon's protestation at face value despite their recognition of his irony.)[6] He expected sophisticated Christian readers, to whom a literal acceptance of the biblical accounts or church tradition was unnecessary and who were able to accept his skepticism without feeling threatened, but who wished to avoid appearing to consent to his views, to find his polite evasion convenient as well as "decent." And in fact, some did so; "I presume you have heard that offence is taken at some passages that are thought unfavourable to the truth of Christianity," wrote Joseph Warton primly, after high praise for the history.[7] Gibbon's mock deference to the "satisfactory" ahistorical explanation, then, would be similar, at least in his own mind, to the behavior of Cicero and other Roman philosophers, who indulgently supported the superstition of the masses as a civic duty, while at the same time making clear their own position to others similarly enlightened.

Very few of the comments in either chapter reflect directly on apostolic times or Christ's own teachings, and Gibbon seems almost mischievous in including those few for the amusement of the fully enlightened. They are in the spirit of the famous footnote (*DF* 1:328, chap. 11, n. 71 [64]) about Apollonius of Tyana, who "was born about the same time as Jesus Christ. His life (that of the former) is related in so fabulous a manner by his disciples, that we are at a loss to discover whether he was a sage, an impostor, or a fanatic." The comment that caused the most indignation was the tongue-in-cheek protestation about the "supine inattention" of the pagans to the Miraculous Darkness at the Passion. Gibbon no doubt believed that the darkness was metaphorical or mythical, but the evidence he cited against it was, as he must have expected every educated reader to know, flimsy; the "distinct chapter of Pliny . . . designed for eclipses of an extraordinary nature and unusual duration," which omits the miraculous darkness, is only one paragraph long. The joke, and indeed the whole concluding passage of chapter 15, turns aside from the historical consideration of the Christians' activities and the spread of their power to support and continue the philosophic campaign against miracles. It is a place to which Richard Porson's comment about the appearance of personal grievance in Gibbon's treatment of Christianity seems particularly to apply,[8] and we recall that it was precisely the acceptance of miracles that had led to his disastrous conversion to Roman Catholicism: "Dr Middleton . . . could [not] destroy my implicit belief, that the gift of miraculous powers was continued in the Church in the first four or five Centuries of Christianity. . . . nor was my conclusion absurd, that Miracles are the test of truth, and that the Church must be orthodox and pure, which was so often approved by the visible interposition of the Deity" (*Memoirs* 59).

Chapter 15 falls into two divisions: the first contains the famous five "causes"; the second surveys the timing and extent of the spread of Christianity prior to Constantine. The five causes—zeal, the doctrine of immortality, miraculous powers, pure morals, union and discipline—are analyzed for fifty-five pages (after a two-page introduction); the "historical view" requires only seventeen pages, beginning and ending with framing portrayals of pagan religion and pagan "philosophy" respectively, to suggest the vulnerability of the superstitious to conversion and the indifference of the intellectual elite. This organization, especially when one is attentive to variations in tone, suggests the covert purpose of this chapter, which is to analyze the quality of civilization promoted by the Christian society, to criticize it in significant ways, and to indict Gibbon's own contemporaries for hypocritical assent to positions in which they really did not believe. But it is important to notice that Gibbon does not condemn or attack all aspects of the early Church in the same way and that he concedes to it admirable qualities, albeit reluctantly.

William Gibson points out that in discussing the first four causes, Gibbon seems to treat the errors of the early Christians as harmless or merely distasteful follies; it is when the church begins to acquire the power to replace or damage Roman culture and to function as a rival "republic" within the failing monarchy that Gibbon takes it seriously, both as a threat and, potentially, as a source of new civilization.[9] The analysis of the growth of the church as a civil organization, however faulty in detail, is a pioneering effort at sociological history fully appreciated by at least some historians of historiography.[10] It prepares the careful reader for Gibbon's admiration of such figures as Athanasius and Pope Gregory I in their roles as civil heroes. But in the period of which he writes in chapter 15, as he himself said only half-jokingly, he wrote with the indignation of a constitutional conservative confronted with revolutionary innovation: "The primitive Church, which I have treated with some freedom, was itself at that time, an innovation, and *I* was attached to the old Pagan establishment" (*Letters* 3:216). As long as Christianity was an other-worldly religion, it had the same faults he had observed already in Zoroastrianism. It was perhaps more foolish than dangerous. But when (in his rather primitive psychologizing) the leaders' self-denial of pleasure led them to compensate by seeking power, they became dangerous.[11] As we shall see, he stands by his assertions about their power-seeking and their foolish, or even irresponsible, neglect of social duties in his subsequent *Vindication of Some Passages in the Fifteenth and Sixteenth Chapters of the History of the Decline and Fall of the Roman Empire.*

It is perhaps significant that the *Vindication* does not defend any passage designed to criticize theological opinions or to impugn the historicity of the Gospels. Theological opinion was precisely what was not worth fighting about, and Gibbon was, in fact, willing to delete at least some of these offensive passages—though he never specifies which—as extrinsic to his argument, both in the French translation (see *Letters* 2:122) and in later English editions. In a note to the *Memoirs* that he decided not to publish, Lord Sheffield says that it was he who advised Gibbon *not* to alter or suppress any of the offending passages in a subsequent edition.[12] It is unlikely that such suppressions would have placated any of his readers. Certainly Christians had every reason to object to his contemptuous tone, and they might also have complained about his rhetorical strategies, for in this section of the history he does not depend on narrative or argument alone to carry his point, but attempts to discredit the Christian position with his readers by arousing their anti-Semitism and snobbery. But his correcting these faults would not have satisfied them. They desired nothing less than to prove him wrong historically, to show that his treatment of Christian history as a natural phenomenon was intrinsically wrong. This Gibbon did not fully anticipate.

In addition to reducing the exaggerated traditional claims about the numbers of early Christian martyrs to something more factual, chapter 16 sought to analyze the conflict between the old Empire and the new Church so as to give a sympathetic appreciation of the perspective of the former, and so as to depict as vividly as possible the most significant moral loss (as Gibbon saw it) that occurred when the Christian world replaced the pagan Empire, the loss of religious toleration. It was a bold move to denounce Christian intolerance in the context in which Christians most clearly were being victimized, and it is clear that Gibbon's effort to dramatize the outrage of Christian intolerance by contrasting it with the rational and humane requirements of the pagan state religion, and by showing that the worst sufferings of the Christians were less severe than they had been painted, failed on two counts. First, he allows himself to seem to treat real sufferings callously and therefore puts himself and his cause in the wrong, however much his intellectual point may be correct; he has been compared to Swift's "Modest Proposer" in his cool calculations of the "annual consumption of martyrs" (*DF* 2:147).[13] Second, he totally fails to understand the reasons for the martyrs' actions. He thinks of them as defending opinions; martyrs, by definition, think of themselves as defending truths.[14] Gibbon sees the verbal conformity required by the magistrates as a perfectly acceptable device, which the Christians had a civic, almost a moral, duty to accept; they testify that they consider such behavior a betrayal of the Living God. He regards dying for an idea with contempt, and killing others for one with indignation. But he does not seem to acknowledge that the killers of those who died for an idea deserved the same indignation. Thus the melancholy and powerful attack on the religious wars of Christian Europe for which he reserved the climax of his first volume escaped the attention, or at least the commentary, of many of his readers.

In his *Memoirs* he claims to have been surprised by the intensity of the reaction these last two chapters evoked. Although he certainly knew that they were controversial, there is no hint in his letters of 1775, while he was revising them, correcting the proofs of the whole volume, and seeing it through the press, that he anticipated a negative reaction strong enough to distract attention from his positive achievements. He seems only to have feared neglect. Fairly early on—when the press had reached page 183—Gibbon received a very flattering commendation in an unmistakably sincere form: the publisher (whose name and record, Gibbon candidly points out, were far more distinguished than the author's) doubled the size of the first edition, from 500 to 1,000 copies. Gibbon was nervous about this decision, he says, "fearing that the junior members of my numerous family would be condemned to inglorious old age in the stock of some shop" (*Letters* 2:105).[15] But he acquiesced in the publisher's judgment and hoped for the best.

With a clear conscience, at least as a scholar, Gibbon was able to take the month of September for a holiday at Sheffield Place with his Aunt Kitty. But at the end of the month, when he returned to London, he received news that caused him to rush to Bath two and a half hours after reaching London: his stepmother was seriously ill (smallpox "of a very bad confluent sort"—*Letters* 2:85). When he arrived, however, he found that the case was much less bad than he had been led to believe, and the invalid well on the road to recovery: "she has at present but in the slightest degree the secondary fever" and is "perfectly out of all danger." But, awkwardly, the doctor thought she should not have the excitement of seeing him for several days. "He knows not the value of time, when the fate of an Empire depends upon it." The cessation of anxiety led Gibbon, indeed, to a certain amount of irritation, as it does so many of us. He considered leaving again for London on Thursday: "Even if I should not see her the attention would be the same. I ought to have acquired some merit at the expence of infinite hurry, twenty pounds . . . and above all of a week's loss of time" (*Letters* 2:86). He did see her, however, two days after his arrival, and he reports to the Holroyds that he has received "regular and favourable" dispatches about her. On the fourteenth, indeed, he received a letter from Mrs. Gibbon herself, "full of health good spirits, and expressions of gratitude. She is much concerned that I had the trouble of coming to Bath, but if I know her would have been much *more concerned if I had* not come" (*Letters* 2:87—underlined by Lord Sheffield). Despite this reprehensible, or understandable, irritation at the loss of time, Gibbon took further time to write an affectionate letter to the invalid, and in his letter to Holroyd devoted a little time to his "domestic war" with Lovegrove and much to America. His impatience for the appearance of his work can only have been increased by a letter from Strahan (his publisher-printer) on October 8:

> The language is the most correct, most elegant, and most expressive I have ever read; but that, in my mind, is its least praise. The work abounds with the justest maxims of sound policy, which, while they shew you to be a perfect master of your subject, discover your intimate knowledge of human nature, and the liberality of your sentiments. Your characters, in particular, are drawn in a masterly manner, with the utmost accuracy and precision; and, as far as I am able to judge, in strict conformity to historic truth. In short, so able and so finished a performance hath hardly ever before come under my inspection: and though I will not take upon me absolutely to pronounce in what manner it will be received at first by a capricious and giddy public, I will venture to say, it will ere long make a distinguished figure among the many valuable works that do honour to the present age; will be translated into most of the modern languages, and will remain a lasting monument of the genius and ability of the writer.[16]

This prophetic opinion cannot have failed to delight Gibbon, and he received similar good news from prepublication readers such as George L. Scott.[17] He could write to his stepmother early in January: "The Public I know not why except from the happy choice of the subject, have already conceived expectations, which it will not be easy to satisfy: the more especially as lively ignorance is apt to expect much more, than the nature and extent of historical materials can enable an author to produce" (*Letters* 2:96). It is apparent that despite his confidence, he had some qualms about his book, principally because he had high ambitions for it: "I knew that my book was good, but I wished it to be excellent" (*Letters* 2:105).

During November and December of 1775 and the first six weeks of 1776, Gibbon remained in London, despairing of the progress of the British Empire in America and rejoicing in the progress of the Roman Empire. The preface to the first volume is dated February 1. In it, he explains "the nature and limits of [his] general plan," an explanation necessary because he has "presumed to lay before the Public a *first* volume only." The first period of his study would extend from "the age of Trajan and the Antonines, when the Roman monarchy, having attained its full strength and maturity, began to verge towards its decline," to the subjection of Rome "to the power of a Gothic conqueror" and would end "about the beginning of the sixth century." "The second period . . . may be supposed to commence with the reign of Justinian" and end with "the elevation of Charlemagne, who, in the year 800, established the second or German Empire of the West." The last extended from "the revival of the Western Empire till the taking of Constantinople by the Turks." The "writer who should undertake" this period, Gibbon adds, "would find himself obliged to enter into the general history of the Crusades . . . and he would scarcely be able to restrain his curiosity from making some enquiry into the state of the city of Rome during the darkness and confusion of the middle ages." He goes on to say that he considers himself committed to the public for the completion of the first period, "probably in a second volume" (*DF* 1:xxxix–xli)

Three things may be observed about this plan. First, the organization of parts 2 and 3 more closely resembles that implied by the "Outlines of the History of the World" (ninth to fifteenth centuries) than the actual organization of the last three volumes of the history.[18] Second, he has already planned to conclude his history with the topic that originally inspired it, the decline and fall of the *city* of Rome. Third, he seems to like to begin each section with a renewed empire and to end it with the elevation of a rival. With his title, this practice identifies his particular understanding of the progress of history: each great civilization tragically loses something of its predecessor's greatness, fortunately preserves portions of it, and in some ways surpasses it. Thus he can combine an elegiac tone with a (qualified and guarded) optimistic theory of history.

On February 17, 1776, *The History of the Decline and Fall of the Roman Empire, Volume the First,* appeared, in 586 quarto pages, plus 88 pages of notes. "History is the most popular species of writing, since it can adapt itself to the highest or the lowest capacity: I had chosen an illustrious subject; Rome is familiar to the school-boy and the statesman" (*Memoirs* 157), said the author modestly. But he hardly expected quite the success that ensued: "My book was on every table, and almost on every toilette." He enjoyed not only the approbation of Hume, Robertson, Ferguson, and Adam Smith, his most qualified readers, but also the delights of being the fashion. He reveled in both, as he admitted to Deyverdun. He begins by telling him of the demand for a new edition, because as horses do not flatter kings, booksellers do not flatter authors. "But you understand that among such a large number of avid readers one can always find a way of capturing some praise, and I admit that as for me, I like it—such praise—very much indeed," whether it comes from "ladies of condition, especially if they are young and pretty," or from "my Masters," Robertson and "le bon David" Hume (*Letters* 2:106).

Horace Walpole was astonished by the book. "Lo, there is just appeared a truly classic work," he wrote to a friend on February 18. After comparing, or rather contrasting, Gibbon with Livy, Tacitus, Clarendon, Robertson, Voltaire, and Montesquieu in general, and preferring his style, "as smooth as a Flemish picture," to Michelangelo's exaggerations and "Dr Johnson's heterogeneous monsters," he speaks of the author, a member of Parliament called "whimsical . . . because he votes variously as his opinion leads him. . . . I know him a little, never suspected the extent of his talents, for he is perfectly modest . . . but I intend to know him a great deal more."[19] In his letter to Gibbon himself, Walpole chooses Gibbon's "amiable modesty" for his principal praise:

> How can you know so much, judge so well, possess your subject and
> your knowledge, and your power of judicious reflection so thoroughly, and
> yet command yourself and betray no dictatorial arrogance of decision? How
> unlike very ancient and very modern authors. . . . The impressions it has
> made on me are very numerous. The strongest is the thirst of being better
> acquainted with you—but I reflect that I have been a trifling author, and
> am in no light profound enough to deserve your intimacy. . . . The best
> proof I can give you of my sincerity, is to exhort you, warmly and earnestly,
> to go on with your noble work.[20]

Gibbon in fact assessed Walpole, as an author, precisely as Walpole politely evaluates himself here—as an "ingenious trifler."[21] But Walpole's social and political importance was far greater than Gibbon's, and his praise of the history was knowledgeable as well as fulsome. He seasoned it, however, with some advice that may have been less welcome to Gibbon: "The strongest, though a presumptuous mark of my friendship, is to warn you never to let your charming modesty be corrupted, by the acclamations your talents will receive. The native qualities of the man should never be sacrificed to those of the author, however shining. I take this liberty as an older man."[22] Most readers of Gibbon will either smile at the notion of his "charming modesty," or assume that Walpole's warning went unheeded. In fact, however, insofar as modesty is a characteristic of the *narrator* of the *Decline and Fall*—Walpole is clearly characterizing the narrator, not the politician or man of society, in the first passage above, though we might prefer to call the quality he points to "urbanity" or "balance"—it is at least as present in the succeeding volumes as in the first. And as a man, though Gibbon became very conscious of his position as an eminence, a star in the world of letters, he was credited throughout his life with avoiding the pose or parade of authorship. We need not assume that the social "modesty" Walpole (and Adam Ferguson) attribute to him was simply timidity and lack of conversational skill. But we must notice that later, when Walpole knew Gibbon better and was annoyed by his politics, he sneered at what he called Gibbon's "absurd vanity" about both his person and his work.[23]

Walpole's incense, though sweet, was by no means the only, or perhaps the best, praise received by Gibbon. The verdicts in which he was most interested, apart from those of the reviewers, came from Scotland (if Rousseau and Voltaire read the *Decline and Fall*, they did not publish their opinions or communicate them to Gibbon). Adam Ferguson and William Robertson provided valuable judgments despite their prudent reservations about the fifteenth and sixteenth chapters. Ferguson wrote that "the persons of this place whose judgment you will value most, agree in opinion, that you have . . . given us what Thucydides proposed leaving with his own countrymen, a *possession in perpetuity*," though he added, "[I] am told many doubt of your orthodoxy. I wish to be always of the charitable side, while I own you have proved that the clearest stream may become foul when it comes to run over the muddy bottom of human nature."[24] Robertson told Strahan (who showed the letter to Gibbon, who copied out the passage twice with his own hand, once to keep and once for Deyverdun's enjoyment) that certain defects of style were "amply compensated by the beauty of the general flow of language, and a very peculiar happiness in many of his expressions. I have traced him in many of his quotations (for experience has taught me to suspect the accuracy of my brother penmen,) and I find he refers to no passage but what he has seen with his own eyes."[25] Though he had not yet read the last two chapters, Robertson was "sorry, from what [he had] heard of them, that he has taken such a tone in them as will give great offence, and hurt the sale of the book."

And Hume's letter, which "over paid the labour of ten years," according to Gibbon in his *Memoirs* (158), said, "Whether I consider the Dignity of your Style, the Depth of your Matter, or the Extensiveness of your Learning, I must regard the Work as equally the Object of Esteem." Hume thought Gibbon had handled the material of the last two chapters "prudently" but warned him to "expect that a clamour w[ould] arise." "In all Events, you have Courage to Despise the Clamour of Bigots."[26] Hume's praise to Gibbon was not merely politeness or kindness; he wrote similarly to others, and he gave practical advice and criticism as well. He strongly urged that the notes be published at the foot of the page and the chapters furnished with chronological shoulder notes and headings and he told Gibbon that "in correcting his history, he always laboured to reduce superlatives, and soften positives."[27]

In Hume's last visit to London, when he was mortally ill, Gibbon seems to have been among those he saw, May 3, 1776.[28] Gibbon was able to tell him that a second edition was in preparation (*Letters* 2:107, n. 4), and Hume warned Gibbon of a fault of which no one else had accused him, excessive concision in the "superficial narrative of the first reigns from Commodus to Alexander" (*Memoirs* 156), a criticism that Gibbon took seriously. Most readers, because of the great length of the history as a whole and because of the stately effect of Gibbon's style, fail to realize that he is almost always economical in his narrative, and when he summarizes instead of dramatizing, he is indeed liable to be almost too concise, rivaling, for the moment, the brevity and occasional obscurity of Tacitus and Montesquieu. Hume, characteristically, was more acute than most readers, but a number of others have subsequently observed the concision, with either approval or disapproval.[29]

Gibbon had been anxious, in his choice of subject, to avoid as much as possible the pitfall of contemporary politics. But "a historian is always, to some extent, a politician," and he was pleased to have been praised for his sound political maxims by politicians from both ends of the spectrum, because such praise proved that he had "observed an honest neutrality" (*Letters* 2:107).[30] He received from David Garrick one report of such praise. Lord Camden, formerly Pitt's Lord Chancellor, was visiting Garrick early in March, when Gibbon's history had been out about three weeks. In the presence of witnesses, Garrick told Gibbon, Lord Camden "declared that he never read a more admirable performance . . . *the author is the only man to write history of the age—such depth—such perspicuity—such language, force, variety, and what not!* I am so delighted with him, continues he, that I must write to thank him—I should be happy to know him. My Lord, I have that honour, and will contrive, if possible to bring you together."[31] Gibbon replied to Garrick's letter accepting the implied invitation promptly and gratefully: "If he were still a Chancellor or a Minister, I might perhaps be inclined to meet his advances with some degree of Coldness and reserve; but as he is now reduced to be nothing more than a great Man, I shall eagerly embrace the first proper occasion of paying my respects to him and shall consider the honour of his acquaintance, as the most satisfactory reward of my labour" (*Letters* 2:99).

To fashionable and learned approbation was added that of the reviewers. The two major British literary journals, the *Critical Review* and *Monthly Review*, began multiple-part accounts of the *Decline and Fall* in February and March respectively. In 1767 Samuel Johnson had told George III that the *Monthly* was the more carefully edited of the two journals and the *Critical* conducted upon the "best principles." In 1776 he further explained their differences:

"The Monthly Reviewers (said he,) are not Deists; but they are Christians with as little christianity as may be; and are for pulling down all establishments. The Critical Reviewers are for supporting the constitution, both in church and state. The Critical Reviewers, I believe, often review without reading the books through; but lay hold of a topick, and write chiefly from their own minds. The Monthly Reviewers are duller men, and are glad to read the books through."[32]

One might expect, therefore, that a book with either political or religious implications would fare differently in the two journals, and that the *Decline and Fall* might be censured by each for different reasons. In fact, however, both reviews recognize the history as a masterpiece and begin by encouraging the author to complete his whole plan. The *Critical* is first in the field, as Johnson's characterization leads us to expect, but the *Monthly* (William Rose) has the stronger and more particular praise. Rose notes that Gibbon's task requires "an uncommon share of learning, judgment, and sagacity. Mr. Gibbon appears in every respect equal to the task he has undertaken; his style is well suited to the dignity of his subject,—elegant, perspicacious, and manly."[33] In May, Rose adds praise of Gibbon's characters, for example, that of Severus, and considers his strategy of providing separate chapters on the rivals of the Romans. Rose approves: these chapters "are no less entertaining than instructive."

When the two reviewers reach the controversial chapters, however, there is some difference between them. According to the *Critical*, Gibbon "seems to be fully sensible of the difficulties attending the prosecution of the subject" in the fifteenth chapter, and his account of the five causes is recommended for perusal "as being replete with interesting sentiments and pertinent observations." Almost alone among reviewers, the *Critical* gets the point of chapter 16: Gibbon "justly observes, that the conduct of the emperors . . . least favourable to the primitive church, is by no means so criminal as that of modern sovereigns, who have employed violence against the religious opinions of any part of their subjects" (41:269). The *Monthly* is less reserved about chapter 15 but hardly mentions 16. According to Rose:

> It is indeed scarce possible for an impartial historian to treat [the subject of the fifteenth chapter] in such a manner as to be approved by all the different denominations of Christians;—such is the diversity of their views, prejudices, and interests! The account, for example, which Mr. Gibbon gives of the rise and progress of the hierarchy, though in our opinion a very just and candid account, must . . . prove unsatisfactory to a very large and respectable class of readers, many of whom may probably censure the whole performance on this account, though they may think it prudent to conceal the *real* ground of their disapprobation. (55:44)

Both reviewers are impressed with Gibbon's accuracy and with the notes with which he supports his statements. Even on religious matters, "the facts, as far as we can judge, are faithfully related," says Rose. He adds, somewhat cryptically, "We only regret that our ingenious Author has expressed himself, on certain topics, with so much

caution and reserve" (55:47). Though it is possible that Rose wished
Gibbon to have expressed more fully his confidence in the "primary"
cause of the success of Christianity, I think he here meant to criticize
Gibbon's failure to avow his skepticism openly. Yet Rose later praises
Watson's polite attack on the *Decline and Fall* and even a churlish
pamphlet by James Chelsum, saying that Chelsum's "*Remarks* . . . are
written in a candid and liberal manner; they shew the Author to be a
scholar and a gentleman, and they contain some things that merit Mr.
Gibbon's attention" (55:462).

Both reviews also indicate that Gibbon was not so out of touch
with British opinion, even on matters of religious history, as has
sometimes been believed. The literary and scholarly public, except
for some clergymen and "a large number of ladies equally respectable
for their age and their learning" (as Gibbon ironically described
them—*Letters* 2:107) could ignore or regret Gibbon's lack of piety and
accept his history, on the whole, as both fascinating and authoritative.
In Burke's *Annual Register*, appearing, of course, after the controversy
was well established, the reviewer says that the *Decline and Fall* has
"justly" received "a more general approbation" than any other book
the reviewer can remember. Gibbon's undertaking requires "great
industry, deep learning, and sound judgment, [with] the rare talent of
rendering . . . obscure times, and forgotten persons, engaging and
delightful. By this first volume now published, the author has shewn
that he possesses all these qualities in a very high degree." But in the
two last chapters, Gibbon shows partiality toward the Roman perse-
cutors and seems to have ceased to be a historian and to assume the
role "of an ecclesiastical critick."[34] This is a balanced representation
of the general view. Indeed, Gibbon does not seem to have known
until June that anyone was *sufficiently* offended to wish to attack his
book in print.

Through February and March, Gibbon enjoyed reports of its success. He spent a good deal of the morning in his library, dispatching
presentation copies and absorbing and replying to letters of praise. By
the end of March, the need for a second edition was already apparent.
"A thousand Copies are sold, . . . which in so short a time is, for a
book of that price a very uncommon event" (*Letters* 2:100). His after-
noons were taken up with "business"—Parliament—and the evenings
with society—whist, chess, dinners, theatre, and one-man performances of French plays by the French entertainer Texier, who was in
England because he had been accused of defrauding the French Ex-
chequer. Gibbon much enjoyed these "wonderful" performances, which
seem usually to have occurred at the Beauclerks' house in Great
Russell Street.[35]

Topham Beauclerk, a member of the Club just two years younger
than Gibbon, and his wife Lady Diana (daughter of the third duke of

Marlborough and divorced from her first husband) appear frequently for a time in Gibbon's correspondence. Beauclerk is more famous as a friend of Johnson's—"Beauclerk could take more liberty with him, than any body with whom [Boswell] ever saw him." Boswell also notes Beauclerk's propensity to satire; Johnson once told him, "You never open your mouth but with intention to give pain." It might seem surprising that he and Gibbon were friends, but Boswell's explanation of the similarly improbable friendship between Beauclerk and Bennet Langton seems perfectly adaptable to Gibbon: Beauclerk "had so ardent a love of literature, so acute an understanding, such elegance of manners, and so well discerned the excellent qualities of Mr. [Gibbon], a gentleman eminent not only for . . . worth, but for an inexhaustible fund of entertaining conversation, that they became intimate friends."[36] Gibbon was sufficiently intimate with the Beauclerks to visit them in Brighton as well as London and to borrow their cook when he wished to give a fine dinner.[37] Though the Beauclerks' was a love match—Lady Diana had been badly treated by her first husband, but it was for Beauclerk that she divorced him—after a time she was apparently abused by Beauclerk as well. His mind and personality were adversely affected by his final illness. Gibbon's sympathies, like those of Edmund Burke, seem to have been with Lady Diana. Fanny Burney reports the following scene in 1782, at Sir Joshua Reynolds's house in Richmond:

> From the window of the dining-parlour, Sir Joshua directed us to look at a pretty white house which belonged to Lady Di Beauclerk [Topham Beauclerk had died in 1780].
> "I am extremely glad," said Mr. Burke, "to see her at last so well housed; poor woman! the bowl has long rolled in misery; I rejoice that it has now found its balance. I never, myself, so much enjoyed the sight of happiness in another, as in that woman when I first saw her after the death of her husband. It was really enlivening to behold her placed in that sweet house, released from all her cares, a thousand pounds a year at her own disposal, and—her husband was dead! Oh! it was pleasant, it was delightful to see her enjoyment of her situation!"
> "But without considering the circumstances," said Mr. Gibbon, "this may appear very strange, though, when they are fairly stated, it is perfectly rational and unavoidable."
> "Very true," said Mr. Burke, "if the circumstances are not considered, Lady Di may seem highly reprehensible."
> He then . . . describ[ed] the misery [Beauclerk] gave his wife, his singular ill-treatment of her, and the necessary relief the death of such a man may give.[38]

In 1776, however, neither the marriage nor Beauclerk's health had begun to deteriorate, and it was a pleasure to Gibbon to have both Beauclerks among the friends "sitting by the fire" in his parlor in

Bentinck Street (*Letters* 2:97). In a rather different way, Gibbon enjoyed the company of Adam Smith, then in London, whose *Wealth of Nations* was published by Strahan and Cadell in March. "What an excellent work is that with which our common friend, Mr Adam Smith, has enriched the public!" Gibbon wrote to Adam Ferguson on the first of April. "An extensive science in a single book, and the most profound ideas expressed in the most perspicuous language. He proposes visiting you very soon" (*Letters* 2:101). In the middle of the month, Gibbon spent a week in Bath, where he—or his book—enjoyed the admiration of the ladies, but from which he "long[ed] to get back to the Library in Bentinck Street," to continue "preparing and correcting (though in a minute and almost imperceptible way)" his new edition (*Letters* 2:102, 110).

Early in April, the successful author had taken several good resolutions. He bought a "pocket book," in which to keep memoranda of his activities and (especially) of his expenditures, and he hired one E. Noble to prepare a catalogue of his library. (This was presumably the "Bentinck Street" catalogue, with entries as late as 1777, thought by G. L. Keynes to have been prepared by Gibbon's valet, Richard Caplen.) Gibbon had in hand £7.1.6 at the beginning of the month and withdrew £100 from Gosling's bank for current expenses. Unexpectedly, on the third, he received £65 from two lottery tickets. These funds sufficed for more than two months, during which he paid Caplen's wages for a year (£35) and reimbursed his two principal servants for some £55 in various housekeeping expenses, including a housemaid's yearly wage (£7.12). During April and May he lost track of £7 (he attended the theatre several times without listing any expenditure for tickets, but he recorded that he tipped the box keepers at Drury Lane a guinea). In addition, he had a net loss of about eight shillings at whist, bought three dozen of champagne for ten guineas, paid the seven-guinea subscription for Almack's club (to which he was elected on May 20), and travelled to and from Bath at a cost of £16.7. He also paid various rates and taxes (including an "Easter offering"—presumably a required parish payment?). His other expenditures were for meals, tips, books, paper, the lamplighter's bill, and a Stilton cheese.[39] This does not seem particularly extravagant, but when it is extended for a year, and to it are added the expenses he paid by bank draft instead of cash, it becomes clear that he required an annual income of at least £1,700 while living in London. This amount includes the £300 paid to his stepmother, but no payments on the debts inherited from his father. The burden of those debts may be estimated from Gibbon's willingness to sell half his inheritance to be rid of them and from his comment, "I am tired of being a Landlord at 2³/₄ and a Tenant at 4¹/₂ per Cent" (*Letters* 1:348).

In this sanguine period, however, with the *Decline and Fall* selling well and two-thirds of its profits belonging to its author, Gibbon seems for once to have been very little worried about his income. After all, even his lottery tickets were for once not blanks. A trip to Bath to visit Mrs. Gibbon occupied him between April 9 and 21, while Parliament was recessed. When he returned, he found that the Neckers had arrived in London on the seventeenth. Of course he was eager to renew his friendship with Suzanne Curchod and with her husband, the rising politician Jacques Necker. He also made a new acquaintance in the family: their ten-year-old daughter, Germaine, later Madame de Staël. In May, therefore, he was "very busy with the Neckers. I live with her just as I used to do twenty years ago laugh at her Paris varnish, and oblige her to become a simple reasonable Suissesse. The man, who might read English husbands, lessons of proper and dutiful behaviour is a sensible goodnatured Creature" (*Letters* 2:109). Though Gibbon assured his stepmother—*still* anxious about his old attachment to Suzanne—that she was "no longer a Beauty" (*Letters* 2:103), it is clear that she had lost little of her charm for him, and that the friendship that survived their romance was a strong one. In fact, so pleasant were the visits that little Germaine offered to marry Gibbon. When asked why, she explained that her parents enjoyed Mr. Gibbon's conversation so much that she wanted to give them that pleasure all the time.[40] Though the anecdote does not mention her own pleasure in his company, they became good friends, and there is ample evidence that Gibbon liked his friends' children and was good with them.[41] Even after obesity, illness, and vanity had stiffened his behavior with adults, he unbent, literally and figuratively, with children.

He gave a "great dinner" for the Neckers on May 7. Probably among the guests was a French friend of theirs, J. B. A. Suard, man of letters and translator of Robertson's history into French. Though Gibbon was still hoping that his friend Deyverdun would translate the *Decline and Fall*, he would remember Suard when it became apparent that Deyverdun was too busy or too lazy to do the translation. Some of the company on these occasions probably spoke only English, for Suzanne (who *read* English well enough to appreciate the *Decline and Fall* long before it was translated) avers that while she was in England, "I understood no one, and no one understood me."[42] She urged Gibbon to come to visit Paris, and when she left in May, he "gave her en partant the most solemn assurances of following her . . . in less than two months" (*Letters* 2:112). Holroyd, who objected to his friend's planning a long absence, seems to have taken this plan seriously; certainly it made him indignant. As long as Suzanne was in London casting her real, if tempered, spell, neither the "voice of indolence" nor those of his English friends and relations could make Gibbon see any objections to an early journey to Paris.

Meanwhile, of course, "business" continued—he records votes on three important motions in late April and May (with his own position underscored; he was in the majority except on the motion not to seat Wilkes for Middlesex.) And in addition to the Neckers, who returned to Paris on May 28, he enjoyed whist, theatre, clubs, and country excursions to Twickenham and Strawberry Hill. At the latter, "Mr W[alpole] read his unpublished Chapter on modern gardening—agreeable." Maybe! Certainly it was agreeable to be among the elect at Strawberry Hill.

On June 3, the second edition of the *Decline and Fall* came out. On June 4, its author at last sat down to begin the second volume. It would prove a false start, interrupted, in the event, by the need to vindicate its "elder brother," to enjoy the fruits of his success, and to meet its responsibilities.

TWO

VINDICATIONS,
1776–1781

Three Capitals

ibbon had composed the first volume of the *Decline and Fall* in obscurity, suffering the self-doubt of the writer who has not yet enjoyed a success and distracted at times by personal and financial problems. He composed volumes 2 and 3 as an acknowledged master among historical writers, a Member of Parliament asked by the Government to write an official statement, a member of the Board of Trade and Plantations, a man sought after not only for his fame but for his company by the social elite of two great capitals. His continuing financial difficulties were soothed and eased by his wealthy and expert friend John Holroyd. He could increase his library more or less at will, and he had organized it in a convenient manner. But also, for the first time in his life, he was not just an individual, but a symbol. And as a symbol, he became the object of anger and attack that was not limited to his work or to his ideas, but included his character— and even his appearance. In June of 1776, however, he was only beginning to realize that the distractions of celebrity would include those of notoriety. He thought that he could proceed expeditiously with volume 2. "I now understand from pretty good authority that Dr Porteous the friend and chaplain of St Secker [archbishop of Canterbury] is actually sharpening his goosequill against the two last Chapters," he wrote calmly (*Letters* 2:111); he expected that the news from America would draw public attention away from all lesser conflicts.

The work on which he was engaged appeared at first to be going well. In June his cash expenditures (he was faithfully keeping up his accounts) reveal only one evening of whist, two dinners and a supper, and two evenings of theatre. Either successfully resisting or untempted by social distractions, at the end of the month he could write to Holroyd, "I am now deeply engaged in the reign of Constantine, and from the specimens which I have already seen I can venture to promise that the second Volume will not be less interesting than the first" (*Letters* 2:112). But Mrs. Gibbon arrived for a visit in mid July, and she and Gibbon went to Sheffield Place on the twentieth. Scholarship necessarily took second place to social life in those circumstances, and Gibbon entered into the country house routine with apparent goodwill. On the 25th, they went to the races at Lewes, and Gibbon lost two guineas. From there, it was on to Brighton to the Beauclerks, where Gibbon lost ten pounds at "Commerce," a card game. He also paid fifteen shillings and sixpence for "Rafles." Nevertheless, after they returned to Sheffield Place on July 31, he put in enough work on the new chapter to record it as "finished . . . without the notes" on August 4. He spent the next week reading the first volume of F. Strada's *De bello Belgico*, a seventeenth-century book that he retained for his Lausanne library, although he does not cite it in the *Decline and Fall*.[1]

He did not begin the notes for this seventeenth chapter until August 24. Though he and Mrs. Gibbon returned to London on August 12, she did not immediately go on to Bath, and while she stayed with him, he had only an hour or so each evening for the *Decline*. Moreover, London had recently received news of the American Declaration of Independence, which seemed to make reconciliation with the colonies impossible. "A tough business indeed; you see by their declaration that they have now passed the Rubicon and rendered the work of a treaty infinitely more difficult," Gibbon wrote to Holroyd. "You will perhaps say so much the better but I do assure you that the *thinking* friends of government are by no means sanguine" (*Letters* 2:114). Clearly he associated himself with this group.

But the duties of friendship were probably even more distracting than filial and political concerns. The Holroyds were coming to London because their baby was due at any time (their second daughter, Louisa, was born September 2). This was a happy but anxious event. On August 15 Gibbon learned of something very disturbing: an old companion and fellow member of the Roman Club, John Damer, had killed himself. Damer was not a particular intimate of Gibbon's, but he was sufficiently troubled by this suicide to underscore the word "death" in the note he made about it. Two days later, he wrote to Holroyd: "Our old acquaintance poor John Damer shot himself last Wednesday night; at the Bedford arms his usual place of resort where he had passed several hours with four Ladies and a blind fidler. By his own indolence rather than extravagance his circumstances were

embarassed, and he had frequently declared himself tired of life"
(*Letters* 2:114). But Gibbon went on to say he was going to "eat turtle
with Garrick at Hampton," so we may conclude that he had quickly
recovered his usual calm spirits. Gibbon was accused by one of his
"Christian" opponents of advocating suicide in the *Decline and Fall*;[2]
his reaction in this instance suggests, I think, that suicide aroused in
him not admiration or horror, but pity and perhaps wonder or mild
contempt. Like Dr. Johnson, Gibbon could not imagine being tired
of London, or of life.

The Holroyds were in London from August 20 to October 3, and
Mrs. Gibbon, although she went to Essex to visit other friends on
August 24, returned to London on the fifth of September for another
week's visit with Gibbon before returning to Bath. In spite of all
distractions, Gibbon began the notes to chapter 17 on August 24, but
there is no record of his having completed them by the end of October, when he ceased to make memoranda in this pocket book. Of
course he might have completed the notes without remembering to
record that fact, but more likely he abandoned them uncompleted. We
do know that the notes and text amounted to some "fifty sheets"
(*Memoirs* 159—by way of comparison, chapters 15 and 16, without the
notes, were "written out in fourteen sheet" in their final form—*Letters*
2:81).

The British capital could fill Gibbon's days and evenings in September without help from Constantinople, the new capital of the
Roman Empire, the subject of chapter 17. In addition to the distractions of visitors, Gibbon was finally able, with Holroyd's "strenuous"
help, to break off (on October 2) the contract to sell Lenborough to
Lovegrove: "The fellow wanted either power or inclination to compleat his agreement, and . . . it was judged most expedient to consent
to a mutual discharge. By this transaction I have lost a great deal both
of time and money, and am now to begin the sale again." He added,
to his stepmother (to whom he often revealed much about feelings he
might have concealed even from Holroyd because they were weaknesses), "It has occasioned me much vexation but Holroyd assures me
that I have [been] *guilty of no fault* and that I may still entertain very
fair hopes. The subject was grown so odious to me, that I could not
bring myself ever to talk to you about it" (*Letters* 2:118; emphasis
added). Several times in Gibbon's later life we see him deal with a
painful or distasteful matter only by ignoring it, most notoriously, of
course, in the case of his "hydrocele."[3] In 1776, however, he was well
able to discuss the unpleasant matter of Lenborough with the appropriate adviser, Holroyd, and thus his denial had no harmful practical
effect.

October was also memorable for its engagements, social and intellectual. Gibbon records a weekend at Burke's "with Sir Joshua [Rey-

nolds], the Provost of Dublin, and Dr Leland," and five days "at Lord Ossory's." He wrote to Mrs. Gibbon about the latter visit:

> I have been some days at this place, and have spent them very agreably. Luckily the weather has been bad, which in a great measure has secured me from excursions, and confined us to an excellent house, conducted on an easy plan and filled with a comfortable society in which the principal part was performed by Mr Garrick. I return to town to-morrow. By the bye you will be so good as not to mention this Bedfordshire journey to Miss Holroyd [John Holroyd's sister, living in Bath]; it might get round to Sheffield place which I have cheated of a promised visit. (*Letters* 2:117)

But the big news of the month, from Gibbon's perspective, was that the long-threatened attacks on his history had begun to appear.

The *Gentleman's Magazine* had assailed the history in its belated review (dated August), warning its readers against the "poison" of this "too fashionable work." "Detesting its principles as much as we admire its style," the reviewer is "surprised by the indiscriminate praise lavished on it by other reviewers."[4] The magazine enjoyed the reputation of being the first to "expose" Gibbon, but only by a narrow margin: on October 16 appeared "an anonymous eighteen penny pamphlet, which will get the author more Glory in *the next World than in this*" (*Letters* 2:117; underlined by Holroyd).[5] This was Gibbon's description to Holroyd. To his stepmother, he wrote (after telling her the American news): "With regard to another great object of hostilities, *myself*, the attack has been already begun. . . . I was afraid that I should be hurt by [the attacks], but if I may presume of my future feelings from the first tryal of them I shall be in every sense of the word *invulnerable*" (*Letters* 2:118). His comment reveals that it was an emotional, not an intellectual, vulnerability, that he had feared and from which, so far, he felt safe. His reactions to his critics confirm his own view of his equanimity, for the only two opponents who aroused him to action and anger, as we shall see, were those who attacked his honor as a scholar and gentleman, Davis and Priestley. Those who merely attacked his irreligious opinions did not trouble him.[6]

Understandably, Gibbon put aside the immense chapter on the reign of Constantine to read the early pamphlets attacking him, and put aside all thought of answering them when he found both unthreatening. James Chelsum's was too shrill and shallow to require rejoinder. The other reply of 1776 was by Richard Watson.[7] It could not be contemptuously ignored, but it was directed to Gibbon's interpretations, not his scholarship, so that Gibbon and Watson might mutually agree to disagree without loss of dignity. Watson's pamphlet was so urbane and civil in manner that it even permitted a friendly acquaintance between Watson and Gibbon. "If any calls of pleasure or business should bring Dr Watson to town, Mr Gibbon would think himself

fortunate in being permitted to solicit the honour of his acquaintance"
(*Letters* 2:119), wrote Gibbon to Watson, who replied, with equal
courtesy and promptness: "Dr. Watson accepts with pleasure Mr.
Gibbon's polite invitation to a personal acquaintance. If he comes to
town this winter, will certainly do himself the honour to wait upon
him. Begs, at the same time, to assure Mr. Gibbon, that he will be
very happy to have an opportunity of shewing him every civility, if
curiosity, or other motives, should bring him to Cambridge."[8]

In November, then, Gibbon turned back to America and to the
problem of a French translator for volume 1. Since there was no
international copyright law to give authors control over translations of
their works, he might have left his history to find its own translator
into French—he made no effort to see that it was translated well into
German or Italian. But French, of course, was his adopted language
and cultural tradition, and he was anxious to appear in it at his best.
Deyverdun had at last written, but not to say, as Gibbon had hoped,
that his translation was complete, but rather to say that he had
decided not to undertake it (he had just completed a translation of
Goethe's *Werther*, and of course he had duties as companion to his
new charge, seventeen-year-old Abraham Hume). Gibbon therefore
turned to a professional, J. B. A. Suard, whom he had met with the
Neckers. Suard had already translated Robertson very successfully.
Gibbon said frankly: "I have always despised the gloomy philosophy
that tries to make us insensitive to glory. I am ambitious for the glory
of being read in France and on the Continent." He therefore hoped
that "the same pen that has so well represented the historic eloquence
of Robertson" would do as much for "a writer his inferior in every
respect, but who has received from the indulgence of his countrymen
a welcome almost equally favorable." Responding, however, to the
clerical complaints, Gibbon goes on to discuss the problem of censor-
ship and to offer Suard carte blanche to "soften [*adoucir*] the expression without weakening the thought" and even to change and suppress
whatever would "wound the delicacy of your Church and your police"
(*Letters* 2:122). Suard politely declined, at the end of the month, on
the basis that Gibbon himself would be the best translator: "You write
our language not only with a rare correctness and purity, but also with
an elegance, a turn of phrase and choice of word, that few of our men
of letters possess."[9] He added that he himself had previously engaged
to translate another Robertson work and that a translation of the first
part of Gibbon's book was already in press at Paris. (The translator—
self-appointed, of course—sent Gibbon a copy of his work early in
December; see below, pp. 87–88.)

Gibbon's thoughts and plans were further fixed on Paris by a letter
from Suzanne Necker, who had urged him to visit the French capital,
and who wrote not only to complain flatteringly of his not having

come, but to praise and criticize the *Decline and Fall* very astutely
(she must have been reading it in English). In November Jacques
Necker was appointed controller of finance. Suzanne's letter, written
at the end of October, though it does not hint at the impending
promotion, has much to say about the delights of celebrity in Paris.
But first, she comments on the history. She has great praise for its
combination of erudition and sensibility:

> You have added to an immense erudition the most profound and the most
> precise knowledge of men and humanity, of nations and individuals of
> every rank. You have united the philosophe and the man of feeling; and
> this period of history, unknown for centuries, will become, I have no
> doubt, the best known and the most often cited. . . . Nature, which had
> refused nothing to Aurelian or Zenobia except a Tacitus, could not bring
> herself to leave her work imperfect; if you have less subtlety than Tacitus,
> in compensation you have a hundred times more, and more varied, ideas.
> One sees that he was the model and perhaps the source for your work,
> but the source was enlarged by the torrents of thought flowing throughout
> the centuries, and you have demonstrated that a fertile and sensitive
> imagination can still add depth and range to the mind. Only philosophers
> read Tacitus, you will be read by everyone: we shall learn to think while
> believing that we are only seeing and feeling.[10]

But she had criticisms to make as well, criticisms that may have made
the praise even more acceptable to Gibbon, as guaranteeing its sincerity. While he tells her that he has "reread a hundred times with
the most lively satisfaction" her "charming letter" (*Letters* 2:126), he
replies most particularly to her criticisms; and on one issue, I think,
he may indeed have been influenced by it. Her objection to the
chapters 15 and 16—"why should a man of genius, who makes Glory
his god and hopes to live eternally in its breast, wish to deprive of the
same hope, those who replace that Glory with virtue?"—he could pass
off. But her other objection seems to have surprised him. She wrote,
"In spite of yourself, Sir, you will count among your readers as many
women as men; I say 'in spite of yourself,' for you have mistreated
women. To hear you talk, all their virtues are artificial; were *you* the
man, sir, who ought to have spoken so of women?"[11] The subsequent
volumes of the *Decline and Fall* portray female virtues more generously, as Gibbon will point out to Suzanne. A swifter response to her
complaint was a new footnote 10 to chapter 7 of the history (*DF*
chap. 7, 1:187 n. 12): "The wife of Maximin, by insinuating wise
counsels with female gentleness, sometimes brought back the tyrant
to the way of truth and humanity. . . . Paulina was the name of this
benevolent empress."

After her rebuke, Suzanne went on to a lively and flattering argument in favor of his coming to Paris to solidify his fame:

You desire and deserve the greatest celebrity: the spirit of your work proves that: but the eagle does not disdain a launching place on earth from which to rise into the air; this launching place is not to be found in London; you are all too much engaged in business; the women there do not talk, and in every country where women are not the center of conversation, fame has only one voice and one ear. It is at Paris that it is pleasant to be a great man, for it is there alone that everyone seeks to please by lively conversation and that feelings are comunicted from one soul to another by the perfected art of exaggeration. . . . I know that your work has made a great deal of noise, but I give you no more than three years of American war before this noise will be heard no longer except in the distance. Your politics . . . suffocate even giants."[12]

Gibbon ingeniously, if unconvincingly, tried to turn her argument in favor of Paris into a defense of his portrayal of women in the history. She who exercised the art of exaggeration so brilliantly was right to praise it, he began, but she forgot, in complaining of his account of women, the country in which he was living,

and the situation of our women, who are not sufficiently considered free and reasonable companions. When one paints remote centuries, one portrays them unconsciously according to the models before one's eyes. Our Englishwomen know how to display only their disorders and follies: graces, talents, even virtues are buried in eternal ice. Please remember that in twelve years, I have spent only six weeks in the society of Mme. Necker. (*Letters* 2:127)

Two could play at the perfected art of exaggeration, but buried in the metaphor of ice is a serious, lifelong desire on Gibbon's part for a "free and reasonable companion."

The conclusion, however flattering to Suzanne, that she, and perhaps others of her countrywomen, are the only women who meet this description, seems to indicate a real obstacle to matrimony for Gibbon. His stepmother was still hopefully proposing candidates for the role of Mrs. Gibbon, but not even their names survive in his letters.[13] Instead, he found himself admiring Englishwomen in socially and even morally anomalous circumstances. His liking for Lady Diana Beauclerk, who had flouted conventional social behavior in divorcing her abusive husband and marrying for love, was the first of several friendships with Englishwomen who had to be admired for their graces and talents even though they were not docile and virtuous homemakers or household ornaments. His complaint here suggests an uncertainty about female potential that he later resolved in ways more generous to the sex as a whole. In this 1776 letter to Suzanne, moreover, the criticism of his English female models is added, almost gratuitously, to two perhaps more serious arguments, first, that as a historian he had to portray the women as they were, and second, that he had represented as artificial only female *courage,* not all female virtues. "Your sex," he pronounces, "was destined to console the human race, always to please it, sometimes to instruct it, never to make it tremble" (*Letters* 2:127).

He was not able to seek the advantages of French society and fame immediately, however. As he told Holroyd, "Parliament visits dinners suppers, and an hour or two stole with difficulty for the Decline leave but very little leisure" (*Letters* 2:119) He explained to Suzanne that he had to postpone his trip to Paris because of duties as his friend Clarke's executor: "He has left some business to disentangle, a very important lawsuit to pursue in the courts, and essential functions to fill that would be neglected if I were away from London at present" (*Letters* 2:127, with n. 2). Possibly he simply invokes Clarke's case as a creditable excuse, for fourteen years later he claimed, when asked by some of Clarke's heirs to intervene in some legal affairs, that he had been only a nominal trustee, with all real duties devolving on his associate (*Letters* 3:200). But as we have seen, he considered himself very much a real trustee immediately after Clarke's death, and Clarke's suit is perhaps the "particular business of serious importance" of which he speaks to Holroyd *"upon my honour"* as the reason for his delay in leaving London in December. It is probable that in 1790— ill, lazy, and expatriate—he preferred to minimize his involvement in the matter. In 1776, when suits over Clarke's estate were still active in Chancery, Gibbon seems still to have considered himself a functioning executor for his friend.

But pious duties to the dead were certainly not his only "business." In nearly every letter to Holroyd, he reports on American affairs and seeks financial advice or action (never loans or gifts, however). In December, when he writes about the business delaying him, he tells Holroyd, "You may say in general in the family (if any should bark) that you are satisfied with my conduct and order them to shut their trap" (*Letters* 2:132). The family, of course, is Holroyd's, but the playfully rough colloquialism shows how much Gibbon identifies himself as a member of it. In the same letter, he reports "confused" news from New York; he had heard that Washington's troops "shew little courage or conduct, but the ground is incredibly strong, and it seems running into a War of posts." And he wants action on Lenborough: "Is the historian of the Roman Empire to write out twenty Copies himself of [an advertisement of] a few acres in Bucks. I should like to have them transcribed or even printed. Why not?"

He made no further progress on the *Decline and Fall* and seems to have done very little serious reading. But he had read two significant new works in manuscript, both by the recently deceased David Hume. In a December letter to J. B. A. Suard, who had asked Gibbon to procure for him a copy of Hume's autobiography, Gibbon, promising to send it as soon as possible, points out that it has not yet been published. "But I have already read this little work in manuscript, and my veneration for the memory of its author made reading it very interesting. His life is only twenty pages long and is written in the style of intimate conversation. There we discover with pleasure a true and honorable nature, the naive vanity of a child, the independence of a philosopher, and the courage of a dying man who loved life without pining for it." Though Gibbon was pleased with this work, it interested him much less than the other manuscript. "He has left a very important manuscript composed quite a long time ago. It is some Dialogues on the Nature of the Gods comparable to Cicero's. M. Hume portrays two believers who argue with each other and a skeptical philosopher who profits very adroitly from their discord to trample underfoot the debris of their opposed systems. The manuscript was entrusted to me for several days, and I do not hesitate to pronounce it the most profound, the most ingenious, and the best written of M. Hume's philosophic works."[14] First refusal of the publication rights of this manuscript had been left to Strahan, and it was undoubtedly he who lent the manuscript to Gibbon.

In December also Gibbon read with great attention another new work—the first volume of the French translation of his history. It reached him on the seventh of December "by the *post* (charged two Guineas and a half)" and contained only the first seven chapters, though it was to be continued. "I did not however regret the money," Gibbon wrote to Holroyd, "as it is admirably well done by M. de Septchenes (Sevenoaks) a young man who has been lately in England and who sent me a very pleasant dose of flattery on the occasion" (*Letters* 2:130). Three days later Gibbon wrote to Leclerc de Septchênes with high praise for his work and directions for avoiding expensive postage in future by sending parcels free via Sir Stanier Porten:

> Imagine the uneasiness of a father over the fate of a child, lost without a guide in the middle of Paris and exposed to the danger of dishonor by liaisons unworthy of the name he bears. If the father learned suddenly that a helping hand, leading the son out of such a sad situation, had presented him to the best society of Paris with a brilliance and advantages not native to him, judge, Sir, the feelings of this father toward his friend and benefactor. (*Letters* 2:131)

Having thus reciprocated Septchênes's flattery, Gibbon promised to provide him with a list of corrections and requested the opportunity to see the proofs of future sections. Septchênes mentions both the praise and the corrections gratefully in his next preface.

Leclerc de Septchênes, in 1776 only about twenty years old, had been an English tutor to Louis XVI, two years older, when he was dauphin, and became one of the king's secretaries when Louis inherited the throne (May 1774). The king himself has been credited with contributing to this translation of the *Decline and Fall*. French bibliographers from 1814 on have accepted the story, of which the "most probable" version is the following: "It passes for certain that Louis XVI, studying English under the direction of M. Leclerc de Septchênes, . . . worked on the first volume of Gibbon's history . . . and that when he arrived at the fifteenth and sixteenth chapters, he gave up the work, which M. de Septchênes revised, continued, and printed."[15] Whatever his part in the translation, if any, it is certain that Louis XVI read the *Decline and Fall* and met its author, and it is morally certain that Gibbon did not know that the king was thought to have participated in the translation, for Gibbon would certainly have mentioned so interesting and flattering a circumstance in his *Memoirs;* and he could have done so without scruple after the king had been deposed and killed.

Gibbon's retrospective view of the translation as a whole was considerably less favorable than this first reaction: "The first Volume had been feebly though faithfully translated into French by Mr Le Clerc de Septchênes a young Gentleman of a studious character and liberal fortune" (*Memoirs* 194). Perhaps Gibbon was influenced not only by his own reflections on the quality of the text, but also by the French critics, who, though they did not criticize the translation, were considerably less flattering to the original than were the critics of England, Italy, and Germany. But at the end of 1776, Gibbon was certainly happy about the fate of his "child," as he went down to Sussex to spend the New Year's holiday at Sheffield Place. When he returned to London in January 1777, he expected an early visit from the Holroyds and believed that everything went "on very prosperously in America. . . . The Continental (perhaps *now* the rebel) Army is in a great measure dispersed . . . but what *I* think of much greater consequence a province [made] its submission and desired to be reinstated in the peace of the King. It is indeed only poor little Georgia" (*Letters* 2:136). His sole anxiety was about some lace made for him by his stepmother that had failed to arrive from Bath.

Yet he did not return to work on the *Decline and Fall*. Instead, he undertook to attend William Hunter's lectures on anatomy at the Royal College of Surgeons. His plan was merely to attend *some* of the lectures, but in fact, he was fascinated by the course and attended "two hours *every day*" (Gibbon's emphasis) throughout the series, even delaying his departure for Paris in May until after the lecture on April 25th (according to Hunter's biography, the lecture series continued into May, but Gibbon seemed to think this lecture climactic—*Letters* 2:141, 144). Gibbon's library throughout his life shows a fascination with natural science. Dr. Hunter's lectures, he remarked to his stepmother, "have opened to me a new and very entertaining scene within myself," and the strength of his interest is further witnessed by his deciding to attend lectures on chemistry as well. "The principles of these sciences, and a taste for books of Natural history contributed to multiply my ideas and images; and the Anatomist or Chemist may sometimes track me in their snow" (*Memoirs* 159—echoing Dryden on the classics).

Gibbon describes his typical day during this period very aptly in a letter to Holroyd, who was in the country: "My life though more lively than yours is almost as uniform; a very little reading and writing in the morning, bones or guts [that is, Hunter's lectures] from two to four, pleasant dinners from five to eight and afterwards Clubs with an occasional assembly or supper." He writes from Almack's, with "Charles Fox . . . at my elbow declaiming on the impossibility of keeping America" (*Letters* 2:140). But Almack's was not the only club he favored; he missed only one supper of the Literary Club at the Turk's Head in 1776.[16] Nor did he neglect Aunt Kitty—"Mrs Porten is as young as ever," he tells Dorothea Gibbon. "I understand the giddy girl has neglected writing to you" (*Letters* 2:141).

In April he received a very satisfactory reckoning from his publishers, who had decided to print a third quarto edition, this time with the notes at the foot of the page. They calculated the expenses of the new edition (1,000 copies) as £310, including five guineas to the corrector of the press for "extra care." If a thousand books sold at 16 shillings each, Gibbon's two-thirds of the profit would be £326.13.4, and the publishers' share would be £163.6.8. Errors would come out of the author's portion.[17] Two and a half thousand copies had already been sold on similar terms. Thus Gibbon thought himself in a position to think of the trip to Paris as "paid by the Roman Empire" (*Letters* 2:141).

Dorothea Gibbon was not at all happy about the proposed journey. Dorothea, who herself had made a love match in middle age, without extraordinary beauty (though she had a beautiful speaking voice and excellent teeth),[18] could not think Gibbon safe from the attractions of Suzanne Necker or the hatred of the French clergy. Gibbon patiently reassured her:

> When you have indulged the exquisite sensibility of friendship, you will, I am sure, make a proper use of your excellent understanding, and will soon smile at your own terrors.
>
> The constancy and danger of a twenty years passion is a subject upon which I hardly know how to be serious. I am ignorant what effect that period of time has produced upon me, but I do assure you that it has committed very great ravages upon the Lady, and that at present she is very far from being an object either of desire or of scandal. As a woman of talents and fortune she is at the head of the litterature of Paris, the station of her husband procures her respect from the first people of the

Country, and the reception which I shall meet with in her house will give
me advantages that have fallen to the share of few Englishmen. When I
mention her *house* I must remove the misapprehension which seems to
have allarmed you. I shall *visit*, but not *lodge* there. . . . So that the
husband will be easy, the world will be mute, and my moral character will
still preserve its immaculate purity.

A moment's reflection will satisfy you that I have as little to fear from
the hatred of the priests, as from the love of Madame N. (*Letters* 2:143)

These alarms quieted, Gibbon turned his attention to settling his
household for the journey and to the last business of Parliament. He
was disturbed by news from his estates in Hampshire, but there was
an easy answer for any such problem. He wrote to Holroyd, compre-
hensively, "Bad news from Hampshire.—Support Hugonin, comfort
me, correct or expell Winton, sell Lenborough and remove my temporal cares" (*Letters* 2:145).

At first Gibbon hoped to wait for the vote on the budget before
leaving for Paris—he reported with amusement that "notwithstanding
the strict oeconomy recommended by Charles Fox and John Wilkes"
(Opposition leaders noted for their personal extravagance), Parliament had "paid the Royal debts" (*Letters* 2:145). But after nearly a
week's extra delay, he set out on May 5. His faithful valet Caplen
travelled in the chaise with him, and he was attended also by a Swiss
footman on horseback. A daring privateer attack and bad weather
delayed him briefly at Dunkirk, but on May 7 he wrote notes to both
Dorothea Gibbon and Holroyd informing them of his safe arrival in
Calais. There he found Lord Coleraine, with whom he had a "good
dinner," and "a Theatre at the end of Dessaints Garden," which led
him to stay at Calais long enough to enjoy a comedy (*Letters* 2:148).
He arrived in Paris on Saturday evening, where he took up residence
in the Hotel de Modène. He wrote a three-line note to tell Dorothea
Gibbon his address and to assure her that he was comfortably settled,
and then—as he had anticipated—his virtues as a correspondent totally lapsed.

We have, however, accounts of this sojourn in Paris from Gibbon's
pen both in his memoirs and in belated letters home, and a few useful
comments from others. He recounts this stage of his life in only one
draft of his memoirs, the one that is most succinct, and he sums up
his life in Paris in one long paragraph describing society at the
Neckers, morning study at the royal library and that of the Abbey de
St. Germain, meetings with men of letters (unsought, he says, but
not declined), and the dispute with one of them, Mably, that led "his
jealous, irascible spirit" to "revenge itself on a work, which he was
incapable of reading in the original" (*Memoirs* 158). His fortunate
friendship with the Neckers is the first object of Gibbon's account:
"As their friend I was introduced to the best company of both sexes:

to the foreign ministers of all nations; and to the first names and characters of France: who distinguished me by such marks of civility and kindness, as gratitude will not suffer me to forget, and modesty will not allow me to enumerate" (*Memoirs* 158). Michel Baridon, oddly, sees this statement as "the most obvious toadyism" (*la flagornerie la plus évidente*).[19] But the sincerity of Gibbon's gratitude in the letters, the necessity of avoiding self-praise, and the desire to please the then unhappy Neckers, who would certainly read the memoirs, at least in manuscript, easily explain his crediting them, rather than the fame of his history, with the introductions he enjoyed.

Baridon, though he thinks Gibbon exaggerates his debt to the Neckers' kindness, acknowledges that the connection really gave Gibbon certain advantages in social circles, such as access to the diplomatic community. Those advantages Gibbon clearly rated very high in 1777. A French noblewoman had a different perspective on the Neckers (who, after all, were bourgeois and Swiss). Mademoiselle de Luxembourg was annoyed that two "women of rank" (her goddaughter and a friend) had "countenanced" the Neckers: "If their manners had approached those of good *ton*, they would only have been ridiculous. But as these women found them completely different from anything they had known before, they believed they were dealing with philosophy."[20] The witticism is sufficiently clumsy and malicious to be genuine, but whatever its intention, in fact it shows that at least two women of rank frequented Suzanne Necker's salons—though she was less interested in attracting people of rank and mere fashion than in the international and intellectual society in which she shone.

Gibbon was more than satisfied. He described his life in Paris to his stepmother with obvious delight:

> My connection with the Neckers who every day acquire more power and deserve more respect first opened the door to me, and perhaps the reputation of a popular writer has contributed a little to enlarge the entrance. I pass my time in the society of men of letters, people of fashion, the higher ranks of *the Clergy*, and the foreign Ministers, and except when I wish to steal a few moments privacy it seldom happens to me to dine or sup at my hotel. The vacancies of my time are filled by the public libraries in the morning and in the afternoon by the Spectacles, and as part of my acquaintance begin to disperse themselves in the environs of Paris, I have contrived . . . to make several very pleasant excursions. (*Letters* 2:155)

This account is not merely reassuring sugarcoating for the anxious elderly lady. Gibbon's report to Holroyd is much the same in effect, though different in tone and more detailed:

> The reception which I have met with from [the Neckers] very far surpassed my most sanguine expectations. I do not indeed lodge in their house (as it might excite the jealousy of the husband and procure me a

letter de cachet), but I live very much with them dine and sup whenever they have company which is almost every day, and whenever I like it for they are not in the least *exigeans*. Mr Walpole gave me an introduction to Madame du Deffand, an agreable Young Lady of eighty two years of Age who has constant suppers and the best Company in Paris. When you see the D[uke] of Richmond at Lewes he will give you an account of that house where I meet him almost every evening. Ask him about Madame de Cambis. I am afraid poor Mary [the duchess of Richmond] is entirely forgot. (*Letters* 2:150)

Surprisingly, those who think that Gibbon was sincerely piqued by Necker's lack of jealousy when they first met have not cited this passage, which is, of course, equally playful. More seriously threatening to Mrs. Gibbon's desire to keep Gibbon safe for Englishwomen, at least according to Madame du Deffand, was the Comtesse de Cambis herself.[21] In August, however, Gibbon wrote "envy[ing Holroyd] Lady Payne and Lady Dy" and with a message for Abigail Holroyd: "Let not the generous breast of My Lady be torn by the black serpents of envy. She still possesses the first place in the sentiments of her slave: [and] the adventure of the fan was a mere accident" (*Letters* 2:158). At forty Gibbon might still have considered himself very much an eligible bachelor, but he seems in fact already most comfortable in the role of wide-ranging and playful gallantry that characterized his relationships with women in the last part of his life.

Gibbon's pleasure in his reception in France is apparent. What, we may wonder, did the French think of him? That "agreable Young Lady of eighty two," Madame du Deffand, was very much taken with him, although she found the *Decline and Fall* tedious. She praised him strongly to Walpole—she wished he would never go home, his conversation was very fluent and put one at ease, he never posed self-consciously as an Author, and—something very difficult in that society—his behavior gave no room for ridicule. This last point suggests strongly that Gibbon had not yet developed any singular habits of speech or action. By the end of his stay, however, he had either acquired an annoying habit, or allowed it to appear in her presence: she says he borders on the ridiculous in trying to make a polished phrase out of everything he says. Her final verdict to Walpole: "He is a very sensible man, who has much conversation, infinite knowledge, you will add, perhaps, infinite intelligence, and you would perhaps be right; I haven't decided on this point. He is too much concerned about our approval, too much desires to acquire it. I always had it on the tip of my tongue to tell him, don't torment yourself, you deserve the honour of being French."[22]

Madame du Deffand's shrewd observation—though perhaps it has less to do with the French nation than with the social world wherever

Gibbon was—is indirectly supported by comments he himself makes. He really was welcomed; he wanted to see in that welcome even more cordiality and personal friendship than he received. "Gradually or rather rapidly I find my acquaintance spreading over the most valuable parts of Paris. They pretend to like me, and whatever you may think of French professions, I am convinced that some at least are sincere. . . . I feel myself easy and happy in their Company" (*Letters* 2:150). The pleasure is clear; so is the wishful thinking: he does not want to see mere politeness in their assertions of friendship. Madame de Genlis later claimed to find him unoriginal as well as immoral, but she says he was praised "to the skies" by "all the philosophes." The abbé de Morellet, something of a philosophe, told an English correspondent that "we" found in Gibbon more wit than depth.[23] Yet, as Gibbon hoped, some of the French protestations of friendship may have been sincere. Madame du Deffand seems to have been the only observer sufficiently acute to recognize that Gibbon's desire to please might be excessive.

She, however, being blind, could not be unduly offended by his appearance, except under peculiar circumstances. A well-known contemporary anecdote supports the view that his features were grossly obscured by fat even at this relatively early period. When Madame du Deffand was introduced to someone for the first time, it was her custom to form a mental picture of the new acquaintance by touching his or her face. When she put her hand to Gibbon's face, she is said to have exclaimed, "Fi donc!" believing that someone was tricking her by presenting instead the behind of a naked baby.[24] Neither she nor Gibbon mentions any such misapprehension, as is certainly understandable. It is not clear, however, just how little he then graced the "silks and silver" with which he had (as usual) hastened to deck himself (*Letters* 2:151). We know that Gibbon was not excessively fat in early youth, or even when he made his Italian journey, and the 1774 portrait was not flatteringly retouched, according to Sheffield, but was an excellent likeness of Gibbon before he became fat. Nor does he seem grotesquely fat in the famous Reynolds portrait, which Malone considered an excellent likeness. But that portrait, as engraved by Hall and published in the second volume of the *Decline and Fall* (1781), struck even a friend such as Lord North as so ugly that he said Gibbon "sold a bargain" in offering it to the purchasers of his history.[25] He certainly had not become so fat as he was eventually to be. While living in Lausanne, he gained so much weight that Lord Sheffield told Dorothea Gibbon that Gibbon was "much more enormous than when he left" when he returned to England in 1787.[26] In Lausanne, but not in England, his tailors' bills constantly include charges for remaking and enlarging garments.

Perhaps it was in Paris that obesity began to get the upper hand.

It has been some time since we heard of Gibbon's walks in Kensington Gardens, and though in Paris his pleasures included "the Spectacles and promenades," we need not infer much exercise from a man
who had "two footmen in handsome liveries behind [his] Coach." He
had invitations both to dine and to sup nearly every day—often
multiple invitations:

> Let me just in two words give you an idea of my day [he wrote to
> Holroyd on June 16]. I am now going (nine o'Clock) to the King's Library
> where I shall stay till twelve, as soon as I am dressed I set out to dine
> with the Duke de Nivernois, shall go from thence to the French Comedy
> into the Princess de Beauvau's loge grillèe, and am not quite determined
> whether I shall sup at Madame du Deffand, Madame Necker's or the
> Sardinian Embassadress's. (*Letters* 2:151)

And he ate—probably in addition to the English breakfast on which
he insisted throughout his life—every meal: "To the great admiration
of the French I regularly dine and regularly sup, drink a dish of strong
Coffee after each meal and find my stomach a citizen of the World"
(*Letters* 2:157). If he did not yet have a "Silenus belly," this was the
way to acquire one.

J. B. A. Suard, after Gibbon's death, used this phrase of him in an
often-cited description:

> The author of the great and superb History of the Roman Empire was
> hardly [five] feet tall [Suard says four feet seven or eight inches, but the
> French inch was 1.066 English inches, so we must add approximately four
> inches to this estimate for English measure]; his huge trunk and Silenus
> belly were placed on the sort of slender legs one calls flutes [shaped like
> loaves of French bread]; his feet, so pigeon-toed that the left toe often
> touched the right, were long and large enough to support a frame a foot
> taller; in the middle of his face, no larger than a fist, the base of his nose
> was buried in his skull more deeply than the nose of a Kalmuck, and his
> eyes, very bright but very small, were lost in the same depths.[27]

But Suard saw Gibbon on numerous occasions, some much later in
Gibbon's life, and this description seems heightened (although Suard's
biographer assures us that he disliked caricature) for effect. It is
confirmed generally, but in some respects contradicted, and I suspect
corrected, by the description of the sharp-eyed young Fanny Burney,
written in 1782.[28] Both descriptions suggest that Gibbon's anxiety
about his ability to please and rather touching pleasure in successes
(and his warning to Holroyd that others should not see "the playful
effusions of friendship" in which he reported these successes—*Letters*
2:151) rested in part on his consciousness that graces of appearance
had been denied him.

His days in Paris were not entirely devoted to frivolous pursuits,
however, as he indicated to Holroyd with his itinerary. He profited

from the generous policy of the "public" libraries, which allowed him to take books to his hotel to study at leisure. He mentions particularly the Abbey de St Germain and the royal library. The experience of this generosity may have contributed to his refusal to join the Protestant bigotry against Catholic scholarship in the remainder of the *Decline and Fall*, though of course it in no way affected his opinion of Catholic religious views or of asceticism, monasticism, and fanaticism. Even the evenings brought him welcome conversation with men and women of letters and culture, the most notable among them being, perhaps, the great naturalist Buffon, "who united with a sublime Genius, the most amiable simplicity of mind and manners" (*Letters* 2:158). Gibbon came to count among his intellectual acquaintances the duc de Choiseul, whose proposed translation of the *Decline and Fall* Gibbon had viewed with alarm—as a rival to the one he then expected from Deyverdun—in 1776 (*Letters* 2:108). In 1777, however, Choiseul *requested* a meeting with Gibbon—an obvious sign of intelligence and good taste—and Gibbon soon concluded that he "deserve[d] attention both for himself and for keeping the best house in Paris" (*Letters* 2:158).

Gibbon's attention to Choiseul's knowledge and judgment is attested by the surviving notebook Gibbon kept in Paris, which deals with materials not from books but from personal testimony (or archival records).[29] In it there are two entries based on information from Choiseul. These and other data in the notebook suggest that Gibbon was instructing himself as a politician as well as a historian, though there is a choice piece of pure gossip as well, according to which the heir apparent to the Russian throne had been fathered by a Count Soltikov instead of the impotent Peter III.[30] Most of the entries concern population, taxes and other sources of revenue, and military establishments and other state expenses in modern European nations. Gibbon's informants included the duc de Duras (director of the "spectacles"), M. de la Reynière (*fermier général*), the président de Cotte, the marquis de Castries, the chevalier de Chastellux, "M. Garnier and the originals of the Controle General," Necker, and others, as well as Choiseul. Some of the information he derived on these subjects is employed in chapter 17 of the *Decline and Fall* (*DF* 2:191 n. 191 [182]) for population and revenue estimates and comparisons, but these perspectives were as valuable to the "senator" as to the historian.

It is clear that in both roles, Gibbon was making good use of his dinners and suppers. On one occasion, however, there was a conflict between the two. Gibbon numbered among his old friends E. L. de Foncemagne, a member of the Academy of Inscriptions. At Foncemagne's table he had an encounter with a well-known French historian, the abbé de Mably. The encounter, political in origin, had consequences for Gibbon's reputation as a writer.

Gudin de la Brenellerie reports the scene this way:

Mably and Gibbon were dining at M. de Foncemagne's with a grand
company. The conversation turned almost entirely on history. During
dessert, the abbé, a profound politician, shifted the talk to the administration; and, as by character, humor, and the habit of admiring Livy, he
valued only republican systems, he began to vaunt the excellence of
republics, thoroughly persuaded that the learned Englishman would approve entirely, and would admire the depth of genius that had made a
Frenchman perceive all their advantages. But M. Gibbon, instructed by
experience in the inconveniences of a popular government, was not at all
entirely of his opinion; he defended generally the monarchical government. The abbé wanted to convince him by means of arguments drawn
from Livy and from Plutarch (in favor of the Spartans). Gibbon, endowed
with the happiest of memories, and having all the facts at his fingertips,
soon dominated the conversation. The abbé became annoyed, then angry,
and said some hard things. The Englishman, preserving the calm of his
country, seized the advantage and pressed the abbé with success increasing in proportion to the abbé's anger. The conversation grew heated, and
M. de Foncemagne broke it up by rising from the table.[31]

To this conversational defeat Gudin attributes Mably's sneers at the
Decline and Fall in a subsequent book, and Gibbon gratefully follows
him in his *Memoirs* (169–70). Next to being called an unscrupulous
scholar, Gibbon most objected to the abbé's charge, dullness.

Politics led Gibbon to some other encounters during his stay in
Paris. These did not, however, reflect the official tension between
England and France. Gibbon wrote to Holroyd:

You may possibly expect from me some account of the designs and policy
of the French Court but I chuse to decline that task for two reasons. 1rst
Because you may find them laid open in every news-paper and 2dly
Because I live too much with their Courtiers and Ministers to know any
thing about them. I shall only say that I am not under any immediate
apprehensions of a War with France. . . . Far from taking any step to put
a speedy end to this astonishing dispute [between England and her American colonies], I should not be surprized if next summer they were to lend
their cordial assistance to England as to the weaker party. (*Letters* 2:157)

Perhaps the final bad guess is simply a joke; perhaps Gibbon was as
deceived by his intimacy with the courtiers as he had said he was.

Several of his political debates were with a fellow countryman, the
duke of Richmond, who, unlike Gibbon, was consistently opposed to
North's policies in America. These arguments, however, were only "a
very few slight skirmishes . . . nothing that deserves the name of a
general engagement." Gibbon adds more seriously: "The extravagance of some disputants both French and English who have espoused
the cause of America sometimes inspires me with an extraordinary
vigour [that is, of opposition to them]. Upon the whole I find it much

easier to defend the justice than the policy of our Measures; but there
are certain cases where whatever is repugnant to sound policy ceases
to be just" (*Letters* 2:157).[32] It is not clear at what Gibbon means to
hint by that last comment, but it is consistent with his fears from the
beginning that though the Government's desire to retain the colonies
was legitimate, it was mishandling the American situation. Baridon,
convinced that Gibbon must have seen the American side as a continuation of the Glorious Revolution of 1688 and therefore as the principled position for Gibbon to support, thinks Gibbon varied his talk to
suit his company and supported the Government because he was
already hoping for preferment.[33] But unless we assume a priori that
such a view must be taken by any intelligent and disinterested observer, this conclusion does not follow. We may wish that Gibbon had
perceived that a concern for freedom should have enlisted him on the
American side, but we would be rash to accuse him of hypocritically
supporting a position he knew to be unprincipled in the hope of
eventual gain.

Perhaps his most interesting political encounter in Paris was an
"accidental" meeting with Benjamin Franklin (*Letters* 2:150—the words
"by accident" are underscored in Gibbon's letter, either by Gibbon
himself or by Holroyd). Gibbon gives no information about this meeting, but there is an anecdote that Franklin invited Gibbon to join
him for dinner. Gibbon replied that he regretted his inablity to dine
with the illustrious Dr. Franklin while he was an enemy of Gibbon's
country. Franklin replied, with equal politeness and wit, "I shall be
happy to furnish materials to so excellent a writer for the Decline
and Fall of the British Empire."[34] This anecdote may well contain a
kernel of truth, but it is rather more probable that if any such exchange had occurred, Gibbon would have told Holroyd about it. The
anecdote is apparently of American provenance.

His holiday in Paris Gibbon ever remembered as one of the happiest periods of his life, and those memories should be recalled in
estimating his response to the French Revolution. To cap all, Paris
was not even expensive—"the ordinary establishment of Coach,
Lodging, Servants [Caplen and two footmen, presumably a coach-
man, and perhaps maids], Eating, and pocket expences does not
exceed sixty pounds pr month," even in an "apartment . . . hung with
damask" (*Letters* 2:151). Gibbon did not forget the pleasures of life in
London—in a letter to Garrick (*Letters* 2:160), he affectionately rec-
ollects the "Society of the Turk's head" and urges Garrick to "assure
Sir Joshua in particular that I have not lost my relish for *manly* conversation and the society of the brown table"—the Club had no female
members and therefore contrasted most strongly with the French
salons. Gibbon also wrote to Mrs. Gibbon about his unabated "relish
for his native Country" (*Letters* 2:161). But it was dutifully, rather than

enthusiastically, that he left the French capital on October 31st, promising to return as soon as possible. In old age as in youth, he came to prefer French civilization as translated to Switzerland. But he long remembered the charms of Paris and its intellectual and social life, going far out of his way to pay them tribute in the *Decline and Fall:*

> If Julian could now revisit the capital of France, he might converse with men of science and genius, capable of understanding and of instructing a disciple of the Greeks; he might excuse the lively and graceful follies of a nation whose martial spirit has never been enervated by the indulgence of luxury; and he must applaud the perfection of that inestimable art which softens and refines and embellishes the intercourse of social life. (*DF* chap. 19, 2:305)

Gibbon himself would never visit that capital again.

Politics and Letters

n his return to London in November of 1777, Gibbon was greeted by attacks from three enemies: hostile Christians, rebel Americans, and the gout. The first he ignored, the second troubled him deeply—not least, perhaps, because of the American war's catastrophic effects on the market for land and stocks—and the third, for a time, conquered him. In the ensuing months, politics, war, lack of money, ill health (his own and his friends'), and attacks on his history made his correspondence unusually gloomy, but there was a saving grace. As he wrote to his stepmother, "Letters (I do not mean Epistles) are in every state of life an amusement, a comfort or a ressource" (*Letters* 2:184). When, in spite of pleasant evenings or even weeks, the normally sanguine Gibbon could write, "My disposition is chearful, my wants not extravagant, my amusements within my own power, and connected with the amusement of many. But the scene before me is horrid" (*Letters* 2:180), the scene may be inferred to be truly "horrid." But the new volume of the *Decline and Fall* was progressing swiftly and smoothly. In some nineteen months between December 1777 and the summer of 1780, Gibbon wrote and revised not only the twenty-two chapters of volumes 2 and 3, but also two "pamphlets," one in French and one in English. His alternative duties and activities, moreover, were far more numerous in 1779–80 than in 1778. Probably, then, he composed a substantial portion of the second volume during the first year of work, and there is indeed evidence (especially in the first half) of the influence of his recent stay in France. But he could not begin work immediately, owing to the irresistible power of his old enemy, the gout.

Gibbon always treats his illnesses (when he discusses them at all) as military campaigns, with appraisals of his "adversary" in both power and honor. This siege of gout was particularly inopportune, for it prevented his visiting either Mrs. Gibbon or the Holroyds. He reacted to it, characteristically, with wit and grim good humor, writing to Holroyd, "I arrived last night: laid up with the gout in both my feet I suffer like one of the first Martyrs, and possibly have provoked my punishment as much" (*Letters* 2:163). A week later he was still unable to walk even with crutches—"I am a Corpse carried about by four arms which do not belong to me" (*Letters* 2:165). But he wrote, with his own hand (though writing was painful), several notes to both Holroyd and Mrs. Gibbon, both of whom were anxious about him. His aunt Catherine Porten he presumably could see—"I love a dutiful aunt," he remarked in another connection. For the first two weeks of November, the gout triumphed, but on the thirteenth he wrote to Mrs. Gibbon, "the enemy appears to be raising the siege . . . and makes a regular and gradual retreat." The next day, he told Holroyd, "the Gout has behaved in a very honourable manner; after a compleat conquest, and after making me feel his power for some days the generous Enemy has disdained to abuse his victory or to torment any longer an unresisting victim" (*Letters* 2:165–66).

Gibbon seems indeed more concerned about Holroyd's uncharacteristic ill health than about his own sickness, though we can get an idea of its severity from his would-be reassuring remark, "the swelling is so amazingly diminished that [my feet] are no longer above twice their ordinary size" (*Letters* 2:166). Holroyd had been suffering fever and rheumatism and a problem with his eyes that forced him to use a secretary. Gibbon, who had seen such a problem worsen into blindness in his father, was greatly concerned about his friend. In fact, this eye problem was recurrent for the rest of Holroyd's life, but it was not progressive. Gibbon's attitude toward illness has a revealing moral aspect: he seems to have assumed that much ill health was the result of ill-judged habits of life. Thus he considered his own illness his own fault, but Holroyd's illness unaccountable, even unjust: "When I consider your temperance and activity I cannot understand why any spring of the machine should ever be deranged" (*Letters* 2:165). In the end, Gibbon prevailed upon his stepmother to allow him to postpone his visit to her in Bath until Easter, so that he could visit the Holroyds in Sussex during the Christmas recess of Parliament.

Parliament was preoccupied with America. "Opposition are very lively, and though in the house we keep our numbers, there seems to be a universal desire of peace even on the most humble conditions," he wrote to Holroyd on December 2. "Are you still fierce?" (*Letters*

2:167). Horace Walpole, a member of the Opposition and therefore not a disinterested witness, is nevertheless probably reliable when he reports that Gibbon told him that he thought that, except for shame, not twenty men in the House would fail to vote for peace. "I did not think it very decent in so sensible a man to support a war and make such a confession," said Walpole.[1] Shame, however, or rather a devotion to "honor," seems to Gibbon in the *Decline and Fall* an adequate motivation for armies, and we must remember that he continued to consider North's policy correct in principle whatever its improbability of success. Two days later, the news was even worse: Parliament learned of Burgoyne's surrender at Saratoga. But Holroyd must have remained "fierce," for Gibbon next wrote, "I congratulate your noble firmness, as I suppose it must arise from the knowledge of some hidden resources which will enable us to open the next Campaign with new armies of 50 or 60000 men. But I believe you will find yourself obliged to carry on this glorious War almost alone" (*Letters* 2:168). These ironic remarks suggest Gibbon's closeness to the Opposition during this period—after Christmas, indeed, he even voted with them on two or three occasions. But the approach was never very close: Gibbon continued to regard England's governing the colonies as just and desirable in principle, though he was willing to pacify them either by conquest or by conciliation. Ironically, when it was published in an American magazine early in the nineteenth century, this letter to Holroyd served Gibbon well with his American readers, the publisher pointing out that it showed him to be more insightful about the American war than his "noble friend." Those who scorn Gibbon's adherence to the Government might well remember this relative insight, especially since it was not easy for Gibbon to reject the practical and active Holroyd's views on matters of action and practice.[2]

Holroyd's illness, combined with bad news from Gibbon's tenant at Buriton, made it necessary for Gibbon to go to Sheffield Place as soon as Parliament recessed. "I arrived yesterday at Sheffield place to enjoy the beauties of the Country which are displayed in a profussion of rain, snow, and fogs" he wrote to Dorothea Gibbon on Boxing Day (*Letters* 2:171). There, plans were rehearsed both for the relief of the country in its American struggles and for the resolution of the financial difficulties left by Gibbon's father and not ameliorated by Gibbon, who lived just within or slightly beyond his income, even as augmented by the earnings of the *Decline and Fall* and despite a *relatively* economical way of life. Both problems were to worsen during 1778.

With the beginning of the year, however, Gibbon returned to serious work on his "long neglected History" (*Letters* 2:169), reducing his unwieldy draft chapter to the five brilliant chapters that begin the second volume, which are only about half the length of the discarded draft, though they undoubtedly include some new material. Comments in the first of these new chapters about what the historian "must" do reveal what at first Gibbon had failed to do:

> The age of the great Constantine and his sons is filled with important events; but the historian must be oppressed by their number and variety, unless he diligently separates from each other the scenes which are connected only by the order of time. He will describe the political institutions that gave strength and stability to the empire, before he proceeds to relate the wars and revolutions which hastened its decline. He will adopt the division, unknown to the ancients, of civil and ecclesiastical affairs: the victory of the Christians and their intestine discord will supply copious and distinct materials both for edification and for scandal. (*DF* chap. 17, 2:149)

These decisions—to abandon strict chronology, to provide a static setting for the changing events, and of course to separate the history of Christianity from strict chronology—make possible a valuable structural relationship between this volume and its predecessor: the first chapter, which describes the founding of Constantinople, its monuments and ceremonies, and its constitution, exactly parallels the first three chapters of volume 1, on the Antonine establishment. The parallels, of course, provide striking contrasts, and Gibbon further emphasizes the decadence or fragility or despotism of the new Empire by contrasts with modern Europe in the notes. Having described the bureaucratic and despotic constitution, Gibbon turns to finances and taxes and observes that, because "despotism . . . tends to disappoint its own purposes," under the new Empire "the agriculture of the Roman provinces was insensibly ruined." He cites the example of the "fertile and happy province of Campania, the scene of the early victories and of the delicious retirements of the citizens of Rome," of which one-eighth, sixty years after Constantine, was reduced to "desert and uncultivated land," well before any external enemies reached Italy (*DF* chap. 17, 2:205). The monsters of the first volume were principally those who attacked the intellectual freedom of the elite and who hastened the loss of Roman culture. In this new volume, Gibbon emphasizes from the beginning the economic disasters threatening "the obscure millions of a great empire." He is concerned not merely about excessive donatives to spoiled troops, but about an establishment with built-in temptations to ruinous levels of taxation and corrupt administrators. Of course, he is not thinking solely or principally of the desperately poor or of slaves, but of landowners, merchants, and manufacturers.

He hesitated at first about delaying the events of Constantine's later reign to portray its constitution, aware that some readers would complain that his narrative flagged: "But the interruption will be censured only by those readers who are insensible to the importance of laws and manners, while they peruse, with eager curiosity, the transient intrigues of a court, or the accidental event of a battle" (*DF* chap. 17, 2:168). And he might expect that even such readers would respond unconsciously to the damning praise in the final paragraph of chapter 17:

> The subjects of Constantine were incapable of discerning the decline of genius and manly virtue, which so far degraded them below the dignity of their ancestors; but they could feel and lament the rage of tyranny, the relaxation of [military] discipline, and the increase of taxes. The impartial historian, who acknowledges the justice of their complaints, will observe some favourable circumstances which tended to alleviate the misery of their condition. The threatening tempest of Barbarians . . . was still repelled, or suspended, on the frontiers. The arts of luxury and literature were cultivated, and the elegant pleasures of society were enjoyed, by the inhabitants of a considerable portion of the globe. The forms, the pomp, and the expense of the civil administration contributed to restrain the irregular licence of the soldiers; and, although the laws were violated by power or perverted by subtlety, the sage principles of the Roman jurisprudence preserved a sense of order and equity, unknown to the despotic governments of the east. The rights of mankind might derive some protection from religion and philosophy; and the name of freedom, which could no longer alarm, might sometimes admonish, the successors of Augustus that they did not reign over a nation of slaves or barbarians. (*DF* chap. 17, 2:213)

Here there are clear and particular echoes of the Age of the Antonines in volume 1, but they echo the points in those chapters at which Gibbon is indicating that decline is imminent. Compare, in chapter 1, the account of the military protection:

> The Roman emperors . . . preserved a military spirit, at a time when every other virtue was oppressed by luxury and despotism. . . . Instead of being confined within the walls of fortified cities, which the Romans considered as the refuge of weakness or pusillanimity, the legions were encamped . . . along the frontiers of the barbarians. (*DF* chap. 1, 1:18)

In chapter 2, the limitations of contemporary analysts and their enjoyment of elegant arts:

> It was scarcely possible that the eyes of contemporaries should discover in the public felicity the latent causes of decay and corruption. . . . The love of letters, almost inseparable from peace and refinement, was fashionable among the subjects of Hadrian and the Antonines. . . . but, if we except the inimitable Lucian, this age of indolence passed away without having produced a single writer of original genius. (*DF* chap. 2, 1:61–62)

And in chapter 3:

> The armies were restrained by the firm but gentle hand of four successive emperors, whose characters and authority commanded involuntary respect. The forms of civil administration were carefully preserved. . . . [Yet]

[t]hey must often have recollected the instability of a happiness which depended on the character of a single man. . . . The ideal restraints of the senate and the laws might serve to display the virtues, but could never correct the vices, of the emperor. (*DF* chap. 3, 1:86)

In short, the causes for distress and symptoms of decay, at the peak of the Principate, were nearly identical with the *alleviating* qualities of the bleak prospect presented by the Constantinean monarchy. Those first three chapters, the most admired and, no doubt, the most often read of the first volume, thus provide Gibbon not only with a background, but with a haunting pattern of decay, in which traits that once represented flaws come to be the beauties of a lesser age. As in a ballad, whose recurrent refrain changes under the pressures of the story in a process called "incremental repetition," so in the *Decline and Fall* events, persons, and processes recur and change not in a rigid scheme or theory, but in a narrative progression that seems inevitable only after the fact. It is striking that the *Decline and Fall* anticipates most of the analyses of the fall of Rome that have adherents in any subsequent period of historical writing, included today. It does so, however, to an extent rarely realized by the subsequent historians, because Gibbon's explicit statements that x or y is "a" or "the" cause of the fall of Rome are unsystematic and mutually inconsistent when treated as separable abstractions. Such remarks do not point to logical causes—things without which the event would not have occurred—but to what we might call narrative causes—things which are inseparably, but not necessarily inevitably, associated with a succeeding event or situation. Gibbon reveals the attributes of decline and their contribution to a fall by "incremental repetition" in narrative and description.

In Gibbon's youthful *Essai* he argues that the "truth" of history is different from that of logic or mathematics. It relates to the honesty of witnesses' statements and to their opportunities for knowledge, not to the reliability of their opinions; and it represents a degree of probability, not of certainty.[3] This line of reasoning is also illustrated in the historian's judgment of the relationships between two events or circumstances. We can discern the most probable relationships among them; we cannot arrive at a set of a priori principles that will allow us either to select among them or to predict further events from them, except in a way that leaves room for many variations. For example, absolute rule will never encourage artistic originality, but the imitative works to which it leads will in one case mark the decline of civilization, in another its survival, and perhaps in a third the first stages of its revival or establishment. In place of hypothetical systems, then, we see Gibbon creating narrative and descriptive echoes (and anticipations) by means of which both narrator and audience can respond coherently to the past. This imposition of multiple chronological perspectives simultaneously becomes more and more prevalent as the history develops, not only by explicit and (much more often) implicit cross-references within it, but also by Gibbon's analogies — again both implicit and explicit—to earlier and later ages.

One instance of this method is his use of paired portraits, and sometimes paired pairs of portraits, in a manner perhaps related to Plutarch.[4] The pairs, however, are not necessarily those we might expect. Either Constantine, as the founder of a new phase of the Empire, or Julian, as a great pagen emperor, might have been paired with Marcus Aurelius Antoninus. But instead, Constantine's portrait is very clearly related to that of Augustus and (in a different way) to that of Julian, and Julian's to those of Constantine and Athanasius. One might also expect that the account of Constantine's reign would begin with the emperor himself; perhaps the rejected version did so. But in the successful version, Constantine's "character" begins the *second* chapter of the volume and is used as the prelude to the tragedy of the Flavians. His establishment of Christianity, moreover, is reserved until the reader has seen not only the weakness and cruelty of Constantine's heirs, but the early career of Julian and his enormous successes as caesar. *Then* the history stops to discuss the conversion of Constantine and the establishment of Christianity as the state religion in the Empire. And before we can learn of Julian's conduct as emperor, we must be initiated into the "mud of the Arian controversy." We thus meet St. Anthanasius, one of the principal combatants in that controversy, before Julian gains the Empire and attempts to return it to paganism. The fifth chapter of the new volume ends with an appraisal of the state of the Church highly comparable to that with which chapter 15 concludes. Only then do we move on to the tragicomedy of Julian as Apostate and Augustus.

Chapters 18 and 19, the narrative chapters of this first section of volume 2, are of course chronologically arranged—but not in a single chronology. Together with the chronological portions of chapters 17 and 20–21, they provide several different perspectives on the events of the first half of the fourth century, and they enact the divisions — damaging, in Gibbon's view—within the power structure of the Empire that occurred during the reigns of Constantine and Constantius II, despite their elimination of their colleagues and rivals. These chronological sequences also provide many opportunities for the kind of comparisons already mentioned and for use of climactic order and telling juxtapositions. Parallel to the character of Constantine with which chapter 17 begins, for instance, is a brief biography cum character of Julian as caesar, with which chapter 19 ends (*DF* 2:214–17; 302–3). And there is a similar account and appraisal of St. Athanasius, whose "superiority of character and abilities . . . would have qualified him, far better than the degenerate sons of Constantine, for the government of a great monarchy," at the end of chapter 21 (*DF* 2:334).

In chapter 19 the first chronological series recounts the military
career of Constantius; the second, the early exploits of Julian. As a
result, Constantius's first victorious actions have faded from the reader's mind in the debacle of the Persian war when we turn to Julian's
campaigns in Gaul—failure at first, owing to inexperience and lack of
support from the central government, followed by triumphant success
comparable, even superior, to Julius Caesar's. Both leaders have experienced both success and failure in the field, but Constantius's
history degenerates, while Julian's progresses.

Though none of the manuscript of the *Decline and Fall* survives,
we do have various sets of fragmentary notes for possible improvements that indicate something about Gibbon's attitude toward completed portions of the history. He seems to have held them in his
mind simultaneously with the new material, making possible the
cross-references already discussed, but also making possible a remarkable freedom from self-contradiction or duplication.[5] For example,
telling of the Persian foray into Roman territory, with its tactical
success and strategic failure, apparently led Gibbon to plan some
revisions to his Persian chapters in volume 1.[6] He made four short
pages of notes, headed "Materials for corrections and improvements
for the 1rst Vol. of my History," most of which are keyed to "p. 240,"
that is, the material on Zoroastrianism and Persian history, though
one note, keyed to "p. 30" and giving the text of Jerome's statement
about the size of Palestine, is utilized in his *Vindication* of chapters
15 and 16. These notes do not refer to new sources, but rather to
material previously overlooked or differently interpreted. They are
entirely unrelated to criticisms by religious opponents or reviewers,
with the exception already noted. At times cryptic in their brevity,
they are chiefly valuable as an insight into Gibbon's workshop and
suggest the kind of work he did in preparing completed drafts for the
printer. But by and large, he swept forward in his new version of the
era of Constantine and his sons with ease and confidence.

Tightly organized as these five chapters—Gibbon's "Age of Constantine"[7]—are, there is one marked break, unsmoothed by any kind
of transition. The account of ecclesiastical history, beginning with the
issue of the effective date of Constantine's conversion, powerfully
integrates religious history with politics. The organization and order
chosen by Gibbon enable him to make plain the contrasts and similarities between the rising Christian "republic" and the declining or
soon-to-decline secular culture and state. The account of the Arian
controversy continues his attack on the absurdity of war and political
conflict over religious dogmas, begun in chapter 16. But despite all
these links to the argument and action of the history, the theological
material has the effect of a digression, as Gibbon himself admits, and
is one of the few passages that justifies his later complaint about his

prolixity in this volume. But in 1778, when compared to the first draft, even this chapter no doubt seemed compressed and condensed.

Gibbon's latter-day critics (or admirers) have too quickly enrolled him among those who anathematized Constantine and all his works. Certainly he has nothing good to say about *Constantius*. But he recognizes the complexity of the character of Constantine as well as any of the emperor's biographers, and Gibbon's view of Constantine's works, though more negative than that of many subsequent historians, does recognize some of Constantine's accomplishments. Much of this is overlooked both because of the enthusiasm of Gibbon's disapproval as compared with the reluctance of his praise, and because, in a work so large as the *Decline and Fall,* it is fatally easy to ignore small but significant distinctions, especially those that differentiate Gibbon from the French *philosophes.* An ironic example: Gibbon is often said to have joined those who accused the Christians of quarreling about a diphthong (*homoousion* versus *homoiousion*). But in fact Gibbon says:

> The profane of every age have derided the furious contests which the difference of a single diphthong excited. . . . As it frequently happens that the sounds and characters which approach the nearest to each other accidentally represent the most opposite ideas, the observation would be itself ridiculous, if it were possible to mark any real and sensible distinction between the doctrine of the Semi-Arians, as they were improperly styled, and that of the Catholics themselves. (*DF* chap. 21, 2:373)

There is certainly no "sensible" (accessible to the senses) difference between "the same" and "similar" divine substance, but the difference is real enough, we may think (compare "the same author," "a similar author"), unless materiality is required for reality. But since there was no way of determining by external and objective means which side had correctly interpreted the point, Gibbon sees this as the kind of issue on which Christians should agree to disagree (as they have subsequently done), without destroying or even anathematizing each other. Gibbon supports his view that the positions were not hopelessly remote from each other by quotations from moderates of both parties who sought to reconcile the two terms. He should be given credit for refusing the cheap point in favor of a serious one, whatever the limits of his theology or metaphysics. That he so often is thought to have been merely derisive is the fault not only of readers inattentive to particles and diphthongs, but also of his own indulgence in skeptical playfulness, especially in the notes—here, for instance, "Philostorgius . . . is inclined to forget the difference of the *important diphthong*" (*DF* 2:373 n. 71; emphasis added).

There is another important respect in which Gibbon's anticipation of his successors in these chapters has been overlooked by those successors. Even Bury fails to credit Gibbon with recognizing the strategic advantages of the founding of Constantinople,[8] though Gibbon explicitly says that the "preservation of the eastern provinces may, in some degree, be ascribed to the policy of Constantine, as the barbarians of the Euxine, who in the preceding age had poured their armaments into the heart of the Mediterranean, soon desisted from the exercise of piracy, and despaired of forcing this insurmountable barrier" (*DF* chap. 17, 2:156.). Gibbon objects to the change of capital both on the rational ground of its cost and on the emotional grounds of its degradation of the old capital, Rome. Yet he criticizes the ancients and moderns, including Montesquieu, who assert that owing to migration to the new capital, "the lands of Italy . . . were at once deprived of cultivation and inhabitants. In the course of this history, such exaggerations will be reduced to their just value" (*DF* chap. 17, 2:165). He sees the grandeur of Constantinople, he reluctantly admires it, but he sees that grandeur as involving a terrible cost and as going far beyond the needs of empire to serve the pride of the emperor. An example is Constantine's imitating the first caesars in supplying such provisions to the poor of Rome as almost to "exempt . . . [them] from the necessity of labour." Augustus, said Gibbon, could claim that the Romans deserved the African harvests they had purchased by conquest, and he "artfully contrived" to replace freedom with plenty. "But the prodigality of Constantine could not be excused by any consideration either of public or private interest; and the annual tribute of corn imposed upon Egypt for the benefit of his new capital was applied to feed a lazy and indolent populace, at the expense of the husbandmen of an industrious province" (*DF* chap. 17, 2:165–66).

Gibbon also criticizes the constitutional innovations that entirely separated the military and civil functions. In his view the advantage of this arrangement, the discouraging of rebellion and internal unrest, was primarily beneficial to the ruler rather than the nation, while the disadvantages, delay and weakness in military defense of the province and multiplication of costs, materially injured the people. "The divided administration which had been formed by Constantine relaxed the vigour of the state, while it secured the tranquillity of the monarch" (*DF* chap. 17, 2:187). Gibbon criticizes several features of the new civil order, including the fragmentation of the Empire into provinces, the loss of liberty in the power granted especially to the Praetorian prefects (he reminds us that the great Marcellus had refused to hold an office so incompatible with the idea of the Republic), and the placing of civil power exclusively in the hands of lawyers. As usual Gibbon acknowledges that certain individuals should be exempted from the (well-nigh universal) distrust of attorneys, but he sees or thinks he sees a real reason to fear that those trained as advocates would be partial in their exercise of governmental offices:

In the practice of the bar, these men had considered reason as the instrument of dispute; they interpreted the laws according to the dictates of
private interest; and the same pernicious habits might still adhere to their
characters in the public administration of the state. The honour of a liberal
profession has indeed been vindicated by ancient and modern advocates,
who had filled the most important stations with pure integrity and consummate wisdom; but in the decline of Roman jurisprudence, the ordinary
promotion of lawyers was pregnant with mischief and disgrace. (*DF* chap.
17, 2:185)

Gibbon does not say what profession or professions ought to have
been preferred—presumably not actors.

But at least since Mommsen, Gibbon has been particularly criticized for failing to appreciate the wisdom of Constantine's military
reorganization. A recent study, however, defends Gibbon's view—
based on the only ancient testimony about the effect of reorganization, that of Zosimus—that the loss to the Empire in the effectivness
and morale of the border troops was far more significant than the gain
represented by a central reserve.[9] To this we may add that Gibbon
stresses not only weakening of the borders in terms of numbers of
troops, but the border troops' treatment as second-rate, especially
their lower pay, their inadequate training and support, and the absence of privileges available to the "Palatines" (Bury points out—n.
135 and Appendix 11—that Gibbon should have distinguished between Palatines and Comitatenses, but since Gibbon is interested
only in the distinction between troops posted on the borders and
those withdrawn into the interior, the distinction would not have
altered his conclusions). And, with Zosimus, Gibbon notes that these
select troops lost their effectiveness as their discipline was slackened:
"The soldiers [stationed in or near cities] insensibly forgot the virtues
of their profession, and contracted only the vices of civil life. . . . and,
while they inspired terror to the subjects of the empire, they trembled
at the hostile approach of the Barbarians" (*DF* chap. 17, 2:188). It is
true that Gibbon does not appreciate the theoretical advantages of a
strategic reserve, but it is not true that he unthinkingly assumes that
the older policy was better; he has reasons for his conclusions.

Gibbon is relatively one-sided in his presentation of Constantine's
personal moral character. Yet two recent full and valuable analyses of
this portrait—those of David P. Jordon and Johannes Straub—reach
rather contradictory conclusions about what Gibbon has said. Jordan
is perhaps too quick to attribute to Gibbon a doctrine of the century
about which Gibbon (among many others) had reservations, that of
the ruling passion. Gibbon's only explicit statement on this idea is
skeptical: "The Ruling passion?. very rare. most passions confined to
times places, persons, circumstances—Love, Hatred, revenge envy
jealousy, Vanity &c—Patriotism seldom even a passion.—Ambition

generally mixed with other passions, often subservient to them—
when pure as in Caesar or Richelieu must succeed or perish—Avarice
perhaps the only permanent ruling passion."[10] There is no logical
connection between a belief that the possibilities of human nature in
general are invariable and a belief that each human being has one
principal and unchanging moral trait. Gibbon found the first principle
a necessary working assumption, the second a dubious and unnecessary hypothesis—"very rare," as he says. Even those—for example,
Pope—who fully believed in the "ruling passion" often explained how
a character was *formed*, that is, see the trait as primary but not as
fixed. In the case of Constantine, Jordan holds that Gibbon sees him
as throughout motivated by the "ruling passion" of ambition, cleverly
dissembled in his youth, but clearly visible once he obtained power.[11]
This seriously oversimplifies Gibbon's characterization, in my opinion, and Straub agrees, seeing Gibbon's "Konstantinbild" as anticipat-
ing the complexity of such a portrayal as Burckhardt's.[12] Gibbon is
demonstrably *not* "anxious to prove" that Constantine's conversion
"was a cynical, callous political move, dictated by overweening ambition."[13] On the contrary, he clearly believes that political convenience was only part of Constantine's motivation and distinguishes
himself explicitly from those who regard it as consciously calculated:

> The protestant and philosophic readers of the present age will incline
> to believe that, in the account of his own conversion, Constantine attested
> a wilful falsehood by a solemn and deliberate perjury. They may not
> hesitate to pronounce that in the choice of a religion, his mind was
> determined only by a sense of interest; and that (according to the expres-
> sion of a profane poet) he used the altars of the church as a convenient
> footstool to the throne of the empire. A *conclusion so harsh and so absolute is
> not, however, warranted* by our knowledge of human nature, of Constantine,
> or of Christianity. . . . As real virtue is sometimes excited by undeserved
> applause, the specious piety of Constantine, if at first it was only specious,
> might gradually, by the influence of praise, of habit, and of example, be
> matured into serious faith and fervent devotion. (*DF* chap. 20, 2:325;
> emphasis added)

Gibbon goes on to justify this conclusion by a lengthy and careful
argument; I do not think (and no one, to my knowledge, has suggested) that this passage can be explained away as irony. Jordon's
method of combining the analysis and portrayal of Constantine from
volume 1 with that in volume 2 has many virtues, but it perhaps
misleads him on this point.

Between volumes 1 and 2, indeed, I think we can see real growth
in Gibbon's own tolerance and understanding. He continues to condemn vigorously moral follies in both individuals and groups, especially those that lead to wars and persecutions, and he does not

develop any understanding that the truth of a metaphysical point could have as much importance to some people as, say, that of a scientific theory. But his psychology is much richer, as Jacob Bernays points out,[14] and his portrayal of the interplay between personal and impersonal conditions affecting history becomes ever more complex. Specifically, he is able, in the account of the Arian controversy, to make such a statement as, "The persecution of Athanasius and of so many respectable bishops, who suffered for the truth of their opinions, or at least for the integrity of their conscience, was a just subject of indignation and discontent to all Christians. . . . The people regretted the loss of their faithful pastors . . . and loudly complained that the right of election was violated" (*DF* chap. 21, 2:403). Such understanding would have been unthinkable in the author of chapters 15 and 16. Certainly Gibbon continues to expose, deplore, and ridicule dogmatic controversy he regards as trivial, superstitious or venal multiplication of miracles, and the cruelties incidental to intolerance and fanaticism. But his tone is quite different from the "sneer" of chapters 15 and 16, and he almost totally abandons the prejudicial techniques by which he attempted to invoke the anti-Semitism, sexism, and class prejudices of his Christian readers against their Christianity. His treatment of the miraculous vision of the cross to which the conversion of Constantine and the success of his troops had sometimes been attributed is an example. His conclusion is that Constantine's *dream* might well have occurred, but that the apparition certainly did not. If Gibbon "gleefully" notes that his Jansenist predecessor Sébastian Le Nain de Tillemont is obliged to reject as spurious a supposed eye-witness report of this miracle,[15] yet he also acknowledges a treatise, in 1774, by a (presumably Catholic) doctor of the Sorbonne, the abbé du Voisin, that "deserves the praise of learning and moderation" (*DF* chap. 20, 2:324).[16]

Gibbon's principal hostility to Constantine seems to rest on his bloody extermination of his rivals, especially his "murder" of his eldest son and possibly of his wife, and on his exploiting the political advantages of Christianity without accepting its moral limits. He objects to what he thinks were catastrophic decisions by Constantine, especially the weakening of civil and military offices and bodies. "The same timid policy, of dividing whatever is united, of reducing whatever is eminent, of dreading every active power, and of expecting that the most feeble will prove the most obedient, seems to pervade the institutions . . . of Constantine" (*DF* chap. 17, 2:189). But it is Constantine's character, as revealed or corrupted by power, by which Gibbon is offended. He invokes the contrast with Augustus, and we have already been instructed by Gibbon in a Tacitean view of Augustus:

In the life of Augustus, we behold the tyrant of the republic converted,
almost by imperceptible degrees, into the father of his country and of
human kind. In that of Constantine, we may contemplate a hero, who had
so long inspired his subjects with love and enemies with terror, degenerating into a cruel and dissolute monarch, corrupted by his fortune, or
raised by conquest above the necessity of dissimulation. (*DF* chap. 18,
2:216)

Everyone remembers that as Constantine "gradually advanced in the
knowledge of truth, he proportionably declined in the practice of
virtue; and the same year of his reign in which he convened the
council of Nice was polluted by the execution, or rather murder, of
his eldest son" (*DF* chap. 29, 2:329). But it is often forgotten that the
decadence Gibbon describes in Constantine's later years is principally
moral, not political—pomp, effeminate clothing, murder of inconven-
ient relatives, jealousy of excellence, vanity, hypocrisy in accepting
pagan honors while attaching himself to the Christians, superstition
(especially in delaying baptism so as to obtain the advantages of its
plenary absolution after as many sins as possible).

Gibbon accepts that Constantine was in various senses "Christian"
long before his deathbed reception into the catechumenate and baptism—in fact, any time after about 311, the only *terminus a quo* for
Constantine's progression toward Christianity to have moved past
neutrality into favoritism; "he persevered till he was near forty years
of age in the practice of the established religion" (*DF* chap. 20,
2:308).[17] Gibbon dates the Edict of Milan, which was forced on
Licinius by Constantine and granted religious tolerance to both Christians and pagans, to 313 and attributes Constantine's increasing favor
toward the Christians to an appreciation of the advantages their obedient society offered to a "prudent magistrate." Gibbon portrays
Constantine's degeneration as accompanied by, undeterred by, his
gradual turn toward Christianity, but in no way suggests that Constantine's adherence to Christianity *caused* this change.

Because the British government was experiencing an imperial crisis
in America at the time when Gibbon was writing the new volumes of
his history, and because Gibbon was a participant in the government,
many readers, both then and later, expected to find parallels to
American issues or reflections on them in Gibbon's second and third
volumes. The Opposition Whigs who took the American side in the
conflict, believing that Parliament had no right to impose laws on a
colony unrepresented in it, had hopes, as we have seen, of enlisting
Gibbon in their ranks. Seeing the praise of freedom in the *Decline and
Fall*, they concluded that Gibbon had changed his views or at least
his practice after being given a post by Lord North's government.
Subsequent scholars have sometimes agreed. J. W. Swain, for instance, sees a difference between Gibbon's attitudes in volumes 2

and 3, which he associates with the period when Gibbon was closest
to the Opposition, December 1777–February 1778, and his attitudes
in volumes 4–6. This theory runs into chronological problems: the
composition of the ostensibly pro-American volumes obviously extended far beyond that brief period, and Swain's "most obvious" example occurs in chapter 31, which was probably written as much as a
year after Gibbon had learned of his government sinecure.[18]

Michel Baridon suggests rather that Gibbon was a "Polybian Whig"
all along, that is, that he thought "freedom" depended on a balanced
government of monarch, aristocracy, and commons.[19] As we have
seen, Gibbon never approved of pure democracy, which he saw as
leading to anarchy and tyranny, first of the many and then of a despot.
A Polybian Whig could accept the imposition of laws by a "free"
government on an unfree colony if the laws were just and the colony
were not able to maintain a balanced constitution on its own. The
Decline and Fall is indeed full of passages that expressed sentiments
congenial to the American rebels and their supporters—the Opposition produced a quotation from the *Decline and Fall* as support for its
motion to abandon the American war after Cornwallis surrendered at
Yorktown.[20] For example, Gibbon deplores the neglect of the senate,
praises friendship rather than tyranny in relation to remote colonies,
and objects to military incompetence; but there is no doubt that such
views were as strongly approved by Lord North and his party as by
Fox and Wilkes. Such ardent Tories and imperialists as Winston
Churchill and Cecil Rhodes found ammunition for their positions in
it as well. In the chapters of the *Decline and Fall* to which Gibbon was
devoting most of his mental energy in early 1778, the faulty principle
that was destroying the Empire was that of weakening by division. It
would be grossly simplistic to say that disapproval of the policies of
Constantine and Constantius drove Gibbon back into the North party;
but the argument could be made, using devices no more arbitrary
than those used to try to show that Gibbon had written a Whig history
that he forgot to edit into conformity with the views he had been
bribed to take. Gibbon was certainly a "Polybian" Whig in some
sense—so too was that notorious Tory, Swift—and L. P. Curtis's view
that Gibbon supported the notion of the great Whig aristocrats,
namely, that a combination of virtue, wisdom, and power was the
ideal polity, is persuasive. But in Gibbon's view, neither party achieved
this idea; these principles, therefore, would not have seemed to him
to rule out a principled support of North's government.

A story current in Opposition circles after Gibbon had become a
Lord of Trade and had written an official paper defending British
attempts at embargo against French complaints, was used to portray
Gibbon as a mere hireling who had abandoned his true principles.
Charles Fox reported that Gibbon had said at Brookes, a short time

before he was made a Lord of Trade, that the conflict with America would not be settled until Lord North's head was lying on the table.[21] But "there are two ways to tell any story," said Lord Eliot, a member of the Opposition, but also Gibbon's cousin. "Gibbon told that story too, but according to him, he said that peace in America would never come until the heads of North and Fox were on the table."[22] This version, stressing Gibbon's discontent with both the practice of North and his party and the theories of Fox and his, is the more probable, if the less entertaining and politically useful, version. Neither version was creditable to Gibbon as an appointee of North's government. There is no doubt that he willingly gave up some of his freedom of opinion to accept the much-needed income of the Lord of Trade. But there is every reason to doubt that he thought of himself as betraying a righteous cause. In his view the Opposition were cleverer, more practical, more realistic perhaps, about the conduct of the dispute with America. But there is no evidence that he ever thought their position more moral, or more consistent with his own advocacy of freedom and balanced government. His strongest statement against the war, when he had just returned from France, stresses the poor success, not the ill-judged and illiberal basis, of the Government's American policy, and even calls British losses in America "miserable news": "I shall scarcely give my consent to exhaust still farther the finest country in the World in the prosecution of a War, from whence no reasonable man entertains any hopes of success. It is better to be humbled than ruined" (*Letters* 2:169).

In some cases, Gibbon's pleasure in the friendship of various members of the Opposition may have been mistaken for approval of their policies. But in any case, his friendships with supporters of the Government were more numerous, longer-lasting, and more intimate. They included especially the friend upon whose worldly wisdom he most strongly relied, Holroyd. His temporary closeness to Opposition members and positions must be interpreted in this light. Of course he was delighted to dine with such entertaining hosts as Fox and Sheridan, to entertain (March 14, 1778) such a galaxy of guests as Beauclerck, Lord Ossory, Sheridan, Garrick, Burke, Fox, and Lord Camden (all except the last friends from the Club as well as members of the Opposition). Gibbon voted with Fox and Co. against the government's concealing from Parliament reports from America, and also for a motion of Fox's forbidding the sending of further troops to America, but the former vote is similar to his vote supporting Wilkes's election, an insistence on the rights of representative government *in England*, and the second is in keeping with Gibbon's grave doubts about the Government's methods and implies no criticism of its intentions. He strongly approved of the Government's conciliation measures, proposed at the end of February, and only feared that they would be too late, or inadequately administered. "Opposition . . . could not refuse their assent to the principles of conduct, which they themselves had always recommended" (*Letters* 2:174). He continues to think that Lord North has conducted the war badly: "In my opinion, Lord N. does not deserve pardon for the past, applause for the present, or confidence for the future" (*Letters* 2:176). But after this comment, Gibbon voted with the Government in the division. Since his vote in this instance could not have been swayed by any anticipation of regard, it seems just to assume that he thought at least as well of the Government's position as of the Opposition's. His dislike of change, "his great respect for order, stability, and the upper layers of society, coupled with his profound contempt for the . . . masses who were swayed by popular passions and not by reason, explain most of his political beliefs";[23] but these beliefs were lifelong, not merely opportunistic.

When Gibbon first entered Parliament, he devoted as much time to educating himself on the issues as to any other activity or concern, even the *Decline and Fall*. Now, however, his political responsibilities were less important to him than his own financial situation. The economic consequences of the war, as they affected his attempts to sell his property and settle his father's debts, were serious. His deteriorating financial position not only troubled but even frightened him. The new problem was that the tenant at Buriton was behaving destructively and had to be removed even though there was no other tenant in sight (and of course the expense of repairs and replacements would have to be met). Moreover, land and stocks were very low and the former almost unsellable. And the Goslings, the Gibbon family creditors and bankers, so long patient about Gibbon's inherited debt, were demanding that part of it be settled by the sale of one portion of its security, the New River stock. Gibbon hated to sell this stock, particularly at a time when stocks were low, because it was the least troublesome and most dependable source of his income. But it had to go. He asked Holroyd to intervene with the bankers to plead for more time, but he was otherwise able to face this painful decision. It was the problems at Buriton that seemed to dishearten him completely. On several occasions he sent letters from his agent, Hugonin, to Holroyd *unread*—unable to bring himself to face them without the support of Holroyd's advice. Dismissing the tenant and refurbishing the estate after his departure required cash, and Gibbon wrote in September, "I am strangely amazed and frightened about Buriton; as I had not the least suspicion of the approaching nay impending demand of so large a Sum" (*Letters* 2:191). Fortunately, a new tenant presented himself fairly soon, and Holroyd persuaded Clive, the officer of Goslings' Bank with whom Gibbon was dealing, to allow him to add the necessary cash to his debt, or rather, to retain £500 from the £7,500 realized by selling the New River Share. But Buriton was still unlet at the year's end. Meanwhile, a visit to inspect the estate— unthinkable without the knowledgeable Holroyd—was necessary. In October, Gibbon wrote to his friend,

> The state of Buriton is uncertain incomprehensible tremendous . . . It has occurred to me that if I *met* instead of *accompanying* you [to Buriton] it would save me a journey of above one hundred miles: that reflection led to another of a very impudent nature, viz, that if I did not accompany you, I certainly could be of no use to you or myself on the spot, that I had much rather, while you examined the premises, pass the time in a horse-pond, and that I had still rather pass it in my library with the decline and fall. But that would be an effort of friendship worthy of Theseus or Perithous. Modern times would credit much less imitate such exalted virtue. (*Letters* 2:195)

Holyroyd was apparently the equal of his ancient models. "I am transported to hear that you will call at Buriton in your way to Bath, and only beg, that considering my situation rather than your spirit you will not leave the place without deciding the business," Gibbon wrote. This was in December, and Gibbon urged Holroyd to approve of the proposed tenant for Buriton—"Consider the bad condition and growing expence which I am so little able to bear" (*Letters* 2:199). But he clearly had no intention of accepting the tenant without Holroyd's "consent," a trust certainly due to Holroyd's heroic friendship.

In the midst of all these difficulties, Gibbon paid his stepmother's jointure faithfully—nearly two weeks late in June, it is true, but quite on time in December. But she was having difficulty making ends meet in Bath without the further income represented by the interest on the loan made to Gibbon in 1772 by her cousin Scott and thus due to her as heiress of Scott's property. Gibbon has been criticized for forgetting this debt, but it is probable that both he and Mrs. Gibbon remembered that it was only legally his responsibility, having been incurred only to pay a debt of his father's. Furthermore, one of the elder Gibbon's debts was inherited by Mrs. Gibbon from her father. "If it was still outstanding in 1769, it perhaps accounts for James Scott's interests being somehow involved in the present troubles."[24] Whatever the origin of the debt, Gibbon, and his father's principal heir, was responsible for it. The interest was clearly Mrs. Gibbon's legal due. But both Gibbon and Dorothea Gibbon seem to have regarded his paying it as optional.

Nevertheless, Gibbon in good times paid the interest as promptly as he paid her jointure. If he thought of the extra £100 as a voluntary expression of affection rather than an obligation, he was willing to bind himself and his estate to pay it as her jointure.[25] But these were not good times. At the end of the year she wrote to propose that she move away from Bath to live with a friend in the country so that she could manage to live on her jointure without his having to pay her the additional sum. "I am not insensible that . . . you have a substantial and even legal claim upon me to a very considerable amount," Gibbon wrote to her early in January 1779, "and while I feel the value of your tenderness on this occasion I must lament that it [is] not in my power to attain even the humble though indispensable virtue of Justice." He cannot sell, he has suffered from the "madness" of the Buriton tenant, and "all credit is so compleatly dead, that in the most pressing exigency I should be at a loss how to borrow a thousand pounds." The *Decline and Fall* had indeed done well, but had not enriched its author, and his establishment, as a Member of Parliament living in London, cost slightly more than his income, given the present high interest and low rents. But he had "well grounded hopes which I build on the assistance of a sincere and powerful friend. I cannot on *this* head explain myself more particularly by letter, but I have the strongest reasons to believe that the year which we have just begun will not end without producing a material improvement in my situation" (*Letters* 2:201–2). He therefore urged her not to make any change in her life. A few more months might see a great improvement, and besides, as he explained later, he could instead retrench *his* expenses by a different way of life. (Since what he had in mind was removing to Switzerland, she was not eager to accept that solution.) But as Gibbon here hints, his appointment to the Board of Trade made it unnecessary for either Gibbon to retire.

At the end of 1778, America too presented more favorable prospects. "In several places the Sky clears a little, and if we could be secure from Spain, we may promise ourselves some success," Gibbon wrote to Holroyd. "You see I am less desponding than usual" (*Letters* 2:197). But it was the *Decline and Fall*, as usual, that most comforted Gibbon. Throughout the year, despite politics, finances, and various junkets, he had made steady progress on it. In February, "notwithstanding the hurry of business and pleasure, I steal some moments for the Roman Empire" (*Letters* 2:176). In March he enjoyed some meetings with William Robertson and some evenings at Almack's. In April he spent two weeks in Bath with Mrs. Gibbon, time necessarily lost from the *Decline and Fall*. Gibbon liked his stepmother, but these visits to Bath were matters of duty, not inclination; he preferred to see her elsewhere, though he found that he enjoyed the dinners given by her physician, a Dr. Delacour. Gibbon described the Bath regime to Holroyd:

> Here I am, in close attendance of my Mamma, who is better in health spirits &c than I have known her for some years. Had I attempted an Easter excuse it would have been very ill received. I am vastly complaisant, *amuse* myself in Routes and private parties and play shilling Whist with the most edifying resignation. . . . Are you acquainted with Dr.

Delacour? In truth there is much kindness in that Jew: and much good
sense likewise; he gives as good dinners as the superstition of the females
of his family will permit and has a proper contempt for all that a reasonable
Man ought to despise. (*Letters* 2:181)

But, as he told his stepmother, "let me say with the utmost truth that
the part of my Bath visit which I recollect with the greatest pleasure,
are the moments which I spent with you and with you alone" (*Letters*
2:182).

Holroyd, in the military zeal of the moment, had taken up duties
as major of the Sussex Militia. Early in July, Gibbon and his aunt
Kitty went to Sheffield Place, where, while Holroyd was at the summer encampment, he "left [Gibbon] Governor of the Castle and
Guardian of his fair Spouse" (*Letters* 2:187). But at Sheffield Place,
progress on the *Decline and Fall* was by no means interrupted. "I carry
[there] a good deal of lumber, and shall work reasonably hard," he
told his stepmother (*Letters* 2:185). There was talk of the whole
family, including Gibbon and Aunt Kitty, following the major to
Brighthelmstone (Brighton); but in the end, Gibbon found Brighton
impractical: "more difficulty and expence than I expected in settling
myself with any degree of comfort, and great inconvenience in being
so long absent and distant from my tools" (*Letters* 2:192). In fact, he
was back in London by the end of August. In his "rural retirement in
Bentinck Street," he found "as much Society as I want for relaxation;
and motives enough to engage me to take more exercise of a morning
than I should any where else; besides the occasional Holydays . . . to
various friends who dwell in Villas adjacent to town. In the mean
time I have the pleasure to see the Sheets of my second Volume
insensibly acquire a respectable or at least a decent size" (*Letters*
2:193).

It is clear that he still did not anticipate that his second volumes
would be "twins," so we may conclude that the respectable pile of
sheets did not yet rival the number required for volume 1. With such
significant progress, however, he had undoubtedly written several
more chapters of the history, including at least part of the famous
account of the emperor Julian, considered by Walter Kaegi in 1965
"still the best short biography [of Julian] in English.[26] Gibbon's account of Julian's career has been much discussed, but it is important
to notice that it is not pure panegyric by any means. Julian is a hero
of the *Decline and Fall*, but a hero not only flawed, but unheroically
flawed—flawed by superstition, fanaticism (in his asceticism), and
misguided ambition.[27] But Julian deserves and receives a far greater
portion of the *Decline and Fall* than chronology would seem to give
him because he attempted to restore not only Roman military pres-
tige, but Roman culture and values. Like nearly all the figures Gibbon

most admired, Julian *combined* the active and contemplative life. He
was not only an excellent writer and thinker, but also an able general,
a statesman of ability and integrity, and thus a man of "business."
Ironically, he failed not only because his subjects (like those of the
Antonines) were no longer capable of enjoying liberty, but because
he himself, despite his many differences from his uncle Constantine,
had like him an "ambitious spirit": "In the cool moments of reflection,
Julian preferred the useful and benevolent virtues of Antoninus; but
his ambitious spirit was inflamed by the glory of Alexander; and he
solicited, with equal ardour, the esteem of the wise and the applause
of the multitude. . . . The successor of Cyrus and Artaxerxes was
the only rival whom he deemed worthy of his arms" (*DF* chap. 24,
2:506–7).

In the course of this war, "the philosopher," Gibbon notes drily,
"retaliated on a guiltless people the acts of rapine and cruelty which
had been committed by their haughty master in the Roman provinces" (*DF* chap. 24, 2:523). "The governor [of another place], who
had yielded on a promise of mercy, was burnt alive, a few days
afterwards, on a charge of having uttered some disrespectful words.
. . . The palaces of Sapor were reduced to ashes, by the command of
the Roman emperor" (*DF* chap. 24, 2:526). Gibbon's comment on this
action reveals not only a single-minded preference for Greco-Roman
culture, but also a sense of the ugliness of war consistent with this
whole account of Julian, and with his gloom about the conflict in
America, but not consistent with the impression some have received,
that Gibbon thoughtlessly admired war as a glorious and sanitary
activity.[28] Gibbon is showing us the decline of Julian even as he
recounts his military victories. Yet Julian's personal virtues, unlike
Constantine's, were undiminished, indeed,

> never more conspicuously displayed than in the last, and most active,
> period of his life. . . . In every useful labour, the hand of Julian was
> prompt and strenuous; and the Imperial purple was [as] wet and dirty, as
> the coarse garment of the meanest soldier. The two sieges allowed him
> some remarkable opportunities of signalizing his personal valour, which,
> in the improved state of the military art, can seldom be exerted by a
> prudent general. (*DF* chap. 24, 2:527)

(This "virtue," of course, ironically foreshadows Julian's doom and,
paradoxically, the mixed blessing of "improved" warfare.) Julian declined the siege of Ctesiphon, whose defenders refused to come out.
They told him, "if he desired to exercise his valour, he might seek
the army of the Great King. He felt the insult, and he accepted the
advice. . . . He resolved to imitate the adventurous spirit of Alexander, and boldly to advance into the inland provinces" (*DF* chap. 24,
2:535). But this heroic plan proved fatal to the Roman cause. Julian's

forces were forced to seek battle on unfavorable ground and were surprised from the rear. Julian, unarmored, hastened to the relief of the rear guard. He was, of course, mortally wounded, and so was his vain, but heroic, attempt to restore Rome to the glories of the Republic. Gibbon's mixed feelings about Julian—his criticism of Julian's faults and the excesses of his virtues, his admiration of Julian's aims and abilities, his ambivalence about Julian's military efforts—suggest once again that we should not oversimplify his response to contemporary leaders and power struggles.

With the end of Julian's career, Gibbon had completed eight of the ten chapters that were published in his second volume. Of course he had far to go before he reached the planned terminus of this portion of the history, the fall of the empire in the West. Yet he could well be content with his work, both quantitatively and qualitatively. In the accounts of Constantine and Julian, with Constantius and Athanasius in between, Gibbon had achieved some of the most admired and longest-lasting portions of his history. He had also acquired a voice for himself as a spectator and judge of the events he describes, not in would-be gnomic universal assertions, or in the sneer of exclusive irony, but as a concerned eyewitness who is somehow both of and detached from the time and place he portrays because of his awareness of many layers of other times and places—the voice of the mature Gibbonian narrator. Gibbon would soon be obliged to leave off this character and the *Decline and Fall* in order to crush a presumptuous adversary. But after a difficult year, politics and letters promised well for 1779.

SEVEN

Counterattacks

ulian had been placed in a parlous situation by the scorched-earth policy of the Persians—"he beheld the melancholy face of a smoking and naked desert" *DF* chap. 24, 2:538)—and by the hot climate; his "hardy veterans, accustomed to the cold climate of Gaul and Germany, fainted under the sultry heat of an Assyrian summer," and Julian himself was fatally unprotected by armor because the "heat of the weather had tempted him to lay aside his cuirass" (*DF* chap. 24, 2:540–41). Under Julian's successor, Jovian, forced (or willing) to make an ignominious peace with the barbarians, the retreating armies were in still worse case: they were safe from their foes, but they "were obliged to traverse a sandy desert, which, in the extent of seventy miles, did not afford a single blade of sweet grass, nor a single spring of fresh water; and the rest of the inhospitable waste was untrod by the footsteps either of friends or enemies" (*DF* chap. 24, 2:552). When Gibbon reluctantly turned from the writing of the *Decline and Fall* to defend his first volume against charges of misrepresentation and plagiarism, these impressions gave him a metaphor for his task.

Unlike his hero, Gibbon was fully armored, and he defended himself against the "swarms" of ecclesiastical critics with spectacular success. These "insects" troubled him less than the morass of debt which still made it impossible for him to live in London, as a Member of Parliament and society, on his earned and inherited income. Neither his doubts of the Government's competence nor the opposition of these enemies prevented his receiving and accepting the timely aid

of the Government post and salary for which he had hoped. In gratitude, flattered by the request, and in general agreement with Government principles, he undertook to counter yet another enemy, not his
own, but the attacker of his Majesty's Government. For Gibbon the
principal events of the eventful year 1779 were the publication of two
editions of his *Vindication of Some Passages in the Fifteenth and Sixteenth
Chapters of the History of the Decline and Fall of the Roman Empire;* his
appointment to, and duties at, the Board of Trade; and the composition and publication of the *Mémoire justicatif* for the North government.
These counterattacks upon critics, debts, and foreign foes provoked
retaliation, but also won Gibbon applause and self-approval. We may
see them as marking a new stage in the development of Gibbon's
character, however—a certain hardening. Subject to new attacks and
increasingly conscious of the dangers of unarmored vulnerability, he
seems somewhat less open to change, to criticism, including self-
criticism, and thus to emotions in general, than in the past. The year
1779 was also that of the Reynolds portrait of Gibbon, and to compare
the clubbable young gentleman of Walton's portrait five years earlier
with the Historian of the Roman Empire portrayed by Reynolds is to
see even more differences than those inevitable from the elapse of
five years and the change of painters.[1]

By the time Gibbon published his *Vindication* (January 14, 1779),
some eighteen attacks on his history had been published, four as
separate pamphlets of substantial length—150 pages or more.[2] Gibbon
had planned to ignore his theological critics, but a 284-page attack in
the spring of 1778 by one Henry E. Davis, a 21-year-old graduate of
Balliol, provoked Gibbon into response.[3] He profoundly regretted the
loss of time and energy. The introductory section of the *Vindication*
ends, "And now let me proceed on this hostile march over a dreary
and barren desert, where thirst, hunger, and intolerable weariness,
are much more to be dreaded, than the arrows of the enemy."[4] The
source of the metaphor is obvious, and where his metaphor was, there
was his heart also. At the end of the work, Gibbon begs his readers,
as soon as they are convinced of his innocence, to "forget my vindication."[5] But his readers have been unwilling to do so; his satire of
pretentious and uncharitable ignorance is so witty and powerful, and
his explanations of his understanding of the art and craft of history are
so interesting, that readers prize the work now, as they did when it
appeared. "If he seriously hoped for [its] oblivion, he should have
written differently: with less irony, less appearance of relish, fewer of
those majestic, devastating phrases."[6]

When Gibbon's opponents had chided or opposed him for lack of
faith or sympathetic understanding of the Christians, he was content
to leave the questions of opinion to the judgment of the reader. It was
those who tried also to discredit him as a historian to whom he finally

felt obliged to respond. Davis's method, and that of others who tried to criticize Gibbon's history rather than his theology, was usually to enumerate many instances of what they considered errors (deliberate or accidental), in no particular order, with no consideration of significance. Gibbon's strategy is to identify the kinds of objection each opponent fixes on, and then to select instances of each kind for refutation or explanation.

For example, a major source of Davis's list of errors and misrepresentations is typographical errors or mistaking editions in Gibbon's references to his sources. Gibbon patiently illustrates the fact that passages triumphantly said not to provide the evidence he attributes to them were actually to be found in adjacent sections or similarly numbered pages or in different editions. He rightly complains of such critics' ingratitude for his documentation: "As I had often felt the inconvenience of the loose and general method of quoting which is so falsely imputed to me, I have carefully distinguished the *books*, the *chapters*, the *sections*, the *pages* of the authors to whom I referred, with a degree of accuracy and attention, which might claim some gratitude, as it has seldom been so regularly practised by any historical writers."[7] Anyone who has read his competitors, at least among the literary and "philosophic" historians, can attest the truth of this statement. Even William Robertson, user of archival sources and attentive, like Gibbon, both to antiquarian and philosophic ideals, falls *far* short of Gibbon in frequency and precision of quotations and citations.[8] The modern reader may be shocked by the informality of Gibbon's references, especially the identification of editions, or by his willingness not merely to cite but to quote from memory; but Gibbon's memory was extraordinary in an age in which memories were commonly better trained than they are today, and he obviously saw no harm in the common practice of educated persons—we have only to consult the modern annotations of any great writer of the age to find evidence that this indulgence was widespread. Even today, an author of encyclopedic range may be unable to verify *all* his supporting evidence: Fernand Braudel apologizes for the "cases where 'reference mislaid' unfortunately replaces an indication of a source which eluded [his] efforts" to reconstruct the notes for an originally unannotated volume.[9]

Davis's charges were unjustifiable by the standards of any age, since he equated an inadequate reference with deliberate falsehood, but Gibbon's reply does more than expose Davis's error. It suggests Gibbon's own goal in the use of his sources and references to them: the historian should make plausible inferences from evidence that, uninterpreted or unjuxtaposed to other information, seems to have none to yield; but readers should be able to retrace the historian's steps and judge for themselves the legitimacy of his interpretation of the evidence. The majority of Gibbon's readers immediately appreciated this approach, which permitted "new" information to be discovered about eras thought to be inaccessible to history. Walpole commented that Gibbon could "melt his materials together, and make them elucidate and even improve and produce new discoveries . . . make an *original* picture with some bits of mosaic."[10] Most of the contemporary reviews of the history note this capacity for shedding light on dark periods, not by the application of theoretical systems of any kind, but by discovering and interrogating the evidence. But the theological critics, at least of these two chapters, were not satisfied unless Gibbon repeated the very words of his source, without amplification, elision, or criticism. Davis goes even further. He assumes that if Gibbon uses evidence already cited by another modern writer, he is guilty of plagiarism—and if his interpretation of that evidence differs from the other modern author, he is *also* guilty of misrepresentation.[11] (Davis was, of course, led to those moderns by Gibbon's own notes.)

In the *Vindication* Gibbon tries to teach such critics, or rather those who might have been impressed by their arguments, something about the process of historical reasoning as he understands it. But their arguments are so feeble that they often fall apart before Gibbon, refuting them, reaches a constructive point. For example, Gibbon had said "The Jews, who under the Assyrian and Persian monarchies had languished for many ages the most despised portion of their slaves, emerged from their obscurity under the successors of Alexander. And as they multiplied to a surprising degree in the East and afterwards in the West, they soon excited the curiosity and wonder of other nations" (*DF* chap. 15, 2:3). The real reason that Gibbon's clerical enemies objected to this passage was, of course, that he clearly treats the Jews not as a Chosen People, but as a tribe and sect subject to conquest and ignominy like any other people. The Bible says far worse, but it says it in a very different tone, and in the context of God's will and plan, not that of the successors of Alexander. Davis and others were not content to prove that Gibbon's attitude was wrong, however; they hoped to show that he was a poor historian. Gibbon quotes Davis: "What a strange assemblage is here. It is Milton's Chaos, without bound, without dimension, where time and place are lost. In short, what does this display afford us, but a deal of boyish colouring to the prejudice of much good history." Here, as elsewhere, Davis's criticism of a passage plays into Gibbon's hand. Every word of the "strange assemblage," as Gibbon shows, is fully verified, from sources that Davis ought to have known from his classical education, or from scripture itself, or from such obvious sources as Josephus.[12]

The connection between evidence and conclusions is very clear throughout this passage. Defending it should have been unnecessary, but to Davis's folly we owe interesting evidence of just how Gibbon thought about a piece of data. The justification for calling the Jews despised slaves has to do, for example, with the unparalleled penalty of the land's remaining uncultivated and uninhabited for seventy years, with the taking of the "most beautiful and ingenious youths" into the personal service of the monarch, with the reduction of population, with the casual permission for genocide in the book of Esther. The Jews' condition under the Macedonians is illustrated by the privileges they still held in the age of Josephus. Unlike Davis, Gibbon sees the difference between national and global history. Davis complains that Gibbon might have seen in the Bible how far from obscure the Jews were. Gibbon points out that the issue is when they "began to act a part in the society of nations, and to excite the curiosity of the Greek and Roman historians." Thus he cites pagan authorities. "If I had designed to investigate the Jewish Antiquities, reason, as well as faith, must have directed my inquiries to the Sacred Books, which, even as human productions, would deserve to be studied."[13]

Other critics, disliking Gibbon's tone, sought to catch him out on the size and fertility of Palestine. Since Jerome as well as modern geographers support Gibbon's view, he has time to toy with his victims and to reiterate the serious point of his sixteenth chapter:

> They seem to consider in the light of a reproach, and of an unjust approach, the idea which I had given of Palestine, as of a territory scarcely superior to Wales in extent and fertility; and they strangely convert a geographical observation into a theological error. When I recollect that the imputation of a similar error was employed by the implacable Calvin, to precipitate and to justify the execution of Servetus,[14] I must applaud the felicity of this country, and of this age, which has disarmed, if it could not mollify, the fierceness of ecclesiastical criticism.[15]

(This comment is echoed and, in effect, revised later in the *Decline and Fall*.)[16]

Gibbon follows up his advantage here with a mock confession of error (a reference in which section and chapter numbers were reversed) and a real attack on Davis for trying to use such a quibble to escape acknowledgment of the inhumanity of Tertullian's gruesome wishes for the damnation of the pagans. A modern writer, or a Richard Watson, would try to show that Tertullian's position was extreme, that such extremity was a response to the horrors of persecution or to an age in which suffering and torture were commonplace experiences, that the Church had repudiated such inhumanity. But he would not try to deny that Tertullian and others happily expected the eternal torment even of virtuous pagans, and he would especially not crow over finding an inaccurate reference in such a context. Davis is so easy a target in this last point that Gibbon's refutation of him gives us no new understanding of Gibbon's methods.

In another instance, Gibbon had ascertained that martyrdoms were newly introduced into Africa by combining information from Thierry Ruinart (his collection of saints' lives) and Tertullian. Not finding the point in the latter's text, Davis says Gibbon has misrepresented Tertullian. Gibbon explains impatiently that it is the two authorities "thus connected" that establish his point and explains exactly how. "Was it my fault if Mr. Davis was incapable of supplying the intermediate ideas?"[17] If readers are inclined to excuse Davis, they soon relinquish that inclination, for in quick succession, Gibbon shows him unaware that Cyprian wrote in Latin, rather than Greek, and failing to read to the end of a sentence. (This is one of the few faults Davis actually acknowledges in his *Reply*.)

One of the most telling arguments Gibbon presents against Davis is quotation from Davis. Davis accuses him of misrepresenting a Latin author and an Italian one, the former from ignorance, the latter from malice. According to Davis, if Gibbon "had looked into the passage, and found that Sulpicius Severus there expressly tells us, that the Apocalypse was the work of St. John, he could not have committed so unfortunate a blunder, as to cite this Father as saying That the greater number of Christians denied its Canonical authority." Gibbon shows that Davis fails to see that Sulpicius's *complaint* about the opinion of the others proves what their opinion was, as well as proving that Sulpicius thought them wrong. In the case of the Italian, Fra Paolo Sarpi, "Mr. Davis has *only* mistaken a motion of the opposition for a measure of the administration." Having demonstrated this, Gibbon ends the section by quoting Davis again: "We have here an evident proof that Mr. Gibbon is equally expert in misrepresenting a modern as an ancient writer"—quite so: he does neither. Gibbon takes the occasion to praise both the historians he is accused of misrepresenting: the "concise and elegant Sulpicius" "has been justly styled the Christian Sallust"; the reader should "give himself the trouble, or rather the pleasure, of perusing that incomparable historian" Sarpi.[18]

A conflict of more moment illustrates the kinds of contention that would continue to separate Gibbon and his antagonists, from time to time, well into the twentieth century. Davis is indignant because Gibbon says one of a group of Christian martyrs was accused of robbery, instead of saying "falsely accused." Gibbon shows that the individual in question received a much harsher punishment than the other Christians and was executed with the robbers. He concludes:

> It is evident that Dionysius represents the religious sufferer as innocent of the criminal accusation which had been falsely brought against him. It is no less evident, that . . . the supreme magistrate considered Nemesion as guilty. . . . The question (*which fortunately is of little moment*) [emphasis added] of his guilt or innocence rests solely on the opposite judgments of

his ecclesiastical and civil superiors. . . . In this doubtful situation, I
conceived that I had acted with the most unexceptionable caution, when
I contented myself with observing that Nemesion was *accused*.[19]

Gibbon disclaims malicious intentions, and here his disclaimers may
be trusted, because his line of reasoning simply shows the result of
treating Christian and pagan evidence equally rather than privileging
either. (He could have said that one martyr was punished for robbery
as well as, or instead of, Christianity.) But since Gibbon needs only
to establish that Roman magistrates sometime thought they were
punishing Christian victims for crimes other than their faith, he may
be guilty of an unnecessary injury to the sensibilities of those to
whom the innocence of *every* accused martyr was important. Similar
replies could have been written to most of the attacks by Hilaire
Belloc in the twentieth century;[20] Gibbon is accused of a serious error
for some passing assertion, important only if the reader thinks the
vindication of the early Church requires the flawlessness of all those
who have been hailed as saints or martyrs. Gibbon's inferences from
the evidence give weight equally to pagan and Christian sources and
allow for bias in both—though Gibbon, too, had unrecognized biases
that made his allowances unequal in some cases. And, in these two
chapters, whenever he has a choice, he permits himself to present
the varying views in the manner most likely to offend the fanatical
modern reader, as the writer of a biology text might go out of his way
to annoy a Creationist (or vice versa). In the *Vindication*, as in the
later volumes of the *Decline and Fall*, this *gratuitous* sneer is less in
evidence.

Much of the rest of the *Vindication* similarly explains Davis's errors
and the lines of thought behind Gibbon's conclusions in various particular instances. "Nothing but the angry vehemence with which these
charges are urged, could engage me to take the least notice of them.
In themselves they are doubly contemptible: they are trifling, and
they are false," says Gibbon wearily.[21] Even from these, however, we
may collect a few general principles by which Gibbon worked. For
example:

The Writer who aspires to the name of Historian, is obliged to consult a
variety of original testimonies, each of which, taken separately, is perhaps
imperfect and partial. By a judicious re-union and arrangement of these
dispersed materials, he endeavours to form a consistent and interesting
narrative. Nothing ought to be inserted which is not proved by some of
the witnesses; but their evidence must be so intimately blended together,
that as it is unreasonable to expect that each of them should vouch for the
whole, so it would be impossible to define the boundaries of their respective property.[22]

Gibbon notes, on the other hand, a unique "principle" held by Davis, "*that* when a modern historian appeals to the authority of the ancients for the truth of any particular fact, he makes himself answerable . . . for all the circumjacent errors or inconsistencies of the authors whom he has quoted."[23] Gibbon's scorn of Davis perhaps betrays that he himself had no clear principles of source criticism, but it also reveals that de facto he made source-critical judgments.

Davis assumes that Gibbon is wrong, or maliciously lying, whenever (by means of Gibbon's notes) he thinks he can spot a discrepancy between Gibbon and another modern authority. Gibbon points out that references are often made to a secondary source, "for the satisfaction of the reader" who might wish to explore a subject further, even when there are minor differences between the conclusions of the other author and Gibbon. Here "the entire sense of this passage, which Mr. Davis first mutilates and then attacks, is perfectly consistent with the original text of the learned Mosheim," but reconsidering it leads Gibbon to decide he was wrong in one item (of five) in the disputed passage. He says he will rectify the expression in future editions (he never did so, however). "Had the error been exposed by Mr. Davis himself, I should not have been ashamed to correct it."[24]

The major point Gibbon makes here is generally applicable to the opponents who attempt to attack his historical, rather than his religious, faith: "What does he mean to establish or to refute?" by his "angry cavils."[25] The real aim of all Gibbon's critics of the Davis school had to be to attempt to discredit Gibbon's reliability, no matter how trivial the point, in the hope that readers would extend their doubts to all his assertions and conclusions. This effort was doomed to failure.

The attack on Gibbon's tone, though thoroughly justified from the perspective, not only of the Christian, but even of those desiring impartiality of presentation, was hardly more successful, as an example will illustrate. Davis had spoken of Gibbon's "*illiberal malignant insinuation*, 'That Christianity has, in every age, acknowledged its important obligations to female devotion'[;] the remark is truly *contemptible*."[26] Now of course Davis is quite right; Gibbon's remark was intended to embarrass and annoy his predictably sexist audience. But obviously Davis lays himself open to a devastating rejoinder: "Religion may accept, without a blush, the services of the purest and most gentle portion of the human species: but there are some advocates who would disgrace Christianity, if Christianity could be disgraced, by the manner in which they defend her cause."[27]

More than 100 pages of Davis's volume had been devoted to what he called plagiarisms. Gibbon does not attempt to refute each—an easy but tedious task, since Davis considers any resemblance to a predecessor a plagiarism, even when there is little resemblance except in "thought" and the predecessor is cited in a note (Davis found all

these sources, indeed, only through Gibbon's notes). "According to
the opinion which he has formed of literary property, to *agree* is to
follow, and to *follow* is to *steal*."[28] To Davis, a striking example of
Gibbon's plagiarism is the following—italics Davis's:

> Middleton . . . says, "These forged books are frequently cited and applied
> to the defence of Christianity, by the most eminent Fathers, as true and
> genuine pieces, *and of equal authority with the scriptures themselves*." Mr. G.
> speaking of these spurious books says, almost in Middleton's words,
> "These *pious forgeries were obtruded* on the Gentiles *as of equal value* with
> the genuine inspirations of heaven."[29]

Instead of showing that each passage is comparable to its predecessors
in information or conclusion, not wording, and that the predecessors
have in each case been credited, Gibbon gives us "three or four short
and general reflexions" about historical discussion: "If my readers are
satisfied with the form, the colours, the new arrangement which I
have given to the labours of my predecessors, they may perhaps
consider me not as a contemptible Thief, but as an honest and industrious Manufacturer, who has fairly procured the raw materials, and
worked them up with a laudable degree of skill and success."[30] Owing
to religious controversy, Gibbon points out, ecclesiastical critics of
every view have closely examined all the evidence about the early
Church, but each has skewed his presentation of the material to
support his own religious views:[31]

> If we skilfully combine the passions and prejudices, the hostile motives
> and intentions, of the several theologians, we may frequently extract
> knowledge from credulity, moderation from zeal, and impartial truth from
> the most disingenuous controversy. It is the right, it is the duty of a critical
> historian to collect, to weigh, to select the opinions of his predecessors;
> and the more diligence he has exerted in the search, the more rationally
> he may hope to add some improvement to the stock of knowledge, the
> use of which has been common to all.[32]

Davis had asserted that Gibbon sometimes "by an unaccountable
oversight, unfortunately for himself, forgot to drop the modern"—
when, for example, he gave a reference to a church father on the
authority of Tillemont. Gibbon points out that the reason he sometimes quotes an older writer on the authority of a modern is that he
has not always had access to the originals: "The greatest city in the
world is still destitute of that useful institution, a public library; and
the writer who has undertaken to treat any large historical subject, is
reduced to the necessity of purchasing, for his private use, a numerous
and valuable collection." This is the context in which Gibbon says
that if Davis "will take the trouble of calling at my house any afternoon when I am *not* at home, my servant shall shew him my library,
which he will find tolerably well furnished with the useful authors . . .

who have *directly* supplied me with the materials of my history."[33]
Michel Baridon regrets that Gibbon in this riposte permits himself
the use of "a Gentleman's sword; to combat what he calls 'the fierceness of ecclesiastical criticism' this kind of *ad hominem* argument would
appear to be a low blow." I confess that a low blow with the flat of
the blade appears to me exactly what Davis deserved for this set of
"accusations," which are not only unworthy of a graduate of any university, but even if true would in no way affect the validity of Gibbon's
arguments. We may agree with Baridon, however, that Gibbon is at
his best when "he uses the arms he has forged for himself."[34] Baridon
illustrates with Gibbon's devastating opening comment on Davis's
manner: "Every animal employs the note, or cry, or howl, which is
peculiar to its species; every man expresses himself in the dialect the
most congenial to his temper and inclination, the most familiar to the
company in which he has lived, and to the authors with whom he is
conversant."[35]

Against the rest of his opponents—East Apthorp, who says almost
nothing; the polite Richard Watson; and the rude James Chelsum and
Thomas Randolph, who took issue with his religious views—Gibbon
contents himself with finding some relatively substantive issues to
discuss. Apthorp, whose title promises "Observations on a late History of the Decline of the Roman Empire" but who mentions it on
only three pages, Gibbon dismisses as having almost nothing to say
about the *Decline and Fall* (Apthorp's critique was reserved for a second
volume that never appeared). As for Watson, both he and Gibbon,
says Gibbon, have delivered their respective opinions about the respective weight of the primary and secondary causes for the Church's
expansion, and the public may make its choice. But one point requires
clarification: Watson objected to Gibbon's saying that the pagan philosophers could not understand the injustice of religious persecution:

> The humanity of Dr. Watson takes fire on the supposed provocation, and
> he asks me with unusual quickness, "How, Sir, are the arguments for
> liberty of conscience so exceedingly inconclusive, that you think them
> incapable of reaching the understanding even of philosophers?" . . . The
> arguments which assert the rights of conscience are not inconclusive in
> themselves, but the understanding of the Greeks and Romans was fortified
> against their evidence by an invincible prejudice. . . . [The pagan] was
> excused, in his own eye, by the consciousness that, in the situation of the
> Christians, he would not have refused the religious compliance which he
> exacted.[36]

Similarly, Gibbon selects issues raised by "the confederate doctors"
James Chelsum and Thomas Randolph that illustrate the errors of
their scholarship, and from the consideration of which, at the same
time, "it may not be impossible to pick up something curious and
useful even in the barren waste of controversy."[37]

The *Vindication* was published—"*in octavo*—for I would not print it in quarto, lest it should be bound and preserved with the history itself" (*Memoirs* 170)—on January 14; a second edition was soon required (its preface is dated February 3), and, as J. E. Norton says, "There seem to be no unfavourable reviews,"[38] though most reviewers were polite enough to Gibbon's opponents to suggest that he should consider their objections in future revisions. Of course he convinced no one that his tone was objective or that his religious opinions were orthodox, and therefore those for whom these points invalidated a priori his writing of religious history continued to believe that his opponent had triumphed. For Gibbon, as he also said in the *Memoirs*, "a victory over such antagonists was a sufficient humiliation." The controversy had some material results for both sides: "I dare not boast the making Dr Watson a Bishop; but I enjoyed the pleasure of giving a Royal pension to Mr Davies [sic], and of collating Dr Apthorpe to an Archiepiscopal living" (*Memoirs* 160); Gibbon and his publishers earned about £20 each on the two editions (1,250 copies).[39] Gibbon certainly enjoyed receiving the praise of such a judge as Horace Walpole, who proclaimed him "the best writer of controversial pamphlets" as well as the first of historians; even in a hurried reading Walpole could "discern, besides a thousand beauties and strokes of wit, the inimitable eighty-third page, and the conscious dignity that you maintain throughout, over your monkish antagonists."[40] This praise was the more welcome, in that Walpole had advised Gibbon "either not [to] reply, or set *your mark* on your answer, that it may always be read with the rest of your works,"[41] and in that increasing political differences between the two men would soon sharply reduce Walpole's willingness to praise Gibbon.

The £20 earned for Gibbon by the two editions of the *Vindication* was obviously no solution to the financial problems that had haunted him in 1778. Early in 1779 Gibbon was forced to acknowledge that the device by which he had expected to end his financial troubles, the sale of Lenborough, was not going to work in time. The *Decline and Fall* only just paid for its own expenses, the much-loved library, and though Gibbon's bachelor establishment in London and his occasional self-indulgences such as gold snuffboxes might have been maintained on the income from Buriton and his minor properties, they could not stretch to include the 5 percent interest due on his father's debts.

Gibbon's gross annual income was now about £1,650, reckoning about £650 from Buriton (*Letters* 3:24), £550 from Lenborough (*Letters* 1:278, 341), £250 from the New River Share (*Letters* 1:344), and £200 from the Copper Share (*Letters* 3:24). From this he had to pay £850 interest to Goslings (5 percent of £17,000), a £200 jointure to his stepmother (to whom also he should have paid £100 as interest on the debt she had inherited from Scott), and living expenses he estimated at £1,000–1,100 while he kept a carriage and a London house and also spent money on "Clubs, public places, servants wages &c" (*Letters* 3:23)—a total of £2,050–2,250. Every Micawber among us can see the problem here. The figure for living expenses, based on Gibbon's estimates of 1785, was somewhat less in 1779 because he had not yet acquired "a breathing place at Hampton Court." On the other hand, the gross income was, of course, subject to reduction for expenses such as the salary of Gibbon's agent, fees and taxes, and tenants' demands, some of which Gibbon undoubtedly failed to include in his estimate of living expenses. The sale of Lenborough, even if nothing were cleared except the sum necessary to pay off the mortgage, would have improved Gibbon's financial picture by more than £300, enough to pay his stepmother the extra £100 which she was owed and which he wanted to give her, and to make his annual income much closer to his annual expenses. But Lenborough could not be sold. Then came the catastrophic loss of the Buriton tenant, the reduction of the debt to £10,000 by the painful expedient of selling the New River Share (which had provided his most reliable minor source of income), and his stepmother's discovery that she could not afford to continue to live in her establishment at Bath without additional income.

Mrs. Gibbon proposed to reduce her expenses by moving away from Bath, but Gibbon, however much he may have been "cut[ting] a figure in town" at her expense[42] was not selfish enough to accept this sacrifice:

> In your last letter you ask whether your remaining at Bath is necessary to my tranquillity. I can answer that question in the clearest manner, and while I answer it I must feel with gratitude how kindly it is proposed. It *is* necessary for my happiness that you should not be *forced* to leave Bath by any difficulties which it would be my duty to remove: nor could I enjoy the comfort of any situation which was purchased at the expence of your ease and happiness. But if your retiring from Bath was the effect of your own inclination, it is impossible that I could be hurt at your leaving a place which I should never visit but on your account. (*Letters* 2:212)

A month later he assured his stepmother that he was "prepared for every possible event. I only beg you to have patience a few months longer, and I give you *my honour* that I will make such arrangements as shall enable you to reside at Bath.—I will likewise add, what I know is material to your feelings, that I shall enjoy myself a very comfortable, if not desirable plan of life" (*Letters* 2:217).

His plan was to take one of two courses: to accept a government post, about which his friend Attorney General Alexander Wedderburn had made overtures and promises, or retire to Lausanne. His sincerity about the latter proposal is clear in a letter to Deyverdun: "I don't know your plans, but I suspect that after having spent the winter in

England you will return to seek repose and happiness in that beautiful land to which they are native. Let us count on nothing, but there are dreams of our youth, which may well be realized. Goodby. I shall be counting the months, the days, and the hours" (*Letters* 2:218). His resolution is clear enough, but in spite of the attitude of optimism appropriate for the letter to his friend, at this point there would have been some cost in the retirement he proposed: "Your affairs and mine: I believe you are rising and I descend. . . . Of the man of letters and the statesman, suffice it to say that the decadence of two empires, the Roman and the British, advance with equal pace. I have, however, contributed much more effectively to the former."

But at the end of June 1779, Gibbon received at last the letter for which he had been waiting, offering him a place on the Board of Trade, with a salary of £750. Gibbon has been much criticized for accepting this place. He was immediately required to defend his action, for all government appointees had to resign their seats and seek reelection in order to occupy their posts, and Gibbon's reelection was dependent upon Edward Eliot, who had moved into Opposition. This is how Gibbon explained himself to Eliot:

> I told [Wedderburn] that I was far from approving all the past measures of administration even some of those in which I myself had silently con-curred; that I saw . . . many essential defects in the character of the Ministers and was sorry that in so alarming a Crisis the Country had not the assistance of several able and honest Men who are now in Opposition. But . . . I did not discover among [the Opposition] such a superiority either of measures or abilities as could make it a duty for me to attach myself to their cause; and that I perfectly agreed with Charles Fox himself in thinking that at a time which required our utmost unanimity, Opposi-tion could not tend to any good purpose and might be productive of much serious mischief. (*Letters* 2:219)

Given these views, he saw no reason to refuse the post if Eliot were willing to continue his support to one who "could never oppose and must *generally* support the measures of Government."

As Gibbon had hoped, Eliot did not see the "addition (if it can be called the addition) of a mute of any great moment to the numerous and regular forces of administration." Gibbon acknowledged, of course, that the salary was his principal inducement to accept the post, but he hoped Eliot would "do me the justice to believe that my mind would not be [easy], unless I were sincerely persuaded that I could accept the offer with honour and integrity" (*Letters* 2:220). Those who do not do Gibbon this justice, or who repudiate his notion of honour and integrity in this instance, should remember that his ideas of political integrity were influenced by the common behavior of his contemporaries and should attempt to judge him not by what his political opinions, in their view, *ought* to have been, but by what they were. In Gibbon's perspective, he sacrificed only the right to vote against the party he preferred on the rare occasions when he considered that party more in error than its opponents. In return, he was delivered from financial alarms, perhaps disaster, without having to sacrifice the writing of his history. As in the case of Suzanne Curchod, no other passion could long compete with scholarship—certainly not political passion.

Before the middle of July, Gibbon was asked to correct the French of an official statement to Spain, and, soon thereafter, to make a more substantial contribution to the work of the government. The French government had issued a manifesto justifying its treaty with the Americans as a separate nation, although it had a treaty with Great Britain that would seem to exclude such friendship with her enemies, and complaining about British attacks on their shipping. The reply to this manifesto needed to be composed with skill and in French; through Holroyd, Gibbon was asked to write it.[43] That the Government thought it appropriate to approach Gibbon through his friend indicates that no one in Government considered Gibbon now a party hireling. The request might have been made, moreover, even if Gibbon had had no post and no prospect of one, and I think he would have accepted the challenge, flattered by the opportunity to address "that free and respectable tribunal which pronounces, without fear or flattery, the sentence of Europe, of the present century, and of posterity. . . . composed of the enlightened and disinterested men of all nations."[44] Gibbon, who admired most the characters who combined active and contemplative virtues, but who was unable to bring himself to speak in Parliament, had at last an opportunity to affect the history of his own time. Certainly he remained complacent about the results and the occasion: "At the request of the Chancellor, and of Lord Weymouth then Secretary of State, I vindicated . . . the justice of the British arms. The whole correspondence of Lord Stormont our late Ambassador at Paris was submitted to my inspection. . . . The style and manner are praised by Beaumarchais himself" (*Memoirs* 160–61).

Gibbon's argument in the *Mémoire justicatif* was that the French had treacherously breached their duties as England's professed ally and that their manifesto tried to claim the irreconcilable rights belonging to peace and to war at the same time. G. O. Trevelyan was perhaps the most enthusiastic reader the *Mémoire justicatif* has ever had: "Compact, lucid, powerfully and fairly reasoned, and glowing with the eloquence of indignant patriotism, it was a composition which, in its own line, has seldom or never been surpassed. . . . Whatever the moral victory might be worth, it had been won by England; for Gibbon, with a single broadside, had blown the case of the allied powers out of the water."[45] Few have equalled this enthusiasm, but the Government was apparently well satisfied, and Gibbon himself was complacent about its reception, though he disclaimed responsibility for the accuracy of the facts. "I spoke as a lawyer from my brief," he says (*Memoirs* 173), and we may recall his opinion of the effects of a legal education on the integrity of the officers of the Roman Empire. But he is quick to point out that those who attacked the facts were themselves inaccurate, and at the time he wrote to his stepmother; "Though I will never make myself the Champion of a party, I thought there was no disgrace in becoming the Advocate of my Country against a foreign Enemy, and the *Mémoire Justicatif* which you may read was the result of that opinion" (*Letters* 2:229).

Once the authorship was known, Opposition writers accused the author of being incorrect, incompetent, venal, and fat. The last charge was irrefutable; the first is a question of political opinion (for example, Wilkes based his attack on the position that the Americans were, in fact, no longer rebels, but an independent nation—surely not obvious in 1779); the second is a matter of literary judgment and taste, and the third is still debated. Gibbon, by now used to attack, appeared able to endure these charges with equanimity. The scurrilous verses in the *Public Advertiser* he could easily ignore, but the wittier attacks of Wilkes and Charles Fox, which emphasized the unworthiness of such pages from the writer of the *Decline and Fall*, might well have troubled him, since he had often enjoyed the company of both. In the *Observer*, Wilkes accused Gibbon of "total want of politeness" and a tedious style, as well as being bribed to change his politics:

> It was hoped that you, Sir, by the most studied urbanity, as well as superiority of argument, would have made England triumph, not have copied, and in some instances exceeded, the low railing accusation of the foreign offices. Has a Lord of Trade been employed to traffick in the grossest abuse? . . . Your facts should have been few, well chosen, strong and pointed: your language not diffuse, flowery, declamatory, but close, nervous, and above all, because it was in the name of your Prince, polite. Could not a single substantive escape without being compelled to marry an adjective? . . . It was indeed wonderful, that when every true lover of his country shrunk from the present ministerial crew, . . . you, Sir, so late as July last, listed under their inglorious banner, and, independent in fortune, unincumbered with a family, joined yourself to corruption, imbecility, and infamy, by accepting a seat on the board of *trade*. . . . I blush for the folly and the prodigality of the age, when I reflect that Mr. *Gibbon* has 1000 l. a year for a contemptible compilation, and *Milton* received only 1000 l. for his noble *Defence of the people of England*.[46]

There are several false statements in this attack, as well as strong differences of opinion, but Gibbon defended himself in only one respect: he pointed out that he could hardly be accused of deserting a cause (Opposition) that he had never espoused. Fox's comment, in verses not published until 1781, is comic in form and spirit but may have done Gibbon's reputation more harm than Wilkes's party attack. Fox's poem premises that King George gave Gibbon a place to prevent his writing the story of England's fall, but the strategem backfired: Gibbon's

> . . . book well describes
>   How corruption and bribes
> Overthrew the great empire of Rome;
>   And his writings declare
>   A degeneracy there
> Which his conduct exhibits at home.[47]

Gibbon retained or regained the friendship of Fox and other attackers for the rest of his life; perhaps he was genuinely able to view their rebukes with detachment. Perhaps, however, a curious error in the *Memoirs* may be attributed in part to residual discomfort either about his actions or his opponents' accusations: he misdates the sequence of the *Mémoire justicatif* and his appointment to the Board of Trade. He says that he was asked to write the *Mémoire justicatif* in May; in fact it was July or August, and he had been expecting the appointment to the Board of Trade or elsewhere for many months before, and had actually received it in June. Thus he himself contributed to the enduring legend that he was appointed to the Board of Trade as a reward for writing the *Mémoire justicatif*.

The writing of the lengthy pamphlet—it is about two-thirds the length of a typical narrative chapter of the *Decline and Fall*—of course interrupted the progress of the *Decline and Fall*. So too, perhaps, did a project to which he was persuaded by his publishers, his portrait by Reynolds (at the "exorbitant price of *fifty* Guineas"—*Letters* 2:215). This portrait was apparently promised by Gibbon to Walpole, but Gibbon's political decisions in the next few months led to a temporary coldness between him and Walpole, which may be why the portrait never became Walpole's. According to Gibbon, his friends said that "in every sense of the word it [wa]s [a] good head."[48] It was completed by May and immediately sent to Hall for engraving. The engraving duly adorned the next volumes of the *Decline and Fall*. Malone considered it an excellent likeness; Holroyd always preferred the earlier Walton portrait.[49] Perhaps their different perspectives result from their different relationships with Gibbon; Malone, though he liked Gibbon, knew only the public man, pleasant, intelligent, companionable, but increasingly stylized in his behavior and conversation, as we shall see. For Holroyd and his family, the grand Gibbon remained also the genial, unselfconscious, spontaneous private person.

The portrait and the pamphlets interrupted Gibbon's pursuit of the *Decline* for a time, and attendance at the House of Commons seriously truncated his working days, but he was otherwise assiduous in the pursuit of the new volumes. "On every account both of fame and interest, it will be highly expedient that the Continuation of my history should appear about this time twelfmonth," he wrote to Dorothea Gibbon at the end of May. "Much is already done, much remains to do; I am well satisfied that by a course of steady temperate diligence, the object may be accomplished; but I shall not be able to lose a week and hardly a day" (*Letters* 2:216). Sticking to his last, he rejected invitations from both Mrs. Gibbon and Holroyd. "I can hardly spare a single day from the Shop" (*Letters* 2:215). Neither the income nor the employment of the Board of Trade began immediately, so in spite of the writing of the *Mémoire justicatif*, he was able to anticipate in September that "in twelve or fourteen months [he should] be brought to bed—perhaps of twins" (*Letters* 2:225). He spent a weekend at Sheffield place in early October but returned to his library and his work despite gout and a "bilious" complaint: "I am always in the right—I knew the journey would be of service to me, and I eat my Pheasant at dinner with a degree of appetite which I have not known for some days" (*Letters* 2:227). The next day he attended a meeting of the Board of Trade. A month later, his "subject has grown so much" that he is certain that "it will form a Second and third Volume in 40, which will probably go to the press in the course of the ensuing summer" (*Letters* 2:233).

Thus the *Decline and Fall* had advanced beyond the bounds of the second volume (chapter 26) and probably at least as far as the end of chapter 32.[50] His position on the Board of Trade, though it was not literally a sinecure and though Gibbon was, especially at first, one of the members most faithful in attendance, cannot have interfered greatly with his literary labors, even if, as Norton suggests, he sometime drew up the minutes and statements prepared by the board.[51] But the value of the post was not limited to the much-needed £750 salary. By giving Gibbon direct insight into the commercial and legal transactions between an imperial power and its colonies, service on the Board of Trade was probably useful to the author of the *Decline and Fall* ("the reader may smile").[52] It was useful, too, in providing another excuse, sometimes perhaps fictitious, for his staying in London rather than losing his working time in Bath or Brighton. On the whole, we can assent to his own judgment of his labors: "I was now master of my style and subject: and while the measure of my daily performance was enlarged, I discovered less reason to cancel or correct. . . . Shall I add that I never found my mind more vigorous, or my composition more happy, than in the winter hurry of society and parliament?" (*Memoirs* 159).

Chapters 25–32 of the *Decline and Fall* encompass much material that was entirely new to Gibbon's readers and contribute strongly to the sense that his work bridges the unfamiliar interval between the ancient and the modern worlds. The heroes and villains upon whom he focuses his narratives, the paradigms of manners and thought he develops in the static chapters, and the psychological, sociological, economic, and constitutional questions he raises are relatively exotic and are familiarized brilliantly and powerfully by means of the relationship Gibbon has now established with his audience. At the same time, of course, he revels in their strangeness, and the immense range of time and space opened up to his readers is nowhere more impressive than in these sections. The faults and weaknesses of Valentinian and his unworthy brother and co-emperor Valens are quickly established, so that Gibbon may dwell on the five theatres of conflict that beset the Empire and on Valentinian's wise measures and Valens's able generals. To chapter 26, on the "Manners of the Pastoral Nations," I shall return in a moment. Civil wars absorb chapter 27 and reintroduce (inevitably, in Gibbon's view) conflicts within the Church. At this point the narrative again pauses, so that in chapter 28 Gibbon may analyze the final defeat of paganism and argue that its superstitious practices in fact invaded Christianity. Republican virtues reappear in the next three narrative chapters, but in the persons of a general, a Gothic king, an empress, and even a pope. The division of the Empire (chapter 32) becomes the occasion less of civil war than of hostile indifference, the prelude, of course, to the different fates of the East and the West.

Every chapter of this section of the history (which has been less often examined than either earlier or later sections) illustrates a new freedom, a remarkable ease in the consciousness of authorial power to construct and judge history. The treatment of the narrator, especially a developing distinction between the impersonally secure "we" and the struggling, concerned "I," gives a new, explicit importance to the issue of the historian's creative and limiting intervention between the past and the reader.[53] Gibbon's narrator, once almost exclusively the "philosophic observer," addressing himself to an Enlightened reader and occasionally playing the faux-naïf to disarm the conventional and deceive the innocent, acquires individuality. Now he feels as well as thinks; he is just to all sides and capable of discerning and applauding human virtue wherever it occurs, though he dismisses with a contemptuous smile the inventions of superstition, flattery, and even fear. He abhors whatever injures individuals or the sum of human achievement.[54] This narrator generates an admittedly subjective text that cannot simply reflect or recreate a real past, but that nevertheless aspires to represent not the creatures of its imagination, or abstracted instances of a general scheme, but reliable *images* of the figures and events that once existed.

The laws, philosophy, and sociology of history, especially as represented in the paradigmatic analysis of cultures and social states or phenomena, on the other hand, serve formal and tonal purposes as much as explanatory ones. No longer principally or necessarily confined to separate chapters, they frame and suspend the action, but they also provide a cultural relativism that contributes greatly to tonal effects, both elegiac and ironic. The metahistorical commentary, in both the notes and the text, complicates both the narrative and the analysis by gradually revealing the tentative, subjective, even "fabulated" aspect of the historian's materials and therefore of his own product. The artifactual nature of a historical work becomes a part of this historian's theme and subject. Every chapter of volume 2 and 3 offers exciting evidence of the new complexity with which Gibbon defined his role as historian; chapter 26, the one that ends the second volume, will serve as illustration.

The narrative of chapter 26 is very obviously the construction of a narrator: it begins with an earthquake ten years before its principal action, and it concludes with openly contrived suspense, "The public safety seemed to depend on the life and abilities of a single man." This conclusion is coupled (in the notes) with a strong rebuke to a predecessor, a rebuke that has generic significance. Montesquieu, says Gibbon, though he was writing on the *causes* of the fall of Rome (Gibbon's emphasis) "seems ignorant that the Goths, after the defeat of Valens, *never* abandoned the Roman territory. . . . The error is inexcusable; since it disguises the principal and immediate cause of the fall of the Western Empire of Rome" (*DF* 3:139 n. 143 [136]). Gibbon himself is writing not a causal analysis, but a history of these events: his own apparently systematic statement of causation must, as usual, be interpreted within the genre of history rather than philosophy of history, that is, it must be read as tentative and incomplete, despite the positiveness of its rhetoric. If the explanatory statement were generically or logically essential to *history*, Gibbon could hardly relegate it to the notes. His conclusion stresses instead a narrative crisis, in which action is directly dependent on character, and at the same time notes the hypothetical nature of this analysis of the past by means of the word "seems." Gibbon seems more and more to reveal to his reader that insofar as the present is concerned, the past, like the present and future, is in flux: it is always subject to reapprehension.

Certain perspectives on experiences of a previous time that are alien to the people of that time, however, become not only available but essential to historical writing. The earthquake at the beginning of chapter 26 was to contemporary observers, with respect to the motion of the earth, exactly what it is to the historian. But its effect and signification were wholly different: in the Roman people, it generated superstitious fear and expectations of loss. The narrator-historian, on the other hand, observes sadly "that man has much more

to fear from the passions of his fellow-creatures than from the convul-
sions of the elements. The mischievous effects of [natural disas-
ters] . . . bear a very inconsiderable proportion to the ordinary calamities of war, [even] as they are now moderated" (DF 3:73). On the
other hand, humankind's egotistical inclusion of all creation in its
calamities is quietly debunked by the same narrator: even if a land
were left utterly uninhabited by man, "the beasts of the forest, his
enemies, or his victims, would multiply in the free and undisturbed
possession of their solitary domain. . . . [I]t is highly probable that
the fish of the Danube would have felt more terror and distress from
the approach of a voracious pike than from the hostile inroad of a
Gothic army" (DF 3:122). The narrator has thus established two
themes that run throughout the chapter as a counterpoint to the
action: the multiplying power of the human imagination as it encounters experience, and the difference between human culture and history and the natural world that surrounds it. Gibbon often complains
of the turgid and misleading metaphors of his sources, and his own
metaphors are relatively sparse and never mistakable for literal statements. When the natural world intrudes, literally or figuratively, it
challenges our perception of human power or importance: "The indiscriminate vulgar was left unburied on the plain. Their flesh was
greedily devoured by the birds of prey, who, in that age, enjoyed very
frequent and delicious feasts" (DF 3:109–10). Similarly, "a formidable
tempest of the Barbarians of Germany seemed ready to burst over the
provinces of Gaul" (DF 3:124), but they are not a natural, but a human
force, and the appointment of Theodosius will prove, for a time, a
sufficient remedy.

The narrative function of this chapter is to introduce the theme of
the Empire's vulnerability to barbarians themselves harassed by more
barbarous, or at least more potent, barbarians. In it, the Goths become
permanent residents of the Roman Empire. They are portrayed first
as victims, then as conquerors, and finally as defeated yet deadly
allies of the Romans, but always henceforth as a presence to be
reckoned with. In order to accomplish this narrative purpose, however,
Gibbon temporarily sets it aside for another kind of history, the kind
lauded or deplored by subsequent historians as sociological history.
The first half of the chapter is devoted to an analysis of the society
of nomadic warrior-shepherds—society, not societies, because Gibbon
believes that societies so close to nature are virtually determined by
that fact and by their environment: "The savage tribes of mankind,
as they approach nearer to the condition of animals, preserve a stronger
resemblance to themselves and to each other" (DF 3:74). They enjoy
great military advantages, and their diets, habitations, and "exercises"
conspire to drive them to and fro between the settled portions of the
world, as those present resistance or prey. "The revolutions of the

North have frequently determined the fate of the South; and, in the conflict of hostile nations, the victor and the vanquished have alternately drove and been driven, from the confines of China to those of Germany" (*DF* 3:78). In addition, the northern shepherds were, Gibbon believed, the lineal ancestors of the Huns who were led by Attila against the Goths, driving them toward Rome, and against the Roman Empire itself.

Bury (n. 10), finding this identification erroneous, assumes that the description of Tartar manners becomes irrelevant, but this misses Gibbon's point. The relevance was always paradigmatic, not causal. He neither asserts nor implies that the activities of the putative ancestors of the Huns in China had any direct relation to Attila's effect on the Empire. The confusion is understandable, however, because Gibbon conducts his analysis by means of narrative and almost scenic description, not just abstract statement. For instance, he argues that the hunter-shepherds are constantly schooled in the skills valuable for war, thus:

> The hunters of Scythia . . . boldly encounter the angry wild boar, when he turns against his pursuers, excite the sluggish courage of the bear, and provoke the fury of the tiger, as he slumbers in the thicket. Where there is danger, there may be glory; and the mode of hunting which opens the fairest field to the exertions of valour may justly be considered as the image and as the school of war. (*DF* 3:80)

In this narrative analysis Gibbon exploits the collective option of the double narrative perspective he uses throughout volume 2 and 3, the "we" in which the reader is securely (and vividly) incorporated, rather than the "I" by which the personality, individuality, and sometimes uncertainty of the narrator are stressed. "We" really means that the reader is imaginatively to travel, to observe; it is not a euphemism for "I": "From the fortieth degree, which touches the wall of China, we may securely advance above a thousand miles to the northward, until our progress is stopped by the excessive cold of Siberia" (*DF* 3:85). And similarly, in the notes, after describing the fierceness of the Alani, whom the Huns had defeated, "We must think highly of the conquerors of *such* men" (*DF* 3:94 n. 56 [54]). Earlier, Gibbon could not rely on the reader's implicit distinction between the clarity and simplicity of a paradigm and the cloudy complexity of history; now, I think, he does. It is perhaps relevant that he produces very few historical maxims—statements presented as if they were universal laws—in this analysis. They would exaggerate the authority of the paradigm, and Gibbon's method is instead to suggest, by narration and description, that even those societies and events that can be reduced to paradigms are not to be understood historically by laws and systems alone.

When Gibbon turns to civilized nations, the experience of China, whose history "ascends, by a probable tradition, above forty centuries" (*DF* 3:84); as well as the conquests, migration, and "Decline and Fall of the Huns [Tartars]" (*DF* 3:88, shoulder caption) and the degeneration of the northern nomads in the modern age, place Roman history in a hugely expanded space and time. The reader's hopes and fears for Rome are inevitably conditioned by this sense of the pettiness and flux of all human things. The history of civilizations, moreover, is much further removed from the comprehensible paradigms that to some extent determine the fate of barbarians, because civilized history is subject also to "moral causes" and to the influence of chance, powerful individuals, and particular institutions.

History as it is known, as it is recorded, is further complicated by the errors, passions, and abilities of historians. To portray it, both the tentative narrator and the assured generalization reappear in Gibbon's text. The reader is implicitly incorporated into the history as a judge, like the narrator, of doubtful, sometimes undeterminable, cases. For example, Valens, already established as weak, cowardly, and incompetent, is forced to make a quick decision. Gibbon comments magisterially, "He was deprived of the favourite resource of feeble and timid minds; who consider the use of dilatory and ambiguous measures as the most admirable efforts of consummate prudence" (*DF* 3:98). There is little risk that the reader will be deceived, however, into granting this comment the authority of a law, for two sentences later, Gibbon shows that this particular decision was one that might have confounded the wisest monarch; he himself does not judge what Valens ought to have done, though he can see that Valens made the worst of his situation. The reader must decide.

The narrator, faced with the complexity of history itself rather than paradigms of history, reacts emotionally and morally as well as intellectually to his material. Perhaps it was unwise to admit the barbarians to the Empire; perhaps it was unavoidable. Having admitted them, perhaps it was excusable to require them to abandon their arms and to give their children as hostages; perhaps it was dangerously inconsistent. But certainly it was both unwise and immoral to mistreat them: "The most lively resentment is excited by the tyranny of pretended benefactors, who sternly exact the debt of gratitude which they have cancelled by subsequent injuries" (*DF* 3:102). Most interesting are the cases in which the apparent maxim is immediately qualified or rejected by the personal reaction of the "I": "The urgent consideration of the public safety may undoubtedly authorise the violation of every positive law. How far that, or any other, consideration may operate to dissolve the natural obligations of humanity and justice is a doctrine of which I still desire to remain ignorant" (*DF* 3:124).

Gibbon comments constantly on the quality of history's witnesses, the historians and their documents.[55] He is aware that the historian's account can influence not only posterity's view of an event, but its outcome: "The splendid narratives which the general [Sebastian] transmitted of his own exploits alarmed the Imperial court by the appearance of superior merit; . . . his valour was praised, his advice was rejected" (DF 3:114–15). The effective power of historical narrative, however, is much less an issue than its unreliability, incompleteness, subjectivity. For example, after a lengthy quotation from Libianus, Gibbon comments—in the text itself—as follows: "The truth of history may disclaim some parts of this panegyric, which cannot strictly be reconciled with the character of Valens or the circumstances of the battle; but the fairest commendation is due to the eloquence, and still more to the generosity of the sophist of Antioch" (DF 3:119). This totally unnecessary tribute, however edged, suggests that Gibbon identifies with Libianus. The historian may merit praise, even when he doubts or errs. Similarly, when Ammianus's narrative ends, exasperated complaints about the "false ornaments, that perpetually disfigure" his style (DF 3:109 n. 83 [81]) are abandoned: "We must now take leave of this impartial historian, and reproach is silenced by our regret for such an irreparable loss" (DF 3:116 n. 93 [91]). Gibbon the historian must often confess that "we are ignorant" of this or that fact. He gratefully credits his fellow workers when they assist him in the struggle to wrest history from the intractable materials left behind by the past: "I should never, without the aid of Tillement . . . have detected an historical anecdote, in a strange medley of moral and mystic exhortations" (DF 3:129 n. 118 [115]); "M. de Guignes has skilfully traced the footsteps of the Huns through the vast deserts of Tartary" (DF 3:91 n. 45). Gibbon also complains about the limitations of his predecessors, even as he demonstrates how he extracts what he elsewhere calls "historical truths," that is, probabilities, from their biased, confused, and inadequate evidence. He complains equally of faults we might consider literary rather than historical—their rhetoric, organization, dullness or vivacity, and so on. Such issues affect the quality of the image they construct, and an image, not the thing itself, Gibbon now seems openly to acknowledge, is what a historical account can achieve.

The effect of this metahistorical commentary is again to bring historical writing to judgment, his own writing as well as theirs. To call attention to another's metaphors is to invite scrutiny of your own. To praise another's ahistorical generosity or ingenuity is to justify or confess your own. In the latter part of the *Decline and Fall*, Gibbon treats the writing of history as a dialogue between himself and his reader and between himself and his fellow historians. The historian, the middle term in these two dialogues, invites the reader to see him seeing the past through these other perceptions and witnesses. Aspects of the past may be fully apprehended in abstract or theoretical paradigms, but to produce those paradigms is not the principal role of the writer of *history;* the historian must resort to the untidiness of narrative, the subjectivity of a particular observer, the exploitation of the probable, and the dangers of the imagination. Associating the reader in the process of judgment, he knows he produces only an image of the past, but he must try to produce an image that is judged to do justice to the particular events and persons that occasion it.

We cannot know the various contributions of financial security, political approval, and successful self-defense and self-definition as historian to Gibbon's new portrayal of his narrator. Swift progress in what he knew to be new portions of the history at least worthy of their predecessor presumably had a reciprocal effect on his demeanor in the living world. In spite of the hostility of Fox, Wilkes, and the other Opposition "Patriots," Gibbon continued to frequent Brookes's and to take there his characteristic pose and role:

> Soon as to Brookes's thence thy footsteps bend,
> What gratulations thy approach attend!
> See Gibbon rap his box: auspicious sign
> That wit and classic compliment combine.[56]

Perhaps he was simply sustained by the knowledge that his Government friends approved him; perhaps, however, his consciousness of the secret power of the narrator gave him this social courage, amounting, in the eyes of the unfriendly, to vanity. In any case, a period that had begun for Gibbon in considerable perplexity concluded with a triumphant sense of accomplishment and success certainly equalled in the narrator's security and dominion in the chapters he was then writing.

EIGHT

Ending Empires

ike many another author, Gibbon's plans to go to press were too optimistic: he hoped for March, but found himself still at work on corrections and improvements throughout the summer of 1780. A few months late, the Roman Empire in the West nevertheless duly fell. The British Empire, on the other hand, began 1780 with such apparent success that the North government decided to risk a general election.[1] In that election, Gibbon's "constituents"—his cousin Eliot—withdrew their support. "If my Seat in the House of C. has not some remote connection with a more valuable seat," he wrote to Dorothea Gibbon—"remote" is of course playful for "direct and essential"—"I should retire without any regret from that scene of noise heat and contention" (*Letters* 2:242). Sensing, perhaps, that he had learned what he could from sitting in Parliament, and valuing the seat on the Board of Trade principally for its income, Gibbon seems more and more willing, or even eager, to devote all his time to his work as historian. But until Burke's reform bill and the fall of North's government eliminated from Gibbon's options not only his lucrative post as Lord of Trade, but the prospects of *any* government post consistent with his historical labors, he was unable to resist the combined lures of wealth and success of a conventional model. Yet whenever the route of "business" (work connected with public affairs) diverged from that of scholarship, Gibbon always selected scholarship, finally turning away from the "noise heat and contention" of contemporary politics to seek a permanent resolution of his economic problems in a new life, away from imperial ambition. In 1780–81, however, the choice was not forced upon him. Indeed, he could see the several milestones in his life not as endings, but as new beginnings. Lord North found an "*almost* gratuitous" seat for Gibbon, the new volumes of the *Decline and Fall* appeared to international praise, and he could rejoice in the triumphs of a friend—John Baker Holroyd, now Lord Sheffield.

The two new volumes of the *Decline and Fall* might have been the final ones. He had announced this possibility in his preface, and in his *Memoirs* (164), he claims that he "long hesitated" about whether to continue his history beyond the epoch to which he had committed himself in the first volume, the extinction of the Empire in the West. But if he hesitated, it was not because he had no more to say, as he was careful to make clear in both the rhetoric and the structure of these volumes. The ending of the third volume—excluding the separate essay ("General Observations"—discussed in chapter 1 above) appended as an epilogue for the sake of closure—makes it very clear that he perceives the decline and fall of the two empires as one subject:

> I have now accomplished the laborious narrative of the decline and fall of the Roman empire . . . to its total extinction in the West about five centuries after the Christian aera. . . . The . . . feeble and imaginary successors of Augustus. . . . continued to reign over the East; . . . and the history of the Greek emperors may still afford a long series of instructive lessons and interesting revolutions. (*DF* chap. 38, 4:170–71)

Thus the tone of the ending of volume 3 of the *Decline and Fall* is far from that of absolute finality. Nor does Gibbon see only catastrophe and loss in the events and processes he recounts. Instead, he observes, in the debris at the end of one empire, the seeds and shoots of many related stories.

The new work of 1780, that is, the last 300 pages of volume 3, carry on and complete not only the history of the Western Empire, but the developments in Gibbon's historiographical practice already apparent in earlier chapters of the new volumes. His conceptions of Roman history and of the nature of historical writing have become, not so much incompatible with his original perspectives, as far richer and more individual than might have been predicted from his earlier work. Walpole, the perpetual dilettante (and in 1781 opposed to Gibbon politically), pointed with discontent to the absence of the finely wrought enamel he had so much admired in volume 1.[2] It is not so much absent, we may say, as challenged. Smooth and polished surfaces, however brilliantly colored, cannot convey Gibbon's developed vision of new life emerging amid Rome's looming ruins.

Gibbon's personal and political life as he wrote the final pages of the third volume seemed relatively smooth. The successes in America and Holroyd's entry into Parliament gave him tranquil pleasure; gout, the Gordon riots, and Burke's efforts to abolish the expensive luxury of the Board of Trade gave him equally tranquil concern. Even the uncertain attitude of Eliot, patron of his seat in Parliament, in the face of a prospective election, did not alarm Gibbon during the first six months of 1780. His mind was far removed in time and space. Parliament was in recess until January 24, and Gibbon had nothing to say concerning modern affairs until February 7, when he wrote calmly to Holroyd (who was planning to enter Parliament as the representative of Coventry in an uncontested by-election): "No news! foreign or domestic. I . . . find people, as I expected, torpid. Burke makes his motion Friday; but I think the rumours of a Civil war subside every day" (*Letters* 2:236). This was Gibbon's response to a turmoil of meetings, associations, petitions, and counter-petitions protesting taxation and demanding more or less radical political reform. Perhaps no one but Gibbon thought there was "no news." Holroyd's response to the same crisis, typically, was to take the lead in organizing a counter-petition in Sussex, as well as to make a maiden speech supporting increased army expenses (April 5) that was so vigorous that he was "several times called to order."[3] Holroyd was more fervent than most, but the extreme contrast between his reaction and Gibbon's clearly suggests how withdrawn, how much that of the historian contemplating current events in the perspectives of many times and places, Gibbon's attitude toward his own times had already become.

He could not be entirely indifferent to Burke's speech, however, for it was designed to eliminate the income from the Board of Trade so essential to Gibbon's continuance in his London way of life. Despite excellent military news from the American war—"We must be glad of these deplorable successes," groaned Walpole,[4] half patriot and half Patriot—the taxation crisis was leading to considerable difficulties for the Government. As Gibbon later described it, the parliamentary session was

> stormy and perilous: County meetings, petitions, and committees of correspondence announced the public discontent; and instead of voting with a triumphant majority, the friends of government were often exposed to a struggle and sometimes to a defeat. The house of Commons adopted Mr Dunning's motion "that the influence of the Crown had encreased, was increasing, and ought to be diminished" and Mr Burke's bill of reform was framed with skill, introduced with eloquence, and supported by numbers. (*Memoirs* 161)

But in his letters of 1780, Gibbon makes no comment on Dunning's motion at all and says of the eventual vote abolishing the Board of Trade: "I can assure you that it has not disturbed my tranquillity. [Burke's bill] will probably be rejected by the House of Lords; and at all events I have reason to expect some equivalent. I hope I am falling asleep" (*Letters* 2:239). The last comment—he was writing at 9:30 P.M. on a Saturday—makes it clear that a night made sleepless by the pain of gout really had bothered Gibbon more than the (as he thought, uncertain or temporary) loss of a major source of income. Indeed, as historian and connoisseur he admired the very instrument by which he was being reduced: "I can never forget the delight with which that diffusive and ingenious Orator [Burke] was heard by all sides of the house, and even by those whose existence he proscribed. The Lords of Trade blushed at their own insignificancy, and Mr Eden's appeal to the two thousand five hundred volumes of our reports served only to excite a general laugh" (*Memoirs* 173). Gibbon's own pleasure in the speech cannot have been diminished by Burke's ironic praise of the Board of Trade as a support of the national literature. Even Burke's barbed compliment to "the historian's labours, the wise and salutary results of deep religious researches,"[5] acknowledged the importance of the first volume of the history in progress. And Gibbon's political assessment or information proved correct: the Lords rejected Burke's reforms, and the Board of Trade was not abolished until 1783.

The Gordon riots (beginning June 2, 1780) received more of Gibbon's attention, but again he responded as a historian, not as an actor or possible sufferer. He was coldly outraged by the outbreak of active bigotry in a civilized age and country, as Lord George Gordon and his mob destroyed property and threatened lives in an attempt to force Parliament to repeal the 1778 acts of relief for Roman Catholics, limited though they were. "The month of June 1780 will ever be marked by a dark and diabolical fanaticism, which I had supposed to be extinct, but which actually subsists in Great Britain perhaps beyond any other Country in Europe," he wrote when all was over (*Letters* 2:245). But his response at the time (June 6) was not only detached, but even in a way amused. "As the old story of Religion has [caused] most *formidable* tumults in this town," he wrote to his stepmother, "and as they will of course seem much more formidable at the distance of an hundred [miles], you may not be sorry to hear that I am perfectly safe and well: my known attachment to the Protestant Religion has most probably saved me" (*Letters* 2:242).[6] Two days later he assured her, "As an individual I do not conceive myself to be obnoxious [that is, to the rioters]. I am not apt without duty or necessity to thrust myself into a Mob: and our part of the town is as quiet as a Country Village" (*Letters* 2:243). Later still (June 10) he was alarmed (sedately) on Mrs. Gibbon's account, owing to reports of an outbreak of rioting at Bath: "I flatter myself that your pretty town does not contain much of that scum which has boiled up to the surface in this huge Cauldron" (*Letters* 2:244).

That "mighty unrelenting Tyrant called the Gout" (*Letters* 2:238) forcibly attracted Gibbon's attention throughout March, but the parliamentary crises forced him to attend Parliament anyway, and the progress of the *Decline and Fall* was so swift that he must also have managed to continue his writing during this siege of illness. In this attack, indeed, the swelling and pain occurred only in his feet, though fever and sleeplessness led to a general weakness. The Easter holidays were necessary to give him "strength and spirits to support a scene [Parliament] which I am heartily tired of," but at the same time, he could announce to his friends that volumes 2 and 3 would go to press in May. Much revision and correction remained to be done, and in June, even though the book was in press, he hoped to obtain new information about Athanasius for the improvement of the fifth chapter of the first of the new volumes. "I will only add that I am in some degree streightened for time; the part of my second volume, that relates to Athanasius, will go to the press very speedily," he wrote to Joseph Warton on June 22. His desire for a sight of the manuscript in question, Sir Isaac Newton's "Paradoxical Questions concerning the Morals and Actions of Athanasius and his Followers," is significant but is also significantly qualified: "By my own diligence and the help of some useful guides, I have gained access to the original documents [that is, the published versions of them] (more especially his own works) that can illustrate the life of Athanasius; but I should think myself inexcusable, if I neglected any opportunity of availing myself of the researches and reflections of Sir Isaac Newton on any subject" (*Letters* 2:244). The manuscript was apparently not available to Gibbon, at least in time for him to consult it for his account of Athanasius, for it is not cited in the *Decline and Fall,* and it is unlikely that he would have failed at least to acknowledge the kindness of its noble owner, Lord Portsmouth, in allowing him to see it, had that kindness occurred. It was probably almost too late when he wrote to request Warton's aid in obtaining a sight of the manuscript, for he was engaged in correcting for the press throughout the summer, a "business [that] fixes me to Bentinck Street more closely than any other part of my litterary labour, as it is absolutely necessary that I should be in the midst of all the books which I have at any time used during the composition" (*Letters* 2:245).

Since he was engaged in correcting the whole, he must have completed the composition of the final chapters, 33–38. These chapters concern the last moments of the Western Empire and its enemies. To them he appended, in revised form, the "General Observations on the Fall of the Empire in the West" that he had composed as an overview to the history some nine years earlier. Thematically and interpretatively, neither the glib organic metaphor borrowed from Montesquieu for the "General Observations" incorporated in chapter

38, nor the equally glib "barbarism and religion" formula used by
Gibbon to describe the conquerors (though not, as often assumed, to
identify the assassins) of the Western Empire, seems adequate to the
perspective of the new volumes completed by these chapters. In these
volumes, and especially the concluding chapters, Gibbon seems to
want to show the complexity and multiplicity of the interrelated
conditions that prevented the Western Empire from surviving. These
include the faults of character of its rulers, the strengths of its opponents, the feebleness of the institutions of empire, the indifference or
distress of the populace, and the total severence of the Western
Empire from the East. These and other "causes" are not represented
as causal in the strong sense demanded by a scientific law, but rather
as associated and contributory factors that may or not be predictive of
the collapse of a nation, government, or culture. Gibbon has been
credited, in later volumes, with at least an embryonic comparative
study of civilizations;[7] in the present volumes, too, he compares
Rome's fate to that of other states, rising, falling, or fallen, but
without making any generalizations about social or historical laws. He
analyzes types and recognizes recurrent patterns, but he seems more
and more to recognize also the intervention of the historian's constructive imagination in these types and patterns.

In chapter 32, the last to deal extensively with the Eastern Empire
in these volumes, Gibbon had begun, "The division of the Roman
world between the sons of Theodosius marks the final establishment
of the empire of the East, which . . . subsisted one thousand and fifty-
eight years, in a state of premature and perpetual decay" (DF 3:378).
This perspective, so justly irritating to subsequent Byzantinists,[8] was,
of course, taken for granted by Gibbon's contemporaries,[9] even though
the paradox of a millennium of decay might well have invited attention. Gibbon explains the reason for his adoption of the opinion clearly
enough. In his view, the "princes of Constantinople measured their
greatness by the servile obedience of their people. They were ignorant how much this passive disposition enervates and degrades every
faculty of the mind. The subjects, who had resigned their will to the
absolute commands of a master, were equally incapable of guarding
their lives and fortunes against the assaults of the Barbarians or of
defending their reason from the terrors of superstition" (DF chap. 32,
3:380). This possibly final chapter on the empire in the East is full
of maxims about public affairs, as if Gibbon felt so contemptuous of
the Eastern regime that he could reduce it, like an uncivilized state,
to general laws, or as if he sought to contain, at least temporarily,
what his present plans did not allow him to pursue. Chapter 32 was
probably completed in 1779.

Chapter 33, written late in 1779 or early in 1780, turns to the
West. Arcadius and Honorius, the sons of Theodosius, had proved

equally unworthy of their father, the Empire, and history. Their sister Pulcheria, who reigned in the East, was Theodosius's most worthy descendant, in Gibbon's view. Another sister, Placidia, now formed the principal link between the empires. Her second husband, the general Constantius, was associated by Honorius to the (Western) Empire, and she became the mother and regent of Valentinian III. After the temporary reign of a usurper, Valentinian III, at the age of six, was confirmed as emperor of the West (A.D. 425) by his cousin Theodosius II, emperor of the East. Theodosius was legally of age (twenty-four) and had married the beautiful, virtuous, and intelligent Eudocia, but in Gibbon's view, it was not by Theodosius, but "by the agreement of the three females who governed the Roman world"— Pulcheria, Eudocia, and Placidia—that the infant emperor of the West was betrothed and later married to the infant daughter of the Eastern emperor (*DF* chap. 33, 3:420). But this dynastic unity did not signify a unitary empire; on the contrary, the alliance was like one between foreign powers. "Theodosius and Valentinian continued to respect the obligations of their public and domestic alliance, but the unity of the Roman government was finally dissolved. By a positive declaration, the validity of all future laws was limited to the dominions of their peculiar author" (*DF* chap. 33, 3:421). This amicable division is attributed by Gibbon to "Theodosius's" emulation of the moderation of his grandfather, but soon Gibbon reckons with the women who were the real decision makers. Unfortunately, "Placidia envied, but she could not equal . . . the elegant genius of Eudocia, the wise and successful policy of Pulcheria" (*DF* 3:421). Gibbon does not appear to blame the final fall of the Western Empire on female rule, but the continuing power of these mothers and sisters, after the young emperors reached mature years, indicates the deplorable weakness of the men. Gibbon does criticize the two mothers for their failures as educators, but no more than he criticizes Theodosius the Great in the same role.

Much more critical than the genders of the rulers are their abilities. The long reign of Placidia, who lacked the talents of her sister and niece, was supported by two generals, Aetius and Boniface, "who may be deservedly named as the last of the Romans," but whose "discord was the fatal and immediate cause of the loss of Africa" (*DF* 3:421). Aetius defeated Attila the Hun, whose "adventures," especially his love of the princess Honoria (*DF* chap. 35, 3:481), suspend and relieve the narrative of the declining Empire. In this account, Gibbon's passing remark about Honoria's extramarital pregnancy—"Her guilt and shame (such is the absurd language of imperious man)"—would bring down upon him the wrath of moralists and self-styled champions of women; it illustrates a shift in his own views, which when he wrote the first volume seemed to adhere to a conventional sexual double standard.

The stories of Attila and the Huns (chapters 34 and 35), Genseric and the Vandals (33, 36 and 37, in part), Count Ricimer the Gothic emperor-maker (36), and finally of Odoacer, Scyrrian king of Italy (36) greatly overshadow the last emperors of the West, with the partial exception of the four-year reign of Marjorian, to which twelve of the last three hundred pages are devoted. The stories of the Huns and Vandals are used to parallel the Roman pattern of self-destruction, but recurrent in their stories and in the others is the theme of emerging nations, variously related to those they replace. Even Attila, "the savage destroyer[,] undesignedly laid the foundations of a republic [Venice] which revived, in the feudal state of Europe, the art and spirit of commercial industry" (*DF* chap. 35, 3:495–96). Only in this context of reconstruction, ironically undesigned, naturally unnatural (Gibbon evokes the story that "grass never grew where [Attila's] horse had trod"), is the structure of the third volume's conclusion understandable, for it does not *end* with the fall of the Western Empire. Indeed, that event is passed over almost parenthetically in the course of chapter 36, and the climax of chapter 36 is a portrayal of the new Gothic kingdom of Italy. In chapter 37 Gibbon's chronological reach extends far beyond the last emperor of the West, as he goes on to analyze the institution of monasticism and the persecution, but final victory, of orthodoxy in its struggle with Arianism.

The final chapter of the third volume, chapter 38, is entirely devoted to new kingdoms, largely, it is true, kingdoms barbarous in deed as well as name. But its conclusion is reserved for the British isles, not merely because of enthusiasm for the historian's own country, but because British history was significantly distinct from that of other Roman possessions: "While the continent of Europe and Africa yielded, without resistance, to the Barbarians, the British island, alone and unaided, maintained a long, a vigorous, though an unsuccessful struggle against the formidable pirates who, almost at the same instant, assaulted the Northern, the Eastern, and the Southern coasts" (*DF* chap. 38, 4:159). As his narrative concludes, Gibbon summarizes the state of the Western world at the end of the fifth century:

> At that unhappy period, the Saxons fiercely struggled with the natives for the possession of Britain; Gaul and Spain were divided between the powerful monarchies of the Franks and Visigoths, and the dependent kingdoms of the Suevi and Burgundians; Africa was exposed to the cruel persecution of the Vandals and the savage insults of the Moors; Rome and Italy as far as the banks of the Danube, were afflicted by an army of Barbarian mercenaries, whose lawless tyranny was succeeded by the reign of Theodoric the Ostrogoth. All the subjects of the empire, who, by the use of the Latin language, more particularly deserved the name and privileges of Romans, were oppressed by the disgrace and calamities of foreign conquest; and the victorious nations of Germany established a new

system of manners and government in the Western countries of Europe.
(*DF* chap. 38, 4:170–71)

He then goes on to propose the consideration of the Eastern Empire
quoted above: "The feeble and imaginary successors of Augustus
continued to reign over the East; . . . and the history of the Greek
emperors may still afford a long series of instructive lessons and
interesting revolutions" (*DF* 4:171). But it is notable that with the
change of a single conjunction, if the "and" introducing the final
clause of the sentence I have just quoted were "yet" or "but," the
conclusion would be obviously optimistic. Without that change, and
without the certainty that there will be succeeding volumes, Gibbon's
tone remains elegiac and even pessimistic. Nevertheless, his conclusion recognizes the existence of a new system, not of chaos.

That this recognition is not merely a concluding gesture is suggested by the stress on new beginnings and preservation of fragments
throughout these last chapters. He utilizes the fable of the Seven
Sleepers (a tale of the Rip Van Winkle type) to make the point that
historical writing, and even the underlying events themselves, are
subject to the system-making habits of the human mind. Many nations
have believed a version of this fable, Gibbon points out, because of
its "genuine merit":

> We imperceptibly advance from youth to age, without observing the
> gradual, but incessant, change of human affairs, and, even in our larger
> experiences of history, the imagination is accustomed, by a perpetual
> series of causes and effects, to unite the most distant revolutions. But, if
> the interval between two memorable aeras could be instantly annihilated;
> if it were possible, after a momentary slumber of two hundred years, to
> display the *new* world to the eyes of a spectator, who still retained a lively
> and recent impression of the *old;* his surprise and his reflections would
> furnish the pleasing subject of a philosophical romance. (*DF* chap. 33,
> 3:439)

In the interval during which the Seven Sleepers slept, government
had moved from Rome to Constantinople, military abuses had been
replaced by "tame and ceremonious servitude," Christianity had replaced paganism, the "union of the Roman empire was dissolved; its
genius was humbled in the dust; and armies of unknown Barbarians . . . had established their victorious reign over the fairest provinces of Europe and Africa." Gibbon's interest in this fable, with its
problematical implications for history itself, is confirmed by a long
note in a manuscript notebook he was keeping in 1783.[10] This note
includes several references not utilized in the *Decline and Fall*, but
like the other entries in this notebook, it appears to have been
written when Gibbon did not have a copy of his history at hand to
refer to, for it gives references only to the appropriate volume, leaving

page and note number blank. In the notebook, Gibbon again stresses the imaginative power of the fable, duplicating or paralleling several points he makes in the *Decline and Fall*.

The Vandals are the first (and, for Gibbon returns to them, the last) foreign power whose history is explicitly and implicitly compared to Rome's in these chapters. Genseric, the terrible and Arian king of the Vandals, took Carthage in 439,

> five hundred and eighty-five years after the destruction of the city and republic by the younger Scipio.
>   A new city had arisen from its ruins, with the title of a colony; and, though Carthage might yield to the royal prerogatives of Constantinople . . . she still maintained the second rank in the West; as the *Rome* . . . of the African world. (*DF* chap. 33, 3:434)

Carthage's prosperity and even its appearance of freedom are stressed in Gibbon's description. It is sacked, looted, and enslaved by Genseric. Genseric's perfidy and his skill in sea battle, as well as the Romans' ineffective opposition, make his future progress to Rome itself seem inevitable. Indeed, in chapter 36, we eventually learn that in A.D. 455 "Genseric boldly advanced from the port of Ostia to the gates of the defenceless city [Rome]" (*DF* 4:5). Gibbon seeks no better way to indicate the decadence of Rome than to portray her defenders— not the emperor and strong young soldiers, but "an unarmed and venerable procession of the bishop at the head of his clergy. The fearless spirit of [Pope] Leo [persuaded] . . . the king of the Vandals . . . to spare the unresisting multitude, to protect the buildings from fire, and to exempt the captives from torture; and, although such orders were neither seriously given nor strictly obeyed, the mediation of Leo was glorious to himself and in some degree beneficial to his country" (*DF* 4:5–6).

This partial and reluctant tribute to Leo is in part perhaps the result of Gibbon's disagreement with St. Augustine, whom he had portrayed fairly favorably in chapter 33 (if due allowance is made for grumblings in the notes about the similarities between Augustine's views and Calvin's, and about Augustine's lack of Greek), but with whose providential explanation of the fall of Rome Gibbon was in total disagreement, as he had indicated in chapter 31 (*DF* 3:341). In general, however, Gibbon now seems willing enough to credit bishops and even saints with their secular virtues. He notes with approval the charity of Leo himself, as well as that of Deodatus, bishop of Carthage. His attitude toward the Christians is now mixed; on occasion, they are Romans; often they deserve pity rather than, or in addition to, censure and contempt; only their intolerance towards each other now arouses Gibbon's hostility. Gibbon, who had once seemed somewhat indifferent to the issue of freedom of conscience in matters of rival superstition, says of the Catholic response to their persecution by the Arian Vandals in Africa, "If the rights of conscience had been understood, the Catholics must have condemned their past conduct, or acquiesced in their actual sufferings. But they still persisted to refuse the indulgence which they claimed" (*DF* chap. 37, 4:91). He carries this controversy forward more than a century after the ostensible terminus of his narrative, into the seventh century: "The cause of Arianism was gradually suppressed by the weight of truth, of interest, and of example; and the controversy, which Egypt had derived from the Platonic school, was terminated, after a war of three hundred years, by the final conversion of the Lombards of Italy" (*DF* chap. 37, 4:102–3).

The triumph of the Latin Christians is, in Gibbon's view, a triumph for civilization, but not, unfortunately, for religious toleration. In Spain, the Catholics owed their triumph in part to the dubious merits of a son who attempted treason against his father, and another who "prudently" betrayed his father's memory. Yet Gibbon does not portray their heterodox opponents as fallen heroes in the cause of religious freedom, even when the virtues of an individual might permit him to do so. For example, the greatest king of the Vandals, Thrasimund, "excelled in beauty, prudence, and magnanimity of soul." He was an Arian, who disguised his persecution of the opposition party with some skill: "he employed the gentle but efficacious powers of seduction" and used cruelty only when "the indiscretion of his adversaries furnished him with a specious opportunity" (*DF* chap. 37, 4:90). Gibbon might have treated him as a latter-day Julian, but instead finds him "degraded by his intolerant zeal and deceitful clemency." In Gibbon's view, there is little to be said for the Arians, except that they were not worse than the orthodox party in their abuse of power. Chapter 37 ends with an account of the persecution of the Jews in Spain, 612–712. After the gradual eradication of heresy and paganism, "the intolerant spirit, which could find neither idolaters nor heretics, was reduced to the persecution of the Jews" (*DF* 4:103). The Jews were suitable victims because of their wealth, and "they might be oppressed without danger, as they had lost the use, and even the remembrance, of arms." Since "injuries will produce hatred and . . . hatred will find the opportunity of revenge," this persecution eventually led to the Jews' assisting the Arabs in their conquest of Spain (*DF* 4:104). Thus in the Western Empire, intestine Christian controversy evaporated. But the East was another story, and at the end of chapter 37, Gibbon prepares his reader for the continuation of his history of Christian controversy. The Nestorian and Eutychian controversies "extend far beyond the limits of the present volume . . . and may afford an interesting and instructive series of history, from the general councils of Ephesus and Chalcedon to the conquest of the East by the successors of Mahomet" (*DF* 4:105).

In chapter 38, Gibbon prepares us for the multiple layers of temporal perspective that will alone permit a sufficiently complex response to the new condition of the Roman world by harkening back to the Republic and noting that the "Romans" oppressed by the new barbarians were descendants of the very barbarians—the Gauls—for whom this fate was predicted by a "lieutenant of Vespasian . . . expressed by the genius of Tacitus" (*DF* chap. 38, 4:106). Throughout this chapter, then, we are reminded that the threatened civilizations had in fact been imposed by conquerors—the Romans—and that they represented the power of civilization itself over mere military might. This power is highly vulnerable and not glibly predictable—Gibbon hardly supports a view of invariable progress in this chapter. What *is* predictable, this chapter would lead us to believe, is a complex interplay between destructive and constructive forces at most moments in history. Clovis, the principal conqueror in this chapter, for example, is brave, inexorable, and prudent: "In all his transactions with mankind, he calculated the weight of interest, of passion, and of opinion; and his measures were sometimes . . . moderated by the milder genius of Rome and Christianity" (*DF* chap. 38, 4:110). But his first exploit is to defeat a Roman-educated leader whose just judgments had made him the popular choice of the Franks and Burgundians and whose reign "seemed to revive the original institution of civil society" (*DF* 4:111). While Clovis's victory is hardly good, the loss is clearly regarded by Gibbon as largely illusory; he compares this "imaginary king" (real person, but imaginary role) to Deioces, the purported founder of the Median Empire, in Herodotus.

Clovis's accomplishments, in all their ambivalence, are also brought forward in time, by a comparison with those of Henry IV of France: Clovis's "savage character and the virtues of Henry IV. suggest the most opposite ideas of human nature," yet both "conquered France by their valour, their policy, and the merits of a seasonable conversion" (*DF* 4:118). Much of the chapter is devoted to a kind of comparative study of the laws and constitution of Clovis as they affected the individual subject. There is, for example, the law by which murder could be recompensated with fines: "Had these laws been regulated by any principle of equity or reason, the public protection should have supplied in just proportion the want of personal strength," that is, the weaker the victim, the higher the fine. Exactly the opposite was true. But to what and how have we progressed since Clovis's time? "The boldest citizen was taught by experience that he might suffer more injuries than he could inflict. As the manners of the Franks became less ferocious, their laws were rendered more severe. . . . Under the reign of Charlemagne, murder was universally punished with death; and the use of capital punishments has been liberally multiplied in the jurisprudence of modern Europe" (*DF* chap. 38, 4:135).

This multiplication of death penalties is hardly clear and obvious progress; Gibbon's own attitude is ambiguous, perhaps ambivalent. But the next stages in the development of law are plainly seen by him as regressive, and their modern replacement, alluded to in an ironic parenthesis, as less sanguinary but not more just. The new developments are trial by ordeal and trial by combat, the latter quickly becoming the more popular among a warlike people. "The tribunals were stained with the blood, perhaps, of innocent and respectable citizens; the law, *which now favours the rich*, then yielded to the strong" (*DF* 4:138; emphasis added).

The theme of the chapter, as of the volume, then, is the ambiguity and often the irony of historical change. It is thus expressed (apropos of wars) by Gibbon himself: "Such is the empire of Fortune (if we may still disguise our ignorance under that popular name), that it is almost equally difficult to foresee the events of war or to explain their various consequences" (*DF* 4:126). Usually, loss and destruction have their compensations, or are less thorough than they appear; progress and construction, on the other hand, are humanly flawed and have consequences unpredicted by men or their theories. Gibbon goes out of his way, in opposition to Montesquieu, to praise the legal code of the Visigoths, which emulated a feature he had admired in the early Empire, in providing equality under law for those they had conquered: "The allegiance of doubtful subjects is indeed most effectually secured by their own persuasion that they hazard more in a revolt than they can hope to obtain by a revolution; but it has appeared so natural to oppress those whom we hate and fear, that the contrary system well deserves the praise of wisdom and moderation." He adds a note, criticizing Montesquieu's "excessive severity" in judging this code: "I dislike the style; I detest the superstition; but I shall presume to think that the civil jurisprudence displays a more civilized and enlightened state of society than that of the Burgundians or even of the Lombards" (*DP* chap. 38, 4:155, n. 132 [125]). It has been suggested that Gibbon judges history not from the perspective either of the past or of the present, but from that of time itself, according to which there is neither progress nor regress, but only change.[11] The only irrevocable and unequivocally destructive change would be one in which a vanished civilization failed to leave its traces in its successor. Gibbon examines the case of Roman Britain to conclude the volume, ostensibly out of mere patriotic curiosity (*DF* 4:156), but actually to explore a possible instance of such a total loss, in instructive contrast with the fallen Empire, still culturally influential in the states rising from its ruins.

After a century of war, the Britons yielded to the Angles and Saxons, except in Scotland, Cornwall, and Wales. "Much courage, and some skill, must have been exerted for the defence of Britain. Yet, if the memory of its champions is almost buried in oblivion, we need not repine; since every age, however destitute of science or virtue, sufficiently abounds with acts of blood and military renown" (*DF* chap. 38, 4:161–62). History has little to say about these years; legend, much; and Gibbon, after playing with the romance of Arthur, remarks, "At length the light of science and reason was rekindled; the talisman was broken; the visionary fabric melted into air; and, by a natural, though unjust, reverse of the public opinion, the severity of the present age is inclined to question the *existence* of Arthur" (*DF* 4:163). But this exotic excursion is only a brief respite; the real story of the Anglo-Saxon conquest is not merely destruction, but "extirpation":

> The arts and religion, the laws and language, which the Romans had so carefully planted in Britain, were extirpated by their barbarous sucessors. . . . The kings of France maintained the privileges of their Roman subjects; but the ferocious Saxons trampled on the laws of Rome and of the emperors. . . . The language of science, of business, and of conversation, which had been introduced by the Romans, was lost in the general desolation. . . . The geography of *England* was universally inscribed with foreign characters and appellations. The example of a revolution, so rapid and so complete, may not easily be found. (*DF* 4:164–65)

Moreover, even "the independent Britons appear to have relapsed into the state of original barbarism, from whence they had been imperfectly reclaimed" (*DF* 4:167), and the Continent lost sight of these former Roman subjects, allies, and enemies. "One of the greatest of the English monarchs was requested to satisfy the curiosity of a Greek emperor concerning the state of Britain; and Henry II. could assert, from his personal experience, that Wales was inhabited by a race of naked [that is, unarmored] warriors." A truly destructive revolution made Britain a fabulous mystery not only to history, but to the contemporary civilized world: "By the revolution of Britain, the limits of science, as well as of empire, were contracted. The dark cloud, which had been cleared by the Phoenician discoveries and finally dispelled by the arms of Caesar, again settled on the shores of the Atlantic, and a Roman province was again lost among the fabulous islands of the Ocean" (*DF* 4:168).

Such a revolution points a moral not only about the vulnerability of (inadequately planted) human cultures, but about that of historical writing: Gibbon presents a fairy-tale account of a land of serpents and spirits from Procopius, "the gravest historian" of the sixth century; "after this dream of fancy we read with astonishment, that the name of this island is *Brittia" (DF* 4:169). Playfully confirming this tacit judgment on the pretensions of historians, Gibbon himself then retells a legendary story of a warrior princess of the Angles—"a singular, though an improbable, adventure"—*without* rejecting it as wholly legendary.

But the devastating loss of history and culture suffered in Roman Britain is clearly in contrast with the fate of the rest of the Roman world. Without much credit either to individual virtues or to wise institutions, humanity for the most part preserved and improved, even as it destroyed and degraded, its own accomplishments and insights. In particular, most barbarians were able to perceive the value of the material culture of the states they conquered, and as they acquired possessions, they acquired also a need for laws: "After the sanguinary Barbarians had secured their dominion, and gratified their revenge, it was their interest to preserve the peasants, as well as the cattle, of the unresisting country. In each successive revolution, the patient herd becomes the property of its new masters; and the salutary compact of food and labour is silently ratified by their mutual necessities" (*DF* 4:166). This is Gibbon's comment on an example of the *worst* case, that of the vulnerable culture uprooted by an unappreciative successor. Even in such a case, some features of civilization have a chance to survive and revive. It is in this context that Gibbon felt willing to round off his work with the old "General Observations," including the limited and highly ironic confidence in certain forms of technological "progress": the "great republic" of Europe now possesses such advantage in warfare that it cannot be conquered by barbarians lacking equivalent technology, and even savages throughout the world now enjoy "the use of fire and of metals . . . domestic animals; the methods of hunting and fishing; the rudiments of navigation; the imperfect cultivation of corn or other nutritive grain; and the simple practice of the mechanic trades" (*DF* 4:180–81).

Following Hume's advice and the model of the third edition of volume 1, the two new volumes of the *Decline and Fall* were to be published with the notes at the foot of the page, so both text and notes had to be ready for the printers at the same time. If the rate of progress at the printer's was similar to that of volumes 3–6, the printing of the two volumes would have required about six months, that is, revisions of at least the first of the two would have had to be complete by the beginning of September. In fact, Gibbon's revisions of both volumes were apparently sufficiently well in hand by the middle of August for him to allow himself a brief holiday. He also turned his attention to the most important of his contemporary political problems. He wrote to Edward Eliot:

It seems to be now universally understood that this Parliament will be dissolved in a few months and possibly in a few days.—and you are not ignorant, Dear Sir, how much the whole colour of my future life will depend on your resolution. Unless I obtain a Seat in the ensuing Parliament I cannot flatter myself with a hope of remaining at the board of trade; such is the unpleasant state of my private affairs that with my office I must resign all future prospect of living in England; and the discontinuance of your favours would be a sentence of banishment from my native Country. My firm assurance that your kindness will allow some weight to these personal considerations will teach me to acquiesce, whatever may be your designs. (*Letters* 2:248)

It is difficult to determine Gibbon's real feelings at this juncture. On the one hand, he is sufficiently agitated to reveal, unintentionally, in the next few sentences, that he believes Eliot already to have decided against him. On the other hand, he had let the matter slide for a long interval; his major interests in his letters of August and September were clearly his own "lying-in" and Holroyd's prospective Irish peerage; he had other powerful friends who might offer him another seat in Parliament; and he tells Abigail Holroyd of his probable dismissal with an effortless series of jokes: "You probably receive my *last* frank. I have *found* reason to believe that I shall never rise again, and I submit to my fate with Philosophic composure" (*Letters* 2:249).

Probably he was genuinely undecided about his own preferences. He may even have anticipated a financial advantage in being "abandoned" by Eliot, the opportunity honorably to avoid paying Eliot half the cost of his 1774 election. In the letter just cited, Gibbon brings up the debt only after ostentatiously assuring Eliot that his delay in telling Gibbon about his plans to take away Gibbon's seat has in no way affected Gibbon's fate. Now this is not what Gibbon told everyone else—of course it would have been helpful to him to know as soon as possible that he needed to seek another seat—and Eliot, who in the past had allowed the seats he controlled to be occupied by people who differed from him politically, must have known that it was inconsiderate not to warn Gibbon of the change. The debt for the 1774 election was not due until 1782, yet Gibbon goes out of his way to request a delay in paying it until he can sell his Buckinghamshire estate and "discharge what I shall always consider as the smallest part of my obligations" (*Letters* 2:249). It is easy to see that on such an occasion, Gibbon might hope that the wealthy Eliot would feel compunction enough to forgive the debt for an advantage he had withdrawn.

In fact, Gibbon never paid this debt. For years his will included a bequest to Eliot's younger son, John, something that had once been mentioned between Gibbon and Eliot as a way of meeting Gibbon's financial obligation, but this bequest is not included in the final draft of Gibbon's will. The debt is not mentioned by either Eliot or Gibbon in further extant letters between them. My own guess is that Eliot forgave Gibbon the debt, as he could well afford to do. In all his full and frank discussions of his financial affairs with Holroyd, Gibbon never mentions it. The bequest to young John Eliot, whom Gibbon liked, might represent a painless gesture of gratitude rather than a quasi-legal obligation. It is certainly possible, however, that in 1791, when Gibbon made his final will, he simply forgot, or chose to forget, this old obligation to a wealthy kinsman.

In September 1780 Edward Eliot certainly did not press Gibbon for payment, and Gibbon was free to look elsewhere for political support without concern about this debt. When he returned from his two-week holiday at Sheffield, he was urged (so he told Holroyd) to apply to Lord North for a seat.

> I fairly stated my public disappointment and private difficulties; and declared to Lord N in the most explicit terms, that "notwithstanding my sincere desire to replace myself in a situation, where I may be serviceable to his M's Government, *small indeed* must be the [financial] effort which I shall be capable of making for that purpose." . . . After some importunity and delay, I saw the Secretary [of the Treasury, John Robinson] yesterday; and he communicated Lord N's resolution of bringing me into Parliament, either for the first meeting, or at the Re-Elections which will immediately be occasioned by the option of those who are returned for two places. He did not mention terms; if any, they must be very light. (*Letters* 2:250)

His dismissal and appeal were seen by others with very different eyes. Lord Edward Bentinck gloated in a letter to the duke of Portland, his brother: "Port Eliot [Bentinck refers to Eliot by the name of his estate] has dismissed Gibbon. Everybody rejoices. He is to be found from 8 in the morning to twelve at night in Robinson's antechamber and once being put into an inward room Robinson went out the back way and the maid not knowing anybody was left locked him in all night. This is the story as told."[12] An extant letter of Gibbon's friend Wedderburn, now Lord Loughborough, however, supports Gibbon's feeling that the administration, harassed though it was with requests for seats and appointments that it found difficulty in meeting, in an election that was not going as it hoped, and in which its powers and influence were greatly exaggerated, truly did value Gibbon. He had reason to be sanguine about his expectations. In this context, then, he may be believed when he writes to Holroyd, "I lament in some sort that [this offer] has disconcerted a very pleasant scheme a sweet vision of *Helvetic* retirement. I know that a prudent man ought not to make himself happy" (*Letters* 2:251).

When Eliot represented to Gibbon that he had withdrawn his support because of Gibbon's parliamentary conduct, Gibbon's reply summarized, from his perspective, his political principles (see chapter

6 above); generally, not to violate positive commitments, to select
the better "system" without being blind to its faults of execution, to
support that system constantly except under extreme pressure, and to
choose the side "upon the whole . . . least reprehensible" (*Letters*
2:253). These principles are hardly heroic, and Gibbon's practice of
them does not indicate historical foresight or, perhaps, great political
wisdom (Gibbon was also certain that Fox would be rejected by the
electors of Westminster—he was elected—and surprised that Government had gained so little in the election). But neither do these
principles represent the betrayal of Enlightenment and liberalism of
which some subsequent writers, moved by their own political views
perhaps, have accused Gibbon.

Gibbon retained his seat on the Board of Trade during the remainder of 1780 even though he had no seat in Parliament. Its business—
"(for there is business)" (*Letters* 2:257)—delayed his holiday visits to
Lord Loughborough and to Dorothea Gibbon. Each day he had a
sheet—eight quarto pages—of the new volumes to review and correct,
as they proceeded towards publication. Holidays, naturally, doubled
this responsibility and may account for the appearance of the volumes
in March rather than February, as originally advertised.[13] When
Gibbon returned to London on January 22, 1781, he found several
"respectful complaints from Mr Cadell," his publisher, awaiting him.

While at Bath, he pursued a new friendship. In mid 1780 the poet
and literary entrepreneur William Hayley had published a versified
history of historiography (with sufficiently voluminous notes to fill a
volume of more than 150 small pages) called *An Essay on History; in
Three Epistles to Edward Gibbon, Esq*. This work stops with Hume,
Voltaire, and George Lyttelton, leaving living authors to posterity. It
is addressed to Gibbon, however, because Hayley desired to champion
him against illiberal and unjust criticism, albeit without defending his
"profaner page." Hayley hopes that when Gibbon's "bright Name, on
History's car sublime, / Rolls in just triumph o'er the field of Time,"
he too will be immortalized, not as the historian's flatterer, but as his
friend.[14] This effusion was well received by the public,[15] and by no
reader more enthusiastically than the historian. His letter of thanks to
Hayley was followed by personal acquaintance, for Hayley's wife Eliza
was making a prolonged stay in Bath when Gibbon arrived on New
Year's Day for his three-week visit. Hayley was one of the very few
friends—*not* including the Holroyds—to whom Gibbon gave a presentation copy of volumes 2 and 3.[16] If Gibbon seems to have found Eliza
Hayley better company at Bath than William in London—he asks
about her several times in letters to his stepmother—he pays William
the supreme compliment of adopting in letters to the poet his breathless and hyperbolic style, at least if the letters available only in

Hayley's *Memoirs* are accurately reported: "Accept, my dear Sir, my kindest Wishes for yourself, and your amiable Eliza!—The delightful Scenes of Eartham are still present to my Mind, and many Days will roll away, before I shall find, in the tumult of the World, those pleasures, which I enjoyed in the familiar Society of the best English Poet of the Age" (*Letters* 2:278). As we shall see, Hayley and Gibbon remained friends until Gibbon's death, and Hayley was one of the committee who edited Gibbon's papers for posthumous publication.

Gibbon also derived much pleasure during the winter from the success and honors of his friend John Holroyd. Holroyd won a disputed election for Coventry: "While I steal in through a postern, you thunder at one of the great gates: knock and it shall be opened to you," Gibbon wrote enthusiastically (*Letters* 2:251). And Holroyd was indeed successful, a welcome addition to the government's strength (he had held Coventry before the election, but he had won the seat in a by-election that was sudden and uncontested). For various services, he was awarded an Irish peerage in November 1780. Gibbon functioned as intermediary:

> Mr Gibbon presents his respectful compliments to Lady Sheffield, and hopes her Ladyship is in perfect health, as well as the Honble Miss Holroyd, and the Honble Miss Louisa Holroyd. . . . Be honest. How does this read? Do you not feel some titillations of vanity? Yet I will do you the justice to believe that they are as faint, as can find place in a female (you will retort, or a male,) heart, on such an auspicious event. When it is revealed to the Honble Miss, I should recommend the loss of some ounces of noble blood. You may expect every post, a formal notification, which I shall instantly dispatch. (*Letters* 2:255)

The formalities were concluded on Tuesday, December 19, and Holroyd's elevation was announced in the *London Gazette* on the 23rd.

Gibbon spent the first three weeks of 1781 in Bath and the next month (with a few recesses for the business of the Board of Trade) in London in anticipation of the appearance of volumes 2 and 3. Advance copies were sent out at the end of February to his stepmother, to Eliot (coals of fire?), to Suzanne Necker, and to Hayley—perhaps to no one else, for Gibbon was trying to limit his presents so as to avoid offending anyone he might accidentally overlook. On March 1, 1781, volumes 2 and 3 were "delivered to the World, for whose inconstant and malicious levity" the author considered himself "coolly but firmly prepared" (*Letters* 2:261). Although Gibbon could look forward to their reception, to a seat in the new Parliament, to secure enjoyment for a while of his income from the Board of Trade, he had really reached the final plateau of this phase of his life. An "interval of suspense" (*Memoirs* 164) of about a year would precede the transition to what, in several senses, was a new life.

THREE

RELOCATIONS,
1781–1788

Interregnum

or a full year after volumes 2 and 3 were published, Gibbon allowed himself a rest from composition. He read his reviews and letters of congratulations, paid £800 for a new seat in Parliament, took a house in Brighton for the summer, acquired new friends, especially that "bewitching animal" Lady Elizabeth Foster, exploited the pleasures of his office and income while waiting for the ax to fall upon them, and turned for intellectual stimulation to Greek literature and philosophy. He was somewhat disappointed by the reception of the new volumes, which created no such stir as their "elder brother"; the clergy were less offended or more cautious than in their response to volume 1, and the Opposition, who now provided the sneers, were less satisfying detractors than the clergy had been; indeed, Gibbon missed the applause he had received from such able judges as Walpole and Fox. Cadell, wise in the ways of book buyers, had divided his press run of 4,000 into two "editions," a common means of puffery that Gibbon, perhaps, had not expected to require.[1]

Playing the role of historian was nevertheless by far the most congenial and successful experience Gibbon had had—not just in the accomplishment, but in the activity itself. He acknowledges frankly in his *Memoirs* that "in the luxury of freedom [he] began to wish for the daily task, the active pursuit which gave a value to every book, and an object to every enquiry" (164). His book purchases during 1781–82 confirm the suspicion that despite his assertions, probably to himself as well as to others, that he might end his history with the fall of the Western Empire, he expected all along to continue it.[2] As he wrote to Lord Hardwicke in October, a little more than halfway through his self-imposed holiday, "I already feel that mere desultory reading will not fill those hours which have been so long devoted to a train of regular composition." It is also clear in this letter that he already planned to take his history as far as the Turks, that is, the taking of Constantinople in 1452, if he resumed it at all (*Letters* 2:280). But he did enjoy his freedom, whether in visits of "amusement and society" or in the bustle and pleasure of service to friends (such as Hayley's protégé Thomas Howell). In November and December, Gibbon and all the Government party were of course concerned about the bad news from America—the news of Cornwallis's surrender at Yorktown reached London on November 25.[3] But Gibbon puts such matters aside easily enough, taking at least an equal interest in his duties as Sheffield's deputy in hiring a house for a London stay; in the hope of finding "the fair Eliza" a fellow visitor at Sheffield Place; and of course in his own attack of the gout.

Enjoying the combination of good dining and good conversation, Gibbon continued to be a faithful attendant at the meetings of the Literary Club at the Turk's Head, and it was he who had the pleasure of writing to inform Edmond Malone of his election.[4] He hoped for the survival of Lord North's administration and his own position on the Board of Trade as long as hope was possible, but when the "thunder-bolts" fell, in March and May respectively, he was prepared. His self-allotted sabbatical over, on the anniversary of the publication of volumes 2 and 3, he returned to his true work and began to write volume 4 of the *Decline and Fall*.

Gibbon always believed that the reception of the second and third volume of his history was cool, at least comparatively. He wrote cheerfully to his stepmother, however, that despite their "quiet and silent" reception, his "vanity [was] so very dextrous" that he was "not displeased" with the change:

> Almost every body that reads has purchased, but few persons (compara-
> tively) have read them; and I find that the greater number, satisfied that
> they have acquired a valuable fund of entertainment, differ [*sic*] the
> perusal to the summer, the country, and a more quiet period. . . . The
> Clergy (such is the advantage of total loss of character) commend my
> decency and moderation: but the patriots wish to damn the work and the
> Author. (*Letters* 2:266)

He was also disappointed not to receive at least a note of thanks from Edward Eliot.

But this impression of less than enthusiastic response was what "no person acquainted with the literary history of that very recent period can remember," wrote Alexander Chalmers.[5] The same writer is of the opinion that these volumes "were written with more caution, yet with equal elegance, and perhaps more proofs of just and profound thinking." This favorable view of the volumes and their acceptance occurs in a retrospective account that is far from uncritical of Gibbon, so it is not likely to be unduly flattering. Yet there was room for another impression. The marquis de Bombelles, writing from Paris in June 1781, asked Adam Smith:

> How are Mr. Gibbon's last two volumes being received? I see some people who fear that he will not have worked on them so much as on the first volume, that a little too much eagerness to talk of religion escapes him, and a little more gallantry or preoccupation with women than is suitable for the gravity of history, especially a history so beautiful so profound and so learned as his.[6]

Perhaps the people to whom the marquis had spoken in Paris had been influenced by Horace Walpole, who admired both Gibbon and his history very much less than in the past. Walpole wrote (not to Gibbon):

> The history is admirably written, especially in the characters of Julian and Athanasius, in both which he has piqued himself on impartiality—but the style is far less sedulously enamelled than the first volume, and there is flattery to the Scots that would choke anything but Scots. . . . David Hume and Adam Smith are *legislators* and sages, but the homage is intended for his patron, Lord Loughborough.[7]

(As Walpole's Yale editors point out, there is almost nothing about the Scots in these two volumes, but Walpole was at this point an irritated political opponent of Gibbon.)

Another early reader in France was Suzanne Necker. She had no such reservations as Walpole or as those the marquis refers to, not even about his treatment of women, about which she had complained apropos of volume 1. Gibbon wrote to her:

> I remember, Madame, that you once asked me whether there would be any illustrious women in this volume. There is one who keenly interested me (Vol III p 318) by a kind of resemblance that will escape no one but you. In the eighteenth century, as in the fifth, fortune may choose from obscurity a rare combination of beauty, virtues, and talents, to place it on the throne or on the steps of the throne, but fortune has little power over souls that she can neither conquer by misfortune nor corrupt by prosperity. (*Letters* 2:263)

The reference is to his account of the Empress Athenaïs, later Eudoxia (*DF* chap. 32, 3:409).

In her reply (April 21, 1781), Madame Necker mixed praise of Gibbon's work and his imagination with reproofs of his laziness as a friend, concluding, however, "I know you, you will have affection for

me when you see me again, and you will not be fully conscious of
your errors until you are no longer guilty of them."[8] It is clear that she
did know him, and that she was willing to regard his failings with
tolerant amusement arising from the knowledge that his affection was
not really to be measured by his intervals of silence during absence.
All of his friends had to learn this lesson. Meanwhile, however, she
could delight, as she always had, in the brilliance and sensitivity of
his intelligence. "I thank you for having filled an immense interval in
history and for having thrown over chaos this bridge that unites the
ancient and modern worlds," she wrote. Delighted at his having "added
five hundred years to [her] existence," she found the new volumes
superior to the first. "You have treated with much wisdom the vain
disputes of the fourth century. I have read you without scandal. For of
what importance is the thought of an author if his writings only give
birth to something that can be blamed or feared?" She notes, uniquely
among Gibbon's early critics, that it gives him more pleasure "to
reproduce the marvels of art than those of nature; and miracles do
not suit you so well as the miraculous efforts of the genius of men;
so true it is that an author cannot escape his own personality."[9] She
sees, in other words, that Gibbon's aim is to celebrate what humans
have created and their capacity to create. In the process, he must
reveal how they destroy, neglect, or abuse their individual and collective powers. But unlike a satirist or reformer, and despite his subject
matter, he portrays the contemptible and destructive as a foil, not as
a primary object or even a prediction.

Suzanne Necker's view was unusual in its insight, but not in its
enthusiasm. The English reviews were not only favorable (even the
Gentleman's Magazine), but ecstatic—more firmly committed to the
classic status of the history than they had been after the first volume,
despite the intervening controversy. Gibbon's *Vindication* had apparently succeeded in reassuring the nonfanatical about the *historical*
reliability of his history, despite the hopes and mutual applause of his
adversaries. In the "List of Books—with Remarks" for April, a reviewer for the *Gentleman's Magazine* opines that the new volumes
contain sufficient "leaven of infidelity" to "disgust the friends of
Christianity," but admits that the history is elegant, important, and
interesting. In "Impartial and Critical Review of New Publications,"
in July and November, however, the praise of the *Gentleman's Magazine*
reviewer (perhaps a different person) is much stronger; he "indulges
the pleasing hope" that Gibbon will continue the history and praises
the "animated and elegant style in which this work is written, though
we could wish that it had been completely in English, 'actual,' for
instance, instead of 'present,' . . . is inexcusable even in a News-
paper." Extracts from the notes, in November, are prefaced with the

comment that "the minuteness and precision of the references add much to the pleasure of every learned and intelligent reader."[10]

The two rival reviews, the *Critical* and the *Monthly*, vied with each other in praising Gibbon. William Rose, in the latter, perhaps wins, in devoting articles in six issues to it. But the *Critical* reviewer, in the first of four articles, asserts categorically that Gibbon is entitled "to the first rank among the historians in the English language" and that even the notes demonstrate not only "the author's minute investigation of historical authorities, but . . . his judgment, his taste and his extensive knowledge of polite literature." In this reviewer's opinion, Gibbon successfully avoids "religious prejudices; . . . he never deviates into superstitious credulity, and seldom into philosophic scepticism." This reviewer is also among the first to praise Gibbon's account of the interpenetration of religious and political history, an accomplishment of great interest to the German sociological historians of the nineteenth century and praised even today by at least two major church historians.[11] Although the *Critical* reviewer praises the style, he observes the occasional intrusions of French (and Latin) idioms. He hopes for a continuation, "for the execution of which [Gibbon] is so eminently endowed by the united qualifications of genius, abilities, and learning."[12]

Rose, in the *Monthly*, finds Gibbon "entitled to a distinguished rank among the most eminent Historians of ancient or modern times." He too praises the style and deplores the occasional French idioms, though he apologizes for mentioning such trifles with respect to "a work of such superior qualities." Rose particularly admires Gibbon's account of Constantine and his analysis of the issue of Constantine's alleged vision of the cross. But Rose, who in past reviews had urged Gibbon to answer more completely the objections of his adversaries, takes the occasion of a comment from Gibbon favoring the Christian system of ethics to hope rather sarcastically that readers and authors will consider "how far it is consistent with the character of good citizens, to endeavour, by sly insinuations, oblique hints, indecent sneer and ridicule, to weaken the influence of so *pure and benevolent* [Gibbon's phrase] a system."[13]

This is an interesting objection, because it raises a point—the *usefulness* of religion—to which Gibbon assented. According to Arthur Young, a friend of Burke's, Burke believed that Gibbon came to regret his contribution to the weakening of the power of Christian belief over the masses: "before he (Mr. G.) died . . . he heartily repented of the anti-religious part of his work for contributing to free mankind from all restraint on their vices and profligacy, and thereby aiding . . . the most detestable of all revolutions."[14] Gibbon's distinction (following Hume) between "enthusiasm"—always detestable because liable to provoke disorder as well as intrinsically irrational—and "superstition"—equally irrational, but conductive to civil obedience and therefore to order—has been valuably analyzed by J. G. A. Pocock.[15] Rose's criticism might therefore have struck home to Gibbon as it regarded good citizenship. It will be clear in Gibbon's treatment of religion in volume 4–6, however, that within the *Decline and Fall*, whatever the possible inconvenience to the magistrate, the historian never ceases to criticize the difference between hypothetical Christian ethics and the cruelty of Christian states to one another and to non-Christians.

The reviewers might well have satisfied Gibbon's desire for praise, but more was available to him: despite his complaint that purchasers were deferring the reading of the volumes till the summer, he received early letters from several astute readers, most notably William Robertson, who wrote on May 12,

> I am ashamed of having deferred so long to thank you for . . . your two new volumes; but just as I had finished the first reading of them, I was taken ill . . . for two or three weeks. . . . I knew enough of your talents and industry to expect a great deal, but you have gone far beyond my expectations. I can recollect no historical work from which I ever received so much instruction; and, when I consider in what a barren field you had to glean and pick up materials, I am truly astonished at the connected and interesting story you have formed.[16]

The high praise from Gibbon's only living rival as a "philosophic" historian concerned also about erudite accuracy did not stop here. Gibbon particularly admired in Robertson the "perfect composition, the nervous language, the well-turned periods" (*Memoirs* 99); it was therefore gratifying to learn that Robertson "like[d] the style of these volumes better than that of the first; there is the same beauty, richness, and perspicuity of language, with less of that quaintness, into which your admiration of Tacitus sometimes seduced you." Since Robertson was a clergyman, his assertion that "even bigots, I should think, must allow, that you have delineated [Julian's] most singular character with a more masterly hand than ever touched it before" helpfully confirmed Gibbon's view that he had portrayed Julian without bias.

There were, of course, others who did not admire the history—not only those who paid tribute to it by fearing it, but more devastatingly, those who simply found it dull. Thomas Newton, bishop of Bristol, found the history "prolix and tedious," uninteresting in its subject matter and affected in its style, but Gibbon cannot have known about this reaction until the publication of the bishop's memoirs in 1782.[17] Perhaps in retrospect the bishop's complaints and his anecdote about one of his fellow bishops returning his copy of the *Decline and Fall* to the bookseller when Gibbon himself was in the shop colored Gibbon's memories of the immediate reception of the two volumes. But it was probably principally Walpole who shook Gibbon's confidence in the merit and reception of the new volumes, who was responsible for his perception of "the coldness and even prejudice of the town" and "a whisper . . . that in the judgement of many readers, my continuation was much inferior to the original attempt" (*Memoirs* 162).

In the letter already cited, Walpole, with his usual brilliant malice, portrays the scene of his discussion of the new volumes with their author. After Walpole had qualified his "incense" by criticizing Gibbon's "disgusting" subject, the conversation continued: "He coloured; all his round features squeezed themselves into sharp angles; he screwed up his button-mouth and rapping his snuff-box, said, 'It had never been put together before'—*so well* he meant to add—but gulped it. He meant *so well* certainly, for Tillemont, whom he quotes in every page, has done the very thing."[18] Gibbon might well have blushed for his sometime friend, for as we have seen, most people were well aware that Tillemont's compilation and Gibbon's history were very different things.[19] But his reaction to this conversation, if we may credit Walpole's report, is more disquieting: "From that hour to this I have never seen him, though he used to call once or twice a week. . . . I well knew his vanity, even about his ridiculous face and person, but thought he had too much sense to avow it so palpably." Walpole's account is clearly exaggerated for comic effect, and his appraisal is poisoned not only by political differences but by a profound snobbery, most clearly revealed in a comment to Lady Ossory in an October letter:

> If an alderman's son [Gibbon], not content with a decent fortune and a large portion of well-deserved immortality, is proud of becoming toad-eater to a Scotch chief Justice, of having a few more words said to him at a levee than are vouchsafed to Dr. Dominiceti, and of being ordered to pen memorials for such boobies as Lord Suffolk and Lord Hilsborough, I do not wonder. But when a gentleman [Lord Cornwallis], a man of quality, sells himself for the paltry honours and profits . . . , he has my utter contempt.[20]

Gibbon, of course, assumed that he himself was a "gentleman, a man of quality," in the old as well as the new sense of those terms.[21] Walpole presumably considered this evidence of his vanity. But there is less biased evidence that vanity—at least in the sense of a thirst for praise, if not in that of overestimating himself—was increasingly a feature of Gibbon's social demeanor.

Gibbon's new friends, the Hayleys, provide an amusing illustration. On January 14 Hayley wrote to his wife Eliza, Gibbon's "tame cat":

> I rejoice you have caught a glimpse of your cherubinical cupid, (as [George] Steevens sarcastically and enviously called our great historian,) for as you

truly say of him, he is always entertaining; but I should quarrel with that
card-table which robbed me of his conversation.

"For sure the fair much joy has mis't,
"Whose cupid sets him down to whist,
"And changing smiles to serious dumps,
"Smothers his wit, to count his trumps."[22]

In her reply, Eliza gives a full and dramatic account of the historian's
vanity (and curiosity) at work:

I also ventured to say [to Gibbon], you had expressed your concern, on
account of the ladies, that so much entertainment should be lost at the
whist table, and that you had given him a couplet: upon which he exclaimed with great eagerness, "O shew me the couplet."

"No! that I cannot; for it was not intended for your inspection, Mr. H.
conceiving that he had already give you couplets enough."

"No indeed! those would make me wish for more."

"That will be very flattering to Mr. H.'s vanity, or rather to his
ambition."

"Well! but my curiosity! you will not be so cruel as to awaken, and
then refuse to gratify it?"

"I cannot suspect Mr. Gibbon of curiosity; and I hardly know why I
mentioned it, unless it were to observe how much the Muse was mistaken
in one line in which she says 'Smothers his wit to count his trumps,' which
I can vouch to be false, as I saw you trump with the ace by mistake.["]
Then he began trying every kind of persuasion, and questioning me why
I would not shew it him. I said I had only a lady's reason with a negative
added, or to polish the language for Mr. Gibbon, because I could not.

"Why! was it too flattering?" "That was impossible." "Was it too
severe?"

"By no means! nor was it (I added) too tender."

"Was it proper for the old woman's inspection?" (for I had given him
Nurse's character [in emulation of Molière, the Hayleys consulted Hayley's
old nurse on literary questions.])

"Yes! I thought it possible she might have seen it:"

"That was indeed very hard, not to allow him the same indulgence."

"Certainly, not to rank you as an old woman."

In short, I had the *curiosity* to try if this great man had any grains of
that feminine endowment, and I am satisfied that he has; though on my
supposing him to be above it, he seemed as if he wished I should think
so; yet, *en badinage*, on supplying Mrs. Holroyd's seat at the whist table,
he charged her to get the secret for him, which she promised to do. After
much entreaty from her, (though she owned she had been a very false
friend, and told Mr. G. almost every thing I had said of him) I at last said,
if I did shew her the verses, it should not be till after Mr. G.'s departure;
upon which she exclaimed, "then Mr. Gibbon I must begin a correspondence with you."

Well, but to conclude my history; he seriously did request Mrs. Holroyd
the next morning to get the verses for him, as she told me after he left

us; but that she told him, honour forbids; and on my reading them to her, and giving her the history of Cupid, or rather of his godfather Steevens, though she was much diverted, she said she did not wish him to know it, as she thought it would hurt him. I make no apologies for all this nonsense.[23]

Nor was such love of praise the only symptom of vanity in Gibbon. His tailor's bills strongly suggest a love of fine clothing that might charitably be interpreted as intended to disguise an unhandsome person, but is more likely to be seen as clear evidence of personal vanity. A partial list of purchases for 1780–81 includes four new frock coats, three with matching waistcoats and one with an accompanying waistcoat that must have presented an arresting sight: the frock coat was burgundy colored cloth; the waistcoat was orange shag velvet "lac'd with gold and silver lace from another waistcoat." The other sets were "beaver" colored, "light-coloured Wilton," and black cloth respectively, and Gibbon also purchased a black cloth dress suit and two pairs of black breeches, one silk and one velvet. But with these relatively subdued garments he wore other new waistcoats: blue and buff figured silk, laced with gold and silver; orange zigzag printed corded dimity; buff and brown zigzag "Janett." His new light-colored mixed kersey coating "Chencile" had a crimson Genoa velvet collar. While six pairs of white ticking drawers were plain enough, he also had a "flannel underwaistcoat new button'd 14-sky blue satin." The tailor also altered—let out—and repaired a "sky blue velvet" waistcoat and breeches, a puce colored spring velvet suit, a spotted feathered velvet waistcoat, a green silk waistcoat with black and white spots, and a violet cloth frock. We might attribute the new down collar on his surtout to a desire for warmth or comfort, but vanity or at least a passion for the colorful certainly influenced the other choices.[24]

On the other hand, in many respects, with his closest friends and relations, his ability to laugh at himself and to relish all the homely pleasures of life remained unimpaired. A visit to London by his pious Aunt Hester inspired a typically playful and gossipy account to his stepmother:

> Mrs Hester Gibbon is now in town. . . . Her old friend Mrs Hutchinson is just dead without leaving her any thing, at which Hester expresses more resentment than seems becoming in the character of a Saint. She is still healthy and sensible, refuses as formerly to enter my house, but appears pleased with my attentions and those of Mrs and Lady Porten and of Lord and Lady Sheffield who have all visited her in Surry Street. She enquired civilly and even kindly into your situation and approved the sentiments which naturally fell from me. (*Letters* 2:266)

Likewise, ten days after finally reentering Parliament, he began a letter to Lord Sheffield with a joking pretence to two affectations,

"O Lord, O Lord—I am quite tired of Parliament and sigh for the Country" (*Letters* 2:270). And most characteristically of all, when he returned to London after his summer's travels, he wrote zestfully to Lady Sheffield:

> Oh ho! I have given you the slip, saved thirty miles by proceeding directly this day from Eartham to town, and am now *comfortably* seated in my library, in *my own* easy chair and before *my own* fire, a style which you understand though it is unintelligible to your Lord. The town is empty, but I am surrounded with a thousand old acquaintance of all ages and characters who are ready to answer a thousand questions which I am impatient to ask. (*Letters* 2:276)

He had continued to serve on the Board of Trade despite his temporary lack of a parliamentary seat, but that situation could not long continue. He was therefore willing, despite his perennial shortage of funds, to pay a modest price for a seat, presumably a good financial investment to protect the income from the Board of Trade. Gibbon's estimate that the Government was willing to go to some trouble and expense to keep him was correct; his new seat, Lymington, "was purchased from Sir Harry Burrard for £3,000, paid from the King's private account."[25] The £800 required of Gibbon (paid to Lord North in July 1781) was relatively moderate. Nevertheless, the bargain was a poor one, financially, for Gibbon received the salary attached to his office for less than one more year, and that salary (£750) was less than £800. For the time being, however, Gibbon thought that his financial future was reasonably secure.

Among the scanty financial records of this portion of his life, we find some evidence of a continued charitable impulse toward those who were ill—in 1778–79, he had not only provided money to a Lieutenant Godefroy "for the use of the Hospital," but also paid the medical bills for one "Richard Cooper Soldier" on two occasions. In 1781–82 he was a subscriber (two guineas per annum) to the Mary Le Bone Medical Asylum.[26] As in youth his charity had extended to the French prisoners,[27] so now it included the Americans: learning from Mrs. Hayley of "an American mother . . . who in a short time had lost three sons, one killed by the savages, one run mad from fright at that accident, and the third, taken at sea, now in England a prisoner in Forton hospital. For *him* something might be done," Gibbon asked his stepmother to obtain dates and circumstances, but not "to raise hopes which it may not be in my power to gratify" (*Letters* 2:283–84). Gibbon's willingness to contribute his time, money, and influence to help those in need is not perhaps a conspicuous aspect of his character, but it is a persistent one, still documentable even at the end of his life. It too militates against the view that

Gibbon had become so self-satisfied as to be merely complacent and selfish.

The success of the *Decline and Fall* as well as his parliamentary seat seemed to justify increasing the great library. It is hard to identify exactly his book purchases for the year, but we know he employed agents to buy for him at sales of private libraries as well as frequenting bookshops. Among the books certainly purchased at this time were a Procopius[28] and H. Stephanus's edition of the Greek Anthology, a book Lord Sheffield already owned but was cautious about lending. Gibbon writes, "Your Greeks were not carried from Brighton through carelessness: but as you are *seriously* absurd about lending books, I have directed Caplen to send them to S P per coach. By way of revenge I may inform you that I have now purchased a Copy of Stephens's Greek Poets compared to which yours is very little more than waste paper" (*Letters* 2:286). Patently Lord Sheffield had allowed his friend to borrow reading material while he was staying in Brighton, which that friend had cavalierly taken away with him. Lord Sheffield has often been assumed to be entirely innocent of classical learning owing to a faux pas about Latin dating that occurred when Gibbon's epitaph was being written, but perhaps he has been underestimated. Certainly he cared to preserve and improve his classical library.

The reference to the Greeks confirms Gibbon's own account of his reading during this holiday year. All attentive readers will notice throughout the *Decline and Fall* Gibbon's habit of juxtaposing the persons and events of various ages: in chapter 36, for example, he had described how the aged bishop of Carthage succored the suffering of the Romans captured and brought back to Carthage by the Vandals, selling the church plate to free, feed, and provide hospitals for the captives, and visiting them, "both in the day and night, with an assiduity that surpassed his strength, and a tender sympathy which enhanced the value of his services. Compare this scene with the field of Cannae; and judge between Hannibal and the successor of St. Cyprian" (*DF* 4:7–8). His rereading "with new pleasure the Iliad and Odyssey, the histories of Herodotus, Thucydides and Xenophon, a large portion of the Tragic and comic theatre of Athens, and many interesting dialogues of the Socratic school" (*Memoirs* 164) cannot be precisely documented in the volumes he was about to begin to write, but its influence can be felt in his allusions and sometimes in his narrative strategies and interpretative comments. "Read and feel the xxiiid book of the Iliad, a living picture of manners, passions, and the whole form and spirit of the chariot race," Gibbon commands the reader of chapter 40 (*DF* 4:233, n. 41). It is similarly impossible to say when he read the natural history for which he had a lifelong taste and which helps to extend the intellectual and geographical domain of the history, but his reading in 1781 may well have included J. S. Bailly's "system or romance," the *Lettres sur l'origine des sciences* and *Lettres sur l'Atlantide de Platon*,[29] as well as the new volumes of Buffon; in the first chapter of the new volume, with very little excuse, he brings up Bailly's discussion of the myths of the phoenix, Adonis, and Osiris. "This ingenious writer is a worthy disciple of the great Buffon; nor is it easy for the coldest reason to withstand the magic of their philosophy" (*DF* chap. 39, 4:197 n. 50 [42]).

Obviously he was reading also the new works of his new friend Hayley, and there is a bill listing his purchase of the poems of Cowper (not listed in Keynes 1980), no doubt on Hayley's recommendation. He purchased Jacob Bryant's 1781 book about the poems of "Thomas Rowley," that is, Thomas Chatterton's medieval forgery.[30] He also owned Chatterton's book (1771). But in the history Gibbon does not even flirt with the idea that it might be authentic, as he does with the work of Ossian. No doubt he had read Malone's cogent strictures on the Rowley poems in the December 1781 *Gentleman's Magazine*. Gibbon also bought Malone's 1780 "Supplement" to the Johnson-Steevens 1778 edition of Shakespeare; perhaps he read this recent work when he welcomed Malone as a new member of the Literary Club (February 5, 1782). The evidence does not permit a precise reconstruction of Gibbon's reading in this year free from writing; we can be relatively sure, however, that it was both wide-ranging and demanding. According to Reynolds, Gibbon said that he read all five volumes of Fanny Burney's *Cecilia* (published June 12, 1782) in a single day.[31] Even if we allow for considerable exaggeration, this claim suggests the great speed with which Gibbon read, and which indeed we might infer from the sheer quantity of material he absorbed in preparation for the history and for his other writings.

But he left himself plenty of time for other activities. These included repairs and improvements to his house and furniture, something that would have been distracting while he was writing, especially since his writing desks required the cabinetmaker's attention. In May, *two* "neat Deal Reading Desk[s]" were stained and polished, and in July Gibbon purchased a strong deal chest "to pack books," as well as having his library steps restained and his library table relined "with the best Superfine pea Green Cloath." While Gibbon was out of the house, the carpenter was engaged in more mundane labors: "Taking Down your bed & thoroughly Cleaning Do. from buggs & putting Do up Compleate"; in August the same necessary service was performed for five servants' beds. The bills also suggest that curtains, carpets, and perhaps oilcloth floor coverings were removed annually for the summer and put back in the fall, at least in the sitting rooms (library, drawing room, and parlor).[32]

Meanwhile, Gibbon was on his travels. "In a few days, as soon as we are released from public business," he wrote to Mrs. Gibbon on July 3, 1781, "I shall go down to my Country house for the summer. . . . [I] have . . . hired for three months a small pleasant house at Brighthelmstone. I flatter myself that in that admirable sea air, with the vicinity of Sheffield place, and a proper mixture of light study in the morning and good company in the evening the summer may roll away not disagreably." He promises her not to swim in the ocean "without due preparation and advice" and notes that his aunt Kitty has been "some weeks at Margate and will scarcely return to town before [his] departure." As with the sea-bathing, he anticipates his stepmother's anxieties and assures her that his aunt has chosen Margate "not for health but [for] pleasure" (*Letters* 2:271). Even so, he did not allow sufficiently for Dorothea Gibbon's tendency to fear for her friends' health: she inquired, by return of post, whether he sought sea air on medical grounds, and he assured her of his health and happiness with a note on the 9th, apologizing that a visit in Surrey to Charles Jenkinson, secretary of state for war, had prevented his writing even sooner (*Letters* 2:272).

He left town about the middle of July, delayed briefly and "not unpleasantly in a round of Ministerial dinners," stopped for a short visit at Sheffield Place, and arrived in Brighton on July 22, where he rented "Cliff House" from a Miss Elliot. He wrote to Dorothea Gibbon:

> My house which is not much bigger than yours has a full prospect of the sea and enjoys a temperate climate in the most sultry days. The air gives health spirits and a ravenous appetite. I walk sufficiently morning and evening, lounge in the middle of the day on the Steiyn [*sic*], bookseller's shops &c and by the help of a pair of horse can make more distant excursions [for example, to nearby Sheffield Place]. The society is good and easy, and though I have a large provision of books for my amusement I shall not undertake any deep studies or laborious compositions this summer. (*Letters* 2:273)

He was not disappointed in his expectations. In August he wrote again, "Notwithstanding our princely visitors (the Cumberlands) who are troublesome, I like the air and society so well that I shall certainly [stay] here at least till the end of September" (*Letters* 2:274). He was able not only to visit Sheffield Place but also to dine with other friends either in Brighton itself or at their nearby estates. For example, his friend Gerard Hamilton, M.P. for Petersfield, invited him to meet Lord Mansfield, the chief justice.

From Gibbon's own point of view, however, the most valuable acquisition of the summer was the acquaintance of Lady Elizabeth Foster, later duchess of Devonshire, whom he seems to have met at Sheffield Place. It is possible that he had met her earlier, for the

Holroyds had long been her friends, but since she now comes up quite frequently in his letters, it is probable that had he become acquainted with her before, she would have been mentioned. On December 29, for example, he suggested to Lady Sheffield, who had invited him to visit, "I have a great [mind] to propose a partie quarrée [in effect, a double date], which might be easily furnished from Ickworth," that is, from the family seat of Lady Elizabeth's father. Playfully complaining to Lord Sheffield of the family's failing to come to London, Gibbon remarks, in a letter dated by Norton January 5, 1782, "If some people would send for the Eliza all might be forgiven" (*Letters* 2:289). Of her, Fanny Burney reports, Gibbon said, "She could charm the Lord Chancellor off his woolsack,"[33] and he asked his stepmother, "Are you acquainted with Lady Eliza Foster a bewitching animal?" (*Letters* 2:294). Clearly she had bewitched Gibbon! She was well qualified to do so—beautiful, charming, intelligent, and safely, though unhappily, married. She was therefore the perfect subject for the kind of gently romantic friendship Gibbon liked to have with women. This friendship, however, did not develop fully until much later in their acquaintance.

A few letters of the summer remind us of qualities of the friendship between Lord Sheffield and Gibbon that are often forgotten. It was not all worldly wisdom on one side and intellectual genius on the other. In the summer of 1781 it was Lord Sheffield who was the author and Gibbon who provided the worldly wisdom on at least one occasion—Maria Holroyd, indeed, would note at Gibbon's death that he was the only person who could control her father when he was led to excesses by his passionate partisanship.[34] In 1781, we see Gibbon counselling his friend to seize an opportunity to avoid a quarrel (with an unidentified person who had, in Lord Sheffield's opinion, violated his confidence by showing about a pamphlet Lord Sheffield had written):

> I have seen the General; you are both wrong; he first in lending your pamphlet without *special* leave, and then in the real or apparent slight of your messages. You in the serious anger which you expressed on so trifling a business. Unless you wish that this slight scratch should inflame into an incurable sore, embrace the lucky opportunity of his illness and confinement which will excuse your dignity and should assuage your resentment. (*Letters* 2:275)

Clearly Gibbon is taking an active role as an intermediary and peacemaker. In the *Decline and Fall*, Gibbon's reason always inclines him to the peace party, but he sees so clearly the possibility that sloth or cowardice can disguise itself as love of peace that his tone in appraising the peacemakers is often ambivalent. In real life, however, he was invariably slow to anger and "philosophical," as he usually called it, about losses and injuries. An anecdote, probably apocryphal, describes a 1779 difference between Gibbon and one of his neighbors about a pump in Bentinck Street. The neighbor complained to Gibbon. Gibbon replied politely, assenting to part of the other's demands but explaining his own needs as well. The neighbor seized the opportunity to write a pamphlet-sized attack on Gibbon's answer, so that he could describe himself as one of those who had written against Gibbon! Gibbon neither replied nor changed the plumbing further.[35] This story is hardly likely to be true as told, but possibly a real difference inspired some wit to invent it. Certainly true is a later difference between Gibbon and one of his neighbors in Lausanne, in which, as well, Gibbon preferred to compromise rather than give offense (see chapter 15 below).

Gibbon spent August and September in Brighton, returning to London by way of the Hayleys: he spent "a very pleasant day in the little Paradise of Eartham" with the "hermit" (*Letters* 2:277). Such was the Hayley style. During this visit, Hayley told Gibbon the romantic story of young Thomas Howell (thought by some to be Hayley's illegitimate son). Howell, according to Hayley, was educated at Winchester, with all that that implies, until at the age of eleven he was left orphaned and destitute and had to take up domestic service. At fifteen, he entered Hayley's employment as a footman. Hayley took an interest in him, procured him a commission in the navy, and when at the age of twenty-one he was discharged with the rank of captain, helped him to become a cadet in the East India Company, upon which he had sailed for India, but, owing to a mishap, was back in England a month later.

Now Howell, about twenty-two, wanted a commission in one of the new army regiments in India. Gibbon promised to assist him, and successfully recommended him to the secretary for war. At this point Gibbon finally met the young man, whom he had known only by repute and presumably by the sketch of him George Romney had made for the Hayleys. Howell wrote to Hayley:

> I waited on [Gibbon] accordingly, & thanked Him for his Kindness to me.—He was pleased with my Account of Lord Amherst's Reception of me, & declared, He never heard an account of so much Politeness in that Minister, who is said to be rather remarkable for his haughty Deportment.—I am indeed particularly fortunate in pleasing Mr. Gibbon, who gave me proof of his desire to serve me by making me a present of some French books, sur l'art militaire, handsomely bound: & also a Map of India. (*Letters*, appendix 5, 2:423)

Gibbon also promised, and provided, a letter of introduction to General James Stewart, one of the Indian commanders. His report on Howell to Hayley was equally favorable: "I am highly pleased with

[his] Address, and Conversation; I was disappointed only in one Instance: I thought Him taller, and thinner; but Heroes have been of
all Sizes. I dreaded an humble Bow, and profuse Thanks; but He is
liberal, manly, and modest; and his Hopes of Fortune seem to be built
on the Resolution of deserving it" (*Letters* 2:281). Gibbon had been
called upon to exercise similar modesty and manliness in the same
week on his own behalf: he replied to the gratifying letter of praise
he had received from the earl of Hardwick, who had also sent him a
copy of his privately published *Athenian Letters* and recommended that
he continue the *Decline and Fall*. "Such is indeed my design as far as
it is consistent with the avocations from which many authors are
exempt, Parliamentary attendance, *some* official business, and the
various dissipations of this immense town." Lord Hardwicke had inquired about Gibbon's opinion of the reliability of Procopius's *Secret
History*, obviously a matter of concern for Gibbon's new volumes.
Gibbon replied, in an anticipation of his views in chapter 40 of the
new volumes, "My opinion of the Anecdotes of Procopius is still
doubtful, with regard to their authenticity, but I am satisfied that the
line of truth may often be drawn in the midway between them, and
the flattering history which is ascribed to the same author" (*Letters*
2:280).

It is apparent, then, that though Gibbon would not allow himself
officially to begin work on the new volumes until his year's holiday
was complete, he was already thinking about the problems and challenges they would represent. It is not equally clear that he had similar
foresight about the political events that were soon to change his
future. He could not be expected to anticipate the devastating news
soon to come from America, of Cornwallis's surrender at Yorktown;
but he might have observed the growing power of the Opposition
Whigs, especially those of Lord Rockingham's group. As late as
March 2, he "still th[ought] that Lord N[orth] [might] survive the
impending storm of the next fortnight" (*Letters* 2:292). As he himself
later summarized North's defeat, with the wisdom of hindsight though
obviously with some remaining party spirit, "The length of a fruitless
contest, the loss of armies, the accumulation of debt and taxes, and
the hostile confederacy of France, Spain and Holland indisposed the
public to the American War and the persons by whom it was conducted. The representatives of the people, followed at a slow distance
the changes of their opinion; and the ministers who refused to bend
were broken by the tempest" (*Memoirs* 163). Gibbon does not mention
the other program of the coalition soon to take over, the financial
reforms advocated by Burke,[36] decidedly including the elimination of
the Board of Trade; but he knew that his own position depended on
the continued existence of Lord North's ministry. "Inconsiderable as

I am, I am sure of being one of the first victims," he wrote to his stepmother. "I shall meet my fate with resolution" (*Letters* 2:292).

Meanwhile, he was more concerned about a domestic crisis: he had resolved to retire the aging family housekeeper, who was at odds at times with Gibbon's indispensable valet, Richard Caplen. She has some fame in literary history, for her name was Phoebe Ford, she was Samuel Johnson's cousin, and her letter to Dorothea Gibbon, complaining of Caplen's encroaching ways, was published among A. L. Reade's *Johnsonian Gleanings*.[37] Gibbon met this crisis by offering her, as a pension, her wages for life, "with which she seems well contented though I am ignorant of her plans." He was ignorant because he had persuaded Aunt Kitty to act as his agent in this delicate matter. "Mrs Porten opened the business to her, but I have not yet sustained the last tender interview which I really dislike very much." But there was a brighter side: "Caplin assumes with pleasure the office of prime minister, and we hope that some lessons at White's will turn the housemaid . . . into a good Cook for private ordinary days" (*Letters* 2:283).

Pursuit of a lodging for the Sheffield family, whose house in Downing Street was lent to Lord North, and the usual winter parties, clubs, and business occupied the remainder of the year. Gibbon spent some time with his carpenter, planning a new sort of writing desk attached to the arm of a chair (it proved unsatisfactory) and ordering two new easy chairs for the library, upholstered in his favorite blue and white.[38] But he spent more time with his friends. The Lucans were among his favorite hosts. At their parties, he could expect companions both select and diverse. Walpole described one such December evening: "I was diverted last night at Lady Lucan's; the moment I entered, she set me down to whist with Lady Bute—and who do you think were the other partners? the Archbishopess of Canterbury and Mr. Gibbon."[39] Though Gibbon's travels and avocations were briefly interrupted by gout, he had recovered in time to participate in the new session of Parliament. There he saw his fate determined with America's and Lord North's, but though he could not be unmoved, he was not distracted. On March 1, 1782, as he had promised himself, he wrote the first words of volume 4.

TEN

Removals

ext Wednesday," Gibbon wrote to his stepmother on May 4, 1782, "I conclude my forty fifth year and in spite of the changes of Kings and Ministers, I am very glad that I was born" (*Letters* 2:294). The whole letter is ebullient, and though he was free of the gout and feeling "five and twenty years" old, apparently because of recent meetings with Lady Elizabeth Foster, the major reason for this cheer in a letter announcing to Mrs. Gibbon that "his Majesty has no farther occasion for my services" (*Letters* 2:293) must be that, his commitment to the history no longer having a serious rival, his early work on the new volume was going well indeed. In the ensuing eighteen months— March 1782–August 1783—Gibbon wrote chapters 39–46 of the *Decline and Fall*, that is, all of volume 4 except its last chapter (and at least some of the notes).[1] Eight chapters in eighteen months may not seem strenuous, but in the first place, they were Gibbonian chapters, some 530 pages in the original quarto; and in the second, they occupied only the time free from the move from one way of life to another, from clubs, Parliament, London, aunts and stepmother, and the Sheffield family, to gardens, library, Lausanne, Deyverdun, and the Sévery family. The history was the constant unflagging pleasure and purpose of his life in both worlds, the bridge between the old and the new. Neither the decision to return to Lausanne for good, nor its implementation, was easy for Gibbon, but, as we shall see, his choice was wholehearted, and he never regretted it.

The first chapter of volume 4 is a brilliant structural tour de force, though Gibbon makes it seem so inevitable that few, if any, have remarked its artifice. Instead of beginning his Byzantine history with Justinian's reign, which would give it, in the new volumes, the position and authority of the age of the Antonines in the first three, he begins indeed with a flawed idyll, as he had in the first three chapters of volume 1; but instead of Justinian, a "Roman" emperor, its hero is Theodoric, the great Ostrogothic king of Italy, "who might have deserved a statue among the best and bravest of the ancient Romans" (*DF* chap. 39, 4:182). To begin his last three volumes with Theodoric, Gibbon must retrace his steps, chronologically: Theodoric's conquests had already been noted (briefly) in volume 3. But doing so has many advantages beyond a spatial and symbolic focus on the old, not the new, Rome. Chapter 39 is organized like many of the early chapters of the history,[2] in which narrative and commentary are framed by contrasting biographies of emperors at the beginning and end of the chapter, but its lessened scale silently embodies Rome's diminished range and perhaps stature: here the framing biographies are not of emperors, but respectively of a king and a philosopher. Of course the reduction from three chapters to one also contributes to the effect of diminishment.

The structural elegance does not end with this tie backward to the Western Empire, however; the chapter also prepares for all the key devices used to portray Justinian and his age, especially the parallel biography of the ornament and victim of Justinian's reign, Belisarius. In addition, this rich chapter presents allusively most of the themes and motifs of the new volume, including "the reign of barbarism and desolation" (*DF* 4:190), "the great republic of the west" (*DF* 4:196), and "female pretensions" (*DF* 4:185); it also establishes the blend of dramatized scenes, morally focused but apparently evenhanded narrative, and personal commentary and metacommentary that characterizes Gibbon's method throughout this volume. Finally, it shows how, even more than in volumes 2 and 3, Gibbon now combines freedom of commentary with powerful points made by silence and indirection. For example, despite the "advantages" of a childhood and youth spent as a Roman hostage in Constantinople, Theodoric was unable to write his name.

Gibbon's overriding concern is the interplay between destruction and construction in both the replacement of Roman power with that of the barbarians and the maintenance of a degenerate despotism (as he sees it) in the East—to what extent, in other words, is the change or maintenance of a political entity coordinate with the civilization and culture that may share or reject its name? Michel Baridon has analyzed at length the "hidden face" of the *Decline and Fall,* the sympathy with the barbarous and "Gothic" that qualifies and complicates Gibbon's "neo-classicism."[3] Baridon does not relate this imaginative sympathy to what he regards as Gibbon's deplorable failures of systematic thought, but if one is willing, with Gibbon, to reject system as a false ideal, it is possible to see this methodological, interpretative, and tonal ambivalence as one of the ways in which Gibbon avoids the trap of unattainable certainty about historical "laws" that has paradoxically made his more advanced rivals— philosophic, scientific, or historicist—seem less modern than Gibbon to subsequent generations.[4] More than half (chapters 40–43) of the fourth volume of the *Decline and Fall* is devoted to a narrative that embodies all the complications and inconsistencies of the historical, social, cultural, and moral significance of Justinian's reign. This is a period of obvious greatness in Byzantine civilization, but to Gibbon this greatness is almost an archetypal instance of historical illusion. In part because the major source of our knowledge of this reign is Procopius, who in three works evinces three different attitudes and degrees of reliability as an historian, the period also illustrates for Gibbon the createdness and tentativeness of the "truths" of history as presented by historians. Gibbon's "Age of Justinian" is much too lengthy and complex to analyze adequately here, and it has rightly received much attention from Gibbon's readers and fellow historians. But Gibbon uses the reign of Theodoric as a kind of brief and local analogue to that of Justinian. To analyze Gibbon's presentation of the "Age of Theodoric" will therefore permit us to appreciate some neglected facets of Gibbon's methods and accomplishments in the rest of the volume.

Theodoric, the near-Roman, is also thoroughly a barbarian, not only in his illiteracy, but in the events of his life and in many of his values. For example, he begins his career (at eighteen), by leading six thousand of his countrymen out to conquer a Sarmatian king, for no better reason (according to Gibbon) than the "quest of adventures," a trait Gibbon sees as characteristic of all brave and idle hunters and nomads (*DF* chaps. 7, 26). But despite the military victory of young Theodoric and his troops, "the invincible Goths were reduced to extreme distress by the want of clothing and food" (*DF* chap. 39, 4:184) and had to sell their services to the court of Byzantium. For a while Theodoric "supported with courage and fidelity the cause of his benefactor" (*DF* 4:186). In describing the events of the next three years, Gibbon demonstrates his peculiar virtues as historian on occasions when he happens to be wrong in detail. During this period (478–81), the Byzantine emperor tried to maintain a balance of power between two Gothic forces, and Gibbon does not accurately present all the changing alliances among the three powers. But he contrives to provide instead the pattern of significance of such a situation, and in the process, despite the chronological errors, he helps us to understand the conceptual qualities of the events.

Bury assumes that Gibbon is "misled by false arrangement of the fragments of Malchus" in the edition he was using (*DF* 4:186 n. 12). This is not improbable, but the inconveniences of representing exactly the correct chronology are such that Gibbon might well have chosen his present order even had he had Bury's information. Instead of following the various alliances and betrayals among these three powers chronologically, Gibbon presents first a *sudden* turn by Theodoric that encourages the reader to regard the barbarian with civilized distaste: not only does Theodoric desert his "benefactor," but he burns cities, and worse: "the agriculture of Thrace was almost extirpated by the wanton cruelty of the Goths, who deprived their captive peasants of the right hand that guided the plough" (*DF* 4:187). Gibbon knew that this ravaging of Thrace was the last act in the first stage of Theodoric's career. But Gibbon places it first, right after the young Goth's sallying forth for adventure and subsequent forced alliance with the civilized Byzantines. In this placement, the real value of the peasants' hands rightly overshadows the dynastic struggles of the Byzantine emperors and the military virtues of Theodoric.

For a moment the transfer of power seems wholly destructive, and barbarism wholly inferior to Roman civilization. But Theodoric will only once more sink so low in our esteem, and Gibbon quickly shows us that we have, in part, misjudged him. He is a victim of the kind of freedom barbarians enjoy: he "reigned, not as the monarch, but as the minister of a ferocious people" (*DF* 4:187). As Gibbon has always shown us in portraying barbarians, there was a price to pay for their personal courage, their energy, and their freedom or license. The civilized purchased their civilization at the cost of those barbarous virtues. It could be a price worth paying. The Goths' "poverty was incurable; since the most liberal donatives were soon dissipated in wasteful luxury, and the most fertile estates became barren in their hands." The ironic play on lost and barren hands is almost, perhaps entirely, accidental, but the contrast between the vulnerable farmers and the powerful but useless warriors is not.

The other charge against Theodoric is perfidy. Bury's chronology of the "complicated triangular duel between the two Theodorics [leaders of the two sets of Goths] and the Emperor [Zeno]" shows that Zeno assumes and drops alliances as lightly as do the Gothic leaders. Bury lists six different alignments in three years. Thus chronology itself indicates that Goths are not the only perfidious allies (*DF* 4:186 n. 12). But Gibbon neither says so nor pursues all these ins and outs. Instead, he portrays the interplay among the parties in a dramatic scene, complete with dialogue.

The scenic presentation of the crucial meeting between the two sets of Goths, led respectively by our Theodoric (Theodoric of Amal) and Theodoric son of Triarus, is a deliberate interpretative technique.

Gibbon of course knows and frequently asserts that the speeches in ancient histories are invented.[5] This is not even one of the cases in which he defends a particular speech as probably representing the gist of what was actually said—his footnote supporting the scene comments instead on the relationship between the passions of the historians who recount the event and what they have to say (*DF* 4:188, n. 15 [12]). The use of dramatic dialogue therefore emphasizes not the factual reality of the scene, but its mythical reality, its place in a pattern of human behavior. The two Theodorics and their followers meet because our Theodoric is "betrayed" by his Thracian guides and his men are exposed to "the arms and invectives" of the other Theodoric, haranguing them from a "neighbouring height" (*DF* 4:187).

" 'Are you ignorant,' exclaimed the son of Triarius, 'that it is the constant policy of the Romans to destroy the Goths by each other's swords?' " He also incites our Theodoric's followers to blame the Romans for their poverty, and these arguments "compell" him "to imitate the example of Roman perfidy" (*DF* 4:188). Thus Gibbon portrays Theodoric as on the one hand unable to avoid deserting Zeno and on the other justified in so doing by the emperor's bad faith. Of the remaining events of Bury's chronology—the alliance of Zeno with Theodoric son of Triarus, that Theodoric's death, and our Theodoric's attack on imperial territory until he is bought off—the first is omitted from Gibbon's account (he thought it preceded the alliance of the two Theodorics). The others are represented swiftly and obscurely by Gibbon, as preparation for Theodoric's attack on Odoacer in Italy, seen by Gibbon as a stroke of moral and political genius: "He prevented the painful alternative of encountering the Goths, as the champion, or of leading them to the field as the enemy, of Zeno" by proposing to reconquer Rome for the Empire. Gibbon asserts that Theodoric "addressed the emperor in the following *words*" (emphasis added), a speech concluding "If I fall, you will be relieved from an expensive and troublesome friend; if . . . I succeed, I shall govern in your name, and to your glory, the Roman senate, and the part of the republic delivered from slavery by my victorious arms" (*DF* 4:189). This "proposal of Theodoric was accepted, and perhaps had been suggested, by the Byzantine court." To support his report of Theodoric's words Gibbon provides the following note (19 [16]): "Jornandes (c. 57, p. 696, 697) has abridged the great history of Cassiodorius. See, compare, and reconcile [four other sources]." Clearly Gibbon is making a point not merely about what happened, but about the kind of truth such an account represents. He acknowledges by the very form of his text, by the rhetoric of his note, and by the relationship between them that his personal choices and judgment have aided him in providing a picture of the past justified by its typical, not its literal, truth.[6]

The next few pages are devoted to Theodoric's campaigns against Odoacer, but they are arranged—and clearly deliberately arranged— to give as little military information as possible. First, Gibbon devotes a long paragraph to establishing how, in barbarian military campaigns, the whole people moved with the army. Military history is subordinated to a portrayal of a culture. Only at the end of the paragraph does he speak of actual combat: "In many obscure though bloody battles, Theodoric fought and vanquished; till at length, surmounting every obstacle by skilful conduct and persevering courage, he . . . displayed his invincible banners on the confines of Italy" (*DF* chap. 39, 4:190). If we have missed the point, on the next page Gibbon tells us in his own person, and in the text, "In the course of this history, the most voracious appetite for war will be abundantly satiated; nor can I much lament that our dark and imperfect materials do not afford a more ample narrative of the distress of Italy" (*DF* 4:191). He does regret, later, the lack of materials on which to base an account and judgment of Theodoric's conduct in victory and of his method of government:

> One record of his fame, the volume of public epistles composed by Cassiodorius in the royal name, is still extant, and has obtained more implicit credit than it seems to deserve. . . . We should vainly search for the pure and spontaneous sentiments of the Barbarian amidst the declamation and learning of a sophist . . . [and] the language of discreet ministers. The reputation of Theodoric may repose with more confidence on the visible peace and prosperity of a reign of thirty-three years. (*DF* 4:193–94)

To bring Theodoric to this point has taken almost one-third of the chapter; the next portion, somewhat longer than a third, is the idyll proper, in which Gibbon describes Theodoric a peacemaker, a "prince who had penetration to discern, and firmness to pursue, his own and the public interest," who "loved the virtues which he possessed and the talents of which he was destitute" and promoted worthy men to civil office. When Theodoric visited Rome and made a public discourse promising just and legal government, "a saint, the spectator of this pompous scene, could only *hope* . . . that it was excelled by the celestial splendour of the New Jerusalem" (*DF* 4:203; emphasis added), and Gibbon himself says, in a note (72 [61]), "In the scale of public and personal merit, the Gothic conqueror is at least as much *above* Valentian, as he may seem *inferior* to Trajan"—contemporaries compared Theodoric to both. Gibbon's use of *is* and *seem* here is quite deliberate.

Gibbon also takes care to note that the Gothic kings, far from ruining the physical monuments of Rome, "were anxious to preserve the monuments of the nation whom they had subdued" (*DF* 4:204). Theodoric also emulated the donors of these monuments. Numerous

Italian cities "acquired under his reign the useful or splendid decorations of churches, aqueducts, baths, porticoes, and palaces. But the happiness of the subject was more truly conspicuous in the busy scene of labour and luxury, in the rapid increase and bold enjoyment of national wealth" (*DF* 4:205) The double purpose of this point, looking back to the age of the Antonines and to Constantine, but also forward, will already be clear to the reader who recalls that Procopius's panegyrical version of Justinian's reign is in his book *On Justinian's Buildings*.

Yet, even more than the splendid panoramas that begin the first and second volumes of the history, this idyll is flawed. Gibbon says so without indirection or irony: "I have descanted with pleasure on the fortunate condition of Italy; but our fancy must not hastily conceive that the golden age of the poets, a race of men without vice or misery, was realised under the Gothic conquest" (*DF* 4:208). The remainder of the chapter is devoted to the real and imaginary grievances, including the "grievance" of religious toleration, that lead to the following paradox: "At the close of a glorious life, the king of Italy discovered that he had excited the hatred of a people whose happiness he had so assiduously laboured to promote; and his mind was soured by indignation, jealousy, and the bitterness of unrequited love" (*DF* 4:210). Theodoric in turn suffers both real and imaginary grievances, and eventually, as a result of the religious intolerance fostered by Justinian (already in power in the East under his uncle Justin), a reciprocal intolerance is awakened in Theodoric: "By the bigotry of his subjects and enemies, the most tolerant of princes was driven to the brink of persecution; and the life of Theodoric was too long, since he lived to condemn the virtue of Boethius and Symmachus" (*DF* 4:211).

The remainder of the chapter is devoted to the biography of Boethius, "the last of the Romans whom Cato or Tully could have acknowledged for their countryman" and one who, in his private life, "might have been styled happy, if that precarious epithet could be safely applied before the last term of the life of man" (4:213). Gibbon records Boethius's death by torture, but goes on to say, "his genius survived to diffuse a ray of knowledge over the darkest ages of the Latin world." As Theodoric revives (in diminished form) the virtues of the Antonines, so Boethius is a new example of the heroic man of letters, serving both his country and posterity. Yet Gibbon is always more willing than able to grant to the contemplative life the value and importance of the active life; here, instead of giving the last words of the chapter to the immortality of genius, he devotes the last paragraph to the remorse, death, and immortality of Theodoric. To represent this final perspective, Gibbon employs a wide variety of tools: a humanist's pious wish, a psychological principle, a malicious

legend, and a neutral account of Theodoric's disposition of his kingdom. Here is Gibbon's last comment on Theodoric, the last sentence
in the chapter: "His spirit, after some previous expiation, might have
been permitted to mingle with the benefactors of mankind, if an
Italian hermit had not been witness in a vision to the damnation of
Theodoric whose soul was plunged . . . into the vulcano of Lipari,
one of the flaming mouths of the infernal world" (*DF* 4:218). To avoid
associating ourselves with the mean and foolish hermit, we must grant
pardon to the killer of Boethius.

Similar interplay among statement, suggestion, and silence characterizes the account of Justinian. The shocking, yet sympathetic,
account of Theodora was perhaps the feature of the account that most
captured the imagination and attention of Gibbon's contemporaries,[7]
but Gibbon himself seems most interested in the relationship between Justinian and his great general, Belisarius, and later in the
power and "manly" virtues of the eunuch Narses. Gibbon's growing
ability to see the merits of historical characters despite conventional
or personal prejudices against their class—women, eunuchs, bishops,
Jews—is certainly evident in the account of Narses, and perhaps also
in his portrayal of Theodora, which gives credit, but by no means
unskeptically, to Procopius's attack on her in the *Secret History*.[8]
Gibbon is also deeply interested in the relationship between Belisarius and his wife. But beyond these issues of character and power, for
Gibbon the story of Justinian's reign is one of spurious achievement,
both military and civil.

Justinian's military successes, or rather those of his generals, were
ephemeral, in part because of the stupidity of Justinian's policies, in
part because of his ingratitude for good service. They were generally
achieved by the *personal* skill and reputation of the generals, and
therefore even more than the peace and prosperity of the age of the
Antonines, depended on the life of an individual. Moreover, their
victories were not victories for civilization and prosperity; when Totila
the Goth recaptured Italy, he "calmly exhorted the senate and people
to compare the tyranny of the Greeks with the blessings of the Gothic
reign" (*DF* 4:424), and Gibbon does exactly that for the reader. In
particular, the Empire imposed extortionate taxes on agriculture. In
striking contrast, "to the husbandmen of Italy, the Gothic king issued
a welcome proclamation, enjoining them to pursue their important
labours" and promising not to impose defense taxation beyond the
ancient level. Totila even helped the starving and ailing masses, and
he took the step of demolishing the fortifications of the cities so that
the people would not have to suffer the calamities of a future siege.
(Gibbon sees this as a clearly humane step, one that prevents war
from being carried on at the expense of civilians.) Ultimately futile

contests, in which the side of civilization is at best indeterminate and often that of the "barbarians," characterize the four chapters (40–43) on the political and military history of the reign of Justinian.

Why then does Gibbon so condemn Justinian's ungrateful treatment of Belisarius, who, after all, was only a general? Why does he seem discontented, even contemptuous, when he contemplates Belisarius's extraordinary patience with both Justinian and Antonina, his sovereign and his wife—"the unconquerable patience and loyalty of Belisarius appear either *below* or *above* the character of a MAN" (*DF* chap. 41, 4:363)? There are perhaps two reasons: Gibbon seems to feel that historical impotence does not devalue or excuse the absence of individual moral virtue; and he sees also that the process of dynastic and military struggle may be powerfully destructive even though it cannot effectively alter the general course of historic change. "The wars, the conquests, and the triumphs of Justinian are the feeble and pernicious efforts of old age, which exhaust the remains of strength, and accelerate the decay of the powers of life. . . . The calamities that followed the departure of Belisarius [and that departure was always the result of Justinian's jealousy and ingratitude] betrayed the impotence of the conqueror and accomplished the ruin of those unfortunate countries" (*DF* chap. 43, 4:415). Some of the Empire's opponents deserved defeat, especially in Africa, where "every step of intestine discord was marked by some deplorable victory of savage man over civilized society" (*DF* 4:419). The conquest of Africa was Belisarius's first accomplishment, but as usual, he was recalled because Justinian feared that a successful subordinate would be a rival. Belisarius was accorded a Triumph but denied the opportunity of becoming a just and peaceful governor instead of the great agent of a destructive policy. The personal ingratitude and ineptitude of Justinian is thus contrasted with the merit already acknowledged in the great, though flawed, Gothic king, Theodoric: Justinian does not rectify his own weaknesses by rewarding the compensatory strengths of his ministers. If "it is difficult to trace the character of a prince who is not the most conspicuous object of his own times" (*DF* chap. 43, 4:459), if the story that the great and loyal Belisarius was "reduced by envy to beg his bread" must be exposed as legend, still the destructive effects of a petty man in a great role deserve to be exposed.

Even nature, Gibbon hints, participates in this exposé. As a coda to his devastating character of the emperor (*DF* chap. 43, 4:459–61), Gibbon provides a description of "the comets, the earthquakes, and the plague, which astonished or afflicted the age of Justinian" (*DF* 4:461). Gibbon stresses the scientific marvel of comet predictability and the popular expectation that they portended disaster, specifically pestilence and war. Earthquakes, he notes, make "the architect . . .

the enemy of mankind" (*DF* 4:465), and their terrors, like those of the comet, are increased by supersition. It was the plague, however, which "depopulated the earth" (*DF* 4:466). "The triple scourge of war, pestilence, and famine, afflicted the subjects of Justinian, and his reign is disgraced by a visible decrease of the human species, which has never been repaired in some of the fairest countries of the globe" (*DF* 4:469). If Justinian could not rationally be blamed for earthquakes or comets, he could be shown to have encouraged, or at least to have failed to alleviate, more devastating scourges. Thus the reign of Justinian, the best candidate for a "golden age" of the Byzantine Empire, is portrayed instead as an age of devastation, not an age of restoration or even of arrested decline. As we shall see, Gibbon reserves for separate treatment the special cases of law and religion.

While Gibbon was exposing the wretched pretensions of the Eastern Empire as a preserver of Roman culture, he was consciously enjoying his own last taste of the way of life he had been brought up to cherish, that of the English gentleman, landowner, and lawgiver. As D. M. Low remarks, "Gibbon never showed himself more equable in temper or more sincerely pleased with [t]his way of life, than in the months when it was becoming increasingly doomed."[9] Low sees this as a paradox; I suspect that the relationship was causal. Gibbon's life in England was certainly pleasant and settled, but it was settled into a pattern that required Gibbon constantly to perform the role of historian and man of affairs for a critical audience, one ready, he seems always to have felt, to catch him out. It is from this period that most of the comic descriptions of Gibbon—vicious or kindly—originate. Notable among them is Fanny Burney's, in a letter to Samuel Crisp (June 1783):

> Fat and ill-constructed, Mr. Gibbon has cheeks of such prodigious chubbiness, that they envelope his nose so completely, as to render it, in profile, absolutely invisible. His look and manner are placidly mild, but rather effeminate; his voice,—for he was speaking to Sir Joshua at a little distance,—is gentle, but of studied precision of accent. Yet, with those Brobdignatious cheeks, his neat little feet are of a miniature description; and with these, as soon as I turned round, he hastily described a quaint sort of circle, with small quick steps, and a dapper gait, as if to mark the alacrity of his approach, and then, stopping short when full face to me, he made so singularly profound a bow, that—though hardly able to keep my gravity—I felt myself blush deeply at its undue, but palpably intended obsequiousness.
>
> This demonstration, however, over, his sense of politeness, or project of flattery, was satisfied; for he spoke not a word, though his gallant advance seemed to indicate a design of bestowing upon me a little rhetorical touch of a compliment. But, as all eyes in the room were suddenly cast upon us both, it is possible he partook a little himself of the embarrassment he could not but see that he occasioned.[10]

I quote this description in full, both because, despite her own self-consciousness, Burney has astutely noticed two aspects of Gibbon's social manner that reveal his remaining social uncertainty—his pre-paring each remark slowly, and his sensitivity to embarrassing situations both for himself and for others—and because she is usually an acute and reliable witness. Gibbon's French acquaintance Suard, whose well-known description has already been quoted (see p. 94 above), gives Gibbon very long feet, possibly a picturesque invention, but otherwise, the two descriptions agree well enough. Though Gibbon's "Silenus belly" (Suard's phrase) had not yet reached its maximum rotundity, his appearance was clearly already grotesque. It was not made less so by his affectations. For example, he tried for a kind of courtly playfulness in a style that prompted his English acquaintances to an amusement that he would have been hurt to know of. We have already seen that George Steevens ridiculed him as "Cupid," that Mrs. Hayley enjoyed his curiosity, and that Fanny Burney found his bow as comical as his cheeks. Another friend, R. O. Cambridge, told Burney about a highly affected letter from Gibbon accepting an invitation for a boating party: "He shall attend him, he says, at Twickenham, and upon the water as soon as the weather is propitious, and the Thames, that amiable creature, is ready to receive him."[11] The cream of the jest, moreover, was yet to come. During this visit, the amiable Thames received him literally: he fell into the water, "a just penalty for his affectation."[12]

But if he was affected, he was also vulnerable, and conscious of the vulnerability of others. Boswell, who in 1779 found Gibbon so "ugly, affected [and] disgusting" that "he poison[ed]" the Literary Club for him,[13] reports a conversation of 1775, in which Johnson, who had been muttering the word "bear" to the suppressed mirth of the company, asserted, "We are told, that the black bear is innocent; but I should not like to trust myself with him." According to Boswell, "Mr. Gibbon muttered, in a low tone of voice, 'I should not like to trust myself with *you*.' This piece of sarcastick pleasantry was a pru-dent resolution, if applied to a competition of abilities."[14] (In this exchange, neither competitor seems to me to achieve a dazzling standard, but it is almost the only remark Boswell admits to Gibbon's having made in Johnson's company.) Boswell notwithstanding, how-ever, it is clear that Gibbon not only participated in conversation at all kinds of gatherings, but also, in his own fashion, shone in this activity. Indeed, other members of the Club found his conversation delightful. According to Malone, for example, "as a companion, Gibbon was uncommonly agreeable. He had an immense fund of anecdote and of erudition . . . and had acquired such a facility and elegance of talk that I had always great pleasure in listening to him. The manner and voice, though they were peculiar . . . did not at all offend."[15] An anonymous contemporary reported that Gibbon's "conversation, though in the highest degree informing, was not externally brilliant. He was by no means fluent of speech; his articulation was not graceful; his sentences were evidently laboured, as if he was fearful of committing himself. It was rather pedantic and stiff, than easy; yet, by some unaccountable fascination, it was always agreeable and impressive."[16]

Combining, according to Gibbon's model, these testimonies, we find that Gibbon had taught himself to be an entertaining conversationalist for those who liked information and anecdote, but not to be spontaneously playful, witty, or profound. His manner was decried or detested by some as affected, especially when his ugly body was attired in a suit of flowered velvet and accoutred with a sword. Yet even in his pretentiousness he had his merits. Young George Colman, about fourteen and socially inept, met Samuel Johnson and Gibbon on the same memorable evening in 1776–77:

> Each had his measured phraseology; and Johnson's famous parallel, between Dryden and Pope, might be loosely parodied, in reference to himself and Gibbon. Johnson's style was grand, and Gibbon's elegant; the stateliness of the former was sometimes pedantick, and the polish of the latter was occasionally finical. Johnson marched to kettledrums and trumpets; Gibbon moved to flute and haut-boys. Maul'd as I had been by Johnson, Gibbon pour'd balm upon my bruises, by condescending, once or twice, in the course of the evening, to talk with me;—the great historian was light and playful, suiting his matter to the capacity of the boy;—but . . . still his mannerism prevail'd;—still he tapp'd his snuff-box,—still he smirk'd, and smiled; and rounded his periods with the same air of good-breeding, as if he were conversing with men.—His mouth, mellifluous as Plato's, was a round hole, nearly in the centre of his visage.[17]

Colman was, of course, a wit, and this recollection no doubt lost nothing in the telling, but the key points, the kindness and the mannerisms, are well confirmed.

Though Gibbon's mannerisms were the same whatever the company, he could count on their being received with pleasure, could relax and enjoy his own weaknesses, among certain selected intimates. These intimate occasions probably still included frequent evenings with Aunt Kitty, though in these years we hear of her principally when she is travelling. They certainly included the evenings with the Sheffield family, as we know not only from the tone of Gibbon's letters to all members of the family, but also from Lord Sheffield's comments to others. For instance, Sheffield writes to William Eden, later Lord Auckland: "Gibbon and I have been walking about the room and cannot find any employment we should like in the intended establishment [of the Prince of Wales]. He agrees with me, that the place of dancing master might be one of the most eligible for him, but he rather inclines to be painter, in hopes of succeeding Ramsay."[18] But on the whole, situations of unselfconscious and playful intimacy seem to have been rare while Gibbon was living in England.

Yet the long-delayed move to Switzerland, to live in the surroundings among which he had first learned to take a place in social life, and in which he still felt most at home, was not yet Gibbon's greatest desire. His English friends, including his stepmother and his aunt, were, of course, anxious to keep him in England. As Hayley put it:

> I still hope, however, that if his revenue is diminished by the annihilation of the Board of Trade, some equivalent will be found to support the dignity of the Roman eagle. I would not have him lose a feather of his wing, or an atom of his nest. If his appointment should be taken from him, without any thing to counterbalance the loss, I apprehend he will retire into France, which would be not only an affliction to his friends, but a disgrace to our country.[19]

And Gibbon was persuaded to make an effort to obtain a new post; "I will not be idle," he assured Lord Sheffield (*Letters* 2:296), and a draft still exists of his letter to Lord Thurlow, offering his services to the peace negotiating team in Paris, a letter probably written in the summer of 1782 (*Letters* 2:303–4). Thurlow's reply is described by Norton as "politely evasive," but it might more appropriately be called "flattering but noncommittal," since Gibbon was a viable candidate for an official post in Paris as late as September 1783.[20]

Even to Thurlow, however, Gibbon could not help emphasizing his pleasure in his private life: "If I consulted only my private interest and inclination I should not be lightly tempted to interrupt the tranquillity and leisure, which I now enjoy, and in which I am never busy, and never idle" (*Letters* 2:303). Gibbon seems to view the turmoil of political life, and even war and peace, with the keen interest of a philosophical observer, but not with the interested concern of a participant. His letter to Lord Sheffield on July 6 sets the tone:

> I sympathize with your fatigues [Sheffield was in camp with his regiment, the 22nd Light Dragoons], yet Alexander, Hannibal &c have suffered hardships almost equal to yours.—At such a moment it is disagreable (besides lazyness) to write because every hour teems with a new lye. . . . [Fox's party] are furious against the Duke of Rich[mond]. Why will he not go out with Fox? said somebody; because, (replied a friend,) he does not like to *go out* with any man. In short three months of prosperity has dissolved a Phalanx which had stood ten years adversity. Next Tuesday Fox will give his reasons, and possibly be encountered by Pitt, the new Secretary or Chancellor at three and twenty. The day will be rare and curious and if I were a light Dragoon I would [take] a gallop on purpose to Westminster. (*Letters* 2:301)

In writing of the changing powers, the selfish or short-sighted decisions, the ingratitude and disloyalty of the important actors in Justinian's reign, Gibbon must have been struck by the similar interplay of personalities and power in his own times. But it is not necessary or desirable to look for specific and literal correspondences. He had long since learned that the sense of individual importance with which he had first taken up his responsibilities as a Member of Parliament was naive; and as a historian, he had long ago learned that such political events as changes of dynasty and leadership made relatively little difference, in most instances, to the majority of the populace, and no difference, in the long run, to the fates of civilization and culture. "The vain titles of the victories of Justinian are crumbled into dust; but the name of the legislator is inscribed on a fair and everlasting monument," Gibbon commented (*DF* chap. 44, 4:470). In this case, Gibbon then proceeds to portray the monument itself unfavorably, but the point is that Justinian's code of law outlasts his buildings, which themselves far outlast his political and military victories.

The portrayal of this powerful and complex story Gibbon calls "a gentle and not unpleasing continuation of my old labours" (*Letters* 2:305). In September he obtained a new setting for them when a parliamentary acquaintance lent him a "country villa" at Hampton Court, a "ready furnished house close to the Palace, and opening by a private door into the Royal garden which is maintained for my use but not at my expence. The air and exercise, good roads and neighbourhood, the opportunity of being in London any time in two hours, and the temperate mixture of society and study adapt this new scene very much to my wishes," he wrote to his stepmother (*Letters* 2:306).

This Hampton Court villa, during the fine weather, "proved no small addition to [his] comforts." Even physical exercise, which had seemed forgotten when he returned to Bentinck Street from France, reenters the picture. This was the way of life at Hampton court: "Every morning I walk a mile or more before breakfast, read and write quantum sufficit, mount my chaise and visit in the neighbourhood, accept some invitations and escape others, use the Lucans as my daily bread, dine pleasantly at home or sociably abroad, reserve for study an hour or two in the evening, lye in town regularly once a week" (*Letters* 2:308). A fine way of life indeed, but already one weaned from "business," public and private. The former concerned him only insofar as the value of his seat in Parliament was at issue; the latter, as always, was a bore and a burden that he turned over as rapidly as possible to his official agent, Hugonin, and his agent de facto, Sheffield.

In mid October 1782 he was "much entertained with the Meta-

physical disputes between Government and secession about the meaning" of the instructions to the British envoy in the American negotiations (*Letters* 2:311). He seems gently pleased also with successes of
British arms and negotiations—for example, General George Augustus
Elliott's successful defense of Gibraltar: "Is not Elliot a glorious old
fellow?" (*Letters* 2:314). At the request of General Sir Harry Clinton,
Gibbon read and made editorial suggestions on Clinton's pamphlet
defending his conduct in the American war (there was controversy
between Clinton and Cornwallis) (*Letters* 2:316–17). But his feeling
himself an observer, rather than a participant, is clear in a letter to
his stepmother:

> The Parliamentary Campaign is approaching very fast and a very singular
> one it must be from the conflict of *three* parties, each of which will be
> exposed in its turn to the direct or oblique attacks of the other two. As a
> matter of curiosity I shall derive some gratification from my silent seat,
> but at present I do not perceive its use in any other light. From honour,
> gratitude and principle I am and shall be attached to Lord N. who will
> lead a very respectable force into the field, but I much doubt whether
> matters are ripe for either conquest or coalition, and the havock which
> Burke's bill has made, of places &c encreases the difficulties of a new
> arrangement. However a month or two may change the face of things, and
> the faces of Men. Among these men, surely Will Pitt the second is the
> most extraordinary. I know you never liked the father, and I have no
> connection public or private with the son. Yet we cannot refuse to admire
> a youth of four and twenty, whom eloquence and real merit have already
> made Chancellor of the Exchequer without his promotion occasioning
> either surprize or censure. (*Letters* 2:314–5)

There is a sort of aesthetic admiration here, of a connoisseur of human
achievements, that strongly resembles Gibbon's praise of another unexpected hero, the eunuch general Narses:

> A feeble diminutive body concealed the soul of a statesman and a warrior.
> His youth had been employed in the management of the loom and dis-
> taff . . . but, while his hands were busy, he secretly exercised the faculties
> of a vigorous and discerning mind. . . . Like Belisarius, he had deserved
> the honours of envy, calumny, and disgrace. . . . it was not by weak and
> mischievous indulgence that Narses secured the attachment of his troops.
> (*DF* chap. 43, 4:440, 452)

Though Gibbon was well aware that his way of life could not
continue without some change, for months he made no decisive move
about his future. He simply drifted, enjoying Hampton Court or his
Bentinck Street library as the seasons required. In February the Shel-
bourne government, which had succeeded Rockingham's on
Rockingham's death (July 3), fell. The vote against it, in which
Gibbon followed Lord North in his coalition with Fox and the Rock-

ingham group, succeeded by a margin of sixteen, including Gibbon, who was so ill with gout that he had to be carried to the House and could get around only on crutches. When Lord North regained office in April, Gibbon expected some acknowledgement—if not an appointment, at least discussion of one. When nothing came, Gibbon seems to have felt quite bitter, for a time, about North's "slow pace and cold heart" (*Letters* 2:327).

He felt far more strongly, however, about a personal controversy during the winter. Joseph Priestley, by whose crowd-unsettling theology Gibbon was repelled and offended, and who in turn found Gibbon's indirection and detachment on religious matters cowardly and offensive, wrote a series of letters to Gibbon to try to provoke him to public controversy. Gibbon's replies were at least as offensive as Priestley's letters, but Gibbon, having made his *Vindication*, constantly refused Priestley's challenges. Finally, Priestley announced his intention of publishing their correspondence. Gibbon wrote, "A single copy of a paper, addressed under a seal, to a single person, and not relative to any public or official business, must always be considered as *private correspondence*, which a man of honour is not at liberty to print, without the consent of the writer" (*Letters* 2:323). Gibbon's resentment reached new heights when, despite all this, Priestley insisted that he had the right to print the correspondence. He did not actually do so until after Gibbon's death, but their publications during Gibbon's lifetime sufficiently attest continued antipathy. Priestley sniped at both Gibbon and his book in a number of publications, and Gibbon produced the following gratuitous note (*DF* chap. 54, 6:134 n. 49): "I shall recommend to public animadversion two passages in Dr. Priestly. . . . At the first of these . . . the priest, at the second . . . the magistrate, may tremble!"[21]

Priestley's last letter was sent to Gibbon at the end of February, the day before Shelburne's resignation. For the next six weeks, "the business of the house of Commons [was] postponed by waiting first for peace and afterwards for Government." When their friends were again in office, Lord Sheffield urgently desired that Gibbon seek a remunerative post in the Customs or Excise. Gibbon himself was not entirely eager to exchange five days a week for £1,000 a year; but he could not seem to overcome his inertia sufficiently to seek an alternative resolution. Finally, in May, he wrote *both* to Lord North (*Letters* 2:331–32) and to his Swiss friend Georges Deyverdun (*Letters* 2:326–30), to ask North if a post might be available, and to discover whether Deyverdun were still interested in sharing a house, or could find a house near his own in which Gibbon could live en pension. He also told Deyverdun about his pursuit of the Customs office and his uncertainty about his real wishes. "If I consulted only my heart and my reason I . . . would leave Parliament, London, England, I would seek . . . in a more tranquil country repose, liberty, ease, and an enlightened and pleasant society" (*Letters* 3:328).

During the spring months when he took no action to secure his future, and now while awaiting replies from North and Deyverdun, Gibbon continued to work on his new volume. After dismissing Justinian and Belisarius, he was ready to consider Justinian's principal claim to "philosophic" immortality, his code of laws. Much of the chapter on law (44) is a brilliant analytical description of the late Roman legal system, in the order of the Institutes, which "proceed, with no contemptible method, from I. *Persons* to II. *Things,* and from things to III. *Actions;* and the article IV. of *Private Wrongs* is terminated by the principles of *Criminal Law*" (*DF* chap. 44, 4:501). As usual in such passages, Gibbon abandons temporal limitations when he abandons chronology, and the account is full of cross-cultural and cross-temporal analogies.[22] There are also many universal propositions, such as, "The perfect equality of men is the point in which the extremes of democracy and despotism are confounded; since the majesty of the prince or people would be offended, if any heads were exalted above the level of their fellow-slaves or fellow-citizens" (*DF* 4:501).

This atemporal analysis is introduced, however, by a long "digression" on the history of Roman law, which is also a meditation on the nature and purpose of laws and on laws as texts—literary works. "Wise or fortunate is the prince who connects his own reputation with the honour and interest of a perpetual order of men. The defence of their founder is the first cause which in every age has exercised the zeal and industry of the civilians" (*DF* 4:470). Legal documents, however, are necessarily and (ironically) properly subject to creative misinterpretation. The civilians' "subtle interpretations concurred with the equity of the praetor to reform the tyranny of the darker ages: however strange or intricate the means, it was the aim of artificial jurisprudence to restore the simple dictates of nature and reason, and the skill of private citizens was *usefully* employed to undermine the public institutions of their country" (*DF* chap. 44, 4:484; emphasis added). When we reach the age of Justinian, however, it is obvious that a millennium of such tortuous and unpredictable courting of nature and reason had produced incoherent results. Gibbon portrays the true authors of "Justinian's" code, Tribonian and his staff, fairly sympathetically; but he sees their accomplishments as significantly limited by Justinian's charge; he desired only a compilation, and he decreed incompatible arrangements of the material: "Since the emperor declined the fame and envy of original composition, we can only require at his hands method, choice, and fidelity, the humble though indispensable virtues of a compiler. . . . as the order of Justinian is different in his three works, it is possible that all may be wrong, and it is certain that two cannot be right" (*DF* 4:495). Gibbon defends the choice of more recent materials rather than those of the Republic— but he credits Tribonian, not Justinian, with the good, though inglorious, judgment involved (*DF* 4:495–96). It is Justinian, however, who is "guilty of fraud and forgery, when he . . . inscribe[s] with [the Antonines'] venerable name the words and ideas of his servile reign" (*DF* 4:496). Justinian does not eliminate the complicated proliferation of laws required by a government of laws, not men; but on the other hand, the laws do not restrain the sovereign. At the end of the chapter, then, we are in a position fully to appreciate Gibbon's final comment: "The government of Justinian united the evils of liberty and servitude; and the Romans were oppressed at the same time by the multiplicity of their laws and the arbitrary will of their founder" (*DF* 4:542).

This chapter on law has led a life of its own as a textbook. A great German legal historian, Gustav Hugo (Gibbon's contemporary), was the first to employ it (in German translation) in this way.[23] Hugo was something of an iconoclast, adopting Gibbon's chapter (heavily fortified with additional notes) despite the official opinion of German reviews such as the *Göttingen Gelehrte Anzeigen* that law was one of the fields in which Gibbon was most handicapped by his autodidacticism, his lack of a good German education.[24] In Hugo's view, Gibbon's technical deficiencies as a legal historian were far outweighed by his virtue of comprehending and conveying the spirit of Roman law, presumably in his analysis as well as his narrative. Gibbon's chapter and Hugo's notes were soon published in French for similar educational purposes (and with more notes), and it was eventually used as an introduction to Roman law in at least seven countries, including the United States.[25] It was even so issued, with a translation of Hugo's notes and an abridgement of his introduction, in Britain.[26] It has the virtues of Gibbon's best analytical chapters, in that it clearly expresses the views of an individual, while convincing the reader that those views are the result of a search for a just evaluation of the objects presented.

It was the last analytical chapter Gibbon wrote in England. Chapters 45 and 46 are narrative. By portraying leaders of unexpected virtue and competence, they complete the task begun by the chapter on Theodoric: they provide an ironic frame for Justinian. Among the figures in chapter 45 whose merits implicitly reproach Justinian are two emperors, both relatively virtuous and one not entirely ineffectual; an almost Byronic hero-villain in Alboin, king of the Lombards, about whose story one contemporary reviewer rhapsodized, "[It] possesses so much of the beautiful wildness of romance, that we are tempted to give it entire";[27] and "Gregory the *Great* [, whose pontificate is] . . . one of the most edifying periods of the church" (*DF* chap. 45, 5:37; this is not irony!). The chapter that begins with a final reproach to Justinian concludes, "in the attachment of a grateful people [Gregory] found the purest reward of a citizen and the best right of a sovereign" (*DF* 5:41). The emperor at the time of Gregory also receives praise, though it is highly qualified: Maurice "reigned above twenty years over the East and over himself" (*DF* 5:21), but he was found cold and avaricious by the people, and he failed to provide for a safe transfer of power (in the next chapter, his death, at the hands of a usurper, delivers almost all of the Empire to two powerful enemies, the Great King, Chosroes II of Persia, and the Chagun of the Avars).

In chapter 46 Gibbon has three themes. Two are explicit: the pointless horror of territorial war and the remarkable character of Heraclius I, the emperor who overthrew the usurper and founded a Byzantine dynasty. The implicit theme is the historian's role as fabricator of meaning, and (because to escape history is often to escape disaster) as bearer of responsibility for the woes he records and judges. For example, Gibbon says that though Damascus has always been a royal city, "her obscure felicity has hitherto escaped the historian of the Roman empire," as if Gibbon himself, by destroying her obscurity, were one of the destroyers of felicity. Nearly every source is evaluated by a phrase or sentence in the note in which it is cited, and many particular facts are reacted to. Gibbon tells us, of course, what we need to know to appraise the probability of his text or to learn how to read history in general, but he also simply chats: "With the Christian daughters [of Maurice], Anastasia and Theoctiste, I am surprised to find the pagan name of Cleopatra." This chat, moreover, is not confined either to the notes or to direct statement, though these are his most frequent vehicles. He alludes to *Julius Caesar* in his text: "In that grave, the faults and errors of Maurice were kindly interred" (*DF* 5:68). Similarly, he both refers and alludes to himself; for instance, by interrupting his own narrative by a question directed to it: "The flight of Chosroes (yet where could he have fled?) was rudely arrested" (*DF* 5:99).

The two explicit themes of the chapter are ironically related. Gibbon gives due credit to the skill and success the Great King and the emperor Heraclius successively enjoy as war leaders, but he hammers home the point that "a war which had wounded the vitals of the two monarchies produced *no change* in their external and relative situations," no advantage at all to either side (*DF* 5:100; emphasis added). Further, "the loss of two hundred thousand soldiers . . . was of less fatal importance than the decay of arts, agriculture and population." Meanwhile, "an obscure town on the confines of Syria was pillaged by the Saracens, and they cut in pieces some troops who advanced to its relief: an ordinary and trifling occurrence," except that "these robbers were the apostles of Mahomet" (*DF* 5:102). With this anticipation of his future subject, Gibbon set aside his history for some time.

In writing to Deyverdun, Gibbon had tried to be completely honest about himself, his recent history, and his hopes for the future, without putting unfair pressure on Deyverdun, with whom he had not exchanged letters for (he says) eight years. In the process he paints himself very unattractively. He forgets his earlier enthusiastic hopes and says, "I entered Parliament without patriotism and without ambition; my views were limited to the convenient and honest place of a *Lord of Trade*." In thinking of his future possibilities, he describes as one of the advantages of moving to Switzerland that he could there await the death of his stepmother and his aunt Hester, after which he could return to England as a man "free, rich, and respectable because of his position as well as his character" (*Letters* 2:327–28). The cynicism of one statement and the calculation of the other have provided valuable ammunition to Gibbon's detractors. To Deyverdun, however, who had lived in the Gibbon house, Gibbon did not have to make clear his fondness for his stepmother. There is much evidence in the letters that, though Gibbon did not really much enjoy his visits to Bath, he sincerely delighted in her good health and wished her well. His attitude toward Hester Gibbon was indeed entirely calculating, but he was hardly acquainted with her, and his designs on her "excessive" share in the family estate were one of his few personal inheritances from his father. It is not nearly so attractive a picture as that of the young man who was grateful for the maternal affection of Mrs. Gibbon and constantly loyal and helpful to her in the trying years of his father's final illness and death, but it is wrong to take these statements out of context to convict Gibbon of monstrous inhumanity.[28]

Certainly Deyverdun did not see him that way. His reply to Gibbon's letter is almost lyrical in its delight at the prospect of their reunion, its description of their future way of life—in beautiful surroundings, among congenial and varied company, combining liberty with domestic companionship—and in its pleasure at a friend's escape from an inappropriate way of life:

> Remember, my dear friend, that I was pained when you entered Parliament and I believe I have proved only too good a prophet; I am sure that this career has made you experience more privations than advantages, many more pains than pleasures; I have always believed, ever since I have known you, that you were destined to live happy in the pleasures of study and society, that any other path was a detour on the road of happiness,

and that it was only the united role of man of letters and amicable man of society that could procure for you glory, honor, pleasures, and a continual series of enjoyments. After a few turns around your room, you will perceive perfectly that I saw well and that the results have confirmed my views.[29]

In the end, Gibbon did see that Deyverdun was the friend who knew him best—not his most active or supportive friend, but the one who most fully understood him.

If a position had been offered by the Government, Gibbon might have had trouble resisting the combined pressures of Sheffield and £1,000 a year, but when he drew up for himself a list of "Reasons for and against" accepting a post (the more attractive post in Paris) if he were offered it, five reasons for accepting occurred to him, but seven against. For: the salary (£1,200); Paris; "obliging a friend in England"; the hope of future financial security; and "the credit of being distinguished and stopped by Government when I was leaving England"— his first reason, which amounts to no more than vanity. Against: the expense; "a rational and agreable scheme on the point of execution"; disappointing a friend in Lausanne; the insecurity of ministerial favor; and (4–6), "Giving up the leisure and liberty for prosecuting my history"; "The engaging without experience perhaps without talents in a scene of business which I never liked"; "Giving myself a Master at least a principal of an unknown perhaps an unamiable character."[30] Obviously, the nays had it.

On June 27, 1783, Gibbon wrote to Deyverdun, "My reason becomes clear, my courage grows strong, and I am already walking on the terrace, laughing with you about all these cobweb threads that seemed to be iron chains." On July 1 he committed himself to Deyverdun with the "sacramental words," "Je pars." (*Letters* 2:339). Six days later, in a gesture curiously like that in which he sought permission from his father to travel rather than enter Parliament,[31] Gibbon communicated his resolve to Lord Sheffield—not in conversation, but in a letter (*Letters* 2:341–43). To enter a new way of life and to detach himself from the old equally required documentation— a "sacred" text in capital letters. For Lord Sheffield, it was "IRREVOCABLE."

ELEVEN

Lion of Lausanne

hose who tried to dissuade Gibbon from moving to Lausanne suggested that he would be bored: "My friends had been kindly apprehensive, that I should not be able to exist in a Swiss town at the foot of the Alps, after so long conversing with the first men of the first cities of the World" (*Memoirs* 178). An English traveller in Switzerland took the opposite view; Gibbon had chosen Lausanne because there he would not be challenged by competition: "Gibbon is the *grand monarque* of literature at Lausanne. . . . His predilection for the Swiss is notorious; and, as a love of pre-eminence may not be classed amongst the least of his failings, he seems to have decided well in the choice of his society."[1] Gibbon thought both friends and foe were mistaken. In Lausanne he would enjoy *more* good company, in better circumstances, than in London:

> Whatsoever may be the fame of learning or genius, experience has shewn me that the cheaper qualifications of politeness and good sense are of more useful currency in the commerce of life. By many, conversation is esteemed as a theatre or a school: but after the morning has been occupied by the labours of the library, I wish to unbend rather than to exercise my mind; and . . . I am far from disdaining the innocent amusement of a game at cards. (*Memoirs* 178)

Moreover, as he goes on to make clear, many eminent persons visited Lausanne every summer. And winter or summer, he could enjoy a way of life that included intellectual, literary, and scientific study and

205

discussion, outings in the beautiful environs of Lausanne, elaborately cared-for gardens, balls and breakfasts and dinners, music and theatre, and, for Gibbon perhaps most important of all, familial intimacy without parental, filial, or marital obligations.

Gibbon arrived in Lausanne, with a complete Homer, several volumes of Lord Clarendon, the nearly completed manuscript of volume 4 of his own history, his dog Muff, and his valet Caplen, on Saturday, September 27, 1783, about ten o'clock in the morning (*Letters* 2:372). He did not return to England until, almost four years later, he had completed the *Decline and Fall*. During these first four years of Gibbon's life at Lausanne, he "found as much happiness as is compatible with human nature and . . . never breathed a sigh of repentance" (*Letters* 3:164). He enjoyed domestic comfort and companionship combined with scholarly independence and privacy: he was welcome in, and enjoyed, the "best" society whether it was defined by rank, intellect, or nationality. After an involuntary holiday, while he waited for the arrival of his books from England, he would find in the *Decline and Fall* itself a new aspect of his subject, a comparative study of the different stages of society, and of their manifestations in different civilizations: in volume 5 and 6, he juxtaposes and connects with the history of the Byzantine Empire and the former Roman territories, the states and conquests of other great peoples, most notably the Arab world.

The interval between Gibbon's decision to leave for Lausanne and his departure, though brief and busy, was filled also with painful suspense. The worst task, of course, was to announce his intention to his closest English friends, Catherine Porten, the "true mother of [his] mind" (*Memoirs* 36); Dorothea Gibbon, and the Sheffields. Of these friends, the Sheffields might easily travel to Switzerland, and since they were of his own generation, neither he nor they feared that they would never meet again. His aunt and stepmother, however, were aging. Catherine Porten was seventy-six years old, Dorothea Gibbon about ten years younger. Both were in good health for their ages, and both were told only that he would be gone for at least a year, a truthful but misleading statement, since he did not expect to return until he had completed his history. They might therefore hope to see him again, but he was keenly aware that his aunt, in particular, might well die before he returned to England.

For years he had lived apart from his stepmother, except for annual or semiannual visits, and "the difference . . . between one, and six, hundred miles" between them was, he believed, to some degree "imaginary" (*Letters* 2:369). But he had been able to see Aunt Kitty frequently, to call on her in domestic crises such as persuading his old housekeeper to retire, and to be comfortably aware of her cheerful, independent way of life. To part with her was even more difficult than he anticipated, as we can tell from the sudden flurry of references to her in the letters, as well as his own acknowledgement that in his preparation, he had "not felt any circumstance more deeply" than her "silent grief" (*Letters* 2:354).

He was touched also by Dorothea Gibbon's offer to surrender two-thirds of her pension to him and live with him as his housekeeper if he would stay in England (*Letters* 2:351). But his attachment to her was by this time grateful and habitual rather than warmly personal, and it was to soothe her feelings rather than his own that he enlisted Lord Sheffield's aid in comforting her. For her, Gibbon believed, there would be comfort in such rational considerations as the healthfulness of the climate and the economy and convenience of the way of life he had chosen. For Aunt Kitty he could only seek to provide affection; the Sheffields took her to Sheffield Place after she had parted from her nephew and even, at his request, founded on her intuited wishes, gave her his very room in their house (*Letters* 2:363). The true friendship of both Lord and Lady Sheffield was demonstrated once again, not only by their assistance in comforting Gibbon's relations, but by their understanding support of what was best for their friend.

Lord Sheffield's letter to Dorothea Gibbon is an example, a masterpiece of sympathetic tact, and that he was capable of it would perhaps have surprised some of those who knew him, as well as most of Gibbon's admirers, who write Sheffield off as solely a man of action.[2] It is indeed possible that Lady Sheffield or Gibbon himself contributed to the content, but the voice is entirely Lord Sheffield's. He writes to the unreconciled Dorothea:

> If it were proper, decorous or fitting, I cou'd indulge in a great Style of swearing or other violence in the migration of your Son. The Idea annoys me as much as it can you. It haunts me & it is particularly unsatisfactory, that after having tryed hard, after having exerted the best disposition to find fault with the Scheme, one cannot find, or detect any thing in it, that is not reasonable on his part, & which one wou'd not eagerly do in his Situation. . . . He always had a vile hankering after Lausanne, Pais de Vaux, Deyverdun &c. & never tasted the Beauties of Parliamentary Business as a true Englishman naturally does. . . . I have some Comfort in thinking that our Friend will however be satiated of this Plan in due time; It is not reasonable to suppose that a man so fitted for Society & so sought for where there is the greatest variety & perhaps the best, should be long content with a Dozen People at Lausanne. . . . But to business, as he is soon going, & I cou'd almost send him to the Great Prince, I am a Candidate to supply his Place in Your Councils. . . . I shall like to be your Chancellor, Attorney General, & agent rather than their Deputy & shall be much gratified by the Correspondence with the Principal. I shall die before I approve the measure he has adopted, but if between ourselves we shou'd think it the best, & I shou'd know that all circumstances consid-

ered, it was irresistible, we may as well acquiesce with a tolerable grace.
He has a Pang about leaving you for any time—to a certain degree he
shou'd suffer, but we may smooth his departure, by adopting such a
System as will give him reason to think that no care or attention to you,
will be wanting, Therefore Pray, Declare by the return of The Post that
you adopt me to all intents & Purposes during his unnatural Absence.[3]

I have quoted this letter at length because I think it reveals much
about Gibbon's friend's kindness, Dorothea's feelings, and Sheffield's
and Gibbon's understanding of them. She did in effect "adopt" Lord
Sheffield (or rather, allow him to adopt her), and in various ways, he
took over Gibbon's duties to the "three old ladies"—Catherine Porten,
Dorothea Gibbon, and Hester Gibbon—Gibbon left behind in
England, that is, his duties as a family man, as well as his duties as a
man of property.

Parting with the Sheffields, however much he anticipated seeing
them soon again, was also more difficult than Gibbon expected. "In
the whole period of my life I do not recollect a day in which I felt
more unpleasant sensations than that on which I took my leave of
Sheffield place" (*Letters* 2:357—he had not yet parted with his aunt),
and in these circumstances, he wavered in his resolution long enough
to write either to Lord Loughborough or Lord North (only the draft
of the letter survives and it is not addressed) asking to be considered
for the vacated post of secretary to the embassy in Paris (*Letters*
2:358). But he was not disappointed at the failure of his request—
indeed, "I should wait with more reluctance did I think there was
much chance of success," he wrote to Sheffield (*Letters* 2:363).

A missing letter from Deyverdun, and the complications incident
to travel by sea, increased Gibbon's discomfort. He delayed his departure from London for more than a week in the hope of receiving a
letter from Deyverdun confirming his welcome, but though the Flan-
ders mails finally arrived, no letter came. Uncomfortable in lodgings,
Gibbon was "impatient to be gone: it is provoking to be so near yet
so far from certain persons. London is a desert" (*Letters* 2:368). When
he finally reached Dover, adverse winds added to his suspense. "What
a cursed thing to live in an island, this step is more awkward than the
whole journey!" he grumbled (*Letters* 2:370) and more seriously wrote
to Deyverdun, "Are you dead? are you ill? Have you changed your
mind? Have difficulties arisen?" (*Letters* 2:364). Finally, on Wednesday
September 17, 1783, "The Triumvirate of this memorable embarka-
tion" (Gibbon, Henry Laurens, and Benjamin Thompson, Count
Rumford) "attended by three horses who are not the most agreable
fellow passengers" sailed for France (*Letters* 2:370).

Gibbon travelled in some style: his French-speaking footman,
Antoine, had been outfitted with boots and saddle jacket so that he
might ride beside the carriage in which Gibbon, his dog, and his valet

travelled. Gibbon was conveyed from Boulogne to Pontarlier, eighty posts, by five horses and two postillions at a cost of 27 French louis, 1 livre, and 10 sous. (Lodging for himself and two servants cost 9-11-10).[4] He travelled from Pontarlier to Lausanne with hired horses (that is, not post horses), a journey of two and a half days. Though Deyverdun's spacious house, with its beautiful view of Lake Geneva against a background of mountains, its splendid terrace and garden, was still occupied by his tenants; though Gibbon's books, sent off on August 18 (*Letters* 2:354), had not arrived; though an attack of the gout immediately after his arrival had prevented him from making visits, part of the pleasure of Lausanne immediately presented itself. "Yesterday afternoon I lay or at least sat in state to receive visits, and at the same moment my room was filled with four different nations" (*Letters* 2:373; September 29, 1783), and on other occasions the variety of visitors was even greater. In profound contrast, when Gibbon was attacked by gout while he was living in London (as he pointed out to his English friends), "my confinement was sad and solitary; the many forgot my existence when they saw me no longer at Brookes's; and the few who sometimes cast a thought or an eye on their friend were detained by business or pleasure. . . . I was proud and happy if I could prevail on Elmsley [his friendly bookseller] to enliven the dullness of the Evening" (*Letters* 3:32).

He was of course more important and more appreciated in a city of seven thousand than in London or even Paris, where he had profited from the Anglophilia of the intellectual circles. In Lausanne, where the noblesse sought him out as a desirable companion and every visiting lord or princeling regarded him as one of Lausanne's tourist attractions, he never had to fear the attitude represented by Horace Walpole, who refused to consider an "alderman's son" a gentleman, much less a "man of quality" (see p. 173 above). In Lausanne, Gibbon frankly acknowledged, "I myself am an object of much larger magnitude" (*Letters* 3:33) than in London. "In London, I was lost in the crowd; I ranked with the first families of Lausanne, and my style of prudent expence enabled me to maintain a fair balance of reciprocal civilities" (*Memoirs* 177). More fundamentally, though Gibbon did not want to tell his British correspondents that the Swiss were kinder than the English, they were, he believed, more interested in the "old and infirm." This pattern of behavior was no doubt the result of Lausanne's reputation as a hospitable place for tourists, combined with its attractions for visiting invalids, its good "air" and excellent doctors, especially the famous Dr. Tissot. Socializing at sick beds was taken for granted—Gibbon himself passed "some delightful hours by [the] bed side" of the "adorable" Lady Elizabeth Foster (*Letters* 3:12). The contrast, and the gratitude and complacency to which it led, provided one strong reason for his preference for Lausanne: "During three months I have had round my chair a succession of agreable men and women who came with a smile and vanished at a nod, and as soon as it was agreable I had a constant party at cards which was sometimes dismissed to their respective homes, and sometimes detained by Deyverdun to supper without the least trouble or inconvenience to myself" (*Letters* 3:33).

To his English correspondents, who had argued that he was cutting himself off from society, Gibbon emphasized the impressive contingents of foreign visitors. But he preferred Lausanne in the winter, when the "natives," who scattered in the summer to their country estates, were in residence. He wrote to Lord Sheffield on November 14 with satisfaction—not to say smugness!—about their respective lots:

> Last Tuesday November 11th [the day Parliament opened] after plaguing and vexing yourself all the morning about some business of your own fertile creation you went to the House of Commons and passed the afternoon the evening and perhaps the night, without sleep or food stifled in a close room by the heated respiration of six hundred politicians, inflamed by party and passion and tired with the repetition of dull nonsense which in that illustrious assembly so far outweighs the proportion of reason and eloquence. On the same day after a studious morning, a friendly dinner, and a chearful assembly of both sexes, I retired to rest at eleven o'Clock, satisfied with the past day, and certain that the next would afford me the return of the same quiet and rational enjoyments. *Which has the better bargain?* . . . After a month of the finest autumn I ever saw . . . the present day is dark and rainy not much better than what you probably enjoy in England. The town is comparatively empty but the Noblesse are returning every day from their Chateaux, and I already perceive that I shall have more reason to complain of dissipation than of dullness. . . . You talk of Lausanne as a place of retirement, yet. . . . all nations and all extraordinary characters are astonished to meet each other [here]. (*Letters* 2:378–79, 381)

With the decision to move Gibbon had developed one of his fits of financial responsibility and had begun to try to keep a double-entry account book (now in the Pierpont Morgan Library, New York). We therefore know that his first expense at Lausanne was his entrance fee for the "Cercle de Bourg" (he next bought an umbrella and repaid Deyverdun for October's household expenses. The society of the rue de Bourg was that of the noblesse of Lausanne, and in earlier years, Gibbon had hardly aspired to it. His entrée resulted in part from Deyverdun's sponsorship, in part from his own increased maturity and status, both as a country gentleman and as a celebrity, "as Edward Gibbon, and as my friend," wrote Deyverdun. He adds, "At first you will be the man of fashion, and I foresee that you will play this role very well, without being annoyed, should you be a little overpraised."[5] This very diagnosis suggests how compatible the two friends were.

In Lausanne, Deyverdun went on to remind Gibbon, winter and summer would present very different scenes, without Gibbon's having to travel into the country or away from his beloved library. It was his invariable habit to spend the morning in it, and in his first years at Lausanne, that habit gave him the way of life he had always sought, the opportunity to balance social pleasure with the private delights of study and writing. Deyverdun had promised, "You will have more time for study than in London; people seldom go out in the morning, and when our common friends come and ask for you, I shall say to them, 'He is no idler like you people, he is working in his study,' and they will be quiet respectfully."[6] He kept his promise.

At first, however, Gibbon's scholarly activities were seriously limited not only by his illness and temporary lodgings, but by his lack of books. Except for those he had brought with him, and those available in the library of the Academy of Lausanne, he was without the "tools of his manufacture" until February 1784, when the first boxes of books he had sent from London arrived. His study was therefore confined to reading the Church Fathers, new purchases,[7] and the chosen companions of his journey. In this period, it has been ingeniously suggested,[8] he may have written the "Outlines of the History of the World" for the period he was about to portray in his history. But the Outlines begin in 800, a year that had long since ceased to seem a turning point to Gibbon, and if they had been a recent composition in 1784, it seems unlikely that Gibbon would have begun chapter 48 with yet another outline for the remaining portion of his history, one that is also as we shall see, to some extent inconsistent with the work that resulted, but in a very different manner.

Even when his books arrived, moreover, and the downstairs rooms in Deyverdun's house that included his library became available, builders and moving made it hard to settle down to serious work.[9] In May, at last, however, he could resume his history, turning first to the final chapter of volume 4, chapter 47, on the history of the doctrine of the Incarnation. As the theme of the accounts of Justinian and his opponents had been the futility of their territorial conflicts, so this chapter illustrates a similar futile and destructive series of religious conflicts. The quarrels of the Nestorians, Monophysites, Catholics, and so on, seem to Gibbon an exact religious parallel of the selfish and empty secular conflicts between the emperor and the Great King of the Persians. In overtly or covertly theocratic states, moreover, religious conflict affected not merely the opinions, but the lives of millions. The rhetoric with which this chapter begins clearly echoes that of the first chapter of the history—pointing out the missed opportunity for, as it were, a Christian age of peace and achievement comparable to that of the Antonines. But in theme and subject, the chapter clearly echoes the infamous chapters 15 and 16:

> After the extinction of paganism, the Christians in peace and piety might have enjoyed their solitary triumph. But the principle of discord was alive in their bosom. . . . It is my design to comprise in the present chapter a religious war of two hundred and fifty years, to represent the ecclesiastical and political schism of the Oriental sects, and to introduce their clamorous or sanguinary contests by a modest inquiry into the doctrines of the primitive church. (*DF* chap. 47, 5:103)

To this statement of purpose Gibbon attaches a despairing footnote, clearly inspired by his previous experience of religious controversy: "By what means shall I authenticate this previous inquiry, which I have studied to circumscribe and compress?—If I persist in supporting each fact or reflection by its proper and special evidence . . . every note would swell to a critical dissertation. But the numberless passages of antiquity which I have seen with my own eyes are compiled, digested, and illustrated by *Petavius* and *Le Clerc*, by *Beausobre* and *Mosheim*" (*DF* chap. 47, 5:103–4, n. 1). He then provides full references for each and comments on their strengths and weaknesses. He had referred to two of his Oxford attackers as the "confederate doctors" in his *Vindication;* here, he provides himself with a confederacy of doctors, and by evaluating them, not only secures them as allies, but places himself in authority over them.

Having established his ground, he proceeds to take on even more than he has promised: not only the controversy from 412 to 661, but also a coda on sixteenth- and seventeenth-century Abyssinia and a prelude that begins in apostolic times. The point, of course, is that such a quarrel never really ends and that it is inevitably decided, temporarily, on the basis of superior power, not superior truth. "Religion was the pretence; but, in the judgment of a contemporary saint, ambition was the genuine motive of episcopal warfare" (*DF* chap. 47, 5:119). As usual Gibbon is horrified by the resultant mutual cruelties: "These were Christians! who differed only in names and in shadows" (*DF* chap. 47, 5:128, n. 53).

Gibbon also seems to reveal some aspects of his own ambivalent attitude toward Christ in this chapter. It is clear that he thinks that Christ was only a man, and one who rarely or never claimed to be more. Of this man's teachings and especially his humanity— specifically, his tears because of Lazarus's death—Gibbon on the whole approves. But he is troubled or offended by Christ's lack of stoicism (as Gibbon sees it) on the Cross, that is, his crying out, "My God, my God, why have you abandoned me?" (Mark 16:34). Gibbon's invidious comparison of Christ to Socrates (*DF* chap. 47, 5:111, n. 16) may be attributed to mere mischief, an easy sneer; but I think Gibbon is also disappointed that Christ, a hero in the contemplative mode, "fails" under active stress. Of course Gibbon knows—and explicitly acknowledges—that Christ is quoting Psalm 22, but that does not satisfy him. It was outside Gibbon's theology and psychology to understand such a perspective as that of St. John of the Cross, that it is this speech through which believers know that Jesus experienced on humanity's behalf the most profound suffering of sin, separation from God. For Gibbon, religious figures ought to have exactly the same virtues as secular heroes; there are no others. Similarly, Gibbon is pleased when Mahomet (I shall adopt his spelling) weeps for the loss of his friend and displeased when the prophet avoids the risk of battle for his own cause (*DF* chap. 50, 5:386, n. 139 [130]).

Gibbon completed this last chapter of volume 4, which returns to Justinian by including an account of his "theological character," but does not treat it as either the center or the climax of the chapter, in June 1784.[10] In July he began what he clearly conceived as a new section of his history. The first half of it had comprised two subdivisions of unequal length, volume 1 and volumes 2–3; similarly, the second part of the second half of his history was to be twice a long as the first part. The outline with which chapter 48 begins makes it clear that the remainder of the history forms a single unit. Yet Gibbon was also conscious of a subdivision within this final portion of the history; he recalled and recorded that he had completed volume 5, that is, chapter 48–57, on May 1, 1786.[11]

For these nine chapters, "after many designs and many tryals," Gibbon "preferred . . . the method of groupping [his] picture by nations; and the seeming neglect of Chronological order is surely compensated by the superior merits of interest and perspicuity" (*Memoirs* 179). In youth, Gibbon had objected to Voltaire's "method (of treating every article in a distinct chapter)" as "vicious, as they are all connected in human affairs, and as they are often the cause of each other, why separate [*sic*] them in History?"[12] Now he considers "excellent" (*Letters* 3:223) the method of Robert Henry's *History of Great Britain* (1771–85), which "was to recount the whole history of each subject together, returning to the starting point with a new subject in each chapter."[13] In Gibbon's own practice, the change of heart is more apparent than real, however, for each of these chapters (except, significantly, the one on the state of the Eastern Empire in the tenth century) is in fact a narrative history of something; the volume is like a collection of related historical works dealing (at least in part) with the same period, but with different places or subjects. One is an overview of the personal and political careers of the Byzantine emperors from 641 to 1204; one portrays the iconoclastic controversy and "the restoration and decay of the Roman Empire in the West"

(Charlemagne); another gives us the history of the Paulician and similar "rational heresies," including the Reformation; one deals with Mahomet and his first five successors; two others give us the rise and fall of the empire of the caliphs (Gibbon's own metaphor [6:53]); and one each recounts the history of the northern barbarians, the Normans, and the Turks. But if this ostensible division by subjects is experienced as parallel narratives in the fifth volume, in the sixth, to which Gibbon also applies this statement about his method, narrative is still more powerfully felt: the first six chapters are quite strictly chronological in organization. They contain his history of the Crusades, with each chapter advancing through the Middle Ages beginning with the eleventh century in chapter 58 and ending in the midst of the fourteenth in chapter 63. Chapters 64–71 return to the same "groupping by nations" of volume 5, that is, they are for the most part a collection of parallel narratives, not synchronic or static pictures.

In describing his plan, Gibbon announces first the chapter (48) to be devoted to the "revolutions of the [Greek] throne," the "tedious and uniform tale of weakness and misery" that he must include because it is "*passively* connected with the most splendid and important revolutions which have changed the state of the world" (5:182), then the chapters on the state of the empire (53) and the Paulicians (54).

> But these inquiries must be postponed till our further progress shall have opened the view of the world in the ninth and tenth centuries of the Christian æra. After this foundation of Byzantine history, the following nations will pass before our eyes, and each will occupy the space to which it may be entitled by greatness or merit, or the degree of connexion with the Roman world and the present age. I. The FRANKS [49]. . . . II. The ARABS or SARACENS. Three ample chapters [50–52]. . . . A single chapter [55] will include, III. The BULGARIANS, IV. HUNGARIANS, and V. RUSSIANS. . . . VI. The NORMANS [56]. . . . VII. The LATINS. . . . VIII. The GREEKS. . . . IX. The MOGULS and TARTARS [64–65]. . . . X. I have already noticed the first appearance of the TURKS [in vol. 4, chap. 42]; and the names of the fathers, of *Seljuk* [57] and *Othman* [68], discriminate the two successive dynasties. (*DF* chap. 48, 5:183–84)

(Topics 7 and 8 turn out to be Gibbon's history of the Crusades, chapters 58–63.)

The chapter numbers I have supplied in square brackets allow us to see that Gibbon was reasonably clear about his plan for volume 5 (chaps. 48–57) when he wrote this summary. Though the Seljukian Turks surprised him by entering his narrative before the Crusades, and though after his opening survey of the Greeks, he indulges himself and us with accounts of the Franks and Arabs before returning to Constantinople, the content, number, and order of the chapters correspond otherwise to his outline. Volume 6, allowing for the reorganization of topics 7 and 8 into a single subject, the Crusades, is also fairly well projected: after the history of the Crusades, we get topic 9, then the portion of topic 10 not treated at the end of volume 5, and, as planned, the whole history ends with a "return from the captivity of the new, to the ruins of ancient ROME" (chap. 71). Chapters 69 and 70, dealing with early Renaissance Italy, were, I think, a later addition to his plan.

Thus though the order of presentation was subject to revision, the materials and especially their thematic evaluation remain constant, with the one major and several minor exceptions (the ampler treatment of the Arabs, the "digression" on the Courtenay family). Nearly every chapter in these two volumes is designed to throw light on the process of cultural loss and on the vexed questions of its connection to military adventures, to religion, and to personal freedom. The very sweep of each chapter makes the point that individuals, dynasties, and even ideas can appear, flourish, and decay without altering significantly the world in which they briefly seem important. The most striking instance, to Gibbon's contemporaries at least, was Charlemagne, who in Gibbon's treatment is not the herald of a new age, but little more than a footnote to the iconoclastic controversy and the temporal dominion of the popes.[14]

Gibbon is particularly interested in the exceptions to this pattern of historical triviality, of course, and he goes out of his way to consider both ephemeral and permanent effects in Islam. Politically, Islam suffers the same process of expansion and fragmentation as other empires. But the religion of Mahomet, Gibbon believes, is a rare instance in which a pure and rational doctrine has not been corrupted with superstitions—to hammer this home, he selects the Paulicians for one of his religious topics, for he sees them as representing the usual case, in which reformers try to abandon the excrescences of a faith corrupted by superstition (and by temporal power) but wind up fettering human freedom as badly as their opponents. By what is presumably a metaphor, Gibbon treats modern reformers as the "successors" of the Paulicians at the end of chapter 54. He feels very little indebted to the reformers for rationality of doctrine: "The loss of one mystery [transubstantiation] was amply compensated by the stupendous doctrines [such as predestination] . . . enforced [by the reformers] as absolute and essential terms of salvation. . . . many a sober Christian would rather admit that a wafer is God, than that God is a cruel and capricious tyrant" (*DF* chap. 54, 6:131–32). But the reformers did (accidentally) introduce individual freedom of belief, because the grounds on which they intended to claim it exclusively for themselves were equally open to others. Even so, the true protection of liberty of conscience is not Protestantism, but modern custom. Gibbon takes the occasion also to speculate about another problem, that is, whether "sublime simplicity be consistent with popular devotion; whether the vulgar, in the absence of all visible objects, will not be inflamed by enthusiasm, or insensibly subside in languor and indifference." Gibbon suspects the latter to be true; in fact, fanatics of "philosophy" (Gibbon here brings up Priestley) may arise and destroy the useful myths that aid reason in the protection of social order without achieving any compensating gain for truth (*DF* 6:132).

The organization of these volumes facilitates such expansion of time and theme. It also encourages self-referentiality, explicit and implicit. In chapter 51, for example, Gibbon repeats almost the sentiments of his description of the Good Emperors of the third century in his portrayal of the Good Caliphs of the seventh:

> Under [Omar's] *reign and that of his predecessor,* the conquerors of the East were the *trusty servants of God and the people;* the mass of the public treasure was consecrated to the expenses of peace and war; a prudent mixture of justice and bounty maintained the discipline of the Saracens, and they *united by a rare felicity,* the dispatch and execution of despotism with the equal and frugal maxims of a republican government. The heroic courage of Ali, the consummate prudence of Moawiyah, excited the emulation of their subjects. (*DF* chap. 51, 5:426–27; emphasis added—cf. *DF* chap. 3, 1:84–85)

In the next chapter, Gibbon points out the parallelism himself: "So uniform are the mischiefs of military despotism that I seem to repeat the story of the praetorians of Rome" (*DF* chap. 52, 6:51). This self-referentiality extends to metahistorical commentary on his own methods. In describing Pope Leo IV, for example, Gibbon says that "the courage of the first ages of the republic glowed in his breast; and, amidst the ruins of his country, he stood erect, like one of the firm and lofty columns that rear their heads above the fragments of the Roman forum." Such developed similes are rare in Gibbon,[15] and he adds the following note: "Voltaire . . . appears to be remarkably struck with the character of pope Leo IV. I have borrowed his general expression; but the sight of the forum has furnished me with a more distinct and lively image" (*DF* chap. 52, 6:43 and n. 104 [87]).

In the very text, not just the notes, the subordination of history itself to the fortune or power of the historian is taken for granted; William of Hauteville's "intrepid companions discomfited the host of sixty thousand Saracens, and left the Greeks no more than the labour of the pursuit: a splendid victory; but of which the pen of the historian may divide the merit with the lance of the Normans" (*DF* chap. 56, 6:185), and we readers are asked to confront the dubiety of our historical knowledge—"the discomfiture of so many myriads will re-

duce the prudent reader to the alternative of a miracle or a fable" (*DF*
chap. 56, 6:200). More simply, though Gibbon sometimes accidentally or deliberately repeats himself in these thematically determined
surveys (for example, *DF* chap. 55, 6:156, and chap. 56, 206, on the
Varangians), he often directs his reader to prior portions of the history.
Pope Gregory VII is "a second Athanasius," and Gibbon continues,
"May I presume to add that the portrait of Athanasius is one of the
passages of my history (vol. ii, p. 383 *sqq.*) with which I am least
dissatisfied?" (*DF* chap. 56, 6:212, n. 101 [83]). Almost every note in
this section of the history is in dialogue not only with the immediate
text, but a larger context. Each chapter in some ways rewrites its
predecessor (it is absolutely baffling to read this portion of the history
in such editions as the Modern Library, which suppresses Gibbon's
shoulder dates), and both text and notes develop the narrator's simultaneous quest to deny absolute authority to historical rules and even
to historical narratives, and to establish his own authority as a wise,
humane, reliable, balanced human being, one with feelings as well as
thoughts, with an environment of his own, with tastes and limitations.

The pleasures and powers of Lausanne and the history were increased during the two years of the composition of volume 5 by
relative good health (the gout visited Gibbon only briefly) and by
satisfaction that he had escaped the "shipwreck" of English politics.
"A regular alternative of Study and society carries away the hours and
days in a smooth and pleasant Revolution, and I have scarcely com-
menced a month before I am astonished to find myself at the end of
it" (*Letters* 3:17). The account book bears silent witness to a possible
source of domestic disharmony, Gibbon's and Deyverdun's differing
notions of household economy, and its resolution: after the first few
months, Gibbon turned over the housekeeping money to Deyverdun
in advance and if Deyverdun exceeded it, he did so without recourse
to Gibbon's pocketbook.[16]

But the financial news from England was uniformly bad, so bad
that Gibbon had difficulty in persuading himself not merely to answer, but even to open and read, Sheffield's letters. "I have intended
every day to write," he writes in March 1785, "and every day I have
started back with reluctance and disgust from the consideration of the
wretched subject" (*Letters* 3:21). Even more starkly, he had written in
the previous October, "The subject is in itself so painful that I have
postponed it like a child's physic from day to day and losing whole
mornings, as I walked about my library, in useless regret and impotent
resolution. You will be amazed to hear that (after peeping to see that
you were well and returned from Ireland) I have not yet had the
courage to peruse your letter for fear of meeting with some gloomy
intelligence" (*Letters* 3:4–5). Though he could "almost promise to land
in England next September twelfthmonth [September 1786—his es-

timate was almost a year short] with a Manuscript of the current value
of three thousand pounds," meanwhile his situation was difficult. In
this emergency he proposed to sell the balance of his library, on the
basis of "[Henry] Payne's valuation," to his friend and bookseller Peter
Elmsley, "who offers on his own account to change the pounds into
Guineas" (*Letters* 3:24). The catalogue of the books remaining in
England was made by one Woodjer.[17] It reached Gibbon on June 20,
1784, costing him an additional seven livres, ten sous Swiss (that is,
about ten shillings) for carriage.[18] Five boxes of books had already
been sent to him; he proposed to select a few more before selling the
library. Fortunately, he was not after all forced to these extremes
(*Letters* 3:37).

The history did not advance with remarkable rapidity in 1784–85.
Gout took three months, but the avocations of Lausanne took more:
"We are now [January 17, 1786] in the height of our winter amusements, balls, great suppers, comedies &c and except St Stephen's I
certainly lead a more gay and dissipated life here among the Alps . . .
than in the midst of London. Yet my mornings, and sometimes an
afternoon are diligently employed, my work advances: but much remains, indeed much more than I imagined but a great book like a
great house was never finished at the given time" (*Letters* 3:40).
Gibbon continued to feel, as he had reported after his first year at
Lausanne: "An excellent house, a good table a pleasant garden are no
contemptible ingredients in human happiness. The general style of
society hits my fancy; I have cultivated a large and agreable circle of
acquaintance, and am much deceived if I have not laid the foundations
of two or three more intimate and valuable connections" (*Letters* 3:12).
And though both he and Deyverdun had "peculiar fancies and hu-
mours," in any family "every moment . . . has not the sweetness of
the honey moon even between the husbands and wives who have the
truest and most tender regard for each other" (*Letters* 3:12–13), and
though the two bachelors agreed that "an house like ours would be
regulated and graced and enlivened by an agreable female Companion
. . . each of us seems desirous that his friend should sacrifice himself
for the public good" (*Letters* 3:13). Slips of the pen in this passage
may indeed betray some uneasiness about their common imperfec-
tions,[19] but on the whole, Gibbon felt what he tells the reader of his
Memoirs: "My friend [Deyverdun] alone was an inestimable treasure. . . . In Switzerland I enjoyed at every meal, at every hour, the
free and pleasant conversation of the friend of my youth" (177).

In Lausanne, Gibbon's growing library was not only a delight to
him, but itself an attraction for people whom he took pleasure in
meeting, "men of information" of all nations. One such visitor in the
eighties was Ernst Langer, librarian of the duke of Hanover and
travelling companion to a rather dim prince of the house. Langer had

attempted to become acquainted with Gibbon when he visited London, but had discovered to his disappointment that Gibbon was preoccupied with parliamentary matters and refused to speak French with his foreign admirer, presumably because other visitors would have been left out of the conversation. In Lausanne, matters were very different. Gibbon enjoyed the opportunity of showing his library to a scholar who shared his interest not only in its content but in its arrangement. After noting the size and range of the collection, Langer comments:

> That with such good fortune and his fine taste in every thing, the elegance of the bindings, the exteriors of his books, bespoke their value, was to be expected. When, therefore, in spite of a sometimes striking idiosyncrasy, he nevertheless granted me the free use of his treasury of learning, I probably owed it to the circumstance that he had previously assured himself of my own love of order. . . . In a word: I could look on this library as my own, and what was more, was often for weeks at a time in possession of a substantial folio-filling catalog of it prepared with his own hand.[20]

There is some mistake here—the book catalogue of Gibbon's library at Lausanne, now in the Pierpont Morgan Library, has a few holograph corrections and additions, but it was prepared by "Bahler."[21] Nevertheless, it is clear that Gibbon could enjoy not only solitary, but sociable pleasures in his library; Deyverdun was not the only person in Lausanne with whom he could discuss literature, history, "science."

In Lausanne, then, intellectual society came to Gibbon, and if he enjoyed it the more when, or because, it came with flattering deference, such deference came from men of every nation, not just from the Swiss. Even Fox, who made wickedly amusing fun of Gibbon behind his back, devoted a day of his Lausanne visit to a tête-à-tête with the historian, as we shall see in chapter 14.

But was it true, in the eighties, as some reported in the nineties, that Gibbon ruled Lausanne society despotically—"Gibbon is very fond of having a sort of court about him"?[22] He objected from the beginning to certain *forms* of opposition in these discussions, which might give color to the assumption that he preferred to avoid competition. Gibbon complained, for example, of his predecessor in the role of Distinguished Historian In Residence, the abbé Raynal, "His conversation which might be very agreable is intolerably loud, peremptory and insolent and you would imagine that he alone was the Monarch and legislator of the World" (*Letters* 2:373). When Gibbon became the monarch, he devised laws to avoid noise.

According to Langer, Gibbon planned his dinner parties even to the conversation; guests were instructed as to the topic: "Further, at his table there was the great convenience, that one's palate was not gratified at the expense of one's lungs. Only *one* of the guests, selected for the purpose, broke into our host's smooth-flowing stream of knowledge and learning, and instead of *one* anecdote, *one* flash of wit, one had the advantage of taking home ten others still more amusing." Where, one wonders, was Deyverdun? Langer last saw Gibbon before Deyverdun's death. Langer also reports that Gibbon's voice, ordinarily "shrill and singsong, would at the least contradiction swell to such a manly bass as would have filled the House of Commons," but the latter part of this description is not confirmed by any other observer, and since Langer is writing after a gap of several years, perhaps his memory deceived him.[23] Most visitors describe instead an excess of calm—slow, prepared speech and an unchanging expression.[24]

What Gibbon particularly liked was the company of charming, intelligent women, something that he found most, he believed, in the native society of Lausanne. He repeatedly asserts that in France and Switzerland, women are intellectually superior to men, and he soon came to feel that the most agreeable women were, in fact, in Lausanne. Even Geneva could not compare: "I found some agreable women, [but] their manners and style of life are upon the whole less easy and pleasant than our own" (*Letters* 3:252). In Lausanne he and Deyverdun could help a charming society actress complete her novel; he could enjoy the readings and acting of the well-born performers and tolerate their concerts with the help of goûters and cards. He was an integral part of their elaborate literary games. In one of these, a Green Bird was questioned by the other participants in the playlet and replied according to their characters. Gibbon's question was, "What is my country?" The bird replied,

> By your pleasant and polished air,
> One would take you for French;
> Your knowledge, your energy,
> Your writings, your success,
> Your wit, your philosophy,
> The depth of your genius
> Make one suspect an Englishman.
> But your true homeland
> Is that to which your heart has brought you,
> Where you are loved, where one tells you so,
> And you must spend your life there.[25]

Gibbon could not but be pleased. In Lausanne, a stately manner, the polite rituals of stylized social forms, neither denied nor concealed warmth of feeling for the participants in those rituals.

In particular, Gibbon came to enjoy with the Séverys of Lausanne a relationship almost as intimate as that he enjoyed with the Sheffields in England, but a relationship more ritualized, perhaps more equal. This, however, is what Maria Josepha Holroyd, Sheffield's intelligent if impertinent teen-aged daughter, wrote of the Séverys when she met them in 1791: "Madame de Severy is called Mont Blanc, and I cannot give you a better Idea of her. . . . There is a great deal of dignity and frigidity in [that family's] composition, which is much increased by Mr. Gibbon's attentions. He dotes upon them."[26] Their coolness was melted by and for Gibbon.

With the inestimable value of near-familial friendships, Lausanne continued to give Gibbon pleasure with its gentle dissipations— assemblies for cards, conversation, and dancing; invitations for every meal, but especially for late evening suppers; and plays and concerts in a dozen theatres—and its beautiful setting. Despite his well-known "indifference" to landscape (of which he himself was unconscious—he writes without any hint of irony, "The glories of the landskip I have always enjoyed; but Deyverdun has almost given me a taste for min- ute observation, and I can dwell with pleasure on the shape and colour of the leaves, the various hues of the blossoms, and successive prog- ress of vegetation [*Letters* 3:43]), he greatly valued the natural beauty of Lausanne. He remarked, for example, of St. Bernard, who had so weened himself from the visible world that, writing in Lausanne, he was unaware that there was a lake nearby, "To admire or despise St. Bernard as he ought, the reader, like myself, should have before the windows of his library the beauties of that incomparable landscape" (*DF* chap. 59, 6:346, n. 34 [30]).

In Lausanne, then, as long as Deyverdun remained healthy and Gibbon could forget the financial exigencies of England, he could proceed with his history at a steady but unrushed pace, enjoying without abusing his position as historian of the *Decline and Fall*. A contemporary report from a Lausannois qualifies Langer's account and suggests that it was influenced by the darker shades of Gibbon's behavior in the late eighties and nineties. "No one had less the air of announcing his celebrity," wrote the Seigneur de Prangins in his journal of 1784, describing Gibbon at a dinner party in Lausanne. "I do not know why, but without his talking more than anyone else, his opinions always dominated; perhaps it was because he himself didn't at all dominate, so that everyone could believe, if he wished, that he was of the same opinion."[27] In Lausanne Gibbon could be dignified without being thought stilted or pompous, affectionate without being thought sentimental, authoritative without being thought vain or pre- tentious, ugly without being thought repellent. But shortly after he had finished the fifth volume, a letter from England "awakened [him] from this dream of felicity." Announcing the death of his "true mother," Catherine Porten, it brought home to him the obligations of affection, the cowardice of his own procrastination, and the proximity of mortality. It may well have helped to inspire the ensuing period of extraordinary effort and energy (May 18, 1786–June 27, 1787) during which he wrote the remaining fourteen chapters of the *Decline and Fall*.

T W E L V E

Farewell to the History

he death of his aunt Catherine Porten was a loss for which Gibbon found himself unexpectedly unprepared—less of the philosopher than he had thought. Since 1770, he had not suffered the death of a family member; since 1774, he had not lost a close friend. Now, once again, as in his early childhood, he began at the age of forty-nine to experience the mortality of his friends. His first response was to finish the *Decline and Fall*, writing the final volume in about half the time required for previous volumes, fourteen chapters between May 18, 1786, and June 27, 1787. He was back in England by August 7, but he was of course too late to see again Aunt Kitty, his oldest friend. These fourteen months are months of accomplishment, but they begin and end with poignant farewells.

Lord Sheffield's letter to Gibbon announcing Catherine Porten's death is not extant. On the same occasion, this is what he wrote to Dorothea Gibbon:

> Poor Mrs Porten continued to treat this life very properly till within a very few days of her death & then she was perfectly tranquil. She died two days before our return from Sheffield Place, I had seen her just before our journey thither & Lady Sheffield had played cards with her two evenings before—She left 30 £ to her nephew E.G. & 20 £ to each of her other Nephews & Neices, the rest to Sir Stanier. Her will begins with thanks to God for enabling her to make such efforts as entitled her to make a will & after mentioning her Kindred she ends with God bless you all.[1]

Though in this letter to Mrs. Gibbon Lord Sheffield calls Gibbon, who had written him only one letter in the past seven or eight months (and none to the "three old Ladies"), "the Wretch the Historian," he broke the news to the "wretch" as gently as possible, judging from Gibbon's reply. "I certainly am not ignorant that we have nothing better to wish for ourselves than the fate of that best-humoured woman as you very justly style her. A good understanding, and an excellent heart, with health spirits and a competency; to live in the midst of her friends till the age of fourscore and then to shut her eyes without pain or remorse." And Gibbon reminds himself of what she had been spared—suffering, weakness, perhaps loss of mental powers. But though this was all "perfectly true," philosophy, as usual, was unable to prevail over "a thousand sad and tender remembrances." Gibbon's very punctuation and syntax, rushed and incorrect and unstudied, reveal how moved he was:

> To her care I am indebted in earliest infancy for the preservation of my life, and health. I was a puny child neglected by my Mother, starved by my nurse, and of whose being very little care or expectation was entertained; without her maternal vigilance, I should either have been in my grave, or imperfectly lived a crooked ricketty monster a burthen to myself and others. To her instructions I owe . . . a taste for books which is still the pleasure and glory of my life, and though she taught me neither language nor science, she was certainly the most useful praeceptor, I ever had. As I grew up, an intercourse of thirty years endeared her to me as the faithful friend and the agreable companion; you have seen with what freedom and confidence we lived together, and have often admired her character and conversation which could alike please the young and the old. All this is now lost, finally irrecoverably lost! I will agree with Mylady that the immortality of the soul is, on some occasions a very comfortable doctrine.

He is very conscious of his own failure to write to his aunt. "When I reflect that my letters would [have] soothed and comforted her decline, I feel more deeply than I can express the real neglect, and seeming indifference of my silence." His final letter had been sent off only the week before, to "a friend, who, when I wrote was already extinct," though it preceded his knowledge of her death. Gibbon imagines here a reproving comment from Sheffield:

> "But it did not precede (you will observe) the information of her dangerous and declining state which I conveyed in my last letter, and her anxious concern that she should never see or *hear* from you again." This idea, and the hard thoughts which you must entertain of me press so hard on my mind, that I must frankly acknowledge a strange and inexcusable supineness on which I desire you would make no comment. . . . The unpleasant nature of business, and the apprehension of finding something disagree-

able tempted me to postpone from day to day not only the answering but
even the opening your penultimate epistle, and when I received your last,
yesterday morning, the seal of the former was still unbroken. (*Letters*
3:46–47)

It is to Gibbon's credit that he could so fully acknowledge his own
fault, not only to himself but to his friend, and it is characteristic of
the relationship between Sheffield and Gibbon that each expected
the other to tell him frankly of his faults and was pleasant when he
did so.[2] Gibbon's request for an exception in this case—"Oblige me
so far as to make no reflections, my own may be of service to me
hereafter"—proves the existence of the rule, and he seems really to
have repented of this habit of evasive procrastination; at least there
are no further instances recorded in the letters.

This letter contains Gibbon's least studied, but not his only, avowal
of his debt to his aunt. His appraisal of her abilities may represent an
involuntary tribute to her value as his nurse and teacher. After his
death, reading the drafts of his memoirs, young Maria Holroyd remarked that others were not so impressed with his aunt's understanding as he: "Indeed he speaks in a higher style of her improved
understanding than I thought it had deserved."[3] Catherine Porten's
own surviving letters, as well as the details of Gibbon's description
of his childhood, show her to have been a woman of wide-ranging
interests and unflagging good temper. Her final illness cannot have
been lengthy: she died on April 23, and Maria Josepha mentions
attending the theatre with a party that included her on March 1. But
if Gibbon admires his aunt and reproaches himself overzealously in
such a moment, it is what he would call an amiable fault, one rather
too soon overcome: by May 12 he is *repeating* in his letter to his uncle,
Stanier Porten, phrases of grief that he had already used to Lord Sheffield, that is, his behavior is once again controlled and even stylized.

A greater tribute to his aunt, perhaps, is the energy and verve with
which he tells the numerous romantic stories that contribute to the
concluding volume of the *Decline and Fall*. This touch of romance in
his nature, like the taste for theological disputation, was directly
related to his reading and conversation with his aunt in his formative
years. The Arabian Nights tales, Pope's Homer, Ovid's *Metamorphoses*
(in translation), and many another romantic or heroic tale were the
substance of their reading and conversation. "I often disputed with my
aunt on the characters of Hector and Achilles," he tells us, though he
did not share her "enthusiasm for the Characteristics of Shaftsbury"
(*Memoirs* 206–7), and "before the age of sixteen, I was master of all
the *English* materials . . . since employed in the chapters of the
Persians and Arabians, the Tartars and Turks."[4] In the sixth volume

of the *Decline and Fall,* many romantic characters first met in his aunt's company return: Saladin, Richard Coeur de Lion, Tamerlane, Genghis Khan.

Sixty thousand Turks found Richard "carelessly encamped before the gates [of Jaffa] with only seventeen knights and three hundred archers. Without counting their numbers, he sustained their charge; and we learn from the evidence of his enemies, that the king of England, grasping his lance, rode furiously along their front, from the right to the left wing, without meeting an adversary who dared to encounter his career. Am I writing the history of Orlando or Amadis?" (*DF* chap. 59, 6:367). The storybook quality of some of the stories Gibbon has to tell in this portion of this history is a powerful foil to his real theme; here, for example, "*if* heroism be confined to brutal and ferocious valour, Richard Plantagenet will stand high among the heroes of the age" (*DF* 6:365; emphasis added).

The motif of the nature of heroism and its relationship to history is recurrent in Gibbon's last two volumes, though not as an organizing theme.[5] He inspects impartially the heroes of Christian chivalry and the heroes of Islam. More often than not, the term *hero* is used with verbal appropriateness and situational irony: for example, John of Brienne, one of the Latin emperors of Constantinople, had only 160 knights and their associated sergeants and archers to defend the city against an army of 100,000 men and a navy of 300 ships. Says Gibbon, "I tremble to relate that, instead of defending the city, the hero made a sally at the head of his cavalry; and that, of forty-eight squadrons of the enemy, no more than three escaped from the edge of his invincible sword" (*DF* chap. 61, 6:452). This eighty-year-old miracle worker inspired the other Latins so much that they "obtained a second victory against the same enemies." The philosophic historian must be unnerved by the success of such unstatesmanlike heroics, and this account forces the philosophic reader to share his discomfort. But our suspicions of this kind of heroism are renewed by the next sentence: "By the rude poets of the age, John of Brienne is compared to Hector, Roland, and Judas Maccabaeus; but their credit and his glory receives some abatement from the silence of the Greeks." Furthermore, the same zeal that may accomplish prodigies is easily diverted; in the next year, John died, "and the dying monarch was ambitious to enter paradise in the habit of a Franciscan friar" (*DF* 6:453).

Despite instigating such heroic follies, ironically, the institutions of chivalry had some civilizing effects.

> In the accompanying character of Tancred we discover all the virtues of a perfect knight, the true spirit of chivalry, which inspired the generous sentiments and social offices of man far better than the base philosophy, or the baser religion, of the times. . . . The abuse of the same spirit provoked the illiterate knight to disdain the arts of industry and peace; to

esteem himself the sole judge and avenger of his own injuries; and proudly to neglect the laws of civil society and military discipline. Yet the benefits of this institution, to refine the temper of barbarians, and to infuse some principles of faith, justice, and humanity, were strongly felt, and have been often praised. (*DF* chap. 58, 6:292, 294)

On the Islamic side, Saladin was regarded as both hero and saint:

In the judgment of his character, the reproaches of treason and ingratitude strike forcibly on *our* minds, impressed as they are with the principle and experience of law and loyalty. But his ambition may in some measure be excused by the revolutions of Asia . . . by the recent example of the Atabeks themselves; by his reverence to the son of his benefactor; his humane and generous behaviour to the collateral branches; by *their* incapacity and *his* merits; by the approbation of the caliph . . . and, above all, by the wishes and interest of the people, whose happiness is the first object of government. (*DF* chap. 59, 6:355)

Saladin's status as hero, then, is defensible. But in Gibbon's view Saladin's sainthood had only bad effects: "The superstitious doctrine of the sect of Shafei was the only study that he deigned to encourage; the poets were safe in his contempt; but all profane science was the object of his aversion; and a philosopher, who had vented some speculative novelties, was seized and strangled by the command of the royal saint" (*DF* 6:356). Thus Gibbon, who seems slightly out of character here; a truly "impartial observer" might credit Saladin's religious zeal with contributing to at least two of the ways in which his virtues exceeded the merely heroic: first, "it was *only* for a kingdom that Saladin would deviate from the rule of equity" (emphasis added); second, "he may deservedly be praised for the glance of pity which he cast on the misery of the vanquished" (*DF* chap. 59, 6:356, 360).

Still, even at its most brutal and fanatical, Gibbon implies, heroism is at least preferable to cowardice and perhaps to apathy. In successive paragraphs, almost in adjacent sentences, Gibbon glances at the extreme exemplars. On the one hand, "Extreme cold has diminished the stature and congealed the faculties of the Laplanders; and the Arctic tribes, alone among the sons of men, are ignorant of war and unconscious of human blood: an happy ignorance, if reason and virtue were the guardians of their peace!" (*DF* chap. 55, 6:146). This rejection of the Laplanders as symbols of a human ideal superior to that of warfare and physical courage is not just a passing comment; in a note, Gibbon goes out of his way to disagree with two of his heroes, Grotius and Tacitus, who attempt to "varnish with philosophy [the Arctic tribes'] brutal ignorance" (n. 37 [28]). On the other hand, the tenth-century Hungarians and Bulgarians receive a still more scathing condemnation:

> Except the merit and fame of military prowess, all that is valued by
> mankind appeared vile and contemptible to these barbarians, whose native
> fierceness was stimulated by the consciousness of numbers and freedom.
> . . . in speech they were slow, in action prompt, in treaty perfidious. . . .
> Their simplicity has been praised; yet they abstained only from the luxury
> they had never known; whatever they saw, they coveted; their desires
> were insatiate, and their sole industry was the hand of violence and rapine.
> (*DF* 6:146–47)

Clearly Gibbon admired only a rational heroism, the middle path
between brutal valor and stolid or fearful inaction.

Indeed, he seems entirely comfortable with a hero only when that
hero is also a statesman *defending* his country; in the last volume of
the history, Gibbon gives unqualified praise only to the last of the
Constantines, a statesman-hero whose death in a lost cause quiets any
scruples of Gibbon's philosophic conscience, especially after he has
portrayed the conqueror, Mahomet II, as an all-powerful and ruthless
tyrant. We wonder whether, in those long-ago contests with his aunt,
Gibbon took the part of Hector or Achilles—I should guess the
former. He certainly took the part of the last Constantine: though
Constantine's "prudent despair . . . cast[s] away the purple" (*DF* chap.
68, 7:201), though he massacres 260 Turkish captives in what Gibbon
calls a "just though cruel retaliation" (*DF* 7:194) for the Turks' slaugh-
ter of forty Christian prisoners, though in his final despair he cries
out for a Christian to kill him, "the distress and fall of the last
Constantine are more glorious than the long prosperity of the Byzantine Caesars" (*DF* 7:197). Leo Braudy makes the valuable observation
that in the *Decline and Fall*, "the new epic hero is the human consciousness that can organize and control the disparate and often chaotic elements that form the onrushing flow of time."[6] But it is important to note that Gibbon portrays that contemplative hero, exemplified,
of course, in the person of the true historian, not in triumphant
isolation, but in counterpoint to heroes and antiheroes of action.

Prominent in the last two volumes is the role of the historian in
creating history; throughout the final portions of his work, Gibbon
uses metaphors that attribute not merely the account or perception of
events to the writer who portrays them, but the events themselves.
"The remaining fragments of the Greek kingdom in Europe and Asia
I shall abandon to the Turkish arms," says the historian of the Roman
Empire (*DF* chap. 68, 7:212). The historian's power (and his use of it)
is here exactly similar to that of the indifferent Christian nations of
Europe, who refused to aid Constantine against the Turks. But the
historian's power is still greater. If he refuses to surpass the limits of
nature, that is a *choice:* "In the uniform and odious pictures of a general
assault, all is blood, and horror, and confusion; nor shall I strive, at
the distance of three centuries and a thousand miles, to delineate a

scene of which there could be no spectators, and of which the actors themselves were incapable of forming any just or adequate idea" (*DF* chap. 68, 7:199). A recurrent joke makes a serious point about the historian's power of life and death: for example, Lupus Protospata and William the Apulian reckon 5,000–6,000 slain in a battle; "Their modesty is singular and laudable: they might with so little trouble have slain two or three myriads of schismatics and heretics!" (*DF* 6:209 n. 94 [76]).

Moreover, Gibbon more and more openly involves himself, in the text as in the notes, with the events he portrays. "I tremble" is only a mild example. "I shall not, I trust, be accused of superstition," he says on another occasion, "but I must remark that, even in this world, the natural order of events will sometimes afford the strong appearances of moral retribution" (*DF* chap. 62, 6:500). The historian goes further, however, when he invokes a first-person plural that involves not only the narrator, but also the reader, in the text.[7] A clear and extended example occurs in chapter 66.

Noting that the Greek and Latin representatives at the Council of Ferrara and Florence had differed on whether the eucharistic wafers had to be unleavened, Gibbon remarks, "We may bestow some praise on the progress of human reason by observing that the . . . question was *now* treated as an immaterial rite, which might innocently vary with the fashion of the age and country" (*DF* chap. 66, 7:114). Except for the assumption that the reader is sufficiently philosophic to rejoice at this tolerance, this passage seems to employ a conventional rhetorical "we," meaning "I." But in volume 6, "we" has become a rare pronoun in the *Decline and Fall,* and three pages later, the role of the reader in the text is further stressed. When Gibbon explains the (to him obviously trivial) difference between Greek and Latin views on the procession of the Holy Spirit, he warns, "I must intreat the attention of the reader (*DF* 7:117). Without the closest concentration, he implies, the reader will be unable to perceive the microscopic distinction. On the next page, he announces that his account of the reception of the Greek negotiators in Constantinople will be delayed until the next chapter. And finally, in the next chapter, clearly already planned as he wrote the passages I have quoted, he informs us that in Constantinople the negotiators repented and recanted their recent steps towards toleration: "and I must retract or qualify the praise which I have bestowed on the growing philosophy of the time" (*DF* chap. 67, 7:142). Gibbon has deliberately forced the reader to experience the series of feelings that a fifteenth-century "philosophic observer" would have suffered: elation at a victory of reason, suspicion about the continued obsession with petty differences, suspense about the reception of the relatively reasonable delegates, disappointment and disgust at their reversion to irrationality.

This example illustrates how conscious Gibbon was, as he wrote the Lausanne volumes, that his decisions about the ordering and emphasis of his materials were instances and proof of the great power of the historian over the past. Of course this is true even when the historian follows the apparently natural order of time, but it is dramatically obvious when even chronology is subject to the will and judgment of the historian. In giving form to his matter, in manipulating how, when, and where a reader encounters the past, the historian in some sense determines its very existence. In these last volumes, Gibbon's competition for this power seems to come less from intractable facts or abstract "laws" of human nature and societies than from other historians; he seems very much aware that he is taking part in a dialogue with his predecessors and contemporaries.

Most striking is his continuing debate with Voltaire, which seems to deal with nothing less than the nature of historical proof. The confrontations usually occur in the notes—for example, Gibbon's notorious comment on Voltaire's bigotry (*DF* chap. 67, 7:146 n. 15 [13])—but they affect the text as well. In describing the huge cannon built for Mahomet II, Gibbon notes that Voltaire dismisses the account of it with contempt, on the apparently scientific grounds that so large a cannon could not utilize gunpowder with sufficient efficiency to project its ball.[8] The "lively philosopher derides, on this occasion, the credulity of the Greeks, and observes, with much reason, that we should always distrust the exaggerations of a vanguished people," says Gibbon. But he continues:

> A stranger as I am to the act of destruction, I can discern that the modern improvements of artillery prefer the number of pieces to the weight of metal. . . . Yet I dare not reject the positive and unanimous evidence of contemporary writers. . . . A Turkish cannon, more enormous than that of Mahomet, still guards the entrance of the Dardanelles; and, if the use be inconvenient, it has been found on a late trial that the effect was far from contemptible. (*DF* chap. 68, 7:177–78)

Both Gibbon and Voltaire make the historian's mind the measure of history; both utilize arguments from human and physical sciences to supply and evaluate data. But in Gibbon's view, Voltaire approaches history with a kind of prejudice against its peculiar materials, the odd, a-rational, unique, and therefore unpredictable occurrences that mark the influence of chance and human choice in human affairs. Such materials cannot be inferred from systematic social laws, but they are what distinguishes history from the other social sciences.

The historiographical debate in these volumes also includes potential readers. Often Gibbon seems conscious that others may think he had digressed from his subject; he anticipates their objections and defends his decision with first-person statements in his text, as well as the notes (for instance, at the beginning of chapter 64, on Zingis Khan and the Moguls, "I have long since *asserted my claim* to introduce the nations, the immediate or remote authors of the fall of the Roman empire; *nor can I refuse myself* to those events which, from their uncommon magnitude, will interest a philosophic mind in the history of blood" [*DF* chap. 64, 7:1; emphasis added]).[9] These statements, as my example illustrates, go far beyond indicating an unnoticed connection with the Roman Empire; they amount to a claim of formal autonomy for the historian, not just as a writer, but as a determiner of the past.

At the same time, the historian seems to have acquired an obligation to share with his readers the critical process by which he makes historical decisions. An extended example is the question of the truth about the celebrated iron cage in which Timour (Tamerlane) was said to have imprisoned the Ottoman sultan Bajazet. On the one hand, the Persian annals recount Timour's gracious treatment of his illustrious prisoner, and Gibbon, having narrated the dramatic scene as those annals present it, comments, "Such is the portrait of a generous conqueror . . . nineteen years after his decease; and a time when the truth was remembered by thousands, a manifest falsehood would have implied a satire on his real conduct. Weighty, indeed, is this evidence" (*DF* chap. 65, 7:65).[10] But though Gibbon sees the testimony of the annals as weighty, there is another side, and he gives it equal space in his text, not as a narrative but as an analysis (7:65–67). The contrary evidence is equally ancient, equally clear evidence of public opinion, and has one powerful feature that is unique: independent sources separately report the "iron cage" (Bury explains that the true explanation of this independent testimony is probably linguistic misunderstanding: Bajazet was placed in a barred litter, like those used for members of the harem [*DF* 7:63 n. 53]). Gibbon concludes that the various accounts can be reconciled if we assume that a first relatively generous interview was followed by disaffection, perhaps an escape attempt; "an iron cage on a waggon might be invented not as a wanton insult, but as a rigorous precaution" (*DF* 7:67). The modern reader will notice that Gibbon has in fact arrived at a conclusion very similar to Bury's: the iron cage has a basis in fact, but has been misinterpreted as a unique and ingenious torture. Yet Gibbon has done so not by knowing *all* the evidence, or using the tools of linguistic analysis, but by a combination of forensic and literary methods, by judging the reliability of the witnesses and then uniting the most probable data in a self-consistent plot. This method, often characterized (and perhaps envied) by subsequent historians as (merely) intuitive, is frequently to be observed in the *Decline and Fall* and is as deliberately utilized as any other means of scrutinizing and evaluating texts and data.

As Gibbon anticipated, many readers were puzzled or offended by his decisions about order and content in this volume (as in earlier ones).[11] Yet, as we have seen, his relationship with his readers is not tyrannical; on the contrary, in this volume, more perhaps than ever before, he invites the reader to evaluate, contemplate, marvel, smile or sigh, in response to rival possibilities or interpretations. "Read, if you can, the life and miracles of St. Louis, by the confessor of Queen Margaret" (DF chap. 59, 6:374 n. 104 [92]), he tells us, for example. And a few pages earlier, he says that *he* "cannot believe" an accusation that in the notes is said to be believed by the Moslems, disinterested witnesses in this instance (DF chap. 59, 6:365, with n. 82 [74]). What readers believe is clearly their own responsibility.[12]

The German classicist Jacob Bernays recognized early how, in later volumes of the history, Gibbon's dialogue with his predecessors and intimacy with his readers increase. Bernays comments, "Many notes, especially in the second triad of volumes, characterize sources. . . . Gibbon appears in person in the notes of his work, but only in the three last volumes, after he was certain of the immortality of his work. The most characteristic example is note 50 to chapter 52, about the number of his happy hours."[13] In this note, Gibbon responds to the mournful comment of the caliph Abdalrahman, "whose magnificence has perhaps excited our admiration and envy," but who says he has enjoyed only fourteen happy hours in his life. "If I may speak of myself (the only person of whom I can speak with certainty)," Gibbon says, "*my* happy hours have far exceeded, and far exceed, the scanty numbers of the caliph of Spain, and I shall not scruple to add that many of them are due to the pleasing labour of the present composition" (DF chap. 52, 6:27 n. 60 [50]). Even more strikingly he lets his readers into his workshop, so to speak, in a note to his description of Mahomet II's naval assault on Constantinople: "I must *confess* [emphasis added] that I have before my eyes the living picture which Thucydides (l. vii. c. 71) has drawn of the passions and gestures of the Athenians in a naval engagement in the great harbour of Syracuse" (DF chap. 68, 7:190 n. 58 [45]). He has acknowledged deliberate echoes of classical models before, but he has not recognized such imitations as part of his personal historical method, as something "I" must "confess." The final and perhaps the most famous instance of his intimacy with his readers is of course the conclusion of the history, to which I shall return.

It seems probable that this combination of personal presentation and openness to dialogue is in part the result of Gibbon's way of life in Lausanne. It is in the Lausanne volumes that he apparently seizes an opportunity to insert a self-portrait, comparable to the portrait of Suzanne Curchod that was the subtext of his portrayal of Athenaïs in volume 2 (see p. 169 above).[14] The scholar Barlaam was "a man of diminutive stature, though truly great in the measure of learning and genius; of a piercing discernment, though of a slow and painful elocution. For many ages (as they affirm) Greece has not produced his equal in the knowledge of history, grammar, and philosophy" (*DF* chap. 66, 7:124). Contrary to earlier belief, including my own, Gibbon was probably about five feet tall, short, but for the age not extraordinarily short—one witness even describes his as of "middle" stature.[15] But in numerous circumstances he had experienced himself as short: he was still short at sixteen, after his years at Oxford; he may well have been shorter than his only love, Suzanne Curchod; he was undoubtedly the shortest member of the Hampshire Grenadiers; and he was conspicuously shorter than his friend Sheffield.[16] And the rest of the description of Barlaam, especially the speech and "piercing" look, fits well enough. Therefore the traditional identification of this description as a self-portrait may be retained. At least for those who had met him, then, this represents yet another way for the historian to enter his text.

Early in the Lausanne volumes, Gibbon comments sententiously, "Conversation enriches the understanding, but solitude is the school of genius; and the uniformity of a work denotes the hand of a solitary artist" (*DF* chap. 50, 5:359–60). As we have seen, Deyverdun provided the conversation and protected the solitude. More significantly, there are at least two explicit pieces of evidence in the *Decline and Fall* that domestic discussions with Deyverdun affected the last two volumes of the history. A note to chapter 57 gives us a picture of a temporary return to the methods of Gibbon's Swiss history, with its German sources;[17] Gibbon cites Marei, "an historian of Egypt, translated by Reiske from Arabic into German, and verbally interpreted to me by a friend" (*DF* 6:264 n. 74 [67]). Deyverdun, a good Germanist, was undoubtedly the friend in question. And it is highly probable that he was also the "ingenious friend" cited in chapter 62, n. 23 [17]. The identity of that friend is relatively unimportant, however; what counts is that Gibbon includes, in the history itself, playful opposition to his own position. This inclusion is evidence that Gibbon was not an intellectual tyrant either in person or in his role as historian.[18]

Openness to doubt and dialogue also seems to reflect a growing and perhaps anomalous discomfort with the ideal of the "eloquent" historian. Of course Gibbon had long dismissed the *merely* eloquent, like mere chronicle, as inadequate to history.[19] If chronicles (and antiquarian treatises that similarly provided only data) could serve the true historian as his raw material, nevertheless they remained "learned rubbish" until transformed by a more skillful writer and thinker into some "elegant piece of history and Philosophy."[20]

We might conclude that, in Gibbon's view, historians of their own times should be chroniclers, while later historians could add the phi-

losophy and eloquence. But that formulation is much too simple. In
writing about a fourteenth-century Hungarian war, Gibbon cites
"Bonfinius, an Italian, who, in the xvth century, was invited into
Hungary to compose an eloquent history of that kingdom." Elsewhere
Gibbon mentions this Bonfinius as one who, "in his division and style,
copies Livy with tolerable success" (*DF* chap. 67, 7:150 n. 26 [23]).
But here Gibbon continues, "Yet, if it be extant and accessible I
should give the preference to some homely chronicle of the time and
country" (*DF* chap. 64, 7:37 n. 92 [60]), thus rejecting the later
addition of "eloquence." In the next note, moreover, he gives the
preference to a lively eyewitness over a dry one: "I should not complain of the labour of this work, if my materials were always derived
from such books as the Chronicle of honest Froissard . . . who read
little, inquired much, and believed all. The original Mémoires of the
Maréchal de Boucicault . . . add some facts, but they are dry and
deficient, if compared with the pleasant garrulity of Froissard." Still
more strikingly, Gibbon praises Sylvester Syropulus, one of the atten-
dants of the Patriarch Joseph at the council of Florence, for his "free
and curious history": "Syropulus may be ranked with the best of
Byzantine writers for the merit of his narration, and even of his style.
. . . the historian has the uncommon talent of placing each scene
before the reader's eye" (*DF* chap. 66, 7:109, with nn. 53, 55 [51,
53]).[21]

Gibbon seems to criticize a Syrian life of Timour "much esteemed
for its florid elegance of style. . . ; this Syrian author is ever a malicious and often an ignorant enemy; the very titles of his chapters are
injurious; as how the wicked, as how the impious, as how the viper,
&c" (*DF* chap. 65, 7:45 n. 5). If that is so, why does Gibbon cite
him? In part because he is, as usual, concerned to obtain witnesses
from both sides of a controversial situation; even prejudiced witnesses
can be useful to the historian:[22] "Timour must have been odious to a
Syrian; but the notoriety of the facts would have obliged him, in some
measure, to respect his enemy and himself." But that is not the only
reason: another value is stylistic and tonal—Gibbon uses a metaphor
of flavor: "His bitters may correct the luscious sweets of Sherefeddin"
(*DF* chap. 65, 7:57 n. 40 [33]).

Yet it is not just prejudice, but elegance itself, or at least the
misguided attempt to be elegant, that can limit the value of a historical witness. "I could wish for some simple authentic memoirs of a
friend of [the Albanian hero] Scanderbeg, which would introduce me
to the man, the time, and the place. In the old and national history of
Marinus Barletius . . . his gaudy and cumbersome robes are stuck
with many false jewels" (*DF* chap. 67, 7:156 n. 40 [36]). The situation
is neatly summed up in one of Gibbon's final chapters, treating the
careers of Petrarch and Rienzi. "The Mémoires sur la Vie de François

Pétrarque (Amsterdam, 1764, 1767, 3 vols. in 4to) form a copious, original and entertaining work, a labor of love, composed from the accurate study of Petrarch and his contemporaries; but the hero is too often lost in the general history of the age, and the author (the abbé de Sade] too often languishes in the affectation of politeness and gallantry" (*DF* chap. 70, 7:265 n. 1). This is at best tepid praise for an authoritative and "entertaining" work.

Gibbon's enthusiasm is reserved for another source; "a particular and authentic life of Cola (Nicholas) di Rienzi . . . printed . . . under the name of Tomaso Fortifiocca. . . . Human nature is scarcely capable of such sublime or stupid impartiality; but whosoever is the author of these Fragments, he wrote on the spot and at the time, and paints, without design or art, the manners of Rome and the character of the tribune" (*DF* 7:269 n. 20). Gibbon adopts the testimony of this anonymous and guileless witness in his text: "A simple citizen describes with pity, or perhaps with pleasure, the humiliation of the barons of Rome. 'Bare-headed, their hands crossed on their breast, they stood with downcast looks in the presence of the tribune; and they trembled, good God, how they trembled!'" (*DF* 7:282, with n. 47 [41]). In his note, Gibbon quotes the original Italian (something by no means inevitable when he quotes in translation) and comments on the anonymous author's naive mimetic skill: "He saw them, and we see them." It is the highest of praise.[23]

Gibbon pays particular attention to certain historians who were actors in the events they portray, a great advantage, he had long believed, "for historians of their own times." In his "Hints" in the mid sixties, he had instanced Thucydides and Francesco Guicciardini:

> Both acquainted with business of peace and war—Their characters procured them every information—had studied the greatest men of their times—better acquainted with them all, than each of them was with the others—Personal knowledge of great men, the chief advantage of their personal Memoirs—Disappointed in those of Caesar—we perceive the Scholar and the Soldier, we lose the man—except in the simplicity with which he relates his greatest actions—the Memoirs of Xenophon much more characteristic.[24]

Two such "noble" historians, Jeffrey of Villehardouin, marshal of Champagne and historian of the crusades, and John VI Cantacuzene, Byzantine emperor (1341–55) and historian of the period 1320–60, are significant in the final volume of the *Decline and Fall*. Of these, the former (who may have been illiterate, simply dictating his history) is much preferred by Gibbon.

Villehardouin's "feelings and expressions are original; he often weeps, but he rejoices in the glories and perils of war with a spirit unknown to a sedentary writer" (*DF* chap. 60, 6:406 n. 68 [55]), says Gibbon, and he pays Villehardouin the honor of adapting his language in the text of the *Decline and Fall* without quotation marks—as a fellow historian, not a naive witness:

> The swelling domes and lofty spires of five hundred palaces and churches were gilded by the sun and reflected in the waters; the walls were crowded with soldiers and spectators, whose numbers they beheld, of whose temper they were ignorant; and each heart was chilled by the reflection that, since the beginning of the world, such an enterprise had never been undertaken by such an handful of warriors. But the momentary apprehension was dispelled by hope and valour; and every man, says the marshal of Champagne, glanced his eye on the sword or lance which he must speedily use in the glorious conflict. (*DF* 6:407–8)

The emperor, on the other hand, is one of three prolix witnesses to his own "languid" times. Gibbon's disgust or fatigue is obvious:

> I reduce into some few pages the enormous folios of Pachymer, Cantacuzene, and Nicephorus Gregoras, who have composed the prolix and languid story of the times. The name and situation of the emperor John Cantacuzene might inspire the most lively curiosity . . . and it is observed that, like Moses and Caesar, he was the principal actor in the scenes which he describes. But in this eloquent work we should vainly seek the sincerity of an hero or a penitent. . . . Instead of unfolding the true counsels and characters of men, he displays the smooth and specious surface of events, highly varnished with his own praises and those of his friends. (*DF* chap. 63, 6:511)

The historian, then, whatever his opportunities (or rank), is no historian unless he can see, show us what was seen, penetrate beneath those surfaces, and answer to the demands of truth.

As an aspirant to the status of historian, not mere witness or rhetor, Gibbon must work out how to give a text he creates by means of such penetration an authority derived in part from materials he has not invented. Lionel Gossman has valuably discussed the nature of the authority Gibbon came to attribute to the historical text, but unaccountably fails to allow for the *history* of Gibbon's practice and opinions, their development over twenty-odd years of experience as a writer of history.[25] Leo Braudy's pioneering study proposes just such a development, but in two essays on the *Decline and Fall* Braudy has time only to suggest, not to pursue, the distinctions that occur, and he has not apparently observed Gibbon's increasing doubts about literary history itself (at least when not in the hands of a Gibbon or a Tacitus).[26] Gibbon discovers these difficulties (and announces the superior value of the naive chronicles) in his most flagrantly artifical and eloquent volumes. We may simply accuse him of inconsistency, perhaps of unwillingness to share the glory of literary conquest of the past. But there is also evidence even in these volumes that he is instead further developing, by precept and example, his conception of history as a genre.

Gibbon no longer is confident that the historian is distinguished from the rhetor by his transparent factuality, his mimetic fidelity to prior material; or even from the naive chronicler by the imaginative qualities of his work. Therefore, to surpass his sources, the historian must not only select and embellish, but, through his invention of the connecting tissues between facts and sources, discover. A historian operates under severe constraints, about which Gibbon is extraordinarily frank in these volumes. He shares his encounter with obstacles ranging from his own ignorance, inability to understand, or lack of books, to recognition of what we might call the historian's condition: "In the fall and the sack of great cities, an historian is *condemned to repeat* [emphasis added] the tale of uniform calamity; the same effects must be produced by the same passions; and, when those passions may be indulged without control, small, alas! is the difference between civilised and savage man" (*DF* chap. 68, 7:205). The acknowledgement and discussion of those difficulties is certainly part of the solution to them. "The epistemological doublet . . . 'real or imaginary' is an integral part of Gibbon's developing style and an index to the nature of his relative and pluralistic vision. . . . Gibbon does not wish to exhaust a world with his polarities. Instead he wishes to convey a sense of the multiplicity of causes that surround any event, some of which at least may be discerned and crudely ranked, without any final judgment."[27] Other solutions involve the choice between narrative and analysis, the interplay between text and notes, transformations of plot (that is, of purposive, emotional, or teleological ordering and linking of events) and manipulations of time. One major example may suffice here.

Gibbon's most flagrant exercise of power in the final volume of the *Decline and Fall*—perhaps in the whole history—is his concluding not with the fall of the last bastion and emperor of the Empire, but with the history of the city of Rome in the Middle Ages (chaps. 69–71). Though these chapters themselves are admirable, and have been duly admired, this ending has been stigmatized as contrived and irrelevant, a merely literary solution to the problem of formal unity.[28] Yet in another sense this decision was the most constrained of the whole history. It was for this that the history was written, according to the autobiography and the concluding coda within the *Decline and Fall* itself: "It was among the ruins of the Capitol that I first conceived the idea of a work which has amused and exercised near twenty years of my life," Gibbon says in the final sentence of the history, and he explains in the *Memoirs* that his "original plan was circumscribed to the decay of the City rather than of the Empire."[29]

His fixed intention to return to the ruins of the city was announced
in his preface (*DF* 1:xi) and is prefigured in chapter 36, near the end
of the first half of the history, in which he comments as follows:

> The [modern] spectator, who casts a mournful view over the ruins of
> ancient Rome, is tempted to accuse the memory of the Goths and Vandals,
> for the mischief which they had neither leisure, nor power, nor perhaps
> inclination, to perpetrate. . . . the destruction which undermined the
> foundations of those massy fabrics was prosecuted, slowly and silently,
> during a period of ten centuries. . . . The decay of the city had gradually
> impaired the value of the public works. . . . The diminished crowds of
> the Romans were lost in the immense space. . . . The degenerate Ro-
> mans, who converted the spoil [materials from the ancient buildings] to
> their own emolument, demolished with sacrilegious hands the labours of
> their ancestors. (*DF* 4:21)

Marjorian, about whose reign (A.D. 457–61) Gibbon was writing in
this passage, attempted to put a stop to these depredations. Gibbon
provides a note to Marjorian's edict, and adds, "With equal zeal, but
with less power, Petrarch, in the fourteenth century, repeated the
same complaints. . . . If I prosecute this History, I shall not be
unmindful of the decline and fall of the *city* of Rome; an interesting
object, to which my plan was originally confined" (n. 52 [43]).

At the beginning of the fifth volume, Gibbon repeats his plan, to
"return from the captivity of the new, to the ruins of ancient ROME;
and the venerable name, the interesting theme, will shed a ray of
glory on the conclusion of my labours" (*DF* chap. 48, 5:185). In the
next chapter (49), he takes a passing look at eighth-century Rome.
The principal magistrates are the popes, whose "noblest title is the
free choice of a people whom they had redeemed from slavery" (*DF*
5:282): "The liberty of Rome, which had been oppressed by the arms
and arts of Augustus, was rescued, after seven hundred and fifty years
of servitude, from the persecution of Leo the Isaurian" (*DF* 5:280).
But

> the ruins of Rome presented the sad image of depopulation and decay;
> her slavery was an habit, her liberty an accident: the effect of superstition,
> and the object of her own amazement and terror. The last vestige of the
> substance, or even the forms, of the constitution was obliterated from the
> practice and memory of the Romans; and they were devoid of knowledge,
> or virtue, again to build the fabric of a commonwealth. (*DF* 5:281)

The ruins here are as much metaphorical as physical, but they are
quite apparent.

Peoples who have left such ruins, Gibbon implies, are the proper
subjects of history.

> If, in the account of this interesting people [the Saracens], I have deviated
> from the strict and original line of my undertaking, the merit of the

subject will hide my transgression or solicit my excuse. In the East, in the West, in war, in religion, in science, in their prosperity, and in their decay, the Arabians press themselves on our curiosity. . . . But the same labour would be unworthily bestowed on the swarms of savages . . . the greater part of these barbarians has disappeared without leaving any memorial of their existence. (*DF* chap. 55, 6:135–36)

A culture that leaves no ruins is excluded from history, has no history. "A fragment, a ruin, howsoever mangled or profaned, may be viewed with pleasure and regret" (*DF* chap. 71, 7:325). When Michael Palaeologus expelled the Latins from Constantinople and returned to the city, "he sighed at the dreary prospect of solitude and ruin. . . . The industry of the Latins had been confined to the work of pillage and distruction" (*DF* chap. 62, 6:486). Still, he could repeople the city and rebuild. Other places were less fortunate:

In the loss of Ephaesus, the Christians deplored the fall of the first angel, the extinction of the first candlestick of the Revelations; the desolution is complete; and the temple of Diana or the church of Mary will equally elude the search of the curious traveller. The circus and three stately theatres of Laodicea are now peopled with wolves and foxes; Sardes is reduced to a miserable village; the God of Mahomet, without a rival or a son, is invoked in the mosques of Thyatira and Pergamus; and the populousness of Smyrna is supported by the foreign trade of the Franks and Armenians. Philadelphia alone has been saved by prophecy or courage. . . . a column in a scene of ruins. (*DF* chap 64, 7:28)

Ruins not only identify, but in a sense restore, the civilization for which they stand, as Gibbon points out in his penultimate chapter on the Greek empire:

The respective merits of Rome and Constantinople are compared and celebrated by an eloquent Greek, the father of the Italian schools. The view of the ancient capital, the seat of his ancestors, surpassed the most sanguine expectations of Emanuel Chrysoloras; and he no longer blamed the exclamation of an old sophist, that Rome was the habitation, not of men, but of gods. Those gods and those men had long since vanished; but, to the eye of liberal enthusiasm, the majesty of ruin restored the image of her ancient prosperity. (*DF* chap. 67, 7:138)

Why did the *expiration* of the Roman Empire, its reduction to ruins, deserve twenty years of Gibbon's life and, in his view, permanent attention from the inhabitants of the world? Because, I have argued elsewhere,[30] its ruins, the fragments of its monuments and institutions, were still functioning in eighteenth-century European culture. Christopher Dawson (1934) saw as one of the unique values of the *Decline and Fall* Gibbon's consciousness of the connection between the ancient and modern worlds. That connection depended, at least in Gibbon's own mind, on the existence and imaginative power of the ruins of the realm, idea, and city of Rome.

Everyone knows the famous account of Gibbon's completion of the *Decline and Fall*, but it nevertheless bears repeating:

> It was on the day or rather the night of the 27th of June 1787, between the hours of eleven and twelve that I wrote the last lines of the last page in a summerhouse in my garden. After laying down my pen, I took several turns in a *berceau* or covered walk of Acacias which commands a prospect of the country the lake and the mountains. The air was temperate, the sky was serene; the silver orb of the moon was reflected from the waters, and all Nature was silent. I will not dissemble the first emotions of joy on the recovery of my freedom and perhaps the establishment of my fame. But my pride was soon humbled, and a sober melancholy was spread over my mind by the idea that I had taken my everlasting leave of an old and agreable companion, and that, whatsoever might be the future date of my history, the life of the historian must be short and precarious. (*Memoirs* 180)

This moving scene so caught the imagination of visitors to Lausanne in the nineteenth century that the summerhouse soon disappeared in the hands of souvenir-takers; Byron contented himself with an acacia leaf (Shelley did not care for one).[31] In Hardy's poem, "Lausanne in Gibbon's Old Garden: 11–12 P.M.," subtitled "27 June 1897 (The 110th Anniversary of the Completion of the 'Decline and Fall' at the same hour and place)," imagination must supply the spirit, "Formal in pose, but grave withal and grand: / He contemplates a volume in his hand, / And far lamps fleck him through the thin acacias."[32]

Gibbon portrays this scene of "final deliverance" explicitly as a pendant to the much-discussed "moment of conception" scene, in Rome, on the ruins of the Capitol, in 1764. Unlike that scene, the historicity of this account of completion has never been challenged. He mentions it not only in the autobiography and the history, but in his private memorandum about the dates of composition of the last three volumes.[33] It is therefore surprising to read in a letter to Lord Sheffield of June 2, 1787, the following: "My great building is, as it were, compleated, and some slight ornaments, the painting, and glazing of the last finished rooms may be dispatched without inconvenience in the autumnal residence of Sheffield place" (*Letters* 3:64). The solemn scene of deliverance, so late at night (Gibbon only reluctantly extended his literary labors past the dinner hour, 2 P.M. in Lausanne), dated three weeks later than this remark to Sheffield, suggests either that one account or the other is false, or that though Gibbon thought he had completed the history on June 2, it then took a form substantially shorter than its present version. I think the latter hypothesis is the true one, and I think also that we can identify approximately what the additions made in June were.

Chapter 68 concludes with the death in 1481 of the conqueror of
Constantinople, Mahomet II: "His lofty genius aspired to the conquest of Italy: he was possessed of a strong city and a capacious
harbour; and the same reign might have been decorated with the
trophies of the NEW and the ANCIENT ROME" (*DF* 7:217). Chapter 71,
the chapter in which Gibbon actually fulfills his frequent promises to
return to the decline and fall of the *city* in the conclusion of his
history, begins thus:

> In the last days of Pope Eugenius the Fourth [1430], two of his
> servants, the learned Poggius and a friend, ascended the Capitoline Hill;
> reposed themselves among the ruins of the columns and temples; and
> viewed from that commanding spot, the wide and various prospect of
> desolation. The place and the object gave ample scope for moralising on
> the vicissitudes of fortune, which spares neither man nor the proudest of
> his works, which buries empires and cities in a common grave; and it was
> agreed that in proportion to her former greatness the fall of Rome was the
> more awful and deplorable. (*DF* 7:313)

Poggius and Gibbon then go on to invoke Virgil's imaginative evoca-
tion of the primeval state of the place where Poggius was sitting. In
the text, Gibbon translates Poggius; in the note, he gives the reference to the *Aeneid* and comments, "This ancient picture, so artfully
introduced and so exquisitely finished, must have been highly interesting to an inhabitant of Rome; and our early studies allow us to
sympathize in the feelings of a Roman" (7:313 n. 3). I believe that
Gibbon's initial impulse was to juxtapose the three scenes: the fall of
Constantinople, the early state of Rome imaginatively created and
preserved by Virgil, and the fallen state of the city.[34]

Chapter 71 is quite independent of its two predecessors, which
deal principally with the heroic, but unavailing, premature efforts of
Petrarch and Rienzi (in their respective domains) to restore the days
of Roman greatness and with the contemporary struggles among the
nobles and between the adherents of the pope and the German
emperor for power in the city. In this final chapter, there are a few
references back to chapters 69 and 70, but because they take the form
of *acknowledging* (rather than avoiding) self-repetition, they are almost
evidence that chapters 69 and 70 did not exist when chapter 71 was
written. For example:

> In a dark period of five hundred years, Rome was perpetually afflicted by
> the sanguinary quarrels of the nobles and the people, the Guelphs and
> Ghibelines, the Colonna and Ursini; and, if much has escaped the knowl-
> edge, and much is unworthy of the notice, of history, I have exposed in
> the two preceding chapters the causes and effects of the public disorders.
> As such a time, when every quarrel was decided by the sword. . . . (*DF*
> 7:326)

The reader of chapters 69 and 70 is already vividly aware that Rome had been afflicted by these quarrels. It is clear that the clause after "Ursini" could have been added later to avoid extensive revision of what had become repetitive. Similarly, on the next page, "The first step of the senator Brancaleone in the establishment of peace and justice was to demolish (*as we have already seen*) one hundred and forty of the towers of Rome" (emphasis added).

Moreover, chapter 71 itself concludes twice, the second time with the famous sentence commemorating the conception of the history and with the date June 27, and the first time, in the immediately preceding paragraph, as follows:

> But the clouds of barbarism were gradually dispelled; and the peaceful authority of Martin the Fifth and his successors restored the ornaments of the city as well as the order of the ecclesiastical state. . . . The map, the description, the monuments of ancient Rome have been elucidated by the diligence of the antiquarian and the student; and the footsteps of heroes, the relics, not of superstition, but of empire, are devoutly visited by a new race of pilgrims from the remote, and once savage, countries of the North. (*DF* 7:336–38)

It seems to me likely that on June 2, when he wrote to Sheffield, Gibbon had already written a version of chapter 71, ending with this sentence, which is most neatly parallel to the last sentence of his very first chapter. He believed that he had completed the *Decline and Fall*, for he had fulfilled all his promises, including the promise to himself to return to the ruins of the city.

Then, even as he began his preparations for travel to London, he realized that an account of the conflicts in church and state of twelfth- and thirteenth-century Italy would permit a greatly strengthened recapitulation of the themes of his history:

> In the first ages of the decline and fall of the Roman empire our eye is invariably fixed on the royal city which had given laws to the fairest portion of the globe. . . . The foundation of a second Rome on the shores of the Bosphorus has compelled the historian to follow the successors of Constantine; and our curiosity has been tempted to visit the most remote countries of Europe and Asia, to explore the causes and the authors of the long decay of the Byzantine monarchy. By the conquest of Justinian we have been recalled to the banks of the Tiber, to the deliverance of the ancient metropolis; but that deliverance was a change, or perhaps an aggravation, of servitude. . . . In the eighth century . . . [the Romans'] bishop became the temporal as well as the spiritual father of a free people; and of the Western empire, which was restored by Charlemagne, the title and image decorate the singular constitution of modern Germany. The name of Rome must yet command our involuntary respect . . . the venerable aspect of her ruins, and the memory of past greatness, rekindled a spark of the national character. The darkness of the middle ages exhibits

some scenes not unworthy of our notice. Nor shall I dismiss the present work till I have reviewed the state and revolutions of the ROMAN CITY, which acquiesced under the absolute dominion of the Popes about the same time that Constantinople was enslaved by the Turkish arms. (*DF* chap. 69, 7:218–19)

This is the last of Gibbon's announcements of his plans for the history. It says little about the subjects of the chapter in which it appears, 69, and its closely linked successor, though it is quite explicit about the contents not only of chapters 1–68, but also of chapter 71. Despite this reticence on the content of 69 and 70, it prepares for all the issues in those chapters: the relationship of the Romans to the powers of the popes (absent in Avignon during much of the period he is about to discuss); the relationship of Rome to the German emperors and of the emperors to the popes; and most of all, the rekindled "spark of national character." Actually there are several such sparks: the revival of the Senate and the attempt to form a new constitution in 1144; the institution, when that failed, of the office of "senator," a magistrate who had to be foreign, and of whom an admirable example was the Bolognese Brancaleone (1252–58); the attempts to control the quarrelsome and destructive wars among the noble families, and most of all the episode of Rienzi, as celebrated by Petrarch, who himself "by precept and example revived the spirit and study of the Augustan age" (*DF* chap. 70, 7:266).

> In the familiar society of Cicero and Livy, [Petrarch] had imbibed the ideas of an ancient patriot. . . . The aspect of the seven hills and their majestic ruins confirmed these lively impressions. . . . in the remembrance of the past, in the hope of the future, [he] was pleased to forget the miseries of the present time. Rome was still the lawful mistress of the world; the pope and the emperor, her bishop and general, had abdicated their station by an inglorious retreat to the Rhône and the Danube; but, if she could resume her virtue, the republic might again vindicate her liberty and dominion. (*DF* 7:268–69)

The last sentence, which is in *indirect style libre* (that is, indirect discourse imitating the style of the original), carries historian and reader into the poet's realm of enthusiasm for a moment; but we are recalled immediately: "Amidst the indulgence of enthusiasm and eloquence, Petrarch, Italy, and Europe were astonished by a revolution which realised, *for a moment,* his most splendid visions" (*DF* 7:269; emphasis added).

Gibbon then turns to a political recapitulation of his theme: "The rise and fall of the tribune, Rienzi, will occupy the following pages" (*DF* 7:269). Rienzi briefly reformed Rome, but having failed to reform himself, he could not expect to succeed for long. The moral failure was certainly not his alone, however: "Could passion have listened to reason, could private interest have yielded to the public welfare, the supreme tribunal and confederate union of the Italian republic might have healed their intestine discord and closed the Alps against the barbarians of the North" (*DF* 7:277). But, as throughout the *Decline and Fall*, they could not.

Instead, Rome acquired essentially the government that Gibbon had encountered when he visited it in 1764; it became an ecclesiastical state.

> In Rome the voice of freedom and discord is no longer heard; and, instead of the foaming torrent, a smooth and stagnant lake reflects the image of idleness and servitude.
>
> A Christian, a philosopher, and a patriot will be equally scandalized by the temporal kingdom of the clergy; and the local majesty of Rome, the remembrance of her consuls and triumphs, may seem to embitter the sense, and aggravate the shame, of her slavery. (*DF* 7:309)

Again the echo is clear: because of their former liberty, the subjects of the first successors of Augustus likewise suffered tyranny with more "exquisite sensibility" than those whose minds were "prepared for slavery" (*DF* chap. 3, 1:87–88).

But Rome's day is over. Now Gibbon goes on to consider the advantages, as well as the disadvantages, of this state of slothful peace. The present regime is "mild, decent, and tranquil," and it is "exempt from the dangers of a minority, the sallies of youth, the expences of luxury, and the calamities of war." Only one pope (Sixtus V) in the past three centuries has, in Gibbon's view, differed from the dull but decent model. If these advantages are no recompense for the practice of drawing the sovereign "from the church, and even the convent; from the mode of education and life the most adverse to reason, humanity, and freedom" (*DF* 7:310), the Romans show no signs of seeking independence, and Gibbon's passionate regret of their loss of freedom is spent. "For myself," chapter 70 ends, "it is my wish to depart in charity with all mankind; nor am I willing, in these last moments, to offend even the pope and clergy of Rome" (*DF* 7:311). I cannot but believe that this sentence was written on the night of June 27th, 1787, in the summerhouse of a garden in Lausanne. Gibbon then had only to turn to the end of what was now chapter 71 and add the autobiographical coda with which the history now ends.

Gibbon had planned to depart for London, with his three volumes, his Swiss valet, his "ideas and his books" (*Letters* 3:71), on July 20. But "the march of heavy bodies such as armies and historians can seldom be foreseen or fixed to a precise day"; he actually departed on July 29, travelling via Besançon, Rheims, and Calais. His friend and bookseller Peter Elmsley had procured or at least recommended lodgings for him in London.[35] On August 7, 1787, about six o'clock in the evening, he arrived, with a "numerous retinue (one Servant)" and the final results of twenty years of arduous but happy work: "the remainder of his history for immediate publication" (*Letters* 3:68).

FOUR

REVOLUTIONS,
1788 – 1794

THIRTEEN

Fathering

ibbon spent a happy year in England, overseeing the printing of his history, refining its notes, and enjoying the position of historian of Rome. Metaphors of parenthood vie in frequency with metaphors of architecture in his references to his works, albeit he is as often their mother as their father.[1] In 1787–88, however, he is more the father; he feels "the strong wish of settling my three youngest children in a manner honourable to them and beneficial to their parent" (*Letters* 3:65).

But from October on, Gibbon was as much concerned about another figurative son, Wilhelm de Sévery, for whom he served as sponsor and surrogate parent during most of the ensuing year. Wilhelm, aged twenty, was the son of "the family that most truly deserve the name of our friends," as Gibbon called them to Deyverdun (*Letters* 3:70). This sponsorship of English experience for Wilhelm was part of a larger plan of Gibbon's. He proposed, and relinquished only with regret, an exchange of children between his two adopted families, the Séverys in Lausanne and the Sheffields in England. Had he persuaded the families to consent, Maria Josepha Holroyd would have lived for a while with the Séverys in Lausanne as a second daughter, but she would also have been in some ways Gibbon's charge in Switzerland, as Wilhelm was in England. Gibbon's affection for both young people—and both, by the way, show themselves to have been lively and intelligent in their extant letters—is obvious in his

249

letters to their respective parents. Despite experiencing, as we shall see, some of the anxieties incidental to the parental role, Gibbon seems greatly to have enjoyed it. Near the end of his and Wilhelm's stay in England, he wrote to Wilhelm's mother, quite gratuitously,

> A propos of this child of ours, I seize the moment of his absence to tell you from the bottom of my heart how pleased I am with him. If I have been able to be of some use to him, I have been very well repaid by the attachment to me that he evinces and by the fatherly pleasures that he has made me feel. I share his enjoyment I am proud of his successes and his conduct has never yet given me an instant of regret or disquiet. (*Letters* 3:116)

Like Wilhelm (and later, Maria), Gibbon's literary children gave him some trouble, but more satisfaction. For more than eight months the presses ran at full capacity, producing 3,000 copies of 256 sheets,[2] and Gibbon made corrections and revisions as necessary—the last ones (on a cancel sheet) to the preface dated May 1, 1788.[3] The volumes were officially published on May 8, a date chosen to coincide with the historian's fifty-first birthday. Like his young Swiss protégé, they succeeded admirably. Reviews and eminent persons alike applauded his achievement. The pleasures and pride of a year of triumphs were capped by recognition, at last, in the chamber in which Gibbons had so long been mute, the House of Commons. One of the greatest parliamentary orators of the age, Richard Sheridan, in the course of the most spectacular political event—the trial of Warren Hastings for his conduct of the governorship of India—referred on the floor of Parliament to "the luminous page of Gibbon."[4] Gibbon "could not hear without emotion the personal compliment which he paid me in the presence of the British nation" (*Memoirs* 181). Yet Gibbon was never tempted to remain permanently in England (*Memoirs* 183). As Wilhelm astutely observed,

> Gibbon has, here in London, the most agreeable acquaintances in the world, everyone most eminent for intelligence; he dines out nearly every day, and, although I hear him talk very often, he has the talent of renewing himself, he is always amusing. However, he doesn't seem settled here; he has the air of a bird of passage, like me, who is waiting for summer to fly away to his country.[5]

The interlude in England was triumphant, even fruitful, but it was only an interlude.

On August 8, the day after his arrival, in his London lodgings, Gibbon was "not a little fatigued," and "devoted th[e] hot day to privacy and repose without having seen any body except Cadell and Elmsley [publisher and bookseller], and my neighbour Batt whose civility amounts to kindness and real friendship" (*Letters* 3:68). Batt, a barrister and government commissioner, was nine years younger than Gibbon. He is a character in Gibbon's story whose personality never becomes known to us, but he was, as we have seen, one of the very few persons who saw part of the *Decline and Fall* in manuscript (volume 1 — not the subsequent volumes); he was an intermediary when one of Gibbon's attackers (James Chelsum) desired to present his book to Gibbon; and when financial business between Gibbon and Sheffield required the formality of a third party, Batt was their choice. With Lord Loughborough, he is frequently mentioned by Gibbon as a dinner companion.

Gibbon's need and gratitude for companionship is apparent. Even when welcomed by Batt and Loughborough, he was glad to conclude his first negotiations with the printers and "bury [him]self at Sheffield place to revise and correct" (*Letters* 3:69). On August 16, 1787, Cadell and Strahan agreed to pay Gibbon, "heretofore at Bentinck St. and now residing in the Adelphi in the Parish of St Martin in the Fields" the sum of £4,000 for volumes 4–6.[6] They also gave him a £500 advance. Though they "grumbled" about their proofs and queries having to travel between London and Sussex, they were apparently resigned to Gibbon's habit of making small changes even while the volumes were being printed, and they recognized the futility of trying to persuade him to remain in "a sultry and solitary metropolis." Soon, therefore, he was restored to a familial atmosphere. As he explained to his stepmother, "I am here very idle and very busy. . . . I have the daily duty of receiving correcting and returning a printed sheet [that is, eight quarto pages] which is sent me from London" (*Letters* 3:76). Whenever he was not at Sheffield Place (or rather, without a "family settlement" with the Sheffield family in either Sussex or London), however, he was decidedly discontented with his English life: "In a lodging I am destitute of a thousand comforts: my books are few, my society precarious, my days long and often tedious, nor is any thing less pleasant than to be left solitary and motionless while the world is flying round and round me. In point of kind civil assiduous attendance of male and female friends Lausanne had quite spoilt me" (*Letters* 3:85).[7] It was at Sheffield Place, therefore, that he continued to revise the *Decline and Fall*.

Apparently (and logically) he left the manuscript of volume 4 in the hands of the printer and carried volumes 5 and 6 away with him. As he had anticipated in Lausanne, upon reaching London he had not only to sign his agreement with Cadell and Strahan and "deliver the first part of the Manuscript," but also to "settle some preliminaries with the printer and corrector, revise the first sheets, procure some necessary books, consult others, and set the machine in motion" (*Letters* 3:66). The action of the machine included the preparation of an index. He had commissioned Cadell and Strahan to find an "intelligent workman" to prepare a general index for the six volumes, and

he had advice to give that workman: "I have thought on the subject
of index-making, and can give him some advice, which will abridge
the size, without impairing the use and value of his alphabetical table"
(*Letters* 3:63). If we compare the style and format of Gibbon's index
to that of another Strahan and Cadell book of the same period,
Robertson's *History of America*, there are only two apparent differences: in Gibbon's book, the headwords of long entries are indicated
in their subheads by indentation and dashes, and when long entries
include material from more than one volume of the history, new
paragraphs are started for each volume. These changes might seem to
enlarge rather than condense the index, but the index to Robertson's
two volumes runs to nineteen quarto pages (nine and a half per
volume), whereas Gibbon's six require fifty-one quarto pages (eight
and a half per volume).

Whether or not Gibbon contributed to the design of his index, he
succeeded in part of his program. "Several rare and useful books, the
Assises de Jerusalem, Ramusius de bello C. P^{ano}, the Greek acts of
the Synod of Florence, the Statuta Urbis Romae &c were procured,
and I introduced in their proper places the supplements which they
afforded" (*Memoirs* 182). The printing of the first volume required
three months,[8] a rate of progress equivalent to six or seven sheets per
week, as Gibbon's description to his stepmother implies. This was a
strenuous rate for the printer, but it was not enough. It was necessary
to speed up, and the printers, and Gibbon, had to get through a sheet
and a half per day in order to complete the impression in time for a
spring publication date. (The publishers felt that such a book could
not "advantageously appear after the beginning, or middle of May"
[*Letters* 3:65].) Fortunately, Gibbon was able to be in London for the
last strenuous months. But during this early period, Gibbon could
indulge in the luxury of improvements as well as corrections. "After
building a great house, a thousand little alterations, improvements,
and ornaments present themselves to the architect, . . . besides the
trouble of painting and glazing some of the last apartments" (*Letters*
3:76).

These changes occur almost exclusively in volumes 5 and 6.
Gibbon's extant papers provide only one possible addition for volume
4, a version of his comment, or rather comments, on Cosmas Indico-
pleustes as edited by Montfaucon in the *Novo collectio patrum*.[9] Since
this draft was written on slips of paper similar to those used in 1787,
it might represent new work. But it is more probable that the notes
on Cosmas were made earlier. If the Maurist collection in which
Montfaucon's edition appeared were something to which he acquired
access only in 1787, Gibbon would probably have included it in his
list of newly available "rare and useful books," and we know Gibbon
had studied Montfaucon's paleographical work while he was in Paris

in 1777. On the other hand, in the two notes on Cosmas, we have a rare instance of Gibbon's unconsciously repeating himself. In chapter 40, he had said,

> Cosmas . . . refutes the impious opinion that the earth is a globe; and Photius had read this work. . . . the most valuable part has been given in French and in Greek by Melchisedec Thévenot . . . and the whole is since published in a splendid edition by the Père Montfaucon. . . . But the editor, a theologian, might blush at not discovering the Nestorian heresy of Cosmas, which has been detected by la Croze. (*DF* 4:250 n. 78 [77]

In chapter 47, we read,

> The entire work of which some curious extracts may be found in Photius . . . Thévenot . . . and Fabricius . . . has been published by father Montfaucon. . . . The Nestorianism of Cosmas, unknown to his learned editor, was detected by La Croze . . . and is confirmed by Assemani. (*DF* 5:158 n. 119 [116]

This forgetful addition might have been made in 1787, especially since the use of the English "father" Montfaucon suggests that Gibbon is thinking in English rather than French. But chapter 47 was written in the first place long after chapter 40—chapter 47 was, we recall, the first chapter Gibbon wrote in Lausanne—so it is certainly possible that it was in 1784 that he was forgetful. If so, in 1787 he made no changes in the first of his three new volumes.

The latter two volumes, however, definitely profited not only from their author's opportunity to examine new books, but from his rereading, and even from his English friendships. A cryptic list of notes headed "Vol v" and "Vol vi." attest the process.[10] Like the fragmentary notes to draft F of his *Memoirs*, they are more memoranda, not drafts. They suggest that among the books to which he had belated access were at least the later volumes of Martin Bouquet's *Historiens des Gaules et de la France* (13 vols. fol., 1738–86), which was eventually in his library at Lausanne, but which is not in the 1785 catalogue.[11] Yet the first six memoranda seem to provide new observations, not new information. For instance, the first two memoranda are "Charlemagne in Bouquet" and "Mecca poems by Jones." Gibbon appears to remind himself to make additions to two existing notes. In chapter 49, n. 95 (Bury 100), the following sentence ends the note: "But I have likewise examined the original monuments of the reigns of Pepin and Charlemagne, in the vth volume of the Historians of France." Similarly, he probably added to n. 41 (Bury 44) of chapter 50 its reference and compliment to Sir William Jones.[12]

It is not clear, however, that Gibbon actually added all the new notes he proposed to himself. He considered, but apparently did not write, an extended note on Greek fire,[13] and if he included a reference

to Andreas Schott's collections of Spanish writings, his most inde-
fatigable indexer, Ronald G. Whitaker, has failed to notice it.[14] There
are fragments related to every chapter in volume 5 except chapter
53, but they do not necessarily occur in chapter order. Some of them
show that Gibbon was working from memory as well as from new
sources; for example, "William. Norman. a lamb, lyon, angel. *perhaps*
Ordericus Vit." (emphasis added).[15] This seems to become the note
that reads, "Gulielm. Appulus, i. ii, c. 12. according to the reference
of Giannone . . . which I cannot verify in the original" (*DF* 6:186 n.
33 [25]). Gibbon had apparently tried to verify it as cited by Giannone,
failed, and now guessed that Giannone's source might actually have
been Ordericus Vitalis, who had also described the Normans. (Gibbon read William of Apulia in L.A. Muratori's *Scriptores rerum Italica-
rum.*) Thus he seems to have derived ideas for this list both from his
perusal of his own work and from the new works that he either
purchased or borrowed. Not all the new acquisitions are referred to in
the fragmentary memoranda, however, so apparently he made some
revisions without making preliminary memoranda.

Gibbon proposed and made more additions to volume 6 than to 5.
Some clearly come from newly available sources, such as the lengthy
final note to chapter 60, about G. B. Ramusio's *De bello Constantino-
politano*, "a modern history . . . which has fallen somewhat late into
my hands" (*DF* 6:430 n. 120 [103]). Five pages of notes from or
suggested by this work, in Gibbon's hand, are extant and were incorporated in various chapters of the last volume.[16]

Interestingly, many of the additions in both volumes include evaluations of previous historians, such as Francisco de Moncada, whose
history "I have read with pleasure, and which the Spaniards extol as a
model of style and composition"; he "may imitate Caesar or Sallust;
he may transcribe the Greek or Italian contemporaries: but he never
quotes his authorities" (*DF* chap. 62, 6:504 n. 65 [50]). In a less good-
humored mood, there is the following: "In one of the Ramblers, Dr.
Johnson praises [Richard] Knolles . . . as the first of historians, unhappy only in the choice of his subject. Yet I much doubt whether a
partial and verbose compilation from Latin writers, thirteen hundred
folio pages of speeches and battles, can either instruct or amuse an
enlightened age, which requires from the historian some tincture of
philosophy and criticism" (*DF* chap. 64, 7:25–26 n. 66 [41]). But
Gibbon is ready to praise where praise is due: "I should quote
Thuroczius, the oldest general historian . . . in the ist volume of the
Scriptores Hungaricarum, did not the same volume contain the original narrative of a contemporary, an eye-witness, and a sufferer . . .
the best picture that I have ever seen of all the circumstances of a
Barbaric invasion" (*DF* chap. 64, 7:6 n. 19 [16]) He even has a kind
word for Johnson's *Irene* (*DF* 68, 7:179 n. 31 [28]. These comments,

and perhaps others not hinted at in the memoranda, may reflect Gibbon's reluctant decision against a concluding review of his sources:

> It was my first intention to have collected under one view the numerous authors . . . from whom I have derived the materials of this history. . . . If I have renounced this idea . . . which had obtained the approbation of a master-artist [Robertson], my excuse may be found in the extreme difficulty of assigning a proper measure to such a catalogue. A naked list of names and editions would not be satisfactory either to myself or my readers . . . a more copious enquiry might indeed deserve, but it would demand, an elaborate volume. (*DF*, Preface to the Fourth Volume of the Quarto Edition, 1:xlv)[17]

Gibbon's use of the *Assises of Jerusalem* is an example of a collaboration with a friend. He gained access to them only belatedly, and they are in "old law French" (*DF* chap. 58, 6:329 n. 140 [132]). Yet he had time to add in the text four paragraphs (the final four of chapter 58) based on this new source, thanks to the availability of expert assistance in interpreting it. "For the intelligence of this obscure and obsolete jurisprudence (c. 80–111), I am deeply indebted to the friendship of a learned lord, who, with an accurate and discerning eye, has surveyed the philosophic history of law" (*DF* chap. 58, 6:333 n. 148 [140]). Though the language of the text and notes are unmistakably Gibbonian, the information is from Gibbon's old friend Lord Loughborough (Alexander Wedderburn), who wrote to William Eden (later Lord Auckland) on January 17, 1788:

> I have passed a month in the country entirely alone, but very much employed. You cannot imagine how valuable a present you made me in the "Assizes of Jerusalem," which I have studied as diligently as ever I did Littleton. The result of it will make its appearance in print in the course of this year, not by my means, however, but through a much better channel. Gibbon had long been in pursuit of this book for a part of his history, and as the language of it was less obscure to me than to him, I have employed myself in furnishing him with an abstract from it.[18]

While Gibbon, the printers, and Loughborough were engaged in their various historical labors, Gibbon had another major responsibility, the welfare of his temporary son, Wilhelm. Even before Wilhelm arrived, Gibbon was busy making arrangements for him (with the invaluable help of Lord and Lady Sheffield). He hired his former valet, Caplen, to stand ready in London to act as Wilhelm's courier to Sussex when he arrived, and he found a suitable family (possibly a connection of his own Porten cousins) two leagues away from Sheffield Place with whom Wilhelm could live while immersing himself in the task of learning English. This family consisted of a widow, Anne Clarke, and her three sons, one of whom Gibbon described as a "man of letters, very suitable for reading good English authors with our student" (*Letters* 3:73, with n. 5). Before leaving London, Gibbon deposited a letter at the office of his friend and bookseller Peter Elmsley and instructed Wilhelm to go there when he reached the city. Wilhelm duly arrived on October 31, found Elmsley's office and Caplen, and came on to Sheffield Place on the first of November.[19] On November 4, Gibbon wrote to Wilhelm's father, "I cannot, Monsieur, let the dispatches of our son go without telling you with how much pleasure I embraced him and what joy I felt in seeing realized the projects that we formed in my little summerhouse in Lausanne. . . . His debut in this little circle of Sheffield place has been very happy: He pleases everyone already, from Mylord down to Milady's little dog" (*Letters* 3:78).

In the same letter, Gibbon delicately assured Salomon de Sévery that though the banker's letter he had sent with Wilhelm was not usable (Gibbon does not explain why), money was no problem: "Permit me to take care of this little matter and when I return to Lausanne, the two fathers can go over the accounts together." He suggests at the same time that Wilhelm tell his father how much money he was spending, so that the father can let him know if he is going beyond suitable limits. "I see in him the wisest and most modest disposition, but in the perilous navigation of great cities there are many shoals" (*Letters* 3:78). Gibbon seems to be trying hard, and with some success, to suggest his pleasure in being allowed to share the parental role, without presuming to usurp the prerogatives of a real parent.

But Wilhelm could not learn English at Sheffield Place, where everyone spoke French, so on November 6 he was sent to Mrs. Clarke, as planned. He was not happy there. In fact, he was so unhappy that three days later, he came back to Sheffield Place, "where he was consoled and persuaded to return."[20] Gibbon, who remembered what it was to lose the power of speech by being isolated in a strange land (*Memoirs* 69), wrote Wilhelm an encouraging note on November 11, the very day after his return to Mrs. Clarke's, in which he promised to visit within two days. Gibbon kept that promise, and when he went to London a week later, Wilhelm was apparently resigned to his fate. Lord and Lady Sheffield, especially the kind "Milady," who reminded Wilhelm of his mother, kept a watchful and friendly eye on the young exile. But they likewise expected Gibbon himself to keep in close touch with them. When he reached London without writing to Sheffield by the first post to let his friends know of his safe arrival, he was duly "growled at" by those friends. Gibbon found such familial solicitude amusing and touching:

> The assurance that neither giants nor dragons were to be feared between Sheffield place and Pall Mall had induced me to leave to your fancy or judgement the well-known circumstances of changing horses, alighting

from the chaise, surveying the lodging (bad and dear) ordering a fowl from
the Cocoa tree &c. &c. . . . You would make me vain; nor am I less
touched by the growlings of Mylady, than by the praises of the Maria.
(*Letters* 3:81).

Gibbon intended this solitary visit to London for "litterary business,"
but he also made a number of calls to old friends—"Crauford, the
Lucans, Sir Joshua &c. I have knocked without success at Lord
Loughborough's door, but shall dine with him before the end of the
week" (*Letters* 3:81). Domestic companionship, the joy of Sheffield
Place and Lausanne, had perforce given way to bachelor ways, no
longer so delightful as they had been to young Gibbon visiting Paris.[21]

He was grateful when old acquaintances sought him out and felt
pleased that "a man has more friends in Pall Mall than in Bentinck
Street" (*Letters* 3:82). "The first evening I passed at home, and had
scarcely dined when, the Poet Hayley was announced: he embraced,
forgave me [for not writing], and we entered on a pleasant conversation of two hours" (*Letters* 3:81). Hayley's account of the same meeting
is fuller and more dramatic:

> I had two hours of most pleasant conversation with the Roman Eagle,
> yesterday evening. My good friend Elmsley informed me that he was to
> arrive from Lord Sheffield's, to a late dinner at a lodging-house in Pall-
> mall. He had requested that courteous and intelligent bookseller to come
> and chat an hour with him alone, and we had agreed to go together; but
> Elmsley being unavoidably engaged with a foreigner of distinction, it was
> my lot to go without any attendant. . . . I luckily arrived at the moment
> when [Gibbon's] dinner had just left the room, and found him in perfect
> solitude on a sofa. He expressed the most flattering kind of surprise at
> the sight of me, and said, with his usual force of expression, "I am both
> overjoyed and ashamed to see you." I told him very frankly my apprehen-
> sions, that some one had poisoned his mind against me, and occasioned a
> silence so unlike our former animated intercourse. He replied, with great
> feeling, "I assure you, on my honour, that no such attempt has been made
> by any person whatever, and if it had been made by a hundred people,
> they would all have failed of success." He then made a very candid apology
> for his habitual indolence in regard to writing letters, and said every thing
> that could tend to assure me of his invariable regard. After these marks of
> his kindness, you will, I am sure, rejoice to hear, that I thought him
> infinitely improved in health. His countenance has much better colouring,
> and his person is not so corpulent as when I saw him on his departure for
> Switzerland.[22]

If there were no dragons between Sheffield and Pall Mall, there
were nevertheless dragons. Gibbon feared them for Wilhelm at
Lewes—"a set of drunken dragoons"—and encountered a familiar one
himself on the very Wednesday that he wrote to Lord Sheffield about
the safety of his journey to London, as he was soon forced to confess:

Last Wednesday evening I felt some flying symptoms of the gout: for two succeeding days, I struggled bravely, and went in a chair to dine with Batt and Lord Loughborough: but on Saturday I yielded to my conqueror. I have now passed three wearisome days without amusement and three miserable nights without sleep. . . . This fit is remarkably painful: the enemy is possessed of the left foot and knee and how far he may carry the war, God only knows. . . . Pity me magnanimous Baron, pity me tender females, pity me Swiss exile and believe me it is far better to be learning English at Uckfield. (*Letters* 3:82–83)

The fit, though severe, was relatively brief, or at least made so by the determination of the sufferer; on December 8, Gibbon declared himself able to travel:

Should no reverse of fortune take place . . . I can promise to ascend my post chaise, painfully enough either friday or Saturday next, the 14th or 15th instant. . . . we will contrive, if I am strong enough some dinner with Lord L, Batt, or elsewhere. I am much obliged to Severy for his letter and Lausanne news: I hope he is somewhat less miserable. Adieu I am tired. (*Letters* 3:85)

And on Saturday, December 15th, Gibbon, Lord Sheffield, and Maria Josepha started for Bath, accompanied by Caplen. They arrived on Sunday afternoon.

Gibbon was still very weak and lame, but he had no object in Bath, a place and way of life he disliked, except seeing his stepmother. Though he appreciated her affection, he seems to have found her undiluted company somewhat wearisome. "I am carried over the way in a chair about one o'Clock, maintain a conversation till ten o'Clock in the evening, and am then reconveyed to my lodging. Lord S with Mrs. [Serena] Holroyd and Maria dined with us yesterday on the haunch of venison, but such reliefs are not always to be expected, and I chearfully perform an act of duty which is necessary and cannot be long" (*Letters* 3:87). It is perhaps better not to inquire whether he meant, in speaking of the brevity of the duty, to refer to his visit or to her life. In the next sentence, he remarks on her astonishing good health; in the following sentence, on how he and Lord Sheffield had dropped hints about "the shortness of our stay, and indispensable business." When Gibbon wrote to his stepmother in May confirming plans for another visit, he betrayed a rather unpleasant conscious virtue: "On my side the promise will be most chearfully performed, and in the prospect of embracing a dear and valuable friend I shall ever esteem fatigue and expence of small account" (*Letters* 3:107)—a sentiment that would be far nobler had it not been voiced! Those who have never visited a still beloved, but now failing, elderly relation with more resignation than pleasure may cast the first stone—unless they have neglected to visit the said relation at all.

Gibbon planned to leave Bath with Maria and Lord Sheffield on December 26th, passing through London to Sheffield Place—hence his hints of a short visit. Bath was far more attractive to Gibbon while his friend and honorary daughter were in residence. Maria, now almost seventeen, was a great resource to Gibbon on this visit. Even through the haze of pain and boredom, he enjoyed her enjoyment of the new experiences. Apparently she was being allowed, as young girls not yet out often were, to test her social wings in the smaller world of Bath. Her beloved aunt "Serena" (Sarah Martha Holroyd), who lived in Bath and was a close friend of Dorothea Gibbon's, was prepared to polish her niece: "Papa and Mama both tell me how much you are improved. I only hear of a certain bad carriage and walk, with a little too fast speaking, which I intend should be quite got rid of before Winter, as you will now in a Manner begin the world, and make your first appearance as being no longer a child."[23] But Gibbon seems to have seen no need for improvement. "Maria to whom every object is new and pleasant, and who begins to undraw the curtain of the great theatre wonders and almost murmurs at our impatience" (*Letters* 3:87), he wrote to her mother. And when gout (as well, perhaps, as his stepmother's disappointment) did not permit him to leave Bath with Sheffield and Maria as he had hoped, he added, "You will admire the triumphant Maria, and your observation will soon discern whether it will be easy to brush the powder out of her hair, and the world out of her heart or to shut her eyes after they have been once opened to the light of pleasure" (*Letters* 3:89).

In the event, Gibbon remained in Bath nearly two weeks after his friends had left, until January 7—indeed, until the 4th, he did not even attempt to go out. But his prolonged stay was not without compensations. Among his visitors were the now blind, but cheerful, Lord North, with whom Gibbon had already spent a day (September 5),[24] the duchess of Devonshire, and "the Aetherial"—Lady Elizabeth Foster; there were visits also from an unnumbered and nameless "&c." Serena wrote to Maria that on January 4 she had dined with Gibbon at Mrs. Gibbon's: "Mr. Gib's first dinner abroad. I staid till nine, and nothing could be pleasanter than the said Gib., tho' he had been two hours in the morn at the feet of his Adorable [Lady Elizabeth]. She being his deity, he did but right to pay her homage the first moment of emerging. I only think how he could be afterwards so agreeable to us poor souls!"[25] Despite this delay, Gibbon was so impatient to leave Bath, or rather "to reach London and S[heffield] P[lace]," that he "escaped" before he was entirely recovered. He could not contain his eagerness to join Lord and Lady Sheffield, to be "happy in the society of two persons (no common blessing) whom I love and by whom I am beloved" (*Letters* 3:87). On January 11, after a mere three days in London, he attained that blessing.

Wilhelm has left us a description of the routine at Sheffield Place. "When Mr. Gibbon was there, every evening there was a reading, for example, Voltaire's *Zaïre*. . . . Mylady has the same tastes as you, dear mother, she likes the society of a few friends . . . she doesn't like the great world. Every morning Mr. Gibbon would chat with her for an hour or two and she feels her loss very much."[26] While Gibbon was away, Wilhelm read with Lady Sheffield the *Letters of Gellert* (a French work) and *The Mirror* (an English magazine). Lord Sheffield furnished Wilhelm with a horse, Lady Sheffield enjoyed his music, and the whole family learned to play a new card game, *triçet*, under his instruction. Thus the environment that Gibbon so much enjoyed at Lausanne—a studious morning, domestic conversation, amateur drama, and card playing—was very nearly duplicated at Sheffield Place.

Sheffield Place to some extent relieved Wilhelm's initial misery at his transplantation to England. According to the *Oxford English Dictionary*, the original word for homesickness (*Heinweh*) was a Swiss invention, and in the eighteenth century the malady itself was strongly associated with the Swiss and included recognizable physical symptoms. But Gibbon seems to have regarded Wilhelm's problem as entirely emotional. He wrote to Wilhelm's parents:

> He felt very strongly the first moments of our separation and his withdrawal. His health was altered to the point of making him unrecognizable, but at the depth of his depression, when as a final consolation I proposed to him a return to Lausanne, he replied proudly, "Rather death." He remained, and he is by no means dead. His health and spirits have regained their strength, and the memory of his first weakness has given him powers to support the tedium of his situation. (*Letters* 3:92)

This was the same letter (January 17, 1788) in which Gibbon proposed his scheme of exchange visits between the two young persons he most loved, Wilhelm and Maria. The scheme would allow Wilhelm more than the three months of enjoyment and practice of his new language anticipated by the present timetable, and it would provide a similar experience for Maria. Gibbon describes her to her perspective hosts as follows:

> In carefully cultivating her talents, she has been so perfectly kept away from the world that she has retained . . . the simplicity and innocence of a child. Without being beautiful, the total effect of her appearance is very good, she is agreeable, intelligent, and a little pride derived from her character and situation will only make her more attentive to the advice of someone whose superiority in every respect she will feel.

Wilhelm also described her to his parents: "Her appearance is good, she is very sweet and kind, full of talents. She plays the clavecin very

well, she draws perfectly, despite spending last winter in the country.
. . . She is, it could be said, a young lady perfectly brought up [*une
jeune fille parfaitement élevée*]."[27] Wilhelm found ten-year-old Louise
Holroyd livelier and prettier than her elder sister, however.

Throughout January and February, as Gibbon continued to struggle
with the aftereffects of his attack of gout (*Letters* 3:95) and to correct
his daily stint of the history, he wrote frequent affectionate notes to
Wilhelm at Uckfield, encouraging him to persevere. At the end of
February Gibbon received a letter from the Séverys, very grateful to
Gibbon and Lord and Lady Sheffield, but unwilling to part with
Wilhelm for so long, or to accept the responsibility of caring for
Maria. Gibbon immediately wrote to give Wilhelm the news and to
suggest that he nevertheless dedicate one more month to perfecting
his English in Uckfield. But he left the choice entirely to his "son":

> You are free, depart, and come to embrace your friend in the city. . . . You
> are awaited with impatience by several of my friends whom you have met:
> you will no doubt see many novel objects, but don't form ideas that are
> too celestial. . . . You will be very much astonished if I assure you that in
> many respects the society of London (the women especially) is not equal
> to that of Lausanne. (*Letters* 3:96)

Wilhelm was not equal to a longer exile. "I cannot be astonished,
my dear friend," Gibbon wrote, "that you have decided to quit the
tedium of Uckfield to fly to your friends who await you with much
impatience" (*Letters* 3:98) And after a short delay for necessary arrangements, Wilhelm arrived in London on March 11. From then on,
Gibbon (with the help of Lord and Lady Sheffield) arranged for him
every species of fashionable party and activity, from visits to military
and naval reviews, to a ticket to the Hastings trial, to theatricals
private and public, music sacred and profane, art exhibitions, artists'
studios, and the royal library, to balls and dinners, to presentations at
court. Wilhelm was staying in lodgings, not at the Sheffields' house
in Downing Street, and little notes about engagements and proprieties
flew between him and his temporary parent. On one evening, invited
to dine at Lord Ossory's, to dance at Lady Mary Duncan's Ball, and
then to attend an assembly at the Lucans, Wilhelm consulted his
mentor about proper dress: might he go to dinner "en frac" (in tails),
explaining and apologizing to his host? "I detest, and it is ridiculous
here, to dance in dinner clothes."[28] Gibbon's verdict: "en frac" by all
means (*Letters* 3:101).

Wilhelm's full and frequent letters home give a lively picture of the
social life of London in 1788.[29] "Yesterday I was presented to the
king, he addressed two questions to me, as he does to all strangers. I
was not as frightened as I would have expected; there were many
people, all men, for it was only a *lever*."[30] On another occasion:

> After the opera, Mr. Trevor took me to the Duchess of Cumberland's, where every one goes after the opera. I was presented to her and she talked to me for some time. A prodigious number of fashionable people met there; it is the best house in London for pleasure, comfort, there was a pharaoh bank where the Louis danced like sous. Lady Ashton bet 3, 4, 5 Louis at a time. It was droll to see. The guests did nothing but arrive and depart, the carriages at the gate were innumerable.[31]

To crown the evening, there was a ball, but young Wilhelm did not go to it, finding that too much for one evening. After a time, he began to find the activities of the London season incomprehensible:

> I can't understand how these men of quality take care of their affairs or rather don't do so; as to the women I am not surprised that they lose their beauty early. A woman goes to four or five assemblies in the same evening, just going in and departing. At an assembly there are very many more women than men; the men are often at their clubs. The other day I saw six ladies playing commerce all alone. I don't understand, either, how the horses can be used so much and at the same time be in such good condition. To trot on the pavement night and day and wait five or six hours in front of a gate is nothing to them, apparently.[32]

Wilhelm saw and greatly admired the great dancer Vestris, the renowned actress Mrs. Siddons, Reynolds's studio, and the queen's library at Buckingham House. "There are 50,000 volumes and the rooms are beautiful. Mr. Gibbon said to me, 'You thought I had a great many books, didn't you? But you see that the king has more.' 'Yes, Monsieur,' I replied, 'he has more than you, but does he read them?' That made him laugh."[33] In April, Gibbon was proposed by Sir Joshua Reynolds for the professorship of ancient history in the Royal Academy. The post was purely honorary and admitted the holder and his guest to the annual banquet and exhibition.[34] Gibbon's guest was his young Swiss friend:

> All the paintings of the different masters, painted during the year, are exhibited in an immense hall, in the middle of which there is a table for 150 people. Lord Sheffield, Mr. Gibbon, M. de Calonne, all the different foreign ministers dined there with a number of distinguished English men. . . . The room, or rather hall, was covered with paintings, and all this formed a majestic and imposing whole.[35]

Gibbon also "had the expensive honour of being elected a fellow of the Royal and Antiquarian Societies" (*Letters* 3:146)—great was his chagrin on discovering the subscription fees: twenty-five guineas for the Royal Society (*Letters* 3:141). But the high point of his stay was surely the birthday party on May 8 for himself and his three new volumes. "The double festival was celebrated by a cheerful litterary dinner at Cadell's house; and I seemed to blush while they read an elegant compliment from Mr. Hayley whose poetical talent had more than once before been employed in the praise of his friend" (*Memoirs* 182).

The author was naturally anxious to know the public's reaction to his new volumes and naturally pleased that they sold quickly. If he was not pleased with the major reviews, he was certainly hard to satisfy. The *Annual Register* saw the new addition as completing a work "justly and . . . universally allowed to be at least among the number of the most valuable literary productions of our time," though the reviewer warns that "wherever . . . the Christian religion [is] in question, Mr. Gibbon is to be read with the utmost caution . . . even his fidelity and exactness as a historian, on this subject, do not by any means stand unimpeached."[36] According to the *European Magazine and London Review*, Gibbon's achievement proves that mankind is not degenerating. In volumes 4–6, says the reviewer, Gibbon is a historian, a lawyer, and a "theologist." In the first two roles he is magnificent; in the third he has been sufficiently opposed.[37]

John Gillies, in the *Monthly*, after calling the history "instructive and splendid," addresses the controversial issue of organization. Gibbon has rejected the annalistic structure in favor of what Gillies calls organization by action. When a writer follows the "rise, progress, and conclusion of one important action" before considering other contemporary events, he best holds the attention and emotions of the reader, Gillies believes. Gibbon has followed that plan "with uncommon industry, and singular success," as well as "minutely accurate" chronology.[38] Gillies was himself a historian. Some who were not historians were baffled by Gibbon's decision. Lady Holland, indeed, felt that the *Decline and Fall* was impossible to read without having the old *Universal History* handy to clarify the chronology.[39] Horace Walpole, too, complained as he praised, "I was a little confounded by his leaping backwards and forwards, and I could not recollect all those *fainéant* emperors of Constantinople, who come again and again, like ships in a moving picture. How he could traverse such acres of ill-written histories, even to collect such a great work, astonishes me."[40] But Gillies admired Gibbon's organizational decisions as much as his style, concluding that Gibbon "unite[d] the splendor of Livy with the energy of Tacitus."[41]

The *Monthly*'s principal rival, the *Critical*, also compared Gibbon to Tacitus. Like Tacitus, Gibbon "formed a new species of historical composition; each expressed the justest and most philosophical sentiments, in a style of expressive brevity, which keeps the attention constantly awake, exercises the judgment, and frequently suggests new topics, which the mind may at its leisure examine, or discussion which it may at a future period renew."[42] The *Gentleman's Magazine* continued its enmity, but with a sarcastic device that rather backfired: it printed "Selections from Mr. Gibbon's learned and entertaining

Notes to the Fourth, Fifth, and Sixth Volumes of the *Decline and Fall of the Roman Empire,*" without comment.[43] The selected notes were often ribald or required the "obscurity of a learned language"; some of the *Gentleman's Magazine's* readers were indignant that its fair pages had been so polluted.[44]

Some other criticism and much significant praise appeared over the next two years; in particular, German criticism, which Gibbon probably did not know, produced some of the most favorable and knowledgeable reviews of his work, for example, that in the *Göttingische Gelehrte Anzeigen.*[45] The chorus of praise from the reviews was varied by two attacks, both published anonymously. In the *English Review,* John Whitaker, who had come to hate Gibbon, either for his attacks on religion (Whitaker's account) or for his lack of admiration for Whitaker's *Mary Queen of Scots* (Sheffield's account), portrays Gibbon as Milton's Belial, criticizes Gibbon's charges against the early Christians, and argues that histories lose in solidity what they gain in splendor.[46] Whitaker explicitly indicted Tacitus as well as Gibbon on this charge; perhaps that contributed to his failing to convince many readers. He himself was sufficiently satisfied with his work to publish it later under his own name.[47] The other attacker, probably Henry Pye, published a pamphlet pointing out four faults in Gibbon's last three volumes: "a very great defect in chronological arrangement, and a want of that *lucidus ordo* which distinguishes the historian from the mere narrator of facts," obscurity and grammatical errors, obscenity and indecent prejudice against Christianity, and "a perpetual display of ridiculous buffoonery" unworthy of "serious history." This attacker admits that there are "many brilliant passages" and regrets that these volumes do not reach the high standard of the earlier volumes. "Of the genius and abilities of Mr. Gibbon there can be but one opinion; but we must regret, that, in the present work, they have not been employed as they ought to be."[48] This small book is not known to have been in Gibbon's library, but such sentiments are represented in his account of the reception of his book:

> The conclusion of my work appears to have diffused a strong sensation: it was generally read and variously judged. The style has been exposed to much Academical criticism; a religious clamour was revived; and the reproach of indecency has been loudly echoed by the rigid censors of morals. Yet upon the whole the history of the decline and fall seems to have struck a root both at home and abroad, and may, perhaps, an hundred years hence, still continue to be abused. (*Memoirs* 152)

For once, the historian was something of a prophet.

One portion of his history, the preface to volume 4, gave him some qualms even before publication. When he left England in 1783, he had felt some bitterness toward his former political leader, Lord

North, who had selected Anthony Storer for an embassy post in Paris in preference to Gibbon, "without even a civil answer to my letter. Were I capable of hating a man whom it is not easy to hate, I should find myself most amply revenged by" North's loss of significance in his own department (*Letters* 2:385). But North was now bravely enduring misfortune, and he remained "one of the best companions in the Kingdom." Under these circumstances, Gibbon was moved to dedicate to him the new volumes of his history. The composition of the compliment cost Gibbons some pains, as can be seen in the cancelled sheet now in the Pierpont Morgan Library.[49] He was afraid that the compliment might be attacked on political grounds, despite North's current powerlessness. He wrote of North as a

> Statesman, who, in a long, a stormy, and at length an unfortunate administration, had many political opponents, almost without a personal enemy: who has retained, in his fall from power many faithful and disinterested friends; and who, under the pressure of severe infirmity, enjoys the lively vigour of his mind, and the felicity of his incomparable temper. LORD NORTH will permit me to express the feelings of friendship in the language of truth: but even truth and friendship should be silent, if he still dispensed the favours of the Crown. (*DF* l:xlv)

Political enemies criticized the wisdom of this view, but not the motivation of the statement. Lord North's reply shows what deep pleasure Gibbon's kindness gave him:

> Upon the receipt of your books and the perusal of your preface, my heart was too full to give you an immediate answer: so kind and honourable a testimony of your friendship and esteem would have afforded me the greatest pleasure in the moment of my highest health and political prosperity; judge then what I must feel upon receiving it in my retirement, while labouring under a calamity which would be severe, were it not for the goodness of my friends.[50]

"As far as I can judge," Gibbon wrote to Dorothea Gibbon, "the public unanimously applauds my compliment to Lord North, and does not appear dissatisfied with the conclusion of my work" (*Letters* 3:107). Those who were personally acquainted with North concurred. Sheffield considered the compliment "beautiful and just."

Gibbon's year in England had been so successful that his friends hoped to retain him there permanently, or at least to persuade him to extend his visit. He mended fences with polite letters to relatives he had not visited,[51] convinced Mrs. Gibbon that the one week available for another Bath visit would simply exhaust and agitate both of them (*Letters* 3:108), and wrote forthrightly to Sheffield,

> After a full and free enjoyment of each other's society, let us submit without a struggle to reason and fate. It would be idle to pretend business at Lausanne but a compleat Year will elapse before my return, Severy and

myself are now expected with some impatience and I will frankly own that I desire to see *my own* house *my own* library, *my own* garden, whose summer beauties are each day losing something. I am grateful for your hospitable entertainment, but I wish you to remember Homer's admirable precept

Wellcome the coming, *speed* the party guest. (*Letters* 3:112)

To the public he would add, in his *Memoirs*, "The tumult of London astonished my eyes and ears: the amusements of public places were no longer adequate to the trouble: the clubs and assemblies were filled with new faces and young men; and our best society our long and late dinners would soon have been prejudicial to my health" (*Memoirs* 183). But young Wilhelm perhaps says it best: "Yesterday, talking with Gibbon, I saw that he rejoiced and that his face grew animated at the idea of seeing again his *home*, for that is what he always calls it. Someone asked him the other day what was the population of Lausanne. 'Well,' he said in his usual tone, 'there may be nine to ten thousand souls, but what is essential is a society of two hundred people, as good as one could wish.' "[52] On July 21, 1788, Gibbon and Wilhelm set out for that home; on the 30th, they arrived.

FOURTEEN

Alone in Paradise:
Remaking a Life

uring a year of friendship and triumph in England, Gibbon's heart had remained in Lausanne. He had written to Deyverdun upon arrival in London, "The mountains have grown smaller, the dragons that bordered the highways have vanished, everything, even the Customs, has proved easy and smooth. . . . I occupy myself in the immense solitude of the Capital in making all my preliminary arrangements, and next week, I will retire to the country. . . . Adieu . . . Love me always, and take care of your health" (*Letters* 3:69–70). The latter injunction was not superfluous: when Gibbon returned to Lausanne, he found "a sad and serious alteration in poor Deyverdun"; less than two months later, Deyverdun suffered two nearly fatal attacks of apoplexy, and less than a year later, he died. "I thought I was prepared," Gibbon would say, "but this blow has overwhelmed me. After thirty-three years—Adieu" (*Letters* 3:156). Thus, relatively soon after his return to Lausanne, and despite an ever-growing friendship with the Sévery family, Gibbon was to find and feel himself to be alone—as lonely in the worldly paradise of Lausanne as in the immense solitude of London. In this emotional emergency, Gibbon tried or contemplated various consolations—he visited friends, remodeled La Grotte (the house he had shared with Deyverdun), thought of returning to England, offered to adopt his young cousin as his daughter, and even considered, once again, the possibility of marriage. But the most successful expedient was autobiography. Even before Deyverdun's death, Gibbon had begun to write the only work other than the *Decline and Fall* with which his name is identified, his memoirs. But after that event, making and remaking an account of himself, an "image of his mind," "My Own Life," was a major resource in his newly lonely bachelor existence.

Gibbon never borrowed trouble. When he first returned to Lausanne from England, he saw that his old friend was not in good health. But Deyverdun was only four years older than Gibbon, fifty-three or fifty-four, and both friends persuaded themselves that Deyverdun's "decline" was not life-threatening. Deyverdun, indeed, saw no need for the restrictions of food and drink recommended by his doctor. So Gibbon could write cheerfully to his stepmother, "The perils of the ocean and the road, imaginary perils, are now over, and I am again seated in the elegant repose of my library and garden: free to enjoy all the pleasures of study, my first pleasures, but no longer chained to the regular performance of a laborious task" (*Letters* 3:125). In August and September Gibbon's most serious problem was the regulating of his engagements, and in September, he enjoyed a particular triumph and pleasure in the visit of Charles Fox, who "gave [Gibbon] two days of free and private society." In Fox Gibbon "admired the powers of a superior man, as they are blended in his attractive character, with the softness and simplicity of a child. Perhaps no human being was ever more perfectly exempt from the taint of malevolence, vanity or falsehood" (*Memoirs* 190). This famous tribute is confirmed and amplified by Gibbon's description in his letters at the time:

> I was informed that [Fox] was arrived at the Lyon-d'or. I sent a compliment, he answered it in person; we returned together to the Inn, brought away the fair Mrs Arm[i]stead, and settled at my house for the remainder of the day. I have eat and drank and conversed and sat up all night with Fox in England; but it never has happened perhaps it never can happen again, that I should enjoy him as I did that day, alone (for his fair Companion was a cypher,) from ten in the morning till ten at night. Poor Deyverdun . . . wanted spirits to appear and has regretted it since. Our conversation never flagged a moment, and he seemed thoroughly pleased with the place, and with his Company. We had little politicks, though he gave me in a few words such a character of Pitt as one great man should give of another his rival: much of book[s], from my own on which he flattered me very pleasantly to Homer and the Arabian nights: much about the country, my garden which he understands far better than I do, and upon the whole I think he envies me and would do so were he Minister. The next morning I gave him a guide to walk him about the town and country and invited some company to meet him at dinner. The following day he continued his journey. (*Letters* 3:132)

Gibbon's glowing picture of Fox, who was twelve years his junior, yet his contemporary in political life, is confirmed by Burke: "the most artless, candid, open, and benevolent disposition; disinterested in the extreme; of a temper mild and placable, even to a fault; without one drop of gall in his whole constitution."[1] Relative to Fox, an absence of gall in Gibbon's own constitution is also to be remarked. It is true that (as Sheffield pointed out) Gibbon never knew that he was passed over for the secretaryship of the Paris embassy by "the act of his friend Mr. Fox, contrary to the solicitations of Mr. Craufurd, and other of his friends."[2] Fox's recommendation on that occasion might be understood as a recognition of what would truly benefit Gibbon, or as a principled decision, rather than as a betrayal of his friend to benefit another candidate for patronage; but Sheffield obviously does not see it in so favorable a light. Unaware of this slight, Gibbon did not have to forgive it. But he did know about, and obviously had forgiven, an earlier attack on him by Fox, Fox's witty verse rebuke for his writing the *Mémoire justicatif*. Gibbon's admiration of Fox was far from uncritical, and he would strongly disagree with Fox once more in 1791, on the French Revolution, but "let him do what he will I must love the dog" (*Letters* 3:313). Fox's reported account of this 1788 visit is much less gall-free than Gibbon's; Fox is not averse to comedy at the expense of his friend: "Gibbon talked a great deal, walking up and down the room, and generally ending his sentences with a genitive case; every now and then, too, casting a look of complacency on his own portrait by Sir Joshua Reynolds, which hung over the chimney-piece."[3] It would spoil the joke to point out that the portrait was the property of Deyverdun, who, ominously, was not feeling well enough to see the distinguished visitor.

Fox's visit was on Thursday and Friday, September 18–19, 1788. They were literally the last days of Gibbon's autumnal idyll; on Saturday, September 20, he was "suddenly recalled from [his] berçeau to the house by the dreadful intelligence of [Deyverdun's] Apoplectic stroke" (*Letters* 3:131). Though Deyverdun was to live for almost a year longer, Gibbon's tone in portraying his enjoyment of freedom and Lausanne is already elegiac in these letters of 1788. His reluctance to accept the darkened reality (he was writing when Deyverdun was convalescent from the first attack) is signaled by a revealing change of tense:

> After having been so long chained to the oar in a splendid galley indeed, I . . . *range* without controul over the wide expanse of my library, converse, as my fancy prompts me with poets and historians, philosophers and Orators of every age and language, and often indulge my meditations in the invention and arrangement of mighty works which I shall probably never find time or application to execute. My garden, *berçeau* and pavillion often *varied* the scene of my studies, the beautiful weather which we have enjoyed exhilarated my spirits, and I again tasted the wisdom and happiness of my retirement. (*Letters* 3:130–31; emphasis added)

The past tense shows his unacknowledged awareness that in losing the pleasure of companionship, he had already lost the perfection of this philosopher's paradise. One of the "mighty works" he contemplated, however, was an account of his own life. This work was inspired or at least spurred on by two things: Gibbon's acquisition of a book that appeared to give him access to a long extension for his family history, and his views about literary biography—that it was a genre valuable to the reader of literature (including, of course, history) and that the most reliable form of literary biography was autobiography. In 1786 Gibbon's friend Ernst Langer had "accidentally found among some litterary rubbish a small, old English Volume of Heraldry, inscribed with the name of *John Gibbon*." Gibbon, then in the throes of composing his final volumes, in which there are several references to the interesting issues of genealogy and hereditary honors, including the "Digression on the Family of Courtenay," could not make much use of this work at the time, but he "soon convinced [him]self that the author was not only my namesake, but my kinsman. . . . in my last visit to England, I was tempted to indulge a curiosity which had been excited by this odd discovery. Some wills, parishregisters, and monumental inscriptions were consulted at my request, and my enquiries were assisted by Mr. *Brooke*, the Somerset Herald."[4]

Gibbon had essayed autobiography once before. In the summer of 1783, probably at the request of Brissot de Warville, Gibbon had written a 1,000-word, third-person account of his life in French (unpublished; see Appendix). Brissot intended to publish it, with an engraving of Gibbon's portrait, in a "historic gallery." Gibbon had consented to provide the account, and Brissot "saw . . . that he was not displeased to transmit to posterity both the memory of his life and the characteristics of his singular face." But Gibbon was too slow in complying, and he was not included in any of the numerous "galleries" examined by J. E. Norton.[5] Gibbon's 1783 French sketch (see Appendix below) is related to the later drafts of the *Memoirs* much as the "Outlines" and the "General Observations" are related to the *Decline and Fall:* it covers the same material, is organized both chronologically and topically, reveals some of the same attitudes as the larger work, but is almost totally devoid of its subjectivity and structural complexity.

Those fearful of psychohistory will be disturbed to see that Gibbon considers worthy of comment, even in this brief account, not just his intellectual development, but his loss of a mother and gain of a loving stepmother, his six deceased siblings, his sickly childhood and his family's expectation of his death. He omits, on the other hand, his aunt, his friends, his love affair, and his conversion to Catholicism. The sketch is not only written in the third person, but expressed as if its author were not Gibbon himself, but rather some friendly, yet dispassionate, well-informed observer. The first paragraph is devoted to Gibbon's birth and parents; the second, to his siblings, sickliness, early education, and youthful sojourn at Lausanne, concluding, "He recognizes with pleasure that it is to Lausanne that he owes the knowledge of the French language, the taste for study, and the development of reason." The third paragraph tells of his two subsequent Continental journeys (clearly Gibbon had not yet returned to Lausanne to live when he wrote this passage), calling the society of Paris that he had enjoyed in 1777 "the pleasantest and most enlightened in the world." The fourth paragraph is devoted to his military and parliamentary careers. "As this battalion never saw the enemy, he did not acquire in some domestic campaigns the reputation of a warrior," he concludes of the former. As for the latter, "During eight years he was present at the most important deliberations, but he never found the courage or the talent to speak in a public assembly." These sentiments, almost in these words, are familiar to readers of his English memoirs, but I translate quite literally.

Only with the fifth paragraph does Gibbon turn to his writing, and there he mentions only the three works he had then published under his name, the youthful *Essai*, the three volumes of the *Decline and Fall*, and the *Vindication*. "A decided taste for history soon engaged him in this career; and after having meditated several subjects, he fixed finally on the decline and fall of the Roman Empire, the idea of which he had conceived in Rome itself. Some years were devoted to the compilation and arrangement of a work so toilsome, and from the year 1772 when he transported his library to London, he delivered himself with ardor to its composition." Pointing out that he does not pronounce on the merits of his work, Gibbon proudly enumerates its editions and translations. "Not having the honor of being a Theologian, he allowed [a crowd of ecclesiatical adversaries] to reason or rave at their ease, but a young man having had the boldness to attack not only the faith but the good faith of the historian, he was reduced to the easy but humiliating task of confounding the calumniator." The final paragraph mentions the recent octavo edition of the first three volumes (May 1783) and Gibbon's present task. "This undertaking demands of him several more years of sustained application, but whatever its success, he finds in this application itself a pleasure continually varied and continually renewed."

This outline of his life was obviously in Gibbon's hands, and sometimes in his mind, as he began to work on his English memoirs. He may also have known another account of his life, published shortly before the last three volumes of the history appeared, in the *European Magazine and London Review* for March 1788. It is not certain that Gibbon saw this anonymous article (the journal is not known to have been in his library), but he was in England when it appeared, and it is unlikely that his friends failed to tell him about an essay that found him "equal to any living foreign author, and but little inferior to the

great historians of antiquity."[6] This piece, however, is principally
appreciative and only secondarily biographical. The biographical material includes references to two of Gibbon's anonymous publications,
the *Critical Observations on the Sixth Book of the Aeneid* and the *Mémoire
justicatif*, thus possibly encouraging him to acknowledge them. But it
is unlikely that this first biography of Gibbon had much influence on
his memoirs.

He probably began to work on draft A in August of 1788. It was
written in his "fifty-second year," that is, before May 1789, and in
fact in 1788, as we know from the reference to his acquisition (1786)
of John Gibbon's book "not two years since."[7] "He took a new 4to
note-book and filled its first page with the full title he had decided
upon, carefully, elaborately composing it."[8] The title thus composed
was "The Memoirs of the life of Edward Gibbon, with various observations and excursions by himself." Under the heading "Chapter I,"
Gibbon then listed the intended contents: "Introduction—Account of
my family—My grandfather—My father—My birth in the year 1737—
My infancy—My first education and studies." His first impulse—the
"introduction"—is to justify the undertaking and define for himself
the demands of the genre:

> I now propose to employ some moments of my leisure in reviewing the
> simple transactions of a private and litterary life. Truth, naked unblushing
> truth, the first virtue of more serious history, must be the sole recommen-
> dation of this personal narrative: the style shall be simple and familiar; but
> style is the image of character, and the habits of correct writing may
> produce, without labour or design, the appearance of art and study. My
> own amusement is my motive, and will be my reward; and if these sheets
> are communicated to some discreet and indulgent friends, they will be
> secreted from the public eye till the author shall be removed from the
> reach of criticism or ridicule.

This statement defines a narrative pose, not literal and unmediated
tenets, as we can tell by the *personification* of the call for simple truth,
and by the announcement that the work will not be published.
Sheffield adds a note: "Mr. Gibbon . . . expressed a determination of
publishing [his memoirs] in his lifetime. . . . In a conversation . . .
not long before his death, I suggested to him that, if he should make
them a full image of his mind, he would not have nerves to publish
them, and therefore that they should be posthumous. He answered,
rather eagerly, that he was determined to publish them *in his lifetime*."[9]

Thus we may infer that we should not take these claims of artless-
ness, simple truth, mere amusement, and above all, absence of audience, too literally. They are, however, reliable as indices of the spirit
in which the memoir was written and in which Gibbon wished it to
be read. The tone and contents of draft A are friendly, frank, com-
plaisant, and complacent. Gibbon discusses matters with his reader

as if the reader were a "discreet and indulgent friend." The nature of this relationship can readily be appreciated by comparing the passage on interest in ancestors as it appears in draft A with a passage very similar in content on one of the detached sheets that were found with the drafts of the memoirs, in a much more impersonal and "philo-sophic" voice. I shall supply one example:

> For my own part, could I draw my pedigree from a General, a statesman, or a celebrated author, I should study their lives or their writings with the diligence of filial love, and I suspect that from this casual relation some emotions of pleasure—shall I say of vanity?—might arise in my breast. Yet I will add that . . . I would rather descend from Cicero than from Marius, from Chaucer than from one of the first Companions of the Garter. The family of Confucius is, in my opinion, the noblest upon Earth. . . . I have exposed my private feelings, as I shall always do, without scruple or reserve——Let every reader, whether noble or plebeian, examine his own conscience on the same subject.

> If any of [our ancestors] have been conspicuous above their equals by personal merit and glorious atchievments, the generous feelings of the heart will sympathize in an alliance with such characters; nor does the man exist who would not peruse with warmer curiosity the life of an hero from which his name and blood were lineally derived. . . . but in the estimate of honour we should learn to value the gifts of Nature above those of fortune; to esteem in our ancestors the qualities that best promote the interest of Society, and to pronounce the descendant of a King less truly noble than the offspring of a man of Genius, whose writings will instruct or delight the latest posterity. The family of Confucius is, in my opinion, the most illustrious in the World. . . . I exhort [the Spencers, the duke of Marlborough's family,] to consider the *Faery Queen* as the most precious jewel of their coronet. . . . Our immortal Fielding was of a younger branch of . . . . the family of Habsburgh. . . . The successors of Charles the fifth may disdain their humble brethren of England, but the Romance of Tom Jones, that exquisite picture of human manners, will outlive the palace of the Escurial and the Imperial Eagle of the house of Austria.[10]

It is surely not necessary to say that the former version is from the intimate, chatty draft A, the latter from the magisterial separate paper.

In this first attempt at his memoirs, written while it still seemed possible that Deyverdun would recover and their pleasant life at Lausanne continue, Gibbon's treatment of his "ancestor" John Gibbon and of the discovery of John Gibbon's book is similarly good-humored and personal. After several pages of quotation and commentary, Gibbon concludes, "But enough of these solemn trifles," quotes a tribute to one ancestress "graced with modesty, manners, innocency, affability, and good parentage: and acceptable to all, and so liberal to the poor as was incredible," and comments archly, "Such women at all times are rare, and it is a pleasure to descend from one of them." Thinking John Gibbon the brother of his great-grandfather, Gibbon discusses John's passion for heraldry in his account of that generation. John, seeing an Indian war dance, believed their war paint to show that "heraldry was ingrafted naturally into the sense of human race." Gibbon comments, "Such an idea . . . displays a degree of enthusiasm for a favourite study, which is at once ridiculous and respectable." The reader is invited to perceive a comic parallel between author John Gibbon and author Edward Gibbon, which reappears in the final draft of the memoirs, when Gibbon says, "In the failure of these hopes [of immortality through his book], John Gibbon has not been the first of his profession, and may not be the last of his name."[11]

Draft A is informal in structure as well as tone. Within the loose limits defined by his chapter heading, Gibbon allows himself to digress, as his title promises. For example, he comments, apropos of his grandfather's fate in the South Sea Bubble debacle, on arbitrary actions of Parliament: "It must be lamented that the Whigs have too often sullied the principles of freedom by the practise of violence and tyranny." Books, relevant and irrelevant, are allowed to redirect by association the progress of this personal narrative. Gibbon's boyhood interview with his father after his mother's death, for instance, reminds the autobiographer—or perhaps reminds Gibbon of a comparison that his younger self was soon to make—between this scene and "the grief of the Marquis on the death of his beloved Selima" in "that interesting romance of the Abbé Prevot d'Exiles, the Memoires d'un homme de qualité," which had then recently been translated into English. As soon as he read Prévost's *Mémoires* he found the resemblance striking, Gibbon says. To describe his father's way of life, he utilizes David Mallet's poem, "The Wedding Day," in which his father, an inconsolable widower but happy farmer, receives six lines in the capacity of wedding guest, but Gibbon adds, "By a wise dispensation, which preserves the balance of riches, idleness is the heir of industry; and the thirst of gain is succeeded by the desire of enjoyment. . . . [My father's] expences soon exceeded the measure of his income," and necessity contributed as much as grief or choice to his retirement to country life.[12]

The most conspicuous example of Gibbon's proceeding in this draft not by design but by literary association is his moving from his father not to his own birth and childhood, as planned, but to the brother and two sisters portrayed in William Law's *Serious Call to a Devout Life.* Family tradition held that these characters were portrayals of Gibbon's father and his two sisters. Chronology (Law's book was published when Gibbon's father was only eighteen) suggests that the characters can hardly be literal portraits of the young Gibbons; "the prophetic eye of the tutor must have discerned the butterfly in the caterpillar. But . . . from my own observation, I can acknowledge the skill of the painter and the likeness of the portrait." Gibbon goes even further astray from his avowed plan, however, in commenting on Law himself, or rather on his works: "I can pronounce with more confidence on his writings than on his person, as I have found and perused several of his books in my father's library,"[13] and, we may add, Gibbon not only preserved six of them in his own library, but also caused them to be transported to Lausanne, perhaps in the seven additional cases of books he had selected during his recent stay in England (*Letters* 3:109, with n. 6).[14]

At this point in Gibbon's composition of his memoirs, he was interrupted. Indeed, I think that all of the genial and consciously artless draft A precedes Deyverdun's attacks of "apoplexy" (I borrow Gibbon's term without vouching for its medical accuracy); certainly draft B, which was definitely written after Deyverdun's mortal illness had become almost undeniable, is very different. Though it is possible that some of draft A was written after the first acute stage of Deyverdun's illness had passed, when Gibbon tried to think his friend's recovery possible and tried to resume his ordinary way of life, it seems unlikely that he was able to achieve its cheerful garrulous spontaneity during this period. He achieved the appearance of his ordinary life only with some effort. His denial, or his selfishness, or both, may be seen in a letter to Catherine de Sévery, dated persuasively by Norton to the period of Deyverdun's first attacks. Here is the whole note, less a few medical details:

> Alas Madame, there is no longer any question of society or amusement. Day before yesterday my poor friend had two attacks of a fulminant apoplexy, and for many hours I was without hope of saving him. But our physicians Tissot and Scholl have employed all the resources of their art and nature has seconded them. Since yesterday evening we have been able to breathe again . . . [there are] only favorable symptoms, but can we allow ourselves to be confident, when any moment a third attack—Goodby my good friends, if you were nearer to me I think I would suffer less.
> Monday morning, nine o'clock
>   We have only one melon. (*Letters* 3:128)

He suffers, true, but he does not forget the shortage of melons in his distress.

Deyverdun's first attacks occurred at the end of September. For the rest of the year, and in the beginning of the next, Gibbon's correspondence includes many references to Deyverdun's health—he is better, he is no worse, this harsh lesson has not taught him temperance—but also dinner engagements, politics, orders for wine and clothing. Gibbon spent three weeks in November with the Séverys at their house in Rolle, during which he joined them in a tour to Geneva (*Letters* 3:135).

In December Sheffield wrote to tell Gibbon of the death of his agent at Buriton, Hugonin, a death sure to result in financial complications for Gibbon. "Poor Hugonin!" Gibbon replied:

> I can assure you that my thoughts, my first thoughts at least when I read your letter turned much more on himself. I knew him from my youth: he was an honest useful friend, and though he could never be much of a companion to me, I always loved and esteemed him. . . . We are now cold and gay at Lausanne. . . . Adieu for the present. Deyverdun is not worse.
> (*Letters* 3:137)

The year 1788 ended very gloomily. Gibbon wrote to Sheffield,

> We are in the midst of the hardest winter I ever felt. . . . A black prospect indeed of public and private affairs. . . . Is it possible that my old friend poor Hugonin should turn out a rogue. . . . You are my only refuge. . . . You wait for my instructions, I can send none. You are an able and active friend, and I shall acquiesce in all you think right. . . . For God's sake, or rather for friendship's sake comfort and extricate me. I am in low spirits. Adieu.
> Ever Yours E G. (*Letters* 3:139)

To this despairing letter Sheffield sent a reply no doubt meant to be bracing, but effectually harsh. Gibbon received it on February 4:

> I feel and confess the true friendship which breathes through the apparent *harshness* of your style but is that harshness absolutely necessary? it can give you no pleasure and it sometimes gives me pain. If Hugonin's debt be desperate I must submit, but there is no *imbecillity* in saying that the loss will derange my plans. . . . On smaller matters you are too earnest and almost angry. . . . Your copiousness on my affairs makes you concise on those of the public. . . . Above all I wish to hear what part you are likely yourself to act in the new regency, your hopes, your wishes, and whether you intend next winter to breathe the free and pleasant air of Lausanne or to tug at the parliamentary and official oar amid the fogs of London. Of my book I have not leisure or inclination to talk. Its genuine reputation will rise or fall without any regard to the barking critics. . . . Poor Deyverdun has had another, a slighter, attack, he is now better, but I fear that his days will be neither long nor happy. A melancholy theme.

Yet Gibbon possessed "a perpetual source of independent and rational pleasure," a "passion which derives fresh vigour from enjoyment," the love of study; and he was "endowed with a chearful temper" (*Memoirs* 186). Thus by the middle of the month, he was sufficiently restored to write to Cadell about his book: "I am happy to find that you express yourself, with some reserve, satisfied with the sale. From some reports of angry criticisms, and from the use and abuse of my name in the papers, I perceive that I am not forgotten. Before a year has elapsed from the time of publication, my History will have been perused by some thousand readers of various characters and understandings." He adds that he has "thrown aside" several plans for new works, "but if the warm weather should ripen any project to form and maturity, you may depend on the earliest intelligence" (*Letters* 3:143).

Among Gibbon's other preoccupations during this period was the sale of Buriton. Complicated by Hugonin's death (a year and a half of rents were lost) and the necessity of changing the security for Mrs. Gibbon's jointure (Gibbon repeatedly reminds Sheffield that he wishes her to be perfectly comfortable about it), the sale was finally accomplished in April: "Well then I have £16,000 pounds [*sic*] instead of Buriton! upon the whole I rejoyce in the exchange" (*Letters* 3:150). Deyverdun, though unable to learn the "lesson of temperance" (*Letters* 3:148) on which his life depended, had been sufficiently aware of his dangerous state to rouse himself to make his will. Gibbon confides to Sheffield, "You will be glad to hear that I am now assured of possessing during my life this delightful house and garden. The act has been *lately* executed in the best form and the handsomest manner" (*Letters* 3:152—it should be noted that the underscores on Gibbon's letters to Sheffield were often made by the latter). But the news about Deyverdun was otherwise more and more disheartening. He had two or three more attacks in the first four months of 1789. "Every time the door is hastily opened I expect to hear of some fatal accident" (*Letters* 3:152), Gibbon wrote. His fears were hardly lessened by two deaths among his circle of friends and relations: in March, the Swiss wife of an English friend died; in June, his uncle Stanier Porten.

It was, I think, in this context of consciousness both of the pressure of death on the historian and of a widening circle of unknown acquaintances for the history that he returned to the memoirs, starting again on a new plan. Internal evidence strongly ties this second draft to June 1789 and the immediately preceding months; less strong evidence suggests that it might have been begun as early as the end of 1788.[15] This draft, draft B, fills seventy-two quarto pages and takes his story down to 1764, just before his departure for Italy and his twenty-seventh birthday. It is probably connected with a sheet of memoranda (similar to the memoranda Gibbon made for the prepublication revisions of volumes 5 and 6—see p. 253 above) in British Library Add. MSS. 34882, f. 284. This unpublished list contains forty-one names, ancient and modern, of which the common denominator is that each left some account of his own life—letters, diaries, apologies, autobiographies. Ten names have been deleted, and some are added to the right of the others, or squeezed in between two previously written names. Most interestingly, all the undeleted names have been assigned a number. Clearly Gibbon made and amended the list and then used the numbers to indicate to himself some plan of classification (in a few cases, a number has been changed). In classification 1 he places the following: Cicero, Josephus (deleted), Frithemius (changed from 2), Pliny, M. Antoninus, and Libanus—possibly St. Augustine—the number is not clear. Classification 2 contains Petrarch and Abelard. Classification 3 contains Erasmus, Cardan, Buchanan, Th. Scaliger (deleted), Wolfius, Montagne, Cellini. The fourth category includes Clarendon, Thuanus, Herbert, Marolles, Bayle and Le Clerc (deleted), Huet, Wood, and Hobbes. Finally we have Reiske (deleted), Goldoni, Whitfield, Duval, Quirini, Cibber, Whiston, Pearce, Newton (the bishop, not Sir Isaac), Rousseau, and Hume. Bentivogli seems to be assigned a "9" and deleted. Gray and Temple and "Gataker"? were deleted without having been numbered.

The classification is roughly chronological, but its eclecticism of genre, country, and period is striking, especially considering the new introduction Gibbon now produced for his autobiography:

> A sincere and simple narrative of my own life may amuse some of my leisure hours, but it will expose me, and perhaps with justice, to the imputation of vanity. Yet I may judge, from the experience both of past and of the present times, that the public is always curious to *know* the men who have left behind them any image of their minds. . . . The author of an important and successful work may hope without presumption that he is not totally indifferent to his numerous readers . . . and I must be conscious that no one is so well qualified as myself to describe the series of my thoughts and actions. . . . it would not be difficult to produce a long list of ancients and moderns who, in various forms, have exhibited their own portraits. Such portraits are often the most interesting, and sometimes the only interesting, parts of their writings; and, if they be sincere, we seldom complain of the minuteness or prolixity of these personal memorials.

He then enumerates writers "known" to their readers by their epistles (Pliny the younger, Petrarch, Erasmus), by their essays (Temple and Montaigne), by their passions or follies at which we "smile without contempt" (Cellini, Cibber), by their confessions (Augustine, Rousseau); by works less interesting than their lives—"the Commentaries of the learned Huet have survived his Evangelical demonstration; and the Memoirs of Goldoni are more truly dramatic than his Italian comedies." Whiston and Bishop Newton play the roles of Heretic and Churchman, and "even the dullness of Michael de Marolles and Anthony Wood acquires some value from the faithful representation of men and manners. That I am the equal or superior of some of these Biographers the efforts of modesty or affectation cannot force me to dissemble."[16]

We infer that in Gibbon's view a biography is a description of "the series of [someone's] thoughts and actions"; sincerity excuses prolixity; biographies can differ widely in form and tone. Lives of individuals can be valuable for insight into various matters: individual experiences, individual or collective psychology, human types, and social history. Above all, the public is legitimately curious about the human beings who have produced "image[s] of their minds." With these positions firmly worked out for himself, Gibbon proceeded to write draft B, now called "My Own Life," beginning with his fortunate birth: "My lot might have been that of a slave, a savage, or a peasant; nor can I reflect without pleasure on the bounty of Nature, which cast my birth in a free and civilized country, in an age of science and Philosophy, in a family of honourable rank, and decently endowed with the gifts of fortune."[17]

This theme of appreciation of his good fortune, which, though moderate enough, was, on the scale of all humankind and human history, bountiful, remains a part of the memoirs hereafter. The destiny of becoming the historian of the Roman Empire is only the culmination—"few works of merit and importance have been executed either in a garret or a palace," we remember (*Memoirs* 153)—of a life in which even misfortunes can be taken as having happy results. Ironically, this theme, which is presented by Gibbon as an instance of the human contribution to human destiny, the capacity to choose whether to regard the proverbial glass as half full or half empty, is later misunderstood as literal fact rather than deliberate interpretation, so that Gibbon's hard-won equanimity is seen as mere luck, and he is even patronized, perhaps unconsciously, by admirers such as Leslie Stephen and Lytton Strachey, for his lack of Romantic Agony.

According to Strachey, Gibbon's life was "an epitome of the blessings of the eighteenth century." Without his struggling, "everything came naturally to him . . . in the correct proportions." In the history, "by the penetrating influence of style—*automatically, inevitably*—lucidity, balance, and precision were everywhere introduced, and the miracle of order was established over a thousand years" (emphasis added).[18] More justly, Stephen, though he regards Gibbon's autobiography as a rare record of a life that was a "complete success" and his apparent misfortunes as blessings in disguise, adds that this is "a fact which does not diminish Gibbon's credit for taking the hints in the right way."[19] But even this misses two key points; first, the facts of Gibbon's life were as easily interpreted as neutral or unfortunate— they have even been seen as tragic—and second, as draft B continually shows, Gibbon sees human choice and character as factors in human fate, as well as general laws and particular chance.

"The chances that I should not live to compose this narrative were, at the time of my birth, in the proportion of above three to one," writes Gibbon. "Such may be the general probabilities of human life, but the ordinary dangers of infancy were multiplied far beyond this measure by my personal infirmities." General laws and particular circumstances conspired, then, to predict his death. But human actions can affect either events or the significance of those events. Gibbon's parents could do little about the probable event of his death, though they provided for him the only protection against childhood dangers then available, inoculation against smallpox. But Gibbon's parents nevertheless protected themselves (he thought) against the loss of what he signified: "after bestowing at my baptism the favourite appellation of Edward, they provided a substitute, in case of my departure, by successively adding it to the Christian names of my younger brothers." They also provided every dubious aid that money could buy: "the fees of Doctors were swelled by the bills of Apothecaries and Surgeons." Human efforts do not necessarily have their planned effect, however: "From these ills and from these remedies I have wonderfully escaped."[20]

Draft B dispatches in five pages the materials of A's thirty-nine pages. It includes no conversation with the reader, no genial confessional comments. It treats the self as subject of the memoir as a figure quite distinct from the self as writer—as a topic for historical study.[21] The memory of the writer is a resource like any other:

> When I strive to ascend into the night and oblivion of infancy, the most early circumstance which I can connect with any known æra is my father's contest and election for Southampton. At that time (1740) I was about three years of age: I had already acquired the familiar use of my mother-tongue, and I was soon instructed in the elements of reading and writing, which in this age of learning are almost as universal as those of language. In the seventh year of my age . . . I was delivered to the care of a domestic tutor. . . . A child is incapable of estimating the learning and genius of his præceptor; but at the end of four and forty years, I can discern them in his writing.[22]

All Gibbon's own experiences are seen as events in general history; that is, at issue in this account is the relationship between his particular experience and human feelings and capacities in general. "The expression may appear burlesque, but there is not in the course of life a more remarkable change than the removal of a child (I was then about eight years old) from the freedom and luxury of a wealthy house to the frugal diet and strict subordination of a school"; "I soon tasted the Arabian nights entertainments—a book of all ages, since in my present maturity I can revolve without contempt that pleasing medley of Oriental manners and supernatural fictions. But it is in rude ages and to youthful minds that the marvellous is most attractive"; and

> When I reflect . . . on the advantages which I gained in a liberal acquaintance with the nations, the manners, and the idiom of Europe, I must rather rejoyce than repine at my early deliverance from the habits and

prejudices of an English Cloyster. But instead of speculating on what *might* have been the colour of my life and opinions, I shall now state with simple sincerity the result of my personal experience of Magdalen College in the university of Oxford.[23]

Examples could easily be multiplied. "Gibbon virtually denies 'the tension between self-image and social recognition.' He seeks in his experience a universal logic. . . . [Draft B is] a memoir in which his role as author . . . dominate[s] his depiction."[24]

Draft B breaks off abruptly in 1764: "And thus was I armed for my Italian journey."[25] The reason that Gibbon stopped writing, clearly, was Deyverdun's death. He had survived long enough to try the waters at Aix-les-Bains, but while he was there, on July 4, 1789, he died. Gibbon was in Lausanne, not in Aix with his friend. Ten days later Gibbon "recollect[ed him]self" sufficiently to write to Sheffield, "I fancied that time and reflection had prepared me for the event, but the habits of three and thirty years friendship are not so easily broken. The first days and more especially the first nights were indeed painful. Last Wednesday and Saturday [post days] it would not have been in my power to write" (*Letters* 3:157). He needed Sheffield's advice about whether to purchase La Grotte outright from Deyverdun's heir at law, or to settle for a life tenancy—the choice was guaranteed to him by Deyverdun's will. A reason for purchase was the possible appreciation of the property, a subject of no interest except to one who plans to sell:

> Should I ever migrate homewards (You stare, but such an event is less improbable than I could have thought it two years ago) . . . the difference would perhaps clear the expences of my removal. . . . Weigh these reasons. . . . But alas when all is determined, I shall possess this house by what-soever tenure, without friendship or domestic society. I did not imagine six years ago, that a plan of life so congenial to my wishes, would so speedily vanish. I cannot write upon any other subject. (*Letters* 3:160)

Clearly Deyverdun's death had interrupted more than Gibbon's writing. In draft B, in describing his youthful studies at Lausanne, Gibbon had said: "Mr. Deyverdun, my friend, whose name will be frequently repeated, had joyned with equal zeal. though not with equal perseverance, in the same undertaking. To him every thought, every composition, was instantly communicated; with him I enjoyed the benefits of a free conversation on the topics of our common studies." In C, the next draft, which repeats long passages of B verbatim, or changes them solely by compression, the account of Deyverdun parallel to this passage has been converted to a little elegy for friend and friendship: "Mr. George Deyverdun, of Lausanne, was a young Gentleman of high honour and quick feelings, of an elegant taste and a liberal understanding: he became the companion of my studies and pleasures; every idea, every sentiment, was poured into each other's bosom; and our schemes of ambition or retirement always terminated in the prospect of our final and inseparable union."[26]

Two years later, Gibbon continued to look back at the dissolution of this union. He speaks of his grief in the past tense, but with vivid recollection. "Before [Deyverdun] expired . . . those who loved him could not wish for the continuance of his life. . . . but the feelings of Nature and friendship could be subdued only by time: his amiable character was still alive in my remembrance; each room, each walk was imprinted with our common footsteps." Thanks to Deyverdun's will, Gibbon points out, "few men of letters, perhaps, in Europe, are so desirably lodged as myself. But I feel, and with the decline of years, I shall more painfully feel, that I am alone in Paradise" (*Memoirs* 184). And for the first few months after Deyverdun's death, Gibbon was not only unable to write, but unable to remain in the house and garden haunted by his memories of his friend.

During his mourning, his other ties seem dearer to him. For instance, he seems somewhat more cheerful in writing to Sheffield on July 22, 1789, but his concern for his stepmother is more marked, perhaps more tender, than usual. "I think she cannot last very long but I should be hurt if her last days were embittered by any fears or scruples" (*Letters* 3:161). He appears to turn to less personal subjects in parts of the letter, "rejoicing," for example, to hear of the marriage of two friends, Sylvester Douglas and Katherine North, but a tender mood is hinted by his hope that they will live with her father, the blind Lord North. He is anxious about Sheffield's portrait by Reynolds, which is to be sent to Lausanne. And it is only in a postscript that he concludes, "Are you not amazed at the French revolution. They have the power, will they have the moderation to establish a good constitution?" (*Letters* 3:161). Three days later, he writes to Sheffield again, not about the revolution in France, but about the possibility of returning to England:

> The prospect before me is a melancholy solitude. I am still deeply rooted in this country: the possession of this paradise, the friendships of the Severys, a mode of society suited to my taste and the enormous trouble and *expence* of a migration. Yet in England . . . I could form a very comfortable establishment in London or rather at Bath. . . . Sir Stanier Porten is just dead; he has left his widow with a small pension and two children my nearest relations: the eldest, Charlotte is about Louisa's age [twelve], and one of the most amiable sensible young creatures I ever saw. I have conceived a romantic idea of educating and adopting her . . . Charlotte would be the comfort of my age and I could reward her care and tenderness with a decent fortune. A thousand difficulties oppose the execution of this plan, which I have never opened but to you; yet it would be less impracticable in England than in Switzerland. (*Letters* 3:164–65)

It is noticeable that, with the loss of Deyverdun, Gibbon sought a family. If he returned to England, it would be at Bath, home of his stepmother and of a small, intimate society—not London, not even Sussex—that he would set up his establishment. In May 1790, ten months after Deyverdun's death, he was still seeking domestic companionship, as we shall see.

Yet in the late summer and autumn of 1789, Gibbon tried to make the best of things and turn to his ordinary life. He planned several alterations to La Grotte, which he decided to lease rather than buy, because buying it would have involved him in legal difficulties and suspense, and followed the Séverys to the country. "They are now at Mex," he wrote, some three weeks after Deyverdun's death, "a country house six miles from hence which I visit to-morrow for two or three days."

> they often come to town and we shall contrive to pass a part of the Autumn together at Rolle. I want to change the scene; and beautiful as the garden and prospect must appear to every eye, I feel that the state of my own mind casts a gloom over them . . . I almost hesitate whether I shall not run over to England to consult with you on the spot, and to fly from poor Deyverdun's shade which meets me at every turn. I did not expect to have felt it so sharply. But six hundred miles! why are we so far off? (*Letters* 3:163)

The summer involved the usual foreign visitors, but "we have escaped the *damned* great ones the Count d'Artois the Polignacs &c who slip by us to Turin. What a scene is France" (*Letters* 3:167; see also Norton's note 5). Late in September, Gibbon set out for Rolle,

> where I shall be settled with cook and servants in a pleasant apartment till the middle of November. The Severys have a house there where they pass the Autumn, I am not sorry to vary the scene for a few weeks, and I wish to be absent while some alterations are making in my house at Lausanne . . . How compleatly, alas, how compleatly! could I now lodge you: but your firm resolve of making me a visit seems to have vanished like a dream. (*Letters* 3:171)

Another of Gibbon's friends, Jean David Levade, seems kindly to have overseen the workers and helped Gibbon with his plans for remodeling. Blondel, Gibbon's valet, and therefore, in Gibbon's scheme of things, also his butler, major domo, and treasurer, took care of the bills and kept the accounts; he was consulted about the remodeling, and, with respect to the kitchen, so was the cook.[27] There were changes also to the entrance and the dining room, and the library, which now had to house some six thousand volumes, had a suite of its own—two libraries and an antechamber—that "close[d] up like a box" (*Letters* 3:173).

Gibbon's first use of these satisfactory—and satisfactorily *new*—

surroundings seems to have been to return, in November, to work on his memoirs. Again, he started afresh instead of editing his previous draft. He even used a new size of paper; draft C is in folio, not quarto. He worked by "keeping his second draft under his eyes, often merely copying it, often altering more or less profoundly what he had first written, omitting many passages, adding a few, and drastically shortening his treatment of all the topics which he preserved."[28] In the Murray edition, draft B is 107 pages long; the portion of C that covers the same period is 56 pages long. B has no subdivisions; C has two complete "sections," the beginning of a third, and outlines for two more.[29] B is called "My own life"; C, "Memoirs of the life and writings of Edward Gibbon." Clearly C is more than a polished and abridged version of B; it represents another rethinking of the possibilities of autobiography and the shape and meaning of his life.

Patricia Spacks provides an excellent characterization of the change: "In Memoir B he had not yet understood what his self-dramatization as historian might mean. In C he evokes more fully the significance of his vocation. . . . Gibbon's interest in generalization has materially diminished. . . . Freedom, in Memoir C, is both a stylistic fact and a psychological issue."[30] Spacks further argues that Gibbon now feels himself to have solved the stylistic problems of autobiography. He is therefore free to use a highly expressive style: metaphors, sentence structure, diction, and tone support his intellectual points. "The confidence of assertion, the reliance on condensation and understatement, and the absence of elaborate explanation point to a new stylistic freedom," and the experience of freedom leads to "increasingly numerous and adventurous metaphors." The stylistic freedom, in turn, enables him to portray his life as one in which "intellectual experience assumes . . . the place that sexuality and religion take in other lives." Both as author and subject, restrictions paradoxically created freedom for Gibbon, through "the opportunity to concentrate; the self-determined choice of narrowness seems very different from the suffering of externally imposed limitations."[31] Whether or not one accepts all the features of this analysis, it is invaluable in pointing to the new qualities of this third draft, the first in which Gibbon clearly perceives his subject—his life and *writings*—and begins to control his materials rather than simply responding to them.

The organization of draft C confirms Spacks's perception that while C is, like B, a history of the historian, that is, an interpretation of Gibbon's life as preparation for the history; and while, also like B, C recognizes the happy irony of the apparent misfortunes that contributed to that preparation, this draft adds the additional theme of the cost or conditions for achievement. His life, Gibbon now saw, fell into several subdivisions. Section 1 extended from his birth to his coming of age and not coincidental recall from his Swiss exile; section

2 comprised the remainder of his life as Edward Gibbon, Jr., ending with his father's death in 1770. Section 3 finds him "in a condition of perfect external freedom" in London in 1772.[32] This section would have ended with the publication and reception of the first volume. Section 4 would have included his holiday in Paris, Parliament and the Board of Trade,

French memorial
Envoy to Berlin
Party attacks.
Diss. and resurrection [a striking metaphor for his change of Parliamentary seats]
Lord Sheffield
ii[d] and iii[d] Vol.

and their reception, ending about 1781 or 82. Section 5, also outlined, would have carried the story as far as his decision to return to Lausanne. But on or about February 9, 1790, he was "seized by such a fit of the Gout as [he] had never known," and the draft abruptly was abandoned. Had it not been interrupted, he might or might not have continued on the same plan. Spacks notes that the fragment of section 3 ends at "a moment full of possibility"; Bonnard finds its manner "comfortable . . . easy and pleasant." Yet its actual subject is Gibbon's "œconomical affairs," and it contains numerous anticipations of the later difficulties Gibbon would have in disposing of his property. Thus Gibbon was wrestling with awkward materials when physical pain interrupted his work, and he had not planned a way of dealing with the happy years with Deyverdun or with the later experience of bereavement. Perhaps he would have abandoned this draft, too, even if it had not been interrupted.

Physical pain, like writing, was a distraction from emotional suffering. "With some vicissitudes of better and worse I have groaned between two and three months: the debility has survived the pain, and though now easy, I am carried about in my chair," Gibbon wrote to Lord Sheffield in May of 1790. And as usual, Lausanne society had rallied to the sufferer. Gibbon had enjoyed "chearful visits" every night that he was able to receive company. Yet he still felt his loneliness. "Since the loss of poor Deyverdun, I am *alone*: and even in paradise, solitude is painful to a social mind. . . . Some expedient, even the most desperate must be embraced to secure the domestic society of a male or female companion" (*Letters* 3:191). The desperate expedients that occurred to Gibbon, who had just turned fifty-three, were, as we have seen, adoption, and—most desperate—marriage.

Gout and its subsequent weakness occupied Gibbon for months; he was not fully recovered until early July 1790. His spirits, too, were aided by good news from England—his friend Lord Sheffield was elected M.P. for Bristol, and his ancient and unloved aunt Hester went "to sing Halleluiahs, a glory which she did not seem very impatient to possess" (*Letters* 3:197). That event might mean for her nephew another step toward financial security, and it is perhaps understandable, if not admirable, that Gibbon, brought up to believe that his Gibbon aunts had been unjustly enriched at their brother's expense, cared only for her estate. She never represented for him the familial warmth for which he continued to feel a need. To fill the gap left in his life by Deyverdun's death, he still thought his "plan of Charlotte Porten is undoubtedly the most desirable. . . . But the mother has been indirectly sounded, and will not hear of such a proposal for some years" (*Letters* 3:196). Sheffield had inferred with alarm that Gibbon might be thinking of marriage and proposed that he find a congenial *couple* to keep him company. Gibbon reassured him:

> I am not in love with any of the Hyaenas of Lausanne. . . . Sometimes in a solitary mood I have supposed myself married to one or other of those whose society and conversation are the most pleasing to me, but when I have painted in my fancy all the probable consequences of such an union, I have started from my dream, rejoyced in my escape, and ejaculated a thanksgiving that I was still in possession of my natural freedom.

Sheffield's plan, "though less dangerous [was] still more absurd" than his own, Gibbon thought (*Letters* 3:196).

Signs of healing, both of gout and grief, may be detected in this letter. Gibbon pictures Charlotte as either "remain[ing] a spinster" or "marry[(ing] some Swiss of my choice, who would encrease and enliven our society." And he does not wish to take her unless she is young enough to be "mould[ed] to the language and manners of the Country" (*Letters* 3:196). His confinement with the gout had been softened, he reports, by books, comforts, company, and "a flow of equal spirits and general good health. . . . My patience has been universally admired, yet how many thousands have passed those five months less easily than myself" (*Letters* 3:197).

He used his recovered strength for some autumn visits in October and November. When he returned to Lausanne, he returned to his memoirs, once more beginning over again from the beginning. The fourth draft, D, is very brief and very closely related to its successor; it may have been written in a very short time, by the end of 1790 or at the beginning of 1791 (*Memoirs*, preface, xix). Why did he not continue draft C? Perhaps, as Bonnard suggests, because Gibbon's experience of interruptions now led him to fear that he would never finish if he continued with the same amplitude as C; perhaps, as Spacks believes, because of "psychic struggles" that led him to try eliminating emotion altogether. "Scanty in its use of figurative language, [draft D] systematically eliminates or distances references to feeling." Spacks points out that it might, if it were Gibbon's last effort, tend to confirm R. B. Mowat's view that in later life, Gibbon stifled emotion before it "disturbed his repose," but because this draft too is rejected, it "suggests, rather, a man struggling to make reason a defense against emotion."[33]

As we have seen, the letters of this period of Gibbon's life, in which he is trying hard to come to terms with Deyverdun's death and his own mortality, strongly support this aspect of Spacks's view. But D, untitled, with (as Bonnard points out) partially unnumbered pages, also suggests a decision that a preparatory study of a less ambitious kind might help him to write his memoirs. Such a study could be complete in itself, yet capable of serving as a preliminary to a greater work—a sort of "General Observations on the Life of Edward Gibbon." The draft contains chronological shoulder captions and preserves, despite its brevity, key epigrammatic observations from other drafts. There are even a few original to this one, such as his account of Deyverdun: "My friendship for Mr. George Deyverdun, a young Gentleman of Lausanne, has ended only with his life."[34] In many respects D is as much an extract from C as a draft for E, though within sections he sometimes reorders the material as well as reducing it— for example, in D he gives the account of his financial difficulties and their fortunate result before reporting his removal to London and Mrs. Gibbon's establishment in Bath. It is obvious that he had decided to write a ruthlessly bare account of his life, almost a witty annals; whether he believed, even as he wrote, that he would remain satisfied with such a record of himself, we cannot know.

Draft E is dated at the end, March 2, 1791. Half again as long as D, it carries Gibbon's story to the moment of writing. Spacks is again the first to appreciate a change within draft E: "At the beginning, Gibbon largely rewrote previously formed material, creating an atmosphere so emotionally denuded that it seems an attempt to deny the importance of the narrative's substance. The last three-quarters of the memoir, on the other hand, displays a new expansiveness."[35] Examination of the manuscript shows, we may add, that many of these expansions occur in the margins, as revisions.[36] The turning point, Spacks argues, is marked by the sentence, "Each year the circle of my acquaintance, the number of my dead and living companions, was enlarged."[37]

Also marking a new expansion of both the text and the story was the addition of notes—twelve manuscript pages of notes, as compared with nineteen of text. These notes may have been written as late as the end of 1792; they refer to Louis XVI as both alive and a former king, but Bonnard notes (*Memoirs* xxvii, n. 2) that Gibbon would have thought of the king as deposed well before the formal abolition of royalty and that he speaks of the *Vindication* (1779) as having been written twelve years earlier. Thus they probably represent expansions and comments made quite close to the original text, just as the notes to the chapters of the *Decline and Fall* had been added within weeks of their original composition. In these notes to draft E, Gibbon permits himself not only personal comments and digressions, but even irrelevances. They contribute strongly to the new atmosphere Spacks notes at the end of E, beginning with the melancholy triumph of the conclusion of the *Decline and Fall*.

Concluding this draft, Gibbon reuses the image he had introduced in B, his "high prize in the lottery of life." But even as he appreciates his good fortune and agrees with the view that the close of life is a happy period, he complicates the concession by observing "reluctantly . . . that two causes, the abbreviation of time and the failure of hope, will always tinge with a browner shade the evening of life" (*Memoirs* 189). As Spacks finely puts it, "Trying always to be rational, he has learned that emotion outlasts reason. Yet he demonstrates rationality's triumph in the act of declaring its defeat: by reason he assesses himself."[38] Not only by reason, we may add, but by art: the very last sentence of draft E, a secular echo, it has been pointed out, of Corinthians 13—"Faith, hope, and charity; but the greatest of these is charity"[39]—utilizes his familiar irony, with himself as both subject and object, to distance and enable his attempt to defeat death by recreating himself: "In old age, the consolation of hope is reserved for the tenderness of parents, who commence a new life in their children; the faith of enthusiasts who sing Hallelujahs above the clouds, and the vanity of authors who presume the immortality of their name and writings" (*Memoirs* 189). To this he adds a disconfirming, tonally jarring note: "This celestial hope is confined to a small number of the Elect, and we must deduct, 1 All the *mere* philosophers . . . 2. All the *earthly* Christians . . . 3. All the *gloomy* fanatics" (*Memoirs* 196).

As Spacks says, it is hard to imagine where Gibbon could go from there, and one reader, Barrett Mandel, has unequivocally condemned draft F, Gibbon's final draft, though on the grounds, incomprehensible both to Spacks and to me, that it is a return to the manner, organization, and content of draft A.[40] Nothing could be further from the truth. Draft F resembles A only in pace—if A and F had been completed, they would have led to books of about the same length. But A would be rambling, bookish, confessional, chatty, actually and ostensibly artless. F is very different: carefully outlined, with a complex relationship between the autobiographer as narrator and the autobiographer as subject, and most of all, with a new purpose: within the structure of the history of the historian's fortunate attainment of intellectual freedom through emotional (and financial) limitation, "for the first time Gibbon discovers how to express the personal."[41] In draft F, the historian of the Roman Empire is not just an intelligence, but a person, and the autobiographer both is and is not that person. The narrator of the memoirs, a famous man, blessed with friends and financial security, and nevertheless aware of his loneliness, now plans to look at *every* period of his life to see not just what it contributed to his achievements, but what it was like to experience that life—what the achievements cost.

Draft F is thus the autobiography one might expect from the author of the concluding sentences of E. It may also have been influenced by Gibbon's reading of Boswell's great *Life of Johnson* (May 1791)—Gibbon refers to it in the fragmentary notes for F. Draft F had probably not been begun when the Sheffield family finally made its long-desired visit to Lausanne, in the summer of 1791. During that visit, for the first time, Gibbon spoke to his friend about the *possibility* of writing his memoirs. It is possible that he even acknowledged the existence of E, which Sheffield considers not "memoirs," but "Annals"; more likely, however, Gibbon simply broached the idea to see whether his friend would think him vain and foolish. Sheffield encouraged the project, but summer and autumn in Lausanne were sociable, as usual, and Gibbon probably did not return to his memoirs until, at the end of December, he wrote to Sheffield, "I have much revolved the plan of the Memoirs I once mentioned, and as you do not think it ridiculous I believe I shall make the attempt: if I can please myself I am confident of not displeasing: but let this be a profound secret between us: people must not be prepared to laugh: they must be taken by surprize" (*Letters* 3:240). He also asks Sheffield to send back the letters Gibbon had written to him—"They may assist me." The implication is both that the earlier drafts do not represent the "Memoirs" Gibbon now plans to write and that among the differences will be the recreation of the responses of Gibbon the subject to the events as they occurred.

Only three chapters of this draft were completed, and only the memoranda for the notes were prepared. It carries Gibbon's story no further than 1753. Yet it is two pages longer than the completed draft E *with* its seventy-two fully developed notes. Clearly Gibbon has reconceived the idea of his memoirs so as to include all sorts of data about his early life that were not formerly considered relevant. I suspect that it was Boswell's *Johnson* that taught Gibbon to solve the problem of proportion that had led him to abandon C's scale. In writing C, he had discovered that the fullness of his materials for his own life (as for his history) was not necessarily proportional to the importance of the events. C ends as he is about to portray a period of his life for which he possessed no commonplace books and journals such as those he had used so far in C. Boswell's method, using other documents and especially letters to bridge gaps between periods he had witnessed, is clearly valuable to Gibbon, but Boswell also solves the problem by characterizing his narrator as actor. This solution, clearly related to Gibbon's methods in the history, was very useful in the new draft.[42] That he intended to continue this draft is strongly indicated by two facts: outlines exist for further work, and he took the drafts with him when he returned to England in 1793. In addition to the plans still preserved from the unfinished draft C (preserved despite the intervening drafts D and E), there is an outline for the unwritten chapter 4 of F.[43]

In draft F, chapter 4 would have had eighteen topics in three chronological subdivisions. The subdivisions are June 1753–December 1754, January–December 1755, and January 1756–April 1758, that is, it would have dealt with his first stay in Lausanne, treating the year 1755 (labeled "mental puberty") and including the "Tour of Switzerland," his first extant extended piece of writing. The climax of the first subdivision would have been topic 5, "Return to the Protestant Church," but more interestingly, even in fragmentary outline, there are indications of the combination of thought and feeling, of introspection and retrospection, that make draft F so different from its predecessors. Point 2 is "First aspect horrid—house, slavery, ignorance, exile"; point 2 is "Benefits—separation, language—health, study, exercises." In section 3, the items treated as equal and parallel tell a story: "13. Taste and compositions—seed of the Essay. 14. Love. 15. Friendship and society. 16. Voltaire Theatre. 17. The World." But the most interesting feature is point 18, "Recall and Estimate," a form of conclusion which has its counterpart in each of the three completed chapters of F, but not consistently in any of the previous drafts. "In Memoir F," Spacks points out, "Gibbon makes a serious attempt—of a kind unprecedented in his own era and rare for long afterwards—to explain, for himself as well as his readers, why, in response to suffering, he turned to books."[44] In his early years, as this judgment suggests, it is particularly pain, physical and emotional, that Gibbon can "recall and estimate." But the outlines show us, I believe, that what he wishes to restore to his account of himself is not just the role of pain, but the roles of pleasure and delight, in defining a person who was indeed the historian of the Roman Empire, but also the product of particular experiences, the subject of particular thoughts, emotions, and beliefs, and an example of human limitation and potentiality.

Even in this last, best draft, Gibbon seems to have remained somewhat ambivalent about the autobiographical process. While he wrote to the *Gentleman's Magazine* in February 1792 in pursuit of more genealogical data for the new draft (*Letters* 3:246), in May he assured Sheffield, who was indignant that Gibbon wished his library to be sold after his death, that he was "not flattered by the Gibbonian collection, and . . . own[ed his] presumptuous belief that six quarto Volumes may be sufficient for the preservation of that name" (*Letters*

3:263). During the summer he was distracted from all work by the usual pleasures, especially the presence of Lady Elizabeth Foster and the duchess of Devonshire. At the end of September he was again in pursuit of his ancestors (*Letters* 3:273); in October, November, and December he had time for nothing but politics and the serious illness of M. de Sévery. In this context, he wrote to Sheffield (January 6, 1793), "Of *the Memoirs* little has been done, and with that little I am not satisfied: they must be postponed till a mature season, and I much doubt whether the book and the author can ever see the light at the same time" (*Letters* 3:312). But this postponement is not abandonment; ten days later he was still seeking information about the Gibbon family, a request pursued again in a letter of April 4, and, as already noted, he took the drafts with him when he left for England in May. We may conclude, I believe, that even though his grief for Deyverdun, and therefore his need to find an absorbing task, had grow less intolerable in his new surroundings and with his new family, and even though his work on the memoirs had not finally satisfied him, his intention of remaking his account of his life to include emotion as well as thought, past and present in dialogue, was ultimately abandoned only because of his death.

FIFTEEN

A Series of Fragments

ibbon's letter to Sheffield reporting the death of Deyverdun is dated July 14, 1789. That date, of course, is associated with an event of far greater importance in public history and one that came to impinge on Gibbon's personal life as well. In the next few years, Gibbon had to come to terms not only with his loss of domestic companionship, but with the French Revolution, which included the political and social devastation of a way of life he had very much admired and the particular sufferings of people he knew and liked. Yet he could not deny that the French system had been unjust and needed reform. He saw, moreover, that the French example might be of importance far beyond that country, affecting especially his natural and adopted homelands. We might expect that hopes and fears about these events would be the most important features of the final period of his life in Lausanne. But in fact, most of the time Gibbon and the other visitors and inhabitants of Lausanne—except the French refugees, more and more a separate social circle—seem absorbed in maintaining a way of life almost defiantly unaffected by politics. Balls, concerts, lectures on natural history, learned societies, plays and dramatic readings, and the simple pleasures of gardens and excursions to the country preserve the values of civilization and even (intellectual) freedom; perhaps that is why Gibbon and his friends so resolutely continued to pursue them as the world changed.

For Gibbon, the most useful support of a sense of meaningful existence had always been a "daily [literary] task, the active pursuit

which gave a value to every book, and an object to every enquiry"
(*Memoirs* 164). The attempt to portray his own life was an absorbing
and recurrent object, but it did not require or reward study; it did not
encourage him to converse with his "intimate friends, among books"
(*Memoirs* 98). Interposed, therefore, among his efforts to write his
memoirs are abortive attempts at several other literary projects. As
he had in his youth, he searched restlessly for a worthwhile historical
project. But he was no longer young; though he was only fifty-two
when Deyverdun died, his physical debility and retrospective attitude
make him seem prematurely old—and in fact he had only four more
years to live. In this old age, while he continued to seek the satisfying
combination of study and society that had always given him happiness, he no longer combined them flexibly and informally.

Now he established a way of life for himself that required the
meticulous ordering of time, violated only for the borrowed pleasures
of family life. Perhaps this rigidity about time—he is said to have
dismissed a hairdresser who arrived *early* for his appointment[1]—helped
him to avoid a sense of vacancy. Perhaps it was a response of courage
or denial to ever-increasing bad health, especially the now all but
crippling swelling in his groin, his "hydrocele." Perhaps it was simply
the self-indulgence of a man unduly revered by those around him.
There are dark shadows over Gibbon's last years in Lausanne, not
only illness and death, but revolution and inflexibility. Instead of a
sustained work, he produced—he even projected—only "a series of
fragments." Yet with T. S. Eliot he might have said, "These fragments I have shored against my ruins," for these last years also
provided for Gibbon a fleeting happiness—some meaningful work,
many pleasant hours, and a few much-loved friends.

The Sévery household did much to ease Gibbon's sense of "com-
fortless solitude" (*Letters* 3:175): "I am encouraged to love the parents
as a brother, and the children as a father. Every day we seek and find
the opportunities of meeting" (*Memoirs* 184). Many brief undated
notes are preserved in the Sévery archives that suggest the ease and
pleasure of Gibbon's relationship to the whole family, despite a society
that seems to us formal. Gibbon could invite and uninvite himself
without embarrassment; for example, "This evening I will have the
pleasure of seeing you. For tomorrow, have the goodness to invite
Monrepos [that is, the current tenants of that house, often English
visitors] and leave me free." Or "I hope, Madame, that you and M. de
Sévery aren't exhausted by all your running about. What are you doing
today. Are you going to the Bois de Vaux? I am still free and willing
to lose my liberty to you alone." Or, "You will find, Madame—or you
have already found—an invitation from Madame Vans, but it seems to
me that we would be better en famille. We have so many things to
say to each other" (*Letters* 3:178, 179, 181). As we shall see, parting

with the Séverys in 1793, when Gibbon made his final trip to England, was so difficult that he delayed an extra day before leaving—and this though he thought he was leaving for a few months only.

Wilhelm de Sévery frequently functioned as Gibbon's "chancellor" or "secretary," writing for him when gout made that painful for Gibbon, or arranging social occasions beyond the scope of Gibbon's staff—in the case of an elaborate concert held at La Grotte in 1792, beyond the scope of Gibbon himself, who was uninterested in music.[2] But the Séverys were not Gibbon's only friends in Lausanne, even excluding "those acquaintance who by courtesy are styled friends" (*Letters* 3:268). Jean David Levade, who was apparently a man very active in serving his friends, and who, as noticed above, more than once undertook to supervise the workmen making alterations in Gibbon's house when he was out of town, was such a true friend, even though he was thirteen years younger and a professor of moral theology. Gibbon gratefully bequeathed to him fifty guineas as a token of friendship.[3] A similar bequest went to Gottlieb Schomberg, of whom Gibbon wrote in August 1790,

> We have now near one hundred French exiles, some of them worth being acquainted with, particularly a Count de Schomberg who is almost become my friend: he is a man of the World of letters, and of sufficient age since in 1753 he succeeded to Marshal Saxe's regiment of Dragoons. As to the rest I entertain them, and they flatter me: but I wish we were reduced to our Lausanne society. Poor France, the state is dissolved, the nation is mad. (*Letters* 3:199)

This near friendship grew; Schomberg seems to have been one of those who valued Gibbon as a person and not just as a celebrity. He wrote to one of Gibbon's Swiss friends, after Gibbon's death: "I can conceive how much this loss for the age and for posterity was more frightful for you than for anyone. I mourn it therefore still more because of the profound and tender feelings that you have inspired in me. . . . All the details that you have given me, in so few words and with so much power, are incessantly before me. Let us believe that the life of the dead is in the memory of the living."[4] And Gibbon had inspired sincere affection also in G. A. d'Erlach, *bailli* of Lausanne, who said to Wilhelm, after Gibbon had gone back to England, "This M. Gibbon—I miss him horribly. I would not have believed that I could miss him so much, I think of him every day."[5]

Among books, Gibbon first sought his beloved Greeks (*Memoirs* 183). A brief note on music in Homer was probably written about this time[6] and almost certainly some extended comments on Pindar. The Pindar notes, in French, are not included in Sheffield's *Miscellaneous Works* but are photographically reproduced in Keynes's catalogue of

Gibbon's library. They are in Gibbon's very late hand. Their subject is the great superiority of Pindar's description of Mt. Etna to Virgil's; Virgil employed the "exaggerations of rhetoric" instead of "power and truth." Pindar astonishes the imagination, yet he satisfies the mind. Gibbon details the powerful visual and auditory images of Pindar—"I see . . . I hear . . ."—and particularly approves Pindar's "sublime" mythology: "I tremble at the name of this Typhon, this hundred-headed monster, whose hairy chest is pressed against the foundations of Etna, and whose limbs extend to the base of Vesuvius. Virgil's Enceladus is cold and small, and the *fama est* seems to me unworthy of a poet instructed by the muses."[7] This delight in Pindar's combination of thought and feeling may have helped to prepare Gibbon to seek a similar power in his own *Memoirs*.[8]

Perhaps even earlier in this period after the *Decline and Fall* were some notes and comments on a favorite Greek historian, written in English. During his sojourn in England Gibbon had acquired the new French translation of Herodotus, by Henri Larcher. He was then inspired to reread the "father of History," a rereading that led first to lengthy marginalia in that volume and then to an extended essay on the supposed circumnavigation of Africa by the ancients. In these comments on Herodotus, Gibbon also makes a number of evaluations of Herodotus as historian. For example, he has this to say about fictional or erroneous history, in the hands of the master:

> Rousseau has wisely observed . . . that the most incredible narratives of Herodotus may be esteemed as moral lessons. In this doubtful history of the Medes we may trace the progress of Civil society. They renounced their freedom to escape the evils of anarchy: their slavery was confirmed and alleviated by the selfish arts, and specious virtues of their first King; but his son was a conqueror, and his great-grand-son a tyrant.[9]

On another occasion, "Plutarch . . . who fondly embraces [a certain] moral tale, derides the vain opposition of *Chronological Canons*." Here Gibbon, instead of either deriding or joining Plutarch, proposes a chronological solution. He objects to some of Herodotus's fables, for example, the rescue of Arion by the dolphin (1.24) as "unphilosophic" or as not sufficiently disinterested. He suspects that Herodotus had been paid off by the Delphic priests. Errors of geography or measurement—the "easy, though wonderful annihilation of time and space"—sometimes allow us to "detect a Romance." He doubts that Herodotus had ever been to Babylon—"We may recollect the Greek historian . . . who had travelled into Armenia, without stirring from Corinth." Yet he praises Herodotus for "discovering two important [geographical] truths, which were disregarded by the false science of succeeding Geographers."[10]

Most significantly, perhaps, Herodotus inspires Gibbon to state two "laws" of their common craft. The first follows a "metahistorical" statement by Herodotus himself: "I shall write [the story of Cyrus] according to the account given by certain of the Persians who do not seek to glorify Cyrus but to tell what really happened. I shall do so although I know as many as three other ways of telling the story of Cyrus" (1.95). Gibbon comments, "Opposite witnesses must be balanced; and we can only deduct the surplus of credibility. But when each weight is positively light, this comparative surplus must be minute."[11] This rather cryptic observation does not take us as far as his many comments about using his witnesses in the *Decline and Fall*. But in the other instance, Gibbon works out explicitly some rules that he apparently had in mind both in evaluating his sources and in composing his own history:

> Without absolutely condemning the composition of speeches so familiar to the ancients, I shall presume to impose the three following laws on this species of historical fiction. 1 That the truth of the leading fact, of the council, debate, orations &c be positively ascertained. 2. That some natural means be suggested through which, the historian (who cannot plead the inspiration of the Muses,) might derive his intelligence. 3. That the language and ideas be strictly adapted to the national and personal characters of his Dramatic speakers.[12]

These laws explain Gibbon's justification for sometimes including in his text speeches that, in the notes, he acknowledges to be fictions or insufficiently supported as historical. Essentially these "laws" are similar to those of realistic fiction—characterization, setting, and point of view must be consistent and probable, though events, which in realistic fiction need only avoid conflict with known historical data, must for history be "positively ascertained." This comment supports Leo Braudy's analysis of Gibbon's attitude toward the "Privilege of Fiction" in the latter volumes of the history—Gibbon can now "accept fiction as a mode of interpretative coherence," at least in certain circumstances.[13]

The reader of the *Decline and Fall* and of the *Memoirs* also notices two comments that might be expected from the author of those works. Gibbon is struck by Herodotus's story of Bias's advising the Greeks to migrate to Sardinia (1.170). He comments, "Had the Ionians removed to Sardinia, that fertile island (obscure and barbarous in every age) might have become the seat of arts, of freedom, and perhaps of Empire. Such a powerful colony might have oppressed the infant fortune of Rome, and changed the history of mankind." And he is interested in the issue of how and when the quality of a human life may be appraised: "Voltaire . . . has ridiculed the observation of Solon, which is clear and judicious, that we should not calculate the good and evil incident to any human life, till death has finally closed the account. A metaphysi[ci]an may perplex himself by contrasting apparent happiness, or misery, with secret pain or pleasure."[14] This story is again alluded to by Gibbon in a later work of this last period of his life, *The Antiquities of the House of Brunswick*. It is clearly related to the question of "autumnal felicity" to which he recurs in the conclusion and notes of draft E of his *Memoirs* (188–89, 196), and also to his repeated rejection of philosophic affectation of envy of unthinking happiness, whether of Gray's schoolboys (*Memoirs* 44) or Frederick of Prussia's old women (*Memoirs* 196). Gibbon repeatedly insists that he has enjoyed *many* hours of happiness, derived in part from "the pleasing labour" of composition (*DF* chap. 52, 5:27, n. 60 [52]; *Memoirs* 187).

These marginal comments on Herodotus occur in seven of the nine books. They surely represent the work of several mornings, even for a man who could read a five-volume novel in a day. In the winter time, when the foreign visitors left Lausanne, most mornings could be devoted to study. On several different occasions following this reading of Herodotus, probably several different days, Gibbon seems to have pursued a project suggested by Herodotus's story of the circumnavigation of Africa by the Phoenicians, doubted by the ancients but believed by the moderns because of "his praevious knowledge of a Geographical truth."[15]

This essay, or rather set of remarks, may well be complete, but Gibbon composed it as a collection of discrete discussions, on separate sheets, each complete with its own notes, but not numbered with respect to the others. Since he was using a stack of paper that had been previously numbered, he doubtless thought that the order of his comments would be unmistakable. Unfortunately, the stack of paper was turned so that the numbers were at the bottom of the sheets, upside down, as he used them, and therefore he often accidentally used versos before rectos, or a higher-numbered sheet before a lower-numbered sheet. As a result, it is not possible to be sure exactly in what order the remarks should run.[16] It is a pity that Gibbon did not more clearly indicate his intentions, because in one sense the essay is not unfinished: he had provided a case against every proposed circumnavigator of Africa prior to the Portuguese as well as an account of the success and the motivation of the Portuguese.

Gibbon may have written this essay soon after he returned to Lausanne, before Deyverdun's death, while he was enjoying his favorite Greek authors in 1788 and 1789. When he returned to his rebuilt library in October of 1790, he had already written, or quickly wrote, a substantial work on another subject. This new work was planned as part of a large historical project that would have been made up of an indefinite number of small projects; such an organization could have been prompted by the knowledge that this circumnavigation essay was already on hand, as well as unpublished or unfinished works on miscellaneous subjects written at earlier periods in his life. Here is his proposal, in a letter of October 12, 1790, to his old friend Langer, librarian of Hanover, who had already assisted the project (unwittingly) by procuring for Gibbon Leibnitz's *Origines Guelficae*, an essential source for the work:

> When I began to find my mind less agitated [after Deyverdun's death], I sought to give myself a stronger, more interesting occupation than simple reading. The memory of my servitude of twenty years frightened me, however, and I promised myself not to embark on such a lengthy enterprise, which I would probably never finish. It will be much better, I said to myself, to choose in every country and every century some historical pieces that I will treat separately, according to their nature and my taste. When these Opuscules (in English I will call them *Historical Excursions*) furnish me with a volume, I will give them to the public: this gift could be renewed, until we are tired, either the public or I; but each volume, complete in itself, will not require a sequel, and instead of being limited, like the Express Coach [Diligence] to the grand highway, I will stroll freely in the field of history, stopping at any place where I find an agreeable prospect. . . .
>
> The choice of my first *Excursion* . . . will explain to you why I had so urgently asked for the *Origines Guelficae*. . . . The antiquity and greatness of the house of Brunswick has excited my curiosity. . . . My researches, in unveiling the beauty of my subject, have made me see its extent and difficulty. [The earlier and later materials are readily accessible.] . . . But between the first Duke and the first Elector of Brunswick there is an interval of four hundred fifty years. . . . As I propose to sketch memoirs and not to compose a history, I would no doubt march at a rapid pace, I would present results rather than facts, observations rather than stories: but you well know how such a general picture requires particular knowledge; how much more learned than his work the author must be. Well this author is two hundred leagues from Saxony, he is ignorant of the language, and he has never applied himself to German history. Far away from the sources, there is only one way for him to bring them into his library. It is to acquire on the spot an exact correspondent, an enlightened guide, an oracle in short, who could be consulted at every need. . . . You are this precious and unique man that I seek. . . . But I do not know if you are disposed to sacrifice your leisure, your cherished studies to an arduous correspondence without pleasure or glory. . . . If you condescend to associate yourself with my undertaking I will send you immediately my first set of questions. Your refusal would decide me to give up my work, or at least to give it a new form. I dare at the same time request a profound secrecy: an indiscreet word would be repeated by a hundred mouths, and I would have the discomfort of seeing in the Journals, and soon in the English papers, an announcement, perhaps distorted, of my literary projects, which I have confided only to you. (*Letters* 3:203–6)

This letter has a number of interesting features, including Gibbon's clearly recognizing a number of different genres of history, especially history itself and memoirs, and also his clear desire for, yet fear of, a lengthy project. Presumably his own ill health as well as the deaths of his contemporaries made him believe or at least fear that he could not hope to complete another long project—in both the drafts of the *Antiquities of the House of Brunswick*, he pays special attention to the extraordinarily long life of the eleventh-century head of the house and notes that fame and longevity are rarely enjoyed by the same person.[17] His recognition and avowal of his own limitations is frank, and he is equally honest about the burden he proposes to place on Langer. Yet it is disturbing that both the admonition to secrecy and the request for a reply are quite manipulative—if you don't help me, I'll give up the project; if it becomes known, it will be because of you. In spite of his honesty and his many compliments to Langer, Gibbon seems egotistically preoccupied with his own desires.

In his reply (November 3, 1790), Langer explained that the project was impracticable. But far from being offended by Gibbon's proposal, he seems flattered. He comments, "Naturally I did not hesitate for a moment to provide my modest service to a writer so meritorious [*verdienstvoll*]." At the same time he warned Gibbon that his services could extend only to printed books and that he himself had found that they were inadequate guides—manuscripts and archival resources were also essential. In an interesting anticipation of nineteenth-century German historiography, Langer told Gibbon that what he really needed, if he were going to write about Germany since the Thirty Years War, was a sense of the "spirit of the nation," which he could only obtain, Langer believed, by visiting Germany himself. Langer concluded that Gibbon found this argument convincing, "for indeed he began to speak of such a trip and finally to plan it in earnest. Unfortunately the French Revolution took such a frightful turn that Germany was soon involved, and shortly thereafter, his own father-land was insulted by hellish anarchists"—Langer's politics are not subtle. But, he goes on, Gibbon at least had to travel along the Rhine and see something of Germany on his way back to England. "Every post day I was expecting to hear something from him, when the . . . news of his death, in all the papers, [informed] me that all, all was in vain."[18]

It is hard to believe that Gibbon would actually have undertaken this trip, but easy to understand that he did not want to give up his project, that he wanted to believe himself capable of mastering the materials for another true history, even though the subject required a new kind of research demanding physical strength (or at least health, good eyesight, and some agility), travel, and additional linguistic and technical skills. He had already written a lengthy draft of the first of three proposed sections for the *Antiquities*, the one dealing with the

Italian descent, and he probably wrote second drafts of several portions of this section, plus studies for parts of the German section, while awaiting Langer's reply.

The *Antiquities* have received very little attention from Gibbon's readers and even his biographers. Jacob Bernays, otherwise so sympathetic and thorough in appraising Gibbon, dismisses them as pompous in style and lacking in philosophical depth. He finds valuable two sentences about Leibnitz, but they are in the "Address" recommending a *Scriptores rerum Anglicarum*, not in the elaborate characterization of Leibnitz in the *Antiquities*.[19] The monograph is certainly essayistic, especially in its first form: Gibbon stops to tell every interesting anecdote, to paint every lively scene, he comes upon, and he seems to have no purpose more profound than simple genealogy— he is not interested in why or even how the house of Este-Brunswick so long survived, or what the consequences of such antiquity may be, either for Europe or for historical writing and theory. He is simply presenting more and less probable information, discussing its reliability with his readers, enjoying the glimpses of human frailty or potentiality it affords.

But the "Italian descent" chapter provides a unique opportunity to compare two of Gibbon's perspectives on the same subject, the struggles of feudal nobles in Italy in the context of the general history of Europe, as portrayed in the *Decline and Fall*, and the same struggles as they take the center of the stage for the adherents and successors of those great families. The various digressions in the *Decline and Fall* itself, in which Gibbon recounts the history of a private individual or family in order to give perspective to pubic affairs, cover the same kind of material but in a very different spirit. There, the life or family is a paradigm; here, it is unique and individual. Also rare is the opportunity to see the various stages of one of Gibbon's works. The "continuous draft" of the *Antiquities*, its fragmentary notes, the revised version, and the fully developed notes to it, are all extant.[20] It is particularly interesting to see his ruthless pruning in revising; it seems clear that with his letter to Langer, he began to take this work more seriously and therefore to prepare it more rigorously to meet the public, not only by adding more precise information, but by eliminating merely decorative material.

One example will suffice. In describing the Marquis Azo, known as "the rich," Gibbon had had occasion to note of rich men in the Middle Ages that after providing for warfare and the Church, "the superfluous wealth which could not purchase the real comforts of life was idly wasted on some rare occasions of vanity and pomp." He then devotes some 350 words to a description of the elaborate nuptials, a century before, of "Boniface Duke or Marquis of Tuscany, whose family was long afterward united with that of Azo by the marriage of their children." The reader might easily be confused about whose "these" nuptials, at which "the bridegroom displayed and diversified the scenes of his proud and tasteless magnificence," were. In the revision Gibbon bites the bullet and relegates this fascinating scene to a brief note.[21] This passage also suggests another interest of the *Antiquities* for readers of Gibbon: the essay contains many and varied *obiter dicta*, especially on human nature and historical writing. But without German, this project could not be completed.

Even before undertaking this project, Gibbon was sorry not to have learned German. A year earlier (October 1789), in his enthusiasm, he had even tried to obtain the services of Friedrich von Matthisson as a German teacher. According to Matthisson, Gibbon was so impressed with the music of a hexameter of Homer translated into German that he decided to attempt to learn the language. Matthisson added, in his autobiography (1818—written in the third person), that he received simultaneously invitations to teach German to Gibbon and to a seven-year-old in Lyon. He decided for the latter, for the child's father "touched his spirit with much warmer eloquence than the cold, courtly, and not seldom a little despotic Gibbon."[22]

Here is Matthisson's account of Gibbon, a month after Deyverdun's death:

> Gibbon has the *ton* and manners of a polished man of the world. He is coolly aloof, speaks French with elegance . . . and almost a Parisian accent. He enjoys hearing himself talk and speaks slowly, because he seems to test each phrase before he pronounces it. His expression is never affected by pleasant or unpleasant things, by happy or tragic occasions, and . . . while we were together, although he was moved to tell a very funny story, he never laughed once. In his house the strictest punctuality and order reign. His servants must carry out their duties nearly at the appointed minute or be in danger of losing their jobs. He himself sets the example, however. His day is organized like the day of the Anglo-Saxon King Alfred. On the stroke of the clock he goes to work, to the table, and into company, and stays nowhere a minute longer than the strict schedule allows.[23]

Though this preference for a rigid schedule may have been exacerbated, when Matthisson met him, by Gibbon's attempts to deal with his grief for Deyverdun—as we have seen, he felt haunted by his friend's presence in the house they had shared—it characterized him throughout his mature years. "You know he is clockwork," said Maria Josepha Holroyd.[24] Reporting on journeys, he usually tells his correspondents how much time each portion of the trip required. But it is only in this period that I have seen references precise to the minute— not an hour and three-quarters, but an hour and forty-four minutes.

Other strangers visiting Lausanne in this period were also critical. Leopold von Stolberg met Gibbon once and described him thus in a letter of 1791: "Intelligence one can see in his face, but he has the demeanor of a man of the world; that is what he wishes to be; he is vain and as chatty as a French abbé; he is very ugly and very fat." Passing visitors from England record similar impressions. For instance, Sir Charles Blagden: "Called on Mr Gibbon: very affected, not civil to me." Blagden admits that Gibbon was "more civil" later, as they grew better acquainted. Blagden visited Gibbon more than once and on at least one occasion "talked with him some time, perfect work of art; piques himself on his fashion evidently: not great mind . . . too much like acting, as if had studied his part.[25] Langer, who knew Gibbon much better, notes Gibbon's willingness to violate his schedule to avoid eating alone and contrasts his manner of speech when he was with intimates with that in "mixed company." Langer observes that Gibbon's spoken French was even better than his written French and believes that his habit of pausing before speaking—in mixed company—was dictated by his desire to avoid embarrassing solecisms.

In English, too, he had a reputation to maintain and, in the company of Burke and Johnson and the other members of the Club, competition to consider. He did not aspire to quickness of repartee—"Wit I have none," he said of himself[26]—but he specialized in the telling of amusing stories, of which he had a great store. Only with his intimates did he unbend enough to joke casually. A few examples of timely retorts in more public circumstances survive to show that he was able to produce what Johnson calls "good things"; but he could not often arrange them in his mind and express them speedily enough to shine as a wit. Sometimes his silence or lack of motion may simply have been a response to pain. Langer observes that "a large hernia" not only prevented Gibbon from walking, but made motion of all kinds difficult for him; in order to minimize this drawback with the least loss of "decorum," Gibbon would find a seat as quickly as possible.

Given these difficulties and the power to order his own house to his own taste, one might expect that Gibbon would rarely go out, preferring to have guests come to him; but in fact his chair was ordered nearly every day when he was in Lausanne in the summer or autumn, and he apparently became so attached to Louis Pache, the carrier who usually transported him, that when Pache died, Gibbon provided four years' support for his son at the local school.[27] He often entertained at La Grotte as well; it was a beautiful setting and well arranged for that purpose, with a large dining room and parlor opening onto a terrace overlooking Lake Geneva and of course the library suite, Gibbon's most impressive setting. "In this bewitching dwelling," says Langer poetically, "whose interior he preserved with taste, and exterior with purity, Gibbon lived a life that would have been considered enviable, if untroubled happiness were the lot of poor earthly pilgrims!"[28] He adds that the interior was not only tasteful but comfortable, and that the gently descending terrace was decked with plants of all kinds.

These plants were the source of some friction between Gibbon and his neighbors. On several occasions, a neighboring family complained that Gibbon's trees were interfering with their view of the lake. A law required that nothing be planted closer than nine feet to the town wall; some acacias and plane trees planted by Deyverdun in the last year of his life had to be removed, and though Gibbon planted others, they had to be kept close-cropped to avoid annoying his neighbors. Gibbon found the shade of these trees essential not only to his taste but to his health: "The promenade in question is essentially necessary to me in the lengthy periods of feebleness that follows my attacks of gout—a promenade of a certain length, well shaded and not far from my house" (*Letters* 3:300). The shortened trees served this purpose, but Gibbon's garden is said to have "suffered from the resulting lack of shade."[29]

But clockwork Gibbon went every morning not to his garden, but to his "work." When he was not engaged with "*the* Memoirs," when he had done as much as he could on the *Antiquities* and was awaiting Langer's reply, what was that work? A letter of November 17, 1790, to Thomas Cadell, his publisher, provides one answer:

> As I am inclined to flatter myself that you have no reason to be displeased with your purchase [the *Decline and Fall*], I now wish to ask you whether you feel yourself disposed to add a seventh or supplemental volume to my History? The materials of which it will be composed will naturally be classed under the three following heads: 1. A series of fragments, disquisitions, digressions, &c more or less connected with the principal subject. 2. Several tables of geography, chronology, coins, weights and measures, &c; nor should I despair of obtaining from a gentleman at Paris some accurate and well-adapted maps. 3. A critical review of all the authors whom I have used and quoted. I am convinced such a supplement might be rendered entertaining, as well as useful; and that few purchasers would refuse to *complete* their Decline and Fall. . . . in plain English, I should expect the same reward for the seventh, as for any of the preceding volumes. . . . I shall instantly renounce the undertaking, if it appears by your answer that you have the shadow of an objection. Should you tempt me to proceed, this supplement will be only the employment of my leisure hours; and I foresee that full two years will elapse before I can deliver it into the hands of the printer.

As with the proposal to Langer, Gibbon places the responsibility for this work on the shoulders of his correspondent. His mixture of reluctance and eagerness is obvious. But he did not wait for Cadell's answer to begin experimenting with the new project.

As noted above, he at some time after the completion of the first six volumes employed someone to make lists of "Authors" and "Places" cited in the *Decline and Fall*. The lists were then alphabetized by the same hand.[30] The lists may have had something to do with Gibbon's plans for indexing the six volumes, but since they include only the *first* reference to each person or place, they more probably represent preparations for this seventh volume. While an amanuensis worked on the lists, Gibbon, of course, could do other things.

There is some probability that he began with a brief, but carefully annotated, observation relevant to the nineteenth line of volume 1, p. 85 of the third and subsequent quarto editions (Bury edition 1:77), on the ancestors of Augustus. For this annotation, Gibbon sets out a full title:

Supplement

to

the History

of

the decline and fall of the Roman Empire

followed by two lines across the page and accompanied by the label "Vol 1" in the top left-hand corner. "I here confound the maternal with the paternal descent of Augustus," the note begins.[31] In Gibbon's writings of this period there are three different comments on Augustus's genealogy: this one, a note to the *Antiquities of the House of Brunswick*,[32] and a correction in a set of changes written on the uncut leaves of a copy of the fourth edition of his history, now in the British Library.[33] Gibbon's annotations of another copy of his history have long been known; this new copy was acquired for the British Library in 1980 and the annotations have not been published. These newly found annotations appear to continue those previously known: they are in volume 1 only, and none refers to the first chapter. The previously known annotations occur in chapter 1 of volume 1 or in later volumes of the history, with one exception, a note on the second page of chapter 2, a page not annotated in the newly discovered copy.

It would be interesting to determine the chronology of the three comments. We would then know whether Gibbon began annotating his copies of his history before or after he made such elaborate preparation for a seventh volume, and how work on revising his history was related to work on the *Antiquities of Brunswick*. Here is the Brunswick passage, from the revised version of "The Italian Descent": "A prudent advocate . . . will dissemble the reproach of Antony, and the apology of Cicero, which may leave a stain on the maternal descent of Augustus."[34] Then there is a cue to note 2: "Ignobilitatem objicit, says the Orator (Philippic iii.6) and we may learn from Suetonius (in Octavio. C 2.) that Antony was still more severe on the paternal ancestors of Augustus. The Emperor himself allowed that his father was the first Senator of the family."

In the "Supplement," Gibbon does not mention any reproach of Antony about the paternal ancestry of Augustus, but instead adopts as his own Antony's assertion (according to Suetonius) that Augustus's great-grandfather was a rope maker. To his sources he adds Cluverius and Cicero *Ad Quintum fratrem*. "The opposite reports of friends and enemies are honestly and doubtfully stated in Suetonius," Gibbon comments, with a reference to "Sueton in Octav. C 1–4." "The father of Augustus was the first Senator and Praetor of his family: his provincial administration of Macedonia is crowned by the impartial praise of Cicero" (here the reference to "ad Quintum fratrem"), "and death alone could have blasted his hopes of the Consulship."[35]

In the annotations in his copy of the history, Gibbon corrects himself about the source of the Octavian family, providing the information from Cluverius in a note and explaining that Antony's attack on Augustus's maternal ancestry was answered by Cicero in *Philippic* 3. He also inserts a second note to "obscure name of Octavianus": "We may observe as an unfavourable symptom, that Virgil never alludes to the Octavian name. . . . The prudent Monarch . . . always declared, that . . . his father was the first who obtained a seat in the Senate. See the accurate Suetonius in the first Chapters of the life of Augustus" (quarto p. 85; Bury edition 1:77). The "Supplement" is the most complete and most precisely supported of the three accounts, but it does not mention Virgil. I conclude that the *Antiquities* passage and note were written before either of the other two, and I think that the "Supplement" is *probably* later than the annotations in Gibbon's copy.

On the same sheet as the elaborate title and correction of the ancestry of Augustus, Gibbon begins an elaborate chronology, entitled (in large letters, centered), "1rst Period," and subtitled (underlined and centered) "From the accession of Nerva to the / death of Marcus Antoninus."[36] In this chronology he gives each emperor's full name on the first line of his section. In the right-hand margin he gives a reference to the history—Vol. 1. p. 91—before beginning his information on Nerva. There are no other references to pages in the history. This absence may point to one of the reasons Gibbon gave up the project; although it is often convenient to have available a strict chronology of Roman history as you read the *Decline and Fall*, specifying exactly where in the text each chronological point becomes relevant could become very difficult. On the other hand, the chronologies need not be keyed to pages in the history at all, given the chronological captions and the elaborate table of contents provided.

In the left margin of this chronology, Gibbon supplies the date—

at least the year and sometimes the day as well. In the content of this chronological table Gibbon attempts to relate different *kinds* of events—for example, the emigration of the Huns and the triumphs of Trajan, and Pliny's governorship with the martyrdom of Ignatius, bishop of Antioch. He also allows himself the now familiar liberties of a philosophic observer: Nerva's "wishes rather than his actions, his virtues rather than his powers announced to the Romans, the first dawn of the Golden Age"; the "virtuous spirit" of Marcus Antoninus, "according to every good system of Religion must have been received with open arms by the Father of the Universe." Such a chronology for the entire *Decline and Fall* would certainly have been a valuable acquisition to the purchasers of that history, but might well have cost the author far more than the two years he anticipated.

On separate sheets there are various memoranda for notes that also seem to be related to the projected "seventh volume."[37] One set of six sheets is entitled "Supplemental notes to the six Volumes of the History of the decline and fall of the Roman Empire" (a title in much the same elaborate format as the "Supplement"); among these notes many of the memoranda are included and developed.[38] Though these notes are less interesting than the other materials for the seventh volume, some do more than provide additional references, for example, "Clairvaux has lately bought and buried a learned library"—an addition to the comment, "St. Bernard would blush at the pomp of the church and monastery [of Clairvaux]; he would ask for the library, and I know not whether he would be much edified by a tun of 800 muids (914$^1/_7$ hogsheads)" (*DF* chap 59, 6:346 n. 33 [29]).

We also see Gibbon considering and rejecting a spurious candidate for inclusion in the notes, a forged "Codice Diplomatico della Sicilia sotto il governo degli Arabi," published in 1790, from which Gibbon takes quite serious notes at first—"Airoldi gives in his preface a tolerable history of the Aglabites and Fatimites," but which he is soon catching out in errors, such as an emir's writing that he had circumcised his newborn son: "Yet the Mahometans do not circumcize their children, till . . . they can repeat, There is but one God and Mahomet is his prophet. . . . Ah you thought of the Jews!" Finally, we seem to have at least one of the proposed "disquisitions" on an author in his account of his "old and familiar acquaintance" Busbequius. Analyzing both the historical value and the literary qualities of the work, this example makes me, at least, deeply regret that Gibbon did not pursue his plan to comment on his authors, because in characterizing them, he would probably have helped us to understand not only his historical practice and literary standards, but also his human affections and values.[39]

Whether the annotations in the two copies of the history were directly related to the projected seventh volume or simply the impulse of an author rereading his own work, they are, of course, of great interest. The recently discovered annotations occur in chapters 2, 3, 6, 8, 9, 11, and 12; the ones previously known occur voluminously in chapter 1; there are two in chapter 64, and single comments in chapters 2, 22, 51, 61, and 70. None of these annotations suggests a major change of heart about the history, with the exception of the first, in which Gibbon considers where he should have begun his history. Even this comment does not have the causal force that Gibbon's use of the verb *deduce* has sometimes been thought to give it; for him "deduce" always means "begin a description"; thus here he means simply that he should have *described* events from an earlier period than the age of the Antonines, not that he should have interpreted them as the *cause* of the decline and fall.

The newly discovered annotations give us new insights into Gibbon's reading and opinions, and a few splendid new Gibbonian sentences. Since some of the pages on which they were written were cut without the cutter's noticing the annotations, some of them are unfortunately mutilated. Like the annotations of chapter 1, they utilize previously written material on one occasion, a long note about the "Patriot Assassin" Brutus, which is in effect an epitome of the separate essay "Digression on the Character of Brutus."[40] This essay, in a copyist's hand, is based on Gibbon's "Hints" of 1765–68, and on that basis I had previously concluded that it was written in the 1760s. With this new indication of relevance (in Gibbon's mind) to the *Decline and Fall* and with the telling title "*Digression* on the Character of Brutus," I now believe that Gibbon either wrote the formal essay in 1789–90, or caused a fair copy of it to be made for inclusion in this seventh volume, with an appropriate title. Such a digression would presumably have replaced its précis in the annotated copy, which itself was composed as a replacement for Gibbon's note 27 to chapter 3 (*DF* 1:78 n. 34). Similarly, the annotations to chapter 1, in the other annotated copy, indicate that Gibbon planned to include an "Excursion" he had written in the 1760s, "On the Succession of Roman Triumphs."[41] He would presumably have rewritten that French essay as he translated it.

Whatever their order, exploring these possible expansions of the *Decline and Fall* obviously helped to keep Gibbon busy in his library in November and December of 1790. In January, alas, all such ambitions had to be laid aside for a time, as Gibbon was laid low by an attack, not of his old enemy the gout, whom "I must hasten, generously hasten, to exculpate," Gibbon wrote to Sheffield, but of "a strong inflammatory *Erisipele* or rash" (*Letters* 3:212). This rash covered his right leg from knee to toe, gave off a great deal of pus, and caused both fever and head and stomach pains. In the letter in which he records his recovery from this illness, Gibbon also expresses a great sense of urgency about the settling of his English affairs—he particularly wanted to complete the sale of Buriton, in progress for almost two years, and had become enthusiastic about selling to Lord Sheffield himself the estate at Newhaven he had recently inherited from Hester Gibbon. "My old scruples against pecuniary transactions with a friend are much diminished by my experience of the delays and difficulties which occur in a treaty with a stranger" (*Letters* 3:213). He also mentions casually that he has made a new will, preferring the poor Porten cousins to the rich Eliot ones (he does not mention the generous legacy to Wilhelm de Sévery, "whom I desire to style by the endearing name of son," also a new feature of this draft). Clearly the illness had been not only painful, but frightening: "I am satisfied that this effort of Nature [the evacuation of pus that "gradually relieved" him] has saved me from a very dangerous perhaps a fatal crisis" (*Letters* 3:212). When we remember the huge chronic swelling in his groin and his obesity, we can perhaps get some idea of the suffering he must have undergone.

In February he felt well enough to write to Cadell expressing his surprise that he had received no answer to his "seventh volume" letter, but no longer well enough to think of undertaking that project. Instead, he hints to Cadell that there may be a "thin quarto on an interesting subject that would be part of "a much larger design," that is, the *Antiquities* and the "Historical Excursions" of which they would have been a part. (He says nothing to Cadell of the subject.) By the end of March, however, he was again enjoying both study and society. He gave a grand ball, which

> opened about seven in the evening, the assembly of men and women was pleased and pleasing, the music good, the illumination splendid, the re- freshments profuse: at twelve, one hundred and thirty persons sat down to a very good support: at two I stole away to bed in a snug corner, and I was informed at breakfast that the remains of the Veteran or young troops, with Severy and his sister at their head, had concluded the last dance about a quarter before seven. This magnificent entertainment has gained me great credit, and the expence was more reasonable than you can easily imagine. This was an extraordinary event, but I give frequent dinners, and in the summer I have an assembly every Sunday evening. What a wicked wretch says Lady Pantile. (*Letters* 3:219)

Gibbon was not the only host who gave memorable parties in Lausanne that spring and summer of 1791. Sophie von La Roche, a German visitor, describes a delightful party to which both she and Gibbon were invited. It was a breakfast at the house of David Levade. The guests ate in the garden room, in which there were many plants on either side of a huge bird cage full of canaries, as well as a pretty white porcelain stove, so that "even inside the room, one already had a beautiful view." Through three great windows and a door, one could see the garden and the lake and the mountains.[42] But despite such entertainments, congenial companions among the locals, and some visitors perhaps more distinguished than congenial among the foreigners, Gibbon urged more and more insistently that his English friends from Sheffield Place fulfill their promise to visit him in Lausanne. In July, they came. Maria Josepha's letters to her aunt Serena describe their reception, their host, and the way of life they found at Lausanne, though allowances should be made for nineteen-year-old intolerance of her elders and also for Maria's preference for the French set, who were, as we have seen, more and more isolated from the Swiss with whom Gibbon identified. Maria was also influenced by Lady Webster, later Lady Holland, then the discontented young bride of an elderly man, who disliked Gibbon and indeed the Swiss. Maria disliked Lady Webster, but nevertheless frequently echoes her opinions.

Lady Webster intensely disliked Gibbon, not only for his partisanship of the Swiss, but because he was the center of attention. "He was treated . . . more as a prince than as an equal," she reminisced in her journal many years later. "Whenever he honoured their *goutees* with his presence every person rose upon his entrance. His whims arranged and deranged all parties."[43] She also found him physically repellent, though again, her account is a memorial reconstruction written years later: "He was a monster, and so filthy withal that one could not endure being close to him. He was buttoned up in the morning, and never *opened* till he was undressed at night; thus every besoin of nature was performed in his clothes."[44] The last assertion would be very surprising, if true, and very distressing for the Gibbon who took care to plan an excellent water closet in his house and who after thirty-five years recalled Mme. de Pavillard's soiled table linens with vivid disgust. No other observer even hints at any such objectionable quality, however, and Gibbon had other enemies who kept journals and were capable of brutal frankness in their contents, notably Boswell. Lady Webster last saw Gibbon in 1793, when his "hydrocele" had grown to enormous size. It seems probable that under those circumstances he might have suffered some leakage from the bladder, exaggerated and misconstrued by the uncharitable and fastidious Lady Webster.

In 1791 the accommodations for the Sheffield family at Gibbon's house were extremely pleasant: "Mama has a Bed-chamber, Dressing-room and Boudoir; we [Maria and Louisa] have two Rooms and two Beds, and the rooms below stairs are entirely at Mama's service to receive her company in. We breakfast in a room [Gibbon] has lately built at the end of his Terrace, which commands a delightful view of the Lake and Mountains."[45] Maria Holroyd, like her father, had plenty of energy. She also had a great taste for sightseeing, a stylish preference for romantic scenery, and a similarly romantic interest in the

noble French refugees in Lausanne. Gibbon arranged numerous expeditions for his guests, which Maria describes—both the destinations
and the adventures in transit—with zest. But Gibbon did not accompany his guests when they took such expeditions; he arranged for
either Wilhelm de Sévery or David Levade to do so. Lady Webster,
her cicisbeo, and her spouse sometimes came along as well, to Maria's
chagrin. "If anybody ever offends you so grievously that you do not
recollect any punishment bad enough for them, only wish them on a
Party of Pleasure with Lady Webster!"[46]

Impatient with the Swiss for their failure to appreciate their own
scenery and their illustrious and unfortunate visitors, Maria makes
them sound rather gluttonous:

> We go to a Party generally every evening; they begin at half past six and
> break up at nine or half past nine. Some are very pleasant, some very
> dull. It is a continual scene of eating. At their Goûter, which is the first
> ceremony in the Evening parties, they eat very heartily of hot puddings
> and pies, fruit, etc., and continue eating Ice and drinking Lemonade
> during the whole time the party lasts.[47]

Later she becomes better pleased, however. One day on the water is
particularly successful:

> The day was uniformly beautiful, and we returned home at eight o'clock,
> better pleased and satisfied than I ever knew so many people with a party
> of pleasure, particularly a water party, the amusement of which depends
> upon wind and weather, as well as Tempers. Mr. Gibbon had some
> thoughts of going with us, but his heart failed him. Luckily, Lady Webster
> is so much afraid of the water that we had not even the alarm of her
> Company.[48]

Maria also sees the Swiss as obsequious to Gibbon, and Gibbon as
partial to their obsequiousness. On her first day in Lausanne, she
writes: "I own my surprise is very great, that Mr. Gibbon should
chuse to spend his days here in preference to England, for there does
not appear to me anybody with whom he can converse on equal terms,
or who is worthy to hear him; but it is a proof how much pleasure
Flattery gives the most sensible people." More than a month later,
she completes a description of "a large dinner" given by Gibbon with
another reference to what she perceives as Gibbon's insistence on
center stage:

> Lally [comte de Tollendal] . . . amused us without ceasing, introducing a
> great many Stories and productions of his own, and did not seem in the
> least alarmed at engrossing the whole Conversation; indeed we all listened
> to him as we would to an Actor on the Stage, and thought as little of
> interrupting him. He is a Companion that would not suit Mr. Gibbon
> constantly, as he does not much like playing a second part. Vive les

Suisses for that! who, when the "King of the Place," as he is called, opens his mouth, (which you know he generally does sometimes before he has arranged his sentence), all wait in awful and respectful silence for what shall follow, and look up to it as an Oracle![49]

Some subsequent biographers have been inclined to adopt Maria's view without question. But Maria was wrong in thinking that Gibbon would not long enjoy Lally's company (she made similar errors on other occasions). Gibbon wrote of Lally, months later, "though Nature might forget some meaner ingredients of prudence oeconomy &c she never formed a purer heart [than Lally's] or a brighter imagination. If he be with you I beg my kindest salutations to him" (*Letters* 3:299). It does not seem to occur to young Maria that she herself was doting on Lally's performance much as she accuses the Swiss of doting on Gibbon's.

Another of Gibbon's performances must have amused everyone: "Mr. Gibbon is desperately in love with Madame de Silva, a pretty Portuguese, who has been some time in England. He courts her at a great rate, and pays her great attention." Madame de Silva was, of course, only the latest in a series of such "desperate loves"; Maria also had the opportunity to meet two earlier ones, Suzanne Necker, and Madame de Montolieu, finding the latter "neither as young nor as handsome as I expected the Woman to be who had put Mr. Gibbon's liberty in danger; for he acknowledges there was a time when he had a narrow Escape. It never occurs to him that she mght have refused him, and if it was mentioned to him, I dare say he would sooner believe a Miracle, than the possibility of a sensible Woman's shewing such a want of Taste."[50] The seriousness of these affairs can be gauged easily enough from Maria's tone, but Gibbon's is better evidence still: "As Mrs Wood [that is, Silva] . . . is about to leave us, I must either cure or die; and, upon the whole, I believe the former will be most expedient. You will see her in London with dear Corea next winter. My rival [Corea] magnificently presents me with an hogshead of Madeira, so that in honour I could not supplant him" (*Letters* 3:236).

On October 4, after a stay of more than two months, the Sheffield family left Lausanne, just as Maria became sufficiently "reconciled" to it to "wish to prolong [her] stay. Indeed, now I am accustomed to dirt and nastiness, and got a little more acquainted with the People here, it is impossible to spend one's time more pleasantly."[51] It was she who wrote to their host about the family's adventures in their return to England via Berne, Coblenz, and Brussels. Gibbon was delighted with her, and with her letters: "I never could understand how two persons of such superior merit as Miss Holroyd and Miss Lausanne could have so little relish for one another as they appeared to have in the beginning; and it was with great delight that I observed the degrees of their growing intimacy, and the mutual regret of their separation (*Letters* 3:234).

Maria's temporary objections to Switzerland were not based on a democratic dislike of its government. "When we came into [Switzerland] from France," Maria tells her aunt, "we imagined we were amongst a happy People who had just sense enough to be satisfied and to have nothing to wish for; but I find we were mistaken, and that the Spirit of Freedom is dispersed over more countries than one."[52] Gibbon, too, was shocked that the spirit of "that strange tragical Romance which occupies all Europe so infinitely beyond any event that has happened in our time" (*Letters* 3:298—so much for America and India!) had invaded Switzerland. His fleeting hopes that the French would take advantage of their opportunity to erect a balanced constitution on the British model soon vanished. But his distress about events in France and even in Switzerland was almost entirely vicarious—he rarely saw himself as affected by it.

There is something of a tradition, following Walter Bagehot, of seeing Gibbon's reaction to the French Revolution as ridiculous—"the truth clearly is, that he had arrived at the conclusion that he was the sort of person a populace kills"[53]—and excessive, though his thinking of wearing mourning for Louis XVI was simply a matter of conforming to British fashionable practice.[54] (He decided not to, since the French refugees in Lausanne, even the Neckers, were not doing so—*Letters* 3:318.) There is really no reason to sneer at his providing himself, at the worst period, with gold and two fast horses in case an army invaded Lausanne (*Letters* 3:282). Not unnaturally, he believed the reports of French and Swiss observers who said that the French army was leaderless and made up of the dregs of the people—"a black, daring desperate crew of buccaneers, rather shocking than contemptible. . . . They . . . call aloud for blood and plunder" (*Letters* 3:291). As we have seen, he had never had any high opinion of mobs and anarchy, seeing them as the tyranny of the many and as the prelude to renewed despotism.

Less understandable is Gibbon's eventually complete disapproval of constitutional innovations. We have already seen the first symptoms, in his objection to the *way* the "clergy [were] plundered"—"a Way which strikes at the root of all property." He considers those who "dream about the establishment of a pure and perfect democracy of five and twenty millions . . . and the primitive rights and equality of mankind which would lead in fair reasoning to an equal partition of lands and money" the "honestest of the Assembly," yet "a set of wild Visionaries" (*Letters* 3:184). He had often made clear in the *Decline and Fall* his strong objections to the Church's accumulation of worldly valuables and even his recognition that theoretical justice would require that all have what was necessary before any enjoyed the luxuries.

But he had also made clear his judgment that the stability of civilization rested on the security of property rights, so these positions on the French situation are not inconsistent with some of his earlier principles.

Now, however, he becomes outrageous in the defense of any status quo. Lord Sheffield even reports a conversation in which he objected to the repeal of the Inquisition, as a now venerable institution![55] Sheffield admits, however, that Gibbon may only have pretended to be serious in this defense; we remember Dr. Johnson's ability to take either side of a case when he "talked for victory." (John Macpherson alludes to this argument as to a joke in a letter to Gibbon of January 1791.)[56] But there is no possibility of mistake in his objection to *any* British parliamentary reform. We can only say that he was appalled by the suffering he *knew* the French Revolution to have brought, and unwilling to purchase a hypothetical good at the risk of such suffering. "I am almost ashamed to complain. . . . A Count d'Argout has just left us who possessed ten thousand a year in the Island of St Domingo, he is utterly burnt and ruined, and a brother whom he tenderly loved has been murdered by the Negroes. These are real misfortunes" (*Letters* 3:240). He does not now "think Burke so very mad" in opposing French constitutional reform (*Letters* 3:243). In August 1792 he describes France as "that inhospitable land, in which a people of slaves is suddenly become a nation of tyrants and cannibals," though he still believes that if they had chosen "to erect a free constitutional Monarchy on the ruins of arbitrary power and the Bastille, I should applaud their generous effort" (*Letters* 3:265). Most significantly, he wrote to Sheffield,

> You have now crushed the daring subverters of the Constitution, but I now fear the moderate well-meaning reformers. Do not, I beseech you tamper with Parliamentary representation. The present house of Commons forms in *practise* a body of Gentlemen who must always sympathize with the interest and opinions of the people, and the slightest innovation launches you without rudder or compass on a dark and dangerous ocean of Theoretical experiment. On this subject I am indeed serious. (*Letters* 3:308)

Knowing, as we do, that the "body of Gentlemen" did not necessarily represent the interest (much less the opinions, which might be a different matter) of the people, and that Gibbon himself had recognized that where grievances existed, if revolution were to be avoided, reformation must be attempted, we may find this attitude not only unenlightened, but inconsistent with Gibbon's own principles. It was a distressing and stressful time. In Gibbon's behalf we can say only that he still rejoiced when his friend Lord Sheffield's motion supporting the slave trade failed, even though he feared that not "an impulse of humanity" but "wild ideas of the rights and natural equality of man" might have motivated the vote (*Letters* 3:257). In Switzerland, he was as troubled by the evidence of arbitrary power the disturbances elicited from Berne as by its occasion: "All are silent, but it is the silence of fear and discontent" (*Letters* 3:254). On the rights of individuals, moreover, he retained his principles in spite of his fears; he was disturbed when well-known local gentlemen, Rosset and La Motte, were condemned and "the proofs and proceedings against them [were] not . . . published, an awkward circumstance which it does not seem easy to justify" (*Letters* 3:254). And finally, he was not the only great man of his age to make the same error: "The last revolution of Paris appears to have convinced almost every body of the fatal consequences of Democratical principles, which lead by a path of flowers into the Abyss of Hell" (*Letters* 3:268).

By mid December 1792 Gibbon could write to Sheffield, "Our little storm has now compleatly subsided, and we are again spectators, though anxious spectators of the general tempest that invades or threatens almost every country of Europe" (*Letters* 3:306). But we must not infer that 1792 itself had been spent in breathless anticipation of French invasion—on the contrary. His ordinary occupations even took new turns. We have already observed the conflict with his neighbor Polier de St. Germain about Gibbon's acacias and plantains. A scholarly paper presented in absentia to the "Wednesday Society" of Geneva, where he had spent the month of March, also generated some conflict. Louis Necker, brother of the famous Necker, read Gibbon's letter and reported that it was very well received.[57] In this paper (not extant), Gibbon had taken issue with some views of H. B. de Saussure on the Greek word *charis*. De Saussure wrote to him anxiously the next day to explain that Gibbon had mistaken the extent of his point. He had meant to deny to the Greeks not the sentiment of gratitude, but a word for it. Like Gibbon, he sees the feeling in the very animals; it would distress him for Gibbon to attribute to him an idea that is not only absurd, but immoral:

> I will not insist further on the literary part of this question, and if you persist in believing that the ancient Greeks . . . expressed gratitude . . . as we do, I shall not be ashamed to have been mistaken relative to you; but what would make me blush eternally, would be to have been able to believe that the sentiment of gratitude is a modern invention, and almost a matter of fashion; that would be like a tiger or a Jacobin, to use, Monsieur, this ingenious comparison that you employ in your letter.[58]

Gibbon also resumed work on his memoirs, on a grander scale (draft F), as we have seen. He considered a trip to England, but left it to Madame de Sévery to decide whether it would be made in the summer of 1792 or 1793 (*Letters* 3:255). Possibly at her request, he decided to postpone it to 1793, when travelling would be easier and, he hoped, safer. And in the summer, he enjoyed one of the best of his flirtations and a charming temporary family during the summer visit of the duchess of Devonshire, her mother, her sister, her little niece Caroline Ponsonby, Lady Elizabeth Foster, and Caroline St. Jules, Lady Elizabeth's (unacknowledged) daughter by the duke of Devonshire. The two little girls were about six. Here is how the duchess of Devonshire described some of their meetings with Gibbon to her own children back in England:

> Mr. Gibbon is very fond of the two Carolines—and Caroline Ponsonby [later the notorious Lady Caroline Lamb] does what she will with him—and would teach him *to do the Kings;* that is, to put her map of the Kings of France together. Mr. Gibbon is very clever but remarkably ugly and wears a green jockey cap to keep the light from his Eyes when he walks in his garden. Caroline was quite entertained with it & made him take it off and twist it about. . . . One day Caroline Ponsonby out of kindness wanted one of the footmen who had been jumping her, to jump Mr. Gibbon, which was rather difficult as he is one of the biggest men you ever saw. . . . She is very naughty and says anything that comes into her head which is very distressing—she told poor Mr. Gibbon . . . that his big face frighten'd the little puppy with whom he was playing.[59]

Though the ladies and Gibbon talked of the revolution and its victims, most of their time together seems to have been spent in a manner almost as carefree and playful as the interludes with the Carolines and their pets, and much less likely to be damaging to Gibbon's amour propre. They attended scientific lectures together (mineralogy and botany), enjoyed his terrace and their place at Ouchy, indulged in charades of courtship and knighthood. One of these charades is the most probable source of a famous legend about Gibbon and Lady Elizabeth. He is said, on the lady's own authority, to have become so bewitched by her, that one day, as she was praising the beautiful view from his terrace, "under pretext of jealousy of the lake and boats" occupying her attention, the ungainly historian fell to his knees before her and asked her to be his wife. She could not help bursting into laughter, and the historian hastily sought to rise, but was unable to do so until she summoned the servants to assist him. The chevalier Artaud de Montor, who reported this story in the *Biographie universelle,* said: "The duchess of Devonshire [Lady Elizabeth succeeded her friend Georgiana in that role] did not tell this singular adventure until long after Gibbon's death. The author of this article heard it from her mouth."[60] Despite this very good authority, the story is not likely to be literally true, principally because the lady's husband did not die until two years after Gibbon himself. Lady Elizabeth was perhaps tempted to improve a real event in this way because such a story had already been told, with other ladies for heroines, by some of Gibbon's enemies.[61] The real event is recounted by Gibbon himself in a letter to Wilhelm de Sévery, who should have been the hero of a mock ceremony of knighthood. Gibbon does not, however, suggest that his fatness created any difficulties:

> You have just received the cockade and the plume but you do not yet know the gracious and solemn manner in which they were given to me, who played in this ceremony the role of your representative. My two sponsors MM. Pelham and Robinson brought me to the Duchess [of Devonshire] who was seated in an armchair. Coming forward I made three bows and I knelt on one knee befoe her. Lady Elizabeth Foster presented a great sword to her. . . . With this sword she gave me the accolade on both shoulders and presented me with the cockade and plume I promised in your name to fulfill all the duties of a brave and loyal Chevalier. (*Letters* 3:278)[62]

Ironically, Wilhelm was not present because he was fulfilling real duties as an officer of the dragoons. Lady Elizabeth wrote to Gibbon from Turin later that month, October 1792, "Pray think kin[dly] of the time spent at the petit Ouchi, forget neither its Philosophy [n]or its folly."[63]

When this entourage had left Lausanne, when Gibbon remembered how empty the downstairs rooms once occupied by the Sheffield family now seemed, and most of all, when he viewed the "approaching dissolution" of his friend Salomon de Sévery, he once again considered leaving his retreat in Lausanne for good. He wrote to Sheffield on January 6, 1793:

> In my letter to Mylady [Lady Sheffield] I fairly exposed the decline of Lausanne, but such an establishment as mine must not be lightly abandoned. . . . in the possession of my library, house, and garden, with the relicks of our society, and a frequent intercourse with the Neckers I may still be tolerably content.—Among the disastrous changes of Lausanne, I must principally reckon the approaching dissolution of poor Severy and his family. . . . I never loved or esteemed him so much as in this last mortal disease which he supports with a degree of courage, patience and even chearfulness beyond all belief. (*Letters* 3:311)

In the same letter he proposes yet another scheme of writing that he himself might undertake:

> the lives or rather the characters of the most eminent persons in arts and arms, in Church and State who have flourished in Britain from the reign of Henry VIII to the present age. This work, extensive as it may be, would be an amusement rather than a toil: the materials are accessible, in our own language, and for the most part ready to my hands: but the subject, which would afford a rich display of human nature and domestic history, would powerfully address itself to the feelings of every Englishman. (*Letters* 3:312)

The volume could be illustrated and popular, he goes on to point out, and asks Sheffield diplomatically to approach George Nicol, the bookseller who did most of the books of this kind, pretending that the idea is his own, "as it is most essential, that I be solicited, and do not solicit."

Gibbon sees himself as having lost his habits of scholarly industry, as needing to "bind [him]self by a liberal engagement, from which [he] may not with honour recede." The work sounds almost like a high-quality coffee-table book, a mere amusement for both reader and author. Nevertheless, fragments of it would be valuable: but there are none. For the first time, Gibbon had proposed a scholarly pursuit that he was not even moved to begin. His own fears about his scholarly habits—or perhaps about his health and energy—seem far too modest. Not a word betrays to his friends any illness or physical difficulty, however, and he concludes, "Shall I be with you by the 1rst of May. The Gods only know" (*Letters* 3:314).

SIXTEEN

Mortal Friendships

n the first of May, 1793, Gibbon was still in Lausanne, though preparing to leave. But his ensuing journey to England was not, as he had planned, a visit of pleasure from one adopted family to another, at a time chosen to minimize the difficulties and dangers of travel. On the contrary, less than a month earlier he had considered the chance of his going to England during the year rather slim, depending on "the events of the [military] campaign; as I am fully resolved rather to remain quiet another autumn and winter in my sweet habitation, than to encounter the dangers of the sea and land" (*Letters* 3:325). The journey also seemed unlikely (though he does not say so to his English correspondents) because he was reluctant to leave the Sévery family: after a long illness, Salomon de Sévery had died on January 29, and Gibbon wanted to offer his mourning friends what they had given him when Deyverdun died: the comfort of loving companionship. When the news of M. de Sévery's death came, Gibbon was at Rolle. He hastened back to Lausanne. Arriving shortly after noon on the 31st, he immediately wrote a note to Wilhelm:

> This moment, my dear friend, I have returned from Rolle, and I return only for you. . . . I share [your] affliction from the bottom of my soul. I wish I could walk the streets of Lausanne without support but I beseech you to receive me in your house at three o'clock and to permit me to stay there part of the afternoon. Madame your mother will not be more troubled with my presence than by her children's; we will moan together in silence around her . . . and try to soften the bitter feeling of sorrow, by

remembering all the virtues of that excellent man who has just been delivered from an intolerable burden. (*Letters* 3:316)

Madame de Sévery was unable to see him that afternoon: "Yesterday I had felt all that I could," she wrote the next day. She had to spend the morning with her attorney. "But after dinner, I await the consolation of seeing you, at any hour that you like—my hours are indifferent to me."[1] Gibbon replied, with a very Swiss mixture of formality and open feeling, "Mr. Gibbon will come to his friend, his sister, if she will permit him this name, about five o'clock, to stay as long as he does not tire her" (*Letters* 3:316). A week later Gibbon wrote to his friends in England, describing the mourners:

> [Madame de Sévery's] firmness has checked the violent sallies of grief, her gentleness has preserved her from the worst of symptoms a dry silent despair. She loves to talk of her irreperable loss, she descants with pleasure on his virtues; her words are interrupted with tears, but those tears are her best relief; and her tender feelings will insensibly subside into an affectionate remembrance. Wilhelm is much more deeply wounded than I could imagine, or than he expected himself: nor have I ever seen the affliction of a son and *heir* more lively and sincere. . . . For myself I have had the misfortune of knowing [Sévery] too late, and of losing him too soon. But enough of this melancholy subject. (*Letters* 3:317)

Poor Gibbon was again astonished, as he had been in the case of his friend Clarke (see p. 25 above), that a son could feel the loss of a father as the loss of a friend. It is noticeable that he had the sensitivity, under these circumstances, *not* to call Wilhelm his son. Gibbon's loving concern for both Wilhelm and Mme. de Sévery reveals itself not only in his language and actions, but in his capacity to divine what was truly comforting to them. He gently claimed Catherine as a sister; and without giving his role a name, he continued to take quasi-parental responsibility for his young friend. A substantial portion of Salomon de Sévery's income had been a pension that died with him, and Gibbon tried to help Wilhelm find a post as a travelling tutor for a young Englishman making the grand tour. One or two such tours, Gibbon believed, would make Wilhelm's fortune "easy" rather than just "respectable" (*Letters* 3:260). (In the event, Wilhelm never took such a post, perhaps in part because of his inheritance from his second "father," Gibbon.) Sévery's death was not a deep personal grief for Gibbon, as Lord Sheffield's or Wilhelm's would have been, but he was saddened by his friends' suffering and by the disruption of a warm and loving family.

Less than three months after that death, he learned of another, more terrible because totally unexpected, and much more painful to Gibbon himself. His friend, his sister, the beloved "Milady," Lady Sheffield, had contracted a pleurisy while working to aid sick and

destitute French refugees and had died in four days (April 4), so
quickly that her family was not even able to be with her. On Friday,
April 26, Gibbon received letters from two friends telling him the
news. Gibbon poured out to Lord Sheffield his own grief and his
keen sense of his friend's much greater suffering:

> My Dearest Friend, for such you most truly are, nor does there exist
> the person, who obtains or shall ever obtain a superior place in my esteem
> and affection!
> After too long a silence I was sitting down to write, when . . . I was
> suddenly struck, indeed struck to the heart by the fatal intelligence. . . .
> Alas what is life and what are all our hopes and projects! When I embraced
> her at your departure from Lausanne, could I imagine that it was for the
> last time? When I postponed to another summer my journey to England,
> could I apprehend that I never, never should see her again. . . . In four
> days! in your absence, in that of her children! But she is now at rest, and
> if there be a future state her mild virtues have surely entitled her to the
> reward of pure and perfect felicity. It is for you that I feel, and I can judge
> of your sentiments by comparing them with my own. I have lost it is true
> an amiable and affectionate friend whom I had known and loved above
> three and twenty years, and whom I often styled by the endearing name
> of sister. But you are deprived of the companion of your life, the wife of
> your choice, and the mother of your children; poor children! . . . I do not
> wish to aggravate your grief, but in the sincerity of friendship I cannot
> hold a different language. I know the impotence of reason, and I much
> fear that the strength of your character will serve to make a sharper and
> more lasting impression.
> The only consolation in these melancholy tryals to which human life is
> exposed, the only one at least in which I have any confidence, is the
> presence of a real friend, and of that as far as it depends on myself you
> shall not be destitute. I regret the few days that must be lost in some
> necessary preparations, but . . . when this letter reaches you I shall be
> considerably advanced on my way. . . . Unless I should meet with some
> unforeseen accidents and delays, I hope, before the end of the month [that
> is, May] to share your solitude and sympathise with your grief. . . . Adieu.
> I could write Volumes, and shall therefore break off abruptly. I shall write
> on the road. . . .
> Adieu. ever Yours. (*Letters* 3:327–28)

Before writing to Sheffield, Gibbon had told the Séverys the sad
news and sought their advice and assistance in planning his travel and
arranging for his household during his absence. They readily agreed
to superintend his domestics, accept his power of attorney, pay his
bills, and otherwise take care of all the problems that arise at home
when someone is suddenly forced to embark on a journey that may
last for months. They too were shocked and saddened by Lady
Sheffield's death; Abigail Holroyd had a quiet gift for inspiring affection. Wilhelm, who had been so grateful for her kindness while he

was in England, was particularly affected: "the poor young Man loved Lady S as a mother," Gibbon says. And Wilhelm proved that love, and also his care and affection for Gibbon, by volunteering to accompany Gibbon as far as Frankfurt or Cologne, that is, through most of the German-language portion of his journey, so that Gibbon would not have to rely on a hired interpreter. Said Gibbon, with perhaps a touch of melancholy pride as well as gratitude, "His attachment to me is the sole motive that prompts him to undertake this troublesome journey, and as soon as he has seen me over the roughest ground, he will immediately return to Lausanne" (*Letters* 3:328).

On May 8, Gibbon's preparations for travel were complete. He wrote to both Sheffield and his stepmother to tell them he would set out on the 9th and to let them know his route and his approximate arrival date. Valiantly he assures them that his health is excellent and that he is sure his journey presents no dangers. In fact, as he later confessed to Dorothea Gibbon, "I must fairly own, that I saw through a magnifyer, and that my resolution to visit Lord Sheffield in his state of affliction was an effort of some courage. But I was most agreably surprized to find the Lyons whom I had seen at a distance become little gentle lap-dogs on a nearer approach" (*Letters* 3:336). May 8 was his birthday, as he noted parenthetically in the dateline of his letter to Dorothea Gibbon. "My fifty sixth," he wrote, deleted "sixth" and continued, "seventh birth-day." It was in fact his fifty-sixth birthday, an error hinting at anxiety and fatigue. It was also his last birthday. In the ensuing months, he repeatedly assures his absent friends that he is in excellent health, but "I am not duped by these remarks about his health," said the astute and affectionate Madame de Sévery.[2]

Gibbon was about to set out without having heard anything further about Lord Sheffield, either from Sheffield himself or from any of his friends in England. This silence added to Gibbon's concern:

> Your own silence announces too forcibly, how much you are involved in your own feelings, and I can but too easily conceive that a letter to me would be more painful than to an indifferent person. . . . What can I think of for your relief and comfort? I will not expatiate on those common-place topics which have never dryed a single tear: but let me advise, let me urge you, to force yourself into business, as I would try to force myself into study. The mind must not be idle; if it be not exercised on external objects, it will prey on its own vitals. . . . Adieu. If there be any invisible guardians may they watch over you and yours. Adieu. (*Letters* 3:331)

With everything prepared for the journey, Gibbon went to spend his last evening in Lausanne with the Séverys. He left two documents authorizing M., Mme., and Mlle. de Sévery to act for him in his absence. The first conventionally empowers them to give instructions to his servants. The second gives them plenary power over his house and garden, including the power to house there persons unnamed whom he has mentioned to them, "and these persons *only*." But suddenly, at the end, it ceases to be a mere legal document—Gibbon says he is "relying with a perfect confidence on the said family, whose friendship I consider as one of the principal good fortunes of my life."[3]

After Gibbon's death, Madame de Sévery wrote a long and detailed description of their last days together. They had spent the evening of Tuesday the seventh with him in his library—just Gibbon and his "family," "in intimacy and sweet confidence," says Madame de Sévery. They discussed all the matters concerning his house that might come up in his absence, and he gave her his will. "How happy I will be to give this back to you," she said. "I hope," he said smiling, "that you won't have any use for it."

On Wednesday, however, they were interrupted. Though Gibbon spent the evening with the Séverys,

> several inopportune people impossible to send away came to torment us; when they went away, Mr. Gibbon who had stayed till the last, talking of his departure which was supposed to be the next day, Thursday, found that he had very little time for completing his business. "Why not stay one more day," he said. "It will be for friendship." . . . I felt as if I had been given a great gift, in getting this day. The four of us spent it together; it was devoted to friendship; who could have told me that it was the last!
>
> The next day, Friday May 10th, he came to see us for one more moment. His carriage was waiting for him before our door. His farewells were very bitter to me. I kissed him. Although already down the steps, he turned back with a touched and disturbed manner. I made a sign to him with my hand, without really knowing what I was doing. He looked at me again with friendship and continued his way toward the carriage. I hurried quickly upstairs to the window and I saw him finish climbing into the carriage, and Wilhelm after him."[4]

If we can believe Gibbon's letters to friends in both England and Lausanne, the trip itself was much less trying than he had expected. But of course that is what he would have told them, whatever his actual difficulties. Yet even in wartime, and on such a journey, there were social opportunities to be seized, and in Gibbon's pursuit of these, especially for Wilhelm, we can see signs that the journey really was not entirely distressing, though they were travelling as swiftly as the circumstances permitted. Every morning they set out soon after sunrise. Wilhelm sent home progress reports from Berne (May 12), Basle (May 14), and Karlsruhe (May 17).[5] En route to Karlsruhe, they spent a night in Schaffhausen, where Gibbon made a deep impression on a young Irishman who chanced to be there, James Roche. Gibbon's appearance, Roche recalled, was what one would infer from the "caricature" decoupage published with his *Miscellaneous Works;*[6] his French accent was poor (Roche had lived in France for some years); but his French conversational style was "perspicuous, racy, and idiomatic," and "the charm of his conversation, short though the enjoyment was, obliterated the impression" of his appearance.[7]

From Karlsruhe they proceeded to Frankfurt via Bruchsal and Darmstadt, reaching Frankfurt around noon on the 19th. There Gibbon could hear the cannons of the siege of Mayence twenty miles away. The British envoy at Brussels, Lord Elgin,[8] wrote a note to Gibbon at 11 o'clock that evening, presenting his compliments and regretting that he had learned only very late that Gibbon was in Frankfurt, especially since Elgin was going out to headquarters very early the next day. He hoped to see Gibbon when he returned: "If Mr Gibbon has any inclination to see the positions of the armies in the coup d'oeil of the environs of Mayence Lord Elgin will, with much pleasure, accompany Mr G. tomorrow morning & bring him back, in the Evening. He can answer for His meeting with an agreeable reception at Head quarters if (as L.E. has reason to suppose) the King of Prussia is now there." Gibbon apparently declined for himself, but asked if Wilhelm could join Lord Elgin. In his reply, also dated Monday evening, Lord Elgin explains that though he "wd. have infinite pleasure in accompanying Mr Severy," he cannot introduce anyone into the king's house except English, and the king's house is the only place to dine. "Lord Elgin cannot be so selfish as propose a simple journey to Mr Severy: while his time can be employed in so much more interesting a way, Even for the same object, by going to *Stockheim,* & Examining the positions from thence—"[9]

Gibbon's interest, albeit for Wilhelm's sake, and his decision to stay over a day in order to meet Lord Elgin, suggest that time and activity had to some extent eased his grief. He took the opportunity to write with his own hand to Madame de Sévery, rather than merely leaving Wilhelm to report to her, because Wilhelm would never tell her "with what truly filial friendship he has taken the most assiduous and delicate care of me. . . . The remainder of my trip, although equally secure will be a little less easy, and much less cheerful" (*Letters* 3:333). To be on the safe side, before leaving Frankfurt on the 21st, he hired a courier who knew German. He reached Cologne on the 24th, Brussels on the 27th. There he found letters from Sheffield and Maria, which "overpaid the Journey" (*Letters* 3:335). Maria's is lost; Sheffield dealt with practical matters, but added, "We shall ever acknowledge that you are a right good friend. I was hardly able to read your letter. This is the first foreign post since its arrival. I had hopes that you would come forthwith, but hardly expected such an effort as your speedy departure require."[10] Gibbon described these letters thus to Madame de Sévery: "The husband let only one cry of pain escape, but it was terrible; the daughter's letter is not dampened with a tear" (*Letters* 3:335).

These reactions prepare us, but did not prepare Gibbon, for a difference between Swiss and British mourning customs that he found difficult to understand and impossible to accept, especially in Maria. The English, comparatively frank and casual in intimate social inter-course, donned masks in moments of great feeling. The Swiss, with stylized and ritualized ceremonies of play, dropped their masks when great occasions authorized great feeling. Gibbon had become Swiss. His friends' masks of fortitude seemed to him inconsistent with gen-uine affection, and as Gibbon could not bring himself to think his best friend, Lord Sheffield, so cold and indifferent, he seems to have centered his criticisms of this attitude—his distress at this failure to pay due tribute to the lost "Milady"—on Maria.

In Brussels he rested for a morning, travelling only to Ghent on the 28th. As far as Ostend, all was easy, but his travel then depended on the winds, and the winds, he wrote to Madame de Sévery, "are capricious like—men" (*Letters* 3:335). In this case, he was fortunate and reached Dover on June 2, only one day later than the earliest day for which he had hoped. Of course he went directly to Lord Sheffield in London, at Downing Street.

He found "Lord S much better and even more chearful than [he] could have expected: he feels his loss, but the new scenes of public business in which he very wisely engaged have alleviated his grief by occupying his mind" (*Letters* 3:337). After about three weeks in Lon-don, the peer and the historian went to Sheffield Place for more than two weeks.

In the middle of July Gibbon finally overcame his habitual lethargy and wrote to his friends in Lausanne. His delay in writing may have had another cause in addition to the familiar demon of procrastination, for he lets slip to his "dear family" at the end of the letter a phrase about something he had perhaps tried not to say, or to see: "Everyone is tranquil and happy; gaiety, even, reigns among us: the *absent* are forgotten a little too quickly in this country. . . . How sweet it is to write to you once one has the courage to set himself to it." Two months later, to Wilhelm, he is much blunter.

> You will be expecting me to speak of the emotional and physical state of the family. . . . I will tell you something about it but the matter is so delicate that you will have to guess, half of it, if you please. I could congratulate myself on the success of my journey, but in truth the patient was nearly cured before the physician arrived. Struck down by a blow as powerful as it was unexpected, the force of his character soon relieved him: business, the world, distractions of every kind, have come to his aid. The storm has ceased, but he is already bored with the calm, and I have every reason to believe that he will try rather promptly to put to sea again

[Lord Sheffield had evidently hinted at his plans to remarry]. This critical moment must have decided the fate of the eldest: it has, but not at all in a favorable way. Her heart has never spoken for a single instant, and as she affects to despise hypocrisy she has even lacked the simplest politeness. All her defects have increased in the last two years, she loves no one, she will not be loved by anyone: what a future. Her taste for any stranger, which she almost no longer dissimulates, only enrages her father, and is only sustained by the indifference of her compatriots. (*Letters* 3:349–350)

Gibbon's own mourning for Lady Sheffield was still quite new in June, while the family had had two months to blunt the edge of their grief. Norton infers, reasonably enough, that comparing the recent mourning of the Séverys made Gibbon underestimate "the more stoical atmosphere at Sheffield Place"; she adds that he was "very unfair . . . to Maria" (*Letters* 3:350).

Certainly, Gibbon's reaction is exaggerated, both by the acute difference in manners and by general discontent or discomfort on his part—he complains about his servants in the same letter and speaks longingly of all the domestic arrangements being made in his house and garden at Lausanne. But Sheffield, it seems, was also furious with Maria. And in her own letters during the months following her mother's death, there is a certain brittle tartness of manner, perhaps particularly connected with Gibbon, and an obsessive interest in the émigrés and French affairs that would confirm Gibbon's impression of her *behavior*, though not of her heart.[11] Gibbon's criticism of her lack of feeling was indeed biased by his Swiss expectations, but it was encouraged by palpable frustration and irritability on her part. In the first letter we have after her mother's death (July 2, 1793), she wrote at her father's request to Ann Firth, family friend and former companion to Lady Sheffield, about his lending their town house to the government:

I wish I had known this for certain before we left Town, for I dare say they will break all our valuable China and Glasses in moving them.

Edward Hamilton came on Sunday, and I suppose will stay till Milord and the Great Gibbon go to London next Monday. I was very glad at his appearance; for I think both the Peer and the Historian began to grow tired of a Tête à Tête after Dinner which always lasted a considerable time, as Gib. is a mortal enemy to any persons taking a walk; I suppose upon the same principle as Satan disliked the situation of Mr. and Mrs. Adam. Moreover he is so frigid that he makes us sit by a good roasting Christmas fire every evening.[12]

Clearly poor Maria had much to try her patience; clearly also her behaviour looked not like unhappiness but ill humor.

Like his daughter's, Sheffield's grieving took an indirect form.[13] He extended invitations to as many guests as he could find, despite the remonstrances of his family and Gibbon, throughout the summer. Though both he and Gibbon made Sheffield Place their headquarters, each and sometimes both were frequently away on visits. In nearly every other stage of her life Maria valued Gibbon's company for her own sake as well as her father's, but in the summer of 1793 she was by no means always pleased to see Gibbon. "We went [to the Camp where maneuvers were being held] yesterday [August 7], all except the Great Gib: who thought himself better at home, in which I perfectly agreed with him."[14]

Fortunately, at the end of August Maria had the pleasure of an excursion that released much more of her restless energy and which she describes with much of her old zest. It was prepared for by an overnight stay with Lord and Lady Pelham—"Nothing could be more pleasant than the whole family was," writes Maria. This was the family from which Maria's first stepmother would come, in December 1794. It is possible that Lord Sheffield may already have hinted as much to Gibbon, to whom he had confided another matrimonial plan that was not realized, but Maria seems to have had no suspicion of it. In any event, she thoroughly enjoyed the Field Day:

> On Thursday morning we set out for the Camp at eight o'clock. . . . Wonder of Wonders! Papa let me mount Mr. Hadden's Horse and I rode the whole morning, about six hours, with the Army. . . . I was amazingly happy to be allowed to ride. . . . It was a very good Horse and so accustomed to such things as Field Days, that all the firing of Cannon did not make him prick up a single ear. Papa took Silver Tail out of the Carriage to ride, and Lord Pelham lent him a Cart Horse to help to draw the Coach containing Mrs. Aunt, Miss Louisa, and Mr. Gibbon. . . . I was so much entertained and pleased with my lot, that I did not suppose we had been three Hours. . . . At three o'clock, when the Army went to dinner, we retired from the Field of Battle and went home; that is, to Stanmer to dinner, and came to S.P. in the evening, attended by a most lovely Moon, and the Day after to be sure I was a little stiff or so, but not in the least tired, or the three Dowagers in the Coach either.[15]

Late in September, a shared social disaster completed the reconciliation of Gibbon and Maria. A few days after his distressed or ill-tempered letter to Wilhelm, they—Maria can tell it best:

> On Tuesday last Papa was engaged to dine at Mr. Sneyd's—a large Party was invited to meet him, and the Carriage was coming out the Door when a letter arrived from Tom Fool [Thomas Pelham, Lady Webster's cicisbeo] to say that Lady Webster meant to come from Battle to S.P. . . . The Dismay of the Family may be more easily imagined than described. Mr. Gibbon vowed if Papa went to Jevington he would immediately set off for Brighton. I was aghast, for as Aunt can claim the Privelege of Invalidism, I should have all the Weight of her Ladyship on my Shoulders. However, after much pro and con . . . Papa stayed. . . . She . . . amused

us very much with her account of the Camp, near Dunkirk. . . . She . . . talked of the dead bodies on the field of Battle she passed over, with as much Rapture as any Vulture might be supposed to do. I do not give her credit for half the unfeelingness she pretends to, or I should begin to question if she were not really an Infernal. . . . But enough and too much of such a woman. . . . Friday, Fred North and Mr. Douglas came. I am glad nothing happened to prevent Mr. D. coming. The Gib. would have been furious, and he was rather grumpy that Papa made him stay a fortnight longer than he intended. . . . However, Mr Douglas with his Greek and Latin, and Fred. North with his Islands of Ithaca and Corfu, have put him quite in good Humour, and they are much more entertaining, *having him to draw them out* [emphasis added].[16]

She adds in a later letter, "Fred North and Mr. Douglas left us on Sunday, after having enlivened us much by their very pleasant conversation. . . . With the addition of Mr. Gib, it was impossible to have selected three Beaux who could have been more agreeable, whether their Conversation was serious or trifling."[17]

Gibbon's various jaunts did not leave him much time at Sheffield Place in this, the last summer of his life, but while he was there, he pursued at least three different literary projects. The first was "*the* Memoirs," or more precisely, the information about his ancestors that Gibbon had long sought through the *Gentleman's Magazine*. In July, at his request, John Nichols asked the author of the articles on the Gibbon ancestry (Samuel Egerton Brydges) to communicate with Gibbon directly.[18] Nichols also offered to lend Gibbon two books about early Kent, one by John Philipot and another by William Lambarde. Gibbon accepted gratefully, asking permission to take the books with him to Sheffield Place and promising that they would be "carefully used and speedily returned" (*Letters* 3:338). The first part of this promise Gibbon may have kept; his notes from Philipot were properly made on a separate sheet of paper.[19] The second part, however, was not kept at all; they were still in his possession when he died; Sheffield thought they belonged to his friend, and they were not returned until 1796, when they were sent back "newly bound."[20] Despite this thirst for information, there is no evidence of Gibbon's working on the actual manuscript of his memoirs, and some evidence that he did not, for Brydges informed him that he was not, after all, closely related to John Gibbon the Herald, yet the correction is not made in any draft. Furthermore, in most of July Gibbon would hardly have had time to do much writing: he was at Sheffield Place for only the first week, then spent a night at Beckenham with Lord Auckland, then went on to London. While there, he sought out his usual haunts, including a trip to Twickenham, and dined at the Royal Society Club.[21] He had to cancel an appointment in London on the 16th because he was exhausted (*Letters* 3:340–41), but after returning

briefly to Sheffield Place, he made a short excursion to visit Lord
Egremont at Petworth and William Hayley at nearby Eartham (*Letters*
3:340, 348).

It was in July also that Gibbon wrote to the current head of
Westminster School, W. Vincent, seeking more information for the
autobiography. Vincent readily consulted the records for Gibbon. On
the 20th of July, he wrote, beginning with a compliment about the
Decline and Fall:

> And now, Sir, permit me to inform you that from Dr. Nichol's book,
> which is in my possession, you were entered at Westminster School, in
> the second form, in January, 1748, the precise day is not noticed, but
> probably from the 10th to the 16th, it was the same year I was entered
> myself in the September following. The time of your quitting the school
> cannot appear from this book. . . . Your age is noticed . . . which makes
> you 9 years old in 1748.

A second letter from Vincent, dated July 22, evidently replies to some
doubts of Gibbon's, not including the issue of his age, about which
Dr. Nichol was misinformed—Gibbon was, of course, ten, nearly
eleven, in January 1748:

> Dr. Vincent is able to assure Mr. Gibbon, from his own entrance in the
> same year, that the year of Dr. Nichol is certainly 1748, and he thinks he
> can bring to Mr. Gibbon's remembrance, facts that will fully satisfy his
> own mind. Boyle, afterwards Earl of Orrery, was one of the principal
> actors in Ignoramus, represented in December, 1747, and would of course
> continue *Captain* till Whitsuntide 1748. Fury succeeded him. These are
> such remarkable epochs in the chronology of boys, that few forget them.
> Dr. Vincent is sure of his own memory likewise, when he asserts that he
> remembers Mr. Gibbon in the 2d form, and at Mrs. Porten's house in
> 1748, as he lived next door.[22]

Although the dates in draft F were not corrected by Gibbon on the
basis of this information, his continuing interest in improving and
continuing his memoirs is obvious.

During his July visit to London Gibbon also made plans to pursue
another literary project. In the first note to chapter 38 of the *Decline
and Fall*, published in 1781, Gibbon had observed, apropos of his use
of Bouquet's *Recueil des historiens des Gaules et de la France*, "Such a
national work, which will be continued to the year 1500, might provoke our emulation" (*DF* 4:106). Apparently the need for such a
collection was one of the subjects Gibbon frequently brought up in
learned and well-to-do circles, "our literary men and our eminent
book-sellers": "As long as I expatiated on the merits of an undertaking, so beneficial to history, and so honourable to the nation I was
heard with attention; a general wish seemed to prevail for its success.
But no sooner did we seriously consult about the best means of

promoting that success, and . . . reducing a pleasing theory into real action, than we were stopped at the first step by an insuperable difficulty, the choice of an Editor. . . . we knew not where to seek our English Muratori in the tumult of the metropolis or in the shade of the University."[23]

In the event, he found his man in the columns of the *Gentleman's Magazine*. In 1788 a series of letters appeared there making the case for an edition of the medieval British historical manuscripts with great energy and fervor. Their author was John Pinkerton, then only thirty but already an historian and antiquarian of great industry and considerable ability, at least in Gibbon's judgment. Like Gibbon, he felt that "next to the glory of national arms, is that of national history"; "our Gibbons and Robertsons perhaps exceed any modern French historians, though no Frenchman will allow this. But historiography is foreign to my subject, which concerns the *foundations* of historiography, the publication and illustration of the original writers and documents."[24] In July 1793, through the bookseller George Nicol, Gibbon learned that Pinkerton was still actively pursuing the idea of a *Scriptores rerum Anglicarum*. It was Pinkerton that Gibbon had planned to meet in London on July 16. The meeting was scheduled for Nicol's shop and was only tentative, for Gibbon was in Twickenham and was not sure he could return in time.

In fact, he did not get back to London until about three o'clock. It was a very hot day, and he was "in such a state of mental and corporeal dissolution as would have rendered [him] very unfit for literary conversation" (*Letters* 3:340–41); therefore the meeting did not take place. Without waiting for another appointment, Pinkerton wrote to Gibbon on July 22:

> I hope you will pardon this [epistolary] intrusion, after our appointment at Mr. Nicol's. . . . I have expressed upon many occasions, that I regarded you as the first of living authors; and perhaps the only one in the world who has united genius, erudition, philosophy, eloquence, all in the most consummate degree. . . . As I hear you will not be in town for some time, I hope you will forgive my impatience in writing to you.
>
> It gave me extreme satisfaction to learn the proposed scheme of publishing our ancient historians, under the auspices of the greatest of modern historians, and whose name alone would ensure success to the work, and occasion the revival of an important study, too much and too long neglected in this otherwise scientific country. Your favourable mention of me as reviser flattered me much. . . . Mr. Nichol expressed his hope that you would consent to give your advice as to the authors employed, and other important points, so he and I warmly join . . . in the request that you will allow your name to appear as superintending the work. . . . It is also hoped that you will spare a few hours to clothe the Prospectus, upon which much depends, with your powerful eloquence, which, like a coat of mail, unites the greatest splendour with the greatest strength.[25]

After reciprocating Pinkerton's compliments, Gibbon, in his reply of the 25th, reiterated his enthusiasm for the project but severely limited his contribution:

> I will embrace every opportunity, both public and private, of declaring my approbation of the work, and my esteem for the Editor. I shall be always ready to assist at your secret committee, to offer my advice with regard to the choice and arrangement of your materials, and to join with you in forming a general outline of the plan. If you proceed in drawing up a prospectus, I will consider it with my best attention, nor shall I be averse to the crowning your solid edifice with something of an ornamental frieze. When the subscription is proposed, I shall underwrite my name for, at least, six copies. . . . But . . . [m]y name, (qualecumque sit,) I could not lend with fairness to the public, or credit to myself, without engaging much further than I am either able or willing to do.

He went on to point out that he was not a specialist in the English historians, that he had other literary projects, that he was going back to Lausanne, and that his publisher was not Nicol, but Cadell (*Letters* 3:341–42).

Negotiations between Gibbon and Pinkerton continued, however. In November they met at last, and eventually a scheme was settled upon under which Gibbon felt willing to be listed as "conjuct editor" (Pinkerton's phrase)[26] of the project. Lord Sheffield's note explains:

> Some of the objections in this letter were overcome: it was agreed that Mr. Cadell, if he chose, should be nominated publisher, &c. The final arrangement was, that Mr. Pinkerton's name should appear in the title-page as sole editor; but that Mr. Gibbon should write a general preface to the work, and a particular preface to each volume, containing a review of the history, and historians of each epoch; for which purpose, on his return to Lausanne, he was to peruse all the ancient English historians in a chronological course, a labour which he mentioned with pleasure, as the last and most favourite occupation of his life. . . . Mr. Gibbon also ageed to write the Prospectus, and to allow it to appear with his name.[27]

It was indeed just such a project as Gibbon had been seeking: continuous but with discrete parts, dependent only upon sources in languages he knew or available in editions with Latin translations, respectful of the antiquarian scholarship for which he had profound regard, yet allowing him to utilize his own talents for narrative and synthesis. Hugh Trevor-Roper has pointed out that Gibbon's "Address" recommending this project and Pinkerton as its editor anticipates one of the major strains of nineteenth-century historiography, the value of, and need for, reliable texts of early sources.[28] It has been said that, though Gibbon died relatively young, he did not die too soon, because his work was complete. Perhaps so, but the "Address," written with unmistakable zest, gives us a hint that the prefaces would have had much to offer. One of the motives for the project is especially interesting to readers of Gibbon's autobiography: "Nature has implanted in our breasts a lively impulse to extend the narrow span of our existence, by the knowledge, of the events that have happened on the soil which we inhabit, of the characters and actions of those men from whom our descent, as individuals or as a people is probably derived."[29] In other words, the historical impulse is allied to the genealogical impulse, in Gibbon's view—and both are innate in the human animal.

In the "Address" Gibbon is no longer a Roman senator, or a citizen of the great republic of Europe, but very English: "Without indulging the fond prejudices of patriotic vanity we may assume a conspicuous place among the inhabitants of the Earth. The English will be ranked among the few nations, who have cultivated with equal success the arts of War, of learning and of commerce: and Britain, perhaps, is the only powerful and wealthy state, which has ever possessed the inestimable secret of uniting the benefits of order with the blessing of freedom."[30] Comically or ironically, this conclusion echoes his comments on Switzerland in the youthful "Letter on the Government of Berne." There he had said that the Pays de Vaud "is the only country in which one both dares to think, and knows how to live. What do you lack? Liberty: and deprived of liberty, you lack everything."[31] In his *Memoirs* Gibbon had learned to see de facto liberty enough in Switzerland: "While the Aristocracy of Bern protects the happiness, it is superfluous to enquire whether it be founded in the rights, of man . . . and the magistrates *must* reign with prudence and equity, since they are unarmed in the midst of an armed nation" (*Memoirs* 185). Since writing those words in February 1791, however, Gibbon had seen that individual liberty might be jeopardized even when an armed populace was ruled by benevolent magistrates (*Letters* 3:318); perhaps that is why it is now England alone that possesses both blessings, or perhaps he was concerned only with "powerful and wealthy" states possessing both.

On historiographic grounds the "Address" is also interesting. Since the best evidence in any issue is that of the first witnesses, the "losses of history are indeed irretrievable: when the productions of fancy or science have been swept away, new poets may invent, and new philosphers may reason; but [a lost fact] . . . can never be restored by the united efforts of Genius and industry." Gibbon even has numerous kind words for the "MONKISH HISTORIANS (as they are contemptuously styled)":

> Our candour and even our justice should learn to estimate their value, and to excuse their imperfections. Their minds were infected with the passions and errors of their times; but those times would have been involved in darkness, had not the art of writing, and the memory of events been

preserved in the peace and solitude of the Cloyster. . . . In the eyes of a
philosophic observer these Monkish historians are even endowed with a
singular though accidental merit; the unconscious simplicity with which
they represent the manners and opinions of their contemporaries: a natural
picture, which the most exquisite art is unable to imitate.[32]

This is the culmination of the movement towards a preference for
naive art in his predecessors that we have already observed in the
Decline and Fall itself.

Gibbon's survey of the previous editions of English historians and
of illustrious foreign scholars who have contributed to such national
collections employs the methods (and the wit) of his evaluations of
his sources for the *Decline and Fall* in the footnotes of the history.[33]
The author of the *Antiquities of the House of Brunswick* reappears for a
moment to praise that subject and its great historians, Leibnitz and
Muratori: "We must explore with respect and gratitude the origin of
an illustrious family, which has been the guardian, near fourscore years
of our liberty and happiness. The antiquarian who blushes at his
alliance with Thomas Hearne will feel his profession ennobled by the
name of Leibnitz." With the recommendation of Pinkerton and the
explanation of the scope of the proposed work—*English*, not *British*,
historical writings, A.D. 500–1500, Gibbon concluded his historical
writings. The last phrase is a description of Pinkerton that might
well be applied to Gibbon himself: "a man of genius at once eloquent
and philosophic who . . . accomplish[ed] in the maturity of age, the
immortal work, which he had conceived in the ardour of youth."[34]

During this last summer, however, Gibbon did take up his pen on
one other literary occasion. He had once employed the classical scholar
Edward Harwood to teach him the English pronunciation of Greek.
Harwood considered him an excellent Greek scholar, though presumably they did not pursue any Byzantine texts or dwell much on the
mysteries of versification and accents (in all of which Gibbon has
been frequently found to err).[35] Now Gibbon found in Lord Sheffield's
library an interleaved copy of Harwood's *View of the Various Editions of
the Greek and Latin Classics*. He did not work his way through all the
entries, but on more than thirty we have Gibbon's characteristic
responses. Many are merely informative, but some, like the notes to
the history,[36] give us a sense of Gibbon's lost conversation: "If Homer
lived within fourscore years of the Trojan war . . . he might converse
with the last companions of Ulysses and Æneas, and the probable
human part of his narrative may be almost read as the history of his
own times"; "I am by no means ungrateful for the discovery of [a
"Hymn to Ceres," attributed to Homer]; yet I should be far more
delighted with the resurrection of the *Margites* of Homer, the picture
of private life and the model of ancient comedy. What an universal
genius! We may think indeed of Shakespeare and Voltaire"; "The

shipwreck of lyric poetry is the heaviest loss the Grecian literature has sustained. . . . The dearest objects of my regret are the better *Iambics* of Archilochus . . . and the pathetic elegies of Simonides, of which such an exquisite specimen has escaped the injuries of time"; in Schweighæuser's edition, "The fragments are disposed in such lucid order, that we seem to have recovered the forty books of the history of Polybius."[37]

Such comments give us an impression of the sense, information, and taste of Gibbon's conversation. But those who knew him valued it for other qualities as well, and those who knew him best, prized it most. Maria Josepha, once reconciled to Gibbon, sees him not only as a delightful conversationalist in himself, but also as adept at "drawing out" others. Gibbon shone, in her critical view, whether his "Conversation was serious or trifling." After his death, she commented, "Papa has read us several parts of Mr. Gibbon's Memoirs, written so exactly in the Style of his Conversation that . . . we could not help feeling a severe Pang at the Idea we should never hear his instructive and amusing Conversation any more."[38]

Gibbon's favorite activity that summer at Sheffield was conversation. "His habitual dislike to motion appeared to increase; his inaptness to exercise confined him to the library and the dining-room," wrote Lord Sheffield:

> and there he joined my friend Mr. Frederick North, in pleasant arguments against exercise in general. He ridiculed the unsettled and restless disposition that summer, the most uncomfortable, as he said, of all seasons, generally gives to those who have free use of their limbs. [Gibbon, though he imagined that his "hydrocele" was invisible and untroublesome, freely acknowledged the problems with his legs and feet he had experienced since his 1791 attack of erysipelis.] Such arguments were little required to keep society . . . within doors, when his company was only there to be enjoyed; for neither the fineness of the season, nor the most promising parties of pleasure, could tempt the company of either sex to desert him.
>
> Those who have enjoyed the society of Mr. Gibbon will agree with me, that his conversation was still more captivating than his writings. Perhaps no man ever divided time more fairly between literary labour and social enjoyment; and hence, probably, he derived his peculiar excellence of making his very extensive knowledge contribute, in the highest degree, to the use or pleasure of those with whom he conversed.[39]

For almost two months, except for excursions with the family, Gibbon stayed put at Sheffield Place. At the end of September, on his way to Bath to visit Dorothea Gibbon, he stopped in London for a few days en route, taking "two small rooms and a closet" for five guineas per week—"clean convenient and quiet" but expensive. His "very agreable" first evening was spent with Peter Elmsley; then he dined at Crauferd's and went on to Devonshire House later. "The

Dutchess is as good and Lady Eliz. as seducing as ever." On the second he was to dine with Madame de Silva, "my Portuguese woman," and expected to see Lady Webster there. On Sunday the sixth he left for Bath (*Letters* 3:351–52).

In Bath he stayed at York House, where he had requested a bed-chamber and dining room *on the same floor* with accommodations for two servants. This specification is an ominous sign, for despite his withered leg and the ever-growing swelling in his groin, he habitually managed to go up and down stairs, both in his house at Lausanne and at Sheffield Place. Yet he had greatly enjoyed the travel by post chaise over good roads, and he seems affectionately pleased with his step-mother as well:

> I reached this place after a very pleasant airing, and am always so much delighted and improved with this union of ease and motion, that were not the expence enormous I would travel every year some hundred miles, more especially in England. I passed the day with Mrs. G yesterday. In mind and conversation she is just the same as twenty years ago; she has spirits, appetite, legs, eyes, and talks of living till ninety. I can say from my heart Amen. We dine at two, and remain together till nine, but although we have much to say, I am not sorry that she talks of introducing a third or fourth actor. (*Letters* 3:353)

He later decided, however, that he and Dorothea were better off without "auxiliaries": "I do assure you that our conversation flows with more ease and spirit when we are alone, than when any auxiliaries are summoned to our aid. She is indeed a wonderful woman, and I think all her faculties of the mind stronger and more active than I have ever known them" (*Letters* 3:354). His original thought of cutting short his visit had been abandoned, though he was still hoping to depart on the 18th, after ten days with his stepmother. "I may possibly reckon without my host, as I have not yet apprized Mrs G of the term of my visit, and will certainly not quarrel with her for a short delay." She accepted his plans as made, however, and he left Bath for Althorp, seat of the Spencers, on Friday the 18th, arriving on the 20th for two weeks with Lord and Lady Spencer and the Althorp Library. On November 5, Gibbon wrote cheerfully, "We have so compleatly exhausted the morning among the first editions of Cicero, that I can only mention my departure from hence to morrow the 6th instant" (*Letters* 3:356). It is obvious how congenial a companion Lord Spencer was, and Lady Spencer's letters make it clear that she too enjoyed Gibbon's conversation and that hers was enjoyed by him.

On November 8, when Gibbon reached London, the word "unwell" suddenly entered the correspondence. The swelling in Gibbon's groin, which made motion difficult for him, was now making sitting in a chair impossible as well. Perhaps only the characteristic pose, with his back planted against the fireplace, snuffbox in hand, was tolerable for him.[40] Others had been shocked or concerned by the swelling for years, but Gibbon insisted on ignoring it. Now, however, it had become "almost as big as a small child" (*Letters* 3:359). The case history supplied by his surgeons to Sir Joseph Banks after Gibbon's death provides details:

> He had a large tumour in his left groin, or rather it should be said that the whole Scrotum was full of an amazing Mass, the contents of which from the most accurate information could not be ascertained.
> The Penis was lost in the lump, and had been so for many years, and the place from which the urine issued was pushed over to the right side near the right Testicle which last was in a sound state. . . . He said he had never felt the least inconvenience from it, till about the month of August or September last [1793], when it began to increase rapidly at the lower part, so as to make him very uncomfortable upon motion and absolutely unable to sit upon a chair from the weight of it dragging & pulling him down about the breast and stomach.[41]

Thus, on November 11, Gibbon at last consulted a physician about the problem (for the first time since 1762—a consultation he himself had forgotten) and wrote to Sheffield a "Most private" letter:

> I must at length undraw the veil before my state of health. . . . Have you never observed through my inexpressibles a large prominency circa genitalia. It was a swelled testicle which as it was not at all painful and very little troublesome I had strangely neglected for many years. But since my departure from S P it has encreased (most stupendously) is encreasing and ought to be diminished. (*Letters* 3:359)

Typically, Gibbon seeks to diminish the effect of his announcement with this joking allusion to John Dunning's famous resolution that "the influence of the Crown has increased, is increasing, and ought to be diminished" (April 6, 1780). Lord Sheffield was astonished that his friend could imagine that no one had noticed his problem, but when they spoke together about it later on, Gibbon was surprised that anyone could have noticed its existence; he himself, he said, "never looked at other people's '*genitures*.' "[42] His self-consciousness even in conversation with Lord Sheffield is suggested not only by his long silence on the subject but by his choice of the rare and obsolete word "genitures" instead of "genitals," and, as we have just seen, he dropped into the "obscurity of a learned language"—circa genitalia—in his "most private" letter.

All of Gibbon's friends were, of course, aware of the problem he thought invisible, and Lord Sheffield did not hesitate to print an account of it in the posthumous memoirs:

> I did not understand why he, who had talked with me on every other subject relative to himself and his affairs without reserve, should never in any shape hint at a malady so troublesome; but on speaking to his valet

de chambre, he told me, Mr. Gibbon could not bear the least allusion to that subject, and never would suffer him to notice it. I consulted some medical persons, who . . . [assumed that it was inoperable and that Gibbon had had medical advice]. He now talked freely with me about his disorder; which, he said, began in the year 1761; that he then consulted Mr. Hawkins the surgeon, who did not decide whether it was the beginning of a rupture, or an hydrocele; but he desired to see Mr. Gibbon again when he came to town. Mr. Gibbon not feeling any pain, nor suffering any inconvenience, as he said, never returned to Mr. Hawkins; and although the disorder continued to increase gradually, and of late years very much indeed, he never mentioned it to any person, however incredible it may appear, from 1761 to November 1793. I told him, that I had always supposed there was no doubt of its being a rupture; his answer was, that he never thought so.[43]

This is a discreet version of what Gibbon said. He actually told Sheffield that his problem developed following a "*lues veneria*."[44] Both Gibbon and his surgeon, according to Gibbon, thought that his complaint was a hydrocele.

This "hydrocele" of Gibbon's has been much discussed. It was long featured in medical literature as a record example of a hydrocele, which, in the loose definition of "an accumulation of serous fluid, usually about the testis," it was—apparently. A surgeon at Lausanne (who, of course, had not examined the swelling) also thought it must be a hydrocele,[45] though friends such as David Francillon and Levade had thought it a hernia. When surgery became necessary and the fluid could be examined, it was not serous, but "clear, transparent, and watery." Sir Gavin de Beer (1949) has provided a technical medical analysis that makes it certain that Gibbon did not have a true hydrocele (because at the autopsy it was determined that the fluid-collecting bag was in communication with the peritoneal cavity) and highly probable that he was suffering both from a "large and irreducible hernia" and cirrhosis of the liver.

De Beer also thought that Gibbon must have known that his disease did not have a venereal origin; he "used this expedient to silence the reproaches which his great friend Lord Sheffield cannot have failed to make to him on account of the culpably long neglect of his condition, and at the same time perhaps to gratify a point of vanity."[46] Now it is impossible to see why Lord Sheffield would be more satisfied with his friend's neglecting a swelling of venereal origin than one of nonvenereal origin, but the issue of vanity may indeed arise—if Gibbon were entirely without sexual experience, he might, as de Beer thinks, have seized the opportunity to claim "credit" for some. But this is the same Gibbon who told his physicians that "for a long time he had used his penis only to urinate," obviously not fearing that they would suspect him of lifelong virginity.[47] It is the same

Gibbon who recommended to the readers of his memoirs the work in which Richard Porson mingled with his praise of the *Decline and Fall* an aspersion on the author's sexuality that might well have stung a man so anxious to exaggerate his sexual experience as de Beer believes Gibbon to have been.[48] It seems to me much more likely that Gibbon really did believe he had contracted a venereal disease in his militia days and *therefore* ignored this alone among all his illnesses and problems. It is striking that none of the physicians' reports mention this theory of a venereal origin for the complaint; it was *only* to his most intimate friend that Gibbon confided this explanation. If he were anxious to demonstrate his manhood, why did he not at least propose it to the physicians? In finding it impossible to believe that Gibbon mistook his symptoms, de Beer forgets that Gibbon's capacity for self-deception about this particular problem was literally enormous.

Whatever the origin of his swelling, it was decided to relieve it by "tapping"—surgical puncture to permit the liquid to drain off. Gibbon seems to have felt liberated by the plans for his operation and his discussion with Sheffield to speak of it to other friends. On the night when Gibbon wrote the revelatory letter to Lord Sheffield, he dined with his friend Sylvester Douglas, later Lord Glenbervie. Ladies, and a stranger, were present, so naturally Gibbon did not discuss his ailment and approaching surgery. On the contrary, Gibbon was especially amusing and, as usual, full of anecdotes, some of them gently risqué. But when Douglas called on Gibbon after the operation, Gibbon "gave [him] the history of his complaint. He seemed to doubt whether I had ever taken notice of it. He was as usual full of anecdote." Prior to the surgery, Douglas commented in his journal, "I shall be very anxious about the event, as he is a very good-natured as well as an ingenious and learned man, and a man of great probity in his conduct, however censurable in his opinions, and he is very kind to me."[49] And Gibbon was also perfectly willing to mention his surgery to John Pinkerton, whom he had never even met (*Letters* 3:364).

The surgeon for whom Gibbon sent on the tenth was Mr. Walter Farquhar, the same who had attended Lady Sheffield in her last illness. Farquhar requested a consultation, "which Mr. G. consented to with great reluctance as he thought the case so very simple and plain"—or perhaps because of his continuing reticence about his condition. Henry Cline, the surgeon consulted, called in a third consultant, Dr. Matthew Baillie, and "a puncture was made at the bottom of the left side of the tumour, on the 16th of November, when four ale quarts of transparent watery fluid were discharged," reducing the swelling to about half its former size.[50] During the operation, Gibbon continued to perform his role as amusing man of the world. Not only did he tell his physicians that he sometimes thought he had lost his

penis altogether, but he joked with them throughout the operation—
for example, "Why is a fat man like a Cornish borough? Because he
never sees his member."[51]

He expected after the operation to be able to "walk about in four or
five days with a truss" but because the physicians cautiously "hinted" at
possible inflammation and swelling, Gibbon correctly thought that
Lord Sheffield would wish to be on hand (*Letters* 3:359). Unfortunately,
the truss was very uncomfortable for Gibbon, and the swelling returned.

> In ten days after the first operation, the parts became again unwieldy
> and troublesome, a second puncture was made by which three quarts of
> fluid like the first were discharged.
>
> The truss was now again resorted to, with every contrivance to support
> the weight, and make it comfortable but that was not possible as from the
> excoriations by the urine wetting the bag every time water was made the
> parts were rendered tender and sore, and at last inflammation and ulcera-
> tions were produced upon many parts of the tumour. These became so
> troublesome as to interfere with general health and to make the nights
> often very restless and unpleasant.[52]

Despite all this, "he enjoyed his usual spirits," said Lord Sheffield.
"He was abroad again in a few days."[53] During this period he "passed
a delightful day with Burke; an odd one with Monsignor Erskine, the
Pope's Nuncio"—odd it must needs have been! The second operation
was "much longer, more searching, and more painful than the former";
it was followed, as we have seen in Farquhar's report, by ulcerations,
inflammation, and sleepless nights, but for a day or so Gibbon felt
much better, and he claimed good health for the rest of the month.
As he wrote to Sheffield, "I do not want dinners," that is, he had
plenty from which to choose (*Letters* 3:365). He even visited Loughborough at Hampstead and Auckland at Beckenham before returning
to Sheffield Place on December 10th (*Letters* 3:367–68). He particularly enjoyed meeting Pitt, with whom he had previously not been
personally acquainted, and the Archbishop of Canterbury, "of whom
he expressed a high opinion" (!)[54] Reassuring letters were despatched
to Bath and Lausanne (*Letters* 3:363–64).

"His discourse was never more brilliant, nor more entertaining,
than on his arrival [at Sheffield Place]," Lord Sheffield recalled. "The
parallels which he drew, and the comparisons which he made, between the leading men of this country, were sketched in his best
manner, and were infinitely interesting."[55] Sheffield himself was perhaps especially appreciative of his friend's company because at the
time Sheffield was suffering from political restlessness and various
physical ills (affecting his eyes and stomach). Gibbon guessed astutely
that his friend's postponed grief was catching up with him (*Letters*
3:368); we may suspect that fears for Gibbon himself also exacerbated
Sheffield's sense of loss:

This last visit to Sheffield-Place became far different from any he had ever made before. That ready, cheerful, various, and illuminating conversation, which we had before admired in him, was not now always to be found in the library or the dining-room. He moved with difficulty, and retired from company sooner than he had been used to do. On the twenty-third of December, his appetite began to fail him. He observed to me, that it was a very bad sign *with him* when he could not eat his breakfast, which he had done at all times very heartily; and this seems to have been the strongest expression of apprehension that he was ever observed to utter.[56]

At least twice during his last six weeks of life, however, Gibbon did consider his own death. During this visit to Sheffield Place, as in all the visits after Lady Sheffield's death, Gibbon enjoyed a number of conversations with Lord Sheffield's sister, Serena, now living with the girls, whom Gibbon refers to as "dear little aunt." Clearly she was moving into the status of "sister" with him. She found him

> a man of the most correct manners, and of the most equal temper,—calm, and rather dignified, and conversing with all the flow of his writings. He was devoted to all the comforts of life, and liked the elegancies and even delicacies of the table, but ate and drank sparingly. A few days before he died, he conversed on a future state with [her], of which he spoke as one having little or no hope; but professed that neither then, nor at any time, had he ever felt the horror which some express, of annihilation.[57]

The other occasion was on the very day before his death. Meanwhile, his friends were very much more alarmed than he appeared to be, about his condition. "Poor Historian!" wrote Maria on New Year's Day, 1794. "He has been very indifferent since yesterday se'en night. It is a great effort to him, going up and down stairs. He fears he shall be obliged to go to Town. . . . Mr. Hayley comes on Sunday or Tuesday, if Mr. Gibbon can stay so long; I wish he may, and yet at the same time, I am very anxious to know he is in London, and within reach of able Physicians and Surgeons. . . . In Face, he is as well as ever; but in other respects looks much worse." Ten days later she adds, "Poor Mr. Gibbon left us on Tuesday [January 7], and I wished him to go long before he did, he seemed so very indifferent. Papa had so much inquietude about him that he followed him on Thursday, and from his Acct. yesterday I suppose if Mr. G. had delayed setting out one day longer, he might have been too ill to recover. Papa says, the Surgeons ordered Bark every 6 Hours and 5 Glasses of Madeira at dinner."[58]

By this time, "the tumour was then much larger than before. The surface of it was considerable inflamed and excorciated all over, with deep ulcerations in many places, particularly where the pressure of the truss had been most felt." Yet Gibbon was well enough for the surgeons to try again on Monday the 13th; this time there were six quarts of fluid: "He thought himself much relieved by the operation. He continued perfectly easy the 14th except feeling some uneasyness at the stomach and a dislike for food. He saw many of his friends this day and had Mr. Elms[l]y with him for four hours in the evening, when he was clear, distinct and accurate as usual."[59] On Tuesday, Gibbon urged Sheffield to keep an engagement he had in the country, saying, "You may be back on Saturday, and I intend to go on Thursday to Devonshire-House."[60] Sheffield duly left to keep his engagement. He did not fear for Gibbon's life, but he did wonder if his friend would ever fully recover; Gibbon, however, optimistic as usual, "talked of a radical cure." Among the friends he saw were Lady Lucan and Lady Spencer. That night he thought himself well enough to do without his "calming" draught (opium). But on Wednesday, January 15, he could not eat his breakfast and

> complained at times of a pain in his stomach. At one o'clock he received an hour's visit from Madame de Sylva, and at three, his friend, Mr. Craufurd . . . called, and stayed with him till past five o'clock. . . . Mr. Gibbon happened to fall into a conversation, not uncommon with him, on the probable duration of his life. He said, that he thought himself a good life for ten, twelve, or perhaps twenty years.[61]

According to Gibbon's servant Dussaut, by six o'clock that evening, this life had begun its final stage. Since Gibbon had not had any meat for several days, chicken had been ordered by the doctor for his supper. He could not bear to look at the whole thing, so Dussaut brought him a wing, cut up into small pieces.

> He himself broke up the piece of bread that he mixed in with them, and the first piece that he took to his mouth cost him a terrible effort, which continued with each piece. In spite of that he managed to eat it all. He took each piece on his plate without looking at it, always asking me if he had not yet finished. He drank three little glasses of Madeira and enjoyed all three. After having finished, he told me that he was very uncomfortable in his armchair, that after I had dined he would like to be moved, but I did that first. . . . He was supposed to see someone at eight and he told me . . . [to explain] that he could not see him until the next day.[62]

At nine he went to bed, taking his opium draught. But he "passed a very unpleasant night having a constant desire to change his position. He complained much of pain in his stomach, was much troubled with flatulence and frequent bursts of wind till towards four o'clock in the morning."[63] He wanted only Dussaut with him, though Dussaut needed help to support him while giving him something to drink. "My poor Dussaut," he said to his valet, "You have a very difficult service with me. I'm afraid you will become ill too."[64] He did not lose consciousness and his mind was apparently clear; even after he could not speak, he could respond when Dussaut asked him to stick out his tongue. He did not ask for his doctor or for anyone else, but at daybreak, Dussaut sent for Farquhar.

Yet "about half past eight" on the 16th, thinking himself no worse than the day before, Gibbon got out of bed and back in again (presumably to use the chamber pot, since Lord Sheffield and Dussaut delicately do not say why), more agilely than he had for some time past. He even wanted to get up and dress at nine, but Dussaut persuaded him to wait for Farquhar, who was expected at 11.[65] When he arrived, Gibbon "was scarcely sensible, had very little pulse and cold extremities."[66] Farquhar took Dussaut out of the room and told him, "Dussaut, you no longer have a master." Dussaut trembled and his hair stood on end—(he wrote this account the next evening at 11 P.M., having been alone in the house with Gibbon's body since 7 in the morning—"Oh my dear master"). He returned to the dying Gibbon, whose last words were (presumably in French), "Dussaut, you leave me."[67] A message was immediately dispatched to Lord Sheffield, but it was far too late. At 12:45 P.M., January 16, 1794, Gibbon died. Twelve hours late, Lord Sheffield and his sister arrived from Sheffield Place. Serena Holroyd wrote to Maria Josepha:

> When Dussot came to the door the picture of despair to tell me *he* was no more, I felt as if it was new to me. Indeed I had somehow hoped it was possible he might be alive and even like to see me. . . . I felt it was worth my coming, for my Brother as we came soothed himself with now and then talking, and indeed the gloom, not to say horror of coming to this Hotel last night required somebody to share it, and by mutually thinking of one another it diverted some of it. There was not a spark of fire in the whole house; nor a maid up. . . . We went to my Brother's bed chamber, and Bull lighted the fire, and in about an hour we got some tea, which was all we desired. We sat up talking and writing till after two.[68]

Mrs. Gibbon had to be told; they sent the message not to her directly, but to her companion, Mrs. Gould. "She bore it with as much fortitude as could be; but . . . her frame was such [that Mrs. Gould] could not answer for the effect. She is gratified with my brother's wish to have poor Mr. Gibbon buried at Fletching,"[69] that is, the parish church near Sheffield Place, where Gibbon is buried in the Sheffield vault. Other reactions were characteristic; Maria regretted him as "a true and sincere friend," and for her father's sake. "There is no other Person who has half the Influence that poor Man had. . . . I am glad Parliament will employ Papa, it will prevent his thinking."[70] Said Lady Elizabeth Foster, "He was always very good to me."[71] Hannah More thanked God that she had not been polluted by his company, and his former friend John Whitaker sneered because despite his pain and his "atheistic" views, Gibbon had not attempted suicide.[72] Sheffield himself was deeply grieved not only by his friend's death, but by his own abscence at the time. And Gibbon's other closest friends, far away in Switzerland, who had just been sent a reassuring note about the results of this third operation? Madame de Sévery, overwhelmed by this second death, wrote,

> O my angel! O my friend! I have lost you both in the same year; who could have told me that this half of myself and this friend with whom I would have spent my life would both have been snatched away from me in such a short space of time? I cannot comprehend it my fate would appear to me a frightful dream from which I will awake, but alas this awakening will be death.[73]

Let this friend, who loved him and could tell him so, have the last word.

Lord Sheffield had the last cares—Gibbon's stepmother, the execution of his will, his simple funeral and elaborate epitaph. And his memory. "Mr. Gibbon has left some Manuscripts that are very curious and interesting, with leave to publish them, if they are thought sufficiently finished. They are Memoirs of his own Life."[74]

GIBBON'S REPUTATION

Miscellaneous Works and Immortal History

hough Gibbon did not fear "annihilation," he did hope for immortality through his history. Those six volumes in folio preserved what he valued most in himself. But as we have seen, he had come to realize both that history itself was in important ways a reflection of the creating mind of the historian and that his own sense of self could not be fully represented by identifying his life with the production of the *Decline and Fall*. Indeed, to those who knew him, the man seemed a greater loss than the historian. To Dorothea Gibbon, the Sévery family, and Lord Sheffield, especially, Gibbon was not solely or even principally a great writer; he was a loving and cherished friend. Although Gibbon had no close relations, he was deeply mourned. His Lausanne obituary mentions that he was loved by his servants,[1] and Dussaut's reaction to his death tends to show that the statement was more than a pious commonplace. But the tone of the *Gentleman's Magazine* obituary is more to the point: it says his works will "probably, last as long as the English language," summarizes his life, praises his conversation, and comments that he "lately, gave a proof of the goodness of his heart in sacrificing every consideration, and quitting his elegant abode, solely to administer every consolation in his power to his dearest friend, who had lost his lady, one of the most admirable women in England."[2]

The obituary ends, however, not with this tribute to Gibbon's heart, but by noting that an autobiography was hoped for. The editing of that autobiography and of Gibbon's other *Miscellaneous Works* was the last active service Lord Sheffield could perform for his friend, and he did so with mournful gusto. But tastes changed with time, and though the autobiography as edited by Sheffield has never been allowed to go out of print,[3] the version of Gibbon as a person perpetuated by Lord Sheffield's editing came to be regarded by many disdainfully or patronizingly. The history, on the other hand, despite various vicissitudes of fortune, has never ceased to hold its place in the great tradition of English letters. It was criticized, it was abridged, it was misunderstood, it was challenged, rewritten, edited, analyzed, and in many ways superseded, but it was not forgotten.

Lord Sheffield had always manifested his friendship for Gibbon in activity, and he now dealt characteristically with his own grief and his responsibilities to that friend. As Gibbon's executor, Sheffield had to cope immediately with practical matters such as the disposition of his body and estate; he could have postponed the task of literary executorship. Instead, he turned to it at once. The *Memoirs* and letters, in particular, gave him a last experience of his friend's conversation and as it were a means of extending his life. But first, Sheffield enabled his friend to make a last contribution to "science" by consenting to an autopsy,[4] and he arranged for his burial (January 23)[5] in the quiet manner Gibbon had desired: "The Funeral was conducted with the greatest Simplicity at his desire, only his own Servants attending the Hearse, and 8 Men with Fletcher and John to carry the Coffin."[6]

Sheffield wrote at once to Lausanne to perform the triple office of telling the Séverys of their common loss, arranging for the legal necessities there, and informing Wilhelm of his inheritance. Though, as we have seen, Gibbon had left a copy of his will with Madame de Sévery, it had not been opened: "The Council refused to open Mr. G.'s Will unless they had an 'Extrait Mortuaire' to prove his Death. It is the custom of the country for all Wills to be opened by the Council."[7] Sheffield also asked Wilhelm to send along all the papers Gibbon had left in Lausanne. The drafts of the most important piece, the autobiography, were already in England.

As the *Gentleman's Magazine* obituary suggests, the fact that Gibbon had left an account of his life was widely known almost immediately. Members of the Literary Club, even those not particularly fond of Gibbon, were impatient for its appearance, for example, Thomas Barnard, who wrote on March 25 to Boswell, "I shall be very impatient for the Publication of Gibbons Private Memoirs, as I hope it will be full of Interesting Anecdote; But . . . His Motives, as well as his Private History, are Equally Indifferent to me, even if they were *Sincerely* display'd, which we have no Reason to Expect."[8] Sheffield began reading it to his own family in early March, and even earlier had apparently shown it to some literary experts, notably Malone, who wrote, on February 20:

He has left a most curious work that will be extremely interesting of which I have [read] a small part. He calls it, "The history of my own mind"; it is, in fact, the history of his life. He enters into all the minutiae of his early years; gives an account of the books he read when he entered on this or the other study, etc., and contrives to make the minutest matters exceedingly interesting. Though he never wrote a foul copy of anything, he has left four different copies of a very large portion of his life, so much pains did he take about it, and so difficult he found it to execute it to his mind. His method of Composition was to turn the subject thoroughly in his mind, and then he filled his paper without a single erasure. Of the first volume of his History there were more copies than one; but he had at length acquired such a facility of style that he told lord Spencer the original copy of the last three volumes was that which went to the press. . . . [Sheffield] has almost promised to put the whole [autobiography] together (for it is not quite finished) and to publish it, as the author certainly intended he should.[9]

In keeping that promise, Sheffield provided the world with Gibbon's final masterpiece and enabled his own generation to do more justice to the man, as well as the historian, than they might otherwise have done.[10] In Sheffield's view, an editor's responsibility was some-what like a physician's: "First do no harm." He must at all costs avoid injuring his friend's reputation by publishing in his name material unworthy of him, either as a scholar or as a gentleman. Malone mentions in the letter just quoted "a great number of cards closely written on both sides, filled with the characters of some of our contemporaries." No such cards now exist among the Gibbon papers; we must conclude either that Malone was mistaken (there are other errors in his letter) or that Sheffield found the "characters" not only unpublishable, but unfit to be preserved. With this possible excep-tion, however, Sheffield not only fulfilled his duty to his friend as he saw it, but preserved the materials for another age to reconsider. He thought he had done no more than allow his friend to speak for himself without embarrassing faux pas. As Sheffield wrote before continuing the narrative past the point at which the *Memoirs* cease with Gibbon's own letters,

The examination of his correspondence with me suggested, that the best continuation would be the publication of his letters from that time to his death. I shall thus give more satisfaction, by employing the language of Mr. Gibbon, instead of my own; and the public will see him in a new and admirable light, as a writer of letters. By the insertion of a few occasional sentences, I shall obviate the disadvantages that are apt to arise from an interrupted narration. A prejudiced or a fastidious critic may condemn, perhaps, some parts of the letters as trivial; but many readers, I flatter myself, will be gratified by discovering even in these, my friend's affec-tionate feelings, and his character in familiar life.[11]

Yet, as J. E. Norton makes clear in her admirable account of Sheffield's editing of the *Miscellaneous Works*,[12] this anxious care for Gibbon's reputation and Sheffield's numerous and varied assistants in the editorial process (who included William Hayley, Maria Josepha, the Miss Harriet Poole who so much admired Gibbon's and Hayley's conversation and talents,[13] the Joseph Jekyll whose conversation was so much enjoyed by Gibbon,[14] and a Mr. More, impartial because he was unacquainted with Gibbon) made some of his editorial decisions whimsical even by the standards of his own time, and his total disregard for the integrity of his text is, of course, distressing to a modern scholar. It is the structure imposed by the Sheffield committee, and its sense of decorum and correctness, that largely determined the public's perception of Gibbon for at least 140 years. The plan, generally, was to combine drafts F, C, and E but to interpolate selected materials from other drafts as desired. Since only draft E was available for the later years, it was supplemented by Gibbon's letters, connected by a narrative by Sheffield himself and concluded by him. Sheffield also freely excised material considered unflattering or indiscreet and even corrected Gibbon's style. Despite criticism by some of his committee, he decided to include many letters by Gibbon that were not necessary to the narrative (as well as some letters *to* Gibbon). He did so because he so much valued Gibbon's conversation. He explained to his readers:

> His letters in general bear a strong resemblance to the style and turn of his conversation; the characteristics of which were vivacity, elegance, and precision, with knowledge astonishingly extensive and correct. He never ceased to be instructive and entertaining; and in general there was a vein of pleasantry in his conversation which prevented its becoming languid, even during a residence of many months with a family in the country.
>
> It has been supposed that he always arranged what he intended to say, before he spoke; his quickness in conversation contradicts this notion: but it is very true that before he sat down to write a note or letter, he completely arranged in his mind what he meant to express.[15]

The committee had in hand not only the drafts of the memoirs, but the papers from Lausanne, which arrived before the end of July. Wrote Maria, "It astonished me to find what sort of Letters he kept. There are several Love Letters of Madame Necker's among them. If the Papers had fallen into the hands of a Boswell, what fun the World would have had! All the papers left at Lausanne were sealed, and directed to Papa."[16]

Perhaps Sheffield's most useful adviser was William Hayley. Hayley, who had been scheduled to visit Gibbon and meet the Holroyd family at Sheffield Place in January, when Gibbon had to go to London for his final surgery, was very much shocked and distressed by Gibbon's death. He wrote to Samuel Rose:

> A new and very bitter affliction fell suddenly upon me, in the unex-pected tidings of Gibbon's death.
>
> Farewell to all the refined pleasures, which I had so vainly projected both for you and myself, in much future conversation with that friendly being, of most exquisite talents, to whose engaging society (though I could not adopt his sentiments on more than one subject of importance) I have still been very deeply indebted for instruction and delight.[17]

Rose, Hayley adds,

> attended him to the house of their friend Lord Sheffield, where they formed his Lordship's little cabinet council, to sit in judgment on the posthumous manuscripts of his illustrious intimate, the departed historian. . . . [Hayley was] much pleased with the warmth of heart and considerate fidelity of friendship, which our noble host exerts in regard to the memory and reputation of the great historian, whose life he intends to publish in the course of the next spring.[18]

The Holroyds, or at least Maria Josepha, were equally pleased with the "Hermit":

> Ten years of common intercourse would not have brought Papa and Mr. Hayley so well acquainted, or made them like and love each other as the cause and subject of this visit of only ten days has done. They were each and almost equally very warmly interested about the fame and character of a common friend who was very dear to both. As to Mr. Hayley, I never figured to myself, much less saw, any person possessing such an animated mind, such Enthusiasm of friendship, and a heart so wholly and entirely divested of every selfish principle. . . . I think I shall not like the conver-sation and manner of any man I meet with for six months to come, as well as I should have done were this dear Poet unseen.

On Hayley's recommendation (derived from William Cowper), Lord Sheffield engaged a secretary. "His name is Socket; he is about 16; has had a good education; can read Latin and French; and is to have £20 a year and to live with the Servants,"[19] We hear no more about this Socket, and most of the editorial markings on the manuscripts of the *Memoirs* are in Maria's hand. It is to be hoped that he is not the person who, using the name of "B. D. Free," communicated to the *Gentleman's Magazine* (September 1805) an English epitaph on Gibbon, which, "Free" says, was written by Lord Sheffield and "fell into my hands, among other papers, while I resided at Sheffield Place as secretary" to him.[20] (In the next issue Lord Sheffield denied his authorship of the epitaph but did not identify its true author, Hayley.) With its sentiments Sheffield was certainly in agreement:

> Formed for the studious and the cheerful hour,
> Here, Gibbon, rest! thy course of glory run!
> Few thy compeers in literary power;
> And in the charm of social converse, none!
> Thy works immortalize th'historian's fame;
> To fond remembrance let this verse commend
> Worth that delighted by a dearer name,
> Thou sprightly guest! thou sympathetic friend.[21]

In Lausanne, the Séverys were not the only ones to grieve for Gibbon. D'Erlach was "in despair" when Wilhelm gave him the news. "I loved Gibbon with all my heart and it was impossible not to love him very much, when one had obtained his friendship. There was not a week in which my wife and I failed to plan for the time when he had promised to come to us to dine here. . . . Poor Gibbon, why not rather these millions of rascals that devastate the earth."[22] Suzanne Necker, already mortally ill, was told the news with great caution. She wrote to Madame de Sévery:

> They had not told me until the moment, Madame, the frightful loss that we have just suffered; in the profound sorrow into which it plunges me, my first care, my first duty, is to mingle my tears with yours; the eternal regrets that I will give to the memory of M. Gibbon will always be accompanied with the memory of all the happiness that you contributed to his life; . . . alas, why did he leave you? why did he leave us? I do not have to reproach myself with having neglected any means to make him renounce this terrible journey, but he is no more, and nothing can replace him for us. If my state had permitted, I would have come to seek with you, madame, the only consolations of which I feel capable, and I am annoyed with M. Necker, who to delay my suffering for a few instants, deprived me of the only means of making it less bitter.[23]

Lord Sheffield, with perhaps surprising delicacy, thought of a means of making the sufferings of both Madame Necker and the Séverys less bitter: he had the materials about them in Gibbon's *Memoirs* copied out and sent to them. Suzanne Necker "had the satisfaction of going out of the World with the knowledge of being Mr. Gibbon's First and Only Love."[24] It was fortunate that the extracts were sent swiftly, because she died within five months of her onetime fiancé.

Publication of the *Miscellaneous Works* took much longer. In mid November, Hayley reports, "Lord Sheffield, with his eldest daughter Maria, and their friend Harriet Poole, returned the hermit's visit, by passing some days with him at Eartham." In a letter to Samuel Rose on November 16, 1794, Hayley described the visit and the committee's work on Gibbon's *Miscellaneous Works:*

> But you will ask, what we have done? in truth we have not been idle: for as I told the lively intelligent Maria, it was a mere excursion of *business*

to her, who read with the diligence of a clerk in office; and she must visit
the hermitage again for *amusement*. She read aloud to us, (and delightfully
she reads,) the whole life and all the letters of the historian, from the
period where the memoirs end; so that our noble editor may now, I think,
keep his word to you of beginning to print very soon after Christmas. He
was pleasant and friendly. Maria and Paulina were as charming as females
should be to a hermit; and the visit seemed to gratify all parties. We
revised his Lordship's Introduction, and I have exhorted him to exert
himself with immediate diligence and spirit, in preparing the important
close of his work.[25]

In the event, other experts had to be consulted in order to perfect
the *Miscellaneous Works*. The abbé de la Rue was employed to correct
the French, which, he said, was very incorrect; Pinkerton was asked
to contribute a conclusion to the account of their common venture,
and other specialists were consulted on other points, including the
correction of the classical quotations, which proved in their unedited
state that Gibbon was not at all fussy about quantities. He himself
had hinted that he lacked "the scrupulous ear of a well-flogged critic"
(*Memoirs* 38), but Sheffield and his committee were determined that
the world should not know of any deficiencies in Gibbon's learning
through their agency. In a draft of his preface Sheffield had acknowledged that the duty of examining Gibbon's papers "became my lot at
a time when I was most severely depressed; within ten months I had
lost the two most intimate companions of my Life to whom I had
been accustomed during the greater part of that life to communicate
every thought as it occurred without reserve or restraint knowing that
they were equally interested in them as myself."[26] The latter part of
this sentence disappears in the published version of the preface, in
part perhaps because of the advice of the committee, in part because
of Sheffield's developing feelings,[27] in part because with experience
he had discovered that the activity of examining the papers was
healing, rather than depressing: as Maria wrote (April 1, 1794), "Poor
dear Pap left us on Saturday; he says he feels low, but I never saw
him so quietly cheerful and good humoured."[28] The first edition of
Gibbon's *Miscellaneous Works*, in two volumes quarto, published by
Gibbon's old publishers as Gibbon had requested (despite many conflicts between publishers and noble lord), appeared on March 31,
1796.[29] Lord Sheffield eventually completed his services to his friend's
memory with a fuller edition of the *Miscellaneous Works* (five volumes
octavo, dated 1814, actually 1815).[30]

The *Miscellaneous Works*, especially the *Memoirs*, were a success at
home and abroad. Despite all his care, some readers thought Lord
Sheffield had allowed things to be published that should have been
suppressed (including compliments to himself and his family).[31] More
readers were fooled by the editing into thinking Gibbon more formal,

more unfailingly correct, more rigid and restrained, than he actually was. They thought the *Memoirs* splendidly sincere, but they found their author a cold and unappealing person. Yet for generations readers nevertheless found the *Memoirs* irresistible. Part of the appeal was the sense of participation in the creation of a masterwork: "In the minute incidents connected with his *Work*, I stand invisible behind him; I steal along his grove of Acacias, and my mind participates in his exultation and in his gloom."[32] King George III "remarked on the egotism and vanity which he had found in them," but also "the strong proof of intense and methodical study."[33] The reviewer for the *European Magazine and London Review* (1815), enjoyed "listen[(ing] to [Gibbon's] discussion of his reading (for we almost fancy we hear him speak)."[34] When Mark Pattison was a lonely and precocious university student, he writes in his own memoirs, Gibbon's *Autobiography* "seized upon my interest in an exceptional way. . . . The minute history of a self-education, conducted on so superb a scale, was just what I wanted. I had long before got hold of a few extracts. . . . I now procured the whole work and devoured it, reading it again and again till I could repeat whole paragraphs. Gibbon, in fact, supplied the place of a college tutor; he not only found me advice, but secretly inspired me with the enthusiasm to follow it."[35] Until the publication of the whole of the six drafts (1896) and the beginnings of modern biography, responses to Gibbon were essentially responses to the version of Gibbon prepared by Lord Sheffield. In that form, Gibbon was credited by all with a classic autobiography, but one that, in the opinion of numerous readers, revealed an unlovable person.

As more and more came to be known about Gibbon, some continued of the same opinion, but many, like myself, would concur with General Meredith Read, the great nineteenth-century Gibbonian, who wrote:

> In scrupulously studying the details of Gibbon's life . . . we attach ourselves to him with warmth. I have had many intimate friends, and Gibbon is one of those whose companionship I have most enjoyed. . . . I have passed days, weeks and months in his company, . . . and in the haunts most dear to his heart. I have learned to love him, to rejoice over his great qualities, and to mourn over his shortcomings. He was very human, with frailties and weaknesses, but he was very lovable to those who knew him best.[36]

I hope that the reader of this biography has formed a similar opinion.

Immediately after Gibbon's death, a few persons still fearful that Gibbon might unsettle the Christian Church tried to believe that his history had died too. One "O," writing in Charles Brockden Brown's *Monthly Magazine and American Review* (April 1799), says that Gibbon excels Hume and Robertson in "malice, dexterity and perseverance" in attacking Christianity, but in nothing else. "No writer is more tiresome than Gibbon."[37] T. D. Whitaker's review of the *Miscellaneous Works* of 1814 admits that Gibbon, "with the defect of a style less chaste and simple, surpassed . . . all preceding historians in the extent and variety of his researches, and produced a work that . . . [in some respects] has no rival in ancient or modern times." But his religious infidelity and "reasoning powers not of the first order" make Gibbon "an English classic who now begins to sleep upon the shelf, and Paley has more readers than the infidel historian."[38] These pious hopes were disappointed. Equally unnecessary were the fears of the ardent atheist Jane Carlile, who published chapters 15 and 16 separately in 1820, "being fully aware that the Christian world would not hesitate to mutilate the writings of one of the best authors this country can boast, if they thought it necessary to protect and preserve their superstition a few years longer."[39] Early in the nineteenth century, Gibbon's history was firmly established as a classic, and as a classic that did not sleep upon the shelf.

Throughout the century, and indeed well into the twentieth century, Gibbon was attacked or defended or praised for his religious positions.[40] The contents of the attacks to 1930 were summarized in McCloy's *Gibbon's Antagonism to Christianity* (1933). Negative qualities—innate coldness of heart, malicious hatred of Christianity, failure of historical imagination—were assumed to account for his not portraying the beauty of Christianity or understanding the Christians' perspective on their experience. But in the course of the century, most readers came to realize that the *Decline and Fall* was not *just* an attack on the Christian church. Virtually all professional historians saw Gibbon's secularization of Christian history as either something to be taken for granted or a positive contribution to historiographical practice,[41] and many other readers agreed, in effect, with John Henry Newman: "It is melancholy to say it, but the chief, perhaps the only English writer who has any claim to be considered an ecclesiastical historian, is the unbeliever Gibbon."[42] Some readers long continued to believe, with approval or disapproval, that Gibbon wrote his whole history as a device to disguise his intention to undermine Christianity; some occasionally attempt to claim that Gibbon did not oppose Christianity itself at all, but only certain aspects of the institutional church; they deny that the concessions to the "First Cause" in chapter 15 are ironic. The latest exponent of this view is Paul Turnbull (1982).[43]

For most readers, however, the treatment of religion in the *Decline and Fall* is now just another historiographical issue. Similarly, the question of the value of Gibbon's style—its role as an asset or liability to the history—has a history of its own, but has recently become again, as it was in Gibbon's own time, subordinated to the issue of the proper role of literary considerations in the writing of history.[44]

The *Decline and Fall*'s peculiarly classic status was early accorded a
unique recognition: it was edited, with explanatory and corrective
footnotes, as if it were an ancient text. Of course even in Gibbon's
lifetime it was being published with polemical notes to counteract its
antireligious tendency, but the new editions were of a different kind.
Paradoxically, the first appeared in France, the Western European
country originally least hospitable to the *Decline and Fall*. Its editor
was F. P. G. A. Guizot.

Whereas the *Esprit des Journaux*, whose mission was to represent
the French critical consensus, complained in 1790 that Gibbon should
have followed Montesquieu much more closely and given him more
credit, that he should have *enumerated* the causes of the fall of the
Empire (the reviewer helpfully does so for him) and avoided digressions into nonpolitical issues such as the role of Christianity,[45] Guizot,
himself a historian, after the obligatory French bow to Montesquieu—
Gibbon is "less strong, less profound, less elevated"—perceives
Gibbon's unique value and makes a statement of it in his 1812 preface
that strikingly anticipates twentieth-century analyses. Like English,
Italian, and German reviewers to the eighteenth century, Guizot
perceives that Gibbon is writing in a different genre from Montesquieu and therefore develops material "whose richness [Montesquieu]
had indicated." In combining the "erudite" or antiquarian critical
methods for dealing with facts with the "philosophic" concern with
connections among actors and events, what Guizot calls the "moral
part" of history, Gibbon provides new insight into the relationship
between political events and other aspects of history, such as finances, opinions, and customs. This is methodologically novel, but
the *Decline and Fall* is also unprecedented in its scope and in its
general accuracy. Gibbon is regarded as an authority, says Guizot,
even by those who disagree with his views or correct particular errors
from a specialist's perspective. Guizot himself had on a first reading
been dazzled by the interest of the narrative; a second reading had
led him to be censorious of numerous errors of detail. But on a third
reading, he found that he had exaggerated the importance of the
errors and had not been just to the "immensity of Gibbon's researches,
the variety of his knowledge, the extent of his insights and especially
the truly philosophic justice of his mind, which judges the past as it
would judge the present."[46]

Of course the English presses had not been idle between Gibbon's
death and 1812, the date of Guizot's first edition.[47] In 1807 Cadell
and Davies issued a new edition of the history with an introduction
by Alexander Chalmers, which was repeatedly reprinted. At the same
time, a different, but anonymous, introduction was supplied for the
edition in "Oddy's Historical Classics," which was issued in seventy
weekly parts, beginning October 31, 1807. The history had already

(1789) been abridged before Gibbon's death; the abridgment, though unauthorized, was, Gibbon thought, a good advertisement: "A translation, an abridgment, or even a criticism, always proves the success, and consequently extends the sale, of any popular work" (*Letters* 3:209). Abridgments and selections, especially chapter 44, flourished alongside the whole history. An opponent, perhaps a Dr. Steuart, grumbled in 1808, "In this very year, three or four [editions] of different size and price have been published in London, and two in Edinburgh . . . in a shape to meet the ability of the humblest purchaser."[48] In the Edinburgh editions of Bell & Bradfute et al., beginning in 1811, the author of a "Life" of Gibbon comments at the end that "the public has long since enrolled [Gibbon] among the atandard writers of the English language."

In England, William Youngman inaugurated a productive line of criticism of Gibbon's history with the concluding sentences of his "Memoir of the Author" in the Robertson, Baynes, and Childs edition of the history. He compares the *Decline and Fall* to an epic. The concept

> was happy and sublime. The Roman republic . . . covered the world, which it had subdued, with its majestic ruins. . . . There was no English history which could throw any satisfactory light upon [this period]. Through this dark and dreary chaos, therefore, Mr. Gibbon undertook to form a safe and open path, and, in the result, he gave to the world the most elaborate and the most accurate history which it had ever possessed. . . . His history is not like that of Hume, a philosophical essay; nor like those of Robertson, a series of biography; but resembles rather a splendid epic.[49]

But perhaps the most important single statement about Gibbon's work in the first half of the century was H. H. Milman's review article in the *Quarterly* in October 1833. "In Gibbon there were wanting . . . a more free and natural style, a purer moral taste, and a philosophy superior to the narrow prejudices of its age . . . but with these grand exceptions, there is everything to be admired in him as an historian," Milman wrote; an annotated English edition of Gibbon, recognizing his classic stature as the French had done, was needed. In 1838 Milman produced that edition. A clergyman, Milman included both in his introduction and in his notes material intended to make the *Decline and Fall* safe for believers, but he did much more. Appreciating with other writers Gibbon's architectonic feat in "bridg[ing] the abyss between ancient and modern times, and connect[ing] the two worlds of history," Milman considers the unity achieved in the *Decline and Fall* the triumph of the historian's ability over intrinsically chaotic material; the creation of an intelligible whole "must be ascribed entirely to the skill and luminous disposition of the historian. It is in this sublime Gothic architecture of his work, in

which the incongruous gorgeousness of the separate parts . . . are all
subordinate to one . . . predominate idea, that Gibbon is unrivalled."
He also notes as a feature of Gibbon's method something previously
noticed, if at all, only as a defect. Gibbon's readers are expected
"sometimes to correct and modify opinions, formed from one chapter
by those of another."[50] Milman's great edition was often reprinted and
finally itself revised by William Smith (1854). An edition with vario-
rum notes designed to rival the Smith-Milman edition appeared in
1853; Gibbon would have enjoyed the passionate scholarly competition
for his remains.

He would have enjoyed still more the testimony of his peers.
F. W. J. Schelling, though he insisted on considering Gibbon an "orator"
rather than a historian, found him the only writer since the ancients
who went beyond the limits of national history; Gibbon's work "is
valuable for its broad conception and for his portrayal of the great
turning point of modern times."[51] B. G. Niebuhr, in the preface and
lecture 77 of his *Römische Geschichte*, said he would end his work where
Gibbon's began, because the *Decline and Fall* renders other versions of
its subject "superfluous and fool-hardy." The history of the empire is
essentially unwritable, in Niebuhr's view, but "all that can be done has
been done by Gibbon, whose work will never be excelled.[52]

Even in America, where Gibbon's support of Lord North's government was known and resented and where his "injustice" and "indecency" were long deplored, William H. Prescott (1828) believed that
Gibbon was the modern historian par excellence, exhibiting the "principles of modern history, with all its virtues and defects." His style
often suffers from "a bloated dignity of expression," but his learning
is equal to his vast range and he is capable of warmth in defense of
Rome or learning. W. B. O. Peabody, in 1847, found Gibbon's narrative method as unattractive as his literary personality, but unequalled
in thoroughness and accuracy: "the verdict of Gibbon is almost decisive in every historical question which he ever undertook to explore."[53]

These Americans respected Gibbon even though they did not like
him; some were not willing to make this concession. Edward Everett,
for example, wrote in 1835:

> The historian must have a noble theme . . . a generous enthusiasm. Look
> at Gibbon, going about his Herculean task and with a giant's strength . . .
> [but] for the purpose [of undermining Christianity]. . . . The result ac-
> cords with the motive. . . . You are fatigued with the soulless beauty of
> the history; exhausted with its dreary learning; and rise from the perusal
> of the twelve admirable volumes, without having experienced one thrill
> of virtuous excitement.[54]

In the same year, however, T. H. Shreve, editor of the *Cincinnati
Mirror and Western Gazette of Literature and Science*, believed that "all"

admit that Gibbon is one of the world's six best historians. Shreve concludes with a magnificent tribute to the history both as a literary and as a historical achievement:

> His incredulity rejects the fabulous and admits nothing which is unsupported by testimony—his imagination is rich, and throws over his descriptions the drapery of fiction, without implicating him in a departure from the truth— . . . he unites the luminousness of Tacitus with the diligence of Herodotus—and we peruse his work with the same activity of imagination and engrossment of feeling, which we experience when we read one of those magnificent epic poems which have glorified genius, and given to fictions . . . the vitality of truth.[55]

A reader after Gibbon's own heart, and, exactly as he and Hume had expected, in the new domain of English-language culture, America.[56]

Gibbon's historical merits were from the beginning very much appreciated in the Catholic countries of Italy and Spain, though evidence on the latter is scanty. Rival Italian translations were published very quickly, with essays to protect the reader against Gibbon's irreligious comments. In the preface to yet another translation (1820), David Bertolotti asserted that Gibbon had all the qualities necessary for impartial history: moderation, dispassionateness, and a middle state of fortune. In his summary of Italian response, emphasizing the nineteenth century, Arnaldo Momigliano explained that though "Italians have never stopped reading Gibbon," they have ignored the question of the origins of Christianity and so "took from Gibbon . . . what Gibbon had taken from his Italian mentors," his view of the Middle Ages, instead of his most original contribution, the "evaluation of Christianity."[57] Like the Americans, they certainly took his information as authoritative and his views as worthy of debate. When the *Decline and Fall* was translated into Spanish (1842—with Milman's notes), the translator, José Mor de Fuentes, assured his readers that Gibbon's work is "absolutely the most instructive and provocative of all ancient and modern literature" and that the "grandeur of its narration, the vivid portraits of its characters, the profound philosophy, the poetic juxtapositions of its sublime pictures, and finally the eloquence of its style . . . make it magnificent, excellent, incomparable."[58]

But it was in Germany that Gibbon was best appreciated in the nineteenth century, in part because it was there that his successors as great historians of Rome were to be found. We have already heard from B. G. Niebuhr. Gibbon was also early appreciated by German historians of culture and of historiography. D. L. Wachler, in a "History of Historical Knowledge" (1820), says that Gibbon's history treats a huge subject without overlooking any relevant factors, internal or external. He puts many matters and data into wholly new perspectives. His research would be exemplary were he not led by his French education occasionally to strive for rhetorical effects that may obscure the truth. There are gaps in his accounts of Byzantium and the Western European provinces, but Gibbon shares with Ferguson the glory of a philosophical-political treatment of ancient history and with Robertson that of a deeper and truer appreciation of the Middle Ages. Johann Wilhelm Loebell, in a sketch of the "Epochs of Historical Writing and their Relationship to Poetry" (1841) also appreciated Gibbon's unmatched sense of proportion and his skill in departing from chronology in order to develop themes; Loebell also repudiates the idea that Gibbon is of the school of Voltaire. Unlike Voltaire, Gibbon has a sense of the nobility of history and a tragic theme, Loebell believes. "The feeling that Gibbon experienced when, sitting under the ruins of the Capitol, he heard the bare-foot monks singing Vespers in the Temple of Jupiter and was inspired to undertake his great composition, sounds throughout the whole work."[59]

The first extended German discussion of Gibbon's work (other than reviews or introductions to his works) that I have seen is that of Wilhelm Dilthey, writing under the name of Wilhelm Hoffner in 1866. He published an essay in *Westermanns Illustrierte Deutsche Monatshefte* designed to persuade the reader to turn to Gibbon's history, "a work of such dimension and such greatness of conception, that in the whole history of historical writing it has no peer." Dilthey sees Gibbon as initiating one of the two species of historical study of Christianity—not, as Gibbon seems to state, of the origins of Christianity, but rather of its effects. Dilthey credits Gibbon with dealing evenhandedly with the various Christian polemics, and he notes that advances in knowledge of particular subjects by specialist historians do not put the *Decline and Fall* out of date. He concludes that it will never be entirely outmoded: "such a deep understanding of the world speaks in his work, that . . . some parts will never be surpassed" (he cites the account of Julian).[60]

When Dilthey wrote these words the first volume of the *Decline and Fall* was already ninety years old. His article raises a continuing theme in subsequent analyses of Gibbon's work and his subject: the extraordinary longevity, modernity, "immortality," of the *Decline and Fall*. By the same token, of course, writers begin to insist that it is out of date, or at least out of date on *their* subjects. I am not a professional historian, and my sympathy is naturally with Gibbon, but I cannot help observing that while Gibbon is indeed corrected on matters of fact or supplemented with specialist studies, on more general grounds the trait that is labeled outmoded by one generation of historians tends to be labeled modern by the next. I shall return to this question as the *Decline and Fall* outlives its century. Meanwhile, it is worth noting that both Mommsen and Ranke paid tribute to it before the end of the nineteenth century (1882, 1883). In addition, Mommsen, too old and busy to attend the 1894 commemoration of the centennial of Gibbon's death, sent greetings to the participants. His letter was read aloud. The *Times* reported (November 16), "He wrote that his view of Gibbon, after years of study, remained the same . . . briefly this—that amid all the changes that had come over the study of the Roman Empire . . . no one would in the future be able to read the history of the Roman Empire, unless he read, possibly with a fuller knowledge, but with the broad views, the clear insight, the strong grasp of Edward Gibbon. That verdict Mommsen placed on record ten years ago, and . . . it remained unaltered."[61]

Throughout the nineteenth century the *Decline and Fall* was not only regarded as authoritative, but even converted into a textbook. The lectures of William Smyth (not Gibbon's editor), who taught "Modern" history at Oxford in the middle of the eighteenth century, were published in 1840. Even though his course dealt only with the later period covered by Gibbon's history, he stopped at the end of the third lecture to explain to the students why he had so often mentioned Gibbon "as the fittest writer to supply you with information in all the earlier stages of modern history, and, indeed, as the only writer that you are likely to undertake to read." Gibbon, Smyth acknowledges, has great faults: indecency, obscurity, irreverence. But, thanks to Gibbon, "The public has been made acquainted with periods of history which were before scarcely accessible to the most patient scholars. Order and interest and importance have been given to what appeared to defy every power of perspicacity and genius."[62] To facilitate such use as a textbook, the editor who had revised Milman's great edition of the history, William Smith, undertook in 1856 to produce a one-volume "Student's Gibbon," of course omitting all indiscreet references to sexuality or religion and abbreviating or omitting "less important material" so as to "narrat[e] at length, and sometimes as fully as in the original work, those grand events which have influenced the history of the world."[63] For more than forty years this edition was reprinted on countless occasions in both England and America, even though it reduces Gibbon's history to a chronicle of events and freely mingles Smith's own language with Gibbon's without any indication that the authorship differs. It was itself revised in two volumes in 1889 and 1901 (to include more of Gibbon's own words) and was succeeded in the age of paperbacks by a series of abridgments on modern principles, in which the editor seeks to represent Gibbon's ideas as well as his information and carefully indicates the difference between his words and Gibbon's.

Despite or perhaps because of these abridgments, there was a continuous demand for the whole history. It was recommended by Sir John Lubbock in his famous list of "the best hundred books" for

working men wishing to educate themselves.[64] and it has been rou-
tinely included in such collections of indispensable works ever since.
In the twentieth century, despite a tendency to decline into "mere"
literature, the history has continued to command the affection of
readers and the attention of historians. In 1901 Charles Francis Adams
wrote in the then young *American Historical Review* that because of
more widespread education, "it is not unsafe to say that twenty copies
of Gibbon's *Decline and Fall* are called for in the bookstores of to-day
to one . . . in 1800."[65] On the other hand, Adams investigated the
circulation of a public library copy of the *Decline and Fall*. Not once
in thirty years had any borrower consecutively borrowed all the volumes. We may hope that interested readers sampled the history and
then acquired their own copies! Not since his own day has Gibbon
been a "popular" writer; yet even today, he has a kind of popularity,
in that many people read him without being forced to do so.

To choose the action that most powerfully testifies to Gibbon's
perennial fascination for the general reader is a matter of individual
opinion. Perhaps it is the touching eagerness of William Butler Yeats
to purchase "a good edition" of the *Decline and Fall* with a portion of
his Nobel Prize for Literature: "As I look at the long rows of substantial backs I am conscious of growing learned minute by minute."[66]
Perhaps it is Cecil Rhodes's attempt to acquire translations of all
Gibbon's Greek and Latin sources so as to appreciate properly his
favorite author. Rhodes spent some £8,000 on typescript translations
of works not available in English, desisting when the project bogged
down in "the apparently endless series of . . . the Fathers of the
Church, from whom Gibbon quarried."[67] Perhaps it is its designation
by many writers of fiction as a symbol of history itself. For example,
when the "Ladies of the Club" in Helen Hoover Santmyer's 1982
novel chose to study the great historians, "Amanda said, 'A good idea:
there are historians enough and to spare: the Greeks, the Romans,
Gibbon.' The . . . committee had little trouble in assigning every
lady a subject: historians were pretty much of a muchness, with the
exception of Gibbon."[68] Gibbon is also the favorite reading of Captain
Horatio Hornblower.

But despite competition from the likes of E. M. Forster and Virgina
Woolf, there cannot be any more eloquent *expression* of Gibbon's power
to educate and delight an intelligent layperson than Winston
Churchill's. As a young army officer stationed in India, desiring to
educate himself after completing Sandhurst, he began to

> read history, philosophy, economics, and things like that. . . . In history,
> I decided to begin with Gibbon. . . . So . . . I set out upon the eight
> volumes of Dean Milman's edition. . . . All through the long glistening
> middle hours of the Indian day . . . I devoured Gibbon. I rode triumphantly
> through it from end to end and enjoyed it all. I scribbled all my opinions

on the margins of the pages, and very soon found myself a vehement partisan of the author against the disparagements of his pompous-pious editor. I was not even estranged by his naughty footnotes.[69]

In addition to this amateur appreciation, however, Gibbon has continued to play a role in professional historical discussions of the issues he virtually defined. The great contemporary historian Hugh Trevor-Roper wrote in a 1987 leading article in the London *Times*, "Gibbon now seems much less dated than his great successors, Macaulay, Carlyle, Froude; nor can anyone, today, discuss the problem—the permanent problem—of the decline of the Roman Empire except in implicit dialogue with him" (May 8). Trevor-Roper was for twenty-three years (1957–80) Regius Professor of Modern History at Oxford and as such an advocate of Gibbon's practice as a historical *model*, not just a historiographical *monument*. "At Oxford, for many years, I gave history undergraduates an opportunity to become acquainted with Gibbon, and so fortify themselves against that narrow specialization which threatens to strangle a noble discipline." He goes on to deplore Gibbon's having been dropped from the curriculum since Trevor-Roper's own departure from Oxford: "He was not a member of the guild, not a professional, not up to date, had not read the latest article. . . . Even by their own standards, I believe, [those who dropped Gibbon] are wrong. . . . His errors are remarkably few. Of course much less has been written on the subject since his time. But his scholarship and his judgement can seldom be faulted." The point is not that no other historian has done well, or that no one has surpassed Gibbon in particular areas of his subject, but that Gibbon still has important insights to contribute to the discussion of that subject, and that such writers as Gibbon must still be read if we are to avoid a new era of divided *erudits* and *philosophes*, in which those who think about the philosophical complexities of historical writing and those who are carefully uncovering reliable information about the past never talk to each other and never find a way of bringing either set of insights into the general culture. Jacob Bernays observed that it would be desirable to have a Gibbon who could use nineteenth-century—we can add twentieth-century—methods and materials for a more complete history, but there was no new Gibbon, and in an age of essays and monographs, said Bernays, one was unlikely to arise. Therefore in practice "the eighteenth-century Gibbon remains indispensable."[70]

Of course, not all historians agree, or have agreed. In perhaps the first influential history of modern historical writing, by the Swiss E. Fueter, Gibbon was treated as a minor member of the school of Voltaire, more successful than Robertson only because he was lucky in his choice of subject. In Fueter's view, Gibbon compares most unfavorably with Voltaire: he took more care to appear impartial, having in his scholarly retreat and leisure little other work to do, but his method is considerably less advanced than Voltaire's: he neglects economic history, has a less developed critical sense, and knows the world less.[71] This ahistorical account was quickly challenged by those who appreciated the erudite tradition and that of Montesquieu,[72] but errors have a long life. Perhaps a clear consensus on Gibbon's importance in modern historiography is no older than Momigliano's seminal address (1952) on "Gibbon's Contribution to Historical Method."[73]

Professional responses to J. B. Bury's great edition (1896–1900) of the *Decline and Fall*, and indeed to his decision to edit it rather than attempt to replace it, naturally considered the issue of its continuing historical value. G. McN. Rushforth, reviewing the completion of Bury's edition in the *English Historical Review*, congratulates the editor on the excellent achievement of an "epoch-making" project; for the first time, we have "a modern historian whose work has not been rewritten . . . but presented again to the world intact . . . almost . . . like an ancient classic." Even editing the *Decline and Fall* is a formidable task; Rushforth doubts "whether any other living historian could have treated the vast field of facts included by Gibbon in his survey with equal versatility and equal sureness of touch."[74] An American reviewer grapples with the peculiarity of the project. Gibbon's "is the only secondary history in the English language which has survived a century of existence." Why? Felicity of style is not the answer, the author, H. M. Stephens demonstrates (we may instantly support this observation for ourselves by remembering that Oliver Goldsmith's utterly forgotten histories are delightfully readable). It is also not the case that Gibbon luckily chose a field in which the material could easily be exhausted; on the contrary, Stephens believes, there is hardly a historical field in which more is being done. Rather, Gibbon's history manages to continue to have, in each generation, the features that "modern historical critics dealing with modern historical works" desire; for Stephens himself, these are objectivity (in the sense that Gibbon has no extrahistorical goal to promote); "conscious master[y]" of all the relevant documents and faithful use of all the authorities; and a clear, unpadded style.[75] Stephens is one of those who notices that despite its great length, the *Decline and Fall* is very economical in its use of language and in its compression of material. Many of the complaints of later scholars about omissions from the history fail to consider that Gibbon knew the material they would have included but recognized that to include it would distort the proportions of his work.[76] Stephens concludes that the *Decline and Fall* offers today's students, as it did "their fathers and grandfathers before them," unrivaled historical scale without compromise on issues of aim and method.

Ninety years later, Trevor-Roper, as we have seen, reached the same conclusion. They are not alone.

In the first half of the present century, historians began to attempt to restate Gibbon's theme, to interpret the significance that the history has in the intellectual development of our present culture. J. B. Black's influential essay (1926) treats the *Decline and Fall* as descriptive rather than analytical and therefore important for its effect on the reader's feelings about the past; Gibbon "stimulates not only the intellect, but the imagination . . . the reader lays down the book with a reflection on the transitoriness of human greatness, the inevitability of decay, and a sense of irreparable loss." Christopher Dawson (1934) understood Gibbon as the "last of the Humanists," who could portray an unbroken link between his culture and that of the ancients no longer accessible to us. L. P. Curtis's "Gibbon's Paradise Lost" (1949) began a tradition of relating Gibbon's history to the politics of his time; its purpose was the education of the political elite. A Canadian scholar, C. N. Cochrane (1942, 1943) argued that despite or because of its greatness, the effect of the *Decline and Fall* is essentially regressive: Gibbon ignores the creation of the modern world and his view of history is essentially static.[77]

An Italian medievalist, Giorgio Falco, in the first sustained appraisal of Gibbon's contribution to medieval history (1933), also considered the history regrettably "static," but credited Gibbon with offering "perhaps for the first time, an ample narrative of the middle ages, apart from universal history, irradiated by an idea." In Falco's view, Voltaire was Gibbon's master, but Gibbon surpassed Voltaire not only in "seriousness," but in allowing political and cultural history to reflect light on each other. Falco sees as a significant methodological contribution Gibbon's solution to the problem of nonchronicle history. Gibbon provides great "pictures"—portrayals of characters, scenes, eras, nations, or discrete events—that allow him to escape from polar interpretations of various issues. For instance, Gibbon sees both faults and virtues in both the Empire and the barbarians, in both "Catholic and Protestant providentialism and crude Enlightenment pragmatism."[78]

Early modern German scholarship, in addition to refuting Fueter's argument exhaustively, explores Gibbon's contributions to cultural or "sociological" history, that is, history that is not merely political or centered on remarkable individuals. Moriz Ritter, in particular, makes an interesting distinction between *two* kinds of cultural history practiced by Gibbon, one focusing on impersonal cultural values, which Gibbon uses for cultural-historical sections not concerned with Christianity, and the other focusing on the personal carriers of those values for sections on Christianity (1911). Friedrich Meinecke, unfortu-

nately, assumes that Gibbon shared what Meinecke saw as the Enlightenment weakness for mechanistic explanations. Since Gibbon
was not a historicist, he could not have grasped in a unified way both
the great tragedy of dying antiquity and its giving new life through
its death. Those who think that the *Decline and Fall* makes this very
point from its first chapter on are obviously mistaken, in Meinecke's
view. "Sentimentality [about the city of Rome and Roman culture]
and intellectual power shaped the *Decline and Fall*, not spiritual pro-
fundity" (1936).[79]

Walter Rehm (1930), Santo Mazzarino (1959), Bryce Lyon (1972),
and Alexander Demandt (1984), who have studied the history of two
problems examined in the *Decline and Fall*, the fall of Rome and the
rise of modern Europe, acknowledge in various ways Gibbon's unique
contribution and continuing importance in the dialogue on these topics. On the other hand, some writers continue to see Gibbon as a
dangerous influence—Byzantinists such as Stephen Runciman, in
particular, but also such a writer as Allen Evans (1973), who contends
that our conception of the problem of late Roman history is still
distorted by Gibbon's search for the internal causes of the empire's
collapse.[80]

Beginning in 1954, a series of important studies of Gibbon by
historians proved that many believe there is still something to be
learned either about Gibbon's subject or about the craft of history
by studying Gibbon's work. Giuseppe Giarrizzo's invaluable *Edward
Gibbon e la cultura europea*, H. I. Marrou's evaluations in *L'Histoire et
ses méthodes* (1961), the 1966 symposium called *The Transformation of
the Roman World: Gibbon's Problem after Two Centuries* (though it should
be noted that that symposium concluded that "our kind of history is
as far advanced over Gibbon's as the present nuclear physics is over
Newton's superb formulations"—reviewers and successors did not necessarily agree), F. C. Scheibe's "Christentum und Kulturverfall in
Geschichtsbild Edward Gibbons" (1968), Karl Christ's *Von Gibbon zu
Rostovtzeff* (1972), the work of Trevor-Roper, David Jordan, and
J. G. A. Pocock in the sixties, seventies, and eighties, the two volumes from the 1976 meetings commemorating the history's bicentennial, and books by Lionel Gossman and J. W. Burrow (1981, 1985)
may sufficiently illustrate the historians' interest.[81] Books and articles
by literary scholars also consider historiographical issues. In short,
Gibbon's history may not be immortal, but clearly it is not dead yet.

Gibbon was gratified by the idea that "one day his mind w[ould]
be familiar to the grandchildren of those who are yet unborn" and in a
note allied himself with Henry Fielding, the author of "the first of
ancient or modern Romances," *Tom Jones*, who enjoyed "this proud
sentiment, this feast of fancy" in book 13, chapter 1 (*Memoirs* 188,
196). Gibbon himself expressed this gratification somewhat ambig-

uously, at the end of a draft of his memoirs, but in the context of a discussion of his history. How did he hope that we would know his mind?

First, certainly, in our respectful, affectionate, and critical knowledge of his portrayal of the past and its observer/creator in the *Decline and Fall*—the understanding of human experience and its discovery over time and space that the great book evolved and presented. Sheridan's compliment to the history incorporated a peculiarly apt adjective, for it is indeed the product of an age of light, but its illumination is not identical to, or solely derived from, the glaring brilliance of the Continental Enlightenment. Moderated by erudition, pragmatism, humanism, and good temper, the history and its historian are, precisely, "luminous."

But though Gibbon desired and expected to be so remembered, I think he wanted us to know him also as Lord Sheffield did—as a man who loved his home and his work and his friends and his Madeira, who hated and feared and sometimes evaded disorder and cruelty, who was susceptible to flattery, especially the flattery of sincere deference, but also appreciated greatness wherever he could find it, who protected himself against certain kinds of painful experience by avoidance, that is, by forgetting, postponing, neglecting, or ignoring what he did not want to see, but who bore unavoidable privations with courage and good humor. These qualities of the man affected, and were affected by, the creation of a great work. Some, perhaps including Gibbon himself, have believed that the man was dwarfed by that work. Certainly, like other human creators of great achievements, he managed to prevent his inevitable human weaknesses from damaging irretrievably the work into which he put his far from inevitable human strengths. But the *Decline and Fall* is the work of a whole man, a whole life, and that man, I have tried to show, is not so small as some would have us think. I find it hard to part with him. Gibbon himself in the numerous portraits in his history put into practice a precept of biographical writing memorably expressed by Samuel Johnson: "If we owe regard to the memory of the dead, there is yet more respect to be paid to knowledge . . . and to truth" (*Rambler* 60). I have of course sought these goals. Yet without presuming to claim for myself so close a place, I would also like to say with Lord Sheffield that in my study of Gibbon, I have tried to serve his memory "with that assiduity which his genius, his virtues, and above all, our long, uninterrupted, and happy friendship, sanctioned and demanded."[82]

Appendix

Autobiographical Sketch, May–September 1783
[British Library Add. MSS. 34874, fols. 130–31]

Edouard Gibbon est né le 27 Avril VS (le 8 Mai) 1737 à Putney dans la province de Surry du marriage de Edouard Gibbon et de Judith Porten. Apres avoir eté élu dans les deux parlements de 1734 et 1741 pour les villes de Petersfield et de Southampton, son pere se retira à la Campagne où il mourit le 10 Novembre 1770 dans sa terre de Buriton dans la province de Southampton. Après la mort de sa premiere femme en 1748, il epousa en secondes noçes en 1755 la demoiselle Dorothea Patton qui vit encore et dont la tendresse fait oublier à M. Gibbon qu'il a perdu sa mere.

M. Gibbon etoit l'ainé d'une soeur et de cinq freres qui sont tous morts dans l'enfance. Son extreme foiblesse et ses frequentes maladies laissoient peu d'esperance de sa vie mais son temperament s'est fortifié avec le tems, et des l'age de seize ans il a joui d'une très bonne santé, sujette depuis quelques années à de legeres atteints de la goutte. Une jeunesse si peu robuste le borna en grande partee à l'institution domestique, qui ne fut interrompu que par des visites courtes et assez inutiles à l'ecole publique de Westminster et au college de Ste Marie Magdalaine dans l'universite d'Oxford. Au mois de Juin 1753, son pere se resolut à l'envoyer à Lausanne en Suisse où il passa près de cinq ans dans la maison de M. le Ministre Pavillard, homme respectable dont la memoire lui sera toujours chere. Il reconnoit avec plaisir que c'est à Lausanne qu'il doit la connaissance de la langue Française, le gout de l'etude et le developpement de la raison.

Depuis son retour dans sa patrie au mois de Mai 1758, il est sorti deux fois de la Grande Bretagne. Apres la conclusion de la paix il courit à Paris au mois de Janvier 1763, d'ou il se rendit au mois de Mai à Lausanne. Les anciens amis l'arreterent près d'une année en Suisse. L'année suivante fut employée dans voyage d'Italie qu'il poussa jusqu'à Rome et à Naples, et il ne revit sa patrie qu'au mois de Juin 1765. Dans l'eté de 1777, il passa six mois à Paris dans la societé la plus douce et la plus eclairée de la terre.

Dans l'avant derniere querre M. Gibbon interrompit pendant quelque tems ses occupations litteraires pour se devouer (en 1759) au service militaire de sa patrie. Il fut successivement Capitaine, Major et Lieutenant Colonel Commandant du bataillon meridional de la province de Southampton: mais comme ce bataillon n'a jamais vu l'ennemis, il n'a pas acquis dans des compagnes domestiques la reputation d'un guerrier. A l'election generale de l'an 1774 il fut elû Membre du Parlement pour le bourg de Liskeard dans la province de Cournouaille. Après la dissolution qui eut lieu en 1780, il ne rentra dans la chambre de Communes qu'au mois de Juin de l'année suivante 1781 pour le bourg de Lymington dans la province de Southampton. Depuis huit ans il a assisté aux deliberations les plus importantes, mais il ne s'est jamais trouvé le courage ni le talent de parler dans une assemblée publique. Au mois de Juin 1779, il fût nommé par le Roi l'un des Lords Commissaires du commerce et des Colonies (*of Trade and Plantations*), l'emploi qu'il continua d'exercer jusqu'au 1ᵉ Mai 1782, lorsqu'il le perdit par le changement du Ministere et la suppresion du consil dont il etoit membre.

Dans sa premiere jeunesse M. Gibbon avoit ebauché a Lausanne quelques reflexions sur l'etude de la litterature. Il ceda enfin à l'autorite de son pere et de ses amis qui lui conseillerent de publier cet l'Essai. Il parut à Londres (en douze) en 1761, et la nouveaute d'une composition Françoise sortie de la plume d'un Anglois lui procura un accueil assez favorable. Mais un gout decidé pour l'histoire l'engagea bientot dans cette carriere; et aprés avoir medité plusiers sujets, il se fixa enfin à la decadence et la chute de l'Empire Romain dont il avoit concu l'idée à Rome même. Quelques années furent consacrées à la compilation et à l'arrangement d'un ouvrage aussi penible, et de l'an 1772 lorsqu'il transporta sa bibliothéque à Londres, il se livra avec ardeur à la composition. Le premier Volume depuis le regne de Trajan jusqua celui de Constantes fut publié au mois de Febrier 1776. Sans prononcer sur le merite de l'ouvrage, quatre Editions assez nombreuse faites à Londres in quarto sans parler des contrefacons irlandoises peuvat etre citées comme la preuve de son succès qui a eté confirmé par des traductions Francoises, Allemandes et Italiennes. Les deux derniers chapitres susciterent à M. Gibbon une foule d'adversaires Ecclesiastiques. Nayant pas l'honneur d'etre Theologien il les laissa raisonner ou deraisoner à leur aise, mais un jeune homme ayant eu l'audace d'attaquer non seulement la foi mais encore la bonne foi de l'historien il se vit reduit à la tache facile mais humiliante de confondre la colomniateur. Sa defense (*Vindication*) de quelques passages du xvme et xvi^{th} [*sic*] Chapitres parut à Londres (in octavo) au mois de Janvier 1779.

Cinq ans apres la publication de son premier Volume M. Gibbon donna (le 1 Mai 1781) le second et le troisieme qui continuent la suite de l'histoire jusqu'a la chute de l'Empire d'Occident. Deux Editions in quarto furent debutées assez rapidement, et le meme libraire (M. Cadell) vient de publier au mois de Mai 1783 une édition en six Volumes in octavo de l'ouvrage entier. M. Gibbon est toujours occupé du meme travail qu'il se propose de processer jusquà la fin de l'Empire d'Orient et la prise de Constantinople par les Turcs. Cette entreprise lui demande encore plusiers années d'une application soutenue, mais quelqu'en soit le succès il trouve dans cette application même un plaisir toujours varié et toujours renaissant.

Notes

Preface

1. Bernays 1885, Morison 1878. I have seen two references to a Russian work by M. Liutov, published in St. Petersburg in 1899, called *Zhizn' i trudy Gibbona* (the life and work of Gibbon), but I have not seen the work itself.

2. Murray 1896; Prothero 1896; Hill 1900; Read 1897; Holroyd 1897; Charrière de Sévery 1911–12. Bury's *Decline and Fall*, 1st ed. 1896–1900; 2d ed., 1909–16; final ed., 1926.

3. Henry James, "London," *Harper's Weekly Magazine* 41 (March 27, 1897):315.

4. Robertson 1907, 271–370; also 1925. On the latter, the *TLS* reviewer commented, "The portrait of the young Gibbon . . . is interesting and will probably be new to many" (November 5, 1925, p. 742).

Chapter 1 Study and Society

1. He later wrote rather unkindly about his meeting with Gibbon (Owen 1796).

2. British Library Add. MSS. 34886, fols. 188–89.

3. Carnochan (1984, 368) calls him a "timid little fat man." If this amusing characterization is ever entirely apt, it is only prior to the success of the *Decline and Fall*, and it is doubtful that Gibbon was then conspicuously fat. But before the history appeared, he was quiet enough to make Horace Walpole think him "modest."

4. "Allein der mindeste Widerspruch, die mässigste Erwärmung hoben es sehr bald zu einem so männlichen Bass . . . solcher gewiss das Haus nicht

weniger gefüllt haben würde, als es gegenwärtig die mächtigen Stimmen eines *Fox*, oder *Sheridan* thun" (Langer 1794, 642).

5. Rousseau's is the first comment in print on Gibbon's "coldness"; see his *Correspondence complète*, ed. R. A. Leigh (Banbury, Oxfordshire: Voltaire Foundation, 1972), 16:280–81. Countless later writers have agreed.

6. According to Lytton Strachey, for example, happiness followed Gibbon throughout his life, sometimes slightly disguised. His life "is an epitome of the blessings of the eighteenth century . . . that most balmy time" (Strachey 1928, 565).

7. Brownley 1976, 23–24; Jordan 1976, 7, 11; Gossman 1981, 118.

8. Gibbon so characterizes her in his *Memoirs*, ed. G. A. Bonnard (1966), 36. This edition will be cited hereafter simply as *Memoirs*. For Catherine Porten's cheerful courage, see Craddock 1982, 36–40.

9. Bagehot 1856.

10. Jordan 1971; Baridon 1977b; Braudy 1970.

11. All comments on Gibbon's library are based on Keynes 1980, supplemented by further examination of Gibbon's manuscript catalogue (dated 1785) in the Pierpont Morgan Library, New York, and by study of bills for book purchases and bookbinding.

12. See Craddock 1982, 284–303.

13. Draft E of Gibbon's *Memoirs* (Murray 1896, 306).

14. *DF:* the 1974 reprint of Bury's second edition. To facilitate the reader's reference to other editions, I also provide the chapter number and (in square brackets) the footnote number in editions that do not include editorial footnotes in the same sequence with authorial notes. Comments in the text (as distinct from citations in parentheses) that refer to volumes by number refer to the original quarto edition.

15. The relationship and the note were apparently first observed by Swain (1966, 122–23). Ghosh (1984) argues for a later date for the extant "Outlines." I do not find his argument convincing, but in any event, the existence of *some* 1771 draft is indisputable.

16. Discussed in Craddock 1982, 269–76.

17. Gibbon 1956 is cited as *Letters*.

18. Heal 1949, 475. They cost a total of 13 shillings. Before his father's death, Gibbon's income was £300 a year. This expenditure on pens reminds us once more that it would have been impossible for Gibbon to support both scholarship and a family on the income then available to him.

19. In his *Memoirs* Gibbon recommends to students his own plan for examining new subjects: after looking over the material, to examine "all that I knew, or believed or had thought on the subject" (98).

20. The first historian-Gibbonian to express such disappointment was undoubtedly John Pinkerton, writing as "Robert Heron":"[Gibbon's] conclusion is pitiably unfortunate" (Pinkerton 1785, 340). Several of the contributors to two volumes celebrating the bicentennial were similarly disappointed. J. G. A. Pocock is representative of modern historian-admirers who find the "General Observations" "puzzling and disappointing" (Pocock 1977, 295).

21. See Jordan 1971, 184–90. The edition of Montesquieu's *Considérations* in Gibbon's library at Bentinck Street was that of Paris, 1755, in 12mo.

Gibbon could have owned it even in the Lausanne years. He refers to it in his youthful *Essai sur l'étude de la littérature.*

22. As David Jordan points out, the last portion of the "General Observations" suggests rather the influence of Voltaire. Jordan 1971, 73.

23. For a brief and brilliant discussion of Gibbon as a member of the "school of Montesquieu" and as a "sociological historian," see especially Trevor-Roper 1968.

24. Ghosh (1984) dates the "General Obserations" some months earlier, to August–December 1772. All of Ghosh's arguments rest on minute confidence in Gibbon's memorial reconstruction of dates and Ghosh's own interpretation of the precise meaning of Gibbon's language about dates, coupled with a rejection of Gibbon's statement that he did not begin the actual writing of the history until he was settled in Bentinck street. This seems to me special pleading of an implausible kind. However, the difference is not very significant.

25. The best evidence of this practice is inspection of Gibbon's manuscripts.

26. Roche 1839, 466.

27. See Garrison 1978.

28. I. W. J. Machin, "Gibbon's Debt to Contemporary Scholarship," *Review of English Studies* 15 (1939):84–88.

29. A. H. T. Clarke, in "Gibbon the Historian," *Nineteenth Century and After* 68 (November 1910):681, recognizes this practice but assumes it is accidental, an "incessant" series of "unconscious plagiarisms."

30. Avant lui, les deux axes de recherche ne convergent pas.

Il y a le droit et il y a les moeurs, Montesquieu et Voltaire; l'un passera de la théorie des institutions à une théorie de l'histoire; l'autre, de la révolte contre l'idéologie dominante à une philosophie de l'histoire." (Baridon 1977b, 424).

31. Montesquieu 1968, chap. 18, 168–69.

32. Montesquieu 1968, chap. 19, 179; chap. 18, 169.

33. Montesquieu 1968, chap. 9, 94–95.

34. Jordan 1971, 184.

35. For an important discussion of Gibbon's treatment of causation, see Giarrizzo 1954, 265–67. "Il lettore . . . avvertirà nella narrazione due piani: quello deterministico, della decadenza di un organismo corrotto avviato alla rovina e alla morte . . . e quello empirico-volontaristico dell'azione individuale, responsabile e consapevole, che colora di toni vari il fondo grigio e inerte delle propensioni naturali. Non quel che è uguale, ma quel che è diverso popola il mondo storico dell'empirisimo: l'esperienza guida sempre la ragione, avvertendola del pericolo di voler sostituire con una metafisica indimostrabile la sociologia relativistica."

36. Jordan 1971, 71.

37. At least in the view of an enthusiast, George Sarton: "The Missing Factor in Gibbon's Concept of History," *Harvard Library Bulletin* 11 (Autumn 1957):278–95.

38. Jordan 1971, 71.

39. Pocock 1977, 297: "A determination to have none of the fashionable thesis that commercial society had degenerated from an agricultural condition helps explain why the 'General Observations' do not consider Europe as threatened from within, but only by a purely conceptual nomad danger from without." See also Pocock 1981 and 1982.

40. Arnold Toynbee (1954) made much of Gibbon's failure to anticipate either Napoleon or proletarian revolutions; the former criticism is debatable, as we shall see, and Gibbon later expresses positions about war much less offensive than this complacency.

41. Gibbon's comment implies that Voltaire might be satisfied if the siege were less costly, whereas of course Voltaire wishes that the money were better spent.

42. Gibbon's side of this controversy may be found in *Letters* 1:327–38; for Hurd's reply see Gibbon 1814, 2:83–94 (followed by a fragmentary reply to the reply, 2:94–5). This note is part of Ghosh's case for dating the "General Observations" in the summer of 1772; I would argue that Gibbon was capable of remembering his interest for several months longer.

43. Notably Swain 1966, 135–36.

44. Only one reader, to my knowledge, has ever tried to argue that Gibbon supports the doctrine of the noble savage, and that reader does so by equating the savage and the barbarian. See B. H. Warmington, *Proceedings of the Classical Association of England and Wales* 53 (1956): 27–28.

45. See Rogers 1856, 77–78.

46. The fullest account of Deyverdun is still that of Read 1897.

47. "Mon aimable et respectable Ami, dont je ne me Separerais jamais Si j'avais une fortune indépendante." British Library Add. MSS. 34887, fol. 194v.

48. Réamur, R. A. F. de., *L'Art de faire éclorre et d'élever des oiseaux domestiques* (Paris, 1749). Keynes 1980, 234.

49. Heal 1949, 474–76.

50. Craddock 1968, 200.

51. Pocock 1976.

52. See, on Gibbon's view of Augustus, Weinbrot 1978, 101–8.

53. E.g., by Leslie Stephen and Arnold Toynbee (among many others). See Ian R. Maxwell, "Gibbon Misread," *A.U.M.L.A.* 3 (August 1959):32–39.

54. Robertson 1769. "If a man were called to fix upon the period in the history of the world during which the condition of the human race was most calamitous and afflicted, he would, without hesitation, name that which elapsed from the death of Theodosius the Great, to the establishment of the Lombards in Italy." Compare *Decline and Fall* chap. 3, 1:85–86.

55. Montesquieu 1968, chap. 16, 154.

56. White 1968, 301.

57. Carnochan, in his fourth chapter, "considers the *Decline and Fall* as prospect" (1987, 3). On the other hand, Oscar Handlin finds the metaphor of mountain peaks "disastrous" for the *Decline and Fall:* "the ascent to the top exposes only a blank." "Living in a Valley," in *Truth in History* (Cambridge, Mass.: Harvard University Press, Belknap Press, 1979), 34–35.

58. Swain 1966, 126.

Chapter 2 Finding a Voice

1. Timetable from J. E. Norton, *Letters* 2:ix–x.

2. James Boswell, *London Journal, 1762-63*, ed. F. A. Pottle (New York: McGraw-Hill, 1950), 154–55. Coincidentally, Gibbon attended the performance Boswell and his friends attempted to damn. Gibbon's party, which included the playwright, was prepared to defend it, if necessary (Low 1929, 202–4).

3. Harold Murdock, "Edward Gibbon," *Proceedings of the Massachusetts Historical Society* 52 (1919):148–52.

4. Low 1960, 8.

5. British Library Add. MSS. 34887, fol. 1.

6. Read 1897, 2:297.

7. For a good discussion of this structure, see Marks 1975, 46–50.

8. Giarrizzo 1954, 259.

9. Braudy 1970, 213–68.

10. *Oxford Classical Dictionary*, 2d ed., s.v. Severus (2), Alexander, 982–83.

11. Baridon 1977b, 583–89.

12. Montesquieu 1968, chap. 12.

13. For attempts to relate specific contemporary British political issues to Gibbon's views in the *Decline and Fall*, see particularly Swain 1940 and Lutnick 1968–69.

14. See Craddock 1982, 18–19.

15. See Norton's notes on Hester Gibbon, *Letters*, passim and especially 1:105; Christopher Walton, *Notes and Materials for an Adequate Biography of William Law* (privately printed, 1854), and Walton MSS. 186, Dr. Williams's Library, London.

16. I have discussed Gibbon's epistolary habits in "Edward Gibbon: The Man in His Letters," in *The Familiar Letter in the Eighteenth Century*, ed. H. Anderson, P. Daghlian, and I. Ehrenpreis (Lawrence: University of Kansas Press, 1966), 224–43.

17. First noticed by Suzanne Curchod Necker, September 30, 1776. Gibbon 1814, 2:177.

18. For example, Black 1926, 162.

19. Extended accounts of Gibbon's relationship to Tacitus, from historical and rhetorical perspectives respectively, may be found in Jordan 1971, 173–83, and Arthur Quinn, " 'Meditating Tacitus': Gibbon's Adaptation to an Eighteenth Century Audience," *Quarterly Journal of Speech* 70 (1984):53–68.

20. See chapter 1, n. 44 above. See also Stewart Crehan, "The Roman Analogy," *Literature and History* 6 (Spring 1980): 30. Gibbon does *not* join those of the late Enlightenment who see the naked Britons as truly civilized and the brutal Romans as the savages. Yet many have observed Gibbon's willingness to give barbarians their due, that is, to use them to criticize the vices of civilization.

21. For example, by John Pinkerton in the eighteenth century and Arnold Toynbee in the twentieth.

22. Braudel 1985, 1:94. And see Walter Goffart, "Rome, Constantinople, and the Barbarians," *American Historical Review* 86 (April 1981):257–306.

23. Milman 1882. xii.
24. Especially "The Middle Ages," in Giarrizzo 1954.
25. I argue this interpretation elsewhere (Craddock 1984).
26. Craddock 1982, 141–64.
27. In draft A and in a detached fragment (Murray 1896, 355, 418–19).

Chapter 3 Ominous Developments

1. A. C. Gupta, "The Historical Pattern," *Itihas* 5 (1950):141–56, as abstracted by N. Sinha, *Historical Abstracts* 1, no. 1750.
2. Letter of Catherine Porten to Dorothea Gibbon, September 24, 1774. Dorothea Gibbon papers, box 3, no. 17. Beinecke Library, Yale University.
3. J. E. Norton, *Letters* 2:35, n. 1.
4. Gibbon 1972, 59–87; Gibbon 1952, 122–41—for date, Louis Junod's preface, 111–21. I consider the evidence for a 1763–64 date much stronger than that for a 1758 date—see Craddock 1982, 187–89, 342.
5. For example: Gibbon as revolutionary, Walter Savage Landor and Peter Gay; Gibbon as admirer of despotism, Leslie Stephen and Arnold Toynbee; Gibbon the man vs. the author of the *Decline and Fall*, Solomon Lutnick and Gavin de Beer.
6. Eduard Fueter (1911), for example.
7. Mortimer Chambers, "The Crisis of the Third Century," in Lynn White, Jr., ed., 1966, 30–58.
8. Quoted by Norton, *Letters* 2:370, from D. D. Wallace, *Life of Laurens* (1915), 381.
9. Swain 1966, 134.
10. Carnochan 1984, 1987.
11. Hutchinson 1883, 1:361–62.
12. Many contemporary testimonials to Gibbon's ability as a conversationalist might be cited, and eighteenth-century criticisms of his conversation are concerned with its manner or accuse him of monopolizing the conversation, not silence. John Macpherson, the Scots historian, said that Gibbon was "the only one capable of examining the current of affairs with a tranquil and clear-sighted eye"—"le seul qui est capable d'examiner le courant des affaires d'un oeil tranquit et clairvoyant" (Gibbon Fonds, Archives Cantonales Vaudoises, letter of November 2, 1791). The *Gentleman's Magazine*'s obituary of Gibbon, derived from Lord Sheffield, praised Gibbon's conversation extravagantly. In the next issue, however, the editor published a correction, obviously derived from someone who was not deeply attached to Gibbon and who may therefore be regarded as more objective than either Boswell or Lord Sheffield:

> His conversation, though in the highest degree informing, was not externally brilliant. He was by no means fluent of speech; his articulation was not graceful; his sentences were evidently laboured, as if he were fearful of committing himself. It was rather pedantic and stiff, than easy; yet, by some unaccountable fascination, it was always agreeable and impressive. (*Gentleman's Magazine* 64 [February, 1794]:178)

13. Carnochan's impression of Gibbon's "shy awkwardness" and essential solitariness seems to me to oversimplify a complex and changing character and to fail to account for many simple matters of fact (1987, 2, 7–21).

14. My count of the "Bn." entries in Keynes 1980.

15. *Letters* 2:45, with Norton's note.

16. Hutchinson 1883, 1:294 and passim.

17. Norton, *Letters* 3:394.

18. Hutchinson, 1:331.

19. See Michel Baridon, "Gibbon, Rome, et deux siècles de plus" *Pensée* (1977):75–93; Lutnick 1968–69; Swain 1966, 71–99.

20. Porson 1790, xxix.

21. Compare Edwin P. Whipple, "Character," in *Harper's New Monthly Magazine* 15 (July 1857):270, with Martine W. Brownley, " 'The Purest and Most Gentle Portion of the Human Species': Gibbon's Portrayals of Women in the *Decline and Fall,*" *South Atlantic Quarterly* 77 (1978):1–14.

22. Hutchinson 1883, 1:358, 362, 364.

23. Gibbon's letters and his conversation as reported by Hutchinson support this conclusion (see especially *Letters* 2:58, 59), but this was also the period of his "Patriotism," his siding with the anti-Government, pro-American party on some issues, notably the Middlesex election, in which Wilkes was elected and the Government wished to expel him from the House. Gibbon sat beside and voted for Wilkes (*Letters* 2:61) and says, "I was a Patriot."

24. East Sussex Record Office AMS 5440, item 23.

25. Hutchinson, for example, thought he would "in general . . . be in Opposition" (June 19, 1775) because of his discouragement about the American fighting (Hutchinson 1883, 1:472).

26. Hutchinson 1883, 1:379.

27. Gibbon was one of those who most assiduously attended the meetings, according to the table compiled by D. M. Low from M. E. G. Duff's *The Club, 1764-1905*, 2d ed.: between 1775 and 1783, before Gibbon moved to Lausanne and Johnson died, Johnson attended twenty-eight dinners, Gibbon eighty (Low 1937, 359).

28. Boswell 1953, 628—April 18, 1775.

29. Or, as Martine W. Brownley suggests, perhaps he shared them, in his way: "Gibbon, Johnson, and the Use of History," *Notes and Queries*, n.s., 27 (225) (February 1980):56.

30. Boswell 1953, 615.

31. Thomas Barnard, letter to James Boswell, March 25, 1794 (Boswell 1976, 399–400).

32. Hutchinson 1883, 1:439.

33. Hutchinson 1883, 1:472.

Chapter 4 Christianity Confronted

1. For surveys of attacks or praise for Gibbon's treatment of Christianity, see McCloy 1936; Norton 1940, chaps. 6 and 7; Craddock 1987a, xv–xx.

2. Letter of May 11, 1776, in Gibbon 1814, 2:151. Whitaker later claimed that Gibbon had deceived him by showing him a copy of the *Decline*

and Fall with the irreligious portions removed and that his moral revulsion when he later read chapters 15 and 16 led to the end of their friendship. It is clear from this letter that Whitaker saw the offending chapters at the same time as the rest of the history and that through he warmly objected to them, he then saw no need to end his friendship with Gibbon. According to Sheffield, Whitaker ended his friendship with Gibbon when he learned what Gibbon thought of his history of Mary Queen of Scots. Whitaker anonymously attacked Gibbon in 1788–89 and published the work under his name in 1791. Macaulay called this attack "pointless spite, with here and there a just remark" (diary entry of October 9, 1850). See *Notes and Queries,* 5th ser., 7 (1877):444–45, 489–90.

3. So much so that some of his religious friends believed that he had returned to the fold: see Read 1897, 2:281. King George III "mentioned that he had been assured by a clergyman who was in Switzerland when he was last there, that he used to go at Christmas and Easter into some of the Catholic countries in the neighbourhood, in order to communicate according to that religion" (Glenbervie 1928, 1-94).

4. Later he undercut Protestant complacency still further with his analysis of the limitations of the Reformation as a victory for reason—see p. 215 above and L. O Frappell, "The Reformation as Negative Revolution or Obscurantist Reaction," *Journal of Religious History* 11 (December 1980):289–307.

5. Oliphant Smeaton, editor's note in Everyman and Modern Library editions of the *Decline and Fall*—note, 1, chap. 15.

6. For example, John Higgins, "The Apologists of the Infant Church," *American Ecclesiastical Review* 70 (May 1924):484–89.

7. Joseph Warton, letter of March 11, 1776 (Gibbon 1814, 2:152).

8. William A. Gibson, "Order and Emphasis in Chapter XV of Gibbon's *Decline and Fall of the Roman Empire,*" in *Rhetorical Analyses of Literary Works,* ed. E. P. J. Corbett (New York: Oxford University Press, 1969), 86–99.

9. Gibbon's perception and treatment of the "great theme" of the clash between two civilizations has often been praised; see especially Walter Rehm (1930, 120–41), who sees Gibbon's work as both the conclusion of a great tradition of universal history and a precursor of Nietzsche's.

10. For example, Ritter 1913; Falco 1933, 191–319; Momigliano 1936; Scheibe 1968; Pocock 1982.

11. Bernays 1885, 2:224.

12. Interleaved copy of the *Miscellaneous Works* 1796, Beinecke Library, Yale University, facing 1:111.

13. See William Frost, "The Irony of Swift and Gibbon: A Reply to F. R. Leavis," *Essays in Criticism* 17 (January 1967):45–46.

14. "They said, 'We have seen,' and extended their throats to the butchers," according to Charles Delalot [pseud. Z], "Le même sujet," *Spectateur français au XIXme siècle* 9 (1809):26–39.

15. For a full account of the printing and the resulting states of the first edition, see Norton 1940, 38–39.

16. Gibbon 1814, 2-138–39. I have suppressed paragraph divisions after each sentence.

17. George L. Scott, mathematician and commissioner of excise, friend of David Mallet and of Gibbon's father, had been consulted by Gibbon as

early as 1762 (when Scott gave Gibbon advice about pursuing his mathematical studies—British Library Add. MSS. 34886, fols. 38–41). For his probable role in the *Mémoires littéraires* of Gibbon and Georges Deyverdun, see Craddock 1982, 253. Scott must have read a portion of the *Decline and Fall* in proof; his letter about it, noting some "slips of the press, or the pen," is dated December 29, 1775 (Gibbon 1814, 2:141–42).

18. Contrary to the contention of P. R. Ghosh (1984).

19. Walpole 1937–80, 28:243–44.

20. Walpole 1937–80, 41:334–35.

21. Gibbon 1972, 122.

22. Walpole 1937–80, 41:335.

23. For example, a letter to Mason of January 27, 1781 (Walpole 1937–80, 29:98–99).

24. Gibbon 1814, 2:161.

25. Gibbon 1814, 2:159–60.

26. Hume 1932, 2:309.

27. Gibbon 1972, 338.

28. Georges Bonnard, editor's note, *Memoirs*, 314.

29. For example, a reviewer in the *Times Literary Supplement* (November 18, 1960), who calls Gibbon "the least garrulous of authors."

30. "Un historien est toujours jusqu'à un certain point, un politique . . . une honnete neutralitè."

31. *The Letters of David Garrick*, ed. David M. Little and George M. Kahrl (London: Oxford University Press; Cambridge, Mass.: Harvard University Press, 1963), 3:108.

32. Boswell 1953, 740.

33. *Monthly Review* 54 (1776):190. I of course owe the identification of all *Monthly* reviewers to the studies of B. C. Nangle.

34. *Annual Register of World Events* 19, pt. 2 (1776):236–38.

35. Information about Texier, or (Le) Tessier, from Norton, *Letters* 3:451— Gibbon's opinion that he was wonderful is from a letter to Holroyd (*Letters* 2:97); Gibbon's attendance at Texier's readings is recorded in his "pocket book for 1776," now in the Pierpont Morgan Library, New York.

36. Boswell 1953, 175.

37. He paid a guinea to "Beauclerk's cook," Monday, May 6, the day before he had a "great dinner at home," according to the notes in his pocket book.

38. D'Arblay 1904, 2:91–92.

39. The pocket book is arranged with two facing pages for each week— on the left, memoranda; on the right, accounts. The first entry is for February 17, the last for October 31. Noble was paid for the catalogue on April 2. The accounts begin on April 1 (on hand, £7.1.6, plus a £100 bank draft), are balanced at the end of May and June (in each case with a small sum unaccounted for) and kept—erratically and unbalanced—until near the end of August.

40. See Pierre Köhler, *Madame de Staël et le Suisse* (Lausanne and Paris: Librairie Payot, 1916), 50.

41. See J. E. Norton, Index I, *Letters* 3:379.

42. Letter of September 30, 1776, Gibbon 1814, 2:180.

Chapter 5 Three Capitals

1. Information about Gibbon's activities and finances were noted by him in a "Pocket Book for 1776," now in the Pierpont Morgan Library. See chapter 4 above. Strada (Keynes 1980, 258) is listed in the manuscript catalog (Lausanne 1785) of Gibbon's library in the Pierpont Morgan Library.

2. Whitaker 1836, 1:99-100.

3. For clarity and convenience I shall adopt the traditional but medically inaccurate term *hydrocele* for the swelling in his groin from which Gibbon suffered.

4. "List of Books—with Remarks," *Gentleman's Magazine* 46 (August 1776):365-67.

5. The author was James Chelsum. It was published by T. Payne and J. Robson and was ninety-two pages long.

6. Various writers accused him of errors, religious infidelity, and unfairness to the Christians. But Davis was the first to include charges of plagiarism and deliberate misrepresentation. Priestley accused him of being cowardly; he considered Gibbons use of irony unmanly and scorned him for not attacking Christianity more openly.

7. Richard Watson, *An Apology for Christianity, in a series of letters addressed to Edward Gibbon, Esq.* (Cambridge: J. Archdeacon et al., 1776), 268 pp. Reprinted in *Gibboniana* (New York and London: Garland, 1974).

8. Gibbon 1814, 2:181.

9. Gibbon 1814, 2:183.

10. Gibbon 1814, 2:177.

11. Gibbon 1814, 2:179, 178.

12. Gibbon 1814, 2:177-78.

13. See *Letters* 2:103 and 130.

14. In French. See Baridon 1971. David R. Raynor has pointed out to me that a report on Hume that appeared in the *Journal de Politique et de Littérature* of 1777 was attributed by Paul Meyer (doctoral dissertation, Columbia, 1954) to Gibbon; it is indeed probable that the source of these remarks, through Suard, was Gibbon.

15. "Il passe pour certain que Louis XVI, étudiant l'anglais sous la direction de M. Leclerc de Septchênes, . . . s'est exercé sur le premier vol. in 4. de l'histoire de Gibbon, publié en 1776, et qu'arrivé au 15e et 16ᵉ chapitres, il abandonna l'ouvrage, que revit, continua et fit imprimer M. de Septchênes" (J. C. Brunet, *Manuel du Libraire*, 4th ed. [Paris, 1842]). Quoted and evaluated in Norton 1940, 120-21. See also Colin Duckworth, "Louis XVI and English History: A French Reaction to Walpole, Hume and Gibbon on Richard III," *Studies on Voltaire and the Eighteenth Century* 176 (1979):385-401.

16. Low 1937, 359.

17. British Library Add. MSS. 34887, fol. 3. See Norton 1940, 44-45.

18. The encomiums of Lady Diana Beauclerk, presumably sufficiently true to be acceptable—*Letters* 2:141.

19. Baridon 1977b, 154.

20. "Si leurs manières avoient approché de celles du bon ton, elles n'auroient été que ridicules. Mais commes ces femmes les trouvioent tout

differentes de ce qu'elles avoient jamais vu jusqu'alors, elles crurent qu'elles tenoient à la Philosophie." Glenbervie 1910, 58.

21. Du Deffand 1912, 3:594–95.

22. "C'est un homme très-raisonnable, qui a beaucoup de conversation, infiniment de savoir; vous y ajouteriez peut-être infiniment d'esprit, et peut être auriez-vous raison; je ne suis pas décidée sur cet article; il fait trop de cas de nos agréments, trop de désir de les acquérir, j'ai toujours eu sur le bout de la langue de lui dire: Ne vous tourmentez pas, vous meritez l'honneur d'etre Français." Du Deffand 1912, 3:376.

23. Both cited in Baridon 1977b, 155 n. 1.

24. Edmond Malone in Prior 1860. See also Roche 1844, 158. Both had experienced Gibbon's appearance personally, though Roche saw Gibbon only once, in 1793.

25. Reported in letter of July 24, 1782 (Auckland 1861, 1:12).

26. Letter of September 23, 1787, interleaved in the proof copy of Gibbon's *Miscellaneous Works* facing 1:675; Beinecke Library, Yale University; this reference was called to my attention by Marvin Stern (1984, 46).

27. Cited in Dominique Joseph Garat, *Mémoires historiques sur le XVIIIᵉ siècle, et de M. Suard* (Paris: A. Belin, 1821), 2:191–2:"L'auteur de la grande et superbe Histoire de l'Empire Romain avait à peine quatre pied sept à huit pouces; le tronc immense de son corps à gros ventre de Silène était posé sur cette espèce de jambes grêles qu'on appelle *flûtes;* ses pieds, assez en dedans pour que la pointe du droit pût embrasser souvent la pointe du gauche, étaient assez longs et assez larges pour servir de socle à une statue de cinq pieds six pouces; au milieu de son visage, pas plus gros que le poing, la racine de son nez, s'enfonçait dans le crâne, plus profondément que celle du nez d'un Kalmouck, et ses yeux, trés vifs mais trés-petits, se perdaient dans les mêmes profondeurs."

28. D'Arblay 1823, 170–71.

29. "Notes on Modern Europe," in Gibbon 1972, 212–25.

30. Gibbon found the account, in a lecture by C. G. de Rulhière, "an entertaining spirited piece of historical composition not unworthy of being compared with Vertot's conspiracy of Portugal." Gibbon heard it twice. But he also itemizes testimony against it. Gibbon 1972, 216.

31. "M. l'Abbé de *Mably* & M. *Gibbon* y [chez M. Foncemagne] dinèrent en grande compagnie. La conversation roula presque entièrement sur l'histoire. L'abbé de *Mably*, étant un profond politique, la tourna sur l'administration, quand on fut au dessert: & comme par caractère, par humeur, par l'habitude d'admirer *Tite-Live*, il ne prise que le système republicain, il se mit à vanter l'excellence des républiques, bien persuadé que le savant anglais l'approuverait en tout, & admirerait la profondeur de génie qui avait fait deviner tous ces avantages à un français. Mais M. *Gibbon*, instruit par expérience des inconvéniens d'un gouvernement populaire, ne fut point du tout de son avis, & il prit généralement la défense du gouvernment monarchique. L'abbé voulut le convaincre par *Tite-Live* & par quelques argumens tirés de *Plutarque* en faveur des Spartiates; M. *Gibbon* doué de la mémoire la plus heureuse, & ayant tous les faits présens à la pensée, domina bientôt la conversation; l'abbé se fâche, il s'emporta, il dit des choses dures. L'anglais, conservant le flegme de son pays, prenait ses avantages & pressait l'abbé

avec d'autant plus de succès que la colère le troublait de plus en plus. La conversation s'echauffait, & M. de *Foncemagne* le rompit en se levant de table." [Gudin de la Brenellerie], *Supplement a la maniere d'ecrire l'histoire; ou response a l'ouvrage de M. l'abbé de Mably* (Paris: Société littéraire-typographique, 1784), 125–27.

32. For accounts of Gibbon's political views see below, chapter 6, note 2.

33. Baridon 1977b, 167–75.

34. Anecdote from (William) Cobbett's *Works*, 7:244, reported in James Parton, *Life and Times of Benjamin Franklin* (New York: Mason Brothers 1864), 2:209.

Chapter 6 Politics and Letters

1. Walpole 1910, 2–11.

2. Z., "Gibbon's Correspondence," *Philadelphia Register and National Recorder* 1, no. 18 (May 1, 1819):295. Full explorations of Gibbon's degree and kind of Whiggery may be found in the following: G. O. Trevelyan, *George the Third and Charles Fox* (London: Longman's, Green, 1912), 1:88, 188–89; Swain 1940; Curtis 1949: G. J. Gruman, 'Balance' and 'Excess' as Gibbon's Explanation of the Decline and Fall," *History and Theory* 1 (1960):75–85; Lutnick 1968–69; A. G. Woodward, "Edward Gibbon: Enlightenment Humanist," *English Studies in Africa* 18 (1975):63–70; Baridon 1977a; Baridon 1977b, especially 167–201, 392–402, 596–626; Dickinson 1978.

3. *Essai sur l'étude de la littérature* (London: T. Beckett and P. A. Dehondt, 1761), chaps. 23–27.

4. But not in valuing moral instruction or parallelism itself more highly than the unique, particular, and contingent: as G. W. Bowersock suggests, Suetonius is a closer model for Gibbon's biographical goals and methods. "Suetonius in the Eighteenth Century," in *Biography in the Eighteenth Century*, ed. J. D. Browning, Publications of the McMaster University Association for 18th-Century Studies, 8 (New York and London: Garland, 1980), 28–33.

5. Milman 1882, 1:xii.

6. Gibbon 1972, 226–27, 569.

7. So denominated by David P. Jordan in his valuable studies of this section of the *Decline and Fall:* in the context of other studies of the period (Jordon 1969); as a turning point in Gibbon's historiographical development (Jordan 1971, 191–212).

8. J. B. Bury, editor's introduction, *DF* 1:xvi.

9. Arthur Ferrill, *The Fall of the Roman Empire: The Military Explanation* (London: Thames & Hudson, 1986), 13–22.

10. Gibbon 1972, 90.

11. Jordan 1971, 198–99.

12. Johannes Straub, "Gibbons Konstantin-Bild," in *Gibbon et Rome à la lumière de l'historiographie moderne* (Geneva: Librairie Droz, 1977, 159–85.

13. Jordan 1971, 199.

14. Bernays 1885.

15. Jordan 1971, 205. Tillemont's *Histoire des empereurs,* a monuments of

seventeenth-century erudite scholarship, was acknowledged by Gibbon as an indispensable source for the *Decline and Fall*.

16. It is interesting to note that some moderns, including the skeptical Bury, seem to believe that there *was* some kind of apparition, explicable, of course, by natural causes.

17. By Gibbon's reckoning, Constantine was 64 when he died in 335; Gibbon therefore implies the year 310 or 311 when he speaks of Constantine as "above 40.".

18. Swain 1966, 135–36.

19. Baridon 1977b, 596.

20. Swain 1966, 136, from *Parliamentary Register* 5:119.

21. Walpole 1910, 2:367.

22. Eliot quoted in *Life of W. Wilberforce* (London: John Murray, 1839), 2:179, cited in Hill 1900, 324.

23. Lutnick 1968–69, 1102.

24. J. E. Norton, appendix to *Letters*, 1:404.

25. See Craddock 1982, 274–75.

26. Walter Kaegi, "Research on Julian the Apostate, 1945–64," *Classical World* 58 (1964):231.

27. Compare Glen W. Bowersock, *Julian the Apostate* (Cambridge, Mass.: Harvard University Press, 1978), 1–2. In his "Acknowledgments," Bowersock says, "My reading of Gibbon and of Cavafy . . . has substantially influenced my understanding of the ancient sources. . . . It is for this reason that I have prefaced the present study with excerpts from these two great writers. My deepest debt is to them" (vii).

28. E. Badian, "Gibbon on War," in *Gibbon et Rome à la lumière de l'historiographie moderne* (Geneva: Librairie Droz, 1977), 103–30.

Chapter 7 Counterattacks

1. Both are reproduced in de Beer 1968, the Walton on page 73, the Reynolds as the frontispiece.

2. See McCloy 1933 and Norton 1940, 78–93, 233–499.

3. Henry Edwards Davis, *An Examination of the Fifteenth and Sixteenth Chapters of Mr Gibbon's History of the Decline and Fall of the Roman Empire. In which his view of the Christian Religion is shewn to be founded on the Misrepresentation of the Authors he cites: and Numerous Instances of his Inaccuracy and Plagiarism are produced* (London: J. Dodsley, 1778). A modern reprint is in *Gibboniana* (New York and London: Garland Publishing, 1974).

4. *A Vindication of Some Passages in the Fifteenth and Sixteenth Chapters of the History of the Decline and Fall of the Roman Empire*, in Gibbon 1972, 236.

5. Gibbon 1972, 313.

6. H. R. Trevor-Roper, preface, *Edward Gibbon's Vindication* (London: Oxford University Press for the Board of the Faculty of Modern History, 1961), viii.

7. Gibbon 1972, 236–67.

8. In the preface to his next work, William Robertson specifically credits Gibbon with encouraging the practice of full and precise reference to sources

in historical writing: "By minute references to [my sources], I have endea-
voured to authenticate whatever I relate. The longer I reflect on the nature
of historical composition, the more I am convinced that this scrupulous
accuracy is necessary. The historian . . . who delineates the transactions of a
remote period, has no title to claim assent, unless he produces evidence in
proof of his assertions. Without this, he may write an amusing tale, but
cannot be said to have composed an authentic history. In those sentiments I
have been confirmed by the opinion of an author* [the footnote reads, "*Mr.
Gibbon"] whom his industry, erudition, and discernment, have deservedly placed
in a high rank among the most eminent historians of the age" (Robertson 1777,
1:xv–xvi).

9. Braudel 1985, 1:565.

10. Walpole 1937–80, 34:131–32, letter to Lady Ossory, November 23, 1971.

11. See Gibbon 1972, 572–73.

12. Davis, *Examination*, 6. Gibbon 1972, 240–45.

13. Gibbon 1972, 246.

14. Gibbon is "more deeply scandalized at the single execution of Servetus,
than at the hecatombs which have blazed in the Auto da Fès of Spain and
Portugal. . . . A Catholic inquisitor yields the same obedience which he requires,
but Calvin violated the golden rule of doing as he would be done by" (*DF* chap.
54, n. 36, 6:133, n. 43). Yet Servetus is also the type for him of the man capable
of better things who insisted on being a religious fanatic—see his advice to
Priestley, *Memoirs* 171.

15. Gibbon 1972, 246.

16. The modern English laws "would still leave a tolerable scope for persecution, if the national spirit were not more effectual than an hundred statutes"
(*DF* chap. 54 n. 41, 6:134 n. 49).

17. Gibbon 1972, 250.

18. Gibbon 1972, 253–54.

19. Gibbon 1972, 256.

20. Belloc, *Dublin Review* 159 (1916):361–76 (replied to by W. H. Kent in *The
Tablet* [a Catholic periodical in London] 128 [1916]:852–53, 887–89); *Studies*
(Dublin) 7 (1918):210–26, 369–84; *Studies* 8 (1919):544–64; *Dublin Review* 169
(1921):265–87; *New Statesman* 30 (February 18, 1928):591–93.

21. Gibbon 1972, 262.

22. Gibbon 1972, 264.

23. Gibbon 1972, 265.

24. Gibbon 1972, 269–70.

25. Idem.

26. Davis, 132.

27. Gibbon 1972, 273.

28. Gibbon 1972, 276.

29. Davis, 110.

30. Gibbon 1972, 277.

31. Wilhelm Dilthey (writing as W. Hoffner) was perhaps the first to analyze
how Gibbon's nonzealous skepticism permitted him to use materials from various
Catholic and Protestant traditions impartially (Dilthey 1866, 144).

32. Gibbon 1972, 278.

33. Gibbon 1972, 279–80.

34. ". . . l'epée du Gentleman; pour combattre ce gu'il appelle 'the fierceness of ecclesiastical criticism' ce genre d'argument *ad hominem* nous apparaît comme un coup bas. . . . des armes qu'il avait lui-même forgées" (Baridon 1977b, 162).

35. Gibbon 1972, 233–34.

36. Gibbon 1972, 284–85.

37. Gibbon 1972, 289.

38. Norton 1940, 87.

39. George K. Boyce, "The Cost of Publishing Gibbon's *Vindication*," *Papers of the Bibliographical Society of America* 43 (1949):335–39.

40. Walpole 1937–80, 42:393.

41. Walpole 1937–80, 42:387.

42. Low 1937, 277.

43. See Lord Weymouth to Sheffield, Sheffield Papers, Yale, quoted in Norton 1940, 25: "As the Chancellor and I have but a very slight acquaintance with Mr Gibbon, I trust to your discretion in the manner of making this proposal to him or of not doing it if you think he will not like it."

44. I quote the *Mémoire justicatif* in the translation published in J. Walker McSpadden's limited edition of Gibbon's *Works* (New York: F. de Fau, 1907) 14:122. The translator is not indicated.

45. Trevelyan 1912, 1:188–89.

46. John Wilkes (The Observer), *To Edward Gibbon, Esq., One of the Lords of Trade* n.p. [1779]), 4–5.

47. *Gentleman's Magazine* 51 (December 1781):584. The theory that these verses were falsely attributed to Fox seems to rest solely on D. M. Low's wishful thinking (1937, 282).

48. Norton notes the report of the sale of another portrait of Gibbon by Reynolds, a "head," to one Jackson at Christie's in 1831. This head is said to have been painted about the same time as the famous portrait. *Letters* 2:216 n. 5.

49. Prior 1860, 382; Sheffield, "Advertisement," in Gibbon 1814, 1:xi.

50. The printing of the two volumes was completed by the end of February 1781; it would have required six months, i.e., would have been begun early in September 1780, and by the end of June 1780 Gibbon was already "pleasantly though laboriously engaged in revising, and correcting for the press" (*Letters* 2:245). He regarded himself as having written volume 6 at extraordinary speed, and he wrote it at the rate of approximately 50 pages per month (see p. 223 above). Thus we can hardly expect him to have written much more than 300 pages in the six months of 1780, and in fact chapters 33–38, exclusive of the "General Observations," occupy the final 302 pages of the third quarto volume.

51. Gibbon was quite faithful in attending the meetings of the Board of Trade. Between July 15, 1779, and April 20, 1780, for example, he missed only four of thirty-seven meetings: *Journal of the Commissioners for Trade and Plantations* (England: Board of Trade, 1920–38), 86. J. E. Norton and the British Library MSS. catalogue credit him with writing some of the Board's minutes. Norton, *Letters* 2:234 n. 2.

52. Baridon 1977b, 178.

53. Compare Gossman 1981, 104–111.

54. Compare Brownley 1978.

55. See Garrison 1978. For Gibbon's *use* of particular sources, exemplary modern studies include those by Glen W. Bowersock and François Paschoud in

Gibbon et Rome à la lumière de l'historiographie moderne (Geneva: Librairie Droz, 1977), 191–213 and 219–45, respectively, and M. Sartori, "Gibbon, l'Historia Augusta e la storia del II e del III secolo d. C.," *Rivistica storica italiana* 94:353–94.

56. Richard Tickell, *Epistle from the Hon. Charles Fox, partridge-shooting, to the Hon. John Townshend, cruising* (London: R. Faulder, 1779), quoted in Prothero 1896, 1:151.

Chapter 8 Ending Empires

1. See Christie 1958.
2. Walpole 1937–80, 29:98–99, letter to Mason, January 27, 1781.
3. J. E. Norton, note, *Letters* 2:241, from *Parliamentary History* 21:334 and *Morning Chronicle*, April 6, 1780.
4. Walpole 1937–80, 2:80.
5. Speech of February 11, 1780.
6. G. B. Hill was outraged that Gibbon thought (or at least told his anxious stepmother) that the Government measures were effectual: "On June 27 Gibbon had the audacity to write, 'The measures of government have been seasonable and vigorous'" (Hill 1900, 208).
7. Grewal 1975, 12–23.
8. Up to and including Stephen Runciman, who continued to believe, in 1976, that Gibbon "killed Byzantine studies for nearly a century" "Gibbon and Byzantium," *Dædalus* 105 (1976):37–48. Archibald R. Lewis, reviewing the *Dædalus* volume, "strongly agrees" (*Journal of Interdisciplinary History* 9 [1978]:338–39). The earliest instance of such a complaint—that is, a complaint not that Gibbon's Byzantine history was wrong, but that it was principally responsible for subsequent misjudgments, is that of E. A. Freeman, in an 1888 letter to Goldwin Smith. W. R. W. Stephens, *The Life and Letters of E. A. Freeman* (London and New York: Macmillan, 1895), 2:380.
9. Compare, for example, George Horne: "The story of the degenerate Greeks, the foolish emperors and profligate empresses, is tedious and tormenting to read." Letter of July 2, 1788, in *The Works of the Right Reverend George Horne*, ed. William Jones (New York: Stanford & Swords, 1853), 1:78. Walpole, too, assumed that "Constantinopolitan history" was a "disgusting subject" (1955, 29:98). Charles Lebeau was the exception—see J. Irmscher, "Charles Lebeau und das deutsche Byzanzbild," *Annales du service des antiquités d'Egypte* 62 (1977): 175–84—abstract in *L'Année philologique*.
10. Gibbon 1972, 324.
11. Oliver 1969. See also White 1968.
12. Christie 1958, 33–34, from the Portland MSS.
13. Norton 1940, 49.
14. William Hayley, *An Essay on History; in Three Epistles to Edward Gibbon, Esq.* (London: J. Dodsley, 1780—photofacsimilie in *Gibboniana* [New York and London: Garland Publishing, 1974]). epis. 3, ll. 417–18.
15. *Monthly Review* 63 (July 1780):30–37 (Edmund Cartwright); *Critical Review* 50 (July 1780):13.
16. See *Letters* 2:261.

Chapter 9 Interregnum

1. Norton 1940, 49–50.
2. Manuscript bills, Magdalen College MS. 359.
3. Walpole 1910, 2:378.
4. Low 1937, 359, and *Letters* 2:291.
5. Alexander Chalmers, "Some Account of the Life and Writings of Edward Gibbon, Esq.," in *The History of the Decline and Fall of the Roman Empire*," 12 vols. (London: Cadell & Davies, 1807). This account is included in subsequent printings of this edition of Gibbon's history, as well as in Chalmers' *General Biographical Dictionary.*
6. Marc Marie, marquis de Bombelles, letter of June 18, 1781, in *The Correspondence of Adam Smith*, ed. E. C. Mossner and I. S. Ross (Oxford: Clarendon Press, 1977), 213.
7. Walpole 1937–80, 29:98–99, letter to Mason, January 27, 1781.
8. Gibbon 1814. 2:246.
9. Gibbon 1814, 2:246–47.
10. *Gentleman's Magazine* 51 (April 1781):184–85; (July 1781):328–32; (November 1781):519–21.
11. Deno J. Geanakoplos and Jaroslov Pelikan.
12. *Critical Review* 51 (March 1781):161–69; (April 1781):249–57; (May 1781):342–51; (June 1781):416–26.
13. William Rose (for the identification I am indebted to B. C. Nangle), *Monthly Review* 64: (March 1781):223–24; (April 1781):228–97; May 1781):357–62; (June 1781):442–53; 65 (July 1781):29–37; (June 1782):459–63.
14. Arthur Young, *Autobiography*, ed. M. Betham-Edwards (London: Smith, Elder, 1898), 258–59 (written 1816).
15. Pocock 1982.
16. William Robertson, letter of May 12. 1781, in Gibbon 1814, 2:249.
17. Thomas Newton, *Works* (London: Rivington, 1782), 1:129–30.
18. Walpole 1937–80, 29:98–99.
19. For a modern comparison and an analysis of Gibbon's "competition" with Tillemont, see David P. Jordan, "Le Nain de Tillemont, Gibbon's 'Sure-Footed Mule,'" *Church History* 39 (1970):483–502.
20. Walpole 1937–80, 33:303, letter to Lady Ossory, October 26, 1781.
21. See Clark 1985, 91–116.
22. Hayley 1823, 1:215–16.
23. Eliza Hayley, in Hayley 1823, 1:219–21. Paragraphing added.
24. Magdalen College MSS. 359, item 91.
25. Norton, *Letters* 2:270, n. 1, from Burrard, *Annals of Walhampton* (1874), chaps. 8 and 9, and *Parliamentary Papers of John Robinson*, ed. W. T. Laprade (1922), 59–60.
26. Magdalen College MSS. 359, items 86, 88, 89, 141, 172.
27. Craddock 1982, 134.
28. Magdalen College MSS. The Procopius was item 52 in the estate sale of Henry Payne—it was bought November 16, 1781, for £1.5.0., and was probably a folio—*Historiarum libri VIII*, opera D. Hoeschelii (Augsburg, 1607)—which is listed in Gibbon's 1785 catalogue at Lausanne (Pierpont

Morgan Library), but not in his Bentinck Street catalogue of 1777 (Keynes 1980, 231).

29. A bookbinder's bill among the Magdalen College MSS. 359 dated April 6, 1782, includes "Lettres de Bailly 8vo"—2 shillings. See Keynes 1980, 61–62, for Gibbon's copies of Bailly.

30. Magdalen College MSS. 359, binder's bill December 1781 and following.

31. D'Arblay 1904, 2:196.

32. Magdalen College MSS. 359, items 108, 123.

33. D'Arblay 1904, 5:30.

34. Holroyd 1897, 269.

35. Joseph Cradock, *Literary and Miscellaneous Memoirs* (London: J. B. Nichols, 1828), 4:317–18.

36. Even after the disposition of sinecures was in their power rather than that of North, "decency compelled the patriots to revive the bill" Burke had proposed (*Memoirs* 164). G. B. Hill calls this a "placeman's sneer" (Hill 1900, 213). We may prefer to see Gibbon's comment as politically astute, and Hill's as a Boswellian's sneer.

37. A. L. Reade, *Johnsonian Gleanings* (1923; reprint, New York: Octagon Books, 1968), 4:46–51.

38. Magdalen College MSS. 359, item 108.

39. Walpole 1937–80, 33:313.

Chapter 10 Removals

1. For instance, n. 128 to chap. 40 speaks of "the mountainous country which I inhabit" (*DF* 4:273). Additional notes and additions to notes could be made, of course, at any point before publication.

2. For a good analysis of the typical structural order within and between chapters in Gibbon's first three volumes, see Marks 1975, chap. 2.

3. Baridon 1977a.

4. For a discussion of this trend in Gibbon criticism, see Craddock 1987a, xxx.

5. See, for example, "Marginalia in Herodotus" (Gibbon 1972, 373).

6. By way of contrast, we may note Bury's reference, in the same note, to the views of a historian contemporary to him, T. Hodgkin. "He is inclined to ascribe this idea of invading Italy to Theodoric." It is perhaps not obvious that the modest Hodgkin makes a much more extravagant claim about the singularity and accessibility of the truth about the past than the confident Gibbon, since Hodgkin implies that he has presented the *res gestae*, while Gibbon acknowledges that however much the historian pursues objective truth, what he writes is always his own *historia rerum gestarum*.

7. See the reviews and comments of contemporary readers summarized in Craddock 1987a, 44–58. John Gillies, in the *Monthly Review*, praises the account but acknowledges that "some fastidious readers" will think Gibbon "dwell[s] too long, and with too little reluctance, on the character and vices of the Empress Theodora" (*Monthly Review* 79 (July 1788):13.

8. Gibbon is so much aware of the importance and complexity of the

issue of Procopius's authority and bias that he honors Procopius with an account in the text (*DF* chap. 40 4:224–26). His skepticism about Procopius's justice to Theodora is even more tellingly revealed in critical asides about his testimony, such as the following note to an account of the alleged cruelties suffered in her prisons beneath the palace, "Darkness is propitious to cruelty, but it is likewise favourable to calumny and fiction" (*DF* 4:231 n. 31).

9. Low 1937, 292.

10. D'Arblay 1823, 2:170–71.

11. D'Arblay 1904, 2:222.

12. D'Arblay 1823, 2:341.

13. Letter of May 3, 1779, to William Temple, in *The Letters of James Boswell*, ed. C. B. Tinker (Oxford: Clarendon Press, 1924), 2:287.

14. Boswell 1953, 615.

15. *Historical Manuscripts Commission* (1870), 13th Report, 28, pt. 2, appendix 1, pt. 8, 230–31.

16. *Gentleman's Magazine* 64 (1794):178.

17. George Colman, *Random Records* (London: Henry Colburn & Richard Bentley, 1830), 1:121–22.

18. Letter of June 13, 1783, Auckland 1861, 1:53.

19. Hayley 1823, 1:269.

20. Thurlow's letter in Gibbon 1814, 2:274. Candidacy in *Historical Manuscripts Commission* (1870), 8th Report, appendix 2, 133. Gibbon was aware of this possibility—*Letters* 2:358, 363.

21. Lord Sheffield reprinted the exchange, starting with Gibbon's first letter, in Gibbon 1814, 2:265–72.

22. I support this generalization in Craddock 1988.

23. Gustav Hugo, *Historisches Übersicht des Römisches Rechts* (Göttingen: Johann Christian Dieterich, 1789). After an 8-page introduction, Gibbon's text and notes require 162 pages, and Hugo's notes require 38.

24. *Göttingische Gelehrte Anzeigen*, no. 205 (December 25, 1788), 2049–56.

25. Germany, France, England, the United States, Greece, Poland, Czechoslavakia.

26. *Survey of the Roman, or Civil Law; an Extract from Gibbon's History of the Decline and Fall of the Roman Empire, with notes by Professor Hugo of Goettingen*, trans. W. Gardiner (Edinburgh: printed for the editor, 1823).

27. *European Magazine* 14 (1788):101.

28. For a contrary view, see E. Badian, "Imposing Gibbon," *New York Review of Books* 24 (October 13, 1977):7–9.

29. Gibbon 1814, 2:282.

30. British Library Add. MSS. 34882, fol. 256.

31. See Craddock 1982, 149.

Chapter 11 Lion of Lausanne

1. Owen 1796, 1:218.

2. Sylvester Douglas, Lord Glenbervie, whose wife was the sister of Sheffield's third wife, described his future brother-in-law thus: "He is of a

very active, bustling temper and turn of mind. But I fear he has mistaken that turn for genius" (Glenbervie 1910, 66).

3. British Library Add. MSS. 34887, fols. 197–98.

4. Gibbon's holograph book of accounts, Pierpont Morgan Library.

5. Gibbon 1814, 2:287.

6. "Vous aurez encore plus de tems pour le cabinet qu'à Londres; on sort peu le matin, et quand nos amis communs viendront chez moi, et vous demanderont, je leur dirai; 'ce n'est pas un oisif comme vous autres, il travaille dans son cabinet,' et ils se tairont respectueusement." Gibbon 1814, 2:301.

7. A bill beginning December 28, 1783 from Lacombe, Libraire, at Lausanne is in British Library Add. MSS 34715, fols. 1–2. But only two of these purchases occurred before Gibbon's books arrived from London, a *Vie des poètes grecs* and a treatise on ballooning.

8. Ghosh 1984. For the "Outlines," see Gibbon 1972, 163–98.

9. Not all the rooms in Deyverdun's house were at the disposal of his tenants, and since he and Gibbon were not living there either, they were able to "arrange some plans of alteration and furniture which will embellish our future and more elegant dwelling" (*Letters* 2:390).

10. A holograph memorandum (British Library Add. MSS. 34882, fol. 175) gives the dates: the fourth volume was begun on March 1, 1782 and completed June 1784; the fifth was begun July 1784 and completed May 1, 1786; the sixth was begun May 18, 1786 and completed June 27, 1787. "These three Volumes were sent to press. August 15th. 1787 and the whole impression concluded April."

11. Everything except the first sentence of this memorandum appears to be identical in ink, pen, and hand; so it is probable that instead of recording his completion of each volume as it was completed, he recorded the dates of volumes 4 and 5 as or after he sent all three to press.

12. Entry for August 28, 1762, Low 1929, 129.

13. J. E. Norton, n. 3. to *Letters* 3:223.

14. In this respect, the history as written spectacularly differs both from the "Outlines" and from the plan announced in the preface to volume 1, but not from the plan announced at the beginning of chapter 48.

15. Patricia B. Craddock, "An Approach to the Distinction of Similar Styles: Two English Historians," *Style* 2 (Spring 1968):122–23.

16. Holograph account book, Pierpont Morgan Library, New York. Gibbon apparently paid for new furniture and decorative items for their common use, such as carpets and china.

17. Elmsley's bill, 1783–84, Pierpont Morgan Library, New York, first page.

18. Account book, Pierpont Morgan Library, New York, 1784. His total expenses for 1784 amounted to about 5,500 livres—£365 at the exchange rate, which was at least 15 livres to the pound and usually somewhat more. Another £100 (1,500 livres) had been prepaid to Deyverdun for routine housekeeping expenses. This £465 included servants' wages, alterations to the house, carriage of books and china from England, tailors' and book bills (though not the large bill to Elmsley in England), charity, and lottery tickets, as well as some purchases, such as new carpets, a new frame for a mirror,

silver candlesticks, and (not the largest sum, but perhaps the greatest single extravagance) nearly £14 for a "A Lyons velvet for a suit of Cloaths."

19. This is Norton's inference, in a note to the passage in *Letters*. Another hypothesis for the psychobiographically inclined is that Gibbon was approaching perilously close to the topic of marriage, with which, indeed, he deals in the next part of the letter, in a safely joking fashion. "Should you be very much surprized to hear of my being married? . . . Not that I am in love with any particular person; I have discovered about half a dozen *Wives* who would please me in different ways and by various merits. . . . Could I find all these qualities united in a single person, I should dare to make my addresses and should deserve to be refused" (*Letters* 3:13).

20. "Dass bey so guten Gluckumstanden, und seinem auf Alles sich erstrekkenden feinem Geschmack, auch die Eleganz der Junen und Aussenseite dem Werthe seiner Bucher entsprach, kann man sich vorstellen. Wenn daher, trotz einer zuweilen wert getriebenen Eigenheit, er mir dennoch den freyen Gebrauch seiner gelehrten Schatze zugestand, so muss ich es vermuthlich dem Umstande danken, dass er sich vorher meiner eignen Liebe zur Ordnung versichert gehabt . . . Mit einem wort: ich konnte diese Buchersammlung wie meine eigne ansehen, und was noch mehr ist, war oft ganze Wochen lang im Besitz seines eigenhandig gefertigten, einem derben Folianten fullenden Katalogs." Langer 1794, 637.

21. Account book, Pierpont Morgan Library, New York, December 20, 1785.

22. Lionel Colmore, quoted in de Beer 1968, 113. De Beer's source not indicated.

23. "Weiter war an seinem Tische die grosse Bequemlichkeit, dass man den Gaumen nicht auf Kosten der Lunge zu kitzeln brauchte. Nur *ein* von dem Gaste hingeworfenes à propos, brachte den Strohm von Kenntnissen und Belesenheit unsers Wirths so gleich in volle Bewegung, und gegen *eine* Anekdote, *einen* witzigen Einfall, hatte man den Vortheil, zehn andere noch unterhaltendere mit nach Hause zu bringen." ". . . gewöhnlich dem Hohlen und Singenden. Allein der mindeste Widerspruch, die mässigste Erwärmung hoben es sehr bald zu einem so männlichen Bass . . . solcher gewiss das Haus . . . gefüllt haben würde." Langer 1794, 635, 642.

24. For example, Friedrich von Matthisson, in a letter of October 11, 1789 (Powell 1938, 346).

25. A ta mine douce et polie
   On te prendre pour un Français
   A ton savoir, ton énergie,
   A tes écrits et tes succès
   Ton esprit, ta philosophie,
   La profondeur de ton génie,
   On soupçonnerait un Anglais.
   Mais ta véritable patrie
   Est celle où le coeur t'a conduit,
   Où l'on t'aime, où l'on te le dit,
   Et tu dois y passer ta vie.
(Charrière de Sévery 1911–12, 1:261).

26. Holroyd 1897, 74.

27. Pierre Köhler, *Madame de Staël au Chateau de Coppet* (Lausanne: SPES, 1929), 21.

Chapter 12 Farewell to the History

1. British Library Add. MSS. 34887, fols. 208-9.

2. Holroyd 1897, 266.

3. Holroyd 1897, 275.

4. Murray 1896, 121.

5. He goes out of his way to cite Sir William Temple's "pleasing Essay on Heroic Virtue" (*DF* chap. 67, 7:156 n. 39 [35]).

6. Braudy 1970, 267.

7. Cf. Braudy 1970, 260-61, and Brownley 1978.

8. Gibbon was irritated by Voltaire's manner as well as his view of evidence; compare a remark in Gibbon's private "Index Expurgatorius" (1768-69) about a well-supported inscription rejected by Voltaire: "I am not insensible that before this question was so acurately examined, some Learned men have had doubts concerning the inscription; but where they doubted, Voltaire decided. Tho his objections are very contemptible, yet I am still more offended at the haughtiness of his unbelief, than at his unbelief itself." Gibbon 1972, 117.

9. He echoes and reverses an earlier comment near the end of volume 5: "From the paths of blood, and such is the history of nations, I cannot refuse to turn aside to gather some flowers of science or virtue" (*DF* chap. 57, 6:236).

10. Gibbon often uses this kind of argument to legitimate using evidence from a biased source; perhaps his assumption that a flagrant lie would be perceived as virtual satire or as criticism of what was actually done is ahistorical. He may have underestimated the power of propaganda and doublethink.

11. For instance, Horace Walpole in the eighteenth century, James Mackintosh in the nineteenth, and P. R. Ghosh in the twentieth.

12. Other interesting examples include chap. 57, 6:238 n. 11 [10] and chap. 56, 6:180-81, n. 15 [14].

13. "Viele Noten, besonders in der zweiten Trias von Quartbänden, geben Charakteristiken [he lists as examples Herbelot, Mariana, Mosheim, Muratori, Petavius]. . . . Persönliches gibt Gibbon in den Noten seines Werks, aber nur in den drei letzten Bänden, nachdem er der Unsterblichkeit seines Werks versichert war. Das bezeichnendste ist ch. 52 not. 50 über die Zahl seiner glücklichen Stunden." Bernays 1885, 2:252. Bernays worked on this study at various periods in his life, beginning in 1853 and again in 1868, 1871, and 1874, but never completed it.

14. Low 1937, 3.

15. J. B. A. Suard estimated his height at four feet seven or eight inches French measure, that is, almost five feet English (Garat 1821, 2:191). Ernst Langer says Gibbon was a man of "middle" height and mentions his "fiery" glance: "*Gibbon* war von mittlerer Statur, die durch zunehmende Corpulenz

immer runder wurde, und sein feueriger Blick kündigte sogleich an, mit wem man zu thun hatte" (Langer 1794, 644).

16. See Craddock 1982, 88, 107, 179. On the grenadiers, including their expected height requirement, see Major R. Holden, "Gibbon as a Soldier," *Macmillan's Magazine* 71 (November 1894):31-38. Silhouettes of Gibbon and Lord Sheffield, to the same scale, are reproduced side by side in de Beer 1968, 101.

17. Craddock 1982, 244-45.

18. "Yet an ingenious friend has urged to me, in mitigation of this practice [trial by combat], 1. *That*, in nations emerging from barbarism, it moderates the licence of private war and arbitrary revenge. 2.*That* it is less absurd than the trials by the ordeal . . . which it has contributed to abolish. 3. *That* it served at least as a test of personal courage" (*DF* 6:483).

19. See Craddock 1988.

20. Gibbon 1972, 117.

21. Gibbon's praise of Syropulus may have been influenced by temperamental similarities: "His passions were cooled by time and retirement; and, although Syropulus is often partial, he is never intemperate" (*DF* 7:109, n. 52 [50]).

22. See Garrison 1977.

23. Literally, the Italian reads, "Then he made them stand in front of him, while he was seated, all the barons standing up with their arms folded and with bare heads. Oh how they were trembling."

24. "Hints," in Gibbon 1972, 94-95.

25. Gossman 1981, 109-13.

26. Braudy 1970 and 1980. See also Grant L. Voth, "The Artist and the Past: Reflections on Two New Gibbon Books," *Eighteenth-Century Studies* 8 (Winter 1974-75):213-21.

27. Braudy 1970, 246.

28. Most recently P. R. Ghosh (1984).

29. Murray 1896, 270.

30. Craddock 1984.

31. George Gordon, Lord Byron, *Letters and Journals*, ed. Leslie A. Marchand (London: John Murray, 1976), 5:81.

32. Thomas Hardy, *Complete Poems*, ed. James Gibson (London: Macmillan, 1978), 105.

33. British Library Add. MSS. 34882, fol. 175.

34. G. W. Bowersock, "Gibbon," *Classical Review* 36 (1986):293, points out that by beginning the final chapter with Poggio's view from the Capitol and ending it with his own, Gibbon "has made himself into the Poggio of the eighteenth century."

35. British Library Add. MSS. 34886 fols. 157-58.

Chapter 13 Fathering

1. For example, "I believe that in twelve or fourteen months I shall be brought to bed—perhaps of twins" (*Letters* 2:225). On architectural meta-

phors, see especially J. W. Johnson, "Gibbon's Architectural Metaphor," *Journal of British Studies* 13 (November 1973):44–63.

2. Norton 1940, 60.

3. Now in the Pierpont Morgan Library, New York.

4. Reported in the London *Morning Chronicle*, June 14, 1788, p. [2].

5. "Gibbon a ici, à Londres, les plus agréables connaissances du monde, . . . tous les gens les plus relevées pour l'esprit; il dîne presque tous les jours dehors et, quoique je l'entende parler bien souvent, il a le talent de se renouveler, il est toujours amusant. Cependant il n'a pas l'air d'être établi ici, il a l'air d'un oiseau de passage comme moi, qui attend l'été pour s'envoler ver sons pays." Letter of Wilhelm de Sévery, in Charrière de Sévery 1911–12, 2:95.

6. British Library Add. MSS. 34887, fol. 10.

7. He would choose the same metaphor of motionlessness to express in the *Memoirs* his frustration during the years between his return from Italy and his father's death (*Memoirs*, 140). And there, too, motionlessness is coupled with solitariness in Gibbon's complaint. As Joan Hartman has pointed out to me, the sentence structure of the passage from the *Memoirs* goes out of its way to stress "alone."

8. Norton 1940, 60.

9. See Gibbon 1972, 315–17, 574–75.

10. Gibbon 1972, 332–35.

11. Keynes 1980, 77. Manuscript catalogue of Gibbon's library, Lausanne, September 26, 1785, in the Pierpont Morgan Library, New York.

12. In revising his first volume, Gibbon made such additions to existing notes, e.g., in chapter 7, in addition to a new note 10 (Bury 12), Gibbon added new material from an old source at the end of note 37 (i.e., first edition n. 36, Bury n. 49): "We are told that Maximin could drink in a day an amphora (or about seven gallons) of wine and eat thirty or forty pounds of meat. He could move a loaded waggon, break a horse's leg with his fist, crumble stones in his hand, and tear up small trees by the roots. See his Life in the Augustan History" (*DF* 1:201).

13. See Gibbon 1972, 570.

14. See Craddock 1987a, 232–33.

15. Gibbon 1972, 332.

16. Gibbon 1972, 333–35.

17. A "naked list" of "Authorities cited," not in his hand, in fact exists: British Library Add. MSS. 34882, fols. 107–37 (discussed above, p. 304).

18. In Auckland 1861, 1:449.

19. Norton, *Letters* 3:77 n. 1.

20. Norton, *Letters* 3:79 n. 1.

21. See Craddock 1982, 167–68.

22. Hayley 1823, 1:356–57.

23. Sarah Holroyd to Maria Josepha Holroyd, in Holroyd 1897, 17.

24. Auckland 1861, 1:458.

25. Holroyd 1897, 21.

26. "Lorsque M. Gibbon y était, on faisait toujours une lecture le soir, par exemple *Zaïre* de Voltaire. . . . Mylady a les même goûts que vous, chère

mère, elle aime la société de peu d'amis . . . ; elle n'aime pas le grand monde. M. Gibbon était tous les matins une ou deux heures à causer avec elle et elle sent bien sa privation." Charrière de Sévery 1911–12, 2:76.

27. "Sa figure et bien, elle est d'une grande douceur et bonté, remplie de talents, elle joue le clavecin fort bien, elle dessine parfaitement, quoique ayant passé l'hiver dernier à la campagne. . . . C'est, on peut dire, une jeune fille parfaitement élevée." Charrière de Sévery 1911–12, 2:76.

28. Je déteste et il est ridicule ici de danser en habit habillé." Charrière de Sévery 1911–12, 2:80.

29. Charrière de Sévery 1911–12, 2:81–97.

30. "Je fus présenté hier au roi, il m'adressa deux questions, comme il fait à tous les étrangers, je n'eus pas aussi peur que je l'aurais cru; il y avait beaucoup de monde, en hommes, car ce n'était qu'un *lever.*" Charrière de Sévery 1911–12, 2:82.

31. "Après l'opéra, M. Trevor me mena chez la duchesse de Cumberland où tout le monde va après l'opéra, je lui fus présenté et elle me parla pendant quelque temps; un nombre prodigieux de monde s'y recontrait, c'est la meilleure maison de Londres pour l'agrément, l'aisance, il y avait une banque de pharaon où les louis dansaient comme des sols. Lady Ashton pontait à 3, 4, 5 louis la mise, cela était drôle à voir. Les invités ne faisaient qu'entre et sortir, les voitures à la porte étaient innombrables." Charrière de Sévery 1911–12, 2:82.

32. "Je ne m'explique pas comment les gens de condition font leurs affaires ou plutôt ne les font pas; quant aux femmes je ne suis pas surpris qu'elles perdent leur beauté de bonne heure. Une femme va dans quatre ou cinq assemblées le même soir et ne fait qu'entrer et sortir, il y a dans une assemblée beaucoup plus de femmes que d'hommes, ceux-ci sont souvent à leurs clubs, j'ai vu l'autre jour six dames jouant au commerce toutes seules. Je ne conçois pas non plus comment les chevaux s'emploient autant et sont en même temps si bien en état. Trotter sur le pavé nuit et jour et attendre de cinq à six heures devant une porte n'est rien pour eux, semble-t-il." Charrière de Sévery 1911–12, 2:83.

33. "Il y a 50000 volumes et les appartements sont beaux. M. Gibbon me dit:—Vous croyiez que j'avais beaucoup de livres, n'est-ce pas? Mais vous voyez que le roi en a encore plus.—Oui, monsieur, lui dis-je, il en a plus que vous, mais est-ce qu'il les lit? Cela le fit rire." Charrière de Sévery 1911–12, 2:88.

34. *Letters* 3:103, with Norton's n. 1.

35. "Tous les tableaux . . . des différents maîtres, peints dans l'année, sont exposés dans une immense salle, au milieu de laquelle se trouve une table pour 150 personnes. Lord Sheffield, M. Gibbon, M. de Calonne, tous les différents ministres étrangers y dînèrent ainsi qu'une quantité d'Anglais de distinction. . . . La chambre, ou plutôt la salle, était tapissée de tableaux, tout cela formait un ensemble magistral et imposant." Charrière de Sévery 1911–12, 2:86–87.

36. *Annual Register* 30 (1788), part 2:198.

37. *European Magazine and London Review* 14 (July–October 1788):19–20, 100–103, 186–90, 253–55.

38. John Gillies, *Monthly Review* 78 (June 1788):468–72; 79 (July–September 1788):12–20, 121–33, 221–37. The last article is the one devoted to the organization of the history.

39. Holland 1908, 2:37.

40. Walpole 1937–80, 34:39–40.

41. *Monthly Review* 79 (September 1788):232.

42. *Critical Review* 66 (July 1788):35. The *Critical* reviewed the new volumes in issues of July, August, September, October, and December of 1788 and also in February 1789.

43. *Gentleman's Magazine* 58 (June 1788):475–78.

44. Such as "Quod Verum"; see *Gentleman's Magazine* 58 (July 1788): 599–600.

45. *Göttingische Gelehrte Anzeigen*, no. 205 (December 25, 1788), 2049–56.

46. *English Review* 12 (1789):241–54, 321–37, 407–24; 13 (1789):1–16, 85–93, 169–82, 241–56, 332–41, 401–14; 14 (1789):9–22.

47. According to a letter from Whitaker to Richard Polwhele (August 19, 1790), he was paid so much for his criticism of Gibbon that he thought of purchasing a silver cup with the money, on which he would have had inscribed, "This vase I owe to GIBBON's genius bold; / Extracted silver from his spurious gold." See Polwhele's *Traditions and Recollections* (London: John Nichols & Son, 1826), 1:249–50.

48. *Observations on the Three Last Volumes of the Roman History by Edward Gibbon, Esq.* (London: John Stockdale, 1788), 4–5, 63. For identification of author, see Norton 1940, 241.

49. Photograph in Norton 1940, 60.

50. Gibbon 1814, 2:418–19.

51. Such as his aging and wealthy aunt Hester Gibbon. She, at least, considered the gesture inadequate; a codicil in her will dated after his return to Switzerland reduced a legacy to him from £100 to £10. See *Letters* 3:117, with Norton's note.

52. "Hier, en parlant avec Gibbon, je voyais qu'il se réjouissait et que son visage s'animait par l'idée de revoir son *home*, car c'est ainsi qu'il l'appelle toujours. Quelqu'un lui demandait l'autre jour quelle était la population de Lausanne. 'Mais, dit-il de son ton ordinaire, il peut y avoir de neuf a dix mille âmes, mais ce qu'il y a d'essentiel c'est une société de deux cents personnes, aussi bonne que l'on puisse souhaiter.' " Charrière de Sévery 1911–12, 2:96.

Chapter 14 Alone in Paradise: Remaking a Life

1. Edmund Burke, speech of February 9, 1790, before his political rupture with Fox; quoted by G. Birkbeck Hill, in Edward Gibbon, *Memoirs of My Life and Writings* (London: Methuen, 1900), 331.

2. Murray 1896, 327n. The manuscripts are in the British Library: Add. MSS. 34874.

3. Rogers 1856, 78. According to Alex Russell (*Notes and Queries*, 10th

ser., 11 [January 16, 1909]:46), "Of the 2136 paragraphs in the seventy-one chapters of the 'Decline and Fall,' 1581 end with a genitive phrase in 'of', a percentage of over 73." It is perhaps relevant that there are three genitive phrases in Mr. Russell's sentence.

4. Murray 1896, 356.

5. Norton 1940, 218, quoting J. P. Brissot, *Mémoires, publiées avec étude critique et notes par Cl. Perroud* (Paris, n.d., 1:385: "Je vis . . . qu'il n'était pas plus fâché de transmettre à la postérité la mémoire de sa vie que les traits de son singulier visage."

6. *European Magazine and London Review* 13 (March 1788):150–51.

7. Murray 1896, 356; date of Langer gift from Charrière de Sévery 1911–12, 2:8.

8. Bonnard 1964, 290.

9. Murray 1896, 354–55.

10. Murray 1896, 354–55, 418–19.

11. Murray 1896, 365, 368, 10.

12. Murray 1896, 378–79, 381.

13. Murray 1896, 383, 388.

14. Keynes 1980, 173–74.

15. He speaks of his seven-year-old self "at the end of four and forty years" (Murray 1896, 113), i.e., near but not after his fifty-second birthday (May 8, 1789); he looks at his *Essai* (June 1761) "at the end of twenty-eighty years" (172); but he refers to his uncle Stanier Porten as "alive, and barely alive," something he could not have written after June 27, 1789, when he knew of Sir Stanier's death. I worked out the internal evidence for the dates of the drafts in my dissertation (Yale 1964–University Microfilms); G. A. Bonnard (1964) reaches the same conclusion and summarizes them in the introduction to his edition of Gibbon's *Memoirs*, xxiii.

16. Murray 1896, 104–5.

17. Murray 1896, 105.

18. Strachey 1928.

19. Stephen 1897, 54.

20. Murray 1896, 112–13.

21. D. M. Oliver's interesting characterization of the strategies of "the autobiography" seems to me most applicable to this draft. See "The Character of an Historian: Edward Gibbon," *English Literary History* 38 (1971): 254–73.

22. Murray 1896, 113–14.

23. Murray 1896, 114, 118, 124.

24. Spacks 1976, 100. The phrase she quotes is from Stephen Shapiro, "The Dark Continent of Literature: Autobiography," *Comparative Literature Studies* 5 (1969):426.

25. Murray 1896, 210.

26. Murray 1896, 140, 238.

27. Correspondence and accounts from this period are in the Archives Cantonales Vaudoises, Lausanne. Many items were published in Charrière de Sévery 1911–12.

28. Bonnard 1964, 209–10.

29. British Library Add. MSS. 34882. fols. 253–54. This outline begins

in 1777 and is headed "Sect. IV." ("Sect. V." would have continued the narrative to the point at which Gibbon decided to move to Lausanne—1783.) The unfinished section III of draft C ends with Gibbon's establishing himself in London to begin the writing of his history (1772). I therefore conclude that Gibbon intended to use the remainder of section III for the writing and publication of his first volume. Draft C is the only one that he subdivided into "sections."

30. Spacks 1976, 104–5. Robert Folkenflik's study of the composite memoir, "Child and Adult: Historical Perspective in Gibbon's Memoirs," *Studies in Burke and His Time* 15 (1973):31–43, provides insights particularly useful in considering this draft.

31. Spacks 1976, 105, 109, 107, 108.

32. Spacks 1976, 108; Bonnard, Preface to Gibbon's *Memoirs*, xxv; Murray 1896, 291.

33. Spacks 1976, 111, quoting Mowat 1936, 277.

34. Murray 1896, 398.

35. Spacks 1976, 113–14.

36. This is true even for the early sections of E—compare the illustration facing page 154, *Memoirs*.

37. Murray 1896, 307. The section is captioned "1773. January—1783. September."

38. Spacks 1976, 117–19.

39. Irma S. Lustig, "On the Conclusion to Robert Folkenflik's 'Child and Adult: Historical Perspective in Gibbon's *Memoirs*,' " *Studies in Burke and His Time* 16 (Winter 1974–75):149–52.

40. Barrett J. Mandell, "The Problem of Narration in Edward Gibbon's *Autobiography*," *Studies in Philology* 67 (1970):553.

41. Spacks 1976, 120.

42. On this subject, see Brownley 1982.

43. Murray 1896, 416–17.

44. Spacks 1976, 122.

Chapter 15 A Series of Fragments

1. Anecdote recorded by Friedrich von Matthisson (Powell 1938).

2. "Je n'aime pas la musique"—*Gibbon's Journey from Geneva to Rome: His Journal from 20 October to 2 April 1764*, ed. G. A. Bonnard (London: Thomas Nelson & Sons, 1961), 16.

3. British Library Add. MSS. 34715, fol. 15.

4. "Je conçois donc combien cette perte du siecle et de la posterité est plus affreuse pour Vous que pour personne. je la pleure donc encore sous ce rapporte vus les sentiments profonds et tendres que Vous m'avez inspirés. . . . tous les détails que Vous me faites, en si peu de mots et avec tant de force, me seront sans cesse presents. Songez que la vie des morts est dans la Memoire des vivants. . . ." Archives Cantonales Vaudoises, 1949 deposit. This letter is said to have been addressed to Levade, but the envelope has not survived.

5. "Ce Mr Gibbon . . . me manque horriblement, je n'aurois pas crû qu'il put me manque autant, j'y pense tous les jours." Letter of Wilhelm de Sévery to Gibbon, British Library Add. MSS. 34886, fol. 372.

6. "Music in Homer," in Gibbon 1972, 359.

7. "des exagerations de Rhetorique . . . à la place de la force et de la verité." "Je tremble du nom de ce Typhon . . . ce monstre a cent tetes, dont la poitrine chevelue est pressée sous les fondemens de l'Etna, et dont les membres s'etendent au loin jusqu'aux racines du Vésuve. L'Encelade de Virgile est froid et petit, et le *fama est* me semble indigne d'un Poete instruit par les Muses." MS. in the collection of Geoffrey L. Keynes (photographic reproduction in Keynes 1980, facing page 16).

8. I owe this observation to Margaret Craddock Huff.

9. "Marginalia in Herodotus," in Gibbon 1972, 367.

10. Gibbon 1972, 365–68.

11. Gibbon 1972, 366.

12. Gibbon 1972, 373.

13. Braudy 1980, 143.

14. Gibbon 1972, 368, 365.

15. Herodotus 4. 42; Gibbon 1972, 371–72.

16. Lord Sheffield's edition ignored the clearest internal indication of order, the existence of sections on Sataspes, Hanno, and Eudoxus, and another section beginning "Of the four circumnavigations of Africa, three have been disproved, and the overthrow of Sataspes, Hanno, and Eudoxus must disturb the easy and early triumph of Necchus." I preserved this order in Gibbon 1972, but I may too hastily have concluded that the section beginning with this sentence should have immediately followed the voyages of Sataspes, Hanno, and Eudoxus; instead, the section presenting the case for Necchus—the final one in my arrangement—might follow immediately the voyage of Eudoxus, and the "four circumnavigations" sentence might introduce the final section. With that arrangement, we would discover a completed essay, with a Gibbonian conclusion already drafted in the margins of his Herodotus: "In the sublime fiction of Camoens, the spirit of the Cape . . . applauds the Portuguese, the first of men who had explored their way round the southern promontory of Africa . . . I WILL TAKE THE GHOST'S WORD FOR A THOUSAND POUNDS!" My order is slightly anticlimactic; Lord Sheffield's is slightly chaotic. Gibbon 1972, 375–97; Gibbon 1814, 5:170–205.

17. *Antiquities of the House of Brunswick*, in Gibbon 1972, 418–19, 525–27.

18. "Man kann sich vorstellen, dass ich keinen Augenblick amstand, einem so verdienstvollen Schriftsteller meine geringen Dienste zuzusagen. . . . denn wirklich fieng er von einer dergleichen Reise zu sprechen, und endlich im Ernste darauf zu denken an. Unglücklicher Weiser nahm die Französische Revolution eine so fürchterliche Wendung, dass Deutschland sehr bald in solche verwickelt, und kurz darauf sein eignes Vaterland selbst von den heillosen Anarchisten insultirt wurde. . . . Jeden Posttag erwartete ich von ihm etwas zu hören, als die in allen Zeitungen . . . Nachricht von seinem Tode, dass alles alles eitel sei, mir . . . predigte." Langer 1794, 646–48.

19. Bernays 1885, 2:252.

20. Relationships among these drafts are discussed in Gibbon 1972, 594–97.

21. Gibbon 1972, 525, 419.

22. "Er entschied sich für das Letztere: den der biedere und joviale Scherer sprach . . . sein Gemüth mit ungleich wärmerer Beredsamkeit an, als der kalt höfische und nicht selten ein wenig despotische Gibbon." Powell 1938, 350n.

23. "Gibbon hat ganz den Ton and die Manieren eines abgeschliffenen Weltmannes; ist kalthöflich; spricht das Französische mit Eleganz and hat . . . fast die Aussprache eines Pariser-Gelehrten. Er hört sich mit Wohlgefallen und redet langsam, weil er jede Frase sorgfältig zu prüfen scheint, ehe er sie ausspricht. Mit immer gleicher Miene unterhält er sich von angenehmen und unangenehmen Dingen, von frohen und tragischen Begebenheiten, und sein Gesicht verzog sich, so lange wir beisammen waren, ungeachtet er veranlasst wurde, eine sehr drollige Geschichte zu erzählen, nicht ein eizigesmal zum Lächeln. In seinem Hause herrscht die strengste Pünktlichkeit und Ordnung. Seine Leute müssen ihre Geschäfte beinahe zur bestimmten Minute verrichten, oder sie laufen Gefahr verabschiedet zu werden. Er giebt ihnen aber auch selbst das Beispiel. Sein Tag is eingetheilt, wie der Tag des angelsächsischen Königs Alfred. Mit dem Klockenschlage geht er an die Arbeit, zu Tische und in Gesellschaft, und bleibt in keiner von ihm abhangenden Lebenslage eine Minute länger, als die festgetsezte Tagsordnung es getstattet." Powell 1938, 346–47.

24. Holroyd 1897, 239.

25. Reported, without documentation, in de Beer 1968, 117, 113.

26. Low 1929, 70.

27. Miscellaneous bills 1784–91, and the final accounting of Gibbon's estate by Wilhelm de Sévery. The cost per year of the Charity School was 120 livres Swiss—about £8. Gibbon Fonds, Archives Cantonales Vaudoises, Lausanne.

28. "In dieser bezaubernden Wohnung nun, deren Inneres er mit Geschmack und ausserster Reinlichkeit unterhielt, führte G. ein Leben, das für beneidenswerth hätte gelten können, wenn ungetrübtes Glück der Antheil des armen Erdenpilgers wäre!" Langer 1794, 634.

29. Norton, citing "Diary of Sir Charles Blagden," *Notes and Records of the Royal Society* 8 (1950):80 (*Letters* 3:237, n. 2).

30. British Library Add. MSS. 34882, fols. 108–59, 60–106, respectively.

31. "Supplement to the History," in Gibbon 1972, 342.

32. *Antiquities of the House of Brunswick*, in Gibbon 1972, 408.

33. British Library self mark C. 135. h. 3. See Jean Archibald and M. J. Jantta, "Recent Acquisitions," *British Library Journal* 7 (Spring 1981):94.

34. *Antiquities of the House of Brunswick*, in Gibbon 1972, 407.

35. "Supplement to the History," in Gibbon 1972, 342.

36. "1rst Period," in Gibbon 1972, 342–47.

37. The relations among these materials are discussed in Gibbon 1972, 587.

38. British Library Add. MSS. 34882, fols. 181–6; "Supplemental Notes," in Gibbon 1972, 348–51.

39. Gibbon 1972, 336–37, 351–52.

40. Gibbon 1972, 96–106.

41. The previously known annotations are in the British Library copy shelf-marked C 60 m l and were published in Gibbon 1972, 338–41. "On the Triumphs" was published in Gibbon 1814, 4:359–98, in English translation. It was written in French, at Rome, November 28–December 13, 1764. In the first edition of Gibbon's *Miscellaneous Works* (London: Strahan & Cadell, 1796), the essay was published in French: 2:361–404.

42. "So hatte man schon in dem Zimmer einen angenehmen Anblick; von den 3 grossen Fensterns und der Thüre konnte man über den Garten hin, die an dem Abhand des Berges liegende Stadt, dem Genser See, die Savoyische Gebirge und das Pays de Vaud grossentheils übersehen." Sophie von La Roche, *Erinnerungen aus meiner dritten Schweizerreise* (Offenbach: Ulrich Weiss und Carl Ludwig Brede, 1792), 136.

43. Holland 1908, 1:2.

44. Holland 1908, 2:39. The second sentence was not published; it is reported by Sir Gavin de Beer from the manuscript of her journal. De Beer 1968, 120.

45. Holroyd 1897, 62.

46. Holroyd 1897. 65.

47. Holroyd 1897, 73.

48. Holroyd 1897, 75.

49. Holroyd 1897, 63, 77.

50. Holroyd 1897, 82, 115.

51. Holroyd 1897, 84.

52. Holroyd 1897, 80.

53. Bagehot 1856, 41.

54. For Lord Sheffield's views, see Prothero 1896, 2:368–369.

55. Gibbon 1814, 1:328–29.

56. British Library Add. MSS. 34886, fol. 229.

57. British Library Add. MSS. 34886, fol. 277.

58. Gibbon 1814, 2:438.

59. Georgiana, duchess of Devonshire, letter of August 7, 1792, quoted in Iris Leveson Gower, *The Face without a Frown* (London: Frederick Muller, 1944), 184–85.

60. A. F. Artaud de Montor, "DEVONSHIRE (Elisabeth Hervey, duchesse d," in *Biographie universelle*, nouv. ed. (Paris: Michaud, n.d.), 10: 604–5.

61. See Low 1937, 307–9.

62. Gibbon adds that though this was only a game, Wilhelm can truly count on the duchess's friendship.

63. British Library Add. MSS. 34886, fol. 294.

Chapter 16 Mortal Friendships

1. "Mais la mesure de ce que je pouvois sentir hier etoit pleine; au dela je n'aurois pu le supporter. . . . mais après diner, j'attends la Consolation de vous voir, a l'heure que vous voudrez, les miennes sont indiférentes." British Library Add. MSS. 34886, fol. 342.

2. "Je ne suis pas dupe de cette force de santé dont M. Gibbon se vante." Letter to Wilhelm de Sévery, July 25, 1793, in Charrière de Sévery 1911–12, 2:31.

3. Gibbon's letters to the Sévery family, box 1, Archives Cantonales Vaudoises, Lausanne. "Me reposant avec une parfaite confiance sur la dite famille, dont je considere l'amitié comme un des premiers bonheurs da ma vie."

4. "dans l'Intimité et la douce Confiance. . . . "que je me rejouir de vous le rendre, lui dis-je; J'Espere, me dit-il en Souriant que vous n'en ferer point d'Usage. . . . plusiers importuns impossibles a renvoyer viennent nous tourments; qd ils furent sortis, Mr Gibbon qui etait resté le dernier, parlant de son départ qui devoit être le Lendemain Jeudi, trouva qu'il avoit bien peu de tems pr finir ses affaires pourquoi pas rester encore un jour dit-il il sera pr l'Amitie; . . . . il me sembloit qu'on m'avoit fait un don immense, en me donnant ce jour. Il se passa efectivement entre nous 4 en fut Consacré a l'Amitié; qui m'eut dit qu'il etoit le dernier! le Vendredi matin 10ᶜ Mai Il vint nous voir Encore un moment, son Carosse l'attedait devant notre porte, ses adieux me furent bien cruèls, Je le baisis, Quoiqu'embas, Il se retournoi d'un air touché et inquiet. je lui fis signe de la main, Sans savoir trop ce que je faisois, Il me regarda Encore avec Amitié et Continua son chemin vers la Voiture, je remontai precipiteusement a la fenetre, et je le vis achever de Monter en Carosse, et Wilhelm après lui." Gibbon Fonds, box 1, Archives Cantonales Vaudoises. See also Charrière de Sévery 1911–12, 2:28–29.

5. Summarized by J. E. Norton, n. 1, *Letters* 3:332, from the letters of Wilhelm de Sévery, Gibbon Fonds, Archives Cantonales Vaudoises.

6. First published in Gibbon's *Miscellaneous Works*, ed. John Lord Sheffield (London: Strahan & Cadell, 1796). Most recently published in de Beer 1968, 101.

7. Roche 1839, 470; Roche 1848, 404.

8. The Lord Elgin later associated with the Parthenon marbles.

9. Gibbon Fonds, Archives Cantonales Vaudoises.

10. Prothero 1986, 2:382.

11. A sad little passage in a letter dated October 12, 1794, hints at the strength of Maria's concealed grief: "To hear of the death of two Relations and one true friend, within four days makes one think, and think seriously; surely few people have lost more friends within a year and a half than I have. God preserve those that remain!" Holroyd 1897, 308.

12. Holroyd 1897, 225.

13. In discussing Holroyd's response to death, Marvin Stern (1984) publishes excerpts from a number of unpublished letters.

14. Holroyd 1897, 228.

15. Holroyd 1897, 234–35.

16. Holroyd 1897, 238–39.

17. Holroyd 1897, 242.

18. "Index Indicatorius," *Gentleman's Magazine* 63 (June 1793):536. Brydges had written under the pseudonym "N.S."

19. "Notes on Philpot," in Gibbon 1972, 360. The conjectural date (1789–91) I proposed there is clearly too early.

20. John Nichols, *Literary Anecdotes of the Eighteenth Century* (London: Nichols, Son, & Bentley, 1814), 8:557.

21. J. E. Norton, n. 4, *Letters* 3:340.

22. Gibbon 1814, 2:488–90. Gibbon's letters to Vincent are lost.

23. "An Address &c," in Gibbon 1972, 541.

24. Gibbon 1814, 3:592.

25. Gibbon 1814, 2:490–91.

26. Gibbon 1814, 3:579.

27. Gibbon 1814, 2:494.

28. H. R. Trevor-Roper, "Historiography 1: The Other Gibbon," *American Scholar* 46 (1976):94–103.

29. "Address," in Gibbon 1972, 534.

30. "Address," in Gibbon 1972, 534–35.

31. "Il est le seul [pays] où à la fois l'on ose penser et l'on sache vivre. Que vous manque t il [?] la liberté: et privée d'elle, tout vous manque" (Gibbon 1952, 124). The most probable date for this unfinished piece is 1763–64—see Louis Junod's introduction in Gibbon 1952, 111–21, and Craddock 1982, 187, 342.

32. "Address," in Gibbon 1972, 535–36.

33. On Gibbon's footnotes, see Michael Bernays, "Zur Lehre von den Citaten und Noten," in *Schriften zur Kritik und Litteraturgeschichte*, ed. Georg Witkowski (Berlin: B. Behr's Verlag, 1899), 4:302–22; Glen W. Bowersock, "The Art of the Footnote," *American Scholar* 53 (Winter 1983–84):54–62; and especially Garrison 1978.

34. "Address," in Gibbon 1972, 539, 545.

35. Reported by Charles Butler, in *Reminiscences of Charles Butler* (London: John Murray, 1817), 2:16–26. It is not clear when this instruction occurred, except that it was undoubtedly later than Gibbon's intensive self-instruction in Greek, during his militia years. When Gibbon first studied the language, with Pavillard in Switzerland, he had presumably been taught to pronounce Greek in the Continental fashion.

36. Leopold von Ranke, *Weltgeschichte* (Leipzig, 1883) 4, pt. 1:212, n. 1. Quoted in Karl J. Neumann, *Entwicklung und Aufgaben der Alten Geschichte* (Strassburg: J. H. Ed. Heitz, 1910), 90–99.

37. "Annotations in Harwood," in Gibbon 1972, 546–48, 550.

38. Holroyd 1897, 239, 252, 242, 273.

39. Gibbon 1814, 1:405–6.

40. Edmond Malone, letter to the earl of Charlemont, February 20, 1794, *Historical Manuscripts Commission*, 13th Report, 231.

41. O'Malley 1943, 206–7.

42. Letter of Timothée Francillon, a Swiss friend of Gibbon's who visited Sheffield Place in December 1793, to David Levade. Jean Charles Biaudet, "L'Hydrocèle de Gibbon," *Revue historique vaudoise* 56 (1948):252–61. Writer identified by Biaudet with the help of Gavin de Beer, "Encore l'hydrocèle de Gibbon," *Revue historique vaudoise* 57 (1949):11–18. Letter cited hereafter as Francillon.

43. Gibbon 1814, 1:414–15.

44. "Cette incomodité existe depuis 31 aneés, et est venue a la suite d'une *lues veneria.*" Francillon.

45. Charrière de Sévery 1911–12, 2:5.

46. De Beer 1949, 79.

47. "depuis fort longtems il ne servît de son *pinus* que pour uriner." Francillon.

48. "If [Gibbon's] history were anonymous, I should guess that these disgraceful obscenities were written by some debauchee, who . . . having survived the practice of lust, still indulged himself in the luxury of speculation." Richard Porson, *Letters to Mr Archdeacon Travis* (London: T. & J. Egerton, 1790), xxx–xxxi.

49. Glenbervie 1910, 58, 80, 66.

50. O'Malley 1943, 207. The actual date was the fourteenth, a Thursday, according to Lord Sheffield, Gibbon 1814 1:415, and Glenbervie 1910, 65.

51. "Il leur a demande pourquoi un home gros, resemblait a un Borough de Cornwailles Il leur a répondu, because he never sees his member." Francillon.

52. O'Malley 1943, 207–8.

53. Gibbon 1814,1:415.

54. Gibbon 1814, 1:418.

55. Gibbon 1814, 1:419.

56. Gibbon 1814, 1:419.

57. James Currie, *Memoirs of the Life, Writings, and Correspondence,* ed. W. W. Currie (London: Longman, Rees, Orme, Brown & Green, 1831), 1:383–84. An account of this dialogue between "H"—Serena Holroyd—and Gibbon is in the British Library: Add. MSS. 34882, fols. 49–50. It is published as Appendix C in Carnochan 1987, 185–86.

58. Holroyd 1897, 257, 260.

59. O'Malley 1943, 208.

60. Gibbon 1814, 1:421.

61. Gibbon 1814, 1:422.

62. "Il a rompu lui-même du pain qu'il a mêlé ensemble, et le premier morceau qu'il a parté à sa bouche lui a fait faire un effort terrible, ce qui a continué a chacun . . . que malgré cela il est parvenu à tout manger. Il les prenait sur son assiette sans les regarder et en me demandant toujours s'il n'avait pas encore fini. Il a bu trois petits verres de vin de Madère qui lui ont fait tous trois plaisir. Après avoir fini, il me dit qu'il était très mal sur son fauteuil, que quand j'aurais dîne je le changerais, mais c'est ce que j'ai commencé par faire. . . . Il devait voir une personne à 8 heures et il m'avait ordonné de lui dire son état et qu'il ne pourrait la voir que le lendemain." Dussaut's letter, written the day after Gibbon's death though misdated January 18. Charrière de Sévery 1911–12, 2:38.

63. O'Malley 1943, 208.

64. "Mon pauvre Dussaut, vous avez un service bien pénible avec moi, je crains que vous ne deveniez aussi malade." Dussaut, in Charrière de Sévery 1911–12, 2:39.

65. Gibbon 1814, 1:423—Lord Sheffield's account, derived from Dussaut.

66. O'Malley 1943, 208.

67. "Dussaut, vous n'avez plus de maître!" "ô mon cher maître" "Dussaut vous me laissez." Dussaut, in Charrière de Sévery 1911–12, 2:39.

68. Holroyd 1897, 264.

69. Holroyd 1897, 266.

70. Idem.

71. Lady Elizabeth Foster, journal, quoted in Dorothy M. Stuart, *Dearest Bess* (London: Methuen, 1955), 64.

72. William Roberts, quoting a diary entry of January 19, 1794, *Memoirs of the Life and Correspondence of Mrs. Hannah More* (New York: Harper & Brothers, 1835), 1:450. Whitaker 1794.

73. "ô mon cher Ange! O mon Ami, Je vous ai perdus tout deux dans la meme année; qui m'eut dit que cette moitie de moi même et cet ami, avec qui je passois ma vie, me seroient ravis tous deux dans un si court Espace de tems? Je ne puis le Comprendre mon sort me paroit un Songe affreux, dont je me reveillerai, mais hèlas ce réveil sera la mort." Gibbon Fonds and Charrière de Sévery 1911–12, 2:29.

74. Holroyd 1897, 267.

Chapter 17 Miscellaneous Works and Immortal History

1. Isabelle de Polier, a Swiss friend to whom Gibbon left fifty guineas in his will, provided "un homage à sa memoire" in "le journal littéraire de lausanne, dont sur le plan que m'en donna Mr Gibbon, j'ai depuis 4 ans entrepris," as she wrote to Lord Sheffield, March 7, 1796 (East Sussex Record Office, Sheffield Park papers, lot 270). The obituary in *Journal Littéraire de Lausanne*, no. 1, 184–87; no. 2, 44–47, is described and quoted by Ernest Giddey, *L'Angleterre dans la vie intellectuele de la Suisse romande au XVIIIe siècle*, in *Bibliothèque historique vaudoise*, no. 51 (1974), 205–6.

2. "Obituary of considerable Persons; with Biographical Anecdotes," *Gentleman's Magazine* 64 (January 1794):94.

3. Though versions based on it may now incorporate some material deleted from his text, e.g., M. M. Reese's edition of 1970 (London: Routledge & Kegan Paul).

4. Gibbon 1814, 1:424.

5. Charrière de Sévery 1911–12, 2:39.

6. Holroyd 1897, 267.

7. Holroyd 1897, 272.

8. Barnard 1976, 399.

9. *Historical Manuscripts Commissions*, 13th Report, 231.

10. For example, L.M.S. in the *Analytical Review* 24 (August 1796) 4:113–223, James Mackintosh in the *Monthly Review*, n.s., 20 (August 1796):437–51, and the French translator of the *Memoirs* (Paris: Décade philosophique, 1797), 1:i–xxx.

11. Gibbon 1814, 1:277.

12. Norton 1940, 182–95.

13. Holroyd 1897, 257.

14. Holroyd 1897, 253.

15. Gibbon 1814, 1:277–78.

16. Holroyd 1897, 293.

17. Hayley 1823, 1:452.

18. Hayley 1823, letter of September 7, 1794, 1:461–62.

19. Holroyd 1897, 286.

20. *Gentlemen's Magazine* 75 (1805):799.

21. Hayley 1823, 1:454.

22. "J'aimais Gibbon de tout mon coeur et il était impossible de ne pas l'aimer beaucoup, quand on était parvenu à obtenir son amitié. Il n'y avait pas de semaines où nous ne calculions, ma femme et moi, le temps où il nous avait promis de nous venir demander à diner ici. . . . pauvre Gibbon, pourquoi pas plutôt ces milliers de scélérats qui dévastent la terre." Charrière de Sévery 1911–12, 2:69–70.

23. "L'on ma laissé ignorer jusqu'à ce moment, madame, l'affreuse perte que nous venons de faire; dans la douleur profonde où elle me plonge, mon premier soin, comme mon premier devoir, est de mêler mes larmes aux vôtres; les regrets éternels que je donnerai à la mémoire de M. Gibbon seront toujours accompagnés du souvenir de tout le bonheur que vous avez répandu sur sa vie; . . . hélas, pourquoi vous a-t-il quittée? pourquoi nous a-t-il quittés? Je n'ai pas à me reprocher d'avoir négligé aucuns des moyens de le faire renoncer à cet horrible voyage, mais il n'est plus, et rien ne pourra le remplacer pour nous; si mon état me l'avait permis, j'aurais été recueillir auprès de vous, madame, les seules consolations dont je me sens susceptible et je sais mauvais gré à M. Necker, qui pour retarder mon affliction de quelques instants, m'a privé du seul moyen de la rendre moins amère." Charrière de Sévery 1911–12, 2:70–71.

24. Holroyd 1897, 288.

25. Hayley 1823, 1:462–63.

26. Sheffield papers, Beinecke Library, Yale University.

27. See Marvin Stern 1984, 32–34, for an analysis of the various drafts of this paragraph in terms of Sheffield's state of mind.

28. Holroyd 1897, 278.

29. Norton 1940, 188–90.

30. Norton 1940, 195.

31. For example, Mary Berry, *Extracts of the Journal and Correspondence from the Year 1783 to 1852,* ed. Lady Theresa Lewis (London: Longmans, Green, 1865), 2:6. She found Lord Sheffield too much the editor and too little the "delicate friend."

32. Gregory L. Way, letter to Lord Sheffield of August 28, 1796, in Gibbon 1814, 2:501.

33. Quoted in Glenbervie 1928, 1:94.

34. "The Miscellaneous Works of Edward Gibbon . . . a new Edition," *European Magazine and London Review* 68 (August 1815):151.

35. Mark Pattison, *Memoirs* (London: Macmillan, 1885), 129–30.

36. Read 1987, 2:285.

37. "O.," *Monthly Magazine and American Review* 1 (April 1799):93.

38. Thomas D. Whitaker, *Quarterly Review* 12 (January 1815):370, 390.

39. Jane Carlile, preface, *An Inquiry into the Causes of the Progress and Establishment of the Christian Religion* (London: Jane Carlile, 1820).

40. For a recent survey, see Craddock 1987a, xvii–xx.

41. For example, Ritter 1913.

42. John Henry Newman, *Essay on the Development of Christian Doctrine* (London: J. Toovey, 1845), 5.

43. William M. Collins, *The Student's Companion to Gibbon* (Melbourne: Hawthorn Press, 1957): Paul Turnbull, "The 'supposed Infidelity' of Edward Gibbon," *Historical Journal* (March 1982):23-41.

44. Craddock 1987b.

45. *Esprit des journaux* [19], no. 1:1-32.

46. "Gibbon, moins fort, moins profond, moins élevé que Montesquieu. . . . du sujet dont celui-ci ont indiqué la richesse." "à l'immensité de ses recherches, à la varieté de ses connoissances, à l'étendue de ses lumières, et surtout à cette justesse vraiment philosophique de son esprit, qui juge le passé comme il jugerait le present." Guizot 1828, 1:3, 8.

47. The following paragraph is based on the bibliography by H. M. Beatty (1914), 7:348-64, as well as on Norton 1940, 114-18.

48. "Memoir of the Author," in David Dalrymple, *An Inquiry into the Secondary Causes which Mr Gibbon has assigned for the rapid growth of Christianity,* 2d ed. (Edinburgh: J. Ritchie for A. Johnstone, 1808).

49. William Youngman, "Memoir of the Author," in *The History of the Decline and Fall of the Roman Empire* (London: J. O. Robertson; Liverpool: A. C. Baynes, 1830; stereotyped by J. R. and C. Childs), xiii.

50. Milman 1833, 273-303.

51. F. W. J. Schelling, "Zehnte Verlesung. Ueber das Studium der Historie und der Jurisprudenz," Vorlesungen über die Methode des akademischen Studiums, *Schriften von 1801-1804, Ausgewählte Werke* (Darmstad: Wissenschaftliche Buchgesellschaft, 1968), 8:546. English translation by E. S. Morgan, *On University Studies* (Athens, Ohio: Ohio University Press), 109.

52. B. G. Niebuhr, *Römische Geschichte*, trans. J. C. Hare and C. Thirwall (Philadelphia, 1844).

53. William H. Prescott, "Irving's Conquest of Granada," *North American Review* (October 1828):302-3; W. B. O. Peabody, "Men of Letters and Science, Art. II," *North American Review* 64 (January 1847):77-87.

54. Edward Everett, "Bancroft's *History of the United States,*" *North American Review* 40 (January 1835):115.

55. Shreve 1835, 128-29.

56. Gibbon's reputation in America is reviewed briefly by Henry F. May, *The Enlightenment in America* (New York: Oxford University Press, 1976), 114, 118-19, and more fully by Meyer Reinhold in a forthcoming article. I am indebted to Professor Reinhold for calling my attention to several American commentators on Gibbon.

57. Momigliano 1976, 132.

58. "Absolutamente la mas instructiva y provechosa de toda la literature antigua y moderna. . . . el raudal siempre grandioso de la narracion, los vivos retratos de sus persona jes, la filosofia profunda, las contraposiciones poèticas de sus cuadros sublimes, y por fin la elocuencia de sus clàusulas: todo la constituye magnìfica, escelente, incomparable." José Mor de Feuntes, "Prologo del Traductor," *Historia de la decadencia y ruina del imperio romano* (Barcelona: Don Antonio Bergnes, 1842), 6.

59. David Ludwig Wachler, "Geschichte der historischen Wissenschaft,"

Geschichte der Künste und Wissenschaften seit der Wiederherstellung derselben bis an das Ende des achtzehnten Jahrhunderts, pt. 5 (Göttingen: Johann Friedrich Römer, 1820), 2:640–43. "Das Gefühl, welches Gibbon, als er unter den Ruinen des Capitols sitzend, Barfüsser mönche im Tempel des Jupiter die Vesper singen hörte, zu dem Entschluss, seine grosse Composition zu unternehem, begeisterte, tönte durch das ganze Werk hindurch." Johann Wilhelm Loebell, "Ueber die Epochen der Geschichtschreibung und ihr Verhältniss zur Poesie: Eine Skizze," *Historisches Taschenbuch*, ed. Friedrich von Raumer, [12] (1841), n.s., 2:360–65.

60. "einer Arbeit von solcher Dimensio und solcher Grösse der Conception, dass in der gesammten Geschichte der Geschichtschreibung keine zweite hierin mit ihr verglichen werden kann. . . . Ein so tiefer Weltverstand spricht aus seinem Werke, dass, wie sich auch Quellen und kritisches Studium mehren mögen, sie Darstellungen . . . nie verdeutlichen werden." Dilthey 1866, 141, 149.

61. *The Times* (London), November 16, 1894, 8.

62. William Smyth, *Lectures on Modern History from the Irruption of the Northern Nations to the Close of the American Revolution* (London: William Pickering; Cambridge: J. & J.J. Deighton, 1840), 163.

63. William Smith, introduction, *The Student's Gibbon* (London: John Murray, 1856), iii–v.

64. To the indignation of Ruskin, who expunged it from the list because "none but the malignant and the weak study the Decline and Fall either of State or organism" and because "Gibbon's is the worst English that was ever written by an educated Englishman." "The Choice of Books," *Pall Mall Gazette* 43 (February 15, 1886):1–2.

65. Charles Francis Adams, "The Sifted Grain and the Grain Sifters," *American Historical Review* 6 (January 1901):227.

66. William Butler Yeats, letter of January 13, 1924, in *The Letters of William Butler Yeats*, ed. Allen Wade (New York: Macmillan), 701–2.

67. Basil Williams, *Cecil Rhodes*, Makers of the Nineteenth Century Series (New York: Henry Holt, 1921), 223.

68. Helen Hoover Santmyer, *And Ladies of the Club* (New York: Putnam, 1982), 626.

69. Winston S. Churchill, "Education at Bangalore," in *A Roving Commission: My Early Life* (New York: Scribner, 1930; paperback reprint 1958 entitled *My Early Life: A Roving Commission*), 111.

70. "bleibt . . . der alte Gibbon des achzehnten Jahrhunderts unentbehrlicht," Bernays 1885, 2:242.

71. Fueter 1911.

72. It was refuted in detail by W. J. G. Ringeling, *Pragmatismus in Edward Gibbon's Geschichte von Verfall und Untergang des römischen Reiches* (Schöneberg: Lehmann & Bernhard, 1915).

73. Momigliano 1954, speech given in London, 1952.

74. G. McN. Rushforth, "Reviews of Books," *English Historical Review* 16 (January 1901):125–26.

75. Henry Morse Stephens, "Gibbon," *Book Reviews* 5 (February 1898):260–65.

76. On this point, see Brown 1976.

77. Black 1926, 165; Dawson 1934; Curtis 1949; Cochrane 1942–43.

78. Falco 1933, 191, 299.

79. Ritter 1913, 126; Meinecke 1936.

80. Walter Rehm, *Der Untergang Roms im abendlandischen Denken* (Leipzig: Dieterich, 1930), 120–41; Santo Mazzarino, *La fine del mondo antico* (Rome: Aldo Garzanti Editore, 1959), trans. George Holmes (New York: Knopf, 1966), 92, 98 114–17; Bryce Lyon, *The Origins of the Middle Ages: Pirenne's Challenge to Gibbon* (New York: Norton, 1972); Alexander Demandt, *Der Fall Roms* (Munich: C. H. Beck, 1984), 132–34; Stephen Runciman, "Gibbon and Byzantium," *Dædalus* 105 (Summer 1976), 103–10; Evans 1973.

81. Giarrizzo 1954; Marrou, 1961; White 1966; Scheibe 1968; Christ 1972; Bowersock, Clive, and Graubard 1976; Ducrey 1977; Gossman 1981; Burrow 1985.

82. Gibbon 1814, 1:425.

Works Frequently Cited

Other works, cited only once, appear in the notes.

Arblay, Fanny Burney d'. 1823. *Memoirs of Dr. Burney.* Philadelphia: Key & Riddle; Boston: Allen & Ticknor.

———. 1904. *The Diary and Letters of Madame d'Arblay.* Edited by Austin Dobson. London: Macmillan.

Archibald, Jean, and M. J. Janetta. 1981. "Recent Acquisitions." *British Library Journal* 7 (Spring):94.

Auckland, William Eden, Lord. 1861. *Journal and Correspondence.* London: Richard Bentley.

Bagehot, Walter. 1856. "Edward Gibbon." *The National Review* 2 (January):1–42.

Baridon, Michel. 1971. "Un lettre inédite d'Edward Gibbon à J. B. A. Suard," *Etudes Anglaises* 24:79–87.

———. 1977a. "Le Style d'une pensée: Politique et esthetique dans le *Decline and Fall.*" In *Gibbon et Rome à la lumière de l'historiographie moderne.* Geneva: Librarie Droz.

———. 1977b. *Edward Gibbon et le mythe de Rome.* Paris: Editors Honoré Champion.

Barnard, Thomas. 1976. Letter to James Boswell, March 25, 1794. In *The Correspondence of James Boswell with Certain Members of the Club.* Edited by Charles N. Fifer. The Yale edition of the Private Papers of James Boswell, Research Edition, Correspondence, 3:399–400. New York and Toronto: McGraw-Hill; London: William Heinemann.

Beatty, H. M. 1974. "Bibliography of Gibbon's History, Minor and Miscellaneous Works, and Letters; and of the controversial Replies to the History." In *The History of the Decline and Fall of the Roman Empire*, edited by J. B. Bury, 7:348–64. 2d ed. London: Methuen, 1914; AMS reprint, 1974.

Bernays, Jacob. 1885. "Edward Gibbon's Geschichtswerk: Ein Versuch zu einer Wurdigung." In *Gesammelte Abhandlungen*, edited by H. Usener, 2:206–54. Berlin: Wilhelm Herz.

Black, J. B. 1926. "Gibbon." In *The Art of History: A Study of Four Great Historians of the 18th Century*, 143–83. London: Methuen.

Bond, Harold L. 1960. *The Literary Art of Edward Gibbon*. Oxford: Clarendon Press.

Bonnard, Georges A. 1964. "Gibbon at Work on His Memoirs." *English Studies* 45 (Supplement): 270–312.

Boswell, James. 1924. *The Letters of James Boswell*. Edited by C. B. Tinker. Oxford: Clarendon Press.

———. 1953. *The Life of Samuel Johnson*. London: Oxford University Press.

Bowersock, G. W., John Clive, and S. R. Graubard, eds. 1976. *Edward Gibbon and the Decline and Fall of the Roman Empire*. Special issue, *Dædalus* (Summer). Reprint. Cambridge, Mass.: Harvard University Press, 1977. Italian translation, Rome: Istituto della Enciclopedia italiana, 1980.

Braudel, Fernand. 1985. *The Structures of Everyday Life: Civilization and Capitalism, 15th–18th Century*. Translated by Miriam Kochan, revised by Siân Reynolds. Perennial Library ed. New York: Harper & Row.

Braudy, Leo B. 1970. *Narrative Form in History and Literature*. Princeton: Princeton University Press.

———. 1980. "Edward Gibbon and the 'Privilege of Fiction.'" *Prose Studies* 3:138–51.

Brown, Peter. 1976. "Gibbon's Views on Culture and Society in the Fifth and Sixth Centuries." *Dædalus* 105 (Summer):73–88.

Brownley, Martine W. 1976. "Gibbon: The Formation of Mind and Character." *Dædalus* 105 (Summer): 13–25.

———. 1978. "Gibbon's Narrative Attitudes and Values in the *Decline and Fall*." *Research Studies* 46 (September):172–82.

———. 1982. "Gibbon's *Memoirs:* The Legacy of the Historian." *Studies on Voltaire and the Eighteenth Century* 201:209–20.

Burrow, J. W. 1985. *Gibbon*. Past Masters Series. Oxford: Oxford University Press.

Carnochan, W. B. 1984. "Gibbon's Silences." In *Johnson and His Age*, edited by James Engell. Harvard English Studies 12. Cambridge, Mass.: Harvard University Press.

———. 1987. *Gibbon's Solitude: The Inward World of the Historian*. Stanford, Calif.: Stanford University Press.

Charrière de Sévery, M. et Mme. William de. 1911–12. *La Vie de société dans le Pays de Vaud à la fin du dix-huitième siècle*. 2 vols. Lausanne: Georges Bridel; Paris: Librairie Fischbacher.

Christ, Karl. 1972. *Von Gibbon zu Rostovtzeff*. Darmstad: Wissenschaftliche Buchgeselleschaft.

Christie, Ian R. 1958. *The End of North's Ministry 1780-1782*. London: Macmillan; New York: St. Martin's Press.

Clarke, J. C. D. 1985. *English Society 1688-1832*. Cambridge: Cambridge University Press.

Cochrane, C. N. 1942–43. "The Mind of Edward Gibbon." *University of Toronto Quarterly* 12 (October 1942):1–17, (January 1943):146–66.

Craddock, Patricia B. 1966. "Edward Gibbon: The Man in His Letters." In *The Familiar Letter in the Eighteenth Century,* edited by H. Anderson, P. Daghlian, and I. Ehrenpreis, 224–43. Lawrence: University of Kansas Press.

———. 1968. "Gibbon's Revision of the *Decline and Fall.*" *Studies in Bibliography* 21:191–204.

———. 1982. *Young Edward Gibbon.* Baltimore: Johns Hopkins University Press.

———. 1984. "Edward Gibbon and the 'Ruins of the Capitol.'" In *Roman Images,* edited by A. Patterson, 63–82. English Institute Essays, n.s., no. 8. Baltimore: Johns Hopkins University Press.

———. 1987a. *Edward Gibbon: A Reference Guide* Boston: G. K. Hall.

———. 1987b. "'Immortal Affectation': Responses to Gibbon's Style." *Age of Johnson* 1:327–46.

———. 1988. "Historical Discovery and Literary Invention in Gibbon's *Decline and Fall.*" *Modern Philology* 85 (May):569–87.

Curtis, L. P. 1949. "Gibbon's 'Paradise Lost.'" In *The Age of Johnson: Essays Presented to Chauncey B. Tinker,* edited by F. W. Hilles, 73–90. New Haven: Yale University Press.

Dawson, Christopher. 1934. "Edward Gibbon." *Proceedings of the British Academy* 20:159–80.

De Beer, Gavin R. 1949. "The Malady of Gibbon FRS." *Notes and Records of the Royal Society* 7:71–80.

———. 1968. *Gibbon and His World.* New York: Viking Press.

Demandt, Alexander. 1984. *Der Fall Roms.* Munich: C. H. Beck.

Dickinson, H. T. 1978. "The Politics of Edward Gibbon." *Literature and History,* no. 8 (Autumn):175–96.

Dilthey, Wilhelm [pseud. W. Hoffner] 1866. "Edward Gibbon." *Westermanns Illustrierte Deutsche Monatshefte* 221:135–49.

Ducrey, Pierre, ed. 1977. *Gibbon et Rome à la lumière de l'historiographie moderne.* Geneva: Librairie Droz.

Du Deffand, Mme. de. 1912. *Lettres de la Marquise du Deffand à Horace Walpole.* Edited by Mrs. Paget Toynbee. London: Methuen.

Evans, Allen. 1973. "The Shadow of Edward Gibbon." In *City and Society in the Eighteenth Century,* edited by Paul Fritz and David Williams, 247–57. Toronto: Hakkert.

Falco, Giorgio. 1933. *La polemica sul medio evo.* Turin: Biblioteca della Societa storica subalpina, no. 143. Reprint, edited by Fulvio Tessito, 191–319. Naples: Guida editori, 1974.

Fueter, Eduard. 1911. *Geschichte der neueren Historiographie.* Munich and Berlin: R. Oldenburg.

Fulgum, Per. 1953. *Edward Gibbon: His View of Life and Conception of History.* Oxford: Blackwell; Oslo: Akademisk Forlag.

Garat, Dominique Joseph. 1821. *Mémoires historiques sur le XVIIIͤ siècle, et de M. Suard.* Paris: A. Belin.

Garrison, James D. 1977. "Gibbon and the 'Treacherous Language of Panegyrics.'" *Eighteenth-Century Studies* 11 (Fall):40–62.

———. 1978. "Lively and Laborious: Characterization in Gibbon's Metahistory." *Modern Philology* 76 (November): 163–78.

Ghosh, P. R. 1984. "Gibbon's Dark Ages: Some Remarks on the Genesis of the *Decline and Fall*." *Journal of Roman Studies* 73:1–23.

Giarrizzo, Giuseppe. 1954. *Edward Gibbon e la cultura europea*. Naples: Istiuto italiano per gli studi storici.

Gibbon, Edward. 1776–88. *The History of the Decline and Fall of the Roman Empire*. 6 vols. London: Strahan & Cadell.

———. 1796. *Miscellaneous Works of Edward Gibbon*. Edited by John, Lord Sheffield. 2 vols. London: Cadell & Davies.

———. 1814. *The Miscellaneous Works of Edward Gibbon*. Edited by John, Lord Sheffield. 5 vols. London: John Murray.

———. 1909–14. *The History of the Decline and Fall of the Roman Empire*. Edited by J. B. Bury. 7 vols. 2d ed. London: Methuen; New York: Macmillan. Reprint. New York: AMS, 1974.

———. 1952. *Miscellanea Gibboniana*. Edited by G. R. de Beer, Louis Junod, and G. A. Bonnard. Lausanne: F. Rouge.

———. 1956. *The Letters of Edward Gibbon*. Edited by J. E. Norton. 3 vols. London: Cassell.

———. 1966. *Memoirs of My Life*. Edited by G. A. Bonnard. London: Thomas Nelson.

———. 1972. *The English Essays of Edward Gibbon*. Edited by P. B. Craddock. Oxford: Clarendon Press.

Glenbervie, Sylvester Douglas, Lord. 1910. *The Glenbervie Journals*. Edited by Walter Sichel. London: Constable.

———. 1928. *The Diaries*. Edited by Francis Bickley. London: Constable; New York: Houghton Mifflin.

Gossman, Lionel. 1981. *The Empire Unpossess'd*. Cambridge: Cambridge University Press.

Grewal, J. S. "Edward Gibbon on Islamic Civilization." In *Medieval India: History and Historians*, 12–23. Amritsar: Guru Nanak University.

Guizot, F. P. G. A., ed. and trans. 1828. *Histoire de la décadence et de la chute de l'Empire romain*. Paris: Ledentu.

Hayley, William. 1823. *Memoirs of the Life and Writings of William Hayley . . . written by Himself*. Edited by John Johnson. London: Henry Colburn.

Heal, Ambrose. 1949. "The Personal and Household Bills of Edward Gibbon." *Notes and Queries* 194 (October 29):474–76.

Hill, G. B., ed. 1900. *The Life of Edward Gibbon . . . by Himself*. London: Methuen.

Holland, Elizabeth, Lady [formerly Lady Webster]. 1908. *The Journal* (1791–1811). Edited by the earl of Ilchester. London: Longmans, Green.

Holroyd, Maria Josepha. 1897. *The Girlhood of Maria Josepha Holroyd*. Edited by J. H. Adeane. London and New York: Longmans, Green.

Hume, David. 1932. *The Letters of David Hume*. Edited by J. Y. T. Greig. Oxford: Clarendon Press.

Hutchinson, Thomas. 1883. *Diary and Letters*. Edited by Peter Orlando Hutchinson. London: Sampson Low, Marston, Searle & Rivington.

Jordan, David P. 1969. "Gibbon's 'Age of Constantine' and the Fall of Rome." *History and Theory* 8:71–96.

———. 1971. *Gibbon and His Roman Empire*. Urbana: University of Illinois Press.

————. 1976. "Edward Gibbon: The Historian of the Roman Empire." *Dædalus* 105 (Summer):1-12.

Joyce, Michael. 1953. *Edward Gibbon*. London: Longmans, Green.

Keynes, Geoffrey L. 1980. *The Library of Edward Gibbon*. Rev. ed. Godalming, Surrey: St. Paul's Bibliographies.

Köhler, Pierre. 1916. *Madame de Staël et le Suisse*. Lausanne and Paris: Librairie Payot.

Langer, Ernst. 1794. "Einige Nachrichten von Gibbon; mitgetheilt von einem Freunde desselben." *Neues göttingisches historisches Magazin* 3, pt. 4:625–48.

Low, D. M., ed. 1929. *Gibbon's Journal to January 28, 1763*. London: Chatto & Windus.

————. 1937. *Edward Gibbon 1737-94*. London: Chatto & Windus.

————. 1960. "Edward Gibbon and the Johnsonian Circle," *New Rambler*, 2–13.

Lutnick, Solomon. 1968–69. "Edward Gibbon and the Decline of the First British Empire: The Historian as Politician." *Studies in Burke and His Time* 10 (Winter):1099–1120.

McCloy, Shelby T. 1936. *Gibbon's Antagonism to Christianity*. Chapel Hill: University of North Carolina Press. Reprinted in the Burt Franklin Research & Source Work Series, no. 144.

Marks, J. W. 1975. "The Narrative Structure of Edward Gibbon's *The History of the Decline and Fall of the Roman Empire*." Ph.D. diss., Georgia State University.

Marrou, H. I. 1961. "*L'Histoire et ses méthodes*." In *Encyclopédie de la Pléiade*, 11:26–28, 15:5–6, 1539. Paris: Librairie Gallimard.

Meinecke, Friedrich. 1936. *Die Entstehung des Historism*. Translated by J. E. Anderson as "Enlightenment Historiography in England, II: Gibbon." In *Historicism: The Rise of a New Historical Outlook*, 186–92. London: Routledge and Kegan Paul, 1972.

Milman, H. H. 1833. "Guizot's Edition of Gibbon." *Quarterly Review* 50 (October):273–303.

————. 1882. Preface to his edition of Edward Gibbon, *The History of the Decline and Fall of the Roman Empire* (1838). New York: Harper & Brothers.

Momigliano, Arnaldo. 1936. "La formazione della moderna storiographia sull'Impero romano." *Rivista storica italiana*, 5th ser., 1, pt. 2:19–29.

————. 1954. "Gibbon's Contribution to Historical Method." *Historia* 2:450–63. Reprinted in *Contributo alla storia degli studi classici* (Rome, 1956) and *Studies in Historiography* (London: Weidenfeld & Nicolson, 1966), 40–55.

————. 1976. "Gibbon from an Italian Point of View," *Dædalus* 105 (Summer):125–34.

Montesquieu, C. L. de Secondat, Baron de. 1968. *Considerations on the Greatness of the Romans and Their Decline* (1734). Translated by David Lowenthal. Ithaca, NY: Cornell University Press, Cornell Paperbacks.

Morison, J. Cotter. 1878. *Gibbon*. London: English Men of Letters.

Mowat, R. B. 1936. *Gibbon*. London: Arthur Barker.

Murray, John, ed. 1896. *The Autobiographies of Edward Gibbon*. London: John Murray.

Norton, J. E. 1940. *A Bibliography of the Works of Edward Gibbon*. London: Oxford University Press. Lithographic reprint. Lewis Reprints, 1970.

Oliver, D. M. 1969. "Edward Gibbon and the Mode of History." Ph.D. diss., University of Illinois.

Oliver, E. J. 1958. *Gibbon and Rome*. New York and London: Sheed & Ward.

O'Malley, Charles D. 1943. "Some Material on the Death of Edward Gibbon." *Bulletin of the History of Medicine* 13:206-7.

Owen, John. 1796. *Travels into Different Parts of Europe*. London: Cadell & Davies.

Parkinson, R. N. 1973. *Edward Gibbon*. New York: Twayne.

Pinkerton, John [pseud. Robert Heron]. 1785. *Letters of Literature*. London: G. J. J. & J. Robinson.

Pocock, J. G. A. 1976. "Between Machiavelli and Hume: Gibbon as Civic Humanist and Philosophical Historian." *Dædalus* 105 (Summer): 153-69.

———. 1977. "Gibbon's *Decline and Fall* and the World View of the Late Enlightenment." *Eighteenth Century Studies* 10 (1977):287-303.

———. 1981. "Gibbon and the Shepherds: The Stages of Society in the Decline and Fall." *History of European Ideas* 2:193-202.

———. 1982. "Superstition and Enthusiasm in Gibbon's History of Religion." *Eighteenth Century Life*, n.s., 8:83-94.

Porson, Richard. 1790. *Letters to Archdeacon Travis*. London: T. & J. Egerton.

Powell, L. F. 1938. "Friedrich von Matthisson on Gibbon." In *German Studies Presented to Professor H. G. Fiedler*, 345-51. Oxford: Oxford University Press.

Prior, James. 1860. *Life of Edmond Malone*. London: Smith, Elder.

Prothero, R. E., ed. 1896. *The Private Letters of Edward Gibbon*. 2 vols. London: John Murray.

Read, J. Meridith. 1897. *Historic Studies in Vaud Berne and Savoy*. 2 vols. London: Chatto & Windus.

Ritter, Moriz. 1913. "Stüdien über die Entwicklung der Geschichtswissenschaft." *Historische Zeitschrift* 112:118-31.

Robertson, John M. 1907. *Pioneer Humanists*. London: Watts.

———. 1925. *Gibbon* Life-Stories of Famous Men. London: Watts.

Robertson, William. 1769. "View of the Progress of Society in Europe." In *History of the Reign of Charles V*. London: Strahan & Cadell; Edinburgh: Balfour.

———. 1777. *The History of America*. London: Strahan & Cadell; Edinburgh: Balfour.

Roche, James [JR]. 1839. "The Historian Gibbon.—His Autobiography." *Gentlemen's Magazine*, n.s., 12 (November):465-82.

———. 1843. "Gibbon's Personal Defects." *Gentlemen's Magazine*, n.s., 21 (February)
:158.

[Roche, James]. 1848. "Gibbon and His Biographers." *Dublin Review* 24 (June):381-408.

Rogers, Samuel. 1856. *Table-Talk*. New York: Appleton.

Scheibe, F. C. 1968. "Christentum und Kulturverfall in Geschichtsbild Edward Gibbons." *Archiv für Kulturgeschichte* 50:240-75.

S[hreve,] T. H. 1835. "Biographical Sketch of Edward Gibbon," *Cincinnati Mirror and Western Gazette of Literature and Science* 4, no. 16 (February 14):128–29.

Spacks, Patricia M. 1976. *Imagining a Self: Autobiography and Novel in Eighteenth-Century England*. Cambridge, Mass.: Harvard University Press.

Stephen, Leslie. 1897. "Gibbon's Autobiography." *National Review* 29 (March):51–67.

Stern, Marvin. 1984. "Death, Grief, and Friendship in the Eighteenth Century: Edward Gibbon and Lord Sheffield." *Advances in Thanatology* 5:1–60.

Strachey, Lytton. 1928. "Four English Historians II—Gibbon." *The Nation and Athenaeum* 42 (January 14):565–68.

Swain, J. W. 1940. "Edward Gibbon and the Decline of Rome." *South Atlantic Quarterly* 39 (January):77–93.

———. 1966. *Edward Gibbon the Historian*. London: Macmillan; New York: St. Martin's Press.

Toynbee, Arnold. 1954. "A Critique of Gibbon's General Observations on the Fall of the Empire in the West." In *A Study of History*, 9:741–57. London: Oxford University Press.

Trevor-Roper, H. R. 1968. "Gibbon: Greatest of Historians," *Journal of the History of Ideas* 1 (Winter):109–16.

Walpole, Horace. 1910. *The Last Journals of Horace Walpole during the Reign of George III, 1771-1783*. Edited by A. F. Steuart. London: John Lane.

———. 1937–80. *Correspondence*. Edited by W. S. Lewis et al. Vols. 2–42. New Haven: Yale University Press.

Weinbrot, Howard D. 1978. *Augustus Caesar in "Augustan" England*. Princeton: Princeton University Press.

Whitaker, John. 1836. Letter of January 25, 1794. In Richard Polwhele, *Reminiscences in Prose and Verse*, 1:99–100. London: J. B. Nichols & Son.

White, Ian. 1968. "The Subject of Gibbon's History." *Cambridge Quarterly* 3:299–309.

White, Lynn, Jr., ed. 1966. *The Transformation of the Roman World: Gibbon's Problem after Two Centuries*. Berkeley and Los Angeles: University of California Press.

Young, G. M. 1932. *Gibbon*. London: Davies. Reprint. New York: Appleton, 1933.

Index

Abdalrahman, 232

Abyssinia, 212

Account book of 1783–84, 210

Adams, Charles Francis, 360

"Address," Prospectus for *Scriptores rerum Anglicarum*, 300, 329–31

Aetius (Roman general), 151

Affectation, 194, 292, 301–2, 312

Affection, 207, 221–22

Alboin (Lombard king), 201

Alexander the Great, 26, 28, 31, 119

Almack's club, 117; Gibbon elected to, 74

Althorp Library, 334

America, 66, 79–80, 82–83, 85–86, 88–89, 96–97, 99–101, 112–14, 117, 119, 134–35, 146–47, 168, 176, 182–83; Declaration of Independence, 80; reputation in, 356–57, 359, 405; Revolution, 13, 24–25, 31, 47, 50–51, 53, 55–59; Revolution as civil war, 58

Anatomy, study of, 88

Anecdotes, 114, 183, 315; store of, 337

Annals, distinct genre of autobiography, 287, 289

Annotations, in the two copies of the history, 304, 306

Annual Register, 72, 263

Antiquarian Society, fellow of the, 262

Antiquities of the House of Brunswick, 297–301, 303–5, 308

Antonina (wife of Belisarius), 191–92

Antonines, age of the, 18–19, 27, 29, 103, 119, 185, 190–91

Antoninus, Marcus Aurelius, 26–27, 40, 105, 305–6

Anxiety to please, 94

Apollonius of Tyana, 62

Appearance, 93–94, 173, 193–94, 220, 233, 257, 293, 295, 299, 301–2, 309, 311, 315, 322

Apthorp, East, 130–31

Arbitrary power, dislike of, 313–14

Arcadius, 150

Archbishop of Canterbury, meeting with, 338

Archilochus, 333

Artaxerxes, 34–35

Arthur (king), 158

Asceticism, disapproval of, 49

Assises de Jerusalem, 252

Athanasius, 63, 105, 111, 120, 149, 169

Athenais, 151, 169

Attacks, untroubled by, 135

Attila the Hun, 141, 151–52

Augustine, 154

Augustus, 16–17, 31–32, 45–47, 103, 105, 108, 111–12; ancestry of, 304–5

Aunt Kitty. *See* Porten, Catherine